THE VICTORIA HISTORY
OF THE
COUNTIES OF ENGLAND

A HISTORY OF
CHESHIRE

VOLUME I

THE VICTORIA HISTORY
OF THE
COUNTIES OF ENGLAND

EDITED BY C. R. ELRINGTON

THE UNIVERSITY OF LONDON

INSTITUTE OF

HISTORICAL RESEARCH

Oxford University Press, Walton Street, Oxford OX2 6DP
Oxford New York Toronto
Delhi Bombay Calcutta Madras Karachi
Petaling Jaya Singapore Hong Kong Tokyo
Nairobi Dar es Salaam Cape Town
Melbourne Auckland

and associated companies in
Beirut Berlin Ibadan Nicosia

Oxford is a trademark of Oxford University Press

Published in the United States by
Oxford University Press, New York

British Library Cataloguing in Publication Data
A History of the county of Chester.—(The Victoria
history of the counties of England)
Vol. 1
Physique, prehistory, Roman, Anglo-Saxon
Cheshire, Domesday
1. Cheshire—History
I. Harris, Brian, 1938–
II. University of London.
Institute of Historical Research
III. Series
942.7′14   DA670.C6
ISBN 0 19 722761 9

Printed in Great Britain
at the University Printing House, Oxford
by David Stanford
Printer to the University

INSCRIBED TO THE
MEMORY OF HER LATE MAJESTY
QUEEN VICTORIA
WHO GRACIOUSLY GAVE THE TITLE TO
AND ACCEPTED THE DEDICATION
OF THIS HISTORY

A HISTORY OF THE COUNTY OF CHESTER

EDITED BY B. E. HARRIS

ASSISTED BY A. T. THACKER

VOLUME I

PHYSIQUE, PREHISTORY, ROMAN,
ANGLO-SAXON, AND DOMESDAY

PUBLISHED FOR

THE INSTITUTE OF HISTORICAL RESEARCH

BY

OXFORD UNIVERSITY PRESS

1987

Distributed by Oxford University Press until 1 January 1990
thereafter by Dawsons of Pall Mall

CONTENTS OF VOLUME ONE

CONTENTS OF VOLUME ONE

LIST OF PLATES

For permission to reproduce photographs in their copyright or in their possession and for supplying prints thanks are rendered to Air Views (M/cr) Ltd., Altrincham, the Bodleian Library, the British Museum, *Britannia*, Dr. J. D. Bu'Lock, Cheshire County Council, *Cheshire Round*, the Grosvenor Museum, Chester, Mr. G. Hutt, Mr. D. M. T. Longley, the Saffron Walden Museum, the Salt Museum, Northwich, and Mr. R. H. White.

Between pages 192 and 193

LIST OF PLATES

LIST OF MAPS, PLANS, AND DRAWINGS

Figures 1–4 were drawn by the staff of the Planning Department of Cheshire County Council from rough drafts by Sheila M. Hebblethwaite, figs. 5–22 by D. M. T. Longley, figs. 36–7 and 43 by the staff of the Planning Department from rough drafts by A. T. Thacker, and fig. 44 by K. J. Wass from a rough draft by A. T. Thacker. Material reproduced by courtesy of the Grosvenor Museum is copyright of the museum (Crown users' rights reserved).

xiii

LIST OF MAPS, PLANS, AND DRAWINGS

EDITORIAL NOTE

THE present volume is the third to be published as a product of the partnership between the Cheshire County Council and the University of London Institute of Historical Research. The course and nature of that partnership, begun in 1971, are outlined in the editorial note to Volume Two of the Cheshire History, which was published in 1978. The University again records its deep appreciation of the generosity of the County Council, which has continued to meet the main cost of compiling the Cheshire History, and of the Leverhulme Trust, which extended its grant towards that cost until 1986. Warm thanks are also offered to the University of Liverpool for its continuing support of the History, particularly in making available for the editorial staff a room in the History Department at Liverpool.

Many people have helped in the course of the compilation of this volume. Some of them are named in the footnotes to the articles with which they were concerned or in the lists of illustrations. They are all most cordially thanked. In particular the help is acknowledged of Mr. T. J. Strickland and other members of the staff at the Grosvenor Museum, Chester, of the County Museum at Weaver Hall, Northwich, and of members of the staff of the Planning Department of the County Council. It is sad to record the death in 1980 of Professor A. R. Myers, of the University of Liverpool, who encouraged and supported the Cheshire V.C.H. in many ways. The retirement of Mr. B. C. Redwood from the office of County Archivist in 1985 provides an occasion to record the debt of the Cheshire V.C.H. for his widespread help.

The structure and aims of the *Victoria History* as a whole are outlined in the *General Introduction* published in 1970.

LIST OF ABBREVIATIONS

Among the abbreviations and short titles used the following, in addition to those listed in the Victoria History's *Handbook for Editors and Authors* (1970), may require elucidation:

Arch. Newsletter	Council for British Archaeology Group 5, *Archaeological Newsletter*
C.I.L.	*Corpus Inscriptionum Latinarum*
E.E.	*Ephemeris Epigraphica* (to supplement *C.I.L.*)
Geol. Macclesfield	W. B. Evans, A. A. Wilson, B. J. Taylor, and D. Price, *Geol. of Country around Macclesfield, Congleton, Crewe, and Middlewich*
Geol. Nantwich and Whitchurch	E. G. Poole and A. J. Whiteman, *Geol. of Country around Nantwich and Whitchurch*
Geol. Soc. Jnl.	*Journal of the Geological Society of London* and variants
Geol. Stockport and Knutsford	B. J. Taylor, R. H. Price, and F. M. Trotter, *Geol. of Country around Stockport and Knutsford*
J.C.A.S.	*Journal of the Chester Archaeological Society*
J.R.S.	*Journal of Roman Studies*
Lawson, 'Schedule'	P. H. Lawson, 'Schedule of the Roman Remains of Chester', *J.C.A.S.* xxvii (2) 163–87
Liverpool Annals	*University of Liverpool Annals of Archaeology and Anthropology*
O.S. Arch. Rec.	Ordnance Survey Archaeological Record, followed by sheet reference
Petrol. NW. Europe	*Petroleum and Continental Shelf of NW. Europe*, ed. A. W. Woodland, i.
R.I.B.	R. G. Collingwood and R. P. Wright, *The Roman Inscriptions of Britain*
R.I.S.S.	R. P. Wright and I. A. Richmond, *Catalogue of the Roman Inscribed and Sculptured Stones in the Grosvenor Museum, Chester*
T.H.S.L.C.	*Transactions of the Historic Society of Lancashire and Cheshire*
T.L.C.A.S.	*Transactions of the Lancashire and Cheshire Antiquarian Society*

PHYSIQUE

CHESHIRE[1] lies centrally within the western lowland of England, which runs from the Severn estuary to Morecambe Bay between, on the east, the Cotswolds, the Midland Plateau, and the Pennines, and, on the west, the foothills of the Welsh upland massif and the Irish Sea. While the county may, physiographically, be considered a representative part of western lowland England it derives cohesion and a distinct identity from the natural features which demarcated its ancient boundaries.[2] On the east, west, and south, an upland rim forms the source area of tributaries of the two major rivers, the Mersey and the Dee, which for the most part delimited the county to the west and north; the boundary thus reflected both the major features of surface relief and the dominant natural drainage pattern.

The highest parts of the county lie along its eastern boundary, attaining 582 m. on Black Hill near Holme Moss, where Cheshire extends its 'panhandle' deep into the Pennine moorlands. The valley of the river Tame contains the textile towns of Hyde, Dukinfield, and Stalybridge; above, the upland surface is dissected by incised tributaries of the Tame, Etherow, and Goyt, streams long used as a source of water power but by the 20th century becoming important elements in the water supply of Manchester and its suburbs, feeding a succession of reservoirs along the deep valley floors.

East of Macclesfield, within the confines of the Peak District National Park, the county boundary follows a watershed of the southern Pennines near Shining Tor (559 m.), a source area for headstreams of the Dane, Goyt, and Bollin. The peat-covered moorlands are bleak and exposed to the prevailing westerly winds, and the roads crossing them are frequently blocked by snow in winter. The Cat and Fiddle Inn, 6 km. west of Buxton (Derb.), claims at 515 m. to be the highest hostelry in England; villages, such as Wildboarclough, Wincle, and Macclesfield Forest, occupy more sheltered positions in the deeply incised valleys. The county boundary, although reaching some of its greatest elevations in that area, follows only minor watersheds among the numerous streams in the glacially modified Pennine slopes. To the south-east, however, along Congleton Edge (229 m.) and Mow Cop (355 m.), the boundary follows a major divide of England, for from that watershed streams flow south-east via the Trent to the North Sea and north-west to the Dane, the Mersey, and the Irish Sea.

South-west of Mow Cop the boundary skirts the Potteries, outpost of the Midland Plateau, between Kidsgrove (Staffs.) and Alsager, and picks its way through the glacially deranged drainage system north and west of Bar Hill (Staffs.). The southern limits of Cheshire, between Bar Hill and Threapwood on the flank of the Dee valley, are marked by a substantial morphological feature of sandy glacial drift with an average elevation of *c.* 100 m., formed during the retreat of the ice which once covered north-west England. Here the county boundary winds through an

---

[1] The help and advice of Professor E. Derbyshire, Dr. B. Ing, Dr. I. B. Terrett, Mrs. S. M. Thomas, and Mr. D. B. Thompson in the preparation of this article is gratefully acknowledged.

[2] The following description relates to the ancient county of Chester, taking no account of changes introduced under local government reorganization in 1974. The history of the county boundary is treated in *V.C.H. Ches.* ii. 2, 94–6.

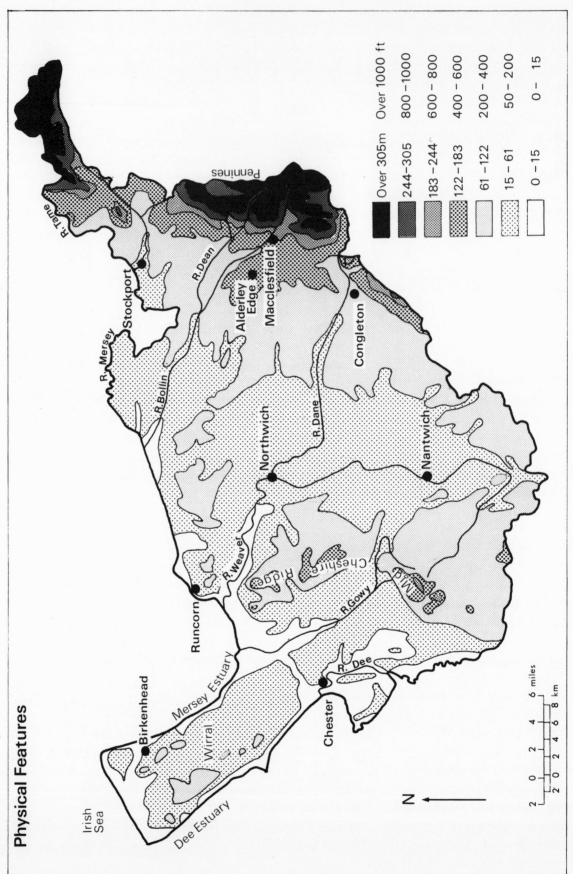

Physical Features

Over 305m		Over 1000 ft	
244–305		800–1000	
183–244		600–800	
122–183		400–600	
61–122		200–400	
15–61		50–200	
0–15		0–15	

FIG. I.

area of sandy hillocks and streams in a predominantly agricultural region. That low watershed, linking the Pennines with the Welsh uplands, forms another major divide, whence streams flow north to the Irish Sea and south to the Severn and Trent. Because of the relatively low elevation of the southern rim, south-east Cheshire forms what has been termed the Midland Gap, an important routeway from north-west England to the Midlands and the south-east, followed by the Shropshire Union Canal, the Chester–Whitchurch, Chester–Lichfield, and Manchester–Birmingham roads, the Crewe–London railway, and the M6 motorway.

After leaving the Welsh foothills near the south-west corner of Cheshire, the river Dee meanders northwards through a flat-floored valley, up to 3 km. wide, which was subject to extensive flooding until artificial regulation of the flow was undertaken near Bala (Merion.). The county boundary generally follows the Dee,[3] diverging from it only to include the civil parishes of Claverton, Dodleston, Eaton, Eccleston, Lower Kinnerton, Marlston-cum-Lache, Poulton, and Pulford south and south-west of Chester. At Farndon and Chester the valley narrows at restrictive sandstone outcrops which have formed historically significant crossing points. The estuary of the Dee formerly extended inland as far as Chester, but was modified by canalization and by subsequent land reclamation in the 18th and 19th centuries.[4] The county boundary parallels the relict cliff of the former coastline, approximately 8 m. above Ordnance Datum, as far as the rocky promontory of Burton Point in south Wirral.

The Wirral peninsula separates the estuaries of the Dee and Mersey and forms a low plateau of c. 50 m. average height, with higher rocky eminences. It is flanked on the west by low cliffs of sandstone and glacial sediments, below which the slow accumulation of silt is building up coastal marshes. The northern shore of Wirral, where low sandy dunes are almost obscured by sea defences, forms the only true coastline of Cheshire; in prehistoric times, when the sea level was lower, that shore was extensively wooded and extended further into Liverpool Bay. Until recently submerged forest beds were visible at low tide off Caldy and Leasowe, and further evidence lies beneath estuarine silt and mud.

The Mersey shoreline from Wallasey to Runcorn forms the western part of the northern boundary of Cheshire. Thence the boundary, until moved to the Manchester Ship Canal, ran along the Mersey as far as Carrington, on the outskirts of the Manchester conurbation. Further east, the towns of north Cheshire merged imperceptibly with the suburbs of Manchester by the late 19th century, the boundary itself following the Mersey and its tributary the Tame. Eastward, it climbs steeply to Swineshaw Moor and follows the northern watershed of the Longdendale valley to Black Hill at the north-eastern extremity of the county.

Thus defined the county consists essentially of an eastern and a western lowland, divided by a north–south sandstone ridge which, as it approaches the Mersey valley, turns east to Alderley Edge, where it abuts upon the Pennine foothills. The lower, western lowland is formed of the shallow valleys of the lower Dee and the Gowy, the undulating surface lying mainly below 60 m., in the rainshadow of the Welsh uplands. Eastwards, that lowland ends abruptly in a succession of escarpments facing west and north-west which form the several summits of the Mid-Cheshire

[3] Locally, where as a result of natural processes river meanders have been abandoned, or where land has been artificially reclaimed, the boundary has moved away from mid stream.

[4] D. Mason, 'Chester: Evolution and Adaptation of its Landscape', *J.C.A.S.* lix. 14–23; *Chester and River Dee*, ed. A. M. Kennett, 7–8, 10–11, 33; maps of Ches. by C. Saxton (1577), and of Chester by G. Braun (c. 1580) from *Civitates Orbis Terrarum*.

Ridge,[5] at Bickerton (212 m.), Raw Head (227 m.), Peckforton (190 m.), Beeston (140 m.), Helsby (141 m.), and Frodsham (146 m.), each the site of an early settlement. The ridge is broken by a number of east–west gaps which give access to the more articulated east Cheshire lowland, of c. 100 m. average elevation, dissected and traversed by tributaries of the Mersey, the rivers Weaver, Dane, and Bollin and their headstreams. Across both eastern and western lowlands the main rivers trend south-east to north-west, converging on the Dee and Mersey estuaries, entry and exit routes for the Cheshire basin.

GEOLOGY

In much of Cheshire,[6] especially at altitudes below 150 m., the solid rocks (those older than the Pleistocene) are obscured by drift deposits[7] up to 90 m. deep left by the glaciers which covered northern Europe during the Pleistocene epoch of the Quaternary period.[8] Such solid rocks as are found at the surface, however, were deposited between c. 380 million and 190 million years ago, during the Carboniferous, Permo-Triassic, and Lower Jurassic periods, when the mobile continental plates were in a different position relative to the poles, the equator, and each other from that of the present. Younger rocks were almost certainly deposited,[9] but have been entirely removed during a long process of erosion which lasted until the start of the Quaternary period.[10] At that time there occurred a widespread lowering of temperatures and several glacial advances which reached as far as southern Britain, so that when the ice finally retreated the whole Tertiary landscape had been blanketed with layers of sands, gravels, and clays released from under and around the ice sheets.

Geologically the Cheshire lowland is a faulted structural basin trending north-east to south-west, floored by considerable thicknesses of Permo-Triassic sediments and bordered and underlain by folded, faulted, and denuded strata of Carboniferous and Silurian age; Silurian rocks do not outcrop within the county boundary. Carboniferous and older rocks in the surrounding uplands dip steeply in a general direction towards the centre of the basin, and are extensively faulted and folded. In a borehole at Wilkesley (SJ 6286 4144) over 1,500 m. of gently dipping Triassic strata have been proved,[11] and the thickness exceeds 3,000 m. elsewhere in south Cheshire.[12]

---

[5] Below, plate.

[6] In writing this section the relevant Brit. Regional Geol. handbooks, the Sheet Memoirs of the Geol. Surv. of Great Brit., and the corresponding 1/63,360 and 1/50,000 solid and drift maps have been extensively used.

[7] F. T. Howell, 'Sub-Drift Surface of Mersey and Weaver Catchment and Adjacent Areas', Geol. Jnl. viii (2), 285–96 and figs. 2 and 3.

[8] Figures of geological age are based on W. B. Harland and others, A Geologic Time Scale. It is generally agreed that the Quaternary constitutes approximately the last 2 million years of geological time.

[9] W. H. Ziegler, 'Outline of Geol. Hist. of N. Sea', Petrol. NW. Europe, i. 178–201 and figs. 13–15.

[10] P. E. Kent, 'Tectonic Development of Great Brit. and Surrounding Seas', ibid. 3–28.

[11] Geol. Nantwich and Whitchurch, 114–35.

[12] V. S. Colter and K. W. Barr, 'Recent Developments in Geol. of Irish Sea and Ches. Basins', Petrol. NW. Europe, 63, 65. Fig. 3 on p. 65 uses data from boreholes at Knutsford and at Prees (Salop.).

SOLID ROCK FORMATIONS

CARBONIFEROUS

The oldest rocks outcropping at the surface in Cheshire are of Carboniferous age and occur in a broad north–south band of general surface elevation over 120 m., parallel to the eastern boundary of the county.[13] Lower Carboniferous (Dinantian) limestone outcrops over a small area at Astbury, south of Congleton,[14] where it forms an inlier of fossiliferous limestone with beds of sandstone and thin coal seams, all of which have been quarried or mined by adit. Associated with those sedimentary water-lain deposits are layers of consolidated volcanic ash. Elsewhere in east Cheshire Lower Carboniferous rocks are present at depth, but do not outcrop; they occur 3 km. east of the boundary on Axe Edge and over a wide area in the centre of the Derbyshire dome around Buxton, where limestone quarrying has been important for agriculture and industry in Cheshire.

The Millstone Grit (Namurian) series are more extensive and form much of the high, bleak moorland country of the Pennines. As the name implies, the coarse resistant sandstones are an economically important rock type within the area, while finer sandstones and argillaceous sediments formed part of a rhythmic sequence of deposition which included thin coal seams in a shallowing marine environment. The massive purple, pink, or grey gritstones and sandstones may be felspathic, and were called 'crowstones' and 'rough rock' by the quarrymen. At the base of the series, flaggy sandstones have been quarried around Marple and Bollington for roofing materials. Thin coal seams have been worked at Billinge Hill and Big Low[15] in the hills east of Bollington, and near Wildboarclough remnants of the old bell pits may still be found. Calcareous beds, while not entirely absent, occur rarely in the Millstone Grit series, and the outcrop as a whole forms a catchment area for soft, lime-free water.

Because of its resistant nature, gritstone tends to form areas of bold topography with whale-back hills, such as Bosley Minn, and prominent escarpments or edges, topped by craggy tors: Cat's Tor and Shining Tor are landmarks on the county boundary east of Macclesfield. Where beds of grits alternate with less resistant shales, the hillsides typically exhibit a stepped profile and may be susceptible to landslides, as in the Pennines east of Tintwistle. Such sequences occur in the upper part of the Millstone Grit series, as the rhythmic pattern of deposition became established.[16]

There is no distinct break between the Millstone Grit series and the Coal Measures (Westphalian); both are characterized by rhythmic deposition, but in the Coal Measures the number and thickness of coal seams increase as beds of gritstone decrease. The Coal Measures represent continued deltaic deposition largely close to sea level[17] in shallowing water, in unstable crustal conditions, on the edge of a land-mass which is thought to have lain to the north-east.[18] The coal seams themselves vary in thickness from a few millimetres to 10 m., but most are between 0.5 and 1.5 m. and on average about 10 m. of sandstone, shale, seatearth, and fireclay lies between the seams.[19] Despite faulting the correlation of individual seams by

---

[13] Geol. Surv. maps; fig. 2.
[14] Geol. Macclesfield, 7–14.
[15] Geol. Stockport and Knutsford, 12.
[16] Geol. Macclesfield, 75, 79.

[17] Petrol. NW. Europe, 7.
[18] Ibid. 170, fig. 6; W. H. Ziegler, 'Tectonic Framework of NW. Europe', ibid. 135.
[19] Geol. Macclesfield, 95–125, 300–7.

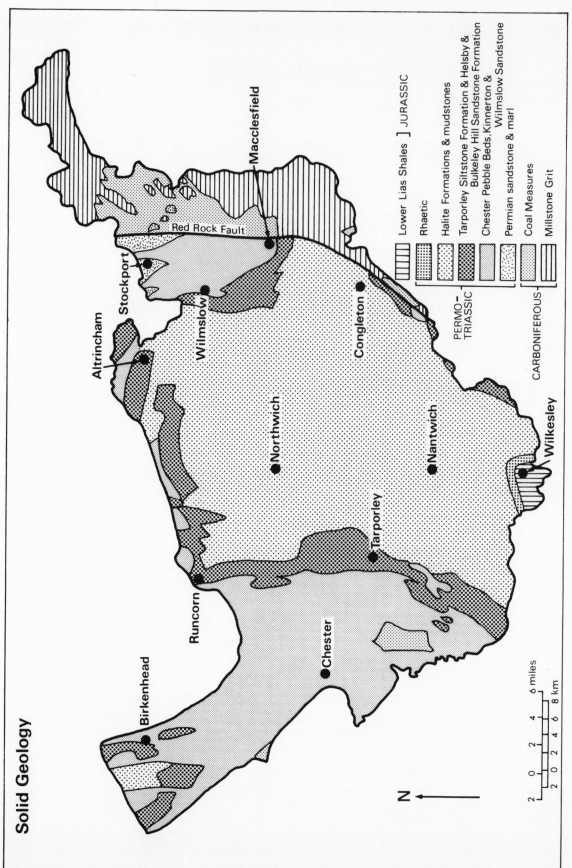

Solid Geology

Lower Lias Shales] JURASSIC

Rhaetic

Halite Formations & mudstones

Tarporley Siltstone Formation & Helsby &
Bulkeley Hill Sandstone Formation

Chester Pebble Beds, Kinnerton &
Wilmslow Sandstone

Permian sandstone & marl

PERMO-
TRIASSIC

Coal Measures

Millstone Grit

CARBONIFEROUS

Macclesfield

Red Rock Fault

Stockport

Altrincham

Wilmslow

Congleton

Birkenhead

Northwich

Nantwich

Wilkesley

Runcorn

Tarporley

Chester

N

6 miles

8 km

FIG. 2.

means of fossil assemblages has been possible and has facilitated exploration and mining.[20] The bituminous coals and cannel are of variable quality and many are suitable only for firing kilns and furnaces. Mining in east Cheshire has taken place in two main areas: the Stockport–Bredbury–Poynton coalfield forms a southerly extension of the South Lancashire coalfield to Macclesfield, while south and east of Congleton the Mow Cop area forms a northerly extension of the North Staffordshire field. Although coal working began in Cheshire in the 14th century or earlier,[21] no pits were operating in east Cheshire in 1985; because the seams are considerably faulted, the exploitation of such small areas within the Coal Measures was no longer an economic proposition. In west Cheshire a small outcrop of Coal Measures over an area 0.5 km. by 3 km. at Neston was the site of the Wirral collieries which closed in 1928. Structurally it forms part of the North Wales or Flintshire coalfield on the western shores of the Dee estuary. East of Aldford a small area of Upper Coal Measures or Erbistock Beds occurs under glacial drift. Elsewhere Coal Measures and older rocks underlie all Cheshire at considerable depth[22] but are covered by strata of Triassic age.

Carboniferous rocks are truncated by an unconformity which marks a major period of tectonic disturbance of a compressive, shearing nature, the Hercynian orogeny.[23] The crustal movement which affected the Cheshire area after the deposition of the Coal Measures resulted in folding and fracturing of the strata, and for the most part the workable coal seams are present only in downwarps or synclines which originated at that time, having been eroded from the summits of the anticlines. Compressive forces formed the Pennines as a monoclinal fold, dipping steeply westward, and a line of structural weakness which may already have existed developed along the western edge of the monocline.[24] That line is still present in the zone of the Red Rock Fault, a quarryman's term, which sharply delimits the Carboniferous rocks of east Cheshire from the Triassic sandstones of central and western parts of the county. Uplift occurred beyond Cheshire's western and southern borders so that what was to become Cheshire took the form of a large crustal downwarp, a tectonic lowland which continued to subside as sediments derived from the newly formed uplands accumulated within it. Thus the separation of upland from lowland Cheshire is fundamental and extends back at least 200 million years.

THE PERMO-TRIASSIC ENVIRONMENT

Apart from the hill areas of east Cheshire, essentially part of upland Britain, and small outcrops of Carboniferous and Jurassic rocks elsewhere, the whole county is underlain by a considerable thickness of Permo-Triassic strata.[25] The source areas of the eroded material which formed those sediments lay in uplifted areas of older rocks. Hercynian crustal deformation was an extended and complicated sequence of events at destructive plate margins which lasted until widespread uplift marked the start of the Triassic and initiated erosion of the uplifted land masses.[26]

Changes in climate occurred between the end of the Carboniferous, with its humid sub-tropical coal forests, and the arid Permian and Triassic periods. They

[20] *Geol. Macclesfield*, 116–17.

[21] H. B. Rodgers, 'Landscapes of Eastern Lancastria', *Manchester and its Region*, ed. I. M. Simpson and F. M. Broadhurst, 68.

[22] L. J. Wills, *Palaeogeography of Midlands*; L. J. Wills, *Concealed Coalfields*; *Petrol. NW. Europe*, 63.

[23] *Petrol. NW. Europe*, 6.

[24] Ibid. 10–11; P. T. Brennand, 'Triassic of N. Sea', ibid. 296.

[25] *Geol. Nantwich and Whitchurch*, 5.

[26] J. Sutton, 'Orogeny', *Understanding the Earth*, ed. I. G. Gass and others, 299.

Stratigraphic Interpretation with revised Triassic terminology for the Cheshire area

GEOLOGY	MAIN SUBDIVISIONS	STANDARD STAGES (CHRONOSTRATIGRAPHIC)	POLLEN ZONE	LITHOSTRATIGRAPHIC UNITS	FORMATION	SURFACE TOPOGRAPHY	SOIL	OLD TERMINOLOGY
					EXPRESSION IN THE CHESHIRE AREA			
DRIFT	HOLOCENE (POSTGLACIAL / RECENT)	RECENT			Alluvium / Blown sand	Flat valley floor, estuary or coastal zone / Dunes along coast	Silt or clay loam with imperfect drainage / Very light but potentially fertile	
		2000 yrs BP	VIII		Peat / River terrace / Submerged Forest / Blown sand and silt	Vegetation debris accumulates in drift hollows / Bench on valley sides (a former valley floor) / Often masked by littoral deposits / Sporadic distribution	Dark, organic but potentially fertile / Fertile, well drained loam / Light, potentially fertile	Shirdley Hill Sand
		FLANDRIAN						
		10000 yrs BP	IV					
	PLEISTOCENE (LATE) GLACIAL	DEVENSIAN	I		Glacial lake clays / Glacial and fluvioglacial sand, gravel, moraine (often associated with) Till	Level with shallow river valleys / Hummocky topography of variable extent / Flat/undulating plain, dissected by streams	Medium/heavy loam / Light sands and sandy loams. Freely drained / Heavy, stony clay slow to dry out	Laminated Clays / Middle Sands / Up/Lr. Boulder Clay
	INTER-GLAC.	IPSWICHIAN			Sand and gravels with organic beds	Poorly developed in Cheshire		
	GLAC.	WOLSTONIAN			Till	Occurs at depth and sporadically in Pennines		Lr. Boulder Clay

U N C O N F O R M I T Y

GEOLOGY	MAIN SUBDIVISIONS	STANDARD STAGES	POLLEN ZONE	LITHOSTRATIGRAPHIC UNITS	FORMATION	SURFACE TOPOGRAPHY	SOIL	OLD TERMINOLOGY
SOLID	JURASSIC	HETTANGIAN	Lower Lias		Calcareous mudstones	Low relief	Clay loam	Pre-planorbis Beds — LIAS
SOLID (RED SANDSTONE)	TRIASSIC LATE	RHAETIAN	Penarth Group		Lilstock Formation / Westbury Formation / Blue Anchor Formation	Calcareous mudstones and shales with limestones give low relief.	Fine clay loam but generally drift covered.	Lilstock / Westbury / Blue Anchor (Penarth Beds) — RHAETIC
		NORIAN	Mercia Mudstone Group		mudstone	Slightly calcareous unresistant	Clay loam or	Up. Keuper Marls
		CARNIAN			Wilkesley Halite Formation	mudstone with saliferous beds	silty clay;	Up. Saliferous Beds
	MIDDLE	LANDINIAN			mudstone / Northwich Halite Formation	cause low relief and subsidence; often masked by drift	imperfectly drained	Middle Keuper Marl / Lr. Saliferous Beds
		ANISIAN			mudstone			Lr. Keuper Marl
					Tarporley Siltstone Formⁿ / Malpas Sandstone	Fine siltstone, with spring lines	Fertile, silty loam	Waterstones
	TRIASSIC EARLY	SCYTHIAN	Sandstone Group / Sherwood Sandstone Group		Helsby Sandstone Formⁿ (locally— Frodsham Member / Delamere Member / Thurstaston Member) / Bulkely Hill Sandstone Formation	Hard sandstones form escarpments, often with prominent summit cap-rocks	Light or loamy, sometimes stony soils. Well drained	Keuper Sandstone / Building Stone Series / Passage Beds
					Wilmslow Sandstone Formⁿ / Chester Pebble Beds Formⁿ / Kinnerton Sandstone Formⁿ	Soft sandstones with hard mineralised or conglomeratic horizons. Undulating terrain with low escarpments, often masked by drift. Important as aquifers	Friable, loamy Sands; often podsolic with iron pan. Well drained	Up. Mottled S'stone / Bunter Pebble Beds / Lr. Mottled S'stone — BUNTER
	PERMO-TRIASSIC	PERMIAN	Permian Lower / Upper		Manchester Marls Facies / Collyhurst Sandstone	Few exposures, often drift-covered	Limited extent	Manchester Marls / Collyhurst S'stone — PERMO-TRIASSIC
	CARBONIFEROUS	WESTPHALIAN			Middle Coal Measures / Lower Coal Measures	Peripheral foothill zones of undulating relief	Loam, variable from sandy to clayey	Mid. Coal Measures / Lr. Coal Measures — CARBONIFEROUS
		NAMURIAN	G₁ R₂ R₁		Rough Rock Group / Middle Grit Group / Kinderscout Grit Group	Bold moorland topography: ridges, cuestas, edges, summit tors. Interbedded shales give stepped profiles	Coarse and sandy; well drained, but masked by drift. Thin on steep slopes	Millstone Grit / Yoredale Rocks
		DINANTIAN (VISÉAN)	D₁		Astbury Sandstone and Limestone	Localised near Astbury in Pennine foothills	Calcareous but drift-covered	Carboniferous Limestone

Fig. 3.

reflect continental plate movements, as the European plate moved across the equator, probably to as far as 20° N. Such movements preceded a world-wide continental break-up by which the ancient giant continent of *Pangea* was resolved into the precursors of present-day continents and land masses.[27] The local manifestation of those tectonic forces was a south–north line of structural weakness and an associated series of fault-controlled blocks and rifts into which waters occasionally spilled from a northern ocean to form the Zechstein Sea east of Britain.[28]

The Permo-Triassic sediments were deposited in such structural depressions. Movements of the fault blocks perhaps kept pace with the accumulation of sediments derived from Hercynian mountains, which formed part of a land area of accentuated relief extending east into central Europe. Transgression from the Zechstein Sea may have begun when those uplands were breached by faults, periodic inundations leaving a succession of salt-water lakes which, cut off from their sources, rapidly became highly saline and were subject to intense evaporation. Such inundations became more frequent and widespread towards the end of the Triassic as the general relief of the whole area was lowered. The addition of eroded evaporite deposits further increased the salinity of the waters, so that the Trias in Cheshire is characterized by well developed beds of rock salt (halite). A line of structural weakness extending northwards from Worcester through Church Stretton (Salop.) into Lancashire was thus the site of deep lakes and evaporite accumulations.[29]

The climate in Permo-Triassic times seems to have been hot and dry, with intermittent wet periods. Sedimentary structures in the rocks suggest that water was periodically abundant and that wind-blown sediments accumulated in it. Torrential river floods brought coarse debris from the denuding uplands, depositing gravelly and pebbly lenses which would eventually form breccias and conglomerates. The river gravels originated south and west of Cheshire, the main river flowing from south to north having been termed the Budleighensis after its probable source area near Budleigh Salterton (Devon).[30] The arid climate was inimical to plant and animal life,[31] and few fossils are preserved, though they may be abundant locally;[32] plant remains have been identified in mudbands, together with the crustacean *Euestheria* (which lived in non-marine environments),[33] fish fragments, and worm tubes. Fossilized mud cracks, raindrops, salt pseudomorphs, and wave ripple marks are frequently recorded. Best known are the footprints of the reptiles *Cheirotherium* and *Rhynchosauroides* from the base of the Keuper, discovered in Storeton quarry, Wirral, subsequently infilled, and other localities.[34] Nevertheless the fossil record is with difficulty used for correlation and classification of Triassic rocks, which must instead be based on lithology, with consequent problems of defining the various rock groups.[35]

The character and classification of Permo-Triassic rocks reflects the environmental conditions in which they accumulated. Coarser stony and sandy sediments

[27] *Petrol. NW. Europe*, 166–9; E. R. Oxburgh, 'Plain Man's Guide to Plate Tectonics', *Proc. Geol. Assoc.* lxxxv (3), 326; M. K. Howarth, 'Palaeogeography of Mesozoic, Pt. V', *The Evolving Earth*, ed. L. R. M. Cox, 194–204.

[28] *Petrol. NW. Europe*, 6; J. C. M. Taylor and V. S. Colter, 'Zechstein of English Sector of Southern N. Sea Basin', ibid. 249–63.

[29] Ibid. 16–18, 296 (fig. 1), 305 (fig. 6), 306 (fig. 7).

[30] Wills, *Palaeogeography of Midlands*; B. A. Hains and A. Horton, *Brit. Regional Geol.: Central Eng.* 66.

[31] G. Warrington and others, *Correlation of Triassic Rocks in Brit. Isles* (Geol. Soc. of London Special Report xiii), p. 3; V. S. Colter and J. Ebbern, 'Petrography and Reservoir Properties of some Triassic Sandstones of N. Irish Sea Basin', *Geol. Soc. Jnl.* cxxxv. 57–62.

[32] G. Warrington, 'Brit. Triassic Palaeontology', *Proc. Usher Soc.* iii. 341–3.

[33] A conch-ostracan crustacean found at Alderley Edge: *Geol. Stockport and Knutsford*, 63; *Geol. Nantwich and Whitchurch*, 22.

[34] W. E. Swinton, 'Hist. of *Cheirotherium*', *Liverpool and Manchester Geol. Jnl.* ii. 443–73.

[35] Fig. 3. Palynological zonal schemes for British sequences were under development at the time of writing: Warrington, *Triassic Rocks*, 18.

are associated with rapid erosion of areas of high relief undergoing contemporaneous uplift, and are most common in the earlier part of the sequence. Conversely the finer sediments (marls) and evaporites indicate a lowered relief, where erosion and deposition occurred in a low-energy environment, with high rates of evaporation. A characteristic feature of all Permo-Triassic rocks in Cheshire is their red coloration, derived in part from generation of iron oxides during burial.

Permian

Permian rocks were laid down as the newly uplifted uplands were eroded, the deposits filling hollows in the rugged Hercynian landscape.[36] Rocks of Permian age appear at the surface between St. Helens (Lancs.) and the country east of Stockport; they are known to exist at depth at Poynton and have been proved in deep boreholes at Prees (Salop.), at Knutsford, and under the Irish Sea.[37] The Collyhurst Sandstone[38] is an aeolian deposit, the lower breccias suggesting rapid erosion of the source area of Carboniferous strata. Overlying sands, fining upwards, were probably deposited in a landlocked basin where the grains were worn round by abrasion and attrition in strong winds. The rock is bright red in colour, owing to a pellicle of iron oxide round each grain, and exhibits large-scale cross-bedding; occasional thin beds of marl indicate the accumulation of micaceous muddy sediments in temporary shallow water. It is not well cemented but erodes easily, so that it underlies areas of low relief and can easily be excavated. Collyhurst Sandstone contains a high proportion of pore spaces, and therefore forms a good aquifer. The Manchester Marl of the upper Permian in east Cheshire is a fossiliferous, red, calcareous mudstone with bands of limestone; it probably formed in an arm of the Permian Sea which did not reach west Cheshire or Wales.[39] In west Cheshire there is no Manchester Marl and therefore no clear demarcation between sandstones of the Collyhurst type and the Sherwood Sandstone (Lower Trias); it has been necessary to classify all Permo-Triassic strata there as Kinnerton Sandstone (formerly known as Lower Mottled Sandstone), which is the lowest formation of the Sherwood group. Poorly developed in east Cheshire but forming a thick member of the sequence in the west, it is well represented in Wirral and the west Cheshire lowland. Lithologically it is a soft, fine, red argillaceous sandstone with round, wind-etched, millet-seed grains typical of fluviatile terrestrial sediments. Cemented by quartz and sometimes calcite, pore spaces are reduced by a clay matrix between the individual grains and its water-bearing potential is consequently limited.[40] The mottling takes the form of yellow, grey, and white streaks and patches, probably due to mineralization, to the presence of pyrite or organic matter, or to reducing processes associated with localized water-tables, themselves the result of thinly bedded micaceous mudstone layers within the strata. The Kinnerton Sandstone is rarely exposed at the surface, apart from small outcrops near Ince and at Burton in Wirral, but like the Collyhurst Sandstone forms areas of low relief extensively masked by drift deposits.

Lower Triassic (Scythian): Sherwood Sandstone Group (formerly Bunter Sandstone)

The Chester Pebble Beds[41] succeed the Kinnerton Sandstone; their base has traditionally been taken to mark the start of the Triassic period. In east Cheshire

[36] E. G. Poole and A. J. Whiteman, 'Variations in Thickness of Collyhurst Sandstone in Manchester Area', *Bull. Geol. Surv. Great Brit.* ix. 33-41.

[37] *Geol. Stockport and Knutsford*, 14, 144; *Petrol. NW. Europe*, 67.

[38] Warrington, *Triassic Rocks*, 30, 34, table 4.

[39] *Petrol. NW. Europe*, 66-9 and fig. 5.

[40] *Geol. Soc. Jnl.* cxxxv. 57, 60, plate 1f.

[41] Warrington, *Triassic Rocks*, p. 31 and table 4.

they outcrop in a faulted band about 2 km. wide extending north–south between Stockport and Macclesfield, abutting the Red Rock Fault. In west Cheshire and Wirral their gently dipping strata are well developed, attaining a maximum thickness of nearly 300 m. The base follows a line from north to south through Chester and Farndon marked by a resistant ridge which locally protrudes through the drift deposits. Southwards they extend into Shropshire; northwards, in north Cheshire and south Lancashire, they contain few pebbles, and it has not been possible to distinguish them from the rest of the Sherwood Sandstone Group.

The Chester Pebble Beds are characterized by the presence of rounded pebbles of white, pink, and brown quartzite varying in diameter from a few millimetres to about 200 mm., often in abundance though in some areas they may be altogether absent. Their source area has been traced to Brittany.[42] Such sandy red-brown sediments, technically conglomerates, represent products of a high-energy terrestrial, mainly aeolian, dune environment, where seasonal torrents brought gravelly deposits. They contain mudstone bands and current bedding, which is sometimes deformed. Current bedding orientation suggests that the source areas of the deposits lay south and south-east of Cheshire and that eroded material was carried by large rivers to be deposited in the subsiding lowland, thus supporting the evidence of a continental origin for the pebbles. Chester Pebble Bed sandstones have been extensively quarried for vernacular building stone in many small quarries where they lie at or near the surface.

Conditions again changed, and the Wilmslow Sandstone Formation was deposited in fluvial conditions with marked aeolian influences;[43] beds outcrop at Carrington, Alderley Edge, Wilmslow, and Macclesfield in east Cheshire but are again best developed in the west, where the sandstone forms the scarp face of the Mid-Cheshire Ridge beneath a capping of Helsby or Bulkeley Hill Sandstone. In the Peckforton area a thickness of 425 m. has been recorded. The Wilmslow Sandstone is a poorly cemented medium- to fine-grained sandstone, normally bright foxy-red in colour but often mottled and stained white, grey, or creamy yellow. In some areas circulating groundwaters deposited barytes in the form of rosettes of crystals which give the rock added cohesion and reduce the rapid rate of weathering.[44] Conversely, the rock in other areas, as south of Congleton, is so poorly cemented and uncohesive that it has been quarried for moulding sand.[45] Weathering gives rise to a whitish sand, and soils tend to develop a hard iron pan or 'fox bench' *c.* 500 mm. below the surface. Exposures of the Wilmslow Sandstone include a number of alluvial sedimentary structures, such as mudstone horizons from which true dips can be calculated, and cross bedding, both typical of deposition in shallow water. The thick strata and high porosity of the rock have resulted in exploitation by water undertakings, supplying industrial and domestic users in north-west England and the north Midlands.[46] Along the Bickerton-Bulkeley fault, where it is faulted against the impervious Mercia Mudstones, the sandstone is highly mineralized; hydrated copper carbonate has been worked at Bickerton.[47]

Locally, above the Wilmslow Sandstone Formation the rocks change to include beds of a coarse, brown, resistant sandstone, the Bulkeley Sandstone Formation formerly called the Passage Beds;[48] they indicate a gradual onset of conditions under which the Helsby Sandstone Formation was laid down. The latter comprises

[42] *Petrol. NW. Europe*, 69.
[43] Ibid.; Warrington, *Triassic Rocks*, table 4.
[44] *Geol. Nantwich and Whitchurch*, 15–17, 111.
[45] *Geol. Macclesfield*, 266.
[46] *Geol. Nantwich and Whitchurch*, 104.
[47] Ibid. 98.
[48] Ibid. 17.

the Thurstaston, Delamere, and Frodsham Members.[49] When fully developed, those uppermost beds of the Lower Trias in Cheshire consist of a hard sandstone underlain by well cemented pebbly sandstone and conglomerate. It forms the summits of the Mid-Cheshire Ridge, of the Frodsham and Helsby escarpments, and of Alderley Edge. The impersistent basal conglomerate, which is associated with an erosion surface, the Hardegsen disconformity, and attains a maximum development of 25 m., is well exposed at the summits of Peckforton, Burwardsley, and Bickerton Hills, where it forms a cap of hard rock on the summits of the escarpment. Lithologically it is a coarse-grained, dark red-brown or grey pebbly sandstone containing angular rock fragments derived from the weathering of underlying Bulkeley Sandstone upon which it lies unconformably. The base is coarser, more open-textured, and usually more massive than the upper flaggy layers, which contain mud partings. Grey, purple, and brown rounded quartzite pebbles are concentrated in lenses or strings at the lower horizons. Well cemented with calcite, haematite, and barytes, it is cohesive and in demand as a building stone. At Alderley Edge the formation is complexly faulted, and weathering has produced a craggy, tor-like profile. The open texture of the basal conglomerate has made the lower layers susceptible to mineralization from percolating fluids, and malachite (copper ore) has been worked.

The Helsby Sandstone has an average thickness of about 200 m., though it may reach 300 m. at Nether Alderley.[50] It is a medium-fine red-brown or buff current-bedded sandstone with angular and sub-angular grains of quartz and mica occurring in association with the conglomerate; generally resistant and well bedded, it is sometimes flaggy. In Delamere the Delamere Member forms the back-slope of the Mid-Cheshire Ridge, while exposures in east Cheshire are faulted in association with the Red Rock Fault. In north Cheshire the Frodsham Member forms the summit of the steep escarpment which overlooks the Mersey valley. Interdigitation of beds of softer Wilmslow Sandstone type may cause lowering of relief, especially near Chester and in north Cheshire; in Wirral the Thurstaston Member, which includes a hard band known as the Thurstaston bed, forms the hills on which Wallasey, Birkenhead, and Heswall are sited. The Helsby Formation is considered to be a mainly aeolian deposit laid down in an arid environment experiencing spasmodic alluvial accumulation in periods of seasonal flood by northward-flowing rivers.[51] There are few fossils, but a well known 'footprint bed' is located 37 m. above the base in Wirral and north Cheshire.[52] At that horizon a layer of marly clay with ripple marks, sun cracks, and plant debris was trampled by giant reptiles, dried out, and was subsequently covered with a layer of fine sandstone, thus preserving the imprints. Fossils[53] were found in Storeton quarry, one of many which have been exploited for building stone in Wirral, Runcorn, Manley, Lymm, and Alderley Edge.

Middle Triassic: Mercia Mudstone Group (Anisian–Landinian)

After the deposition of the Helsby Sandstone an abrupt environmental change brought about by a marine transgression[54] resulted in the accumulation of a series

[49] Warrington, *Triassic Rocks*, table 4; the attributes are summarized in *Geol. Soc. Jnl.* cxxxv. 58-9 and in D. B. Thompson, 'Stratigraphy of So-Called Keuper Sandstone Formation', ibid. cxxvi. 170, 176, and fig. 6.
[50] *Geol. Stockport and Knutsford*, 63.
[51] *Geol. Soc. Jnl.* cxxvi. 176, figs. 6, 16.

[52] *Liverpool and Manchester Geol. Jnl.* ii. 443-73.
[53] Preserved in geol. section of Liverpool Mus.
[54] G. Warrington, 'Stratigraphy and Palaeontology of "Keuper Series" of Central Midlands of Eng.' *Geol. Soc. Jnl.* cxxvi. 205.

of chocolate- or grey-coloured argillaceous and micaceous siltstones and fine sandstones called the Tarporley Siltstone Formation, which attain a maximum known thickness of 275 m. in north Cheshire and south Lancashire.[55] They may be banded, fine-bedded, or flaggy, and may show ripple marks, rain pittings, salt pseudomorphs, sand-filled mudcracks, or small scale cross stratification structures;[56] fossils include footprints, small brachiopods, crustacea, fish, and plant remains, all indicative of deposition in shallow water within the zone of wave action. Dolomite and gypsum may be present as cementing substances. The Tarporley Siltstone is regarded as a deposit in shallow water of intermittent turbulence due to wave action.[57] The *Muschelkalk* formation of Europe, where the Trias, as its name implies, develops its three components of Bunter, *Muschelkalk*, and Keuper, is not recognized in Britain, but conceivably the Tarporley Siltstone in north-west England was deposited by a marine transgression which correlates with the Muschelkalk Sea.[58] Nevertheless that concept does not appear to be supported by microfossil evidence.[59] In Cheshire the Tarporley Siltstone outcrops in a band 2–4 km. wide parallel to the Helsby Sandstone, forming low plateaux on which Pensby, Greasby, and Irby are sited, and in areas east of the summits of the Mid-Cheshire Ridge, often obscured by drift deposits and exposed only in stream sections. In south Cheshire about 180 m. of massive bright red fine- or medium-textured crossbedded aeolian sandstone, similar to the Wilmslow Sandstone, replaces the Tarporley Siltstone near Malpas, and has been termed the Malpas Sandstone.[60]

The upper part of the Mercia Mudstone Group, formerly called the Lower, Middle, and Upper Keuper Marl and Lower and Upper Keuper Saliferous Beds, consists of two main interbedded rock types, each of uniform lithology, mudstones and saliferous beds. Those rocks underlie extensive areas of central Cheshire and, where fully developed, attain 1.5–2 km. in thickness. Their maximum development within the British Isles occurs in Cheshire,[61] where they overlap older rock types unconformably. Although often termed 'marl', which implies a high content of calcium carbonate, the Cheshire marls are noted as being rarely calcareous but containing beds of dolomitic siltstone.[62]

Above the Tarporley Siltstone, the Mercia Mudstone Group consists of the lower Northwich Halite Formation which underlies south-east and east Cheshire, and the upper Wilkesley Halite Formation which occurs in south Cheshire, centring on Sandbach, Elworth, and Nantwich. The halite formations are underlain, separated, and overlain by mudstones. Unresistant and susceptible to solution and erosion, they form areas of low relief covered with thick sequences of brecciated mudstones and glacial and postglacial sediments: their extent, faulting, and thickness remain uncertain. The soluble nature of halite precludes the possibility of outcrops of saliferous beds in a humid climate; solution occurs, and adjacent mudstone beds subside and become brecciated, in which form they are difficult to differentiate from deposits of glacial till. Borehole evidence suggests that the three groups of impermeable mudstone may contain horizons of evaporite minerals, while the two halite formations consist of rock salt with variable layers of mudstone.[63] Structurally, south Cheshire is a synclinal, faulted outlier, additional faulting having established an extended area of outcrop.

[55] Warrington, *Triassic Rocks*, p. 33 and table 4.
[56] *Geol. Soc. Jnl.* cxxvi. 170–1.
[57] F. J. Pettijohn, *Sedimentary Rocks* (2nd edn.), 594.
[58] D. V. Agar, 'Triassic System in Brit. and its Stratigraphical Nomenclature', *Geol. Soc. Jnl.* cxxvi. 10; *Petrol. NW. Europe*, 71.

[59] *Geol. Soc. Jnl.* cxxvi. 200, 212.
[60] Warrington, *Triassic Rocks*, table 4.
[61] *Petrol. NW. Europe*, 296, fig. 1.
[62] *Geol. Macclesfield*, 131.
[63] At Wilkesley: *Geol. Nantwich and Whitchurch*, 114–35.

The Mudstones are unfossiliferous and exhibit red-brown, chocolate, or grey-green mottling. The lower series contain sedimentary structures, salt pseudomorphs, ripples, and sun cracks, together with some evidence of current bedding. Locally there are skerries, bands and lenses of fine dolomitic sandstone, which weather out to form small hills and give variety to the surface relief. The upper beds are more massive and blocky, and contain sandstone and anhydrite bands and silty patches, becoming more greenish in colour towards the top of the series. Secondary gypsum, black dendritic manganese dioxide, salt veins, and nodules of anhydrite occur within the banded beds.[64] It has been suggested that the banding is primary in origin and represents an irregular rhythmic depositional sequence;[65] mottling, mainly secondary in origin, may be due to the emission of radiation and the removal of haematite.[66] The fine sediments of which the mudstones are formed probably derived from aeolian dust or washed mud eroded during periodic storms from tropical lateritic soils covering the surrounding hills. Analysis indicates a bimodal sediment with identifiable cyclothems within the sequences; elements of wind- and water-transported particles suggest that the fine loessic dust accumulated in and near standing water.[67] The marls, though essentially argillaceous, contain evaporite minerals of mainly primary origin, and seem to have been deposited in extensive inland fault-bounded lakes, replenished continually by highly saline sea water in an extreme arid continental climate where evaporation was continuous.[68] Such conditions might be expected to prevail in the arm of a sea whose main body was at a distance, beyond a broad shelf area.[69]

Northwich and Wilkesley Salt Formations

The saliferous beds consist of two main sequences where bedded rock salt dominates over mudstone beds. A total thickness of 610 m. was proved in the Wilkesley borehole, of which 80 per cent was halite or rock salt.[70] The series consists of alternating beds of massive rock salt, up to 30 m. thick, and beds of chocolate-coloured or grey-green mudstone. When pure, the halite is transparent, but impurities impart pink, orange, or brown coloration. Both members of the series are very persistent and can be correlated in widely separated boreholes,[71] a feature consistent with deposition over a wide area in homogeneous conditions and at similar rates and times. Secondary salt deposits take the form of red-vein salt or 'beef' often accompanied by veined gypsum. Salt beds may be associated with brecciated mudstone of nearly contemporaneous or recent origin. From records of boreholes it has been possible to construct isopachytes, or lines of equal salt thickness: maximum development is at Byley, the probable centre of the depositional basin, with 275 m. of salt, while Northwich, Middlewich, and Winsford all have a thickness in excess of 244 m.[72]

It is thought that such thicknesses of halite could not have accumulated as the result of evaporation from shallow, geomorphically stable desert lakes and coastal

[64] Geol. Nantwich and Whitchurch, 19–21.

[65] Geol. Macclesfield, 134–7.

[66] F. J. Fitch, J. A. Miller, and D. B. Thompson, 'Palaeogeographic Significance of Isotopic Age Determination in Detrital Micas from Triassic of Stockport-Macclesfield Area, Ches.', Palaeogeog., Palaeoclimat., Palaeontology, ii. 281–313.

[67] L. J. Wills, 'Triassic Succession in Central Midlands in its Regional Setting', Geol. Soc. Jnl. cxxvi. 232–3.

[68] Ibid. 279–80; Petrol. NW. Europe, 71.

[69] Geol. Soc. Jnl. cxxvi. 279, fig. 17; Petrol. NW. Europe, 296, fig. 1.

[70] The Wilkesley borehole (SJ 6286 4144) provides the type section of the Wilkesley Halite formation, and a full sequence of the Northwich Halite formation: Geol. Nantwich and Whitchurch, 123–5; Warrington, Triassic Rocks, 60, 62. Further evidence from boreholes at Byley and Holford suggests that the thickness of saliferous beds is greater elsewhere in Ches.: Geol. Macclesfield, 132; Geol. Stockport and Knutsford, 77.

[71] Geol. Macclesfield, 133.

[72] Ibid. 134.

lagoons or 'sabkhas' as occur around the Red Sea and Caspian Sea today, because there is little evidence of the other evaporites normally found in association with halite formed under such conditions.[73] More recent hypotheses favour accumulation in a deep, probably fault-guided trough, where the earth's crust was unstable and subsidence more likely:[74] such a trough could be formed by an arm or embayment of a neighbouring sea, receiving a continuous supply of saline water and subjected to intense evaporation under arid conditions. Supersaturated brine accumulated in the deepest parts of the trough under relatively high pressure; it is postulated that crystallization and deposition occurred as the salinity varied above and below saturation point, owing to fluctuations in rates of surface deposition, water supply, and temperature, one salt bed conceivably forming in a single season.[75] Sedimentation of marl bands, by wind-blown dust or water-borne clay particles, is likely to have occurred continuously, but at a much slower rate, the sediments either being incorporated with the crystallizing halite or forming mudstones.[76]

The depth at which ground water circulates varies with local conditions but may be as much as 150 or 200 m.: all salt beds within that zone may undergo solution along underground watercourses, causing a lowering and collapse of overlying strata and ground subsidence at the surface. Although measures, both preventive and precautionary, have been taken to mitigate the problem, subsidence continues to occur, and the exact locality is often unpredictable since underground channels bear little relationship to surface drainage. Many surface springs, such as those along the Weaver valley, are saline and originally formed the source of brine supplies.

From the Roman period and perhaps earlier salt formed a basis of trade and industry in central Cheshire.[77] In the 17th century an unsuccessful search for coal at Marbury[78] revealed the presence of thick salt beds, the Northwich Top Rock, and initiated the period of 18th- and 19th-century industrial development based on salt and brine. The results of that activity could still be discerned in the late 20th century, although the derelict industrial sites had mostly been eradicated. By that time several of the meres thought to be subsidence hollows, such as Rostherne Mere, had become stable, but others had extended. Large lakes or 'flashes' originated in the Northwich and Winsford areas in the late 19th century, and without warning, smaller subsidence craters spectacularly engulfed houses, roads, and farmland. In the 20th active subsidence was reported from Tatton, Tabley, Knutsford, Hough, and Marbury. Subsidence resulting from commercial extraction largely ceased with the introduction of controlled brine pumping by I.C.I.,[79] but natural ground-water circulation has continued to dissolve rock salt beds, collapse being most likely at the source of the brine run, before the water becomes saturated, often many kilometres from its issue as a spring. Where brine runs occur near the surface, linear subsidence causes a succession of elongated depressions or lakes, bounded by miniature stepped fault scarps and extending for several kilometres. Such

[73] *Geol. Soc. Jnl.* cxxvi. 277–80; L. J. Wills, *Palaeogeography of Midlands*; *Geol. Stockport and Knutsford*, 74–6.

[74] *Petrol. NW. Europe*, 16.

[75] *Geol. Macclesfield*, 142.

[76] Evidence exists of layers of saturated brine in the deep basins of the Red Sea: J. C. Swallow, 'Hot Salty Water', *Oceanus*, xi. 3–5; J. C. Swallow and J. Crease, 'Hot Salty Water at Bottom of Red Sea', *Nature*, ccv. 165–6. It is discussed in *Geol. Macclesfield*, 142–3.

[77] J. D. Bestwick, 'Excavations at Roman Settlement at

Middlewich (*Salinae*) 1964–74', *Ches. Hist. Newsletter*, viii. 8–9; W. B. Crump, 'Saltways from the Ches. Wiches', *T.L.C.A.S.* liv. 84–112.

[78] Coal exists at depth under the accumulations of Permo-Triassic sediments, but even with modern technology is exploited only as it approaches the surface on the periphery of the Ches. basin. The 17th-cent. search demonstrated logical thinking but little else.

[79] *Geol. Macclesfield*, 263; J. C. Collins, *Ches. Minerals Local Plan: Written Statement*, 61–73.

topography created problems for farming and communication in the Sandbach area in the mid 20th century.

Until the industrial era salt was used mainly for culinary purposes. By the late 20th century the bulk of the salt obtained was used by the chemical industry, with smaller amounts going to manufacture agricultural fertilizers, domestic salt, and road salt. The only rock salt mine remaining in operation in 1985 was at Winsford and lay below ground-water level.

The highest unit of the Mercia Mudstone Group shows a change of colour from predominantly red to predominantly grey or green, and the salt beds are replaced by fossiliferous calcareous mudstones and siltstones with gritty bands, occasional suncracks, and minor erosion surfaces, suggesting that conditions of aridity and high salinity had been replaced by an environment in which fish, worms, and other fauna flourished.[80] Those deposits, the Blue Anchor Formation, formerly known as Tea Green Marls, are well exposed in the Weaver valley, and have been proved in the Wilkesley borehole, where they reach a thickness of about 15 m. and are topped by an erosion surface.

The Penarth Group (Rhaetic) forms the topmost rocks of the Triassic and consists of a lower Westbury Formation (9.5 m. thick) and an upper Lilstock Formation (4 m. thick), the former predominantly fossiliferous dark grey mudstones and shales showing small-scale current bedding, the latter grey-green mudstones with limestones and algal remains.[81] They occur as a restricted outcrop in south Cheshire near Wrenbury in the Weaver valley bordering the northern part of the Jurassic outlier.[82]

JURASSIC TO TERTIARY

Lower Liassic (Hettangian) rocks of the Jurassic system, a highly fossiliferous group of dark grey, fissile, silty mudstones and siltstones with limestone and sandstone bands, which become more calcareous in the upper layers, are preserved in the centre of the large syncline which covers south Cheshire, and occur in a faulted outlier at Frith Farm south-west of Nantwich and again near the southern boundary at Burleydam, Audlem, and Wilkesley.[83] They attain a thickness of 598 m. at Prees (Salop.) just south of the Cheshire boundary where major crustal downwarping resulted in thick accumulations in a transgressive marine episode which marks the onset of Jurassic sedimentation.[84]

Liassic sediments, like the Mercia Mudstone group, are masked by thick drift deposits. They are the youngest solid rocks to occur in Cheshire; although later sedimentation almost certainly occurred, evidence has been removed, so that glacial drift lies unconformably on an ancient land surface cut on mainly Triassic rocks. It is suggested that widespread changes in sediments in the Liassic may be attributed to tectonic warping on the eastern margins of the developing Atlantic ocean.[85] Nevertheless the timespan between the Lower Lias and the Quaternary was significant in terms of landform evolution, and in that context the area which became Cheshire may be placed in its regional and global setting.

Over 200 million years separate the Lower Liassic deposits from the glacial drift.[86] For about two thirds of that time, sediment accumulation occurred in mainly

[80] *Geol. Nantwich and Whitchurch*, 14, 21, 120.

[81] Warrington, *Triassic Rocks*, 60, 62; *Geol. Nantwich and Whitchurch*, 21–3, 119.

[82] *Geol. Nantwich and Whitchurch*, 40.   [83] Ibid. 44.

[84] D. T. Donovan and others, 'Transgression of Lower Lias over Northern Flank of London Platform', *Geol. Soc. Jnl.* cxxxvi. 165–8.   [85] Ibid. 172.

[86] Harland, *Geologic Time Scale*, 4, 5, charts 1.1 and 1.2.

marine conditions of the Jurassic and Cretaceous periods, as clays, sandstones, limestones, and chalk were deposited in marginal seas.[87] The rocks derived from those sediments occur in Britain mainly in the south Midlands and south-east, though it seems probable that at one time they also covered most of northern Britain.[88]

The Tertiary period was marked by the formation of the Alps in southern Europe,[89] as the European and African crustal plates approached each other and the Atlantic continued to widen and extend northwards by sea-floor spreading.[90] Mountain-building on a global or continental scale is likely to be associated with mobile convergent margins of crustal plates and involves slow, imperceptible warpings of the crustal rocks and rapid, sometimes frequently repeated slippage along fault lines as rock stresses are released, causing earthquakes. As a result, the crust over a wide area may be subjected to uplift, depression, or lateral movements, which in aggregate may amount to many hundreds of metres over the geological time periods involved. Intrusions and vulcanicity characterize the plate edges and marginal basins, where terrestrially derived sediments accumulate. The two plates came into close contact at first in the Pyrenean area, and later in south and east Europe, and in those zones rock deformation was intense, creating fold mountain ranges, while clastic sediments accumulated in great thicknesses in narrow troughs in front of the rising mountains.[91] Parts of the plates far removed from the orogenic belt, such as Britain, experienced pulses which caused mainly gentle tilting and flexuring of the rocks into synclines and anticlines, though significant crustal movements occurred in south Britain until the late Tertiary or later. Meanwhile, off the western approaches, the opening northward of the Atlantic resulted in zones of tension and crustal weakness, and the extrusion of basaltic lava flows and other volcanic phenomena, in western Scotland and northern Ireland.[92]

In Cheshire the repercussions were at a maximum in mid-Tertiary times, about 20 to 30 million years ago, and were accompanied by faulting, possibly along pre-existing lines such as the Red Rock Fault, and mineralization, which particularly affected fault planes and adjacent porous sediments.[93] Complex faulting occurred in the Triassic rocks, and secondary faulting in the already fractured Carboniferous rock strata and coal seams, creating future problems for their exploitation. Conversely, some mineralization along and adjacent to faults, as at Alderley Edge and Bickerton,[94] produced workable copper and other ores there, while the occurrence of mineral veins of lead in the Pennines is also attributed to those movements.

Crustal instability, block faulting, and the intense erosion which removed post-Triassic sediments, affected northern Britain, which was generally subject to pulsatory uplift, while in the south deposition continued intermittently as the Tertiary sea transgressed crustal downwarps.[95] In Cheshire one result was the removal by erosion of all rocks younger than the Lower Lias,[96] leaving the Triassic saliferous beds nearer the surface where they were easily exploited. Erosion not only effected a fault-scarped landscape of sharp relief, whose higher parts are visible in the Mid-Cheshire Ridge, but also excavated river valleys whose presence has been proved

[87] *Evolving Earth*, ed. L. R. M. Cocks, 197-220.
[88] *Petrol. NW. Europe, passim*, especially pp. 178-85.
[89] *Evolving Earth*, 221-36.
[90] D. G. Roberts, 'Tectonic and Stratigraphic Evolution of Rockall Plateau and Trough', *Petrol. NW. Europe*, 77-91.
[91] *Evolving Earth*, 223.
[92] *Geol. Macclesfield*, 180; D. V. Ager, 'Geol. Evolution of Europe', *Proc. Geol. Assoc.* lxxxvi (2), 127-54. For a general explanation of the processes referred to above, R. J. Chorley,

S. A. Schumm, and D. Sugden, *Geomorphology*, caps. 5-6; *Understanding the Earth*, caps. 19-21.
[93] *Geol. Nantwich and Whitchurch*, 53-7.
[94] *Geol. Stockport and Knutsford*, 121; *Geol. Nantwich and Whitchurch*, 58-9; O. W. Jeffs, 'Occurrence of Copper in Keuper of Peckforton Hills', *Proc. Liverpool Geol. Soc.* v. 139-44.
[95] *Petrol. NW. Europe*, 183-4.
[96] *Geol. Nantwich and Whitchurch*, 6.

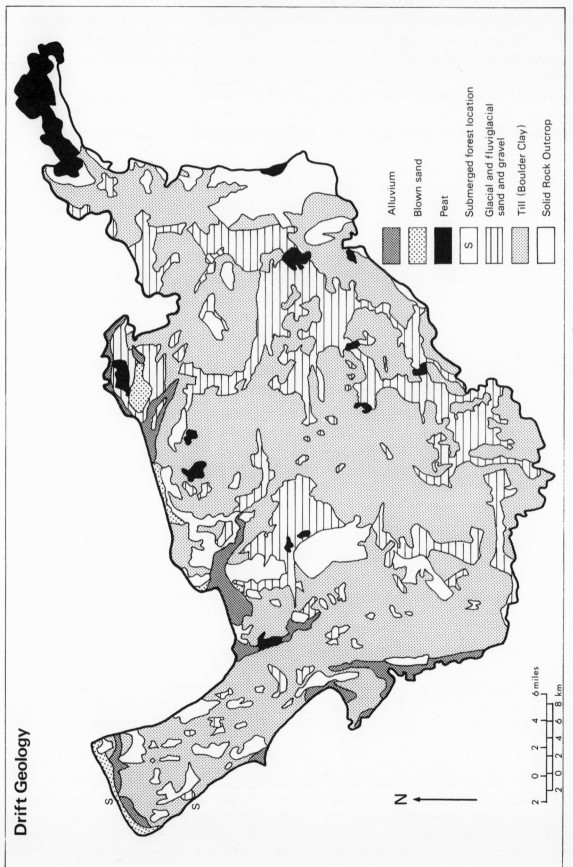

Drift Geology

Alluvium

Blown sand

Peat

S Submerged forest location

Glacial and fluviglacial
sand and gravel

Till (Boulder Clay)

Solid Rock Outcrop

FIG. 4. (This map is a generalized statement of the drift cover. The complexity and interdigitation of the deposits in Cheshire is such that for detailed information reference should be made to larger-scaled maps published by the Geological Survey.)

under the widespread drift deposits.[97] It has also been argued that parts of the land surface were affected by marine and sub-aerial erosion, which initiated bevelled beach and inland platforms at different levels, perhaps related to the pulses of uplift.[98] Dissected remnants of such surfaces have been identified as areas of consistent height which cut across the underlying rock structures. In the Pennine hills of east Cheshire such levels, discernible as benches or interfluve and ridge summits, are postulated at approximately 300, 400, and 600 m.,[99] while in Wirral and west Cheshire, associated particularly with outcrops of harder rocks of the Helsby Sandstone Formation, lower plateaux at 45, 70, 100, and 150 m. may also exemplify such bevelled surfaces.[1]

DRIFT GEOLOGY

QUATERNARY: GLACIATION IN BRITAIN

The Quaternary period is usually considered to date from c. 2 million years ago,[2] and because of the short time that has elapsed since deposition most sediments remain unconsolidated. Two main series of 'soft' rocks or drift deposits accumulated in the north-west lowland and its bordering upland rim. The older Pleistocene series consists mainly of a number of distinctive glacial sediments, while the Holocene series includes postglacial peat, alluvium, and sands, many of which continue to accumulate. The latter, being little altered, are easily interpreted, and give valuable indications of landscape changes occurring in historical times.[3] Conversely, the glacial sediments, despite investigation on an ever-increasing scale, have remained since the 19th century the subject of argument, conjecture, and thesis, by virtue of their variability of genesis in space and time. The term 'drift' itself derives originally from the belief that debris had been deposited in marine or flood conditions,[4] and even after the acceptance of the Glacial Theory many 19th-century geologists continued to attribute the movement of erratics[5] and rock particles to icebergs during a period of marine submergence, convictions apparently substantiated by the presence of marine shells high in the Pennines.[6] Not until the end of the 19th century was the existence of an ice sheet over land areas generally accepted,[7]

[97] Geol. Nantwich and Whitchurch, 6; D. E. Owen, 'Lower Mersey', Proc. Liverpool Geol. Soc. xx. 144; F. T. Howell, 'Sub-Drift Surface of Mersey and Weaver Catchment and Adjacent Areas', Geol. Jnl. viii (2), 285–96. It should be noted that further subglacial erosion occurred later and accentuated the sub-drift relief.

[98] A. A. Miller, 'Pre-Glacial Erosion Surfaces round the Irish Sea Basin', Proc. Yorks. Geol. Soc. xxiv. 31–51; R. J. Small, Study of Land Forms, 262–86; C. D. Ollier, Tectonics and Landforms, 151, 244, 309; G. F. Adams, Planation Surfaces (Benchmark Papers in Geol. xxii).

[99] J. T. Parry, 'Erosion Surfaces of SW. Lake Dist.' Trans. Inst. Brit. Geographers, xxviii. 39–54; R. H. Johnson and R. J. Rice, 'Den. Chron. of SW. Pennine Upland', Proc. Geol. Assoc. lxxii. 21–31; F. Moseley, 'Erosion Surfaces in Forest of Bowland', Proc. Yorks. Geol. Soc. xxxii. 173–96.

[1] R. K. Gresswell, Sandy Shores in S. Lancs. and Liverpool, 7; R. K. Gresswell, 'Origin of Dee and Mersey Estuaries', Geol. Jnl. iv. 77–86; R. K. Gresswell and R. Lawton, Merseyside (Brit. Landscape through Maps, vi), 6–9; C. A. M. King, Northern Eng. 30–59.

[2] Harland, Geologic Time Scale, 26.

[3] J. McN. Jackson, 'Geomorphology of Halton Brow, Runcorn, Ches.' J.C.A.S. lviii. 88–9.

[4] E. Hull, Geol. of Country around Oldham; T. M. Reade, 'Drift Beds of NW. Eng., Part 1', Geol. Soc. Jnl. xxx. 27.

[5] i.e. stones or boulders of distant provenance, whose lithology differs from local strata, suggesting transport by moving ice during a glacial episode.

[6] W. Shone, 'Discovery of Foraminifera, etc., in Boulder Clays of Ches.', Geol. Soc. Jnl. xxx. 181. The 19th-cent. literature on the subject is discussed in Geol. Stockport and Knutsford, 93. One worker considered the area of the Mersey estuary to have been 'covered with a mantle of boulder clay and sand containing erratic blocks, from northern sources, during the period it was under water': G. H. Morton, 'Pleistocene Deposits of District around Liverpool', Rep. Brit. Assoc. (1861), sec. 5, p. 120.

[7] R. H. Tiddeman, 'Evidence for Ice Sheet in N. Lancs.' Geol. Soc. Jnl. xxviii. 471–91; A. Geikie, 'Phenomena of Glacial Drift of Scot.' Trans. Geol. Soc. Glasgow, i. 1–190; G. H. Morton, 'Geol. of Country around Liverpool' (3rd edn). The early work of L. Agassiz and others on the Alps is discussed in R. J. Price, Glacial and Fluvioglacial Landforms, 2–3, and a summary of the conceptual and theoretical development of glaciation is in D. Q. Bowen, Quaternary Geol. 2, table 1.2.

and even up to the mid 20th the presence of clay or stony clay was taken to indicate an ice front advance, while sand and gravel accumulations were considered to be outwash deposits laid down beyond the ice front during warmer retreat phases, though correlation within quite short distances had always presented problems.[8] Recent research using contemporary Arctic glaciers as models has based investigations on stratigraphical sequences and sediment analysis,[9] and has largely invalidated that supposition; it has been realized that the complexity of sediments and morphological features, such as occur in Cheshire and adjacent areas, indicates deposition in an environment of rapidly downwasting and often stagnant ice.[10] That assemblage has been termed a 'supraglacial landform association',[11] indicative of climatic amelioration, at the end of the glacial phase, in a locality close to an oscillating ice front.

The centres of glaciation in Britain lay over the mountains of Wales, the Lake District, and Scotland, though Britain lay at the edge of an extensive continental ice sheet extending to Scandinavia and the polar regions.[12] Britain was affected by a number of ice advances and retreats. Eight interglacials, or periods when deglaciation within the region was complete, are known to have occurred during the last 700,000 years, and 17 are postulated in the Quaternary as a whole,[13] though evidence of only the last three has been found at or near the surface. In northern England the final glaciation, the Devensian, was responsible both for surface features of erosion and deposition and for obliterating evidence of earlier advances. The start of that glaciation occurred well over 60,000 years ago.[14] Ice entered the Cheshire basin from a north-westerly direction, via the Mersey and Dee estuaries, and to a minor extent from the Pennines and Wales, spreading south as far as the Midlands. During its retreat several fluctuations and halt phases occurred before final dissipation, when the ice disappeared from the Cheshire area possibly about 14,500 years B.P.[15]

Estimates suggest that the thickness of ice over the Cheshire plain was about 450 m.[16] at the Devensian glacial maximum, and there is evidence that it reached a height of 425 m. on the slopes of the Pennines in east Cheshire.[17] It has been postulated that during the retreat of the ice from south-east to north-west, c. 18,000 years B.P., a marginal oscillation of considerable dimensions occurred, known as the Irish Sea Re-advance, when the thickness of ice over Cheshire again built up to 210 m.,[18] and the ice front lay across south Cheshire, causing a sandy terminal moraine to accumulate. The glacial conditions were short-lived and the ice downmelted rapidly, leaving the deposits and landforms which give much of the present surface relief in lowland Cheshire.[19]

[8] E. W. Binney, 'Notes on Lancs. and Ches. Drift', Geologist, p. 112; E. W. Binney, 'Geol. of Manchester and its Neighbourhood', Trans. Manchester Geol. Soc. iii. 359–65; E. Hull, Geol. of Country around Prescot, Lancs.; De Rance, 'Glacial Phenomena of Western Lancs. and Ches.' Geol. Soc. Jnl. xxvi. 641–5.

[9] Based mainly on the size and surface texture of particles and on study of fabric; the latter is defined as the summation of all directional properties of a sediment.

[10] G. S. Boulton, 'Modern Arctic Glaciers as Depositional Models for Former Ice Sheets', Geol. Soc. Jnl. cxxviii. 361–93; S. M. Hebblethwaite, 'Devensian Tills of NW. Ches.: An Examination of Sequences and Environments of Deposition' (Keele Univ. M.Sc. thesis, 1980), 317–20.

[11] G. S. Boulton and M. A. Paul, 'Influence of Genetic Processes on some Geotechnical Properties of Glacial Tills', Qtrly. Jnl. Eng. Geol. ix. 159–94.

[12] Literature and controversy on the subject summarized in A. A. Aseev and others, 'Exogenic Landforms of Europe', Geomorphology of Europe, ed. C. Embleton, 40.

[13] Bowen, Quaternary Geol. 193.

[14] G. F. Mitchell and others, Correlation of Quaternary Deposits in Brit. Isles (Geol. Soc. Lond. Special Report no. 4). The lower Devensian lies beyond the reach of reliable Carbon 14 methods which cannot accurately date deposits older than 45,000 B.P.: Geol. Nantwich and Whitchurch, 65.

[15] R. H. Johnson, 'Last Glaciation in NW. Eng.' Amateur Geologist, v. 18–37; Hebblethwaite, 'Devensian Tills', 52. In a crater subsidence hollow at Bagmere peat is ascribed by Carbon 14 dating to Pollen Zone I, but the base of the zone has not been defined: H. J. B. Birks, 'Late Glacial Deposits at Bagmere, Ches., and Chat Moss, Lancs.' New Phytol. lxiv. 270–85.   [16] Geol. Stockport and Knutsford, 106.

[17] Geol. Macclesfield, 185.

[18] Geol. Stockport and Knutsford, 106.

[19] Hebblethwaite, 'Devensian Tills', 24–9, 135, 320;

The effects of a glacial episode may be categorized as erosional or depositional, as a result of the action of both ice and meltwater under a variety of thermal conditions. Bedrock or pre-existing frozen sediments are eroded by the rasp-like action of debris-laden basal ice, and finely ground rock flour or clay, stones, and boulders from within the ice mass are deposited, to form boulder clay or till, as a flat sheet of irregular thickness, as irregular mounds, or as drumlins.[20] Till is also derived from debris which accumulates on the surface of the ice. Such deposits may later be reactivated in the cold and watery downwasting environment, and may move down-gradient to form spreads of flow till, while a standstill of the ice front over a period of time results in a thick accumulation at one locality, forming a terminal moraine. Streams of subglacial, supraglacial, and proglacial meltwater deposit deltaic gravels and sands, silts, and muds in proglacial lakes. Such sediments may be laminated because of seasonal textural variation in the transported debris. As meltwater seeks to escape, channels are eroded by high-energy streams through or along the contours of containing upland rims. Those channels temporarily, and sometimes permanently, modify the normal drainage system, and often take the form of deep rocky gorges.

Evidence of bedrock erosion by ice sheets was discovered in the late 19th century during building operations, when striae aligned in a north-west to south-east direction were revealed under a cover of soil or till, on the surface of resistant sandstone formations.[21] Later evidence from boreholes has proved deep drift-filled channels under the Dee, Mersey, and Weaver valleys, to depths greater than 60 m. below O.D. Such troughs may be preglacial in origin, but may alternatively be due to the scouring action of fast-flowing basal ice or debris-laden subglacial meltwater; they have little surface expression, but are aligned in the same north-west to south-east direction.[22] Further evidence of the direction of the ice flow from the north-west has come from detailed analyses of the composition and fabric of the boulder clays or tills.[23]

GLACIAL DEPOSITS IN CHESHIRE

The map of drift geology illustrates the complex surface distribution of sediments. Vertical sequences in the environment of an ice margin are likely to vary over distances as small as a few metres, and prediction about the drift at depth is therefore largely conjectural. The upland rim, when free of ice, experienced a periglacial climate, with much frost-shattering of rock surfaces providing loose debris but no true glacial deposits apart from a single thin sheet of till on the slopes below 425 m. and in the valleys, where it is sometimes responsible for drainage diversions. Erratic boulders found above the upper limit of the till are thought to represent remnants of an earlier and more extensive glaciation.[24] The surface of the lowland areas of Cheshire is characterized by both till and sandy deposits, the former tending to dominate in the western lowland, while the sands and gravels

T. W. Freeman, H. B. Rodgers, and R. H. Kinvig, *Lancs., Ches., and Isle of Man,* 17–18.

[20] Drumlins are elipsoid hummocks of till, sometimes with a rock core, and sometimes showing layering; they are normally up to *c.* 1 km. long and may occur in swarms as 'basket of eggs' topography.

[21] D. Mackintosh, 'On a Number of New Sections around Estuary of Dee', *Geol. Soc. Jnl.* xxiii. 730–9.

[22] Boreholes sunk by local authorities, water undertakings,

industrial concerns, etc., continue to yield new evidence of the processes. Summaries and maps in F. T. Howell, 'Sub-Drift Surface of Mersey and Weaver Catchment and Adjacent Areas', *Geol. Jnl.* viii (2), 285–96; R. F. Grayson, 'Buried Bedrock Topography of S. Lancs. and N. Ches.' (Manchester Univ. M.Sc. thesis, 1972).

[23] Hebblethwaite, 'Devensian Tills', pt. 2.

[24] *Geol. Macclesfield,* 242.

are more frequently encountered in east Cheshire. Bordering the county on the south, and lying between the plain and the uplands in the east, is an arcuate belt of intercalated clays, sands, and gravels in places more than 100 m. thick marking the standstill positions of terminal ice.[25]

Proglacial lakes lay south and east of the ice margin near Nantwich and Crewe and near Bollington (in Prestbury), possibly forming extensions of the large Lake Lapworth which covered much of midland England.[26] It seems that ice-front lakes of various sizes, both fresh-water and marine, existed at different stages over most areas of Cheshire during ice retreat, and were the sites of accumulations of complex sequences of laminated clays, lacustrine silts, and bedded sands. Water from those lakes drained southwards, carving out valleys parallel to the front and sides of the ice lobe and, because the Mersey and Dee outlets were blocked by ice, eventually drained into the river systems of the Severn and Trent. Rudyard Lake and the Biddulph valleys (Staffs.), the gorge at Disley, and valleys at Poynton and Lyme Park are examples of such channels in the Pennine foothills,[27] while similar origins may be ascribed to the Urchin's Kitchen in the sandstone ridge south of Kelsall and to valleys at Bickerton and Peckforton.[28] Larger transverse channels at Mouldsworth, Tarporley, and Beeston probably contained lobes of ice when the ice front lay along the western side of the ridge at a late stage in deglaciation, but were later blocked by meltwater accumulations of thick sand and gravel, which attain 25 m. in Beeston Castle sandpit.[29] Beyond the county boundary, but of profound significance to the drainage pattern which evolved during glacial episodes, lies the Ironbridge Gorge on the river Severn. It may predate the Devensian glaciation, but during glacial retreat served as the main outlet for ponded meltwater which normally would have flowed north via the Dee and Mersey systems.[30]

Till

Sheets of till or boulder clay[31] cover most of the surface of west Cheshire and Wirral, where they form gently undulating plateau surfaces and completely mask the subglacial bedrock relief. In many localities an upper and a lower till have been recognized, often separated and topped by layers of sand and gravel. The tripartite sequence was first recognized in 1862 in the Stockport area, where it has been named the Stockport Formation.[32] Originally thought to be the product of two glacial episodes with their overlying meltwater and outwash deposits, the sequence has more recently been attributed to processes operating near the edge of the ice during deglaciation, though in some instances it may represent two separate

[25] *Geol. Nantwich and Whitchurch*, 60.

[26] Ibid. 87–90.

[27] R. J. Rice, 'Some Aspects of Glacial and Post-Glacial Hist. of Lower Goyt Valley, Ches.' *Proc. Geol. Assoc.* lxviii (3), 217–27; *Geol. Stockport and Knutsford*, pp. vi, 102, 106–9, plate 7a; R. H. Johnson, 'Glacial Geomorphology of W. Pennine Slopes from Cliviger to Congleton', *Essays in Geog. for Austin Miller*, ed. J. B. Whittow and P. D. Wood, 58–94.

[28] Personal observation; P. Worsley, 'Glaciations of Ches.–Salop. Lowlands', *Glaciations of Wales and Adjoining Regions, ed.* C. A. Lewis, 35; *Geol. Nantwich and Whitchurch*, 86–7.

[29] Personal observation; R. K. Gresswell, *Sandy Shores of S. Lancs.* 44; E. G. Poole and A. J. Whiteman, 'Glacial Drifts of S. Part of Ches.–Salop. Basin', *Geol. Soc. Jnl.* cxvii. 95, 114 and fig. 4; *Geol. Nantwich and Whitchurch*, 71–6, 90, figs. 10–12.

[30] It is maintained that the Severn was at one time tribu-

tary to the Dee and that the Ironbridge Gorge was cut when the lower Dee valley was icebound to allow the escape of waters accumulating in the southern part of the Ches.–Salop. lowland: L. J. Wills, 'Late Glacial and Post-Glacial Changes in Lower Dee Valley', *Geol. Soc. Jnl.* lxviii. 180–98; L. J. Wills, 'Devt. of Severn Valley in Neighbourhood of Ironbridge and Bridgnorth', ibid. lxxx. 274–314.

[31] Till is a sediment deposited directly from ice in various ways, the most important in Ches. being by lodgement at the ice/bedrock interface of debris carried in the lowest layers of active ice; by melt-out as downwasting interstitial ice slowly melts *in situ* to release its debris; and by flow as till exudes from partially melted ice surfaces. Maps of Geol. Survey refer to till as boulder clay.

[32] E. W. Binney, 'Geol. of Manchester and its Neighbourhood', *Trans. Manchester Geol. Soc.* iii. 350–65; Mitchell, *Quaternary Deposits*, 30; P. Worsley, 'Problems in Naming Pleistocene Deposits of NE. Ches. Plain', *Mercian Geologist*, ii. 51–5.

marginal advances.[33] Only rarely as in deep boreholes at Arclid and Burland, have sediments been found which may be of pre-Devensian age.[34]

The tills of west Cheshire have a fine-grained clay matrix, which contains stones of angular to rounded shape, both erratic boulders from widely separated sources in Scotland and northern England, and blocks of local bedrock. The red-brown clay is heavy and glutinous, difficult to differentiate from the underlying Triassic mudstones; where it overlies Triassic sandstones in west Cheshire the lower horizons have a sandier matrix and in east Cheshire tills may locally be characterized by a matrix of very coarse texture. Protruding as islands through the till are outcrops of sandstone bedrock forming hills and small relief features. Largest is the Mid-Cheshire Ridge, but many of the smaller examples form drift-free sites throughout west Cheshire and Wirral, as at Chester, Tarvin, Eccleston, and Willaston.

Sands and Gravels

Sands and gravels are deposited in close contact with ice, either as fluviglacial outwash in front of the ice or as lacustrine sediments in glacial lakes. Many of the accumulations are overlain by boulder clay subsequently deposited from ice during marginal fluctuations as a supraglacial melt-out till or as a flow till moving on ice or frozen sediments. In east Cheshire glacial sands dominate the topography; at Gawsworth an extensive area of red-brown sand is ascribed to the 'middle' sands, may be subglacial in origin, and passes laterally into till;[35] hummocky topography north of Alderley Edge has been interpreted as an esker, a sandy infilling of the tunnel of a subglacial stream.[36] Rudheath consists of a sandy deltaic fluvio-glacial deposit formed on top of laminated clay, which appears to be a late glacial lacustrine sediment linking with newly forming river terraces along the Dane valley, and contains till pellets and frost wedges.[37] It is ascribed to the Upper Sands, formed during the final retreat of the ice as the present drainage pattern became established.[38] In west Cheshire and Wirral an upper layer of flow till and melt-out till sometimes as little as 2 m. thick is underlain by variable thicknesses of bedded sands which are occasionally visible at the surface. That layer, often termed the Middle Sands, is well exposed in the Wirral cliffs near Thurstaston, and probably projects out of the till at Upton-by-Chester. It overlies an eroded surface of till with occasional deposits of aeolian silt and laminated lacustrine clay, and may represent a marginal oscillation,[39] the sands and gravels being outwash material deposited by streams emerging from the ice front which at one stage during deglaciation lay across the Dee estuary.[40]

Delamere Forest is an extensive tract of deltaic outwash sands deposited during the late Devensian, carbon-dated from molluscan shells in gravel underlying an upper till to 28,000 years B.P.[41] It is sited where the Mouldsworth drainage channel opens on the plain of east Cheshire, and accumulated in a proglacial lake at a time when the ice front lay along the western slopes of the Mid-Cheshire Ridge. Its hummocky surface, at an average altitude of 75 m. above O.D., is pockmarked with

[33] Hebblethwaite, 'Devensian Tills', 319–20; *Qtrly. Jnl. Eng. Geol.* ix. 159–94; M. A. Edwards and F. M. Trotter, *Pennines and Adjacent Areas*, 67–72.

[34] Mitchell, *Quaternary Deposits*, 32–3 and table 5; *Geol. Nantwich and Whitchurch*, 6.

[35] *Geol. Macclesfield*, 183, 193–4.

[36] *Geol. Stockport and Knutsford*, 105.

[37] Frost wedge: vertical fissure opened by freeze-thaw processes, which becomes infilled with distinctive sand or silt sediment.

[38] *Geol. Macclesfield*, 184, 216; *Mercian Geologist*, ii. 51–5; Mitchell, *Quaternary Deposits*, 30–2.

[39] *Geol. Stockport and Knutsford*, 95.

[40] Ibid. 98.

[41] D. B. Thompson and P. Worsley, 'Late Pleistocene Molluscan Fauna from Drifts of Ches. Plain', *Geol. Jnl.* v. 197–207; G. S. Boulton and P. Worsley, 'Late Weichselian Glaciation of Ches.–Salop. Basin', *Nature*, ccvii. 704–6; *Glaciations of Wales*, 101–2.

hollows formed as buried ice blocks melted *in situ* and ground-water began to circulate once more to dissolve the underlying saliferous beds, forming subsidence depressions on the surface.

Light-coloured sands at Congleton and Chelford are early to middle Devensian in age and thought to predate all deposits of till presently at or near the surface.[42] Within the complex lie a river channel and a bed of peat carbon-dated to *c.* 60,000 years B.P.,[43] and the whole has been assigned to an interstadial, a period shorter than an interglacial but long enough for flora and fauna to become established.[44] A cold climate would have favoured alluvial and aeolian sandy accumulations under a vegetative cover of boreal forest similar to that now in Finland.[45] The sands rest on bedrock or an eroded surface of till which, though undated, is thought to be earlier than other tills in the area and may be pre-Devensian. Patches of sands in the Pennine foothills are greyish in colour and contrast with the reddish or light-coloured sediments of the plain. They are derived from erosion of Carboniferous sandstones and often take the form of small fans or deltaic deposits where glacial drainage channels emerged from their gorges.

In south and east Cheshire the sandy area of low morainic hills which stretches as an arcuate lobed zone about 10 km. wide from Wrexham (Denb.) through Whitchurch (Salop.) to Bar Hill (Staffs.), and extends northward along the flanks of the Pennines in the Congleton and Macclesfield areas, constitutes one of the thickest glacial sequences in Cheshire. In places those hills attain an altitude of 150 m., being formed of a complex area of sands, gravels, and tongues of till, but their age and origin remain controversial.[46] Many authorities consider the zone to be a true moraine marking the site of the ice margin at a time of standstill during the final downwasting of the ice sheet from the north-western lowland.[47] A similar ridge has been identified at Duckington, Hanmer (Flints.), Cholmondeley, Chorlton, and north of Chester.[48] All such features tend to have a thin covering of flow tills, and that in the Chester area is associated with a distinctive valley cut partly in solid rock at the base of the Wirral peninsula. That channel, termed the Deva Spillway,[49] may represent the remnant of a drainage channel at the ice margin, which carried ponded water from the east Cheshire lowland to the Dee estuary and thence to the Irish Sea at a time when the lower Mersey estuary was still blocked by ice.[50]

Laminated Clays

Laminated clays are variable and impersistent, often merging laterally with tills and suggestive of deposition in ephemeral lakes. Lithologically they range from dominantly silty to dominantly clayey, and contain variable amounts of organic remains, small erratics, and pebbles but tend to thin towards the north-west and become impersistent. When on the surface they form the level topography of south Cheshire near Nantwich and Crewe, where they attain their greatest development.

[42] Mitchell, *Quaternary Deposits*, 32 and table 5 (p. 30).

[43] I. M. Simpson and R. G. West, 'Stratigraphy and Palaeobotany of a Late Pleistocene Organic Deposit at Chelford, Ches.', *New Phytologist*, lvii. 239–50. A full discussion of radiocarbon datings within the Chelford Sand Formation is in F. J. Shotton, D. J. Blundell, and R. E. G. Williams, 'Birmingham Univ. Radiocarbon Dates, IV', *Radiocarbon*, xii. 385–9.

[44] P. Worsley, 'Ches.–Salop. Plain', *Wales and Ches.–Salop. Lowland* (I.N.Q.U.A. Field Guide A8/C8), 53–6.

[45] R. G. West, 'Pollen Zones in Pleistocene of Gt. Brit. and their Correlation', *New Phytol.* lxix. 1179–83.

[46] For controversy on relative age of this feature see *Glaciations of Wales*, 93–4; E. A. Francis, *Quaternary Research Assoc. Field Handbk.* 63; E. M. Yates and F. Moseley, 'A Contribution to Glacial Geomorphology of Ches. Plain', *Trans. Inst. Brit. Geog.* xlii. 117–20.

[47] *Geol. Nantwich and Whitchurch*, 60, 79–83; *Wales and Ches.–Salop. Lowland*, 57.

[48] *Geol. Nantwich and Whitchurch*, 66–9; Hebblethwaite, 'Devensian Tills', 158, 317.

[49] *Geol. Stockport and Knutsford*, 110.

[50] Ibid.; Hebblethwaite, 'Devensian Tills', 60, 159.

Similar clays are revealed in boreholes in most parts of the county, but are overlain by later till deposits, as at Crewe station and in the Dane valley.[51]

DEGLACIATION

The late glacial period, characterized by melting ice blocks, streams laden with outwash sands, and ponded meltwater, merged imperceptibly into the postglacial period as rivers began to establish regular channels between remnant blocks of ice and accumulating debris.[52] The landscape was clothed first with a tundra vegetation and later with forests. Peat began to form in hollows on the till surface, or where drainage was impeded, as at Carrington Moss, Lindow Common, Flaxmere, and the Gowy valley. In many areas accumulation of peat has continued to the present, attaining a considerable thickness, as at Dane's Moss where 10 m. has been recorded. Datings suggest that the peat began to form during Pollen Zone I at Bagmere, a salt subsidence hollow,[53] and during Pollen Zone II at Hatchmere.[54]

During the transitional period[55] a periglacial climate existed in upland Cheshire, freeze-thaw and solifluction[56] causing the accumulation of weathered rock debris in the form of head deposits, as on the slopes of Mow Cop.[57] Solifluction lobes can be discerned when the sun is low in the sky on many slopes of the sandstone ridge. Cold, dry winds blowing outwards from the glaciated areas to the north and west picked up loose silt-size particles from the dried-out surface, depositing them as a thin cover of loess on the flanks and summits of the Pennines and other hills,[58] and extensively in the Mersey and Dee valleys.[59] In most respects the windblown silts and sands compare with the Shirdley Hill Sands of south Lancashire.[60]

THE POSTGLACIAL PERIOD

Much of the sand and gravel carried by the Mersey was deposited on its valley floor in extensive spreads which have since been uplifted, as a result of isostatic equilibrium,[61] to form the High Terrace at 9 m. above O.D. At the time of their deposition, the Mersey flowed to the Irish Sea through the Deva Spillway and the Dee estuary, but at an unknown later date the ice-blocked Mersey estuary became free and the river was able to resume its shorter normal course to the sea. That change initiated a rapid downcutting along the Mersey valley and its tributaries, and the formation of a series of lower alluvial terraces.[62] Similar valley-side features occur along the Dee valley; varying in height and degree of preservation, they can be located along the Dee at c. 1.5 m. and 5 m., and along the Weaver at c. 1 m. and

[51] *Geol. Macclesfield*, 215-16, 234.
[52] Deglaciation may extend over 5,000-6,000 years: Hebblethwaite, 'Devensian Tills', 319; M. A. Paul, 'Supraglacial Landsystem', *Glacial Geol.* ed. N. Eyles, 71-90.
[53] *New Phytol.*, lxiv. 270-85; *Geol. Macclesfield*, 148, 218, 238.
[54] *Nature*, ccvii. 704-6; J. H. Tallis, 'Terrestrialization of Lake Basins in N. Ches.' *Jnl. Ecol.* lxi. 537-67.
[55] Although the base of Pollen Zone I has not been defined, both it and Zone II are earlier than the closing stages of the Devensian at c. 12,000 B.P. That corresponds to the estimate that the Ches. basin was ice free by c. 14,500 B.P.: *Proc. Geol. Assoc.* lxxii. 21-3. The Flandrian began c. 10,000 B.P.: Mitchell, *Quaternary Deposits*, 5. It is approximately coincident with the base of Pollen Zone IV.

[56] Solifluction: seasonal creep and flow down-gradient of waterlogged slurry released by the spring thaw of ground ice.
[57] *Geol. Macclesfield*, 189.
[58] P. C. D. Cazalet, 'Correlation of Ches. Plain and Derb. Dome Glacial Deposits', *Mercian Geologist*, iii. 71-84; Mitchell, *Quaternary Deposits*, 32.
[59] Hebblethwaite, 'Devensian Tills', 154.
[60] *Geol. Stockport and Knutsford*, 111.
[61] Isostatic equilibrium: the balance of crustal plates on plastic or semi-liquid underlying layers. A weight of ice tends to cause the surface to be depressed; ice-melt results in a slow rebound over several millennia. The process can be observed in the gulf of Bothnia (Finland) today.
[62] *Geol. Stockport and Knutsford*, 110-11.

2 m.[63] At Churton by Farndon a well drained alluvial fan marks the point where a tributary stream entered the Dee valley.[64]

During the postglacial period the coastline of Wirral and its bounding estuaries were subjected to a fluctuating sea level and intermittent inundation. Ice melting over the globe as a whole caused sea level to rise steadily, but many areas which had been under a weight of ice experienced isostatic rebound which offset that effect. The overall result in north-west England was twofold. Submerged forest beds off Leasowe, Meols, and Thurstaston, once visible at low tide, were originally formed when the sea level was low and the coastline was west of Liverpool Bay. At times of high sea level, however, wave action notched a succession of reputed raised beaches, including the so-called Flandrian or Hill House coastline at 5.2 m. above O.D.[65] which has been traced from topographic and stratigraphic evidence in north Wirral and west of Chester, indicating a former marine limit inland from the present coastline.[66] While many authorities favour the concept of a single inundation, the Flandrian Transgression has been questioned.[67]

Apart from peat, contemporary accumulations include blown sand forming dunes along the north and west Wirral coasts, a process much reduced by coastal defences and dredging, and alluvium resulting from deposition in times of flood along the main river valleys. Areas of marine alluvium in the Dee estuary have extended rapidly since the straightening of the river in the 18th century and the subsequent reclamation of tidal flats at Sealand north-west of Chester.

No short descriptive account can fully describe the variety of Quaternary sediments which form a surface mosaic over Cheshire. Their outstanding characteristic is a variable stratigraphy, lithology, and morphology, which has exerted controls on topography, soils, settlement, and landscape evolution. The surface drift deposits cover all but a few areas, mainly on the sandstone ridge and in the Pennines, with a patchwork of clays, silts, sands, gravels, and peat. Any consideration of the landscape on which man established his earliest settlements must take into account their heterogeneous nature and impersistent distribution, for in detail they have strongly influenced the selection of settlement sites, the clearing of the forest, the routes of early migrations, overland travel, and economic development throughout historical time.

THE CONDITIONS OF SETTLEMENT

SETTLEMENT SITES

Late Palaeolithic hunters moved into an inhospitable environment of cold and exposed tundra-like conditions during the closing stages of the Devensian.[68] Vegetative cover consisted of an open, stunted growth of dwarf birch scrub in expanses of moss, lichen, herbs, and hardy shrubs. As temperatures rose dwarf willow and

[63] *Geol. Nantwich and Whitchurch*, 78.
[64] SJ 40 56: Geol. Surv. Map 1″, drift edn., sheet 109 (1965).
[65] R. K. Gresswell, *Sandy Shores in South Lancs.* 11–16.
[66] M. J. Tooley, *Sea Level Changes in NW. Eng. during*

Flandrian Stage.
[67] Gresswell, *Sandy Shores*; Tooley, *Sea Level Changes*; summary in Hebblethwaite, 'Devensian Tills', 62–3.
[68] W. J. Varley, *Ches. before Romans*, 8 and table 2; below, Prehistory.

juniper became established. Pine, an indigenous conifer, spread northwards into Cheshire to establish with birch the pre-boreal forests of early Flandrian times. Subsequent rapid amelioration of climate in the Boreal period favoured colonization by deciduous species, initially hazel, but closely followed by wych elm, oak, and finally small-leaved lime, as summers became warm and dry: the average July temperature is estimated to have been *c.* 2–3° C above those of the mid 20th century.[69] A plant-climax community of mixed deciduous woodland with extensive peat development became established in the warmer and wetter Atlantic period, between six and seven thousand years B.P.[70] On the wetter clay soils the pedunculate oak, *Quercus robur*, was dominant, while the drier sandstone outcrops were vegetated by the sessile oak, *Quercus petraea*, with intermediary species apparently established in many areas. By the mid 20th century remnants of mixed deciduous forest had become rare in Cheshire, though some areas, such as Peckforton and the Weaver and Bollin valleys, have remained wooded throughout their postglacial history.[71] It seems likely that the woodland was subjected to continuous modification by Mesolithic man who used the available timber resources as building material and fuel.[72] At higher altitudes in the Pennines and on sandy soils the mixed woodland contained a larger proportion of birch and ash, and was probably more open in character, facilitating penetration.[73] Throughout prehistoric times peat accumulated in poorly drained areas, trapping and preserving pollen grains from the surrounding plant species so that palynological studies of the 20th century can trace the development and decline of surface vegetation.[74]

Late Mesolithic and Neolithic inhabitants actively destroyed the oak community as they established primitive systems of grazing and cultivation.[75] A climatic optimum, when average July temperatures were *c.* 2° C warmer than in the mid 20th century,[76] heralded the shifting agriculture of the Bronze Age, which was apparently concentrated in the drier, sandy areas of the Mid-Cheshire Ridge and the eastern foothills; there is evidence of a major clearance of oak forest.[77] River valleys were used extensively as routeways, the advantage of easy waterway penetration outweighing the effort of negotiating heavily wooded valleys or treacherous peat bogs. Other early routeways followed the Mersey valley and the plateau-like crest of the Mid-Cheshire Ridge, where drier conditions ensured a lighter oak woodland and open heathland,[78] so that the trackway had excellent lookout points and was presumably in frequent use.[79] Along the same high-level track linking northern and southern parts of the county, Iron Age settlers established impressive defensive hillforts on sandstones of the Bulkeley and Helsby Formations at Maiden Castle, Kelsall, and Helsby, though the dwellings of that people, presumably in densely wooded lowland areas, have not been located.[80] Evidence of less substantial early domestic buildings has inevitably been obscured in later surface modification for agriculture and to provide building materials and fuel. Only on the exposed Pennine

[69] H. Goodwin, *Hist. Brit. Flora* (2nd edn.); W. Pennington, *Hist. Brit. Vegetation* (2nd edn.); G. R. Coope, 'Climatic Fluctuations in NW. Europe since Last Interglacial indicated by Fossil Assemblages of Coleoptera', *Ice Ages Ancient and Modern*, ed. A. E. Wright and F. Moseley, 153–68; A. G. Tansley, *Brit. Isles and their Vegetation*, i–ii; R. G. West, *Pleistocene Geol. and Biol.* (2nd edn.).

[70] N. Pears, *Basic Biogeography*, 166.

[71] A. Newton, *Flora of Ches.* 24–8.

[72] P. Ashbee, *The Ancient British*, 50–69.

[73] Newton, *Flora of Ches.* 28.

[74] West, *Pleistocene Geol. and Biol.* 343–413.

[75] Below, Prehistory.

[76] West, *Pleistocene Geol. and Biol.* 218–23, 241; H. H. Lamb, 'Changes of Climate', *Ice Ages Ancient and Modern*, 169–88.

[77] Sedimentary deposits are examined as indicators of agricultural practice and the location of settlements in J. Schoenwetter, 'Environmental Archaeology of Peckforton Hills', *Ches. Arch. Bull.* viii. 10–11; O. J. Bott and S. R. Williams, *Man's Imprint on Ches.* 7.

[78] Erica-vaccinium (heather-bilberry species) with dwarf birch and stunted oak species.

[79] Bott and Williams, *Man's Imprint on Ches.* 7.

[80] Ibid. 9; *Ches. Arch. Bull.* viii. 10–11.

and central ridge slopes, on dry thin infertile soils, has a less intensive agriculture allowed preservation of settlement sites.[81]

The selection of sites for early settlement was determined by access, bedrock, relief, and vegetative cover. Elevated areas of more resistant strata and sands of mainly glacial origin could most easily be cleared by early man with limited technology. Such sites were located on bevelled outcrops of the more resistant Triassic sandstones, on the Carboniferous rocks of the Pennines, and on mounds of sandy glacial outwash. Few such sites remain as significant settlements. Lower, but probably more densely wooded, were the ridges and knolls of Chester Pebble Beds and Kinnerton Sandstone which have retained significant settlements, including the city of Chester. They constitute a distinctive element in the settlement pattern of Wirral[82] and west Cheshire, and though other factors were involved the geological drift map provides sufficient evidence to infer the influence of bedrock on the siting of early settlements such as the villages of Tarvin, Christleton, Willaston (Wirral), and Storeton. In east Cheshire with its thick covering of drift a preference for sandy sites beside the through-ways of main river valleys is discernible at Cranage, Sandbach, Goostrey, Macclesfield, and Nantwich.

Well drained and gravelly high terraces, often covered with a fertile layer of windblown sand, lie above the Mersey valley and have provided prime sites for 19th- and 20th-century housing in the Manchester suburbs, while smaller river terraces of later origin are variously used by tracks and isolated settlements, for they lie above the flood-prone alluvial valley floors, often marked by changes in land use.

Heavily wooded and with dense undergrowth and uncertain drainage, claylands were late to be settled, though evidence from other parts of England suggests that settlement may have taken place earlier than was once supposed.[83] In west Cheshire areas of till, unless underlain at a shallow depth by 'middle' sands, are characterized by small dispersed farmsteads, hamlets, and modern housing estates. Southern Cheshire contains many small townships in the rural areas near Nantwich, often centring around small patches of glacial sand as at Acton by Nantwich and Faddiley.[84] Significantly, the 19th-century railway town of Crewe is sited on an area of laminated clays.

In Wirral bevelled plateau surfaces on outcrops of the Thurstaston Sandstone and the Tarporley Siltstones have been settled at Heswall, Irby, Grange, Birkenhead, Wallasey, Frankby, Greasby, Caldy, Thurstaston, and Thingwall, some of whose names indicate Norse settlements on coastal locations with an unrestrictive and lightly vegetated, if less fertile, plateau surface.[85] Such topography did not appeal as strongly to Anglian colonists, who settled in south Wirral and west Cheshire after crossing the Midland Gap on their migrations from the south-east.

Any consideration of the geological influence on settlement is incomplete without reference to the period after the Second World War. Large-scale building has found it increasingly necessary to assess the hazards of unpredictable drift sequences, underground water courses, and potential subsidence zones where saliferous beds lie near to the surface in the groundwater zone. In the late 19th century and early

[81] Bott and Williams, *Man's Imprint on Ches.* 9.
[82] E. Rideout, 'Sites of Ancient Villages in Wirral', *T.H.S.L.C.* lxxvii. 54–69.
[83] Bott and Williams, *Man's Imprint on Ches.* 8.
[84] Close perusal of Geol. Surv. Maps 1/63,360 and 1/50,000, drift edn., reveals details of settlement pattern and is particularly informative in rural areas.
[85] Newton, *Flora of Ches.* 13, 24; Freeman and others, *Lancs., Ches., and Isle of Man,* 29; below, Anglo-Saxon Ches.

20th catastrophic collapses occurred in towns of central Cheshire and, while they have not recurred, those areas still susceptible to subsidence have been defined and building has been restricted.[86]

WATER

The availability of a pure and reliable water supply indirectly reflects geological and physical controls. In Cheshire, while some settlements are associated with surface watercourses, many have relied for centuries on spring and well water, often adjacent to or within the confines of dwellings.[87] Thick sequences of porous and fissured Permo-Triassic sandstones ensured a plentiful and free-flowing supply in west Cheshire while the water table was higher, up to the late 19th century. Glacial sands were also tapped in shallower wells,[88] but yielded less reliable supplies, for they tended to run dry in summer and became susceptible to contamination as population increased. Large private and public water undertakings have tapped the Sherwood Sandstones in west Cheshire and Wirral to provide industrial and domestic supplies to users in the Potteries and Merseyside, frequently lowering the water levels in local wells in the process.[89] The flow of water from those sandstones may be as much as ten times that from the Mercia Mudstone Group in east Cheshire.[90] The area between Farndon, Threapwood, and Broxton constitutes an excellent resource on account of the porosity and fissuring of the sandstone, and is exploited by the Staffordshire Potteries Water Board at Peckforton Gap and near Fuller's Moor; distinctive but unobtrusive features in the Mid-Cheshire Ridge are the small hip-roofed pumping houses which dot the fields above deep boreholes. Less common in west Cheshire are water seepages from the Tarporley Siltstone, sometimes influencing the site of a spring-line village as at Eaton near Tarporley and Irby in Wirral.

The water potential of east Cheshire is due to high rainfall in the Pennines, over 1,700 mm. a year, which ensures a reliable supply of soft water from Millstone Grit outcrops, while narrow, steep-sided valleys, formed by streams which drained the ice margin or by river incision, are well suited to damming and storage.[91] Bosley, Langley, and Longdendale are three which since the 19th century have supplied the needs of towns in east Cheshire and the Manchester conurbation. Earlier the same streams had been tapped to provide water power for industrial activities, particularly textile mills located in the upper valleys of the Tame, Etherow, Goyt, Dane, and Bollin.[92] In west Cheshire the Dee has likewise been used as a water supply, a source of power, and a natural aqueduct for water from Wales.

[86] The Ches. Brine Pumping (Compensation for Subsidence) Act, 1952, followed the recommendations of the Weekes Report, 1934, in amending the limits of areas prone to subsidence originally defined in an Act of 1891: J. F. N. Collins, *Salt: A Policy for Control of Salt Extraction in Ches.* 26–7.

[87] e.g. J. Hemingway, *Hist. Chester*, i. 430–1. Wells can be seen within the confines of Beeston castle.

[88] *Geol. Nantwich and Whitchurch*, 82.

[89] R. J. Ireland, 'Hist. of Groundwater Devt. in NW. Ches.' (paper presented to Liverpool Univ. School of Exten-

sion Studies conference on groundwater, 10 Nov. 1984), 8.

[90] Yields are recorded as follows: Wilmslow Sandstone Formation: up to 50,000 gall. per hour; shallow drift (sand or gravel) wells: up to 2,800; Mercia Mudstone Group, including Tarporley Siltstone: up to 1,000; Millstone Grit (rough rock): up to 20,000. *Geol. Nantwich and Whitchurch*, 104; *Geol. Macclesfield*, 268.

[91] *Geol. Macclesfield*, 190–1.

[92] Freeman and others, *Lancs., Ches., and Isle of Man*, 68 and fig. 15; G. Unwin, A. Holme, and G. Taylor, *Samuel Oldknow and the Arkwrights*.

BUILDING MATERIALS AND FUEL

Ubiquitous woodlands ensured a plentiful supply of building materials and fuel.[93] The continuing use of timber in building resulted in a high proportion of timber-framed structures, particularly in the south. Local clays were used for daub and for making bricks. Where Chester Pebble Beds or the Helsby Sandstone Formation occur at or near the surface, red and pink sandstone has been extensively used for all types of building, the larger quarries, as at Runcorn, supplying first-class stone to Liverpool. Similarly, Carboniferous sandstones, flags, and gritstones have been exploited in east Cheshire, for example at Kerridge and Tegg's Nose quarries near Macclesfield, providing a wide range of building materials as well as millstones. Some of the finest stone is that which has been subjected to mineralization, possibly during the Alpine orogeny, often with barytes, giving the stone a desirable hardness and an elegantly distinctive surface texture.

Fuel supplies were traditionally obtained from deciduous woodland and from peat mosses. Small coal seams in the upper strata of the Millstone Grit series provided useful but restricted coal supplies in the Pennine foothills and were exploited from adits and small bell pits, some of which remain visible on the moorland slopes near Wildboarclough. By the late 17th century timber resources had been so depleted by salt-pan owners and shipbuilders that a search for coal supplies began in central Cheshire.[94] All that was found was rock salt, a discovery which was to have profound effect on the future development of central Cheshire but did nothing to relieve the demand for fuel, which had to be imported from south Lancashire by barge.[95] Easily accessible coal seams in folded and faulted Carboniferous rocks at Stockport, Poynton, and Mow Cop in east Cheshire were exploited during the 19th century and supplied growing industrial centres in Manchester, north-east Cheshire, and the Midlands. Many seams were worked out, while others proved too faulted or too thin for exploitation, so that in the 20th century coal output from Cheshire gradually declined.[96]

MINERALS

The rock salt proved at Marbury north of Northwich during the search for deeply buried coal was part of the Northwich Halite Formation; its discovery marked the beginning of 18th- and 19th-century industrial development. Salt is pre-eminent among the mineral deposits of Cheshire, and its ease of exploitation is attributable in part to the effect of geological faulting and tilting followed by surface erosion during the Tertiary period, which had the overall effect of bringing the saliferous beds nearer the surface. Glacial processes removed more of the Triassic strata by further erosion and finally over wide areas sealed off the soluble beds with a layer of impervious till, leaving the saltfield in approximately its present form.

The salt trade may have flourished from pre-Roman times, and established routeways are known to have existed. It was extensively active in Norman times. Exploitation was essentially small-scale and involved evaporation of brine obtained

[93] J. Beck, *Tudor Ches.* 34, 58; W. H. Chaloner, 'Salt in Ches. 1600–1870', *T.L.C.A.S.* lxxi. 61; Freeman and others, *Lancs., Ches., and Isle of Man*, 53; B. G. Auty, 'Charcoal Ironmasters of Ches. and Lancs.' *T.H.S.L.C.* cix. 71–124; Bott and Williams, *Man's Imprint on Ches.* 24.

[94] Beck, *Tudor Ches.* 57–8; *T.L.C.A.S.* lxxi. 66.
[95] Coal has since been proved at a depth exceeding 3,000 m. in central Ches.: *Petrol. NW. Europe*, 65 (fig. 3).
[96] *Geol. Stockport and Knutsford*, 114; *Geol. Macclesfield*, 263–4.

from saline springs, in small timber-fired pans. Expansion in the 18th and 19th centuries was closely linked with growing maritime activities in the Mersey estuary and with improved transport along the new canals, providing much wider trade links and high profits. New brine pits were sunk and new salthouses built at an unprecedented rate, transforming urban and rural landscapes in much of central Cheshire. The industrial development caused subsidence of buildings, flooding, the formation of large flashes, and a desolate and ravaged landscape, all owing their origin to excessive and indiscriminate extraction of salt and brine and to the inability to dispose of waste materials derived from the manufacture of salt and associated chemicals. Development of the industry was based at first on an extension of the old brine evaporation process to produce salt in greater quantities as the expanding port of Liverpool, accessible by barges on the canalized river Weaver, provided new and profitable markets outside the British Isles. Later developments saw the introduction of the heavy chemical industry of the mid Mersey valley near Runcorn and Widnes, on which the area was dependent in the late 20th century.[97]

Associated with post-Triassic faulting, copper ores and to a lesser extent lead and cobalt were deposited probably in Tertiary times in the Wilmslow, Bulkeley Hill, and Helsby Sandstone Formations by circulating hydrothermal fluids, the principal localities being at Alderley Edge, Mottram St. Andrew, and Bickerton. Although it is possible that ores were extracted in Roman and earlier times, there is no unequivocal evidence of mining before the late 17th century; several individuals attempted to work and extend the mines, including specialists from Germany. Activity reached a zenith in the mid 19th century, but most of the accessible ore in the narrow lodes was worked out and the mines closed, leaving as visible evidence only adits and an old boiler-house chimney at Bickerton.[98]

Widespread sand and gravel resources are a direct result of the suites of glacial deposits which accumulated in association with a fluctuating ice margin.[99] Together with adjacent parts of Shropshire, Flintshire, and Lancashire, Cheshire can claim some of the most important reserves in Britain, and conservation precautions are necessary to prevent scenic and agricultural despoliation after extraction.[1] The purer silica sands at Chelford and Moore are in demand as refractory and moulding materials; some soft silica sands are also obtained from poorly cemented sandstones, as in the Mouldsworth area. Particularly large sand quarries have worked thick outwash sequences in the Beeston gap and near Delamere station, where a reputed esker has slowly been erased, while quarries in glacial lake sands at Chelford and Sandiway have yielded datable organic material which has helped the interpretation of Pleistocene history in the north-west.[2]

Glacial clay deposits, especially when relatively free of clasts, have been the basic raw material for local brickworks, many in use until the 20th century but then superseded by national suppliers. Those at Hoole, Tattenhall, and Wallasey all at some time contributed significant archaeological or geological evidence. Brickworks near Hooton remained potentially viable in 1984.[3] Tiles and various types of

[97] Salt production in Roman and later times is described below; treatment of the later development of the salt and chemical industries is reserved for another volume. See *Hist. of Co. Palatine of Chester: Short Bibliog. and Guide to Sources*, ed. B. E. Harris, 33–4.

[98] *Geol. Nantwich and Whitchurch*, 56–9, 98–9; H. Dewey and T. Eastwood, *Copper Ores of Midlands, Wales, Lake Dist. and Isle of Man* (Mem. Geol. Surv., Mineral Resources, xxx); *Geol. Stockport and Knutsford*, 121–2; G. Warrington,

'Copper Mines of Alderley Edge and Mottram St. Andrew, Ches.' *J.C.A.S.* lxiv. 47–73.

[99] M. A. Paul, 'Supraglacial Landsystem', *Glacial Geol.* ed. N. Eyles, 71–90.

[1] Collins, *Ches. Minerals Local Plan: Written Statement*, 21.

[2] *Geol. Stockport and Knutsford*, 122–3; *Geol. Nantwich and Whitchurch*, 90, 103; *Geol. Macclesfield*, 266–8; *Nature*, ccvii. 704–6.

[3] Collins, *Ches. Minerals Local Plan: Written Statement*, 99.

earthenware have also been produced throughout the county, using both glacial clays and Mercia Mudstones.[4]

As elsewhere in Britain, prospectors were active in the 1980s in the search for untapped reserves of coal and hydrocarbons, using both seismic survey and borehole probe methods. Economically viable supplies of coal were thought to exist in the Mersey and Dee valleys, and licences for exploitation and production of hydrocarbons were granted within the county.[5]

AGRICULTURE

The spreads of heavy till are one of Cheshire's greatest assets. That glacial deposit forms the parent material of the clay or clay loam soils which support some of the best known grassland pastures in the world.[6] Although inherently difficult to cultivate on account of their tenacious and often stony nature, they produce first-class pasture which can survive summer drought when sandier areas are burnt dry. In 1977 more than 80 per cent of the land area of Cheshire was down to grass.[7] Although water-retentive, most Cheshire tills drain naturally through their extensive fissure system,[8] supplemented artificially by field drainage pipes and ditching. As a result the pastures in such a relatively mild western maritime location can be used for a large proportion of the year. The long history of Cheshire cheese making and trade directly reflects the pastoral potential of the glacial clays.[9]

By contrast, those parts of the county which are characterized by lighter sandy soils, developed both on Triassic sandstones and on glacial outwash sands and gravels, have been easily worked, and their porosity enables them to drain rapidly and dry out quickly in spring for early cropping. The same property, however, means that plant nutrients are quickly leached out and must be replaced with fertilizer if crop yields are to be maintained.[10] Mineral substances so removed may accumulate at a depth of about 0.5 m. to form a hard impermeable layer or 'fox-bench', which must be broken up before deep ploughing is possible. Characteristically in Cheshire the hard 'pan' of sandy podsolic soils has a rusty red colour owing to the presence of iron oxides. Similar 'hungry' soils develop on sandstone outcrops and on soliflucted material at the foot of the sandstone escarpments in mid and east Cheshire. Light, easily worked soils, predominantly in arable use, occur on river terraces which are normally well drained; where peat accumulations are present, particularly in the north of the county, artificial drainage produces a soil of high fertility.[11] By contrast, upland peat soils developed on outcrops of Millstone Grit in the Pennines are acidic with low agricultural potential and support only poor quality permanent pasture. Even with frequent applications of agricultural lime they remain marginal.[12]

[4] *Geol. Nantwich and Whitchurch*, 97; B. A. Hains and A. Hinton, *Brit. Regional Geol.: Central Eng.* 105–6; below, The Roman Period.

[5] Collins, *Ches. Minerals Local Plan: Written Statement*, 86, 121, figs. 15 and 21.

[6] R. R. Furness, 'Intro. to Physical Background and Soils of Ches.' *Proc. N. of Eng. Soils Discussion Group*, xiv. 13.

[7] A. Finn, 'Farming in Ches.' ibid. 1.

[8] Hebblethwaite, 'Devensian Tills', 290–3.

[9] Beck, *Tudor Ches.* 41; D. M. Woodward, *Trade of Eliza-*bethan Chester (Hull Univ. Occasional Papers in Econ. and Soc. Hist.); R. Craig, 'Some Aspects of Trade and Shipping of River Dee in 18th Cent.', *T.H.S.L.C.* cxiv. 99–128; *Chester and River Dee*, ed. A. M. Kennett, 12.

[10] R. R. Furness, 'Soils of Ches.' *Soil Survey Bull.* vi. 29.

[11] *Proc. N. of Eng. Soils Discussion Group*, xiv. 15.

[12] E. S. Simpson, *Agric. in W. Ches.* (Liverpool Univ. Geog. Dept. Research Paper 5), 39.

Marling

The need to modify and improve both heavy and light soils led to the practice of marling, which may date from the 12th century.[13] By 1808 marl was considered 'unquestionably one of the most important of the Cheshire manures . . . found in many parts of England, but in peculiar abundance in Cheshire'.[14] Geologically marl is a clay deposit containing a proportion of lime or calcium carbonate. In Cheshire both calcareous tills[15] with up to 15 per cent of calcium carbonate and non-calcareous marls are present. When calcareous marl is added to clay soil, the lime improves the soil structure by causing flocculation of the clay particles, with enhanced porosity and ease of working. Conversely, when added to sandy soils the resultant mixture of sand and clay particles, termed a 'loam', has a reduced pore content and greater water retention, the lime tending to counteract the natural acidity of podsolic soils. Hence organic and mineral components of the soil are conserved rather than washed out, and soil fertility is enhanced. The effect of marling is both chemical and physical, improving composition, texture, and soil structure. When non-calcareous marls were used the beneficial effect was limited to textural changes. For almost seven centuries, and possibly longer,[16] all types of glacial clays as well as Triassic marls have been exploited, the practice being facilitated by the close juxtaposition of glacial and Triassic sands, clays, and marls. Though a continuous process of infilling has operated since earliest times, the surface of west Cheshire in particular remains pockmarked with old marl pits, often one to each field.[17]

Less convenient until the advent of canal transport, but nonetheless significant, was the burning of limestone in kilns to produce lime, which was done mainly near the outcrops of Carboniferous Limestone in the Pennines but also near the Wirral coast, where the limestone arrived by sea from north Wales.[18] Although the practice lapsed late in the 19th century as chemical fertilizers became available, it retained a counterpart in the fertilizer industry at Winnington.

COMMUNICATION

Lines of communication[19] into and across Cheshire have been influenced by geological, physical, and historical controls of ancient origin. The principal trend is north to south or north-west to south-east, partly attributable to a drainage pattern which evolved in Tertiary times and which may be preserved in greater relief at the sub-drift surface. The present modified form of that river system on the drift-covered surface provided lines of access for early settlers who approached from the north across the Irish Sea, and from the south across the Midland Gap and the low morainic watershed. Of more recent glacial origin are those gaps and gorges, used by early salt traders and livestock drovers, which facilitated east–west movement across the county between Wales and the Pennines.[20] The saltway from Nantwich to Wales was later followed by a road, originally part of the turnpike system in Cheshire, through a gap in the Bickerton Hills. To the north, the course of the Gowy at Beeston is a through-route on the site of a drift-choked glacial

[13] Freeman and others, *Lancs., Ches., and Isle of Man*, 165.

[14] H. Holland, *Gen. View of Agric. of Ches.* 221.

[15] Hebblethwaite, 'Devensian Tills', App. 4, p. 348.

[16] M. F. Thomas, 'Delamere Forest', *Ches. Hist. Newsletter*, Nov. 1976.

[17] See especially O.S. Maps 1/25,000.

[18] Holland, *Agric. of Ches.* 226; O.S. Map 1", sheet 79 (1st edn., 1840) marks limekilns at Thurstaston and Caldy.

[19] Below, The Roman Period: Roads; treatment of the history of communications in Ches. is reserved for a later volume.

[20] *T.L.C.A.S.* liv. 92, pl. 21.

drainage channel, and was followed not only by an early turnpike road but also by Telford's 18th-century canal (for which instability in the soft glacial sands necessitated locks of cast iron), by the 19th-century railway from Crewe to Holyhead, and by the modern Whitchurch–Warrington road. The Chester–Manchester railway uses another glacial channel at Mouldsworth cut through the sandstone ridge, negotiating peaty infilling of iceblock hollows on embankments: the resultant problems are clearly shown where the railway crosses Linmere Moss, 1 km. west of Delamere station, on an embankment (SJ 545 706).

In Wirral, where the summits of a well drained plateau follow the same trend as the high-level trackways of the Mid-Cheshire Ridge, parallel longitudinal 'grooves' initiated by subglacial erosion have been followed by the mid-Wirral motorway. In contrast, the builders of the motorway from Ellesmere Port to Manchester necessarily used the flat peaty marshland of the Mersey estuary; the earlier turnpike engineers had been more cautious, building on soliflucted scree deposits linking Frodsham and Helsby at the foot of the sandstone escarpment. Also on the line of the ice 'grooves' lie the port installations of Liverpool, Wallasey, and Birkenhead, to which much of Cheshire is tributary. Docks bordering the Mersey were easily excavated from 1715 in restricted deposits of till flooring the creeks which occupied the grooves, and adjacent to deep estuarine channels with a high tidal range, in part attributable to their physical evolution.[21] Across the base of the Wirral peninsula the Deva Spillway, a transverse valley which originated at the ice margin, is followed by the 18th-century canal from Chester to Ellesmere Port.

Gorges formed by glacial meltwater in the Pennine foothills of east Cheshire have provided routeways and settlement sites, for example in the Goyt valley at New Mills (Derb.) and Marple and at Broadbottom in the valley of the Etherow. The railway from Macclesfield to Leek (Staffs.) follows a similar channel which at one time drained the proglacial Lake Macclesfield.[22] In south Cheshire the Adderley drainage channel, which carried the meltwaters from proglacial lakes in Cheshire to the Severn across the Whitchurch moraine near Audlem,[23] is followed by road, rail, and canal.

SILTATION OF THE DEE ESTUARY

Most spectacular of the topographical changes of historical times has been the transformation of the Dee estuary. In its early form the sheltered and shallow estuary of the Dee was probably attractive to man, for it lacked the tidal scour of the Mersey. Complaints of silting at Chester were recorded in the Middle Ages; by the 14th century sand and gravel deposits had become a serious problem, for sand and silt accumulation is a natural process in a coastal inlet of that type, receiving sediment-loaded streams from an easily denuded hinterland. Until the 17th century the port of Chester was pre-eminent in the north-west for local and continental trade and included not only outports along the shores of the estuary but also the minor port of Liverpool. Progressive silting and coastline changes along the Wirral coast from Chester to Hoylake are attributable both to physical processes and also to attempts at coastal control, dredging, and straightening of the Dee below Chester.[24]

[21] Freeman and others, *Lancs., Ches., and Isle of Man*, 87.
[22] *Geol. Stockport and Knutsford*, 101–2.
[23] *Geol. Nantwich and Whitchurch*, 75–7.

[24] M. E. Marker, 'The Dee Estuary: Its Progressive Silting and Saltmarsh Development', *Trans. Inst. Brit. Geog.* xlii. 65–71; *Chester and River Dee, passim*.

PHYSIQUE

In Roman times access for the small ships then in use presented no problem as far as Chester, and trade continued to thrive in the medieval period. Siltation progressively affected the channel on the Cheshire side of the estuary, and to accommodate the needs of increasingly large vessels outports along the Wirral shore were established before the 15th century, to be followed in turn by the Old Quay at Neston in the 16th and Denhall and Parkgate in the 18th. The Dee New Cut of the 1730s attempted to restore the waterway to Chester, thus diverting the deep navigable channel from the Cheshire side near Burton to Connah's Quay (Flints.). While seagoing vessels could use the Dee and unload at Chester until the early 20th century, the problem of the estuary itself was exacerbated and tidal reaches on the Cheshire side retreated at an accelerating rate as saltmarsh developed. By the mid 19th century substantial areas of new fertile farmland at Sealand, administratively in Wales, had been reclaimed below the ancient cliff-line which extended from Chester to Burton, thus cutting off completely the old port of Shotwick. In the 1920s the saltmarsh cord grass *Spartina anglica* (Hubbard) first appeared on sand and mud flats along the Wirral coast, its rapid spread finally sealing the fate of Parkgate.[25] Further north, from the mid 19th century, moving sediment in Liverpool Bay resulted in the gradual disappearance of the ancient Hoyle Lake. The mouth of the Mersey, because of its narrow bottleneck shape and resultant tidal scour, has persisted as a deep channel serving the port of Liverpool, but between Runcorn and Ellesmere Port the estuary has experienced infilling comparable to that in the Dee below Chester.[26]

RECREATION

In recent decades, as the physical landscape has become a resource for recreation and pleasure, a natural heritage has become recognized. Within the Peak District National Park the amenity value of the high Pennine slopes, bleak, exposed, infertile, and reluctantly settled, has been realized as the magnificent windswept horizons are appreciated by the inhabitants of the neighbouring conurbations. The ancient forest of Delamere is located on glacial sands admirably suited to light oak woodland; the same hummocky surface, clothed in conifers planted by the Forestry Commission, provides amenities and open space for visitors and residents from adjacent areas. Long distance footpaths, the Gritstone Trail, more than 30 km. from Disley to Rushton (Staffs.), and the Sandstone Trail, more than 50 km. from Frodsham to near Malpas, have provided extended access to the Pennines and the Mid-Cheshire Ridge respectively. Remnants of natural landscape on heaths or in the hills are preserved by national and local bodies as accessible and irreplaceable open spaces. Randomly throughout the county the ravages of 19th-century industrialization and mineral extraction have been remedied and the sites used to advantage for nature reserves and wildlife sanctuaries; examples include the Whitegate Way and Wirral Country Park, following former railway lines, Tegg's Nose Country Park in a former quarry, and Styal Country Park in grounds associated with an industrial settlement. Footpaths along the network of canals provide amenities for walkers and fishermen, while cruising has from the mid 20th century brought some traffic back to the canals.[27]

[25] Newton, *Flora of Ches.* 173; *Jnl. Ecol.* lvi. 795–809. The sequence is demonstrated by successive edns. of O.S. Maps 1″ and 1/50,000.

[26] W. A. Price and M. P. Kendrick, 'Field and Model Investigation into Reasons for Siltation in Mersey Estuary', *Jnl. Inst. Civil Engineers*, xxiv. 473–517.

[27] Some of the sites are described in Ches. County Council, *Out and About in Ches.*

PREHISTORY

HUNTERS AND GATHERERS: THE PALAEOLITHIC AND MESOLITHIC PERIODS

TO 4500 B.C.

LOWER Palaeolithic[1] or Old Stone Age groups from the Continent were exploiting hunting grounds in Britain during the Hoxnian interglacial of the Pleistocene Ice Age around 200,000 years ago, and the earliest hunters may have arrived considerably earlier.[2] At the height of that period temperatures were comparable with those of the present day and a cover of mixed oak forest predominated. The ensuing Wolstonian glaciation may have seen the return of ice as far south as the Severn estuary, and ice covered Cheshire again during the most recent glaciation, the Devensian. The Ipswichian interglacial c. 100,000 years B.P., on the other hand, allowed the return of vegetation of temperate type, and shorter 'interstadials' within the periods of glaciation witnessed milder conditions. Such an interstadial during the last glacial period, characterized by a type of northern coniferous forest, has been identified in Cheshire by pollen analysis at Chelford, Withington, and dated c. 59,000 b.c. by radiocarbon measurement.[3]

No evidence has yet come to light of human activity in Cheshire during those early periods, although there is abundant evidence from south-eastern England, principally in the form of flint 'handaxes' (multi-purpose tools):[4] perhaps the erosive effects of the last glaciation and subsequent deposition have contributed to the lack. Conversely, the distribution of known material may reflect a preference for lower ground and the exploitation of flint resources in the manufacture of large tools. Cave occupation, if only on a seasonal level, is known from Pontnewydd (Denb.) and Cresswell Crags (Derb.),[5] and it may be supposed that Lower and Middle Palaeolithic hunters were ranging west of Cheshire too.

Pollen analysis from Mother Grundy's Parlour (Derb.), a cave site east of the Pennines, suggests a landscape virtually devoid of trees during the last full glacial, and herb and moss tundra also prevailed in Cheshire when it was not under ice. The period from c. 12,000 B.C., however, saw an improvement in climate with an increase in trees and shrubs as the ice sheets melted and receded. At Mother Grundy's Parlour herbs and grasses were substantially replaced by birch, juniper,

[1] The help and advice of Miss G. Chitty, Mr. J. V. H. Eames, Mr. A. Fergusson, Mr. P. Hough, Mr. R. Loveday, Miss F. Lynch, Miss R. McNeil, Dr. E. Morris, Dr. S. Needham, Mr. D. F. Petch, Mr. K. Smith, Mr. R. J. Turner, Mr. P. Wagstaff, Mr. J. Walker, and Mr. S. R. Williams in the preparation of this article is gratefully acknowledged.

[2] D. A. Roe, *Lower and Middle Palaeolithic Periods in Brit.* 270; A. Morrison, *Early Man in Brit. and Ireland*, 32–8. Dates in the text, except for the Chelford date below, are quoted in calendar years A.D./B.C. Those derived from radiocarbon measurements are calibrated by reference to dendrochronological scales which extend back to c. 7,000 years B.P., to take account of a distortion in the radiocarbon time-scale arising from past variations in the rate of production of Carbon 14 in the atmosphere. Uncalibrated determinations have been cited as a.d./b.c.: cf. J. Klein, J. C. Lerman, P. E. Damon, and E. K. Ralph, 'Calibration of Radiocarbon Dates', *Radiocarbon*, xxiv (2), 103–50.

[3] I. M. Simpson and R. G. West, 'Stratigraphy and Palaeobotany of a Late Pleistocene Organic Deposit at Chelford, Ches.' *New Phytol.* lvii. 239–50.

[4] D. A. Roe, *Gaz. of Brit. Lower and Middle Palaeolithic Sites* (C.B.A. Research Rep. viii).

[5] H. S. Green, *Pontnewydd Cave*; P. A. Mellars, 'Palaeolithic and Mesolithic', *Brit. Prehist.* ed. C. Renfrew, 55–6, 65.

willow, and thermophilous trees during the late glacial and early post-glacial period.[6] A framework for post-glacial climatic and vegetational change in Cheshire has been provided by pollen evidence and radiocarbon dating at Hatchmere in Norley.[7] On a human level, radiocarbon dating together with a succession of artefact assemblages shows a long, if interrupted, use of Mother Grundy's Parlour from the Palaeolithic period to the Mesolithic.[8] The Parlour is only one of a number of cave sites which show such recurrent occupation: nearer the Cheshire border, caves at Dowel Hill and Fox Hole (Derb.), and Ossum's Cave, Elder Bush, and Thor's Fissure (Staffs.) were used on a seasonal basis from the late glacial to the post-glacial period by hunting parties who were perhaps following herds of deer to the higher ground in summer.[9]

The meltwater released from the retreating ice sheets caused a rise in sea level and the final isolation of Britain from the Continent c. 6000 B.C. Precipitation increased, attributable to the establishment of oceanic circulation around Britain, and with the spread of woodland and the establishment of deer, boar, and aurochs, low-lying areas provided a rich resource of game with winter camps attracted to the shores of many lakes and ponds.[10]

A changing environment might be expected to provoke a change in tool production. Nevertheless the distinction between the late Upper Palaeolithic and the Early Mesolithic is not clear cut. Blades struck from flint cores and scraping tools for butchery and the working of organic materials tend to become smaller. Very small flints (microliths) and their waste products (micro-burins) characterize later Mesolithic industries and seem to have functioned as points and barbs, set with resin into the shafts of arrows, spears, and harpoons. The Mesolithic period also saw the introduction of the tranchet axe, hafted in wood, a precursor of a long succession of hafted heavy stone implements.[11]

In Cheshire the Mesolithic period is best represented as an element in the very dense concentration of upland Pennine sites above 370 m. between Rishworth Moor and Broomhead Moor (both Yorks. W.R.). The majority of finds, which include blades, scrapers, microliths, cores, and waste products, have been located as surface concentrations in eroded patches of moorland. A lower, but prominent, location at c. 195 m. at Alderley Edge, where sandstone outcrops from the Pennines to overlook the Weaver basin, has produced a series of blades, flakes, scrapers, and cores in chert and flint. West of Alderley an excavation at Tatton Mere has demonstrated low-lying occupation on the banks of what was once a marshy stream. Microliths, scrapers, awls, and cores are the principal components of the assemblage. Nearby, at Tatton village 1 km. to the north, activity involving the use of three hearths has produced a radiocarbon date in the 6th millennium B.C. The evidence from central Cheshire is sparse. Nevertheless, several worked flints including small scalene triangles and rods, retouched scrapers, and borers have been recovered from garden soil and as surface finds after ploughing in the Ashton (by Tarvin) area, below the western slope of the central sandstone ridge at c. 35 m. Further north, at Frodsham, a number of locations on the ridge at c. 120 m. have produced Mesolithic material as surface finds. Rod forms, retouched blades, scrapers, cores, and waste material are represented. A further aspect of the hunter-gatherer economy for

[6] J. B. Campbell, *Upper Palaeolithic of Brit: A Study of Man and Nature in Late Ice Age*, ii, fig. 76.

[7] *Radiocarbon*, xvii. 39–40, 303–4.

[8] Campbell, *Upper Palaeolithic*, i. 173.

[9] Ibid. 173–5; ii, map 41.

[10] J. G. Evans, *Environment of Early Man in Brit. Isles*, 75, 86–7.

[11] *Gaz. of Mesolithic Sites in England and Wales*, ed. J. J. Wymer (C.B.A. Research Rep. xx), fig. 2.

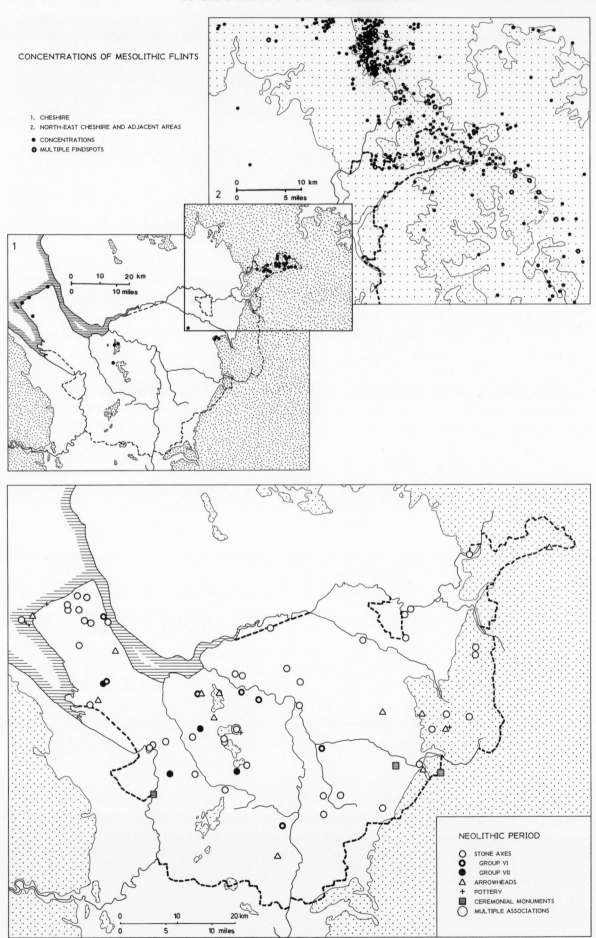

CONCENTRATIONS OF MESOLITHIC FLINTS

1. CHESHIRE
2. NORTH-EAST CHESHIRE AND ADJACENT AREAS
● CONCENTRATIONS
◉ MULTIPLE FINDSPOTS

NEOLITHIC PERIOD

○ STONE AXES
◉ GROUP VI
● GROUP VII
△ ARROWHEADS
+ POTTERY
▦ CEREMONIAL MONUMENTS
◯ MULTIPLE ASSOCIATIONS

Fig. 5. (Contours at 400 ft. and 800 ft.)

which evidence becomes available during the Mesolithic period is the exploitation of the resources of the coastline, perhaps in part a consequence of the spread of forest cover inland but perhaps also reflecting the transitory nature of Mesolithic man, whereby the potential of a range of environments was used to the full at different seasons of the year. Concentrations of Mesolithic flintwork have been recovered on the Wirral peninsula at Hilbre Point, Thurstaston, and Red Noses in New Brighton.[12]

Flint was used for making tools for a considerable period beyond the Mesolithic, and several stray finds which appear to lack diagnostic features are known from Cheshire. Their chronological position remains uncertain, as must further refinement of the chronology of the accepted Mesolithic assemblages noted above. With the exception of Tatton Mere, none of the groups can be regarded as a closed find from a stratified archaeological context. Although early partial excavation has sometimes taken place, as at Castle Rock Field, Alderley Edge, c. 1900, most of the material has been recovered as surface scatters.[13] Deliberate selection of the more diagnostic forms inhibits assessment on the basis of a full range of products, and when manifestly later artefacts, such as a barbed and tanged arrowhead and a polished stone axe at Ashton, are included, the integrity of an assemblage as the product of a single industry comes into question. Sometimes, too, the exact provenance of flints subsequently acquired by museums is no longer known.

GAZETTEER OF MESOLITHIC ASSEMBLAGES

ALDERLEY

ALDERLEY, NETHER. Alderley Edge, sandstone outcrop reaching 195 m. (a) Castle Rock Field (SJ 856 779), partially excavated 1894–1905. Blades (highest frequency), scrapers, cores, flakes, borers. (b) centred SJ 860 776. Miscellaneous flints including flakes 'tiny' and 'large'; cores, scrapers, and a 'hammer head' from various locations. (c) SJ 851 776. Flint flakes and blades found 1904 after erosion from rock ledge. Finds in Manchester Mus., Grosvenor Mus., and private possession.[14]

FRODSHAM

(a) Harrol Edge (SJ 522 754). Cores, rod-like flakes, and waste material from area of c. 0.5 ha. on northern central ridge. Finds in Grosvenor Mus. (b) SJ 51 75. Retouched rods, borers, scrapers, and retouched blades from various locations on the sandstone ridge S. of Frodsham. Most finds in Grosvenor Mus., some in private possession.[15]

KIRBY, WEST

(a) SJ 203 885. Various collections from coastline at Hilbre Point and Red Rocks. Cores, blades, flakes, obliquely blunted point, and notched blade. Finds in Grosvenor Mus. and Manchester Mus.[16] (b) SJ 231 906. Possible Mesolithic material from coastline at Dove Point, Meols. Finds in Merseyside County Mus.

MOTTRAM IN LONGDENDALE

HOLLINGWORTH. (a) Boar Flat (SK 010 990). Partial excavation on moorland. Blades, flakes, cores, microliths, scrapers, and waste; in Cambridge Mus. of Archaeology and Ethnography, Manchester Mus., and Tolson Memorial Mus., Huddersfield.[17] (b) SK 017 998. Cores, microliths, retouched flakes, and waste from eroded patch above Ogden Clough; in private possession.[18]
STAYLEY: Brushes Moor. Collections from a number of locations and limited excavation. Cores,

---

[12] Where no other reference is given, details of finds and published sources are to be found in the gazetteers below.
[13] Fig. 5.　　　　[14] *T.L.C.A.S.* xxiii. 17–20.
[15] *J.C.A.S.* xl. 63; *Ches. Arch. Bull.* iii. 59.
[16] *Gaz. of Mesolithic Sites*, 33.
[17] Ibid. 34.　　　　[18] Ibid.

blades, flakes, scrapers, retouched flakes, microliths, and waste. Finds in Manchester Mus. and Tolson Memorial Mus., Huddersfield.[19]

TINTWISTLE. (a) Arnfield Moor (SK 024 994). Retouched flakes, microlith, and waste from eroded patch; in private possession.[20] (b) Crowden. i. Butterley Cross (SE 089 013). Blades and flakes from moorland erosion. ii. Hey Clough (SE 085 008). Blades, flakes, and microliths from eroded patch. iii. Heydon Moor (centred SE 103 022). Blades, flakes, and cores from eroded patches in area of Britland Edge Hill. iv. Flats in vicinity of Crowden Great Brook and Oaken Clough (centred SE 058 010). Blades, flakes, and cores; small number of scrapers and microliths. v. Westend Moss (SE 083 012). Blades and flakes from erosion in peat. Finds all in private possession.[21] (c) Ironbower Moss (SK 118 999). Core and blades; in private possession.[22] (d) Longdendale. Retouched flake, microlith, and core from peat erosion; in private possession.[23] (e) Little Clough (SE 059 037–060 035, exact location unknown). Core and blades; in private possession.[24] (f) Low Moor (SK 020 970). Microlith; in Merseyside County Mus.[25] (g) Oaken Clough (SE 054 011). Retouched flakes, microliths, cores, and scraper from peat erosion; in private possession.[26] (h) Ormes Moor (SE 029 004). Blades, flakes, core, and microlith from moorland erosion; in private possession.[27] (j) Red Ratches (SE 056 037). Microliths; in private possession.[28] (k) Shiny Brook (SE 062 007). Blades, flakes; in private possession.[29] (l) Tintwistle Knarr (SK 030 990). Blades, flakes, microliths, cores, scraper, tranchet axe, sharpening flake, and waste; in Tolson Memorial Mus., Huddersfield. (m) Tooley Shaw Moor (SE 092 029). Cores, blades, and flakes from erosion of moorland; in private possession.[30] (n) Tooley Shaw Moss (SE 085 035). Blades, flakes, microliths, and retouched flake; in private possession.[31] (o) Torside Reservoir (SK 072 989). Flint scatter; in private possession.[32] (p) Woodhead Reservoir (SK 090 996–094 999). Flint scatter; in private possession.[33]

ROSTHERNE

TATTON. Tatton Mere (SJ 757 803). Microliths including obliquely blunted points, scrapers, awls, a possible sandstone rubber, a saw, an axe sharpening flake, and cores from excavation of mereside site, possibly a marshy stream valley in antiquity. Finds in private possession.[34]

TARVIN

ASHTON (c. SJ 50 69). Miscellaneous flints from garden and plough soil over a wide area below western scarp of central sandstone ridge. Small scalene triangles and rod forms, scrapers, and borers but also later material mixed. Finds in Grosvenor Mus.[35]

THURSTASTON

SJ 243 846. Blades, flakes, and waste from area rising above coastline. Finds in Merseyside County Mus.[36]

WALLASEY

New Brighton, Red Noses (SJ 299 940). Blades, flakes, and waste from coastline. Some finds in Merseyside County Mus. but lost in bombing, others in Manchester Mus.[37]

EARLY AGRICULTURALISTS: THE NEOLITHIC PERIOD
4500–2000 B.C.

CHRONOLOGY, ASSOCIATIONS, AND DISTRIBUTION

Forest cover extended over most of Cheshire, as over much of Britain below *c.* 600 m., at the beginning of the Neolithic. The earliest farming colonists are likely, on the evidence of radiocarbon dating, to have crossed to Britain during the 5th

[19] *Gaz. of Mesolithic Sites*, 34.
[20] Ibid.
[21] Ibid. 33.
[22] *N. Derb. Arch. Cttee. Rec.* (1914).
[23] *Gaz. of Mesolithic Sites*, 34.
[24] *N. Derb. Arch. Cttee. Rec.* (1926).
[25] *Gaz. of Mesolithic Sites*, 34.
[26] Ibid.
[27] Ibid.
[28] Ibid.
[29] Ibid.
[30] Ibid. 33.
[31] Ibid. 35.
[32] *N. Derb. Arch. Cttee. Rec.* (1914).
[33] Ibid. (1916).
[34] *Ches. Arch. Bull.* ix. 95.
[35] *J.C.A.S.* xxxv. 53–8, 60–2.
[36] *Gaz. of Mesolithic Sites*, 34.
[37] Ibid. 35; *T.H.S.L.C.* xiv. 123–30.

millennium B.C., although it was not, perhaps, until the earlier part of the 4th millennium that forest clearance and the growing of crops began to make much impact on the environment.[38] On lighter, well drained soils permanent clearances were established, while small temporary clearances (*landnam*) of woodland, followed by short-term cultivation, abandonment, and regeneration, have been identified through the analysis of tree, cereal, grass, and other pollen grains contained in differential proportions within sequential deposits. Such a *landnam* has been identified in the Hatchmere (Norley) lake pollen sequence between *c.* 4200 and 3500 B.C.[39] Clearance of woodland is known during the Mesolithic period and a symbiotic relationship between man and animals may already have been achieved; the indigenous population may therefore have made a significant contribution to the new developments which led to the proliferation of settled farming communities.

The distinguishing characteristics of Neolithic society include mixed farming, with cattle particularly important but with sheep or goats and pigs also represented, and cereal cultivation. Ceremonial and funerary monuments became permanent features of the landscape. The manufacture of pottery vessels, plain at first in Britain but becoming increasingly decorated, arrived with the introduction of agriculture. Flint continued to be used for a variety of tools, among which leaf-shaped arrowheads are characteristic of the period. A new development in stone technology is represented by axes flaked or pecked to the desired shape and completed by grinding to a smooth finish and sharp cutting edge. Rocks were selected for their resilience and flaking properties, and a relatively small number of 'factories', where such rocks could be exploited, produced considerable quantities which were widely distributed.[40]

A lack of firm associations from Cheshire hinders the interpretation of such types of artefact as leaf arrowheads and polished stone axes, which enjoyed popularity over a long period during which they changed little. Nevertheless the Bridestones chambered tomb indicates activity in the area during the Earlier Neolithic, and some at least of the arrowheads and axes may probably be assigned to that period. Other examples may belong to a later phase. If the implied associations of stone axes with shafthole axes at Birkenhead and Beeston are genuine, a late use of the former type may be represented. The use of Group XV greywacke in making one of the Delamere axes found near the hillfort of Kelsborrow Castle may again suggest a late date. Later Neolithic activity in Cheshire is confirmed by the occurrence of decorated Peterborough pottery at Meols and Gawsworth and by the use of Grooved Ware in a funerary context at Eddisbury Hill. Those associations are considered more fully below.

The role of stone axes in clearing land for settlement is disputed. Pollen analysis has indicated a significant decline in the relative proportion of elm after *c.* 3000 b.c. (*c.* 3700 B.C.), and while the decline was first attributed to climatic changes, it is now, together with the opening up of the forest canopy and the spread of grassland and heath, considered to be anthropogenic.[41] The fate of the elm in particular has been explained by the usefulness of its leaves as cattle fodder. In the Lake District, evidence of elm decline and finds of isolated axes have been correlated, but in areas where clearance and domestic settlement are indicated axe finds are infrequent. An extreme reading of this correlation suggests that axes may have played little part in

[38] I. F. Smith, 'The Neolithic', *Brit. Prehist.* ed. C. Renfrew, 101, 103, fig. 12.

[39] *Radiocarbon*, xvii. 39–40, 303–4. Uncalibrated dates are 3319±80 b.c. and 2743±90 b.c.

[40] W. A. Cummins, 'Neolithic Stone Axes, Distribution, and Trade', *Stone Axe Studies* (C.B.A. Research Rep. xxiii), 5–12.

[41] Evans, *Environment of Early Man*, 113.

clearance itself, being used primarily for lopping elm branches for fodder; what is clear is that they could be used and lost well away from contemporary sites.[42] It may be significant that the distribution of Neolithic axes in Cheshire,[43] with few exceptions, avoids the lighter, more freely draining sands and gravels of the central ridge and western Pennine slope which might be supposed to be the more favoured areas for Neolithic settlement.

Those axes which are known from the central ridge have all, except for the Tarporley axe, been found at or near prominent topographical features which became centres of later prehistoric activity. A polished axe was found near the hillfort at Helsby and a leaf arrowhead was recovered from washed-out soil in a gully on the slope. Two polished stone axes have been found on separate occasions near the hillfort of Kelsborrow Castle. Two axes were found, with an Early Bronze Age shafthole axe, on the same occasion in draining a field near Beeston Castle. The 13th-century castle is sited on a prominent sandstone crag: excavations have demonstrated Late Bronze Age activity near the summit and have revealed a defensive line, of prehistoric date, pre-dating the castle's outer bailey. Five stone axes were discovered in a hoard at the foot of Castle Ditch hillfort, Eddisbury: a cremation cemetery involving the use of Late Neolithic Grooved Ware had earlier been uncovered during quarrying below the same site. Such associations may well be fortuitous; nevertheless the occurrence of Grooved Ware and stone axes at Eddisbury, types known to be associated regularly at ceremonial sites elsewhere, suggests that Eddisbury Hill may probably have acted as a focus for Late Neolithic communities on the northern part of the central ridge, while the Earlier Bronze Age certainly saw marked activity in the area. The details of finds from the central ridge, the clustering of axes as at Eddisbury and Beeston, the circumstantial association of axes with later, defended enclosures, and the location of those sites in areas of more favourable subsoil, suggest a 'home base' in contrast to the isolated finds of axes in clay areas.

A concentration of Neolithic finds in north Wirral, mostly polished axes but including small flintwork and a single sherd of Peterborough Ware from the coastline at Meols, attests activity in that area. That the coastline was formerly wooded is known from the observation of forest peat beds, particularly at Meols, over a long period.[44] Clearance of the woodland, either through human activity or through the deposition of blown sand, probably resulted in the stabilization of fixed dune pasture. Nevertheless at Meols a regeneration of woodland seems to have occurred before the Roman period.

SETTLEMENT AND BURIAL

Structural evidence of Neolithic activity in Cheshire is scarce. A moderate distribution of flint and stone implements hints at the presence of farming communities, while a very small quantity of pottery from three locations suggests settlement in their vicinity. Perhaps the most tangible structural evidence is the group of post and stake holes and the pit containing charred barley and a single grain of oats at Tatton, radiocarbon dated to the later 4th millennium B.C.[45] Elsewhere in Britain

[42] Evans, *Environment of Early Man*, 128; R. Bradley, 'Prehistorians and Pastoralists in Neolithic and Bronze Age Eng.' *World Arch.* iv (2), 200.
[43] Fig. 5.
[44] G. Chitty, *Wirral Rural Fringes Survey Rep*.
[45] N. J. Higham, 'Excavations at Tatton', *Ches. Arch. Bull*. ix. 89. Uncalibrated dates are 2530±60 b.c. (HAR 5146), 2590±70 b.c. (HAR 4495).

structures associated with purely domestic occupation have proved similarly elusive, though, as in Cheshire, substantial ceremonial and funerary monuments provide evidence of Neolithic construction. Considerable communal effort, which may also imply nearby settlement, was needed for building them. Three such sites have been claimed in Cheshire: the chambered long cairn at Bridestones House, Congleton, a mortuary enclosure in the Dee valley near Churton, and a possible long barrow or cairn at Loachbrook Farm, Somerford.

The Bridestones (SJ 906 622)

The Bridestones comprise an important though dilapidated example of a chambered long cairn.[46] Impressive and often elaborate constructions of monumental nature were erected in many parts of Britain from early in the Neolithic period. They are generally regarded as tombs, and indeed burial, often involving a number of individuals, is always an element in their make-up. Both the number and the character of the burials vary, and such a monument was perhaps equally important as a focus for related ceremonies. Regional and chronological variations also appear, with a tendency towards increasing elaboration. In southern and eastern Britain long earthen mounds predominate, while in the west and north stone construction was the rule, with megalithic chambers covered by round or long mounds of stone rubble (cairns). Many chambered cairns underwent modification and enlargement over a long period of use:[47] in its present condition, however, the stages of development of the Bridestones cannot be isolated.

The site is at c. 275 m. on the west flank of the Cloud, a ridge which forms a prominent northern extension of Biddulph Moor detached from the Pennines proper. The contour turns east–west in the immediate vicinity of the cairn where the ridge falls to a slight saddle: the general trend is a fall away to the west, affording extensive views. The cairn entrance faces rising ground. The final form of the monument appears to have comprised the following elements: (i) an elaborate crescentic forecourt defined by orthostats with two free-standing stones set within the forecourt and two further stones beyond the eastern open end aligned on the chamber; (ii) a rectangular chamber 4.9 m. by 1.8 m. by approximately 1.5 m. high internally, immediately west of the forecourt, divided into two segments by a septal slab pierced by a small porthole, and capped by long flat stones; (iii) a small chamber '2½ yd. by 2½ yd. by 3 ft. 2 in. high', '55 yd. distant' from the main chamber; (iv) a possible third chamber; and (v) a very long cairn '120 yd. long and 12 yd. broad' covering the chambers and almost certainly on an east–west alignment from the forecourt. Elements (iii)–(v) no longer survive.

The earliest description of the Bridestones is an account based on observations following the removal in 1764 of several hundred tons of stone from the cairn during the construction of Dial Lane turnpike road.[48] It is the sole source of information on the elaborate nature of the forecourt, on the subsidiary chambers, and on the monumental size of the cairn, which, if the measurements are correct, was one of the longest in Britain. It also provides important information on the contents of the main chamber. A layer of broken stones 2½ in. thick overlay a 6-in. deep deposit of pounded white stones, the upper portion black-tinged. The floor thus formed was covered with a 2-in. thickness of ashes, oak charcoal,

[46] Fig. 6; below, plate.
[47] J. X. W. P. Corcoran, 'Multiperiod Construction and Origins of Chambered Long Cairn in Western Brit.'
Prehist. Man in Wales and the West, ed. F. Lynch and C. Burgess, 31–63.
[48] T. Malbon in H. Rowlands, *Mona Antiqua Restaurata*, 319–20.

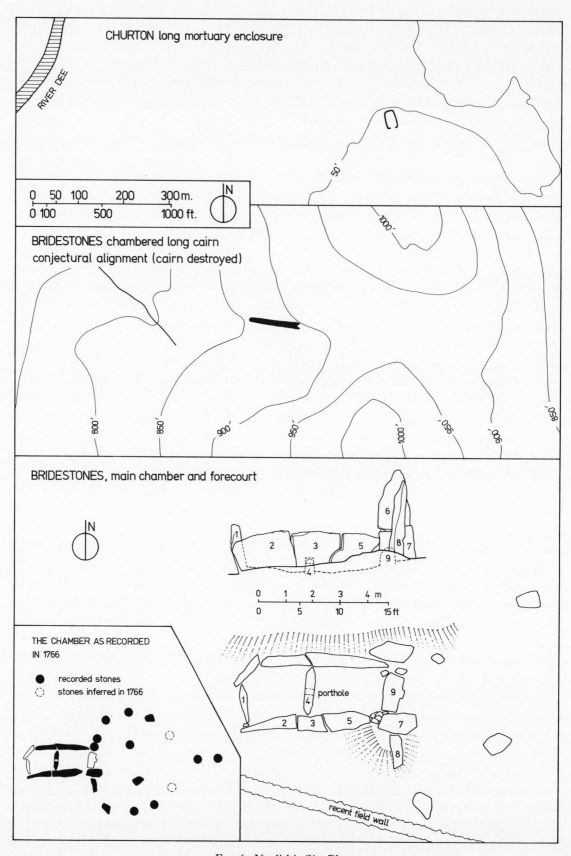

FIG. 6. Neolithic Site Plans.

and very small and indeterminate bone fragments. Ashes and oak charcoal were also recognized near the central monoliths. The north and south walls of the chamber were originally constructed of single large orthostats which had each fractured in two. The rear orthostats may well have been concealed by cairn material at the time, and the blocking of the entrance was not mentioned. The capstones of the main chamber had been removed before 1766, and by 1843 further damage had made it impossible to plot more than four or possibly five stones of the façade and portal or to record the cairn, although its prior existence was known.[49]

The southern orthostat of the chamber was further split by fire in 1823, and by 1854 the porthole stone was reduced to a height of a few inches, though temporarily restored in 1877.[50] In 1936–7 limited excavation was carried out in the area of the main chamber and forecourt, attended by some reconstruction of the monument.[51] Some previous excavation had apparently taken place within the chamber, which had become filled with debris from a nearby cottage. Evidence was found of rough cobbling in the forecourt and of a flat triangular stone centrally placed with charcoal immediately adjacent. A large fallen stone across the entrance to the chamber which appears to correspond to one described in the 19th century in that position[52] was erected, with little apparent justification, on the stump of the southern portal stone. A further fallen stone was uncovered, slightly removed from the north-eastern angle of the chamber, and repositioned to correspond to its southern counterpart.[53] The reconstruction appears over-elaborate in view of the strong possibility that the two fallen stones represent the original partners, on the north side, of the existing southern pair. On the same occasion the fallen fragment of the chamber's southern orthostat was re-erected.

The depredation and, to some extent, the reconstruction that have attended the monument hinder close analysis. Nevertheless it is reasonably clear that constructional details and the arrangement of forecourt and chamber have affinities with northern Irish Sea traditions of megalithic architecture and ritual. A crescentic forecourt of orthostats fronting a trapezoidal cairn is a feature of the latest elaborate 'Clyde cairns' of western Scotland and of the 'court cairns' of northern Ireland whose architecture may have influenced the Clyde tombs. Monoliths have been recognized within the forecourts of some of those tombs, for example at Browndod (Co. Antrim) and beyond the forecourt at Ballyalton (Co. Down).[54] On the evidence of depressions on the projected eastern circumference, the arcing stone settings at the Bridestones have been thought to have originally completed a circle. A freestanding stone beyond the cairn façade at Carn Ban, Arran, has similarly suggested a complete circle, partly recessed into the cairn's façade and partly free-standing beyond it.[55] In their most elaborate form some Irish cairns incorporate fully circular courts, although enclosed within the body of the mound or the recurved horns of the façade. The Bridestones chamber, entered directly from the forecourt between portal stones and across a low sill, is in the tradition of the Clyde cairns, having a septal slab butting against the chamber walls, whereas the builders of the Irish court cairns invariably interposed projecting jambs. The Bridestones septal slab was unusually tall (5 ft. 6 in. as recorded) and probably reached the capstones.

[49] J. Ward, *Hist. Stoke-on-Trent*, 2–6.
[50] J. Sainter, *Scientific Rambles round Macclesfield*, 26 sqq.
[51] M. Dunlop, 'The Bridestones', *T.L.C.A.S.* liii. 14–24.
[52] By Sainter, *Scientific Rambles*, 26 sqq., and possibly by Ward, *Hist. Stoke-on-Trent*, 2–6.
[53] *T.L.C.A.S.* liii. 14–24.
[54] J. G. Scott, 'Clyde Cairns of Scot.' *Megalithic Enquiries in W. of Brit.* ed. T. G. E. Powell and others, 175–222; J. X. W. P. Corcoran, 'Chambered Cairns of Carlingford Culture', *Megalithic Graves and Ritual* (3rd Atlantic Colloquium), 105–16.
[55] A. Henshall, *Chambered Tombs of Scot.* ii. 381–3.

Limited communication between the segments of the chamber was, however, effected by a small porthole 'about 19½ in. diameter' in the slab, a feature encountered in many diverse traditions of megalithic sepulchral architecture. The burial evidence from the chamber appears to compare with Irish practice, where token cremations in a fragmentary state are mixed with charcoal and what seems to be domestic refuse; in the Clyde area, by contrast, inhumation, involving on occasion more than 40 individuals, is more common. Paving or cobbling on the floor of the chamber can be paralleled in Ireland and Scotland, as at Browndod and at Cairnholy Island (Kirkcuds.), while the use of layers of paving to separate burial deposits, evidenced at Ballyalton, may find an echo in the 'black tinge' of the upper parts of the pounded layer of white stone at the Bridestones. Cobbling in the forecourt is known at a number of sites, and hearths, too, as at Cairnholy Island, flanking a central stone-hole, recall the Bridestones evidence and hint at the ceremonies associated with the cairn's use.[56]

The Bridestones, while not fitting neatly into either the Clyde or the court cairn series, has nonetheless been influenced by both. The geographically intermediate cairn, Cashtal-yn-Ard (Isle of Man), displays similarities: its deep forecourt of comparable dimensions; the projection of its portal stones beyond the façade and into the forecourt area; the monolith within the forecourt; the forecourt cobbling; the 'Clyde' construction of the septals and porthole stone.[57] Those features attest the spread and merging of ideas around the northern Irish Sea during the Earlier Neolithic period.

Churton (SJ 411 558)

The cropmark site 800 m. south-west of Churton may represent an important addition to the evidence for Neolithic funerary practice in Cheshire.[58] The most distinctive feature visible represents a rectangular ditched enclosure c. 33 m. by 18 m. with bowed sides and rounded corners aligned approximately north–south. The southern end is pierced by a wide (c. 10 m.) gap. Regular linear features crossing the field are a result of recent drainage. Other irregular lines may, however, reflect ancient demarcations. The location overlooks the flood plain of the Dee, 730 m. from its east bank.

It may cautiously be suggested that the rectangular feature represents a class of monument known as long mortuary enclosures. Timber mortuary structures, of various dimensions and connected in some way, perhaps, with the exposure or storage of the dead before sealing the structure under an earthen long barrow, are known from a number of excavated sites.[59] Timber structures may also have provided the inspiration for stone ones with the appearance of 'protomegaliths', themselves initiating the elaboration of the sepulchral monument into the full chambered tomb.[60] While both small mortuary houses and relatively large mortuary enclosures of dimensions comparable with that of Churton are known to precede mound construction on the same site, the larger long mortuary enclosures can also occur as free-standing monuments. The Churton site is toward the lower end of the long mortuary enclosure scale, but finds morphological parallels at Barford (Warws.) and Sonning (Berks.). Although neither site has been dated by associated material, stratigraphical evidence at Barford and proximity to a sub-rectangular enclosure

[56] Megalithic Enquiries, 175–222.
[57] H. J. Fleure and G. J. H. Nealy, 'Cashtal-yn-Ard, Isle of Man', Antiq. Jnl. xvi. 392–5.
[58] Fig. 6; below, plate.
[59] D. D. A. Simpson, 'First Agric. Communities', Intro. to Brit. Prehist. ed. J. V. S. Megaw and D. D. A. Simpson, 91–4.
[60] Megalithic Enquiries, 206–7.

producing Peterborough Ware at Sonning suggest an Earlier and perhaps Later Neolithic date respectively.[61]

Loachbrook Farm, Somerford (SJ 830 634)

An earthen mound approximately 107 m. long and 25 m. wide in Somerford parish has been claimed as a long barrow.[62] The site is on marshy ground near the Loach brook, 3 km. west of Congleton. It is under grass and the identification is not confirmed.

ARTEFACTS

Other than the monuments already discussed, most of the evidence for Neolithic activity in Cheshire is provided by artefacts, single or in groups, without recognized structural associations. Although in most instances the circumstances of discovery inhibit the recognition of such associations, they should not be assumed never to have been present. No pottery of the Earlier Neolithic period is known from the county; stone technology is better represented, and two classes of artefact, polished stone axes and leaf-shaped points of flint, can be regarded as diagnostic.

Polished stone axes

Although artefacts resembling the type have occasionally been found in Mesolithic contexts, production reached a high level during the Neolithic period over more than 1,500 years between the middle of the 4th millennium B.C. and the beginning of the 2nd. The axes were designed to be set into wooden hafts, which survive very rarely in British contexts. The range in size supports their suggested use in forest clearance, fodder collection, and carpentry. Igneous and metamorphic rocks were favoured, and at a limited number of locations in northern and western Britain where suitable rock outcrops, production reached industrial proportions, supplying much of the demand for such tools over a wide area. Isolation of those 'factory' products has been made possible through microscopic identification of the raw material, and occasionally fieldwork and excavation have revealed flaking floors.[63] Of the 28 Cheshire axes that have been petrologically examined, 14 can be assigned to specific groups.[64] The products of Group VI, the epidotized tuffs of the Borrowdale Volcanic series, exploited at Scafell Pike (Cumb.) and Great Langdale (Westmld.), are dominant (7 or possibly 8 axes), as they are over much of England north of the Thames. A further 5 axes derive from north Wales: 4 from the important Group VII (augite–granophyre) flaking sites at Graig Lwyd above Penmaenmawr (Caern.) and a single example from Group XXI, the baked shale of Mynydd Rhiw on the Lleyn peninsula which seems otherwise to have been of relatively local importance. Cornish products are represented by 3 axes, although only one has been satisfactorily identified as Group I, a greenstone from the Penwith area. The remaining grouped axe is of Group XV, a greywacke from the Lake District. Very few axes of Neolithic form are known to have been produced from that rock, and none have datable associations.[65] In the Early Bronze Age, however, Group XV greywacke was a major raw material employed in producing numerous shafthole axes, with a particular concentration in the north-west.[66] The polished axe from

[61] *Arch. Jnl.* cxxii. 19, pl. 1a; *Berks. Arch. Jnl.* lxi. 4–19.
[62] *Ches. Arch. Bull.* iii. 60.
[63] R.C.H.M. (Wales), *Caerns.* i, pp. xli–l.
[64] Some of the identifications are listed by D. J. Robinson,

'Implement Petrology in Ches.' *Ches. Arch. Bull.* iv. 2–6.
[65] I. F. Smith, 'Chronology of Brit. Stone Implements', *Stone Axe Studies*, 19.
[66] F. Roe, 'Typology of Stone Implements', ibid. 23–48.

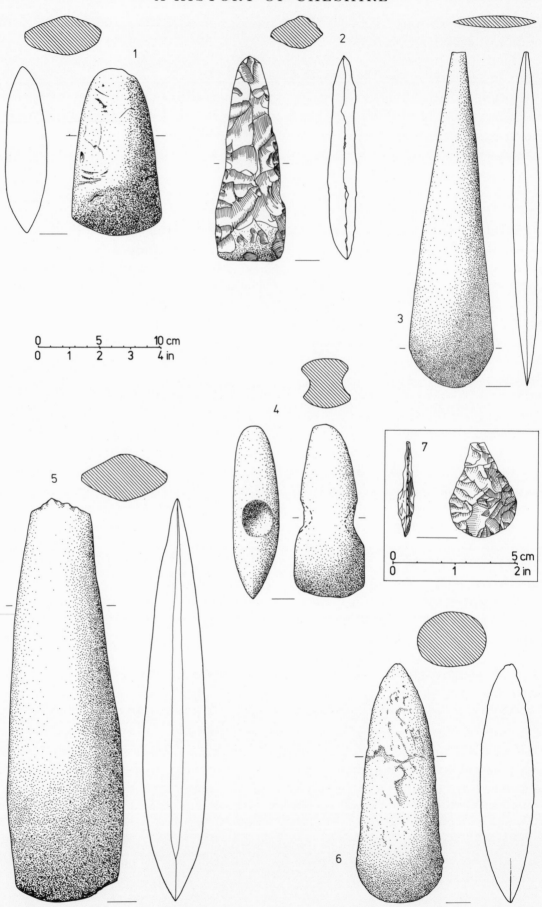

Fig. 7. Neolithic Axes and Flintwork: 1. Tarporley; 2. Elton; 3. Lyme Handley; 4. Church Lawton; 5. Crowton; 6. Foulk Stapleford; 7. Helsby.

Delamere of Group XV rock is further anomalous in that, for its length, it is both exceptionally wide (along the blade axis) and thick: it is wider than any other Cheshire axe, while only the very long axes from Crowton (324 mm.) and Birkenhead (257 mm.) are thicker.

Five Cheshire axes are of flint, which was exploited widely by mining techniques in southern Britain; the products have not yet been differentiated petrologically.[67] Two at least of those axes, one from Elton and the other from Stockton Heath, have been flaked to shape, with only the cutting edge ground.

The material of two further axes calls for comment: those made of jadeite from Lyme Handley and Chester, which were certainly imported from the Continent. Jadeite was used from at least the mid 4th millennium B.C. for a range of tools and decorative attachments, both functional and ceremonial, on account of its resilience and its decorative qualities. The Chester axe, found during the excavation of a Roman site, though well made, has the proportions of a functional axe. The Lyme Handley axe, found in clay during drainage works, is exceptionally long in proportion to its width and particularly to its thickness. Despite some damage to the butt, at 264 mm. it is the second longest in the county; it is finely worked, and was probably fashioned for some ceremonial or ritual purpose.

Both fine-grained rocks and medium-grained basic igneous rocks were used in making axes; the former could be worked as an extension of flint-working techniques by flaking into shape before grinding and polishing, whereas the latter were first shaped by pecking. The distinction can be apparent in the finished form of the implements.[68] The axe from Crowton is very characteristic of the long Cumbrian axes, flaked from the volcanic tuffs of Group VI. Conversely, the axe from Foulk Stapleford, with its circular cross-section, pointed butt, and slightly expanded curving blade, is of Bridlington (Yorks. E.R.) type, pecked to shape from Cornish greenstone.

Although the small number of petrological identifications available urges caution in considering the distribution of factory products in the county, north Welsh axes have a marked western distribution, in Wirral and west of the central Cheshire ridge, while Group VI products occur in the Mersey hinterland and the Weaver valley area of central Cheshire. In three instances polished stone axes have possible associations with other artefacts. Five polished axes were found together in a group at the foot of Eddisbury Hill: none can now be traced, although one, photographed while in private possession, was the smallest found in Cheshire. Two axes were found during the drainage of a field near Beeston Castle. Again, neither can be traced: one was broken on discovery, while a cast of the other is in the Grosvenor Museum. A shafthole axe of Early Bronze Age date was discovered at the same time, although it is not recorded whether the three axes were found in association. An axe with its wooden haft from Tranmere Pool, Birkenhead, is also reported to have been found with an Early Bronze Age shafthole axe during dock works, although close association is not confirmed. No weight should be placed on such associations, which, even if genuine, need cause no surprise. The making of polished stone axes in the Neolithic fashion continued beyond the introduction of metal working and into the first quarter of the 2nd millennium B.C.[69] Shafthole implements replaced them in terms of lithic technology but not, it must be stressed, as functional equivalents, as the major type of stone tool during the Early Bronze

---

[67] Cf. P. R. Bush and G. de G. Sieveking, 'Geochemistry and Provenance of Flint Axes', *Stone Axe Studies*, 87.

[68] G. R. Coope, 'Influence of Geol. on Manufacture of Stone Implements', ibid. 90–101.

[69] Ibid. 14–15.

Age. In two instances in Cheshire an attempt was made to convert polished axes into shafthole implements. From Wallasey what appears to have been a faceted stone axe was converted into a shafthole adze by drilling a perforation at right angles to the cutting edge, while an axe found at Porthill (Staffs.) in quarry material from Church Lawton has depressions pecked into opposing edges in an unfinished attempt to make a shafthole.

Neolithic flint arrowheads

Archery was practised during the Neolithic period and, while it may be assumed that the bow and arrow were used in bringing down game, a growing body of evidence suggests that they were also used in warfare.[70] Bows have been preserved only in exceptional circumstances; those that have survived are long bows.[71] Flint points, however, originally set as the tips of wooden arrows by resin, are distinctive and relatively common finds. The earliest single-piece arrowheads are pressure flaked flint points of leaf form, which occur in a range of sizes and have a long chronology extending into the 2nd millennium. Larger forms are thought to have been used as spear heads, while smaller points may have been set as drill bits or for some similar use. During the Later Neolithic new forms of transverse, oblique, and hollow-based flint arrowheads were developed and used contemporaneously with leaf forms into the 2nd millennium. Oblique forms, of which there is one possible example from Congleton, have particular associations with the Late Neolithic period. The occurrence of a number of hollow-based arrowheads on or near the western coast of Britain suggests contact with, or importation from, Ireland, where they are widely distributed; the Hoylake arrowhead may be considered in that light.[72]

Two leaf arrowheads have been recovered during the course of excavations. Both, however, had been incorporated into the mound material covering Early Bronze Age burials. The first, from Henbury, formed part of a large flint assemblage from the mound erected over a cremation burial which was contained within a Collared Urn. The second, from Woodhouse End, Gawsworth, was damaged and comprised an element in a large residual assemblage of flints and Late Neolithic pottery in a mound which sealed the burial of a Step 6 Beaker (after Lanting and Van de Waals's classification)[73] and five cremations, including at least two contained within Collared Urns. There is a strong possibility that both arrowheads were lost on the ground before the Early Bronze Age burials and became incorporated in the material quarried up to cover them. Transverse arrowheads from the Lower Withington barrow may similarly represent residual material from earlier activity there, though the possibility of near-contemporaneous loss cannot be excluded.

Later Neolithic pottery

Pottery manufactured during the Earlier Neolithic, while often well made, was generally plain and round-based. By the 3rd millennium new forms had been introduced, becoming increasingly decorated with bone and whipped cord impressions and with incisions. Rim forms were elaborated and flat-based pottery became more common. Over the greater part of southern Britain such styles are

[70] H. S. Green, *Flint Arrowheads of Brit. Isles* (Brit. Arch. Rep. lxxv), pt. i, 178–9; P. Dixon, 'Crickley Hill', *Current Arch.* lxxvi. 145–7.

[71] J. G. D. Clark, 'Neolithic Bows from Somerset and Pre-

hist. of Archery in NW. Eur.' *Proc. Prehist. Soc.* xxix. 50–98.

[72] Green, *Flint Arrowheads*, pt. i, 141–2.

[73] J. N. Lanting and J. D. Van der Waals, 'Brit. Beakers as seen from the Continent', *Helinium*, xii. 20–46.

collectively termed Peterborough Ware; in Scotland and Ireland other forms of impressed and similarly decorated pottery predominate.[74]

The single whipped-cord impressed body sherd from Meols is in the Peterborough tradition, though little can be added to the fact of its presence other than to note the relatively high density of Neolithic finds in north Wirral. Conversely, the assemblage from Gawsworth comprises one of the largest groups of Peterborough pottery from the north Midlands: 162 sherds representing at least 23 different vessels were recovered from the fill of quarry ditches and the body of a mound sealing the primary deposit of an intact Beaker of Step 6 (Lanting and Van der Waals). The Gawsworth pottery embodies characteristics of the Mortlake style of the Peterborough series and may be considerably earlier than what is essentially a late Beaker. Many of the sherds are very small and severely abraded and, together with the leaf arrowhead discussed above, a quantity of flints, and small fragments of animal bone, may represent occupation debris scraped up from the original ground surface during the construction of the mound. The concentration of Peterborough Ware through the north-west quadrant of the mound suggests that a pre-existing Neolithic settlement nearby might be sought in that direction. The pottery itself is thick-walled and gritted, varying in colour from buff through red to dark brown. Rims are heavily moulded and decoration takes the form of closely spaced tooled designs carried out with the articular end of a bird bone. Incised herringbone and lattice also occurs and whipped cord 'maggots', though present, are rare. The assemblage is one of the very few tangible clues to the location of Neolithic settlement, in contrast to ceremonial or funerary practice, in the county.

In addition to the Peterborough series, during the course of the 3rd millennium poorly fired, slab-sided, flat-based bucket- and barrel-shaped vessels became popular throughout Britain from north Scotland to the south coast. Decoration of these rather more basic vessels consists of grooved lines closely set and arranged in geometric patterns: common ones were filled triangles, chevrons, or herringbone, and plastic decoration in the form, for example, of converging bands and vertical panels. Rinyo (Orkney), Durrington (Wilts.), Woodlands (Wilts.), and Clacton (Essex) sub-styles have been identified by variations in the arrangement of decorative elements, though all may be encompassed within the classification 'Grooved Ware', so termed because the grooved line decoration predominates.[75] Both Peterborough and Grooved Wares were in use through much of the 3rd millennium B.C. and into the earlier 2nd. A distinction can be drawn between the occurrence of Peterborough Ware in both domestic and burial contexts, and the virtual restriction of Grooved Ware to 'domestic' sites, although the latter is, significantly, also associated with a number of ceremonial sites including three of the great Wessex enclosures, Marden, Avebury, and Durrington (all Wilts.). Of the large number of sites on which Grooved Ware has been found, in only two instances was it in direct association with burial: in both, at Winhill (Derb.)[76] and Delamere, Grooved Ware vessels were used as cinerary urns, the former apparently under a cairn, the latter as part of what seems to have been a large cremation cemetery. Both cremations are anomalous.

The Delamere find was made in the spring of 1851 by workmen digging near a quarry below and to the east of Castle Ditch hillfort, Eddisbury. A number of urns

[74] C. Burgess, *Age of Stonehenge*, 37–41.
[75] G. J. Wainwright and I. H. Longworth, *Durrington Walls* (Soc. Antiq. Research Rep. xxix), 55–71, 235–8; T.

Manby, *Grooved Ware Sites in N. Eng.* (Brit. Arch. Rep. ix).
[76] T. Bateman, *Ten Years' Digging in Celtic and Saxon Grave Hills*, 254–5.

containing calcined bone are reported to have been found, though only three sherds representing the rim and upper portion of one vessel now survive: it was 'found full of bones' and located in 'the Sandhole Field'. The urn was barrel-shaped with an external rim diameter of 30 cm. Its fabric is heavily gritted with large inclusions, only a few of which protrude from the outer face. It may contain some grog, but that could not be confirmed by macroscopic analysis. The outer face has been fired light brown and become blackened. Decoration is in the form of close-set 'maggots' of impressed whipped cord, horizontal rows of which frame 'maggot'-impressed filled triangles below the rim. Below this an applied cordon and pendant strips are filled with 'maggot' impressions arranged in zig-zag form or vertically. The inner face is brown and blackened. A zig-zag of 'maggots' is ranged round the inside of the rim and an irregular groove runs along the top. The vessel has affinities with the Durrington Walls sub-type of Grooved Ware,[77] although whipped cord impressions are restricted to a single sherd at Durrington and are infrequent elsewhere. Radiocarbon samples associated with pottery at the Wiltshire type-site give a calibrated range of dates from c. 2600–2300 B.C.

The Eddisbury cremations represent a departure in two respects. First, the pottery is in a Late Neolithic tradition. Cremation was practised in the Neolithic period but the ashes are not contained within pottery vessels. Secondly, Grooved Ware is thought to be an essentially domestic pottery. A changing attitude to burial at the end of the 3rd and beginning of the 2nd millennium is reflected in the appearance of specialized sepulchral pottery, not simply to accompany burial but to contain the ashes of the dead. The new range of cinerary urns, of which Collared Urns are the most important, developed out of the Peterborough series and accentuated the distinction between funerary and domestic ceramics. 'Domestic' Grooved Ware gave rise to bucket- and barrel-shaped vessels of the Deverel–Rimbury tradition in the south with analogues further north and west, although both Grooved Ware and Deverel–Rimbury related material are rare in Wales and the Marches.[78] While the cinerary urns and accessory vessels seem to have been restricted to funerary use, Deverel–Rimbury and related vessels were used in both domestic and funerary contexts. The Eddisbury cemetery therefore appears to stand at the transition between the Neolithic tradition in ceramics and burial and the innovations of the Bronze Age. A new burial rite had been adopted in a context where traditional forms of pottery continued to be produced, or at least to be available.

GAZETTEER OF NEOLITHIC FINDS

Stone Axes[79]
(Length, width, thickness in mm.)

ACTON

HENHULL (SJ 633 534). Polished axe; faceted sides; blue-grey, fine-grained stone. Group VI (110, 52, 21). Grosvenor Mus. 79.P.55.

ASTBURY

CONGLETON (SJ 869 637). Polished axe; 'Bridlington' type; Group I. Not located.[80]

---

[77] Wainwright and Longworth, *Durrington Walls*, 59.
[78] J. Barrett, 'Deverel–Rimbury: Problems of Chronology and Interpretation', *Settlement and Econ. in 3rd and 2nd*
Millennia B.C. (Brit. Arch. Rep. xxxiii), 289–307.
[79] Fig. 5.2.
[80] *Ches. Historian*, ix. 3.

PREHISTORY

BARROW

SJ 480 682. Polished axe; mottled black, brown, grey dolerite (193, 64, 40). Grosvenor Mus. 61.P.51.[81]

BIDSTON

BIDSTON CUM FORD (c. SJ 28 89). Polished axe; basalt (129, 44, 21). Merseyside County Mus. 1969.219.

BIRKENHEAD. (a) SJ 326 882. Polished axe; faceted; originally found with wooden haft; Group VI; found in uncertain association with shafthole axe (below, Early Bronze Age Gazetteer) (146, 67, 27); Merseyside County Mus. M 6385. (b) c. SJ 33 87. Polished axe (145, 50, 16); Merseyside County Mus. 64.158.

MORETON. Polished axe; faceted sides; butt broken; Group XXI (84, 60, 20). Wallasey Public Libr.

BOWDON

ASHLEY (SJ 773 842). Polished axe (168, 67, 37). Manchester Mus. 0.978.[82]

BUDWORTH, GREAT

ANTROBUS (SJ 643 798). Polished axe; grey-white flint (174, 62, 34). Private possession.[83]

BUDWORTH, GREAT (c. SJ 66 77). Polished axe; dark green Borrowdale tuff (101, 50, 22). Manchester University Mus. 0.5046.[84]

NORTHWICH. Polished axe; faceted sides. Not located.[85]

BUNBURY

BEESTON (c. SJ 53 59). Two axes found in uncertain association with stone shafthole axe (below) (94, 56, 23). One lost; cast of other in Grosvenor Mus.[86]

BURTON

SJ 302 737. Polished axe; faceted sides; light grey-green fine-grained rock (103, 69, 29). Grosvenor Mus. 27.P.1975.[87]

CHEADLE

(a) c. SJ 85 89. 'Stone celt'; possibly a Neolithic axe. Stockport Mus. IX.31.[88] (b) c. SJ 84 88. Polished axe. Not traced.[89]

CHESTER

(a) Polished axe; faceted sides; grey-green rock (137, 45, 31). Brighton Pavilion Mus. 1934/67. (b) SJ 403 665. Polished axe; faceted sides; very finely made; jadeite? Found during excavation of a Roman site in 1914 (133, 54, 17). Grosvenor Mus. cc 277.1910.[90]

CHESTER, ST. OSWALD

SAIGHTON (SJ 440 620). Polished axe; butt damaged; pink-grey, fine-grained stone; Group VII (132, 89, 33). Grosvenor Mus. cc 284.09.

COPPENHALL

COPPENHALL, CHURCH (SJ 704 586). Polished axe; faceted sides. Light grey fine-grained rock (108, 57, 19). In private possession.

COPPENHALL, MONKS, i.e. Crewe (c. SJ 70 55). Polished axe; some damage to surface; light grey stone (166, 57, 30). Manchester Mus. 323.[91]

---

[81] *J.C.A.S.* xxxix. 109.
[82] W. Shone, *Prehist. Man in Ches.* 37, 92.
[83] *Ches. Arch. Bull.* viii. 70, fig. 10.
[84] *T.L.C.A.S.* xxxix. 195.
[85] Ibid. l. 74.
[86] *J.C.A.S.* iv. 110.
[87] *Ches. Arch. Bull.* iii. 59.
[88] Shone, *Prehist. Man in Ches.* 38, 98.
[89] *T.L.C.A.S.* l. 74.
[90] *J.C.A.S.* xxvii. 62, 80.
[91] *Ches. Arch. Bull.* i. 3.

DELAMERE

(a) SJ 535 673. Polished axe; badly damaged grey-buff greywacke; Group XV (160, 109, 49). Grosvenor Mus. 85.P.65.[92] (b) *c.* SJ 55 69. Five polished axes found at foot of Eddisbury Hill, 1896. One, of 'drab clay-slate', was photographed in private possession, 1906 (82, 57, 15). Not located.[93] (c) SJ 533 676. Polished axe; surface rough above blade end. Dark grey stone (140, 72, 40). In private possession.[94]

FRODSHAM

HELSBY (SJ 491 755). Polished axe; faceted sides; fine-grained stone; Group VI (117, 55, 29). Merseyside County Mus.[95]
KINGSLEY (SJ 562 759). Polished axe; faceted sides; greenish brown fine-grained stone; Group VI (126, 62, 26). Grosvenor Mus. 63.P.56.[96]
SUTTON (SJ 551 789). Polished axe; fine-grained grey-white stone (172, 61, 27). In private possession.

GAWSWORTH

SJ 890 696. Finely polished axe; light grey flint (207, 80, 39). In private possession.[97]

KIRBY, WEST

MEOLS, LITTLE (SJ 185 879). Stone axe; oval section (120, 70, not known). Not located.

LAWTON, CHURCH

c. SJ 80 56. Polished axe with unfinished perforation showing intended conversion to shafthole axe (fig. 7.4). Grey, mottled tremolite schist, Cornish? (138, 57, 38). Stoke-on-Trent Mus. 11.31.

MIDDLEWICH

SJ 701 664. Polished axe; faceted sides; butt damaged; light grey fine-grained stone; Group VI (95, 55, 26). Grosvenor Mus. cc 279.1912.[98]

MOTTRAM IN LONGDENDALE

STAYLEY (*c.* SJ 95 98). Wedge-shaped ?Neolithic axe; grey-brown dolerite; weathered. Ashton colln.

NESTON

WILLASTON. (a) SJ 330 775. Polished axe; faceted sides; grey-green fine-grained stone; Group VI (132, 56, 29); Grosvenor Mus. 163.P.67. (b) SJ 328 772. Polished axe; possibly Group VII (153, 77, not known); in private possession.[99]

PRESTBURY

LYME HANDLEY. (a) SJ 965 831. Polished, dark brown, flint axe (125, 70, 13); in private possession.[1]
(b) SJ 967 819. Polished axe (fig. 7.3); greenish grey, mottled jadeite (264, 66, 22); in private possession.[2]
MACCLESFIELD (SJ 916 720). Polished axe. In private possession.[3]
MACCLESFIELD FOREST (SJ 955 716). Axe. Not located.[4]

RUNCORN

ASTON (*c.* SJ 56 78). Polished axe, badly damaged; fine-grained grey rock (142, 52, 23). Warrington Mus., Acc. 216.09.
STOCKTON HEATH (SJ 616 862). Flaked grey flint axe with cutting edge polished. Found during excavation of a Roman site, 1902 (114, 42, 22). Warrington Mus. 222.06.[5]

[92] *Ches. Arch. Bull.* iv. 35.
[93] *T.L.C.A.S.* xxiv. 115.
[94] *Ches. Arch. Bull.* iv. 35.
[95] *N.W. Naturalist*, v. 92.
[96] *J.C.A.S.* xliv. 51.
[97] R. Richards, *Manor of Gawsworth*, 5.
[98] *Ches. N. & Q.* lx. 59.
[99] *Ches. Arch. Bull.* i. 3.
[1] *J.C.A.S.* xlii. 48.
[2] *Antiq. Jnl.* xii. 167.
[3] *T.L.C.A.S.* l. 74.
[4] Ibid. xl. 209.
[5] Shone, *Prehist. Man in Ches.* 41.

PREHISTORY
SUTTON, GUILDEN

c. SJ 434 675. 'Stone axe from Piper's Ash.' In private possession.

TARPORLEY

RUSHTON (SJ 572 635). Polished axe. In private possession?[6]
TARPORLEY (SJ 555 625). Polished axe (fig. 7.1); faceted sides; brown-grey fine-grained rock; Group VII (133, 75, 34). Grosvenor Mus. 37.P.53.

TARVIN

FOULK STAPLEFORD (SJ 485 620). Polished axe (fig. 7.6); weathered Cornish greenstone (190, 71, 44). Grosvenor Mus. 191.P.1903.[7]
HORTON CUM PEEL (SJ 495 696). Polished axe; cutting edge damaged; light grey fine-grained stone; Group VII (121, 68, 33). Grosvenor Mus. 92.P.52.[8]

WALLASEY

(a) SJ 263 894. Polished axe; faceted sides; grey weathered stone (86, 36, 18). Wallasey Public Libr.
(b) SJ 280 918. Polished axe; faceted sides; siltstone. Re-used as shafthole adze (145, 80, 29). Earlston Libr., Wallasey. (c) SJ 297 915. Polished axe. Not located.[9]

WARMINGHAM

ELTON (SJ 733 587). Flaked, brown-yellow flint axe (fig. 7.2); some polishing of cutting edge (163, 58, 24). In private possession.[10]

WEAVERHAM

CROWTON (SJ 593 744). Large polished axe (fig. 7.5); faceted sides; greenish grey, fine-grained rock; Group VI (324, 98, 54). Grosvenor Mus. 24.P.52.[11]

WOODCHURCH

BARNSTON (SJ 282 836). Polished axe; not located.
OXTON. (a) SJ 291 878. Polished axe; rhyolite (180, 66, 30); Merseyside County Mus. 1976.605.
(b) SJ 303 872. Polished axe; grey-green dolerite (257, 76, 54); Grosvenor Mus. 53.P.56.

WILMSLOW

POWNALL FEE. Styal (*c.* SJ 847 847). Mottled grey flint axe; polished at cutting edge. Provenance uncertain as findspot was in load of soil from Wilmslow. In private possession.[12]

Flint Arrowheads[13]

ASTBURY

CONGLETON (SJ 874 628). Oblique or 'lopsided' flint arrowhead. Weaver Hall Mus. Z 80.

BEBINGTON

SJ 346 825. Leaf-shaped flint arrowhead. Merseyside County Mus. 1975.330.[14]

BURTON

SJ 317 742. Transverse arrowhead. Grosvenor Mus. 102.P.1978.[15]

[6] *Ches. Arch. Bull.* vii. 57.
[7] Shone, *Prehist. Man in Ches.* 34.
[8] *J.C.A.S.* xxxv. 58, 61–2.
[9] O.S. Arch. Rec. SJ 29 SE 8.
[10] *Ches. Arch. Bull.* i. 4.
[11] *Antiq. Jnl.* vii. 60–1.
[12] *Ches. Arch. Bull.* v. 36.
[13] Fig. 5.2.
[14] *Ches. Arch. Bull.* ix. 35.
[15] Ibid. vii. 57.

FRODSHAM

FRODSHAM (SJ 52 75). Leaf-shaped flint point. Grosvenor Mus. 75.P.57.
HELSBY (SJ 492 755). Leaf-shaped flint arrowhead (fig. 7.7). Grosvenor Mus. 105.P.1967.[16]

GAWSWORTH

SJ 915 696. Leaf-shaped flint point, tip missing, from make-up of Beaker mound. Grosvenor Mus.

KIRBY, WEST

MEOLS, LITTLE (SJ 202 885). Hollow-based flint arrowhead. Grosvenor Mus. 153.P.67.

MOTTRAM IN LONGDENDALE

TINTWISTLE. Leaf-shaped flint arrowhead. In private possession.[17]

PRESTBURY

HENBURY (SJ 874 720). Crudely shaped leaf arrowhead from make-up of Early Bronze Age burial mound. Grosvenor Mus. 3-4.P.1967.[18]
WITHINGTON, OLD (SJ 807 724). Transverse arrowheads from make-up of Early Bronze Age burial mound.[19]

TARVIN

MOULDSWORTH (SJ 518 714). Leaf-shaped flint arrowhead. Grosvenor Mus.

WRENBURY

SOUND (SJ 628 483). Leaf-shaped flint arrowhead. Not located.[20]

Later Neolithic Pottery

DELAMERE

c. SJ 55 69. Three sherds from single surviving vessel. One of a number of urns containing cremations. Grooved Ware. Warrington Mus. 28-30.[21]

GAWSWORTH

SJ 915 696. 162 sherds representing at least 23 vessels. Peterborough Ware. From body of mound covering Beaker pit. Grosvenor Mus.[22]

KIRBY, WEST

MEOLS, GREAT (*c.* SJ 23 90). Single body sherd in red-brown gritted fabric. Whipped cord 'maggot' impressions in parallel lines. Grosvenor Mus. 115.P.67.

THE FIRST METALWORKERS: THE EARLY BRONZE AGE
2500–1500 B.C.

CHRONOLOGY, ASSOCIATIONS, AND DISTRIBUTION

The later 3rd millennium B.C. and the early 2nd appear to have seen an amelioration of the somewhat wet conditions of the Earlier Neolithic period: the climate was warm and dry and some opening up of the forest cover may have taken place.

---

[16] *Ches. Arch. Bull.* iv. 36.
[17] *N. Derb. Arch. Cttee. Rec.* (1916).
[18] *Ches. Arch. Bull.* iv. 28.
[19] Ibid. vi. 67.
[20] O.S. Arch. Rec. SJ 64 NW 1.
[21] *T.H.S.L.C.* iv. 99.
[22] *J.C.A.S.* lx. 1–34.

Arable exploitation of highland zone areas beyond the limit of present-day cultivation certainly began during the early 2nd millennium, to reach perhaps its fullest extent by the 15th century B.C. Stone circles and stone alignments, first erected during the earlier 3rd millennium, continued to be constructed in greater numbers during its latter part: they imply terrestrial and celestial observation, needing clear skies and still air conditions, as an element of their design and function.[23]

The first metal tools appear in Britain in the mid 3rd millennium, some two thousand years after the earliest metalworking in south-east Europe. The coincidence of metal and of distinctive pottery vessels, termed Beakers on the supposition that they contained drink, has been taken to indicate the appearance of immigrant groups. Beakers often accompany inhumation burial, and their bearers have been credited with initiating cultural changes which included a new burial rite, that of single, crouched inhumation under a small round mound.[24] Evidence of new physical types to support the argument for immigration has been sought in the skeletal remains; nevertheless the magnitude of any Beaker-bearing immigration, or succession of immigrations, has been seriously questioned.[25] Only the very earliest vessels from a thousand years of Beaker use can be confidently identified as imports. Furthermore the funerary evidence does not support the hypothesis that Beaker users initiated the single grave tradition: while individual inhumations accompanied by Beakers are well attested, Beakers have also been recorded in other well established funerary and ceremonial contexts including multiple inhumations, chambered tombs, and henge monuments. The evidence of burials is by no means consistent in confirming a sudden appearance of broad-headed, more robust physical types; for, while a greater proportion of brachycephalic types are indeed represented in Early Bronze Age burials compared with the dolichocephalic, more lightly built, skeletons from Neolithic long barrows and chambered cairns, the question of regional, social, and chronological variations requires fuller consideration.[26]

The early use of metal appears to have had little effect on society, apart from opening up new areas to those prospecting for copper and later, as the bronze alloy replaced copper, for tin. Tanged daggers and flat axes were among the few artefacts made first in copper, while gold was available for producing more precious ornaments. Bronze replaced copper before 2000 B.C., and Early Bronze Age metalworking is characterized by developments in axe, dagger, and spearhead types whose changes of design reflected improved methods of hafting.[27] Polished stone axes continued to be produced and traded in considerable numbers until c. 2000 B.C. The manufacture of perforated stone implements, particularly shafthole axes, using specific and new sources of rock on a large scale, began before the end of the 3rd millennium to become the major type of stone tool of the Earlier Bronze Age. Smaller, more finely produced 'battle-axes' of similar form, which may indeed have been weapons rather than tools, frequently appear as grave goods accompanying burial.[28] Archery continues to be well attested, and, while the characteristic Earlier Neolithic leaf-shaped flint arrowhead is known from Early Bronze Age contexts, and transverse and hollow-based forms continued to be used well into the 2nd millennium, the newer barbed and tanged variety frequently accompanied Beaker

[23] C. Burgess, 'Bronze Age', *Brit. Prehistory*, ed. C. Renfrew, 196.

[24] C. Burgess, *Age of Stonehenge*, 70.

[25] Ibid. 62–5.

[26] Ibid. 160–1.

[27] Ibid.

[28] F. Roe, 'Typology of Stone Implements with Shaftholes', *Stone Axe Studies*, 23–48.

burial both in Britain and on the Continent, along with other presumed items of archery equipment such as wrist guards.[29]

Beaker-using immigrants have traditionally been credited with innovations in burial practices and at ceremonial monuments. Long chambered tombs had ceased to be constructed during the 3rd millennium, although the final blocking of some did not take place until nearer 2000 B.C. Round mounds came into vogue, and while their use, like individual inhumation, can be shown to pre-date the Beaker rite, a number of single or multiple burials, in cists or graves under mounds or in flat graves, have been distinguished by the accompaniment of a Beaker and frequently of a small number of prestigious grave goods. After c. 2000 B.C. Beaker burials continued; other inhumation burials, however, were accompanied by a variety of Food Vessels, and an extensive range of specialized funerary pottery was developed to contain the ashes of the dead as the rite of cremation became more widely used.[30]

The Later Neolithic period, from c. 3000 B.C., saw the construction of bank-and-ditch 'henges' and of stone circles, which continued beyond the earliest use of metal into the Early Bronze Age. A range of size is represented, with a distribution extending throughout Britain, and while a variety of functions may be involved the ceremonial aspect is always present, and the larger examples are engineering achievements of monumental proportions. Stone circles are found mainly on the older hard rocks of the west and north; the Peak District has several, but the one claimed for Cheshire, only '7 ft.' in diameter, is unlikely to have been a free-standing circle and may have been associated with a cairn.[31] Ring cairns and what may be termed variant circles, where circular stone settings are incorporated in a burial monument which may comprise a cairn, appear to be a development during the early 2nd millennium of the tradition of free-standing stone circles. The latter, although burial may have been an element of the ritual practised there, were primarily ceremonial constructions.[32]

Ceremonial and funerary monuments have tended to dominate Earlier Bronze Age studies, and Cheshire is no exception. A large number of burials are known, concentrated particularly along the western flanks of the Pennines and the northern central ridge, and mostly avoiding the boulder clays and alluvium of the Dee and Weaver valleys and the Wirral peninsula. Few have been excavated, and fewer still to acceptable standards, and while burial under a round mound may have been introduced to Cheshire as elsewhere in a Neolithic context, the earliest datable mound is that which covered the Step 6 Beaker (early 2nd millennium) from Woodhouse End, Gawsworth, with its secondary burials in Collared Urns. Cremation was the dominant rite in Cheshire and the relatively prestigious though widespread Collared Urn the favoured receptacle. Diagnostic artefacts associated with burial are few; the bronze dagger and dagger pommel from the Wilmslow cremations are exceptional. Barbed and tanged arrowheads found at Sutton near Macclesfield and at Manley are consistent with an Early Bronze Age date, while radiocarbon dates from Withington place the cremations without urns under a round barrow there in the earlier 2nd millennium B.C.[33]

Although highly organized landscapes of field systems and farms are known from elsewhere in Britain, while evidence of settlement has also been preserved in

[29] H. S. Green, *Flint Arrowheads of Brit. Isles* (Brit. Arch. Rep. lxxv), 92–7.
[30] Burgess, *Age of Stonehenge*, 84–95.
[31] Below, gazetteer of mounds and burials: Delamere (b).

[32] e.g. Druids' Circle, Penmaenmawr (Gwynedd): *Proc. Prehist. Soc.* xxvi. 303–39.
[33] *Ches. Arch. Bull.* vi. 66–8.

adjacent upland areas of Derbyshire and north Wales,[34] the settlements which gave rise to the Cheshire burials have proved elusive. Nevertheless, major episodes of forest clearance in the Bronze Age, followed by cultivation, have been identified by pollen analysis at Bar Mere, Bickley.[35] There are no direct associations of stray artefacts in the immediate vicinity of burials, such as might provide clues to the location of settlement, though there is a general correlation between the concentration of shafthole axes and of burials between *c.* 60 m. and *c.* 120 m. above sea level, which may reflect the distribution of better agricultural land on the sands and gravels. That association is perhaps supported by the negative correlation between burials and shafthole axes on the one hand and Neolithic polished stone axes on the other, a point discussed more fully below.

SETTLEMENT AND BURIAL

Considerable effort was expended on the burial monuments of the Early Bronze Age, which may nevertheless have commemorated only a proportion of the population. What that proportion was must remain guesswork: estimates have varied from an average population of 2,000 for the whole of England and Wales, based on the assumption that every individual received barrow burial, to a maximum of 2,000,000 for the whole of mainland Britain by the mid 1st millennium B.C.[36] The lower estimate suggests an average population for Cheshire of between 13 and 20 people, whereas an upper estimate based on a carrying capacity for good land of 10 per square kilometre suggests a Cheshire population in excess of 5,000. A figure mid way between the two extremes best fits the extensive evidence of Early Bronze Age activity in the county including upstanding monuments and stray finds of artefacts. The relationship of burial to settlement is likewise unknown. Burials have been recorded overlying or in the vicinity of earlier occupation layers, as, for example, in the Brenig valley on the Denbigh moors, where a platform cairn was constructed over occupation debris containing Beaker sherds,[37] and in Cheshire at Gawsworth where abraded Peterborough pottery was incorporated in the mound covering a Beaker burial. At Gawsworth animal bone fragments, ash, and charcoal were also incorporated in the fill of the latest of the quarry ditches, as were Collared Urn fragments and fragments from another Bronze Age vessel. The Neolithic pottery presumably represents the disturbance of an older occupation deposit in the construction of the Beaker mound. Whether the material from the outer ditch represents occupation adjacent to and contemporary with the burials, or activity associated with the burial ritual itself, remains a matter of conjecture. The circumstances which gave rise to the abandonment of occupation and the establishment of funerary monuments on such sites, the length of the interval between the two, and the frequency with which such a pattern occurred, await clarification; radiocarbon results from Brenig suggest that the interval was not necessarily long.

The evidence of burial in Early Bronze Age Cheshire constitutes the largest single category of prehistoric material from the county. Over 100 sites are involved.[38] Ninety mounds of earth (barrows) or stone (cairns) may on morphological grounds be accepted as burial monuments of the period, although only 31 have,

---

[34] e.g. Swine Sty (Derb.); Brenig (Clwyd): *Trans. Hunter Arch. Soc.* x. 5–13; *Denb. Hist. Soc. Trans.* x. 204–11.

[35] J. Schoenwetter, 'Environmental Arch. of Peckforton Hills', *Ches. Arch. Bull.* viii. 10–11.

[36] R. J. C. Atkinson, 'Burial and Population in Brit. Bronze Age', *Prehist. Man in Wales and the West*, 107–16; Burgess, *Age of Stonehenge*, 171–2.

[37] *Denb. Hist. Soc. Trans.* xxiv. 14–16.

[38] Fig. 8.

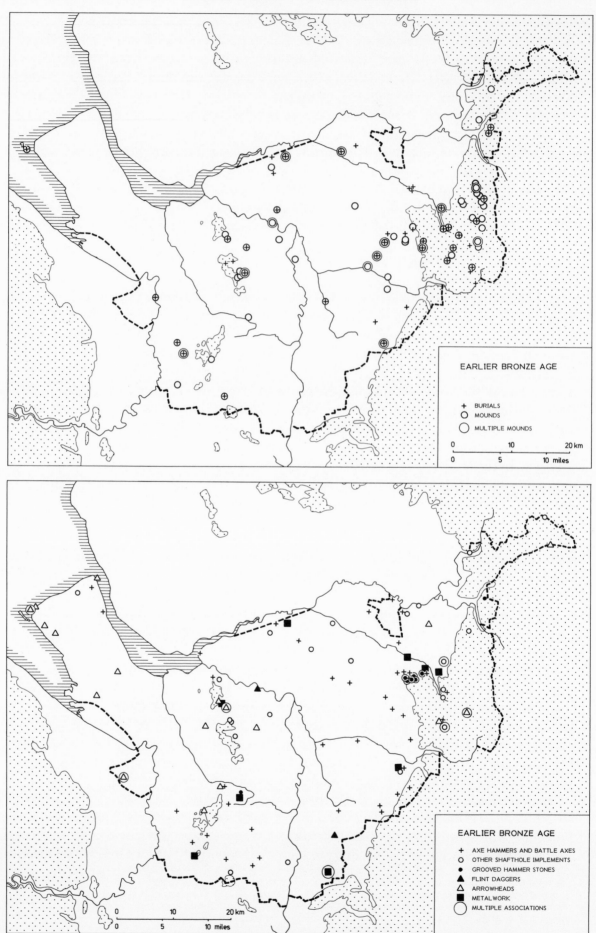

FIG. 8. (Contour at 400 ft. in both maps.)

through excavation or other disturbance, produced evidence of burial. A further 24 sites, without evidence of a mound, are recognized as burial sites by the association of diagnostic pottery; some may have had mounds since destroyed, while others may originally have been incorporated in flat cemeteries. The dominant rite is cremation. Inhumations are recorded only at Little Eye, Hoylake (crouched under a cairn), at Lower Withington (outside the perimeter of the barrow and therefore not necessarily contemporary with it), and at Appleton; at the last several extended inhumations were recorded in the early 19th century from at least two stone cists near Early Bronze Age cremations, but the details are not clear. At Gawsworth the primary pit containing the Beaker had been badly damaged and no human remains survived in that context. At Church Lawton a pit 1.35 by 0.75 by 0.5 m. had been filled with sand flecked with charcoal, and contained no body.

The burial evidence is not distributed randomly across the county. Seventy-two per cent of the burials can be shown to occur within altitude bands representing only 37 per cent of Cheshire's surface area, in the upper ranges of altitude. The large number of burials at heights of 60–120 m. may reflect the agricultural potential of the freely draining sands and gravels of the eastern flank of the central ridge and the west flank of the Pennines; more significant is the tendency to avoid the lower, heavier boulder clays and alluvium of the Dee and Weaver valleys. The coincidence of lighter soils and burials near Warrington (Lancs.), along the Wirral coast, and in the Weaver valley near Northwich enhances the pattern. Significant also is the high relative density of burials at altitudes between 240 and 425 m. in areas which were to become agriculturally marginal after the climate worsened during the later 2nd millennium.[39]

The burial mounds of the Early Bronze Age are all round and, although such mounds are known to cover Neolithic burial in some areas, the earliest datable round mound in Cheshire is the Gawsworth cairn covering a relatively late Beaker of *c.* 2000 B.C. The choice between cairns and barrows appears to have depended simply on which materials were available. Some monuments, however, incorporated circles of stakes or stone in their construction, while other circular stone settings of the period, associated with burial but with no accompanying mound, may be a development of the free standing stone circle of primarily ceremonial rather than burial function. Four Cheshire sites, Church Lawton (iii), Grappenhall, Delamere, and the Bullstones, at Wincle in Prestbury, have produced evidence of circular stone settings.

The monument at Church Lawton (south) was originally constructed as an open ring, 22–3 m. in diameter, of nine massive boulders with entrance gaps on the north and south perimeter. Seven of the stones were laid lengthwise along the circumference; the other two stood upright. A small rectangular turf and daub structure of *c.* 2.5 by 1.5 m. stood within the area so defined. Two fragments of cremated bone were associated with that feature, which itself appears to have been burnt. The function of such a monument can only be guessed at: exposure and cremation of the dead might reasonably be an element. After some time the site was closed by the construction of a low mound contained within the stone ring. That development is not isolated. At Balbirnie (Fife) a comparable one can be traced from open stone circle with rectangular stone setting to closed cairn. Church

---

[39] Anomalies in distribution of sites can often arise through differential survival of the evidence, or through activities which make recovery of certain categories of information more likely. Nevertheless the distribution above is considered to reflect genuine locational preference: D. Longley, 'Stray Finds, Prehist. Settlement, and Land Use in Ches.' *Ches. Arch. Bull.* vi. 84-7.

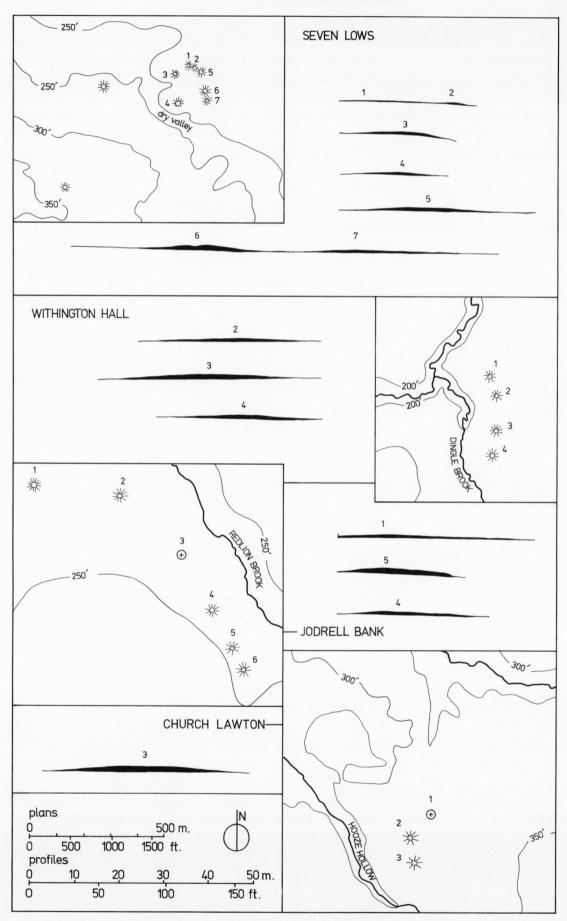

Fig. 9. Site Plans of Early Bronze Age Barrow Cemeteries.

Lawton (south) was not used for burial; conversely at Balbirnie a phase of cist burial preceded the construction of the cairn and cremations were also incorporated into the cairn material itself. At Balbirnie that transition spanned the Late Neolithic and Early Bronze Age.[40]

At Grappenhall two cairns appear to have been bordered by stone kerbs. Although the excavations of 1931–4 have never been adequately published, and the details are somewhat obscure, it seems that one cairn incorporated a central stone cist 'with cremations outside' and several secondary cremations in the body of the mound, one in association with urn fragments. The other cairn produced a Food Vessel with a primary burial of unspecified nature together with a saddle quern. A second Food Vessel was recovered from the outer margin of the cairn on the original ground surface, and secondary cremation burials were recovered from the body of the mound. A bone pin can no longer be assigned to its original context. A number of cremations, in excess of five, were recorded from outside the area of the cairns in association with two Collared Urns and an Enlarged Food Vessel.

At Delamere a possible stone cist and cremation were disturbed by ploughing in 1937; later excavation revealed a circular stone setting '7 ft.' in diameter. No trace of a mound was recognized although regular ploughing may well have obliterated the evidence and the observation that several cartloads of stone and two barrowloads of soot were removed is suggestive. Three pits were located outside the circle of stones, one of which contained the cremated remains of an infant in an inverted Collared Urn together with a small fragment of bronze.

At the Bullstones, Wincle, a circle of stones 8.5 m. in diameter encloses, off-centre, a much larger, broad, standing stone 1 m. in height. The precise character of the ring, which has become obscured by vegetation, is uncertain. A 19th-century illustration depicts a ring of contiguous small stones, broken to form an entrance and extending beyond it to form a short avenue with returns to the circle itself. A cremated infant burial within an inverted urn was found near the centre of the circle in 1867 together with a flint 'knife' and what has been claimed as an arrowhead. Only fragments of the urn survive, including one small sherd with incised decoration.

While individual burial is frequently held to be characteristic of the period, the Grappenhall cemetery and Church Lawton (ii) barrow provide an indication of the complexity of Early Bronze Age burial. In the second cairn at Grappenhall the primary burial, the one central to the cairn's construction, was within a stone cist accompanied by a Food Vessel. Secondary cremations were inserted into the body of the mound without the accompaniment of urns. Further cremations, some contained in urns, were buried outside the circuit of the cairn, and the cemetery as a whole comprised at least one other cairn with a similarly complex make-up.

At Church Lawton (ii) a ditch marked out an area 15.5 m. in diameter within which a sand dump mound was constructed to a height of c. 2.25 m. The focal point, dug within the body of the mound, was a pit 1.35 by 0.75 by 0.5 m., which although sealed by a carbonized wooden lid appeared to contain no burial. A Collared Urn with no cremation and c. 10 unurned cremations were incorporated within the mound. Two further vessels, a Collared Urn containing a cremation and an inverted Food Vessel, may have been buried at that stage. In addition, on two occasions, bags seem to have been used to contain the cremated remains, in one instance accompanied by a flint knife and in the other by a stone battle-axe.

---

[40] Grooved Ware is associated with the construction of the stone circle at Balbirnie; the earliest cist contained a Beaker and at least one of the other cists has a Food Vessel association: *Arch. Jnl.* cxxxi. 1–32.

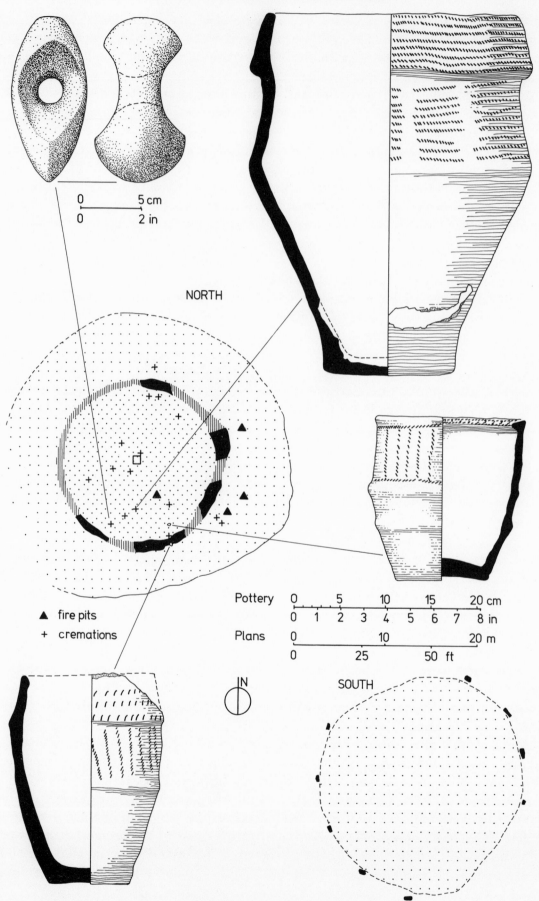

NORTH

0   5 cm
0   2 in

▲ fire pits
+ cremations

Pottery   0   5   10   15   20 cm
       0   1   2   3   4   5   6   7   8 in

Plans   0   10   20 m
      0   25   50   ft

N

SOUTH

Fig. 10. Church Lawton: Site Plan and Artefacts.

Scatters of cremated bone and pot sherds attest further, disturbed burials. A fire pit in the south-west quadrant seems to have been used as a funeral pyre. A second phase saw the original mound enlarged to a diameter of *c.* 30–2 m. by the addition of sand capped by turf, and, while three fire pits or pyres are appended to that, there is no certain evidence of the continued use of the barrow for burial.

Secondary burials in such contexts may imply the periodic re-use of the cairn for burial long after its original construction. Alternatively they may represent contemporary burials which for some reason, such as status, were not afforded a prime position in the grave. Status may also have dictated the appropriate accompaniment for burial which was, most commonly, a pottery vessel. Other grave goods are as rare in Cheshire as they are generally, the bone dagger pommel and bronze dagger blade from two Wilmslow sites and the battle-axe from Church Lawton being exceptional, and no groups approach the richness of the Wessex Culture graves of Salisbury Plain and the Marlborough Downs.[41]

Funerary pottery: accessory vessels

Two categories of pottery vessel are associated with Early Bronze Age burial: accessory vessels accompanying inhumation and cinerary urns containing cremated remains. Although pottery vessels were sometimes included with Neolithic burials, the beginning of the 2nd millennium B.C. saw the evolution of a range of specialized funerary pottery, and the use of urns as receptacles for ashes was a new departure.[42]

The earliest and finest inhumation accessories are to be found in the Beaker series. The first Beakers, well made and decorated with horizontal bands of cord impressions or panels of comb or cord impressions, are Continental imports.[43] During the course of the later 3rd millennium the British Beaker series developed its own regional variations, and the single intact[44] Cheshire Beaker, from Gawsworth, belongs to a relatively late stage in that development, Step 6 in Lanting and Van der Waals's classification, of the early 2nd millennium B.C. Decoration has been impressed into the pot with a six-toothed comb, in three panels separated by two cordons, one below the rim and one at the waist. The metopic arrangement is typical of that stage of Beaker development. Geometric arrangements of vertical floating lozenges above the waist and horizontal lozenges below it have been formed with the comb, leaving saltires or zigzags of undecorated clay. The cordons and the rim have been impressed with a wedge-shaped tool. No burial was found in association with the Beaker, perhaps because a substantial portion of the pit containing the deposit had been destroyed. A layer of black ash lined the base of the pit, over which a small cairn had been constructed before a larger earthen mound was raised over the deposit.

Beakers were so named because it was felt that they may have contained drink, possibly alcoholic. Similarly, Food Vessels may have contained a food offering. Food Vessels are generally small; characteristic forms include bipartite or tripartite vases and globular bowls with thick rims and internal bevel. Decoration of impressed cord, comb stamps, and incised lines is common, with zigzags and herringbone a recurring feature. The vessels generally, though not invariably, accompany inhumation burial, although there are marked regional variations and in north-west

[41] *V.C.H. Wilts.* i (2), 352–75.
[42] Burgess, *Age of Stonehenge*, 84–95.
[43] D. L. Clark, *Beaker Pottery of Great Brit. and Irel.*; *Helinium*, xii. 20–46.
[44] Sherds of Beaker pottery were recovered from the ground surface upon which the Church Lawton (ii) barrow was constructed.

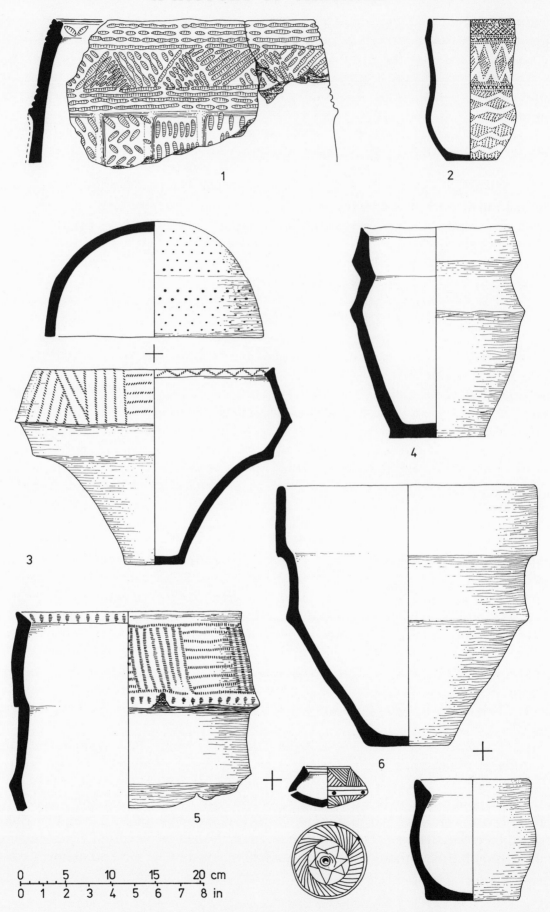

FIG. 11. Early Bronze Age Pottery from Burials: 1. Delamere; 2. Gawsworth; 3. Henbury; 4. Tytherington; 5. Betchton; 6. Gawsworth.

England and in Wales the reverse seems to be true.[45] At the Gawsworth burial referred to above, an inverted plain globular vase with outcurving and bevelled rim accompanied a cremation contained within a plain inverted Collared Urn. A corrugated hollow-cone clay 'mouth-bellows' was associated with the burial in the urn, which was inserted, with three others, into the quarry ditch of the Beaker mound.

South of Warrington two sites, Grappenhall and Appleton, in Great Budworth, have revealed Food Vessel burials in unusual circumstances. The second of the two Grappenhall cairns, discussed in general terms above, covered a primary burial accompanied by a Food Vessel and a saddle quern. Neither the nature of the burial nor whether it was in a cist, like that of the first cairn, was recorded. The Food Vessel is 12 cm. in height, of bipartite vase form with out-turned rim internally bevelled. A groove on the shoulder gives the impression of two ridges and a cordon runs below the rim. Impressed twisted cord decoration covers the vessel, horizontal above the shoulder and on the rim bevel and diagonal below the shoulder. A second Food Vessel, of tripartite bowl form with impressed whipped cord 'maggots' in herringbone arrangement, a common North of England combination, was found near the edge of the cairn.

At Appleton in 1829 workmen disturbed a number of burials near the main road from Stretton to Stockton Heath. Several extended skeletons lay in two stone cists, each formed of four upright slabs. Early accounts record the presence of two urns containing bones, ashes, and charcoal lying nearby. A third urn was later found on the opposite (west) side of the road. The only surviving vessel is a small bipartite pot with out-turned flattened rim; it is labelled 'Burial urn found with another *in* a stone grave at Stretton near Warrington' (author's italics). It appears that at Appleton a vase of Food Vessel type was in use as a cinerary urn. No trace of a mound was recorded, but there need not necessarily have been one. The mixture of inhumation and cremation in the same cemetery, and even in the same grave, is recorded elsewhere.

At Church Lawton (ii) a tripartite 'ridged-bucket' Food Vessel was inverted in a conical pit within the mound. No burial was associated, although charcoal and ashy soil surrounded the vessel in the pit.

A class of accessory vessel which came into vogue during the later Early Bronze Age, towards the mid 2nd millennium B.C., was the miniature 'Pygmy Cup'. Vessels of the type are frequently perforated, as the Betchton example is, and the alternative name 'incense cup' has been coined in respect of their supposed function as containers of incense or some similar substance. Two Pygmy Cups are known from Cheshire. At Manley in Frodsham the round earthen mound called Glead Hill Cob was levelled in 1879; ten or twelve cremation urns were disturbed in the process, of which three Collared Urns and the base of a fourth urn survive. Two barbed and tanged arrowheads, a bronze pin, and a Pygmy Cup, all since lost, were recovered from the mound. The Pygmy Cup had a squat barrel shape with two horizontal zones of incised hatched triangle decoration bounded by horizontal lines. The base had a cross arrangement of incised hatched squares. The second Cheshire Pygmy Cup was found in Betchton in Sandbach in association with a cremation burial contained within a Collared Urn. The site had been under cultivation and no mound was recorded. The cup is biconical in shape with incised hatched triangle

---

[45] D. D. A. Simpson, 'Food Vessels, Associations, and Chronology', *Studies in Ancient Eur.* ed. J. M. Coles and D. D. A. Simpson, 197–211; Burgess, *Age of Stonehenge*, 82.

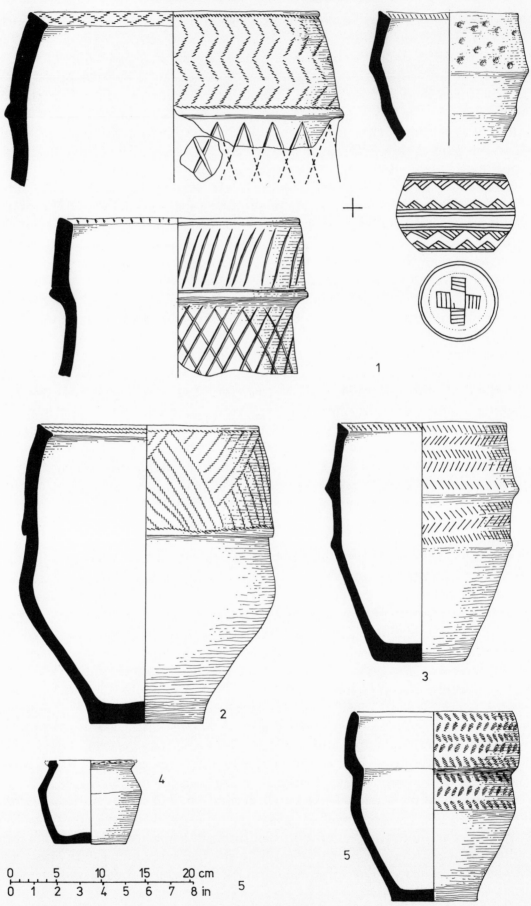

FIG. 12. Early Bronze Age Pottery from Burials: 1. Manley; 2. Delamere; 3. Delamere; 4. Appleton; 5. Newbold Astbury.

decoration above the carination and diagonal incisions below. The two zones are isolated by horizontal incised lines. A six-pointed star motif radiates out from a slight omphalos at the base. Two perforations are located immediately below the carination on one side of the vessel.

Cinerary urns

The most common form of urn that was developed, it appears, specifically to contain the ashes of the dead was the Collared Urn. Such vessels have their antecedents in the Peterborough series of the Late Neolithic, particularly those in Fengate style, and derive their name from the distinctive overhanging collar above a generally, though not invariably, carinated shoulder. Decoration is applied to the collar and internal rim bevel, which occasionally extends down the interior to the external depth of the collar, and frequently to the neck of the vessel.[46]

The Collared Urn, the dominant form of cinerary urn in Cheshire, is represented by 20 examples out of a total of 24 identifiable vessels. More than 30 additional cinerary urns of unspecified form are recorded, the details of which have been lost. The Cheshire urns embody most of the decorative traits occurring commonly on Collared Urns from other areas of north Britain, including whipped cord 'maggots' in herringbone arrangement at Wincle, Sutton, and Newbold Astbury, whipped cord impressed lines forming alternating horizontally and vertically hatched squares at Betchton, incised cross hatching at Manley, and incised herringbone at Delamere. Twisted cord impressions are more common, occurring in lattice arrangement at Grappenhall, in herringbone at Grappenhall and Manley, and in horizontal and vertical lines on each of the two Church Lawton urns. The urns from Delamere (Seven Lows), Henbury, and Wilmslow and probably that from Over Alderley have twisted cord impressed filled triangles. Impressions made with a stick or the articular end of a bird bone decorate the collar of one Church Lawton urn and the collar and shoulder of the Wincle and Sutton urns, and occur on the shoulder only of the smallest of the Manley urns. The smaller of the two Collared Urns from the Grappenhall cemetery has vertical rows of dots impressed with a sharp point on its neck. The rows begin very neatly but deteriorate into a row of slashes by the time the decoration has completed the circuit of the vessel. Many of those motifs and techniques of decoration occur in differing combinations on the same vessel.

There seems to be no regional differentiation, although the plain urns from Gawsworth and Tytherington were found within 5 km. of each other, as were, apparently, the typologically similar urns from Wincle and Sutton. The Wincle urn poses a problem, in that it is claimed to be the vessel associated with the Bullstones cremation.[47] Pottery sherds from another, incomplete vessel, which include one with incised decoration, certainly came, with flint work, from the Bullstones excavation. The confusion over the attribution of the two vessels awaits resolution.

The contexts of deposition of the urns are varied. Five mounds have produced a total of 11 urns. In no instance can it be demonstrated that those urns were in a primary position, although it remains a possibility at Glead Hill Cob, Manley, where only 3 Collared Urns survive out of an important cemetery group of 10 or 12 urns, a Pygmy Cup, 2 barbed and tanged arrowheads, and a bronze pin or awl. At Delamere, a Collared Urn was recovered from one of the Seven Lows. The urn contained a cremation and was inverted on a flat stone at the north-eastern perimeter

---

[46] I. H. Longworth, *Collared Urns of Bronze Age in Great Brit. and Irel.*   [47] *Congleton Chron.* 29 Oct. 1976.

of the mound. At Henbury an unusual Collared Urn, containing a cremation and capped by a round-based vessel, was also located near the perimeter of the mound in an ash-filled pit. The two Collared Urns from Church Lawton (ii) have been mentioned in discussion of that barrow, where burials were incorporated within the mound rather than dug into the underlying subsoil, including the rectangular pit without human remains which appears to have been the focus of the barrow. Excavation of the Woodhouse End barrow at Gawsworth has produced the best stratigraphical sequence for Collared Urn burial within a mound. There a primary Beaker burial (with no record of a body, the burial pit having been disturbed) was capped by a small cairn and a mound, into the quarry ditch of which four cremations were later inserted, two inurned cremations in separate pits and two further cremations, one in a Collared Urn set upright on the floor of the quarry ditch and the second in an inverted Collared Urn in association with an inverted Food Vessel. The clay 'mouth-bellows' was associated with this burial. After the quarry ditch had become filled, partly with material which may have eroded from the Beaker mound including abraded Peterborough pottery and other domestic refuse, a fifth cremation in an inverted urn was set into the cobbles of the quarry ditch infill. The mound was raised again and enlarged in diameter with material from an outer quarry ditch. Finally the outer ditch became filled with stones and domestic debris which included fragments of a Collared Urn. The presence of domestic debris, including charcoal ash and animal bone fragments, in the quarry ditch infill may represent contemporary occupation in the immediate vicinity or, on the other hand, may suggest activities associated with the burial ritual.

It appears that, on occasion, barrow-like mounds of natural origin were used for the interment of cremations either mistakenly or deliberately. A possible instance may be seen at Birtles Hall, Over Alderley. An urn, since lost but seeming from an ambiguous engraving to have been a Collared Urn, was recovered during gravel digging. A partially quarried, apparently natural, mound in the grounds of Birtles Hall may have been the site of the discovery.

None of the remaining Collared Urns show evidence of having been buried within a barrow or cairn although in many cases the circumstances of discovery and prior land use do not preclude the possibility. At Betchton, for instance, the site had been under intensive cultivation before the discovery of the burial, while at Tytherington an inverted urn was discovered on a site that had previously been levelled. Flat cemeteries of the period are known, apparently either unenclosed or demarcated by a bank or ring of stones. Some circular stone monuments may represent, in the first instance, a continuation of the tradition of free-standing stone circles and may have been focal points of ritual activity rather than cemeteries even though they incorporated burials. The Bullstones, Wincle, with its elaborate entrance, central cremation, and off-centre monolith may belong to the category.

The Grappenhall complex has been discussed above. Several cremations, two of which were contained within Collared Urns, were excavated outside the area of the two cairns. Similarly at Delamere three pits were located outside a formal monument with a central cist; one contained an infant cremation in an inverted Collared Urn.

Other specific types of urn recorded from Cheshire include a Cordoned Urn from West Kirby and a Food Vessel Urn from Grappenhall. Cordoned Urns are characteristically barrel shaped with two horizontal cordons around the girth. They have generally late associations within the Early Bronze Age and may have continued to be used for cremation into the later 2nd millennium. The West Kirby urn was one of several found inverted and containing cremations in an apparently flat cemetery. It has short incisions on the rim bevel, short diagonal incisions in horizontal rows not quite achieving a herringbone effect on the upper part, and horizontal incisions irregularly arranged amongst an incised zigzag between the two cordons.

Food Vessel Urns belong to the same ceramic family as Food Vessels except that they are sufficiently large to hold cremations.[48] Both classes of Food Vessel have their counterpart in the domestic repertoire and, in common with Collared Urns, have their origin in the Peterborough Ware of the Late Neolithic. The Grappenhall urn contained a cremation and was located just outside the second of the two cairns. It stands over 26 cm. tall and is of high-shouldered bucket form. The deep bevel of the rim has three horizontal rows of diagonal whipped cord 'maggot' impressions; the outer face from the rim to the shoulder has six horizontal rows of impressed knotted cord or very short, almost circular, 'maggots'.

It is possible that, as at Grappenhall, cairns, in addition to attracting their own secondary burials, acted as the focal points of more extensive burials in less durably marked graves. Only excavation will resolve the possibility. By contrast, additional burials in some cemeteries apparently called for the erection of new mounds, and such grouping into 'barrow-cemeteries' is particularly noteworthy at the Seven Lows (Delamere), Jodrell Bank (Goostrey, Swettenham, and Twemlow), Withington Hall (Prestbury), and Church Lawton.

The Seven Lows

The Seven Lows are a cluster of seven earthen mounds (there are two others close by) which overlook a dry valley south of Delamere.[49] They were known to John Leland, the antiquary, who in the 16th century described them as 'the works of men of warre'.[50] Early in the 19th century one of the mounds was removed to form the adjacent road; another had been opened some time earlier. In 1845 a third mound was quarried, revealing a cremation contained within a Collared Urn inverted on a flat stone near the perimeter. Sandstone rubble formed part of the make-up of the mound. Although that barrow was said to have stood 6 ft. (1.8 m.) high, all are now reduced to slight circular rises in the ground.[51]

Jodrell Bank

The six barrows in the group form a curving line through the parishes of Goostrey, Twemlow, and Swettenham, following the course of the Redlion brook along its south bank.[52] They are in varying degrees of preservation. One mound was partially excavated in 1867 to reveal an inurned cremation. The urn 'soon crumbled away'. The largest surviving mound is consistently under the plough and in 1977 cremations were ploughed up in the course of potato planting.

Withington Hall

In the 18th century a line of imperfect barrows was reported between Astle Hall and Withington.[53] In the 19th three mounds were recorded near Withington Hall.[54]

[48] T. G. Cowie, *Bronze Age Food Vessel Urns in N. Brit.* (Brit. Arch. Rep. lv); H. N. Savory, *Guide Catalogue of Bronze Age Collections in Nat. Mus. of Wales*, 80–2.
[49] Fig. 9.
[50] Leland, *Itin.* ed. Toulmin Smith, v. 82.
[51] Ormerod, *Hist. Ches.* ii. 2.
[52] Fig. 9.
[53] B.L. Add. MS. 11338, f. 72, quoted by W. T. Watkin, *Roman Ches.* 76.
[54] Ormerod, *Hist. Ches.* iii. 3.

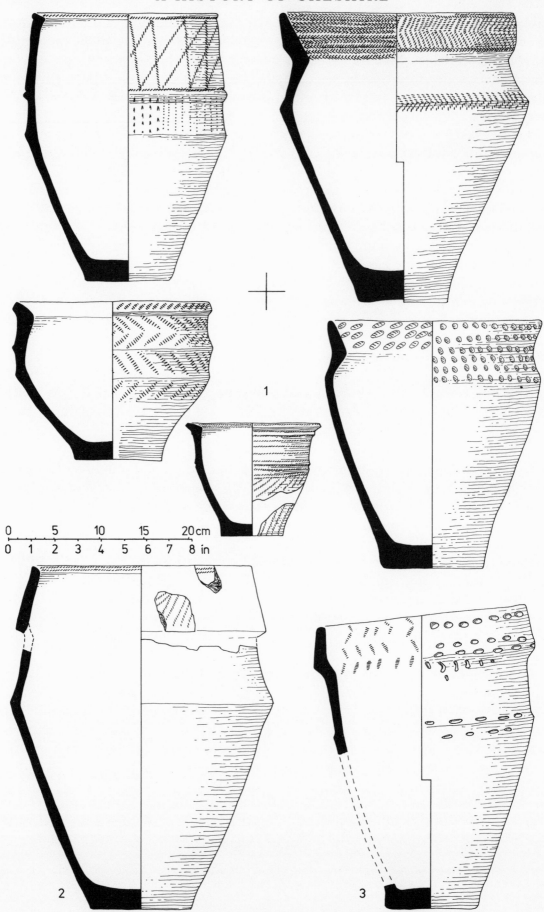

FIG. 13. Early Bronze Age Pottery from Burials: 1. Grappenhall; 2. Wilmslow; 3. Wincle.

A fourth was identified in 1972.[55] As at Jodrell Bank, all are dispersed along a curving line, which follows the course of the Dingle brook on its east bank. All are under pasture. An inurned cremation is recorded on an Ordnance Survey map to have come from mound (iii). The northernmost mound was excavated during 1976–7 and revealed the cremated remains of an 18-year-old female, who appears to have died from a blow on the head, in a primary position under a stacked turf and sand mound. No urn was present but the burial may have been interred in a leather container. Two inurned secondary cremations, one above the primary, the other in the north-east quadrant, were also present. An inhumation burial was located outside the perimeter of the barrow to the south-east. An elaborate ritual, sealing off the primary cremation pit, seems to have involved capping the pit with successive layers of turf, sand and gravel, and charcoal. Transverse flint arrowheads among other used flints were recovered from the body of the mound. Radiocarbon determinations of 1490 b.c. ± 100 (c. 1900 B.C.) and 1350 b.c. ± 100 (c. 1700 B.C.) for one of the secondaries were obtained. The presence of the inhumation, of which too little survived for radiocarbon dating, is unusual: inhumations very rarely occur in a secondary relationship to cremations in a single burial complex.[56]

Church Lawton

A 19th-century source records the recovery of 'urns etc.' from one of three mounds overlooking Hooze Hollow north-east of Alsager. The northernmost no longer survives.[57] Excavation of (ii) and (iii) revealed a complex and varied history of ceremonial and burial practice described above.[58]

PERFORATED STONE IMPLEMENTS

Some basically unaltered pebbles with hourglass perforation may have been used as tools during the Mesolithic period. Those apart, stone-working technology developed, from the 3rd millennium onwards, a range of perforated stone artefacts designed to be set with wooden hafts through the perforation. They can be conveniently classified under four headings, mace heads, shafthole axes, shafthole adzes, and a miscellaneous group. As in the making of Neolithic polished stone axes certain rocks might be preferred. The makers of mace heads tended to use rocks familiar from Neolithic axe production such as Group VI (Great Langdale) and Group VII (Graig Lwyd). The majority of perforated axes and adzes, however, were made from medium-grained rocks more suited to the pecking and drilling techniques required to form a shafthole. New sources of rock with that property were therefore exploited, such as picrite from the Welsh Marches (Group XII) and quartz dolerite from Whin Sill (Group XVIII). Lake District greywacke (Group XV) was also used extensively and accounts for the majority of petrologically identified Cheshire shafthole axes. Group XV products concentrate in the source area, with a distribution that extends south into Lancashire and beyond into Cheshire and Derbyshire, tailing off into Staffordshire and Shropshire.[59]

[55] T. Clare, 'Aspects of Stone Circles and Kindred Monuments in the North-West of Eng.' (Liverpool Univ. M.A. thesis, 1973).

[56] D. Wilson, 'Lower Withington', Ches. Arch. Bull. vi. 66–8.

[57] Figs. 9–10.

[58] R. McNeil, unpublished excavation rep. Thanks are due to Miss McNeil for access to illustrative material in advance of publication.

[59] Figs. 14–15.

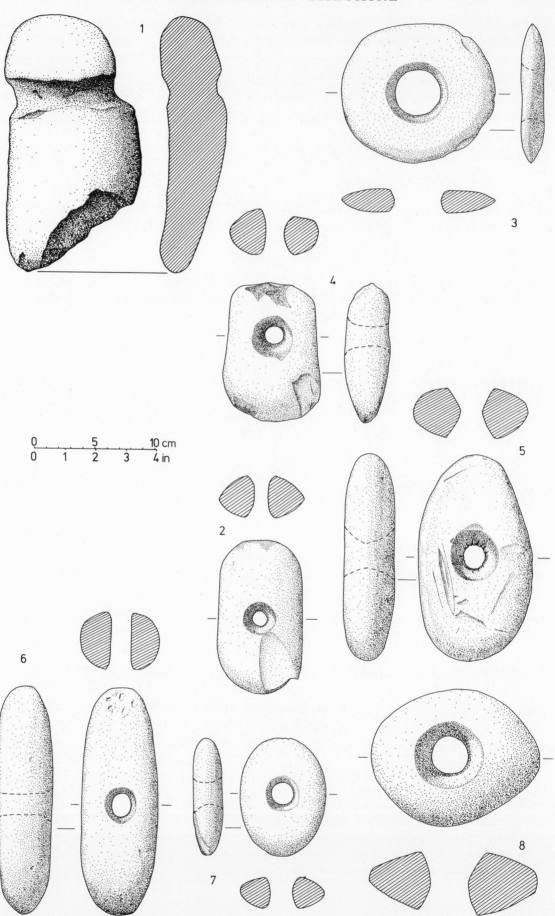

FIG. 14. Early Bronze Age Stone Shafthole Implements and Grooved Hammer-Stone: 1. Alderley Edge; 2. Knutsford; 3. Delamere; 4. Weaverham; 5. Wirswall; 6. Macclesfield; 7. Delamere; 8. Adlington.

Mace heads

Common features of mace heads include the fine quality of workmanship and the generally attractive nature of the rock chosen; a recurring feature is the placing of the shafthole, invariably cylindrical, offset from the centre slightly towards the narrower end of the implement. The consistent lack of evidence of their damage through use suggests a symbolic or ceremonial function. They have been classified on the basis of their ovoid, pestle, or cushion form, though none of those well defined forms are immediately recognizable from Cheshire contexts.[60] The elongated artefact from Tytherington Fields, in Prestbury, is of polished Group XV rock with a central cylindrical perforation. The rounded ends have suffered some damage, but whether as a result of performing the original function of the implement cannot be ascertained. A second implement of Group XV greywacke, from Appleton, though ovoid in form and with a slightly off-centre shafthole, has an hourglass perforation. Neither that nor the use of Group XV rock is characteristic of the classic series of mace heads. A mottled grey polished stone from Weaverham with a shafthole nearer the narrower end has something of the proportions of an ovoid mace head. The distal end, however, thins ambiguously to a blunted edge in the fashion of a shafthole adze. Both extremities show severe damage which may have resulted from the nature of its find spot, on the bed of the river Weaver.

Shafthole axes

Among shafthole implements with a cutting edge at one end along the axis of the haft, and a hammer head at the other, battle-axes may be distinguished from axe-hammers. Battle-axes are well made, smaller, and generally well proportioned, and, even if not used as weapons, are nevertheless likely to have conferred status or prestige on their owners, as their grave associations testify. Axe-hammers, on the other hand, are larger and can be more crudely fashioned, suggesting a utilitarian function as tools. In most cases the distinction is clear cut, but nonetheless some implements appear to fall between the two groups, and certain metrical criteria have been suggested as an aid to classification.[61] Eight battle-axes have been recorded in Cheshire. Insufficient information is available on three (Church Hulme, Tabley Inferior, and Pickmere) to confirm that they are indeed battle-axes, and of the other five only that from Church Lawton conforms entirely to the requirements of that classification. Nevertheless the Odd Rode axe, found near Little Moreton Hall, and the Tarporley axe of Cornish greenstone found on Peckforton Farm may confidently be assigned to the class. The Bickley/Norbury implement of Group XV greywacke, polished with flattened butt and expanded blade, is amongst the smallest of all Cheshire axes but lacks the graceful proportions of the classic battle-axes. The Haslington axe, on the other hand, is at the upper limit of size for a battle-axe. Its present rather dumpy proportions are a result of a regrinding and shortening of length at the blade end after damage, while the hammer end also appears to show slight signs of use. Raised ribs decorate the sides of the axe.

Only battle-axes and mace heads have satisfactory associations, as in the barrow burials at Church Lawton and at Winwick (Lancs.) just outside the county boundary.[62] The chronology of shafthole axe development has therefore relied on the battle-axe series, with the typology of axe-hammers apparently mirroring the

[60] F. Roe, 'Stone Mace Heads and Latest Neolithic Cultures of Brit. Isles', *Studies in Ancient Eur.* 145–72.

[61] F. Roe, 'Battle-Axe Series in Brit.' *Proc. Prehist. Soc.* xxxii. 199–245.

[62] R. McNeil, 'Church Lawton', *Ches. Arch. Bull.* viii. 46–9; *Jnl. Brit. Arch. Assoc.* xvi. 295–6.

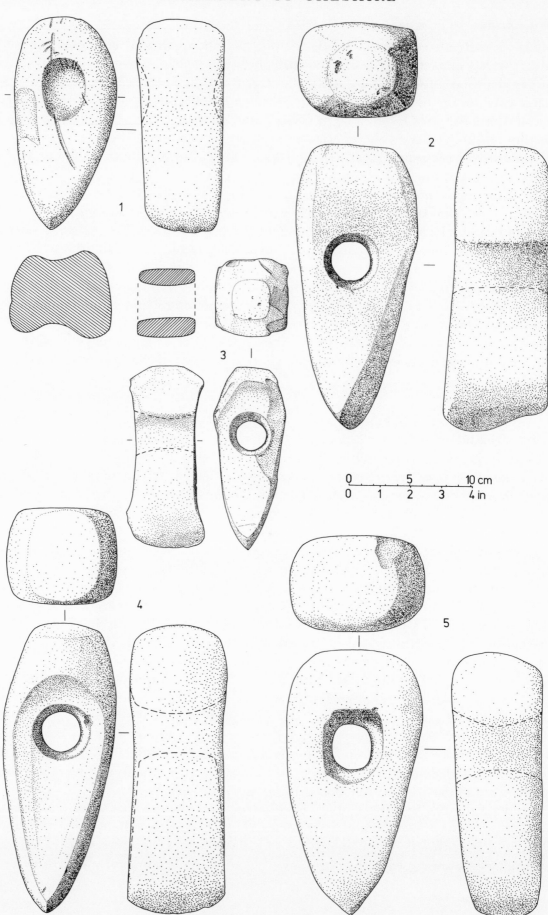

FIG. 15. Early Bronze Age Stone Shafthole Axes and Battle-Axes: 1. Congleton; 2. High Legh; 3. Odd Rode; 4. Middlewich; 5. Alderley Edge.

progression. The earliest battle-axes, and therefore axe-hammers, have slightly convex side profiles with the greatest depth, along the shafthole axis, at the hammer end. The earliest associations are with late Beakers, from the turn of the 3rd to 2nd millennium, and the production of shafthole axes continued to the end of the Early Bronze Age. Gradually concave profiles were introduced, with the blade and butt becoming more expanded, in their most developed form, in relation to the slender body.

Group XV greywacke alone among the grouped rocks has been positively identified as the material used for making shafthole axes found in Cheshire, though the possible battle-axe found at Church Hulme may be of Whin Sill quartz dolerite (Group XVIII), and the Tarporley battle-axe is of Cornish greenstone. While new medium-grained rocks capable of being drilled or pecked relatively easily were sought out for manufacturing axe-hammers, in contrast to the fine-grained and flakeable rocks of many Neolithic axes, the shafthole series cannot simply be seen as a straightforward replacement of polished stone axes resulting from a technological improvement in the hafting method. Axe-hammers have their densest concentration within the altitude range, between c. 60 and 120 m., that accounts for the least dense concentration of polished stone axes. In addition, the two groups are geographically separated, with polished stone axes predominant on Wirral, the north central ridge and the north Gowy and Weaver valleys and shafthole axes along the west Pennine slope and the south part of the central ridge. Such anomalies in distribution are difficult to explain in terms of chronological displacement alone, and some functional distinction may be responsible, a possibility supported by the marked difference in the size of the implements. Large polished stone axes occur, but axe-hammers are generally very much more massive. The Early Bronze Age also saw the appearance of new forms of axes in metal which copied the basic shape of their Neolithic stone prototypes.

The lack of good associations for axe-hammers has been noted. In two instances, at Beeston and Birkenhead, they have been found in uncertain relationships to polished stone axes. The Neolithic axe from Church Lawton, with its unfinished attempt to create a perforation for intended re-use as a shafthole axe, has been discussed above. A second unfinished implement from Congleton, originally conceived as an axe-hammer, also has depressions pecked into both faces as the beginning of an attempt at perforation which was not concluded. Its surfaces present a similarly unfinished and roughly dressed appearance.

Shafthole adzes

Shafthole adzes have a perforation at right angles to the axis of the blade and cannot have been used in the same manner as shafthole axes. They are elongated with a central hourglass perforation, and have a narrow profile thinning to a blade which is frequently blunt; whether they were used as adzes in woodworking, as hoes, or for some other purpose has not yet been established. Their chronology appears from the rock sources exploited to be linked to that of the axe-hammer series and the Early Bronze Age.[63] A polished stone axe from Wallasey has been reworked, through the provision of a shafthole, into an artefact of that type, and it is possible that other stone axes were hafted as adzes during the Neolithic period. Other than the Wallasey find, only three shafthole adzes are known from Cheshire. That from Knutsford is apparently an adze, though polished and provided with

[63] *Stone Axe Studies*, 23–48.

a more regular perforation than is usual. The Coole Pilate adze has one blunt 'hammer' end.

Miscellaneous perforated implements

A number of perforated or imperfectly perforated stone implements from the county cannot readily be assigned to any of the well defined groups discussed above. Some may be of Early Bronze Age date; for example, the ovoid stone with hourglass perforation from Appleton is of Group XV rock. Others need not be of that date, while some with depressions worked in one or both faces may never have been intended to be completely perforated. The pebble from Chester with a shallow depression worked in one flattened face could have been used as the chuck of a drill. A group of six ovoid quartzite stones with hourglass perforation, displaying some evidence of damage at either end, was found at Adlington. Perforated stones need not be hafted, but could be used suspended as weights on thatch, nets, or looms, or as flywheels on drills or spindles. The present catalogue, however, does not purposefully include such implements.

GROOVED HAMMER-STONES

Large numbers of grooved hammer-stones have been recovered from the vicinity of Alderley Edge. Nineteenth-century copper mining on the Edge revealed traces of earlier workings, and the occurrence of hammer-stones in the backfill and spoil from the workings raises the possibility of early exploitation of copper along the sandstone outcrop.[64] The implements were not apparently used in the mining process but to pulverize the mined material in order to separate the ore from its gangue or matrix. The activity apparently took place close to the source of ore, although access to water was necessary for the next stage of the process, washing. The finding of hammer-stones below the Edge at Kirkleyditch may therefore be significant. The Alderley Edge hammer-stones are roughly made, apparently of local rock, ranging in size from 15 to 20 cm. in length and up to *c*. 9 cm. across. A groove, often shallow, is pecked round the girth. They have close typological affinities with implements associated with copper mining in Austria, southern Spain, the Pyrenees, and southern France.[65] The date of exploitation at Alderley Edge remains uncertain, however, as similar implements apparently continued in use through much of later prehistory and conceivably until superseded by wind-powered machinery in the relatively recent past.[66] Isolated finds of grooved hammer-stones also appear to have been made at Marple and possibly at Bunbury.

FLINT DAGGERS

Flint daggers reflecting the form of early metal blades appear with predominantly late Beaker associations from the turn of the 2nd millennium. The implements are leaf-shaped with a finely pressure-flaked blade tapering to a tang which might form the core of an organic hilt. The daggers are concentrated in the southern and eastern counties of Britain, although there is a notable cluster of find spots in the Peak

[64] G. Warrington, 'Copper Mines of Alderley Edge and Mottram St. Andrew, Ches.' *J.C.A.S.* lxiv. 47-73.

[65] J. G. D. Clark, *Prehist. Eur.: The Econ. Basis*, 188.

[66] *J.C.A.S.* lxiv. 49-53.

District.[67] A single example has been recorded from Cheshire, as a surface find at Basford, while a second is known from just north of the county boundary at Winwick.

In Scandinavia an elaborate series of flint daggers was developed during the Early Bronze Age, and examples sometimes occur in British contexts either as imports or as indigenous copies.[68] A very fine example was found at Acton Bridge in 1974; bones of an unspecified nature were found at the same time but have since been lost. The Acton Bridge dagger is characteristic of the Scandinavian series in the high quality of its execution and the marked distinction between the flat leaf-shaped blade and the narrower, more solid, lozenge-sectioned hilt. The pointed tip of the blade was broken after discovery, and the extremity of the hilt appears to have been lost in antiquity. An expansion of the hilt terminal is a typological feature of certain of the Scandinavian daggers but cannot be demonstrated in the Acton Bridge example.

BARBED AND TANGED FLINT ARROWHEADS

The second half of the 3rd millennium B.C. witnessed an innovation in arrowhead design that can reasonably be attributed to the users of Beaker pottery. Barbed and tanged arrowheads are the only form of arrowhead to be included in Beaker graves and occur there with other items of archery equipment such as stone wrist-guards. The new form did not entirely supplant the leaf, transverse, and hollow-based arrowheads of the Neolithic which continued in use throughout the Early Bronze Age. The enhanced status of the barbed and tanged points, however, suggested by their occurrence with Beaker burials is confirmed by the predominant selection of that form as an accompaniment to Food Vessel burial, which includes a high proportion of the finest arrowheads.[69]

The increase in numbers and importance of archery equipment, together with a corresponding scarcity of wild animal bones on domestic sites, might support the view that the inferred use of archery during the Neolithic period[70] continued into the Early Bronze Age. Nevertheless there is equally a scarcity of human skeletal evidence of wounding during the period, and the importance of archery equipment in prestigious graves perhaps reflects an increase of interest in hunting as a social activity of some status, a sport, rather than a necessary source of meat.[71]

The majority of barbed and tanged arrowheads from Cheshire are stray finds; nevertheless on two occasions they have been found in association with burial. Two were recorded from the burial mound at Glead Hill Cob, Manley (Frodsham), along with (though not necessarily in association with) three Collared Urns and a Pygmy Cup. Two further arrowheads, one barbed and tanged, the other probably of that form, were contained within a Collared Urn together with a cremation at the side of Ridgegate reservoir, Sutton.

METALWORK

The first British metallurgy coincides with the appearance of some of the earliest (Step 2) Beakers, and it is reasonable to ascribe its introduction to the users of that

[67] W. F. Grimes, 'Early Bronze Age Flint Dagger in Eng. and Wales', *Proc. Prehist. Soc.* (1931), 340–55 and fig. 2.
[68] J. G. D. Clark, 'Flint Daggers of Scandinavian Type from Brit. Isles', *Man*, xxxii. 186–90.

[69] Green, *Flint Arrowheads*, 92–7.
[70] *Current Arch.* lxxvi. 145–7.
[71] R. Bradley, *Prehist. Settlement of Brit.* 84.

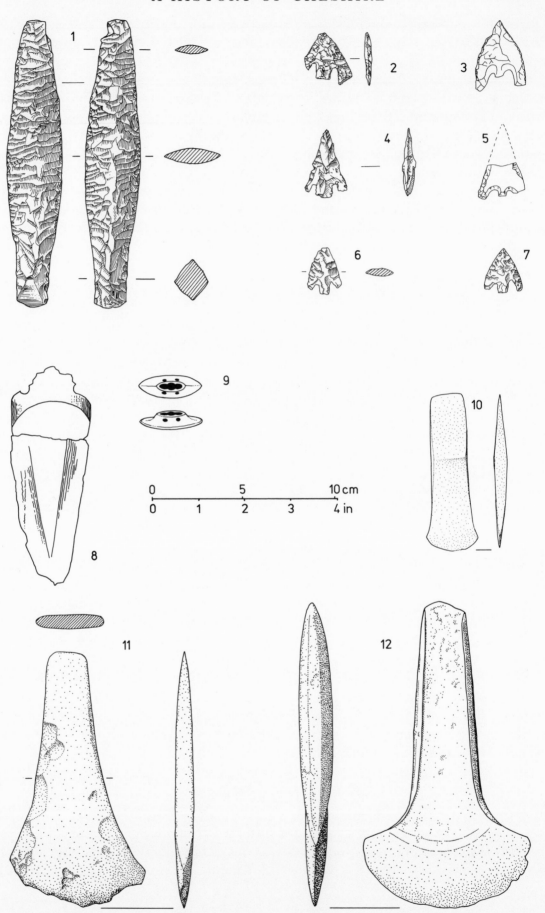

FIG. 16. Early Bronze Age Metalwork and Flintwork: 1. Acton Bridge; 2. Macclesfield; 3. Marton; 4. Horton; 5. Ashton; 6. Bickerton; 7. Manley; 8. Wilmslow; 9. Wilmslow; 10. Newbold Astbury; 11. Grappenhall; 12. Bridgemere.

pottery. The earliest tools, of copper, include flat axes, tanged knives, and double pointed awls. Ornaments were also produced in copper and in gold.[72] No metalwork of that earliest phase is known from Cheshire; it is doubtful whether the 'small fragments of copper' associated with an inurned cremation in a cist at Prestbury were in reality from a copper artefact.

Bronze, the alloy of copper and tin, had replaced copper by the end of the 3rd millennium, following the lead of European metallurgy, and bronze artefacts show both developments of their precursors in copper and an increased range. The earliest flat axes had a strongly trapezoidal shape with thick butt and straight sides. Developed forms show a concave curvature of the sides and a thinning of the butt. Bronze forms continued the process, with narrower thin butts. The Mottram St. Andrew, Malpas, and Grappenhall axes belong to that earliest phase of bronze working. A further development within the Early Bronze Age was the raising of slight flanges along the edges of the faces of axes and the provision of a ridge or bevel transversally. The small axe or chisel from Astbury, slender and only 84 mm. in length, has such a transverse bevel but appears not to have been provided with flanges. Such features, together with the thin butt, allowed a novel form of hafting in which a haft with a right-angle bend was split vertically down either side of the axe and held in place. The latest Early Bronze Age axes had slender bodies, cast flanges, and expanded blades. The development is represented by an axe from Spurstow, decorated with transverse furrowing on the body and diagonal fluting on the flanges, and by the cast-flange axes in the Bridgemere hoard.

A fourth bronze flat axe is known from Cheshire. Found amongst a 'heap of bones' at the Tattenhall bone works, it has a strong trapezoidal shape with almost straight sides and a rather thick butt. Typologically those features are early in the axe series. The unusual circumstances of its discovery, however, urge caution in accepting the axe as necessarily of local origin.

The development of knives and daggers is also an important chronological indicator during the Early Bronze Age. Tanged daggers, and tanged daggers with rivet holes for the attachment of the organic hilt, gave way to rivetted daggers, initially with residual tang or 'languette'. Daggers with multiple slender rivets were replaced by those with fewer thick 'plug' rivets towards the mid 2nd millennium. An unusual dagger with two slender rivets was included in the Bridgemere hoard together with the three cast-flange axes mentioned above. Although the organic hilts of those daggers seldom survive, decorative studs or wire sometimes do, as do pommels of more durable material. A group of burials from near Wilmslow railway station has produced evidence both of a dagger and of a bone pommel of that late phase of the Early Bronze Age, though much of the material has been lost and the records are confused. In the first burial to be disturbed, an urn was found to contain a cremation and a bronze dagger of Gerloff's 'Aylesford' group. Two further burials were subsequently recorded, one c. 400 m. south-east of the railway station involving an inverted Collared Urn whose mouth was sealed by coarse cloth, the other c. 100 m. east of the station with an inverted Collared Urn containing a bone dagger pommel. It is nowhere expressly stated that the urn containing the dagger was a Collared Urn, though it was regarded as similar to the others. The cremated remains associated with the pommel were recognized as those of 'a young person of about 14 years of age'. The dagger appears to have had a flat blade with V-shaped grooved decorations. The heel, although badly damaged, may have had two rather than four

---

[72] Early Bronze Age metalworking developments are summarized in Burgess, *Age of Stonehenge*, 71–3 sq.

rivets. The pommel, with an expanded flange narrowing to a truncated cone, was pierced laterally by two sets of opposed rivet holes and has a slot formed by three conjoined circular perforations for a dagger tang.

EARLY BRONZE AGE GAZETTEER

Mounds and Burials

ALDERLEY

ALDERLEY, NETHER (SJ 842 739). Sodger's Hump. Round earthen mound on large natural knoll in pasture land; diameter 65 m., height 2 m. Originally capped by pine trees, of which only one survives.

ALDERLEY, OVER. (a) Inurned cremation found near Macclesfield Road during gravel digging in 19th cent.; urn described as having small perforated lugs at intervals around upper part; neither site nor urn located (but see following).[73] (b) SJ 857 745. Large ?natural mound with irregular disturbance; ?Collared Urn found during 19th-cent. gravel digging may be associated; site is a large depression now under grass; urn in private possession in 19th cent., subsequently lost.[74] (c) SJ 856 746. Round earthen mound on top of natural rise; diameter 24 m., height 1.2 m.; in wooded parkland.

ASTBURY

NEWBOLD ASTBURY. (a) SJ 843 616. Several cremations including one within a Collared Urn (fig. 12.5) revealed during grave-digging, 1941; urn is Grosvenor Mus. 20.P.60; site a modern cemetery.[75] (b) Inurned cremation; urn kept at Astbury school for some years; not located.[76]

SOMERFORD (SJ 812 645). Earthen mound. Several unsuccessful attempts to locate a burial. Site destroyed.

BOWDON

DUNHAM MASSEY (SJ 734 876). Existence of barrows and finding of urns in Dunham Park recorded in 18th cent. Neither site nor urns can be located.[77]

BUDWORTH, GREAT

APPLETON. (a) SJ 617 839. Several extended inhumations in at least two cists; three urns, two containing cremations, found nearby; only one small bipartite vessel survives (fig. 12.4): Warrington Mus. RA 26; site occupied by housing estate and golf course.[78] (b) SJ 614 854. Round earthen mound; original diameter 23 m., original height 1.5 m.; ploughed out 1964 and built over.[79]

BUDWORTH, GREAT (SJ 622 778). Robin Hood's Butts. ?Mound. Arms of man in upright posture reported to have been found there 1661. Site under grass with no trace of mound.[80]

BUNBURY

ALPRAHAM (SJ 575 599). Robin Hood's Tump. Round earthen mound excavated 1940 with no evidence of burial. Diameter 17 m.; height 2 m. Site disturbed and covered by trees and grass.[81]

CHEADLE

SJ 858 885. Three cinerary urns, broken during house building. Site occupied by housing and urns untraced.[82]

CODDINGTON

SJ 453 553. Round earthen mound from which bones and 'articles of some sort' are recorded. Site wooded, with 19th-cent. disturbance.[83]

[73] *Proc. Soc. Antiq.* (1843–9), 31.
[74] Ibid. 36.
[75] *T.L.C.A.S.* lix. 155–9.
[76] *Ches. Historian*, ix. 23.
[77] J. Horsley, *Britannia Romana*, iii. 415.
[78] *T.H.S.L.C.* ii. 33.
[79] W. Beamont, *Account of Roman Station at Wilderspool*.
[80] Bodl. MS. Ashmole 854, f. 322, quoted by Shone, *Prehist. Man in Ches.* 95.
[81] *T.L.C.A.S.* l. 97.
[82] Earwaker, *E. Ches.* i. 185.
[83] Ormerod, *Hist. Ches.* ii. 371.

PREHISTORY
DAVENHAM

MOULTON (SJ 653 694). Round earthen mound; diameter 35 m., height 1.5 m. Previously surmounted by water tower.[84]

DELAMERE

DELAMERE. (a) The 'Seven Lows' barrow cemetery: seven earthen mounds (fig. 9). i. SJ 567 671. ii. SJ 567 670. iii. SJ 567 671. iv. SJ 567 670. v. SJ 566 670. vi. SJ 567 671. vii. SJ 566 671. Site severely denuded by ploughing, quarrying, fencing, and gardening; a cremation within a Collared Urn found during quarrying (fig. 12.2); urn is British Mus. 53.4-5.1.[85] (b) SJ 536 688. ?Cist and burial within 7 ft.-diameter circular stone setting; three external pits, one containing cremation and small bronze fragment within inverted Collared Urn (fig. 12.3); site is ploughed; urn is Grosvenor Mus. 30.P.52.[86] (c) SJ 548 690. Cist containing cremation and urn (possibly same site as following); site under grass; urn, formerly in Liverpool Mus., was lost before 1939.[87] (d) c. SJ 55 69. A number of inurned cremations, one at least of which was within a Grooved Ware vessel (fig. 11.1); finds are Warrington Mus. RA 28-30.[88]

OAKMERE (SJ 570 713). Gallowsclough Cob. Round earthen mound; diameter 22 m., height 0.5 m. Excavated 1960, revealing two unurned cremations. Site plough-damaged.[89]

ECCLESTON

SJ 414 628. Round earthen mound; diameter 20 m., height 3 m. 'Many human bones and, according to some, coins' found in late 18th cent. Mound was badly disturbed c. 1770 and 1850.[90]

FRODSHAM

KINGSLEY (SJ 534 734). Castle Cob. Round earthen mound; diameter 25 m., height 4 m. 'Excavated' in early 19th cent. without result; site in private garden surmounted by water tank and summer house.[91]

MANLEY (SJ 538 726). Glead Hill Cob. Round earthen mound levelled 1879. Ten or twelve urns containing cremations were disturbed, including at least three Collared Urns. A Pygmy Cup, two barbed and tanged flint arrowheads, and a bronze 'pin' were also found (fig. 12.1). Site is farmhouse and garden. Many finds subsequently lost; remainder are Grosvenor Mus. 149.P.67.[92]

GAWSWORTH

SJ 914 695. Round sand and cobble mound, excavated 1966-8; diameter 20 m., height 1 m. Primary pit contained Step 6 Beaker; secondary burials include two inurned cremations within Collared Urns, one inverted and with Food Vessel, a third inurned cremation, and two cremations without urns (figs. 11.2, 11.6). Mound, damaged by Home Guard dug-out, restored to its original condition after excavation.[93]

GRAPPENHALL

(a) Two cairns and an associated cremation cemetery discovered 1930, excavated 1931-4. i. SJ 637 866. Cairn 11 m. diameter, central cist; several secondary cremations. ii. SJ 638 865. Food Vessel with primary burial; uncertain number of secondary cremations; Food Vessel from outer margin on original land surface. Several cremations from area adjacent to cairns, including two Collared Urns and an Enlarged Food Vessel (fig. 13.1). Site occupied by housing estate. Finds are Warrington Mus. 45.33/1-5.[94] (b) SJ 639 865. Small pot, not located, broken during building work 1932.[95] (c) SJ 640 867. ?Cairn. Sandstone blocks uncovered 1927. Site occupied by housing estate.[96]

KIRBY, WEST

(a) SJ 189 875. Inverted, damaged urn in pit exposed by sea erosion 1965. No trace of cremation. Urn is Grosvenor Mus. 5.P.65.[97] (b) Several inverted urns are recorded containing cremations, also a crouched burial under a cairn and a partly cremated burial dug into forest peat. None of the sites have been located.[98]

KNUTSFORD

KNUTSFORD, NETHER (SJ 756 785). Round earthen mound; diameter 20 m., height 0.5 m.

[84] Ibid. iii. 137.
[85] Ibid. 3.
[86] J.C.A.S. iv. 109-10.
[87] T.H.S.L.C. iv. 99.
[88] Ibid.
[89] T.L.C.A.S. lxx. 74-83.
[90] Ormerod, Hist. Ches. ii. 829.
[91] Ibid. 2.
[92] J.C.A.S. iv. 103.
[93] Ibid. lx. 1-34.
[94] T.L.C.A.S. l. 96-101.
[95] S. Grealey, Arch. of Warrington's Past, 27.
[96] Ibid.
[97] Ches. Arch. Bull. iv. 37.
[98] Shone, Prehist. Man in Ches. 51.

LAWTON, CHURCH

Three earthen mounds (figs. 9–10): i. SJ 809 559. Destroyed. ii. SJ 808 558. Diameter 35 m., height 1 m.; finds of 'urns etc.' reported in early 20th cent. but urns cannot be traced; two phase mound, the second (*c.* 32 m. diameter) greatly enlarging the first, which had been constructed within a marker ditch of *c.* 15 m. internal diameter. Focus of Phase 1 was a rectangular pit with no associated burial. Cremation in Collared Urn; Collared Urn with no cremation; Food Vessel with no cremation; 10 unurned cremations; cremation in sack with flint knife; cremation in sack with battle-axe outside; all probably to be associated with Phase 1. No burial certainly associated with Phase 2 although fire pits and pyres on east margin. iii. SJ 809 557. Diameter 37–58 m., height 1 m. Phase 1: circle of 9 massive boulders, 2 erect, 7 recumbent, *c.* 23 m. diameter with entrance gaps N. and S., enclosing rectangular (2.6 by 1.7 m. max.) turf and daub structure. Phase 2: low mound covering central feature but making use of original stone circle as an element of circumference.[99]

MALPAS

BICKERTON (SJ 511 527). Banky Field. Round earthen mound; diameter 20 m., height 0.5 m. Site is ploughed field.

MALPAS (*c.* SJ 53 46). 'Tumulus', not located, yielding 'the usual evidence of prehistoric burial'.[1]

MOTTRAM IN LONGDENDALE

STAYLEY (SJ 989 980). Cairn; diameter 16 m., height 1 m. Summit and southern limit damaged.

PRESTBURY

BOLLINGTON (SJ 940 788). Round mound. Centre is quarried; mound is capped by trig. point and field boundary.

CHELFORD (SJ 811 738). Several urns and calcined human bones discovered during garden landscaping in 18th cent. Site not traced.[2]

HENBURY CUM PEXALL. (a) SJ 872 713. Three round earthen mounds; one excavated 1967 revealed five cremations; horizontal plank of carbonized wood at centre of mound; site destroyed by mineral extraction. (b) SJ 874 720. Round mound; diameter 22 m., height 1.5 m.; excavated 1955–6; cremation within Collared Urn capped by round based vessel in ash-filled pit near perimeter of mound (fig. 11.3); site tree-capped and crossed by field boundary; finds in Grosvenor Mus.[3]

KETTLESHULME (SJ 977 788). ?Barrow, not located.[4]

LYME HANDLEY. (a) SJ 964 816. Supposed cairn on Knight's Low, not located.[5] (b) SJ 964 818. 'Three small tumuli', not located.[6] (c) SJ 970 802. Round earthen mound, grass covered. (d) SJ 978 798. Cairn; diameter 16 m., height 1 m.; excavated in 19th cent. and 1911, revealing two cists; site badly disturbed.[7]

MACCLESFIELD. (a) SJ 907 745. Cairn; possible cist; calcined human bones; large and small urn; possible saddle quern destroyed during levelling in 19th cent.; site is part of modern cemetery.[8] (b) *c.* SJ 93 73. 'Tumulus', not located, opened at Macclesfield Common in 18th cent. revealing cremation.[9]

MACCLESFIELD FOREST. (a) SJ 968 726. Round earthen mound; diameter 12 m., height 0.8 m.; sectioned 1906, no finds; under grass; some disturbance.[10] (b) SJ 968 726. Round earthen mound; diameter 12 m., height 0.75 m.; disturbed. (c) SJ 969 718. Round earthen mound surmounted by standing stone; diameter 9 m., height 0.5 m.; under grass.[11] (d) SJ 971 749. Brock Low: round earthen mound, partially quarried.[12]

POTT SHRIGLEY. (a) SJ 939 791. Round earthen mound; diameter 30 m., height 0.3 m.; site partially enclosed by stone wall. (b) *c.* SJ 96 80. Possible barrow intercepting linear earthwork; not located.[13]

PRESTBURY. (a) SJ 907 784. Round earthen mound; diameter 34 m., height 1 m.; ploughed. (b) *c.* SJ 90 78. Cairn cemetery disturbed and excavated 1808: cist containing inurned cremation, human bones, and small fragments of 'copper'; site and finds not located.[14]

RAINOW. (a) SJ 959 766. Round earthen mound; diameter 20 m., height 1 m.; under grass. (b) SJ 964 760. Yearnslow: round earthen mound; diameter 20 m., height 1.5 m.; bones and 'Roman' coins and glass beads found in 19th cent.; depression in summit of site.[15] (c) SJ 971 764. Round

[99] *Ches. N. & Q.* i. 51.
[1] *J.C.A.S.* iv. 103.
[2] Earwaker, *E. Ches.* ii. 364–6.
[3] *Ches. Arch. Bull.* iv. 28.
[4] Ibid. 36.
[5] Sainter, *Scientific Rambles*, 148.
[6] Marriott, *Antiq. of Lyme*, 238–9.
[7] *T.L.C.A.S.* xxx. 184–94.
[8] Sainter, *Scientific Rambles*, 69.

[9] J. Whitaker, *Hist. Manchester*, 368.
[10] *2nd Ann. Rep. Manchester and Dist. Branch, Classical Assoc.* supplementary vol. (1909).
[11] Sainter, *Scientific Rambles*, 19.
[12] Ibid. 16.
[13] Marriott, *Antiq. of Lyme*, 314–15, 335.
[14] Sainter, *Scientific Rambles*, 4, 156; Ormerod, *Hist. Ches.* iii. 3, 537.
[15] Sainter, *Scientific Rambles*, 16.

earthen mound; diameter 35 m., height 1.3 m.; site more or less disturbed by 19th cent.; trenched 1972.[16] (d) SJ 971 791. Round earthen mound; diameter 16 m., height 1.3 m.; site disturbed by moles.

SIDDINGTON. (a) SJ 843 729. Round earthen mound (?recent landscaping); diameter 25 m., height 1.5 m.; surmounted by pedestal. (b) SJ 845 726. Round earthen mound (?recent landscaping); diameter 20 m., height 2 m.; tree- and turf-covered.[17]

SUTTON. (a) SJ 923 701. Round earthen ?artificial mound. (b) SJ 925 713. Cairn; diameter 20 m., height 1.1 m.; cremations recorded during excavation 1962; site tree- and turf-covered.[18] (c) SJ 953 719. Collared Urn containing cremation, barbed and tanged arrowhead, and fragments of a second arrowhead; site a reservoir; finds not located.[19]

TYTHERINGTON. (a) SJ 914 747. Cremation within inverted Collared Urn (fig. 11.4); no record of mound; site levelled; urn is Grosvenor Mus. 150.P.60.[20] (b) SJ 914 749. Round earthen mound; plain pottery sherds and bone fragments; site tree- and turf-covered; Home Guard disturbance; pottery is Grosvenor Mus. 64.P.73.[21]

WINCLE. (a) c. SJ 95 67. Collared Urn and cremated bone alleged to be from Bullstones site (fig. 13.3); urn in *Congleton Chronicle* offices.[22] (b) SJ 956 676. Bullstones kerb circle with off-centre standing stone and elaborate entrance: diameter 8.5 m.; cremation within inverted urn excavated 1870-1; site under grass, overgrown; finds are Grosvenor Mus. 232.P.55.[23] (c) SJ 958 681. Cairn within irregular circle of grass covered stones; diameter 15 m., height 1 m.; inurned cremation excavated c. 1875; cairn disturbed; recent dog burial near summit; finds not located.[24] (d) c. SJ 96 65. Urn containing bones and a large number of stones laid in a cruciform pattern discovered before 1886; not located.[25]

WITHINGTON, OLD. (a) Withington Hall barrow cemetery: four earthen mounds, all lowered by ploughing (fig. 9). i. SJ 807 724. Diameter 20 m., height 1 m.; excavated 1976 and 1977 revealing a primary and two secondary cremations without urns and an inhumation outside the perimeter of the mound. ii. SJ 807 723. Diameter 35 m., height 0.6 m.; under grass. iii. SJ 807 722. Diameter 27 m., height 0.7 m.; under grass. iv. SJ 807 721. Diameter 30 m., height 0.5 m.; under grass. (b) SJ 823 732. Round earthen mound; diameter 40 m., height 2 m.; ploughed.[26]

RUNCORN

STOCKTON HEATH (SJ 614 864). Cinerary urn reported to have been found in late 19th cent. Site ?built over.[27]

SANDBACH

BETCHTON (SJ 792 591). Cremation contained within Collared Urn (Grosvenor Mus. 390/30/507-28); Pygmy Cup (ibid. 391/30/508) and perforated calcined bone pin associated (fig. 11.5). Worked flint reported to have been found in urn. Pin and flint lost; site is a private garden.[28]

TWEMLOW (SJ 781 683). Two 'tumuli' levelled by ploughing 1921-39 and destroyed.[29] See also below, Sandbach and Swettenham: Jodrell Bank barrow cemetery.

SANDBACH AND SWETTENHAM

GOOSTREY, TWEMLOW, and SWETTENHAM. Jodrell Bank barrow cemetery: six earthen mounds in various stages of denudation (fig. 9). i. SJ 791 704. Diameter 45 m., height 0.9 m. ii. SJ 794 703. Diameter 55 m., height 3 m. iii. SJ 796 701. iv. SJ 797 699. Diameter 35 m., height 0.6 m. v. SJ 798 698. Diameter 35 m., height 1.7 m. vi. SJ 799 697. Diameter 35 m.; height 0.5 m. Mounds (i), (ii), and (vi) damaged by ploughing, and (iii) destroyed by landscaping; (iv) 'opened' 1867 and bulldozed 1950; (v) is tree-covered.[30]

STOCKPORT

MARPLE. (a) SJ 988 909. Brown Low cairn: diameter 24 m., height 2 m.; excavated 1809 revealing 'speiks of bone' and fire-blackened stones; site disturbed; turf- and tree-covered.[31] (b) SJ 990 913. Cairn; diameter 20 m., height 2 m.; robbed by treasure hunters; apparently concentric internal divisions with central inurned cremation; badly disturbed; urn broken; not located.[32]

WERNETH (SJ 969 929). ?Cairn on highest point of Werneth Low.[33]

[16] Ibid.
[18] O.S. Arch. Rec. SJ 97 SW 16.
[19] Sainter, *Scientific Rambles*, 22.
[20] *J.C.A.S.* xlviii. 43–5.
[21] *Ches. Arch. Bull.* ii. 36.
[22] *Congleton Chron.* 29 Oct. 1976.
[23] Sainter, *Scientific Rambles*, 35–6.
[24] *Mins. Macclesfield Scientific Soc.* (1877), 37–8.
[25] Watkin, *Roman Ches.* 305.

[17] Ibid.

[26] Ormerod, *Hist. Ches.* iii. 3; *Ches. Arch. Bull.* vi. 66–8; Clare, 'Stone Circles', 708.
[27] H. Boscow, *Warrington: A Heritage*, 12.
[28] *J.C.A.S.* xxxiii. 40.
[29] *T.H.S.L.C.* xci. 205.
[30] Uhthoff-Kaufman, *Arch. of Jodrell Hall*, 3–9.
[31] Marriott, *Antiq. of Lyme*, 375–84.
[32] Ibid.
[33] Ibid. 272.

SWETTENHAM

SJ 814 667. Round earthen mound, diameter 26 m., height 0.7 m., spread by ploughing. See also above, Sandbach and Swettenham: Jodrell Bank barrow cemetery.

TARPORLEY

UTKINTON. (a) SJ 555 662. High Billinge: round earthen mound; diameter 32 m., height 4.4 m.; tree- and turf-covered. (b) SJ 562 667. Round earthen mound; diameter 22 m., height 2 m.; ploughed. (c) SJ 563 670. Round earthen mound; diameter 26 m., height 0.8 m.; under grass.[34]

TILSTON

CARDEN (SJ 463 535). 'Roman urns' discovered in one of a group of mounds in 19th cent. Site not located.[35]

HORTON (SJ 455 483). Round earthen mound; diameter 20 m., height 1.5 m. Oak plank at base of mound. Site plough-damaged and 'dug into'.[36]

WARMINGHAM

SJ 705 624. Earthen mound levelled in 19th cent.; 'Roman urn' found. Site a garden; urn not located.[37]

WEAVERHAM

(a) SJ 628 727. Gibbet Hill. Mound; diameter 6 m., height 0.5 m. Crossed by field boundary; under grass and cereal crop.[38] (b) c. SJ 61 75. Two considerable tumuli, not located.[39] (c) c. SJ 61 75. 'Large mound', not located.[40]

WILMSLOW

(a) SJ 850 810. Urn containing cremation and bronze dagger found during excavation of railway cutting, 1839–40. Finds not located.[41] (b) c. SJ 85 81. Collared Urn inverted over cremation (fig. 13.2). Site a housing estate. Urn is Manchester Mus. 6941.[42] (c) SJ 851 810. Collared Urn inverted over cremation and bone dagger pommel (fig. 16.9). Site destroyed; finds not located.[43]

Perforated Stone Implements
(length, width, thickness of implement, diameter of perforation in mm.)
'*Sceptres*'

DELAMERE

SJ 556 679. Ovoid (fig. 14.7); flattened section; brown stone (95, 74, 24, 18). Grosvenor Mus. 38.P.63.[44]

PRESTBURY

MACCLESFIELD (SJ 913 757). Elongated (fig. 14.6); damaged at both ends; grey-brown fine-grained rock (Group XV) (183, 64, 45, 17). Grosvenor Mus. 276.1910.[45]

'*Shafthole Adzes*'

ACTON

COOLE PILATE (SJ 648 470). Small (99, 42, 27, 11). Not located.[46]

KNUTSFORD

KNUTSFORD, NETHER (SJ 754 805). Damaged at butt end, and more severely at blade end (fig. 14.2); buff fine-grained stone (123, 69, 35, 12). Tatton Hall Mus.

WALLASEY

SJ 280 918. Polished stone axe re-used.[47]

[34] Shone, *Prehist. Man in Ches.* 60.
[35] Ormerod, *Hist. Ches.* ii. 584.
[36] *Ches. Arch. Bull.* iv. 28.
[37] Watkin, *Roman Ches.* 71.
[38] Ibid. 314.
[39] Ormerod, *Hist. Ches.* ii. 2.
[40] Watkin, *Roman Ches.* 314.
[41] *Jnl. Brit. Arch. Assoc.* xvi. 288–9, pl. 25, fig. 6.
[42] Earwaker, *E. Ches.* i. 145–6.
[43] *Jnl. Brit. Arch. Assoc.* xvi. 288–9.
[44] *Ches. Arch. Bull.* ii. 36.
[45] Shone, *Prehist. Man in Ches.* 38, 99.
[46] *J.C.A.S.* xxxviii. 173.
[47] Above, Gazetteer of Neolithic Finds: Stone Axes.

PREHISTORY
WEAVERHAM

c. SJ 61 75. Both extremities damaged (fig. 14.4); mottled grey stone (112, 81, 38, 15). Grosvenor Mus. 89.P.1969.[48]

Miscellaneous Perforated and Incompletely Perforated Implements
ASTBURY

CONGLETON (SJ 840 624). Perforated stone implement in private possession.[49]

BOWDON

AGDEN (SJ 724 869). Small ovoid stone of flat section with depressions worked in each face (84, 65, 27). Grosvenor Mus. 43.P.57.[50]

BUDWORTH, GREAT

APPLETON (SJ 615 850). Ovoid stone with hourglass perforation. Polished light grey, fine-grained rock (Group XV) (92, 74, 38, 18). Warrington Mus. 125-21.[51]

CHEADLE

(a) SJ 870 898. Perforated 'macehead', circular and thin. '5 in. wide, perforation $1\frac{1}{2}$ in. diameter.' Not located.[52] (b) *c*. SJ 84 88. Perforated 'macehead', circular and thin; 'fine-grained micaceous sandstone; $4\frac{5}{8}$ in. × $4\frac{1}{2}$ in. × $\frac{7}{8}$ in. thick'. Not located.[53]

CHESTER

SJ 403 658. Pebble with small (16 × 6 mm.) depression worked in one, flattened face (63, 60, 37). Grosvenor Mus. 78.P.1970.

DELAMERE

SJ 549 701. Perforated stone disc (fig. 14.3) with sharp ground edge (128, 113, 18, 38). Grosvenor Mus. 78.1.GM.[54]

FRODSHAM

FRODSHAM (SJ 529 773). Disc with depressions worked on both faces; greywacke (96, 90, 27). In private possession.[55]
MANLEY (SJ 525 735). 'Macehead' in private possession.[56]

GAWSWORTH

SJ 914 695. Two 'unfinished stone hammers' incorporated in quarry ditch fill associated with Beaker mound and Collared Urn cremations: (a) mudstone (160, 85, 75); (b) gritstone (112, 75, 68).[57]

MOTTRAM IN LONGDENDALE

STAYLEY (SJ 959 986). 'Perforated pebble hammer', '6 in. diameter', not located.[58]
TINTWISTLE (*c*. SE 08 04). 'Early Bronze Age macehead.' Bradford Mus., Turner Collection L71/47.[59]

PRESTBURY

ADLINGTON. Ovoid stone with hourglass perforation (fig. 14.8); evidence of damage at both ends (138, 108, 49, 30). Found 1898 with five others which were left *in situ*. Manchester Mus. (25951) o. 1483.[60]
MACCLESFIELD (SJ 912 746). Badly chipped and irregular, thick, perforated disc (101, 96, 33, 30). British Mus. 63.3.25.1.[61]

[48] *Ches. Arch. Bull.* i. 4.
[49] Author's notes.
[50] *J.C.A.S.* xlv. 71.
[51] W. J. Varley, *Ches. before Romans*, fig. 25.5.
[52] *N.W. Naturalist*, xi. 114.
[53] Ibid.
[54] *Ches. Arch. Bull.* vii. 57.
[55] *J.C.A.S.* xliv. 52-3.
[56] Author's notes.
[57] *J.C.A.S.* lx. 1-34.
[58] *T.L.C.A.S.* v. 331.
[59] *Bradford Arch. Gp. Bull.* iv. 54.
[60] *T.L.C.A.S.* xxiii. 25-6.
[61] C. E. de Rances, *Superficial Geol.* 95.

ROSTHERNE

Legh, High (SJ 686 824). Thick disc with flattened side and depressions worked in both faces. Black or dark grey stone (93, 93, 33). Warrington Mus. 7.60.69.

STOCKPORT

Marple (SJ 956 855). 'Perforated hoe or hammer.' Stockport Mus. 1.32.58.

WHITCHURCH (SALOP.)

Wirswall (SJ 550 452). Large perforated stone, flattened section; hourglass, grooved, perforation (fig. 14.5). Light grey, fine-grained stone (167, 94, 42, 18). Weaver Hall Mus. Z 158.[62]

Stone Shafthole Axes

ACTON

Faddiley (SJ 58 52). Perforated stone implement; square sided, thin butted. Not located.[63]

ALDERLEY

Alderley, Nether (c. SJ 83 78). Shafthole axe '8½ in. by 4½ in.'; not located.[64]

ASTBURY

Congleton (SJ 843 624). Unfinished (fig. 15.1); beginning of perforation pecked on both faces; light grey volcanic rock (173, 85, 74). In private possession.[65]
Newbold Astbury (SJ 856 595). Crystalline stone, ?gabbro (144, 81, 45, 38). In private possession.[66]
Rode, Odd (c. SJ 83 58). Battle-axe (fig. 15.3); greenish brown fine stone (146, 60, 69, 26). In *Congleton Chron.* offices.

AUDLEM AND WRENBURY

Dodcott cum Wilkesley (SJ 588 464). Light grey fine-grained greywacke (186, 82, 75, 23). Grosvenor Mus. 94.P.61.[67]

BARTHOMLEY

Haslington (c. SJ 73 55). Battle-axe; blade and one side reground; fine-grained ?dolerite (162, 91, 66, 29). At Buglawton school.[68]

BIDSTON

Birkenhead (SJ 326 882). Porphyritic basalt; found in uncertain association with polished axe (199, 71, 83, 18). Merseyside County Mus. M6671.

BOWDON

Altrincham (c. SJ 78 88). 'Perforated stone hammer', not located.[69]

BUDWORTH, GREAT

Pickmere. Flattened butt; 'length 4½ in., width 3¾ in., thickness 1¼ in.'; not located.[70]
Tabley Inferior (SJ 721 774). Shafthole axe; flint; found in clearing moat at Tabley Hall, 1725; not located.[71]

BUNBURY

Beeston (c. SJ 53 59). Brownish grey fine-grained greywacke (Group XV), found in uncertain association with two polished stone axes (243, 90, 84, 30). Grosvenor Mus. 26.P.55.[72]

CHEADLE

c. SJ 84 88. 'Perforated stone hammer.' Owen's College Mus., Manchester.[73]

[62] *Ches. Arch. Bull.* iv. 38.
[63] W. J. Varley and W. Jackson, *Prehist. Ches.* schedule II.
[64] *T.L.C.A.S.* v. 328.
[65] Author's notes.
[66] *Ches. Arch. Bull.* viii. 74, fig. 15.
[67] *J.C.A.S.* xlix. 57.
[68] *Antiq. Jnl.* vii. 522–3.
[69] *T.L.C.A.S.* xiii. 192.
[70] *N.W. Naturalist*, xi. 113.
[71] W. Stukeley, *Itinerarium Curiosum*, 57.
[72] *J.C.A.S.* iv. 110.
[73] *T.L.C.A.S.* v. 327.

PREHISTORY

CODDINGTON

c. SJ 45 55. Dark grey greywacke (Group XV) (180, 72, 75, 27). Grosvenor Mus. cc 364 A.

FRODSHAM

c. SJ 517 778. Grey, fine greywacke (Group XV) (213, 87, 78, 29). Provenance uncertain as find-spot is garden rockery. Grosvenor Mus. 48.P.1964.[74]

GAWSWORTH

SJ 911 709. Limestone; not located.[75]

KNUTSFORD

KNUTSFORD, OVER (SJ 751 770). Greenish greywacke (197, 81, 86, 34). At Knutsford library.[76]

LAWTON, CHURCH

See above, Gazetteer of Neolithic Stone Axes; Gazetteer of Early Bronze Age Mounds and Burials.

MALPAS

EDGE (SJ 481 501). Medium greywacke (200, 78, 84, 50). In private possession.[77]
LARKTON (SJ 506 515). Light grey fine-grained stone; ground flat on one face (184, 85, 83, 30). In private possession.[78]

MARBURY

NORBURY (SJ 542 473). Battle-axe; brown-grey fine-grained greywacke (Group XV) (95, 54, 56, 23). Grosvenor Mus. 46.P.61.[79]

MIDDLEWICH

c. SJ 70 66. Dark greywacke (Group XV) (232, 91, 81, 32). St. Helens Mus. 1950/2/1 (fig. 15.4).

NORTHENDEN

SJ 82 90. 'Perforated stone hammer.' Possibly in Manchester Mus.[80]

PRESTBURY

CHELFORD (*c.* SJ 81 74). Group XV (231, 122, 78, 46). Manchester Univ. Mus. 0.7898 (25939).
MACCLESFIELD (SJ 914 757). Fragment; light grey, fine greywacke (Group XV). Grosvenor Mus. cc 301.[81]
MARTON (SJ 859 674). Shafthole axe (210, 83, 81, 30). Manchester Univ. Mus. 0.1599 (25921).[82]
MOTTRAM ST. ANDREW (*c.* SJ 88 78). Expanded blade and truncated conical butt; not located.[83]
SIDDINGTON (*c.* SJ 84 71). 'Gritstone' (190, 90, 63, 35); not located.[84]
WITHINGTON, OLD (*c.* SJ 82 72). Not located.[85]

ROSTHERNE

LEGH, HIGH (SJ 664 837). Dark, fine-grained stone (229, 100, 86, 33). Warrington Mus. 109 977 (fig. 15.2).

RUNCORN

RUNCORN (SJ 498 817). Damaged; greywacke (245, 120, 87, 40). Weaver Hall Mus. 3428 1978.[86]
STOCKTON HEATH (*c.* SJ 62 86). Brown-grey fine stone (259, 111, 68, 27). Warrington Mus. 7/60/27.[87]

SANDBACH

HULME, CHURCH (SJ 768 671). Group ?XVIII; in private possession.[88]

[74] *Ches. Arch. Bull.* iv. 36.
[75] Sainter, *Scientific Rambles*, 119, 148.
[76] *J.C.A.S.* xli. 85.
[77] Ibid.
[78] *Ches. Arch. Bull.* iv. 37.
[79] *J.C.A.S.* xlix. 57.
[80] O.S. Arch. Rec. SJ 89 SW 9; SJ 89 SW 12.
[81] *Ches. Arch. Bull.* iv. 5.
[82] Sainter, *Scientific Rambles*, 119.
[83] *T.L.C.A.S.* ii. 172.
[84] *Geologist*, vii. 56.
[85] *J.C.A.S.* xlvii. 33.
[86] *T.H.S.L.C.* lv–lvi. 326.
[87] *Proc. Prehist. Soc.* vii. 429.
[88] *Ches. Arch. Bull.* iv. 36.

TARPORLEY

c. SJ 54 56. Battle-axe; Cornish greenstone (114, 48, 46, 24). Grosvenor Mus.[89]

WALLASEY

SJ 305 923. Not located.[90]

WILMSLOW

ALDERLEY EDGE. (a) *c.* SJ 84 78. Brownish grey fine-grained stone (Group XV) (213, 112, 74, 33); Grosvenor Mus. 37.P.1951 (fig. 15.5). (b) *c.* SJ 85 78. In private possession (222, 95, 72, 37). (c) In Manchester Mus. (d) *c.* SJ 85 77. In private possession (225, 76, 83, 29).[91]
POWNALL FEE: Styal (SJ 837 835). Fine stone (191, 90, 54, 32). In private possession.[92]

WRENBURY

WRENBURY CUM FRITH (SJ 600 477). Shafthole axe (224, 92, 81, 35). At Wrenbury school.[93]

Grooved Hammer-Stones
ALDERLEY

ALDERLEY, NETHER. (a) SJ 860 775. Found near old surface workings at Engine Vein; in Manchester Mus., Grosvenor Mus., and private possession.[94] (b) Windmill Wood (SJ 856 776). 2 complete, 4 fragmentary from spoil heap; in Merseyside County Mus., Manchester Mus., and Grosvenor Mus.[95] (c) SJ 856 773. More than 100 recovered from backfill of old workings after discontinuation; in Merseyside County Mus., Manchester Mus., and Grosvenor Mus. (fig. 14.1).[96] (d) *c.* SJ 85 77. Three from 'earthen circle'; in private possession.[97]
ALDERLEY, OVER: Dickens Wood (SJ 862 778). 5 complete, 12 fragmentary from spoil below mining levels. In Grosvenor Mus.[98]

BUNBURY

c. SJ 56 38. Provenance uncertain; in Bunbury school.

PRESTBURY

MOTTRAM ST. ANDREW: Kirkleyditch (SJ 875 784). 12 complete, 20 fragmentary. In Grosvenor Mus.[99]

STOCKPORT

MARPLE (SJ 981 907). 'Waisted stone hammer' found 1930 in stream bed. In private possession.[1]

Flint Daggers
WEAVERHAM

ACTON BRIDGE (SJ 594 756). Scandinavian; blade point and hilt terminal broken, bifacially pressure-flaked blade (fig. 16.1); grey flint. Length 153 mm., width 31 mm. In private possession.[2]

WYBUNBURY

BASFORD (SJ 727 515). Tip broken; notched at base of blade; bifacially flaked mottled grey flint. Grosvenor Mus. 29.P.1963.[3]

Barbed and Tanged Flint Arrowheads
BUNBURY

BEESTON (*c.* SJ 53 59). Not located.[4]

BURTON

c. SJ 31 74. In private possession.[5]

[89] *J.C.A.S.* viii. 106.
[90] Shone, *Prehist. Man in Ches.* 32.
[91] Author's notes.
[92] Ibid.
[93] Varley, *Ches. before Romans*, fig. 25.
[94] *T.L.C.A.S.* xix. 83, 87–8; xxiii. 24.
[95] Ibid. xix. 83, 87–8.
[96] *Jnl. Anthrop. Inst.* v. 3–5.
[97] Author's notes.
[98] *T.L.C.A.S.* xix. 83, 87–8.
[99] Ibid. xix. 83, 87–8; xxiii. 24.
[1] Author's notes.
[2] Ibid.
[3] *Ches. Arch. Bull.* iv. 35.
[4] Author's notes.
[5] *Ches. Arch. Bull.* vi. 75.

PREHISTORY

DODLESTON

SJ 361 609. Two; lost in fire.[6]

EASTHAM

Hooton (SJ 352 784). Grosvenor Mus. 87.P.1969 (fig. 16.4).[7]

FRODSHAM

Manley. (a) SJ 527 736. In private possession (fig. 16.7). (b) SJ 538 726. Two from Early Bronze Age cemetery-barrow; not located.[8]

KIRBY, WEST

Meols, Little. (a) SJ 200 888. Two; Grosvenor Mus. CSNS 32 61. (b) SJ 200 888. Not located.[9] (c) SJ 225 862. In Grosvenor Mus.[10]

MALPAS

Bickerton (SJ 503 553). Extreme tip missing (fig. 16.6). Grosvenor Mus. 110.P.60.[11]

MOTTRAM IN LONGDENDALE

Tintwistle (c. SK 092 998). In private possession.[12]

PLEMSTALL

Hoole (SJ 419 677). Found with another worked flint in garden of no. 48 Oaklea Ave. Grosvenor Mus. 259.P.55.

PRESTBURY

Macclesfield (SJ 906 704). One barb damaged (fig. 16.2). Grosvenor Mus. 33.P.70.[13]
Sutton (SJ 953 719). One and fragments of a second found with cremation inside Collared Urn; not located.[14]

STOCKPORT

Bramhall (SJ 889 869). Lost.[15]

TARVIN

Ashton (c. SJ 50 69). Tip missing (fig. 16.5). In Grosvenor Mus.[16]

THURSTASTON

SJ 243 848. Grosvenor Mus. 76.P.61.

WALLASEY

SJ 315 940. In Liverpool Mus. but lost in bombing.

WHITEGATE

Marton (SJ 592 693). Tang damaged (fig. 16.3). In Grosvenor Mus.[17]

Metalwork

ASTBURY

Newbold Astbury (SJ 840 625). Small flat axe, slender with transverse bevel; length 84 mm. (fig. 16.10). In private possession.[18]

---

[6] Shone, *Prehist. Man in Ches.* 34.
[7] *Ches. Arch. Bull.* i. 4.
[8] *J.C.A.S.* iv. 109–10.
[9] *T.L.C.A.S.* xxxii. 245–6.
[10] Author's notes.
[11] *J.C.A.S.* xlviii. 43.
[12] *N. Derb. Arch. Cttee. Rec.* (1916).
[13] *Ches. Arch. Bull.* i. 4.
[14] Sainter, *Scientific Rambles*, 22.
[15] *Ches. Arch. Bull.* viii. 70.
[16] *J.C.A.S.* xxv. 53–8, 60–2.
[17] Ibid. xliv. 53.
[18] *Ches. Arch. Bull.* iv. 35.

BUNBURY

SPURSTOW (*c*. SJ 56 57). Flanged axe; low flanges, expanded blade, curved transverse furrowing on body, diagonal furrowing on flanges. In private possession.[19]

FRODSHAM

MANLEY (SJ 538 726). 'Bronze pin' found in association with cremation burials under a barrow (*see* above, Mounds and Burials); not located.[20]

GRAPPENHALL

SJ 642 868. Flat axe; expanded blade, cutting edge damaged; length 136 mm. (fig. 16.11). Warrington Mus. RA 6.[21]

MALPAS

c. SJ 488 479. Flat axe; blade damaged, butt missing, extant length 44 mm. In private possession.[22]

PRESTBURY

MOTTRAM ST. ANDREW (*c*. SJ 88 78). Flat axe, length 99 mm., possibly derived context. In private possession.[23]

PRESTBURY (*c*. SJ 90 78). 'Small fragments of copper' from cist (*see* above, Mounds and Burials); not located.[24]

TATTENHALL

c. SJ 48 58. Flat axe; possibly derived context; length 82 mm. Grosvenor Mus. 164.P.67.[25]

WILMSLOW

SJ 850 810. Rivetted dagger (fig. 16.8) found with cremation in urn 1839–40 (*see* above, Mounds and Burials); not located.[26]

WYBUNBURY

BRIDGEMERE (SJ 716 454). Hoard comprising: cast-flanged axe, length 156 mm. (fig. 16.12); cast-flanged axe, cutting edge of blade missing, length 144 mm.; cast-flanged axe with weak curved bar-stop and less pronounced flanges, length 147 mm.; dagger with grooved decoration on blade and 2 small rivet holes in arched butt, in 5 fragments through recent damage, length 292 mm. All items were found stacked together, except for the dagger, which had been spread by the plough.[27]

THE LATER BRONZE AGE

c. 1500–*c*. 700 B.C.

The distinction between the earlier and later phases of the Bronze Age is based in particular on an apparent change of emphasis from concern with ceremonial practices and funerary monuments to an intensification of secular activity. The catalyst of change may have been a deterioration in climate.[28] As a result of cooler and wetter conditions, perhaps combined with soil erosion, upland areas such as those flanking Cheshire, which had witnessed their fullest exploitation *c*. 1500 B.C., were soon taken out of arable cultivation. The concept of a distinction between highland and lowland zones in Britain first becomes valid as a consequence of that process. The response to the reduction of the amount of land available for cultivation appears to have been an increasing organization of the landscape, involving

[19] *Ches. Arch. Bull.* viii. 74, fig. 17.
[20] *J.C.A.S.* iv. 109–10.
[21] Shone, *Prehist. Man in Ches.* 66.
[22] *Ches. Arch. Bull.* ix. 98.
[23] Ibid. viii. 24.   [24] Sainter, *Scientific Rambles*, 4, 156.
[25] *J.C.A.S.* xxxv. 53–62.
[26] *Jnl. Brit. Arch. Assoc.* xvi. 288–9.
[27] Thanks are due to Mr. R. C. Turner, Principal Archaeologist, Ches. Co. Council, for supplying this inf.
[28] Evans, *Environment of Early Man*, 142–50.

the demarcation of territories or areas of land use and a greater emphasis on the defensive aspects of large enclosures entailing, perhaps, greater political as well as economic control. There is little evidence of the earlier variety and elaboration of burial monuments, or of the range of specialized funerary pottery familiar from Early Bronze Age graves. Mounds might still be erected, though on a reduced scale, and existing mounds were re-used, while flat cremation cemeteries are widely recorded.[29] Nevertheless the latest phase of the Bronze Age, from *c.* 1000 B.C., provides very sparse evidence of traditional burial; indeed, human bones have been found scattered among domestic refuse. A very great quantity of prestigious Late Bronze Age metalwork has been recovered from major river systems and other watery contexts. In some instances such finds can be accounted for by the erosion of riverbank settlements, though their richness might also perhaps reflect the introduction of ritualized burial by water.

It is possible that the same argument can be extended to the numerous bodies recovered in remarkable states of preservation from north-west European peat bogs. Many bear the marks of a ritualized death, perhaps sacrifice, with dates throughout the 1st millennium B.C. The discovery of a man's body at Lindow Moss, Wilmslow, in 1984 provides the first British example from a prehistoric context. Although discovered in and preserved by peat the body originally lay naked, face down in the water near the edge of a shallow pool. The victim was well built, *c.* 25 years of age with well trimmed moustache and beard and manicured fingernails. He had been struck twice on the head by a narrow bladed instrument with sufficient force to drive bone deep into the cranium. A thong neatly tied round the neck and a laceration to the right of the larynx have suggested to those seeking a ritual explanation that garrotting and a slit throat may have completed a grisly ritual. A single radiocarbon determination indicates a date in the 7th century B.C.[30] Analysis of the palaeoenvironment at Lindow suggests that the deposition of the body coincided with a period of greater waterlogging of the bog, corresponding to a more widely spread phenomenon of renewed wetness recognized as a recurrence surface in peat (RY III) and dated elsewhere to the 7th century B.C.[31] The increasingly wet climate and overcast skies may have led to a transfer of allegiance from the celestial deities implied by the structures of the Early Bronze Age to those of rivers, streams, and lakes for which there is documentary evidence in the Later Iron Age.[32]

In material culture improved casting techniques and a greater range of more sophisticated bronze products accompanied a decline in the specialized stone and flint industries.[33] Conversely, the ceramic repertoire lost the variety of the earlier burial urns. Coarse bucket-shaped vessels often decorated with applied cordons and finger-tip impressions were used both in domestic and in funerary contexts. In southern England such pottery, together with barrel urns and the more finely made and decorated globular urns, has been characterized as an element of the Deverel-Rimbury complex, taking its designation from the Deverel barrow and the Rimbury flat cemetery (both Dors.). Its origins may be recognized as the domestic counterpart of the familiar Early Bronze Age cinerary urns, perhaps with antecedents in the Grooved Ware of the Late Neolithic.[34] Where Deverel-Rimbury cremations

[29] A. Ellison, 'Deverel-Rimbury Urn Cemeteries: Evidence for Social Organization', *Brit. Later Bronze Age* (Brit. Arch. Rep. lxxxiii), i. 115-26.

[30] I. Stead and R. C. Turner, 'Lindow Man', *Antiquity*, lix. 25-9.

[31] Ibid.; Evans, *Environment of Early Man*, 145.

[32] A. Ross, *Pagan Celtic Brit.* 46-59.

[33] C. Burgess, 'Later Bronze Age in Brit. Isles and NW. France', *Arch. Jnl.* cxxv. 1-45.

[34] J. Barrett, 'Deverel-Rimbury: Problems of Chronology and Interpretation', *Settlement and Econ. in 3rd and 2nd Millennia B.C.* (Brit. Arch. Rep. xxxiii), 289-307.

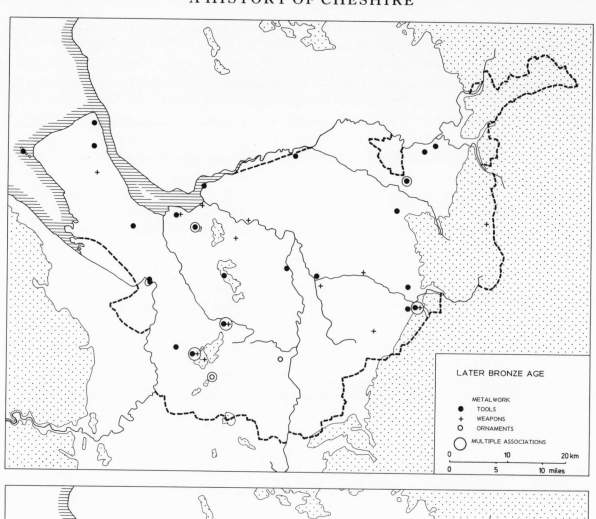

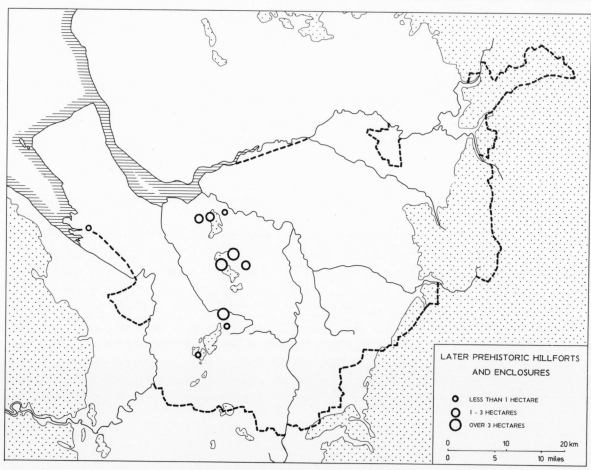

FIG. 17. (Contour at 400 ft. on both maps.)

occur secondary to Collared Urns it is possible that the relationship may be one of status rather than of chronology. The Deverel–Rimbury complex is fundamental to Bronze Age studies, and analagous material, of bucket-jar form, has been recognized outside the core areas of Wessex, Hampshire, Sussex, and the Thames valley. Nothing comparable has yet been recognized from Cheshire; nevertheless a cremation cemetery at Bromfield (Salop.) and a pit group from Rhuddlan (Flints.) admit the possibility.[35] At the Breiddin hillfort (Mont.) related pottery appears in a domestic context during the early 1st millennium B.C.[36] At that time many areas of southern and eastern Britain were developing a new ceramic repertoire in which Deverel–Rimbury and related pottery was replaced by a range of novel plain-ware forms which became increasingly decorated at a date now recognized to be well before the conventional start of the Iron Age.

LATER BRONZE AGE METALWORK

The range of metal types increased during the Later Bronze Age, as did the sophistication of metalworking technology and its products. Although a very great quantity of material has been recovered nationally, little is associated with stratified contexts, and analysis has tended to be typological, the chronology relying heavily on comparison with Continental material. Technological advances during the period included the development of bivalve moulds and core-casting techniques, both features which had begun to appear by the end of the Early Bronze Age. The addition of lead to the bronze alloy, to facilitate casting and perhaps to economize on the use of tin, was introduced in North Wales early in the period and became universal after c. 1000 B.C.[37]

The best indicators of the development of metal types are the axe, sword, and spear series, the industrial phases of which have taken their names from representative hoards.[38] The expansion and consolidation of central European communities before 1500 B.C. spread a uniform burial rite and technology over a very wide area, initiating the Tumulus culture. That phase of European metalworking (Reinecke B1) is matched by the production of new forms of tools and weapons throughout Britain. The major innovations included the production of trapeze-butt dirks and rapiers, replacing rivetted knives and daggers; developments in socketed spearheads with side-loops on the socket; and the logical development of the cast-flanged axe with transverse bevel into haft-flanged axes and palstaves.

North Wales was in the forefront of the developments; an early phase of the transition from Early Bronze Age types is named after the Acton Park hoard from Wrexham, 8 km. west of the Dee.[39] That phase is represented in Cheshire by all the new forms. The haft-flanged axe improved on the Early Bronze Age flanged axe in restricting the more pronounced flanges to the upper, haft end of the implement. The haft-flanged axe from Grappenhall is provided with a minimal medial ridge or stop to cushion the thrust of the butt into the forked haft in use. The Wallasey axe of the same class exhibits that feature in a more marked form, together with a shield pattern below the stop, a detail also encountered on the earliest

[35] S. C. Standford, 'Excavations at Bromfield, Salop.' *Proc. Prehist. Soc.* xlviii. 279–320; H. Miles, 'Rhuddlan', *Current Arch.* xxxii. 248.

[36] C. R. Musson, 'Excavations at the Breiddin, 1969–73', *Hillforts*, ed. D. Harding, 464, fig. 4.

[37] J. P. Northover, 'Analysis of Welsh Bronze Age Metalwork', *Guide Catalogue of Bronze Age Collections in Nat.* *Mus. of Wales*, ed. H. N. Savory, 229–43.

[38] *Arch. Jnl.* cxxv. 1–45; a more recent assessment of the chronology is in C. Burgess, 'Bronze Age in Wales', *Culture and Environment in Prehist. Wales* (Brit. Arch. Rep. lxxvi), 243–86.

[39] *Guide Catalogue*, ed. Savory, no. 262, fig. 30.

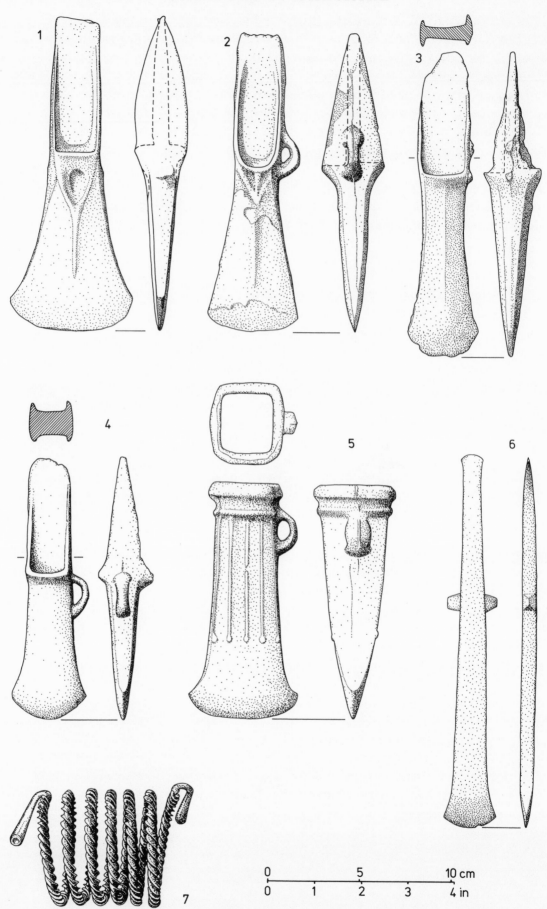

FIG. 18. Later Bronze Age Metalwork: 1. Hulme Walfield; 2. Winsford; 3. Wilmslow; 4. Runcorn; 5. Ince/ Ellesmere Port; 6. Broxton; 7. Hampton.

palstaves which formed the next typological stage of axe development. Palstaves merged stop-ridge and flanges to provide a secure setting for the haft; north Welsh palstaves are amongst the first produced in Britain.[40] Shield-pattern palstaves are the earliest in the series; examples have been found at Adswood, Cheadle and Gatley, and Alderley Edge. A faint shield survives on the Delamere palstave. That, and the shield and midrib decorated palstave from Hulme Walfield, are both of the Acton Park phase. Dirks and rapiers of Burgess's Groups I and II with trapezoidal butts and two-rivet attachment replaced the arched heel, rivetted daggers of the Early Bronze Age.[41] A rapier discovered at Wallasey in a consignment of sand from Storeton quarry, Bebington, is of Group II form with lozenge-sectioned blade and bevelled edges. The chronological development of spearheads cannot be defined precisely, as some forms were particularly long-lived. Nevertheless it is possible that fully socketed leaf-bladed spearheads with loops on the sides of the socket ('side-looped') replaced tanged and end-looped socketed Early Bronze Age forms during the course of the 15th century B.C. in mainland Britain and continued in use until the end of the millennium.[42] Cheshire examples are known from Twemlow, Frodsham, and Ellesmere Port. Two indentations round the base of the Twemlow spearhead's socket, producing a raised rib between them, may be the result of securing the spearhead to its shaft.

The next industrial phase, Taunton, emerging during the course of the 14th century B.C., introduced new types of palstaves which were first developed in southern Britain and reflect the close Continental connexion of the Later Bronze Age.[43] The low-flanged palstave from Ellesmere Port, provided with a loop for thonging to the haft, represents that phase. New rapiers were in circulation too, although Cheshire has not as yet produced an example. Side-looped spearheads remained popular, but were joined around that time by a class of larger spearhead, leaf-shaped with loops at the base of the blade ('basal looped').[44] The Broxton hoard included such a spearhead together with two looped palstaves with trident decoration and a trunnion chisel. Trunnion tools, with lugs projecting from the sides of the implement, first appeared towards the end of the Early Bronze Age, as seen in the hoards from Westbury on Trym (Glos.) and Ebnal (Salop.).[45] Good parallels for the Broxton chisel occur in the Voorhout (Holland) hoard, together with early north Welsh palstaves of the Acton Park phase, and in the Bishopsland (Co. Kildare) hoard which gives its name to the Irish phase of metalworking corresponding to Taunton in England.[46] A feature of Taunton metalworking in southern Britain is its emphasis on bronze ornaments, such as torcs and armlets, many originating from or inspired by developments across the Channel. Versions of those ornaments were also produced in gold in Ireland during the Bishopsland phase, and the two armlets from Hampton are almost certainly of Irish origin.[47] One is complete, while the other lacks one third of its length. Each was formed from a rod of gold from which flanges were beaten out in a cruciform cross-section; the armlet was then coiled into a spiral, with the terminals left as plain bars.

[40] *Culture and Environment in Prehist. Wales*, 261; the chronology and development of Later Bronze Age metalwork is summarized in *Brit. Prehist.* 165-232.

[41] *Arch. Jnl.* cxxv. 12-15.

[42] *Culture and Environment in Prehist. Wales*, 262; M. Ehrenburg, *Bronze Age Spearheads from Berks., Bucks., and Oxon.* (Brit. Arch. Rep. xxxiv), 8.

[43] Burgess, *Age of Stonehenge*, 149-55.

[44] Ehrenburg, *Bronze Age Spearheads*, 10.

[45] D. Britton, 'Traditions of Metalworking in Later Neo-lithic and Early Bronze Age of Brit., Pt. 1', *Proc. Prehist. Soc.* xxix. 286-9, 316, fig. 18; C. Burgess and J. D. Cowen, 'Ebnal Hoard and Early Bronze Age Metalworking Traditions', *Prehist. Man in Wales and the West*, 167-81.

[46] G. Eogan, 'Later Bronze Age in Irel.' *Proc. Prehist. Soc.* xxx. 273-7, fig. 5; *Prehist. Man in Wales and the West*, 173, fig. 4.

[47] P. J. Davey and E. Foster, *Bronze Age Metalwork from Lancs. and Ches.* (Liverpool Worknotes, i), discussion (unpaginated).

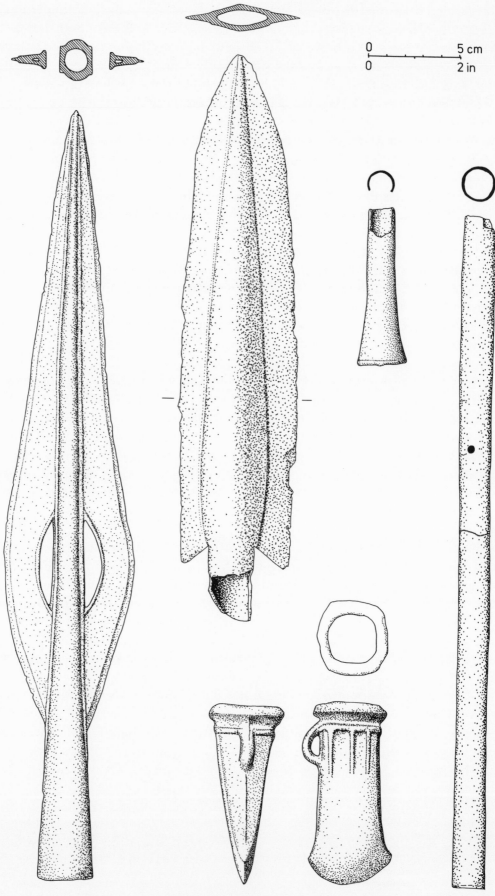

FIG. 19. Congleton Hoard.

Central Europe entered a period of change towards the end of the 13th century B.C. The widespread adoption of a new burial rite identifies the new 'Urnfield' phase of European prehistory, although metallurgical innovations were possibly of greater significance. Raiding perhaps brought contact with Mediterranean technology and important new developments took place in the range of prestigious products, especially weaponry and body armour.[48] The repercussions of the rise of Urnfield Europe are reflected in Britain in the Penard (Glam.) metalworking phase.[49] The first true swords appeared, with hilts cast integrally with the blade; imported at first, they found a British response in Lambeth, Chelsea, Ballintober, and Hammersmith swords, the type-findspots accurately reflecting the area of greatest Urnfield influence along the Thames valley and Ireland axis.[50] In common with much of the north-west, Cheshire has produced no example of such novel swords, or even of the Group IV rapiers with a flattened midrib. New palstaves were also produced, termed 'transitional' in anticipation of later developments and showing a tendency towards a more slender form. The palstave of questioned provenance from Chester is a transitional type, as is one from Winsford, and the two from Wilmslow which may be imports from Brittany.[51]

Penard innovations were taken further in southern Britain, after 1000 B.C., during the Wilburton phase, with the development of leaf-shaped, peg-hole, socketed spearheads, of socketed axes which no longer needed a split haft for attachment, and of leaf-bladed swords, all forms with precursors in the Penard tradition.[52] The widespread adoption of a lead-bronze alloy facilitated the casting of thin-walled products and a number of hollow or socketed artefacts were produced showing that characteristic. Northern England and Scotland, conversely, preserved a more archaic tradition both in type and in technology, with tin-bronze as standard. Despite the adoption in the south of axes with socketed haftings, palstaves remained the dominant type of axe; late ones are characterized by their narrow form, low flanges, and projecting stop-ridge. A Cheshire example is known from Runcorn.

The final phase of full bronze metallurgy before the advent of iron has been designated 'Ewart Park' after the swords from the eponymous Northumbrian find.[53] Ewart Park leaf-bladed swords are the most widespread of all bronze swords. Only one fragment, from Beeston, has certainly been identified from Cheshire, though swords of all types are generally scarce in north-west England. Records of a bronze sword blade found together with the horns of wild cattle at Pott Shrigley, of a bronze sword fragment from Kingsley, and of a 'rapier', unusually long at 58 cm., from Dutton leave some uncertainty as to their correct classification. In fact the spear rather than the sword may have been the pre-eminent weapon in the area during the period. Cheshire is on the northern periphery of an area, extending from the Thames valley to the Welsh Marches, within which characteristic hoards dominated by spearheads occur and which is defined as the 'Broadward Province' after the Shropshire hoard.[54] The hoard from Congleton, which evidently represents the personal equipment or offering of a warrior, comprised two spearheads, two spearshaft ferrules, and a socketed axe. The larger of the two spearheads is a fine example of a lunate-opening type with leaf-shaped blade cast hollow. The other

[48] S. Piggott, *Ancient Eur.* 150–5, 158–60.
[49] Burgess, *Age of Stonehenge*, 155–7.
[50] *Arch. Jnl.* cxxv. 3–9.
[51] S. Needham, 'A Bronze from Winterfold Heath, Wonersh', *Surr. Arch. Colls.* lxxii. 38–9, fig. 1.
[52] *Arch. Jnl.* cxxv. 3–17.
[53] Ibid. 17–26 and appendices; *Brit. Prehist.* 209–11; C.

Burgess, 'A Find from Boynton, Suff., and End of Bronze Age in Brit. and Irel.' *Bronze Age Hoards* (Brit. Arch. Rep. lxvii), 269–83.
[54] C. Burgess, D. Coombs, and D. G. Davies, 'Broadward Complex and Barbed Spearheads', *Prehist. Man in Wales and the West*, 211–83.

is a substantially complete barbed spearhead with lozenge section. The function of such barbed forms has been much debated, attempts having been made to see in the rather blunt point, long blade, short socket, and barbs, a differentiation of hunting, harpooning, and fighting implements.[55] It can hardly be denied, however, that the Congleton spears would have conferred great prestige upon their possessor. Of the two spearshaft ferrules, one, short and with an expanded foot, has been lost; the other is a long tubular ferrule broken into two pieces, with a slightly dished terminal and a peghole for attachment to its wooden shaft. Dating from the Ewart Park phase of the 9th–8th centuries B.C., the Congleton finds nevertheless betray their Wilburton ancestry in many respects; in particular the lozenge section and thin casting of the barbed spearhead and the hollow blade of the lunate spearhead can be traced back to Wilburton innovations. Lunate spearheads were introduced towards the end of the Wilburton phase in the south and were taken up slightly later in northern England and Scotland. A fragment from a second lunate opening spearhead has been found at Bickerton.

Socketed axes are known from Cheshire assemblages at Helsby and Beeston. The Helsby hoard, which comprises a three-ribbed axe with a fragment of a socketed gouge wedged into its socket, was probably once part of a metalworker's hoard of scrap. More direct evidence of Late Bronze Age metalworking has been found on the hill at Beeston from within the area that was certainly enclosed by ramparts during the Iron Age. There, three socketed axes of three-ribbed form, a fragment of a fourth plain axe, a swordblade fragment, and a leaf-bladed peg-hole spearhead were dispersed over an area which also produced clay moulds and fragments of crucibles for casting bronze objects. It may be inferred that the metalwork is, as at Helsby, the debris of a bronzesmith's stock of scrap. Further socketed axes of the Ewart Park phase include a second from Congleton, found near the river Dane, and axes from Byley and from Hilbre Island. The Congleton and Byley axes are three-ribbed; the Hilbre axe is very small, of oval section with horizontal ribbing below the collar, and probably of Irish origin.

An important discovery made *c.* 1700 at Coddington, of which only crude sketches survive, was of a 'kurd' bucket of beaten bronze with high rounded shoulders and, apparently, slightly everted neck. The bucket was seemingly made in sections which were afterwards rivetted together. Eight T-shaped strengthening plates were rivetted around the circumference of the base and the bucket was suspended by two ring-handles secured, it seems, to the inside of the rim. Continental kurd buckets were imported into Britain in the Later Bronze Age in apparently limited numbers, giving rise to a Hiberno-British series of vessels. The bucket from Arthog (Merion.) is a unique example in mainland Britain of the Continental prototype of such prestigious items which were used at feasts.[56]

Although introduced on a small scale earlier, ironworking became accepted in southern Britain *c.* 700 B.C.[57] In spite of the suggestion that iron was adopted rapidly, many of the basic craftsmen's tools that had proliferated during the Ewart Park phase continued to be produced in bronze, as did some larger forms, though in reduced numbers. The Llyn Fawr (Glam.) hoard gives its name to that phase of metalworking, designated Hallstatt C in Continental terminology and chronology, and well illustrates the perpetuation of minor types in socketed bronze gouges, the

---

[55] *Prehist. Man in Wales and the West*, 226–8; Ehrenburg, *Bronze Age Spearheads*, 23.

[56] *Guide Catalogue*, ed. Savory, nos. 256, 58, 114–15, pl. 4a; C. F. C. Hawkes and M. A. Smith, 'On Some Buckets and Cauldrons of Bronze and Early Iron Ages', *Antiq. Jnl.* xxxvii. 131–98.

[57] *Bronze Age Hoards*, 269–83.

development of others in the form of massive rib- and pellet-decorated socketed axes, and the appearance of novelties, an iron Hallstatt C sword, an iron spearhead, and an iron version of a socketed bronze sickle, all of which were included in the hoard.[58] A massive socketed axe, the largest from Cheshire, from the Manchester Ship Canal at Ince was made during the Llyn Fawr phase. It has a decoration of five vertical ribs terminating in pellets below a horizontal rib beneath the collar, and finds parallels in axes in the Llyn Fawr hoard itself. A further late characteristic is the orientation of its rectangular socket, at right angles to the blade axis rather than along it, a possible derivation from 'Breton' socketed axes of the period.[59]

GAZETTEER OF LATER BRONZE AGE METALWORK[60]

ACTON

HENHULL (SJ 634 539). Gold bracelet, round sectioned bar beaten into flat ribbon except for terminals, which are slightly expanded; opened out of shape. Diameter of bar 4 mm.; ribbon 6 by 1 mm.; total length 173 mm.; reconstructed diameter *c.* 65 mm.[61]

ASTBURY

CONGLETON. (a) SJ 864 626. Hoard (fig. 19) comprising lunate-opening, hollow-bladed spearhead, length 398 mm.; barbed spearhead, length 293 mm.; spear-shaft ferrule with expanded foot, extant length 83 mm.; long tubular spear-shaft ferrule with dished foot and peg-hole (two fragments), extant length 347 mm.; socketed axe, three-ribbed, length 95 mm.; Weaver Hall Mus. 3430 (except the spear-shaft ferrule with expanded foot, which is lost).[62] (b) *c.* SJ 85 62. Three-ribbed socketed axe; in private possession.[63]
HULME WALFIELD (SJ 850 660). Unlooped palstave, shield and midrib decoration, length 166 mm. (fig. 18.1). Weaver Hall Mus. Z 421.

BEBINGTON

STORETON (*c.* SJ 314 845). Rapier, Group II flattened lozenge section with bevelled edges; length 204 mm. Provenance uncertain; Liverpool Mus. 25.126.[64]

BIDSTON

BIRKENHEAD (SJ 309 889). Unlooped palstave; apparently plain but badly corroded. Length 160 mm. Williamson Art Gallery and Mus. 2491.[65]

BUDWORTH, GREAT

DUTTON (*c.* SJ 579 768). 'Bronze rapier', length '23 in.', probably a sword. In private possession.[66]

BUNBURY

BEESTON (SJ 538 592). Bronze Age metalwork spread over area producing crucible and clay mould fragments, although not directly related. Some dispersed by later (Iron Age) occupation of hillfort.[67] Three three-ribbed socketed axes; fragment of ?plain socketed axe; fragment of sword blade; plain peg-hole spearhead. In private possession.[68]

CHEADLE

(a) *c.* SJ 87 88. Unlooped palstave, shield pattern; length 138 mm. In private possession.[69] (b) *c.* SJ 89 89. Unlooped palstave, shield pattern; length 182 mm. At Wythenshawe Hall.[70]

[58] *Guide Catalogue*, ed. Savory, nos. 291–4, figs. 7, 46, pl. 4b.
[59] *Arch. Jnl.* cxxv. 43–4.
[60] Fig. 17.
[61] *Ches. Arch. Bull.* ix. 98, fig. 32.
[62] *Antiq. Jnl.* viii. 62–4.
[63] Davey and Foster, *Bronze Age Metalwork*, 88.
[64] Ibid. 64.
[65] Ibid. 40.
[66] *T.L.C.A.S.* ii. 5–6.
[67] Below.
[68] P. Hough, 'Beeston Castle', *Current Arch.* xci. 245–9.
[69] *N.W. Naturalist*, ii. 115–16, fig. 2.
[70] Shone, *Prehist. Man in Ches.* 80, fig. 13.

CHESTER

(a) SJ 405 666. North Italian palstave. Grosvenor Mus. 166.P.67.[71] (b) SJ 405 664. Transitional palstave, looped, slight midrib; length 172 mm. Uncertain provenance. In Liverpool Mus.[72]

CODDINGTON

c. SJ 45 55. Bronze bucket with high round shoulders and slightly everted neck; not located.[73]

DELAMERE

c. SJ 531 675. Unlooped palstave, faint shield pattern, length 150 mm. Manchester Mus. o 7874.[74]

EASTHAM

Sutton, Great (SJ 378 755). Looped palstave, low-flanged single midrib, length 155 mm. Grosvenor Mus. 76.P.51.[75]

FRODSHAM

Frodsham (*c.* SJ 49 79). Side-looped spearhead, length 154 mm. Grosvenor Mus. cc 283.1908.[76]
Helsby (*c.* SJ 48 75). Hoard comprising socketed axe, three-ribbed, length 105 mm.; socketed gouge fragment. Grosvenor Mus. 88.P.58.[77]
Kingsley (SJ 554 738). Bronze sword fragment. Grosvenor Mus. 596.50.

GRAPPENHALL

SJ 655 875. Haft-flanged axe, vesicular texture on cutting edge and flanges; length 152 mm. Warrington Mus. 27/61.[78]

INCE

(a) *c.* SJ 45 77. Side-looped spearhead, length 170 mm. Warrington Mus. 217/09.[79] (b) *c.* SJ 45 77. Socketed axe, five ribs with pellet decoration; length 126 mm. (fig. 18.5). Weaver Hall Mus. 1978.[80]

KIRBY, WEST

Meols, Little (SJ 189 875). Socketed axe, small, fragmentary. In Liverpool Mus. but lost in bombing.[81]

MALPAS

Bickerton (SJ 502 533). Lunate spearhead fragment. In private possession.[82]
Broxton (*c.* SJ 48 54). Hoard comprising trunnion chisel, length 200 mm. (fig. 18.6); two looped palstaves with trident decoration, length '6 in.'; basal looped spearhead with leaf-shaped blade and lozenge-faced loops, '10½ in.'. In private possession 1881; not now located.[83]
Hampton (*c.* SJ 51 50). Hoard comprising twisted gold spiral armlet, round-sectioned expanded terminals intact (fig. 18.7); twisted gold spiral armlet, terminal and four coils. Manchester Mus. 148B.[84]

MIDDLEWICH

Byley (SJ 696 675). Three-ribbed socketed axe, damaged; length 82 mm. Grosvenor Mus. 432-49.[85]
Middlewich. Socketed bronze spearhead.[86]

OVER

Winsford (SJ 641 689). Transitional looped palstave, trident decoration, length 159 mm. (fig. 18.2). Weaver Hall Mus. 3538.1981.[87]

[71] *J.C.A.S.* xl. 63.
[72] Shone, *Prehist. Man in Ches.* 53.
[73] *Antiq. Jnl.* lvii. 90–1, 97.
[74] Ormerod, *Hist. Ches.* (1st edn.), ii. 3.
[75] *J.C.A.S.* xxxix. 110.
[76] Shone, *Prehist. Man in Ches.* 69.
[77] *J.C.A.S.* xlvi. 79.
[78] Davey and Foster, *Bronze Age Metalwork*, 25.
[79] Ibid. 73.
[80] Shone, *Prehist. Man in Ches.* 68.
[81] *T.H.S.L.C.* lxxxviii. 143.
[82] *Ches. Arch. Bull.* vi. 75.
[83] J. Evans, *Ancient Bronze Implements*, 90–1, 169, 330–1.
[84] *Archaeologia*, xxvii. 400–1.
[85] *Ches. Life*, May 1934, 19.
[86] *T.L.C.A.S.* l. 74, 89.
[87] *Ches. Arch. Bull.* viii. 76.

PRESTBURY

POTT SHRIGLEY (c. SJ 98 76). 'Bronze sword blade' and horns of wild cattle; not located.[88]

RUNCORN

SJ 499 824. Late palstave, looped, plain, low-flanged; length 141 mm. (fig. 18.4). Cast in Grosvenor Mus. 119.P.53.[89]

SANDBACH

BETCHTON (c. SJ 79 58). Peg-hole, socketed, leaf-bladed spearhead; ribbed moulding below peg-hole and expansion at base of socket. Length 117 mm. Warrington Mus. RA 24.[90]
TWEMLOW (SJ 773 680). Side-looped spearhead, lozenge-shaped loops, ribbed and indented socket mouth; length 155 mm. Not located.[91]

WALLASEY

SJ 309 928. Haft-flanged axe, stop ridge; length 131 mm. In Wallasey public library.[92]

WILMSLOW

ALDERLEY EDGE (SJ 830 786). Unlooped shield pattern palstave, length 158 mm.[93]
WILMSLOW (c. SJ 84 83). Hoard comprising transitional looped palstave, loop damaged, low-flanged, length 164 mm. (fig. 18.3); transitional looped palstave, loop damaged, low-flanged single midrib, length 164 mm. Stockport, Vernon Park Mus., LX 281-2.[94]

LATER PREHISTORY

c. 700 B.C.–c. A.D. 50

While it is convenient to discuss the last phase of British prehistory under an Iron Age heading in recognition of the technological advances brought about by the new metal, many of the features traditionally held to be characteristic of the Iron Age had their origins in an earlier period. Nevertheless the arrival of exotic bronze metal items of the Hallstatt C phase on southern British and east coast sites in association with apparently new forms of pottery, coinciding with the appearance of the first recognizable iron artefacts, has suggested that the innovations were brought by new cultural groups from the Continent.[95] Furthermore it appears likely that the Celtic language was introduced to Britain during the first millennium B.C. Such factors have seemed to come together to define a horizon initiating the Iron Age and held by some to be characterized by a phase of innovation in types of settlement and in the production of artefacts.[96] Nonetheless it is by no means clear that new developments in diverse crafts and changes in social organization occurred simultaneously, or that all were due to outside influence, although it has been suggested that the adoption of ironworking itself may have spread relatively rapidly thoughout Britain after its introduction.[97]

The latest phase of prehistory is characterized by an increased recognition of settlement sites and, except in a number of important though localized instances, an apparent lack of interest in formal burial. The trend can be traced back to the transition between the Earlier and Later Bronze Ages and has led to a greater emphasis on the nature of settlement and on the artefactual and economic evidence

[88] Ormerod, Hist. Ches. iii. 772.
[89] Shone, Prehist. Man in Ches. 68.
[90] Ibid. 66-7.   [91] Watkin, Roman Ches. 312-13.
[92] T.L.C.A.S. xxix. 222.
[93] Inf. from Mr. R. C. Turner.

[94] T.L.C.A.S. xxxi. 149-50.
[95] C. F. C. Hawkes, 'ABC of Brit. Iron Age', Antiquity, xxxiii. 170-82.
[96] B. Cunliffe, 'Iron Age', Brit. Prehist. 255.
[97] Bronze Age Hoards, 269-83.

to which it gives rise. The ceramic sequence of Iron Age lowland Britain has proved particularly important both from an archaeological viewpoint and in defining areas of regional interaction, while a hierarchy of settlement sites can be recognized with the proliferation of hillforts as one of its more significant manifestations.[98]

An important manifestation of later Cheshire prehistory concerns the recognition that fragments of 'Very Coarse Pottery' (V.C.P.) occurring on sites in the Welsh Marches and north Wales represent the debris of vessels used for evaporating and transporting salt. The results of petrological analysis and the occurrence of natural brine springs coincide to suggest the Middlewich–Nantwich area as the probable source of V.C.P. and the centre of salt production. The Romans knew and used the salt springs at Middlewich from the 1st century A.D.[99] Cheshire salt was reaching the Wrekin hillfort (Salop.) as early as the 5th century B.C.[1] The occurrence of V.C.P. at Beeston may be equally early and closer to the source of production than any association yet recognized. The V.C.P. industry continued until the end of the Iron Age with an extended distribution of the product into north Wales and the southern Marches.[2]

Wales and north Britain do not have the range and variety of domestic pottery that distinguishes assemblages from southern British settlements. Conversely the southern Welsh Marches do have a tradition of decorated pottery, although the upper Severn effectively marks the limit of distribution of such wares.[3] While little excavation has been carried out on Cheshire sites which might give rise to such evidence, it remains to be seen whether further work will reveal more in material culture than the undistinguished pottery and paucity of metalwork that characterize the excavated Iron Age sites of north-east Wales.[4] At Meols, on the north tip of the Wirral peninsula, progressive erosion by the sea has destroyed a potentially significant site. Numerous finds, washed out of buried land surfaces, attest substantial settlement throughout the Roman period beyond the present shoreline.[5] Two swan's-neck pins, three Carthaginian silver coins, two Armorican silver coins, and a small gold Celtic British coin point to an earlier origin of the settlement. It has been suggested that the exotic finds from Meols represent trading connexions with the Mediterranean by way of the western seaways during the Iron Age. The principal object of the trade may have been the mineral wealth of north Wales, certainly exploited during the Roman period, with Meols operating as an entrepôt.[6]

Structurally the evidence from Cheshire is more revealing, although the lack of modern excavation hinders full interpretation of the evidence of settlement. Fieldwork and in particular aerial survey may extend the range of types of settlement and perhaps of their associated farming systems. A field system extending over 12 acres across the north end of a long ridge west of Longley Farm, Kelsall, may be of the prehistoric or Roman rather than of the medieval period.[7] The fields are demarcated by low scarps or lynchets formed by ploughsoil slipping downhill from the upper portion of a field and accumulating against its lower boundary. Lynchets were recorded by 19th century historians on the south, west, and east sides of Storeton Hill but can no longer be identified. On the exposed rock of Bidston Hill,

[98] For a survey of pottery styles and settlement types on a regional basis see B. Cunliffe, *Iron Age Communities in Brit.*

[99] Below, The Roman Period.

[1] Uncalibrated date 390±70 b.c.

[2] E. Morris, 'Prehist. Salt. Distributions: Two Case Studies from Western Brit.' *Bull. Bd. of Celtic Stud.* (forthcoming). Thanks are due to Dr. Morris for showing the author her paper.

[3] D. P. S. Peacock, 'Petrological Study of Certain Iron Age Pottery from Western Eng.' *Proc. Prehist. Soc.* xxxiv. 414–26.

[4] G. Guilbert, 'Moel y Gaer, Rhosesmor, 1972–3', *Hillforts*, ed. D. Harding, 316.

[5] Below, The Roman Period.

[6] J. and L. Laing, 'Mediterranean Trade with Wirral in Iron Age', *Ches. Arch. Bull.* ix. 6–8.

[7] J. D. Bu'Lock, 'Possible Remains of Celtic Fields at Kelsall, Ches.' *T.L.C.A.S.* lxiv. 24–6.

common land since the Middle Ages, cross-ploughing has been claimed: again, prehistoric agriculture may be suspected but cannot be demonstrated.[8] Evidence of prehistoric cultivation appears also to have been preserved near the Roman fortress of Chester, attested by the discovery of plough marks sealed beneath the parade ground and from within the area of the fortress itself. A number of prehistoric pottery sherds have been recovered from the make-up of one of the fortress ramparts.[9] Cropmarks delineating circular (9 m. diameter) and rectangular features observed near Rawhead Farm, Bickerton, while possibly representing prehistoric settlement, cannot with any certainty be assigned to a specific phase.[10] Analysis of the sedimentology of Bar Mere, Bickley, indicates a high rate of soil erosion, suggestive of agriculture, during the Iron Age, while further analysis of the pollen sequence at Peckforton Mere suggests continuing forest clearance and cultivation in the vicinity of the mere from the Roman period onwards, although the chronology of the adjacent earthwork enclosure has not been established.[11] In default of much further evidence for farms and field systems, discussion must rely heavily on the more conspicuous features of the Iron Age landscape, the hillforts.

The term hillfort covers a range of enclosed sites in a variety of locations. Nevertheless a common feature shared by all is an emphasis on the defensive characteristics of the enclosure provided by a strong rampart of stone or earth accentuating natural advantages such as steep slopes. Most hillforts occupy elevated positions, although low-lying locations, perhaps taking advantage of other forms of natural defence, as in the lakeside fort at Oakmere or on the coastal promontory at Burton Point, may legitimately be considered within the classification. Hillforts vary in size. Excavated examples have shown that the chronology of their construction spans one and a half millennia, from the Late Bronze Age to the early medieval period. Since hillforts vary in size and span some 1,500 years their functions are likely to have been diverse, including economic exploitation and interchange, defence, and political control. Larger sites may have been tribal capitals with multiple functions, long-lived sites may have changed in the emphasis of their use, and small sites may have been little more than defended homesteads. The hierarchy of settlement, which extends beyond those enclosed sites which might be regarded as hillforts, reflects an increasing stratification of society dominated by a warrior aristocracy, an over-riding feature of the Celtic Iron Age.

The scarcity of diagnostic artefacts from excavated hillforts in Cheshire hinders the establishment of a chronological sequence for their occupation. Morphology and the typology of structural detail are no surer guides. There are, however, one or two pointers. Excavations at Beeston Castle have for the first time demonstrated the existence of prehistoric settlement on the hill. Bronze working, attested by clay moulds and crucibles, together with Ewart Park phase bronze metalwork of the 9th–8th centuries B.C., a considerable quantity of later prehistoric pottery, and structural evidence in the form of post-holes and post-pits, is known from the area of the medieval outer ward. Two radiocarbon determinations centring respectively on the 9th and 5th centuries B.C. are an indication of the minimum chronological range to be expected from the settlement area, while a third date centring on the 12th century B.C. is a tantalizing indication of potentially earlier activity.[12] The

---

[8] G. Chitty, *Wirral Rural Fringes Survey Rep.* 4. Cross ploughing has been recorded as early as the Neolithic period in Wilts. and continued throughout prehistory. Lynchet formation as an indicator of prehistoric fields can be supposed to have equally early origins: C. Taylor, *Fields in Eng. Landscape*, 24–31.

[9] J. McPeake, 'Abbey Green', *Ches. Arch. Bull.* vi. 58.
[10] D. J. Robinson, 'Rawhead Farm', ibid.
[11] Ibid. viii. 10–11; below, gazetteer (Peckforton Mere).
[12] P. Hough, 'Beeston Castle', *Current Arch.* xci. 245–9. Uncalibrated dates: 910±60 b.c., 660±60 b.c., 330±60 b.c.

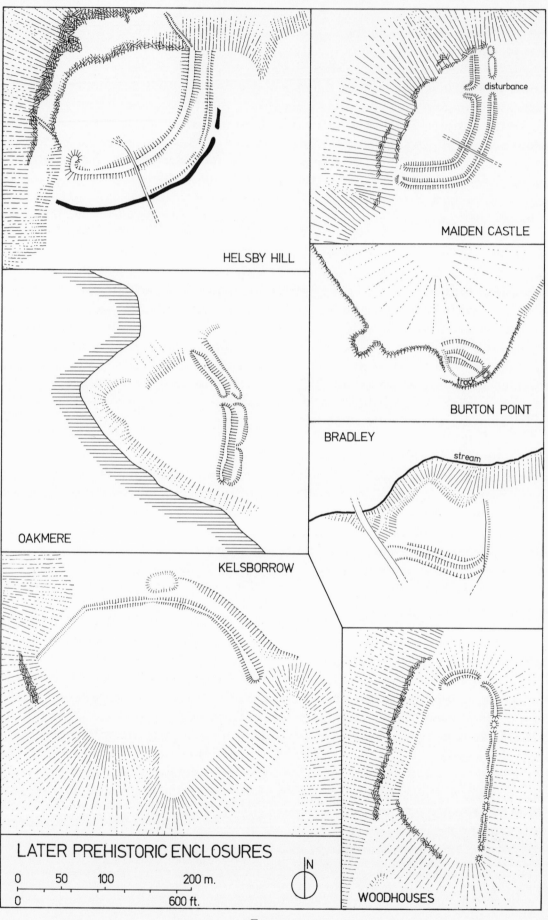

LATER PREHISTORIC ENCLOSURES

FIG. 20.

latter determination was derived from timber at the base of the prehistoric bank near the gate of the outer ward, the context of which did not allow sufficient precision to confirm that it was actually built into the bank rather than simply sealed by it; it can therefore only provide a *terminus post quem* for the bank's construction. While the origins of hillforts are to be sought within the later Bronze Age, it is equally clear that certain hilltop sites which were occupied then were not provided with defences until well within the Iron Age as conventionally defined. The nature and complexity of the Beeston outworks suggests a date later rather than earlier in the 1st millennium B.C., though there may have been a sequence of earlier defensive constructions around the hill.

The rampart at Beeston incorporated timber uprights in at least one phase of its history. Some of the earliest hillfort defences employed a box framework of timber uprights, front and rear, tied laterally by horizontal members, the whole retaining a rubble core and presenting a vertical face to the outside. In stone-using areas the same effect might be achieved with dry stone revetments retaining a core laced with horizontal timbers; the inner rampart at Maiden Castle, Bickerton, is of such construction. While the single published pottery sherd from the site, from a high-shouldered bucket-jar, would not be out of place in an Early Iron Age context, it would be unwise to emphasize that single piece of evidence.[13]

It has been argued that inturned corridor entrances are a relatively late phenomenon in the Iron Age.[14] The existence of free-standing timber corridors at the entrance of enclosures in the later Bronze Age and in the early phases of certain hillforts, however, allows at least the possibility that earthwork inturns could be an early development in some areas.[15] Both Maiden Castle, Bickerton, and Eddisbury have inturned entrances, the latter at both the west and the east gates.

North Wales and the Marches exhibit a concentration of a particular type of hillfort entrance that incorporates a guard-chamber or pair of guard-chambers at the gateway.[16] Such a provision would necessarily create a corridor of approach whether the guard-chambers were recessed into an expanded rampart terminal or set behind the rampart flanking the access. Eddisbury has such a guard-chambered entrance at its east gate. The sequence is by no means clear, but there is a suggestion of an original single timber guard-house which was replaced by a pair of rectangular stone chambers. Upright timbers were recessed into the dry-stone revetment along the corridor of approach in front of and behind the chambers; the forward posts may have supported a bridge linking the rampart terminals. Some 30 miles to the west at the northern extremity of the Clwydian hills, excavations at Moel Hiraddug have revealed a gateway sequence whereby a single guard-chamber was replaced by paired ones behind a putative bridge.[17] The best dated parallel for that phase at Moel Hiraddug is at Rainsborough (Northants.), where radiocarbon determinations suggest that the guard-chambers may have been built as early as the 7th century B.C.[18] Croft Ambrey (Salop.) was provided with stone guard-chambers at an almost equally early date, although its bridge may not have been built until very much later.[19] Guard-chambers appear to have continued in fashion for a considerable

[13] Varley, *Ches. Before Romans*, fig. 38 (4).

[14] Cunliffe, *Iron Age Communities*, 262–3.

[15] R. Bradley and A. Ellison, *Rams Hill* (Brit. Arch. Rep. xix), 39–47.

[16] G. Guilbert, 'Northern Welsh Marches: Some Recent Devts.' *Iron Age in Brit.* ed. J. Collis, 44–5, fig. 4.

[17] Ibid. 46, fig. 5.

[18] M. Avery, J. E. G. Sutton, and J. W. Banks, 'Rains-borough, Northants., Eng.: Excavations 1961–5', *Proc. Pre-hist. Soc.* xxxiii. 207–306; *Radiocarbon*, xvii. 228–9 for dates of 540 ± 35 b.c., 480 ± 75 b.c.

[19] S. C. Stanford, 'Invention, Adoption, and Imposition: Evidence of Hillforts', *Iron Age and its Hillforts*, ed. M. Jesson and D. Hill, 44, fig. 10. Uncalibrated date is 460 ± 135 b.c.

period in the northern Welsh Marches and caution should be displayed in assigning the east gate at Eddisbury to an early phase in the sequence. Nevertheless some corroboration may be sought in the similar constructional technique of the dry-stone and timber revetment at Eddisbury to that of rampart A at Moel-y-Gaer, Rhosesmor, some 20 miles to the west. Radiocarbon evidence from Moel-y-Gaer might be taken to suggest a construction date for rampart 'A' *c.* the 5th century B.C. and provides the earliest possible context for a guard-chambered entrance at that site.[20]

The single published sherd from Eddisbury is in an uncertain stratigraphical relationship to the defences. Sherds with similar decoration to that high-shouldered bucket-jar with fingertipping below the rim and on the shoulder were recovered from the layer of occupation debris sealed by the stone revetted rampart on the north side, however, and would not be out of place in a latest Bronze Age or Early Iron Age context. Dressed stone in the fill of the inner ditch presumably derives from the rampart revetments. Roman tile and pottery of the 2nd century A.D. is mixed with the ditch fill and has suggested a deliberate dismantling of the defences during the Roman period. The Roman road from Chester to Northwich passes within 230 m. of the hillfort. An occupation floor of the Saxon period overlies the fully silted inner ditch and a stone hut foundation overlies the denuded rampart near the former west entrance, suggesting that the hillfort defences, in this area of the site at least, remained out of commission until their refurbishment under Aethelflaed in the early 10th century A.D.[21]

Activity in the Roman period at the foot of the hill at Beeston cannot as yet be related with certainty to the occupation of the hillfort.[22] Contact with the Roman world introduces written evidence to the understanding of later prehistoric society. The people of Cheshire were known to the Romans as the Cornovii, their name perhaps attesting adherence to the cult of the 'Horned God', Cernunnos, if not topographically derived from the horn which is the Wrekin.[23] The administrative centre of Cornovian territory in the Roman period was *Viroconium* (Wroxeter) on the upper Severn, which probably replaced the Iron Age hillfort on the nearby Wrekin as tribal capital. Ptolemy records that the legionary base at Chester fell within Cornovian territory, which may have extended north to the Mersey and east to the Pennines, embracing modern Cheshire. The Dee probably constituted a western boundary separating the Cornovii from the Deceangli in the Clwydian hills beyond. The Dee, known in the Iron Age by the Celtic name of *Deva* ('the goddess'), gave its name to the Roman fortress on its banks.[24] The sandstone outcrop in the clay vale of the Dee may have influenced the siting of the fortress at Chester; the recognition, slight as yet, of prehistoric activity in the vicinity suggests that the location may have been equally attractive during the Iron Age. Whether or not Ptolemy's reference to *Deva* as a *polis* of the Cornovii can be taken to refer to a major pre-Roman settlement is, however, extremely uncertain.

[20] G. Guilbert, 'Guard-Chamber Gateways at Dinorben and Moel Hiraddug Hillforts', *Bull. Bd. Celtic Stud.* xxviii (3), 519. Radiocarbon dates are published in *Arch. in Wales*, xiv. 14; xv. 33; xvi. 23. The calibrated date suggested for Rampart A is based on the assumption that the gridded 4-poster, the stake wall round house, and the rampart are broadly contemporary as part of a planned layout. Thanks are due to Mr. Guilbert for discussing the dating while reserving his own interpretation.

[21] Below, Anglo-Saxon Ches.

[22] Below, The Roman Period.

[23] A. L. F. Rivet and C. Smith, *Place Names of Roman Brit.* 324–5.

[24] Ibid. 336–7.

PREHISTORY

GAZETTEER OF LATER PREHISTORIC ENCLOSURES[25]

In addition to the nine stone and earthwork enclosures described below, a denuded enclosure adjacent to Peckforton Mere may mark a tenth,[26] while another, Finness or Finborrow, said to be on one of the elevations of Delamere forest, cannot now be identified.[27]

BUNBURY

BEESTON CASTLE (SJ 538 592) ?4 ha.

The sandstone crag at Beeston, rising to a height of 160 m. above O.D., forms a conspicuous landmark detached from the central ridge.[28] The summit is crowned by the inner ward of a 13th-century castle, protected on the south-west, north, and west by steep slopes. The south-eastern approach is more gentle, and that flank is occupied by the extensive outer ward of the castle.

While finds of prehistoric material have occasionally been made near the hill, the first recorded instance from the hill itself was the discovery in 1978 of a Late Bronze Age socketed axe. Later excavations in the area of that find, in the outer ward, have brought to light five more bronze implements, clay moulds and crucibles used in bronze casting, a considerable amount of later prehistoric pottery, and structural evidence in the form of numerous post-holes representing a sequence of building phases.

Excavations at the outer gateway of the castle since 1978 have demonstrated that the medieval masonry wall was preceded by a prehistoric defence comprising a rampart, external ditch, and counterscarp bank. Timber and stone elements have been recognized in the construction of the rampart, and the prehistoric entrance, overlain by the medieval gateway, demonstrates some complexity in the deployment of its outworks.

The bronze implements found at Beeston, including three three-ribbed socketed axes, a fragment of a plain socketed axe, a leaf-bladed peg-hole spearhead, and a fragment of a sword blade, fit within the Ewart Park phase of bronze metallurgy of the 9th–8th century B.C. The chronology of the pottery is more difficult to assess in the absence of comparable assemblages from other sites within the region. Plain high-shouldered jars with straight necks are present and much of the pottery is rough and heavily gritted. Nevertheless finer, thin-walled vessels are also represented. 'Very Coarse Pottery', used in transporting salt, has been identified among the ceramic repertoire.

The surface evidence for the prehistoric defences appears to have been totally obscured by the medieval works, although a circuit commensurate with the medieval outer ward would accord with the topography of the hill. The interior is overgrown with trees and scrub, and terracing within the outer ward is said to have been caused by activities associated with Bunbury parish fair.

PECKFORTON MERE (SJ 543 577) 0.6 ha.

A small, sub-rectangular ditched enclosure partly encircles a low knoll at 75 m. above O.D. adjacent to Peckforton Mere.[29] The bed of the stream formerly entering the mere, and the mere itself, perhaps originally completed the circuit. The site has been severely levelled by ploughing and the ditch is barely visible as a slight depression. The age of the earthwork is unknown; on morphological grounds it would not be out of place in an Iron Age context.

BURTON

BURTON POINT (SJ 302 736) 0.1 ha.

The enclosure is sited on a low but rocky south-facing promontory of Keuper sandstone above and overlooking the eastern shore of the Dee estuary. The Dee at one time undoubtedly reached the foot of the cliffs but has since receded, leaving marsh and mud flats to the west and reclaimed pasture land to the south. The enclosure is itself immediately overlooked by ground rising northwards to c. 23 m. above O.D.

A single bank and external ditch describe an arc c. 60 m. in length enclosing an area between the bank on the north and the cliff edge on the south. The bank is composed of fine-grained, predominantly sandy, glacially derived material, and stands to a maximum height of 3.5 m. above the base of the ditch and 2.5 m. above the internal ground surface; in places, however, it reaches only 0.5 m. above the interior, and is overshadowed by the rising ground to the north. A shelf of land a little below the cliff top slopes down from east to west to the old coastline on the south side of the site.

The area enclosed is small, and may have been truncated as the cliff-line has been eroded by the past action of the sea. Quarrying is evident some 50 m. to the west and may also have affected the area. A stone wall revets a section of the cliff face south of the site. The bank has been cut through near its eastern end to allow access to the field beyond, and the track so formed is a source of erosion. The western boundary of the field cuts the eastern end of the ditch and possibly part of the adjacent

---

[25] Figs. 17, 20–2; below, plates.
[26] Aerial photo. RAF/CPE/UK/1935, no. 1100.
[27] Ormerod, *Hist. Ches.* ii. 11.
[28] P. Hough, 'Beeston Castle', *Current Arch.* xci. 245–9.

Thanks are due to Mr. Hough for discussing aspects of the prehist. of Beeston with the author in advance of full publication of his report.
[29] Aerial photo. RAF/CPE/UK/1935, no. 1100.

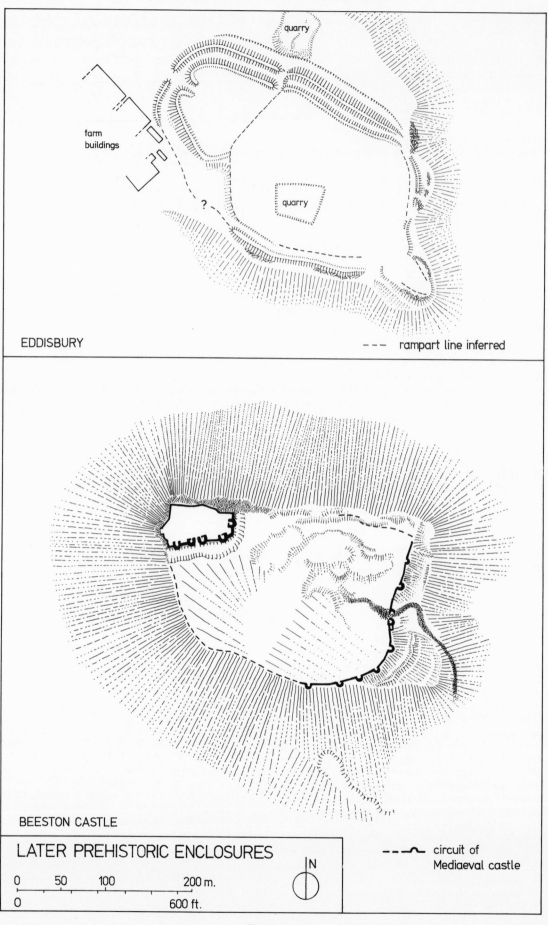

EDDISBURY

--- rampart line inferred

BEESTON CASTLE

LATER PREHISTORIC ENCLOSURES

N

----⌐ circuit of Mediaeval castle

0   50   100   200 m.

0   600 ft.

Fig. 21.

bank. Plough erosion there is severe, while tree growth and rodent burrows present a continuing threat over most of the site. There is no evidence of archaeological examination.

DELAMERE

Castle Ditch, Eddisbury (SJ 553 694) 2.8 ha., extended to 3.5 ha.

Eddisbury hillfort occupies a sandstone eminence at *c.* 152 m. above O.D. projecting from the east flank of the central ridge and overlooking the sand and gravel fans that dip eastward to the Weaver valley. Relatively steep slopes surround all sides of the fort except the north-west, where a saddle of generally gently rising ground connects the spur with the hill of Pale Heights.

A double bank and associated ditches can be traced round the western and northern circuits of the fort, while it is possible to recognize only a single bank over much of the southern and eastern circuits. The surviving condition of the defences along the north and west sides is reasonably good; in the south-east angle, however, medieval building has obscured much of the original arrangement, while modern field boundaries appear to have denuded stretches of rampart along the south and east flanks and impinge on the ramparts at many other points. The 10th-century refurbishing of the defences under Aethelflaed of Mercia may also present a false impression of the surviving extent of the prehistoric alignments. The building of Old Pale Farm has truncated the outer rampart at the western angle; there are indications that the rampart originally continued to join the surviving southern bank and complete a bivallate defence on the south side.

An old stone quarry occupies part of the interior, which is ploughed consistently, while stone has been quarried from the flanks of the hill. Cremation burials of the Late Neolithic/Early Bronze Age were uncovered near one of the quarries in 1851; further evidence of early activity in the immediate vicinity was provided by the discovery in 1896 of five Neolithic stone axes at the foot of the hill.[30] The earliest defences, however, belong to the later prehistoric period, with evidence of no constructional phase earlier than the Iron Age. Nevertheless the chronology of occupation is prolonged. The history of the defensive construction is complex and many aspects remain unsolved despite excavations on the site:[31] the following proposed outline of events is therefore tenuous.

The eastern portion of the hill appears to have been enclosed first, the original enclosure being strengthened by a second, outer bank at least along the north flank. The nature of the original eastern entrance has been obscured by later modifications, but may at some stage have incorporated a timber guardroom on the south side of an internal corridor flanked by timber uprights. An additional area was subsequently enclosed to the west. It appears to have been a bivallate extension, the clay ramparts seemingly set on a flagstone foundation along the north side. The western end was provided with a timber revetted and inturned gateway, and a gap between the original and extended fort may have been retained on the north side at that stage. The timbers of the west entrance were found to have been burned. A considerable amount of occupation debris was allowed to accumulate over rampart material on the north side, although the proximity of the recorded section providing that information to the postulated gap through the rampart introduces the possibility that the debris had built up over slipped rampart material rather than over the rampart itself.

Stone revetments, to front and back of a rubble and sand core, were added to the entire bivallate circuit, ultimately, though perhaps not initially, closing the gap between western and eastern areas. Rear revetments are not clearly visible in the published sections of the northern circuit, though said to have been present at the eastern entrance. Perhaps at that stage rectangular twin stone guard-chambers replaced the putative timber one. The dry-stone revetment of the rampart terminal is interspaced with timber uprights, part recessed into the revetment; that arrangement appears to continue into the interior and is employed in the guard-chambers and extended along the interior corridor. The four paired posts in advance of the guard-chambers may be imagined supporting a bridge connecting the two rampart terminals, with the gate suspended from the rear pair. The ditch between the outer and inner ramparts was recut and later became filled with rampart material, including clay and dressed stone. Incorporated in the filling along both northern and western circuits is Roman pottery and roofing tile perhaps of the early 2nd century A.D. A sub-circular stone house apparently overlying the inner stone revetted rampart near the western entrance may represent a phase of occupation at a time when the defences were no longer maintained, while an occupation floor established over the silted ditch fronting the western inner rampart may, from its stratigraphical position and the association of an annular baked clay loom-weight, be of Saxon date. Those later apparently undefended phases of activity take the story of Eddisbury beyond the prehistoric period, though the defences were to be refurbished once more, along the outer circuit, with a recutting of the ditch and superimposing of a rubble rampart with stone revetment on the earlier line.

Kelsborrow Castle (SJ 532 676) 3.3 ha.

The fort is sited on a south-facing promontory *c.* 122 m. above O.D. extending from the western flank of the central sandstone ridge and overlooking the plain beyond. The promontory is formed between two now dry valleys dropping from the ridge. The southern slopes are steep, but the ground is relatively flat to the north, and that approach is defended by a single arcing bank constructed, perhaps, in three relatively straight stretches with external ditch traceable along the

---

[30] Above, gazetteers. [31] W. J. Varley, 'Excavations of the Castle Ditch, Eddisbury, 1935–8', *T.H.S.L.C.* cii. 1–68.

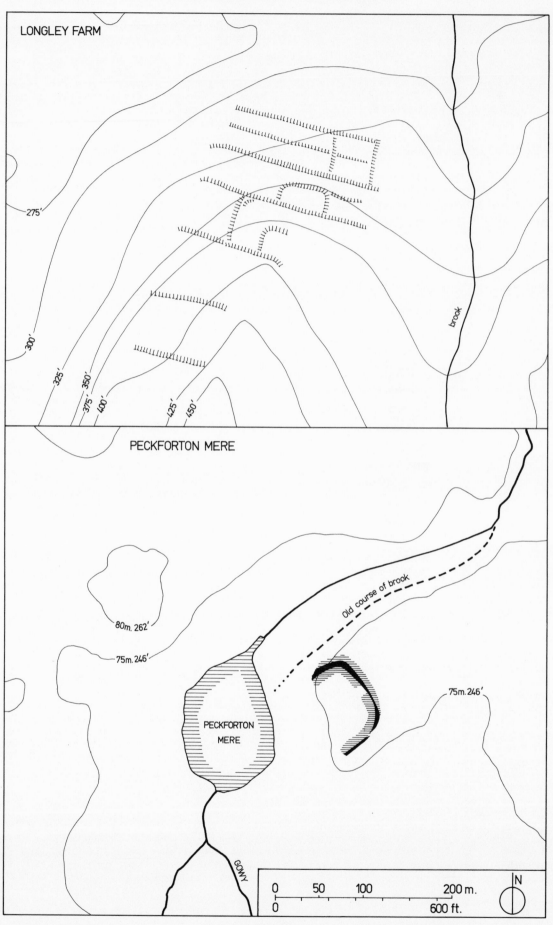

LONGLEY FARM

275'

300'

325'
350'
375'
400'
425'
450'

brook

PECKFORTON MERE

80m. 262'

75m. 246'

Old course of brook

75m. 246'

PECKFORTON
MERE

GOWY

| 0 | 50 | 100 | 200 m. |
| 0 | | | 600 ft. |

N

Fig. 22.

eastern half of its length.[32] The fort is overlooked by higher ground immediately to the east, although slightly set back from the scarp edge.

At the eastern end the rampart terminates immediately before the break of the slope, and it has been suggested that the narrow gap so formed could have accommodated an entrance way.[33] Nevertheless, an earlier record made when the site was better preserved recognized two gaps through the bank and ditch at approximately one quarter of the total distance from either terminal.[34] A field track once used a more gentle gradient in the southernmost angle of the promontory to gain access to the site from the plain below.

The site is at present under grass and transected by field boundaries, while further boundaries have been removed in recent years. Past ploughing has reduced the defences, particularly in the western field where they are barely traceable and the ditch no longer survives as an earthwork. A quarried depression serving as a pond truncates the ditch at the northern apex of the circumference.

An early palstave was discovered within the defences in 1810, and on the same occasion a fragment of an iron sword, which cannot now be traced, was found.[35] A limited excavation of the rampart has been carried out, but the results are unpublished.

OAKMERE (SJ 576 678) 1.4 ha.

A promontory of glacial outwash sands and gravel protrudes from the eastern bank of Oakmere. The surrounding area is relatively low-lying, though gently undulating, and the landward approach is level. A single bank with external ditch describes an arc across the neck of the promontory.[36] The bank no longer meets the water's edge at its northern extremity; the deficiency may be explained by the presence of a scarp dropping to the mere at that point and continuing around the promontory approximately along the 76 m. contour. The water level in the mere may well have been higher in the past, so completing the defences. Approximately midway along its length the ditch has been interrupted by a causeway, and the adjacent bank is broken at that point. Those have been thought to be modern disturbances effecting entrance to the site, and it is believed that the original entrance way was in the south, in the short gap between the rampart terminal and the crest of the scarp down to the shore. The ditch itself has been irregularly dug, although both bank and ditch are reasonably well preserved, the bank standing to c. 2 m. in places. A section of the bank taken in 1960 showed it to be composed of earth, with no evidence of a stone revetment. The site is at present under grass, with tree cover round the periphery of the promontory and gorse on the ramparts.

FRODSHAM

BRADLEY (SJ 539 768) 0.7 ha.

The enclosure is sited above the 30 m. contour on ground sloping down from the northern central ridge to the river Weaver some 730 m. distant.[37] The steep bank of a brook forms the northern limit of the site, while a single curving bank and outer ditch face northwards and uphill. The site has been regularly ploughed and the defences severely damaged, leaving the bank standing to a maximum height of 0.5 m. above the base of the ditch. At its eastern end the line of the defences is obscured by an embanked field boundary and adjacent drainage ditch. That relatively recent feature appears to supersede the ancient defences, although such an interpretation necessitates a sharp angled turn of the rampart and ditch at its junction with the field boundary. No surface evidence survives for an extension of the enclosure into the adjacent eastern field, although there are indications of past ridge and furrow ploughing in an area now under grass. No obvious entrance survives, though much of the defensive circuit has been obliterated by the above-mentioned activities on the eastern side and by a sunken cart track to the west.

HELSBY HILL (SJ 493 754) 1.7 ha. with 0.5 ha. annexe

The fort is sited at c. 140 m. above O.D. on a promontory at the north end of the central sandstone ridge overlooking the Mersey. To the north-west, cliffs drop almost vertically to a flat expanse of marshland forming the southern flank of the river, which lies some 3 km. distant. To the south the ground slopes more gently, and that approach is defended by two ramparts describing an arc across the promontory. Two subsidiary banks have been identified enclosing the rock ledge on the cliff face just below the summit on the north side; excavation on the north-east bank revealed a wall 4 m. wide with a sand and rubble core revetted front and rear by dry stone walling. A deposit of burnt sand, burnt pebbles, and charcoal was recorded behind the wall.[38] Approximately 1.7 ha. was enclosed by the main ramparts, with a further 0.5 ha. on the rock ledge.

Accounts have differed over the original complement of defences, the most recent stressing the univallate character of the site.[39] The rampart, though much denuded, can be traced reasonably clearly along its entire length. It is apparent from early aerial photographs, however, that the hill was provided with at least one further rampart beyond and concentric with the existing line.[40] A distinct band, interpreted as a ditch line, has been recorded in root crop and parched grass, and

[32] J. Forde-Johnston, 'Iron Age Hillforts in Lancs. and Ches.' *T.L.C.A.S.* lxxii, fig. 27. Aerial photo: RAF/CPE/UK/1935, no. 2042.   [33] *T.L.C.A.S.* lxxii. 21.

[34] Ormerod, *Hist. Ches.* ii. 3.

[35] Ibid.; above (gazetteer) for palstave.

[36] *T.L.C.A.S.* lxxii. 21-3.   [37] Ibid. 19-20.

[38] J. D. Bu'Lock, 'Hillfort at Helsby, Ches.' *T.L.C.A.S.* lxvi. 107-10.

[39] J. Forde-Johnston, *Hillforts of Iron Age in Eng. and Wales*, 139, fig. 70; but cf. *T.L.C.A.S.* lxvi. 107-10; lxxii. 15-17.

[40] R.C.H.M. (Eng.), N.M.R. SJ 8876/1/1-2.

a contour survey confirmed the existence of an internal bank along the greater part of its length.[41] A difficulty in associating the two features is, however, encountered towards the western end of the defences, where the crop-mark ditch line appears to intersect the alignment of the earthwork visible in aerial photographs taken in the 1930s. At the western end, the inner rampart turns in to cover access to the interior gained between the rampart and the cliff edge.

The defences have suffered very badly through ploughing. The inner rampart at its western end is in the care of the National Trust and is the best preserved portion of the site, though visitor traffic in the interior has eroded some areas down to the sandstone bedrock.

WOODHOUSES (SJ 511 757) 1.6 ha.

The enclosure is situated on sandstone at the northern end of the central ridge at c. 137 m. above O.D.[42] Relatively gentle slopes fall from the summit area on the north and east sides, and there defences can be traced. The gradient on the south is steep, and on the west precipitous. It has been suggested that a scarp, continuing the recurve of the northern rampart and set back some 20 m. from the western cliff edge, constituted the remains of a former bank. The break in slope along that western flank is at present a natural feature, as it is also along the southern flank, though the beginnings of a return have again been recorded in the south-eastern angle. Where the rampart is traceable, it consists of an irregular bank varying in height from 0.5 to 2 m. varying in spread and with frequent interruptions, some used as footpaths. At the north-eastern curve of the bank a slight inturn occurs on the eastern side, and there is a gap of c. 9 m. before the rampart continues westward. There is no evidence of a ditch. Excavation in 1951 across the eastern bank recorded dry stone revetments to front and back of a 4 m. rampart.[43]

The summit of Woodhouses Hill is heavily overgrown with mixed small trees, shrubs, bracken, and heather and is crossed by many footpaths, from which traffic has diverged in places to form wider areas of erosion. A number of small rounded sandstones recovered from the site have been interpreted as slingstones.[44]

MALPAS

MAIDEN CASTLE, BICKERTON (SJ 498 529) 0.7 ha.

Towards the southern limit of the central sandstone ridge the Bickerton hills command extensive views to the west over the Dee valley. The bivallate fort is at one of the highest points on the sandstone against the steep north-western scarp of the ridge 211 m. above O.D. The subsoil is sandy glacial drift. The ground slopes more gently to the south-east and two concentric ramparts were erected to obstruct that approach. The ramparts curve eastwards from their southern junction with the scarp face to make a sharp angled turn at about one third of their length, curving northwards to rejoin the scarp edge. There appear to be no associated ditches. Two thirds of the way along the south–north sector a break in both ramparts defines an entrance. The inner rampart displays a marked inturn, along the 15 m. length of which the entrance gap narrows from c. 5 to c. 2.5 m. Excavation has revealed opposed gate posts set into the inturn revetment c. 5 m. from the inner end. In 1980 a possible subsidiary entrance was identified between the southern termination of the ramparts and an outwork on the cliff edge.[45]

The entrance and parts of adjacent defences were excavated in 1934 and 1935, and in spite of apparent contradictions the published sections allow some attempt to interpret the sequence.[46] The chronological relationship of the inner and outer ramparts was not resolved. The inner one, as recorded, demonstrates no evidence for more than one phase of construction. An inner and outer revetment of vertical dry stone walling retained a core of sand and timber. The timbers, of varying dimensions, were arranged lengthways, crossways, and diagonally in distinct layers alternately with the sand, and set into the back of the outer and inner revetments. The timbers did not protrude to the exterior of the rampart. The outer rampart has a more complex history. The earliest demarcation on the line appears to have been a timber palisade, partially dug into the subsoil and supported by a minimal, drift-derived clay bank. The free-standing palisade was replaced by a dump bank which was ultimately enlarged and strengthened by the addition of a dry stone revetment to its outer face. The insertion of the revetment involved cutting back the front face of the existing bank.

A rock-cut feature behind the palisade line presents a problem. Stones associated with it were interpreted by the excavator as a built wall. The feature as a whole pre-dates the construction of the outer rampart but not, apparently, the palisade. An alternative interpretation is that the hollow provided a quarry for the revetment of the inner rampart; it implies priority for the inner rampart, perhaps with a contemporary outer palisade, followed by a strengthening of the outer line of defence.

A single sherd from a plain, high-shouldered jar, and a fragment of iron from an occupation surface pre-dating the collapse of the inner rampart revetments, are uncertain chronological indicators.[47] Numerous quarry mounds and hollows within the defences, together with rock-splitting wedges and hammer stones, are likely to be of relatively recent date.

[41] Author's unpublished original contour survey.

[42] *T.L.C.A.S.* lxii. 17–19.

[43] T. G. E. Powell and G. Webster, unpublished excavation.

[44] Grosvenor Mus. 197.P.1953.

[45] J. J. Taylor, 'Maiden Castle, Bickerton', *Ches. Arch.*

Bull. vii. 34–6.

[46] W. J. Varley, 'Maiden Castle, Bickerton', *Liverpool Annals*, xxii. 97–110; W. J. Varley, 'Further Excavations at Maiden Castle, Bickerton', ibid. xxiii. 101–12.

[47] The sherd is illustrated in Varley, *Ches. Before Romans*, fig. 38 (4).

THE ROMAN PERIOD
THE ROMAN OCCUPATION

CHESHIRE[1] was not thickly inhabited at the time of the Roman conquest. Several defended sites certainly or probably Iron Age in date exist, but of settlements and cultural affinities little is known. Ptolemy's reference to *Deva* as a *polis* of the Cornovii may recall something of the state of affairs late in the Iron Age.[2] The major concentration of that tribe is believed to have lain in the hill country of southern and western Shropshire; whether the inhabitants of pre-Roman Cheshire were Cornovians remains uncertain, for in creating a system of local government based on the tribal canton or *civitas* the Roman authorities took care to create units of the right size, neither so large as to be unwieldy or too powerful, nor so small as to be incapable of effective management of their own affairs. The consequent submergence of some small independent tribes by larger neighbours may have taken place in Cheshire.[3] To the west lay the Deceangli[4] of what is now Clwyd, and to the east and north the powerful tribe of the Brigantes. Although Cheshire was thinly populated, control of the east–west corridor between the Pennine uplands and the northern Welsh Marches was strategically important.

It is not entirely clear why Ptolemy assigned the legionary fortress at *Deva* to the *civitas* of the Cornovii, or why he termed it a *polis*, unless his reference is in effect to the *canabae*. As much of his information about Roman Britain appears to be pre-Flavian it might be thought that the term was being used of a native settlement, but archaeological evidence of such a site either under or near the fortress is lacking. Plough-marks were sealed by the fortress parade-ground and the site may not have been uninhabited when the Roman army arrived.[5] The ploughing could not be precisely dated, but may be late pre-Roman Iron Age.[6] Plough marks have been reported from the interior of the fortress, and also scraps of prehistoric pottery.[7]

The name *Deva* is Celtic, and comes from the name of the river; six river names derive from *Deva*, 'the goddess', in Britain alone, and the name is widespread in Europe in various forms. A variant, *Deva Victrix*, used in the Ravenna Cosmography, borrows the second element from the titles of Legio xx. According to Bede the British name for the site was *Caerlegion*, closely comparable with

[1] The help and advice of Mr. J. D. Bestwick, Mr. J. V. H. Eames, Dr. A. K. B. Evans, Mrs. K. M. Hartley, Mr. J. Hinchcliffe, Professor G. D. B. Jones, Dr. G. Lloyd-Morgan, Miss R. McNeil, Dr. D. J. P. Mason, Dr. E. L. Morris, Lady Rochester, Mr. T. J. Strickland, Dr. J. J. Taylor, Dr. G. A. Webster, Mr. J. H. Williams, and Mr. S. R. Williams in the preparation of this article is gratefully acknowledged; thanks are also offered to the County Planning Officer, Cheshire County Council, the Curator of the Grosvenor Museum, and the Director of Merseyside County Museums for allowing access to the sites and monuments records under their control, and to the University of Liverpool for granting the writer an honorary research fellowship in the Dept. of Ancient History and Classical Archaeology.

[2] Ptolemy, *Geography*, bk. II, 3, 11, compiled *c*. A.D. 140–50.

[3] I. A. Richmond, 'The Cornovii', *Culture and Environment*, ed. I. Ll. Foster and L. Alcock, 252–4 and fig. 55; G. Webster, *Cornovii*, 20–3. The suggested derivation of the name from the horned shape of the Wirral (*Culture and Environment*, 251), conflicts with archaeological evidence of the point of balance of the tribe.

[4] The name is discussed in A. L. F. Rivet and C. Smith, *Place Names of Roman Brit.* 331, and *Welsh Hist. Rev.* iv (2), 165.

[5] *Arch. Newsletter*, ix. 12. The marks lay below a layer of turf which was subjected to pollen analysis.

[6] A similar pollen spectrum from a pit at Tallington (Lincs.) was dated on archaeological grounds to the late Iron Age or early Roman period: *Rural Settlement in Roman Brit.* ed. C. Thomas (C.B.A. Research Report vii), 18 and fig. 4.

[7] *J.C.A.S.* lxiii. 15. The pottery was found in the turf rampart.

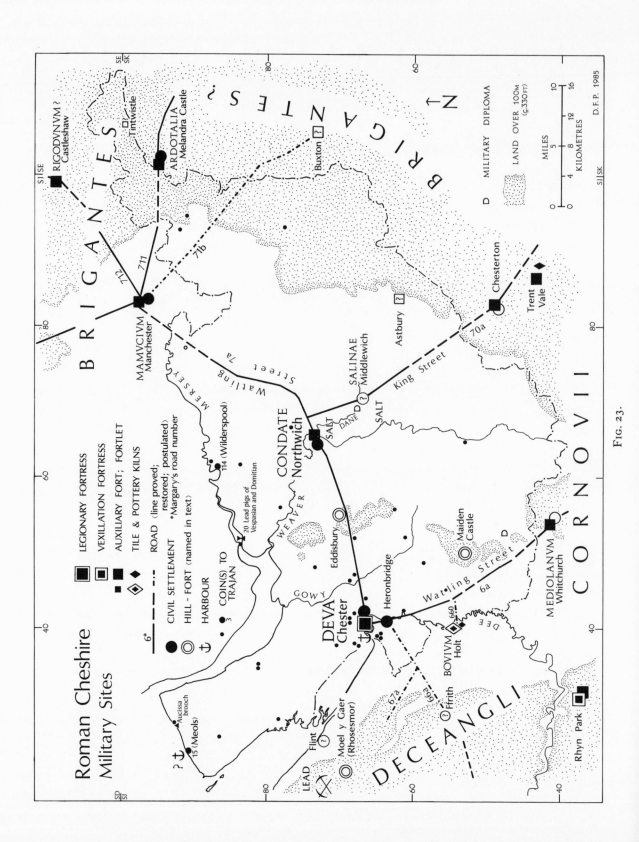

Roman Cheshire Military Sites

FIG. 23.

Caerleon (*Isca*), meaning literally 'the legionary fortress'. The naming of the fortress after the river on which it was sited is in itself a fair indication that there was no pre-existing native settlement whose name could be used.[8]

'Conquest' is perhaps an inappropriate word to describe the Roman occupation of Cheshire.[9] There is no literary or archaeological evidence of resistance by the native population; the slighting of hillfort defences need not imply desperate resistance, and indeed it is difficult to say which of the Cheshire hillforts were still in use in the Claudian period.[10] The rulers of Cheshire were probably among the kings and chieftains who submitted to Claudius and entered into treaty relations with Rome. Within a very few years a frontier was established for the new province which left Cheshire in what may be termed 'free Britain'. Only five years after the invasion, however, the second governor of Britain, Ostorius Scapula, mounted a campaign against the Deceangli, and part of his forces presumably passed through Cheshire. When the Roman forces had almost reached the Irish Sea disturbances among the Brigantes necessitated intervention on Queen Cartimandua's behalf, and the attack on the Deceangli was abandoned.[11]

For the next decade Cheshire remained ungarrisoned, although perhaps not entirely unvisited by army patrols or enterprising merchants. Under Nero a decision was apparently taken to conquer and subdue the hostile tribes of Wales. In north Wales the crucial campaign was that of A.D. 60, when Suetonius Paullinus led an army to Anglesey. Such a campaign, mounted over difficult terrain, required preparation beforehand; it has been suggested that the landing craft in which the army crossed the Menai Straits may have been built on the Dee estuary, and a possible fort and supply base of the period at Chester has been postulated.[12] The bulk of the supplies which Paullinus's large force required presumably went by sea, and a harbour was needed. That the main part of his army took the overland route may be demonstrated by the campaign base at Rhyn Park (Denb.) some 28 km. south of Chester, though the site cannot be precisely dated.[13] Once again the campaign was nullified by rebellion, this time within the province; it was followed by a further decade of consolidation during which little interest appears to have been shown in expansion beyond existing frontiers. Cheshire was within the sphere of influence of the Roman province and was still ungarrisoned only, perhaps, because its people were too few and too poor to warrant it. The assassination of Nero, and the struggle for the purple which followed, brought peace to an end. At about the same time Cartimandua was with difficulty rescued by the Romans from her own people. When Vespasian became emperor in A.D. 69 Brigantian hostility precipitated a decision to adopt a more aggressive frontier policy.

CHESTER: THE LEGIONARY FORTRESS

The first of Vespasian's governors of Britain, Q. Petillius Cerialis, seems to have confined his attention in the main to the Brigantes. Recognition of forts built during

[8] Rivet and Smith, *Place Names of Roman Brit.* 336–7; *Archaeologia*, xciii. 31.

[9] F. H. Thompson, *Roman Ches.* 6. For the historical background to the conquest see S. S. Frere, *Britannia: A Hist. of Roman Brit.* (2nd edn., 1978), P. Salway, *Roman Brit.* and the sources there cited.

[10] *J.R.S.* xxix. 206. Eddisbury cannot have been slighted before the Flavian period. See also W. J. Varley and J. W. Jackson, *Prehist. Ches.* 84.

[11] The two events may well have been related, since the driving of a wedge between Wales and north Britain could have been construed as a hostile act by some of the Brigantes. Scapula's real intention may have been to gain access to the deposits of lead, and the silver ore which they contained, in NE. Wales.

[12] Thompson, *Roman Ches.* 7; Frere, *Britannia*, 104.

[13] *Antiquity*, li. 58–60; *Britannia*, ix. 436.

his period of office (A.D. 71–4) is not easy and his campaigns may have been largely punitive in character. If Cerialis established the legionary fortress at York, as is supposed, some Brigantian territory was annexed to the province. Whether the Romans also campaigned west of the Pennines at that time remains unproven. The next governor, S. Julius Frontinus, was apparently responsible for the subjugation of Wales, which had not quite been completed when he was succeeded, probably in A.D. 78, by the best known of Vespasian's appointments, Cn. Julius Agricola.

While the pre-Flavian fortress at Wroxeter (Salop.)[14] was excellently placed for operations in the Marches and mid-Wales, it lacked access to the sea and did not overlook the corridor which Cheshire provides between Wales and northern England. A military presence at or near Chester accorded with the new strategic requirements of the Flavian period, for possession of a harbour with good land communications was necessary for operations both in north Wales and west Brigantia, and a fort or fortress in that position drove a wedge between the two areas, preventing concerted military action by the Brigantes and Ordovices. Whether Frontinus or Agricola chose the site for the fortress of Chester is difficult to say. Tacitus, having credited Frontinus with the subjugation of the Silures,[15] implies that the Ordovices had already been subdued, and their territory garrisoned, before Agricola succeeded him. It seems reasonable to infer that the conquest of the Silures was Frontinus's main concern, and that he turned his attention to the Ordovices relatively late in his governorship, the restoration of order among the Ordovices and the conquest of Anglesey occupying Agricola in his first short campaign of A.D. 78. The fortress at Caerleon (Mon.) dates from Frontinus's governorship, and Chester was started at latest at the beginning of Agricola's, since building work was proceeding in A.D. 79. During its construction, and for several years thereafter, its garrison was the Legio II Adiutrix. Recently raised from the Adriatic fleet, that legion is thought to have been transferred to Britain under Cerialis and had for a short time been quartered at Lincoln, where the tombstones of two of its soldiers survive.[16] Eleven of those found at Chester can certainly also be assigned to it. Legio XX at first remained at Wroxeter, but is generally assumed to have provided the garrison for Inchtuthil (Perths.) until its abandonment, by which time Legio II Adiutrix had left the province.[17] Vespasian's reign thus saw the establishment of the fortresses at York, Caerleon, and Chester; they were the bases for the legionary garrison of Britain for most of the Roman period.

The Siting of the Fortress

Chester is at the north-western extremity of the Midland Plain, on the edge of the Highland Zone lying to west and north. It bestrides an easy route of access into north Wales along the coastal plain, and is situated at the head of a navigable tidal river. Land communications with the rest of the province were also important, and the crossing of the Dee at Chester was one link in a chain of military communication extending from Caerleon in the south to York in the north.

Examination of the topography of the fortress site[18] indicates some of the factors which dictated its choice. The relatively narrow gorge which the river has cut through the sandstone ridge determined the effective limit of navigation upstream and ensured a good crossing point, whose precise position was dictated by con-

---

[14] *Trans. Salop. Arch. Soc.* lvii. 113; *J.R.S.* liv. 165.

[15] *De Vita Agricolae*, 17, 2.

[16] *R.I.B.* i, nos. 253, 258.

[17] Inchtuthil cannot have been evacuated before A.D. 87,

and Legio II Adiutrix left Britain before A.D. 92, perhaps in 86 or 87, for service in Dacia: Salway, *Roman Brit.* 150.

[18] D. J. P. Mason, 'Chester: Evolution and Adaptation of its Landscape', *J.C.A.S.* lix. 14–19.

venient gulleys on both banks. The fortress is in effect a bridgehead site securing the crossing, and enjoys the protection which the river affords on its south and west sides. Although a more level site could have been obtained to the east, and a slightly more elevated one to the north, the chosen site was preferred because of the tactical importance of the river crossing and the need to control it. The site was adequate for the large fortress planned, and its sand and sandstone base gave it good drainage and probably slight tree cover.[19] The availability of building stone was also in Chester's favour, since several large masonry buildings were planned from the fortress's inception. The river water was brackish except at dead low tide, but east of the fortress good springs supplied sufficient drinking water for a fortress and its *canabae*.

Other Related Sites

The fortress was the nodal point in a system of dependent forts garrisoned by auxiliary units. Recruited usually at that time from among those in the empire who were not Roman citizens, such units were nominally 500 or occasionally 1,000 strong, and either cavalry, infantry, or mixed in composition. It is relatively easy to see which of the forts in Wales came within what has been termed 'Chester Command', and Chester was also presumably responsible for posts in the Pennines. From military *diplomata*, discharge documents issued to soldiers of the *auxilia*, dated to A.D. 98 and 105 respectively,[20] 16 units can be named which appear to have been under the authority of the legate of Legio XX in the early Trajanic period.[21] Forts for most of those units have long been known, but new ones are still being recognized, as at Northwich[22] and Whitchurch (Salop.),[23] while forts at Rhyn Park[24] and at Prestatyn (Flints.)[25] were recognized from the air only in 1975 and 1976 respectively. Not all Flavian forts had a long life; Pen Llystyn (Caern.) is thought to have been evacuated before the end of the 1st century.[26] The forts were linked to the fortress and each other by roads whose alignments are generally predictable, even if their precise position is not known. In the Highland Zone the known road system is more likely to reflect that which the army laid down when the forts were first built than in the Lowland Zone where the requirements of the civil authorities, the local population, and trade might eventually produce a different system. Several of the forts in north Wales were placed conveniently for supply from the sea; that was desirable in view of the hostility of the natives and the difficulty of the terrain.

A site of *c.* 24 ha. was enclosed by a rampart and ditch forming 'a perfect parallelogram' at Wallfield in the parish of Astbury. The site, sought in vain at Hulme Walfield 3.5 km. north of Astbury,[27] is thought to have been rediscovered at Bent Farm, Astbury. The defences were sectioned, revealing a V-shaped ditch 2.4–3.4 m. wide and *c.* 1.2 m. deep and a clay rampart not less than 2.4 m. wide. Trial trenching in the interior located post-holes and slots of timber buildings aligned on the defences.[28] Of the eastern defences 100–150 m. remain upstanding, but the remainder of the circuit cannot be discerned on the ground. As no datable finds have been reported it is impossible to be sure when the earthwork was constructed. Its size is appropriate to a legionary fortress, but a marching camp or temporary field work capable of holding auxiliaries as well as a legion would have

[19] Thompson, *Roman Ches.* 10.
[20] *C.I.L.* xvi. 43, 51.
[21] V. E. Nash-Williams, *Roman Frontier in Wales* (2nd edn.), 14–16.
[22] Below.
[23] *Arch. Jnl.* cxxv. 200–2.
[24] *Antiquity*, li. 55–60; *Britannia*, viii. 394.
[25] *Britannia*, viii. 358–9.
[26] *Arch. Jnl.* cxxv. 145.
[27] *T.H.S.L.C.* xxix. 84–5, xxxix. 56; Watkin, *Roman Ches.* 298–9.
[28] *Northern Hist.* iii. 3–4, 26; *Britannia*, ii. 255.

seemed more likely had timber buildings not been found in the interior. In view of the estimated size a practice camp seems an unlikely identification.

A possible camp has been observed from the air at Blacon, near Chester.[29] A site at Halton Brow[30] had a V-shaped ditch on three sides; a size of *c*. 61 m. by *c*. 64 m. was estimated, giving an area of under half a hectare. No internal structures were found, and very little dating material; occupation was dated to the late 3rd or 4th century. In further investigation undertaken when the site was threatened by house-building,[31] the single ditch was found to have enclosed an irregular pentagon 106 m. by 73 m.; there was no sign of a bank or rampart, and it seems unlikely that the site was military as was initially thought. A small amount of pottery was dated to the 2nd and 3rd centuries. The old belief that Halton castle occupied one corner of a larger Roman site, of which the defences 'in the form of a parallelogram' were still thought to be visible in the 18th century, seems to have no basis in fact.[32] A vertical air photograph shows what appear to be the defences of a military site at Manley, but a site visit proved negative. Pottery and a quern are recorded as having been found close by at Crossley Hospital, Manley.[33]

The Defences of the Fortress

The earliest comprehensive review of Roman Cheshire could not, from lack of evidence, define the defences of the fortress with accuracy. It was supposed that the 'quay wall' on the Roodee formed part of the curtain wall, or, alternatively, that the defended area was smaller than that accepted today.[34] The salient features of the plan were, however, perceived: angles were postulated near the Newgate and south-east of St. Martin's church, for example, and the southern defences therefore followed the north side of Pepper Street and ran between White Friars and Cuppin Street. It was noted that 'none [of the streets] can be traced *in a continuous line* west of Nicholas Street, Linenhall Street, and St. Martin's', which indicated the likely line of the wall on the west side, with a gate on the line of Watergate Street near Holy Trinity church. A curve in the city wall at Morgan's Mount betrayed the position of the north-west angle.[35] The fortress enclosure now revealed on every side confirms the accuracy of those observations and deductions; the city wall and the Roman defences follow the same line on the north and east sides. The defences underwent development, for initially they consisted of a turf rampart at least 6 m. wide at the base, exceeding 2 m. in height (and possibly twice that measurement), with timber towers and gates. Only later were a stone wall, which followed the rampart line precisely, and stone gates and towers built. The Flavian ditch was relatively slight, *c*. 1.5 m. deep, and perhaps 3.6 m. wide, and was enlarged to virtually double that size, *c*. 6 m. wide and up to 3 m. deep, presumably when the stone defences were built. Indirect evidence bearing on the date of the turf rampart can be recovered from the earliest deposits at the rear which have produced Flavian finds on a number of sites.[36] Dating evidence otherwise is far to seek: the curtain wall could structurally be as early as the turf rampart, and the towers have yielded nothing of use. Discussion of the same point in relation to the very much better documented fortress at Caerleon[37] revealed a similar lack of evidence; a date before

[29] *Ches. Arch. Bull.* vii. 11.

[30] *Liverpool Annals*, xxiv. 165-8; *J.R.S.* xxvii. 232.

[31] *J.R.S.* lviii. 183; *J.C.A.S.* lviii. 85-8.

[32] Watkin, *Roman Ches.* 295, quoting Foote Gower. The site was thought to be nearly 16 ha. in area.

[33] Thanks are due to Mr. K. Jermy for drawing the aerial photograph to the writer's attention and for visiting the site with him. See also *T.L.C.A.S.* xxiv. 121-2.

[34] Watkin, *Roman Ches.* 88, 90.

[35] Ibid. 88-9, 92-4; the author suggested that there had been an earlier, smaller site, and a larger late Roman enclosure.

[36] e.g. Linenhall Street, 1949 and 1961-2: *J.C.A.S.* xl. 5; lvi. 7.

[37] G. C. Boon, *Isca*, 38-9.

c. A.D. 120, though perhaps not long before, is suggested for the stone wall and towers. A sherd of samian found embedded in a turret foundation could, nevertheless, have been Hadrianic or even Antonine in date.[38] In the circumstances it is unwise to press a Trajanic date for Chester's stone defences.

It is perhaps surprising to find that one at least of the 22 interval towers was demolished as early as the Severan period, and then covered by a wider rampart which has been identified on every side save the east. Some towers remained, for that in Abbey Green was substantially rebuilt, and it seems likely that the curtain wall and gates were repaired at the same time. It might further be suggested that a recutting of the ditch which to some extent restored the original profile should be assigned to the Severan restoration: the slight amount of dating evidence would not be at odds with that conclusion.

Despite doubts[39] there is every reason to suppose that the fortress was occupied throughout the 2nd century, though at a reduced level until Scotland was abandoned early in the 160s. It has been argued that the repair of the curtain wall incorporating re-used masonry implies that *Deva* continued at that time to be garrisoned, and of some military significance. Without evidence to the contrary, occupation of the fortress must be assumed to have continued for most of the 3rd century, and perhaps into the 4th. A number of the fortress buildings had been demolished by the time the late repairs were undertaken: it seems unnecessary to defend a largely empty enclosure, and a post-Roman date has been preferred for the work.[40] The supposed late defences lack bastions, and another feature consistently found in southern Britain in late Roman defences is the broad flat-bottomed ditch. Such new devices do not, however, appear on the military sites of the north, and at York are conspicuously absent, even from the grand reconstruction facing the Ouse, for which a Constantian date is generally accepted.[41] The problem is resolved by indications that the rebuilt wall probably does not represent a unified scheme of reconstruction at all, but rather one stage of a process of patching and rebuilding of lengths of wall over a long period.

On present evidence the enclosure established in the Flavian period continued to be defended until at least the end of the Roman occupation without either enlargement or reduction in size.

The Turf Rampart

The Flavian turf rampart was first observed at the south-east angle, where the outer face was found to be vertical for a height of 1.5 m.[42] Timber strapping seen towards the base of the rampart consisted of some rather short isolated slabs of oak 10–15 cm. wide 'so reduced by pressure and decay that none was more than half an inch [1.25 cm.] thick', laid 'horizontally and somewhat obliquely to the rampart wall'. Later there were found to be two layers of strapping 38 cm. apart, each of 15-cm. logs. The turf was concentrated towards the front of the rampart.[43] The rampart lay immediately behind the later stone wall on every side of the fortress, and the size of the defended enclosure therefore remained the same during the fortress's life. The details of construction are not identical at every site. Excavation

[38] Ibid. 38 and n. 122.

[39] T. J. Strickland, '3rd Cent. Chester', *Roman West in 3rd Cent.* ed. A. King and M. Henig (Brit. Arch. Rep. Internat. Ser. cix), 415–19; *Welsh Hist. Rev.* vii. 93.

[40] J. C. McPeake, 'The End of the Affair', in *New Evidence for Roman Chester*, ed. T. J. Strickland and P. J. Davey, 41.

[41] R.C.H.M. *City of York*, i, p. xxxiii.

[42] R. Newstead, 'On a Recently Discovered Section of Roman Wall at Chester', *J.C.A.S.* xvi. 9–24; R. Newstead and J. P. Droop, 'SE. Corner of Roman Fortress, Chester', ibid. xxix. 41–8; Newstead was the first to recognize the turf rampart for what it was: ibid. xxxvi. 57.

[43] G. Webster, 'Excavations on Legionary Defences at Chester, 1949–52 (Pt. 1)', ibid. xxxix. 21–7.

on the site of the cathedral bell tower revealed the rear half of the rampart standing 1.75–2 m. high: while individual turves could be observed and measured, no timber strapping was revealed either in or under the rampart.[44] The turves were *c*. 30 cm. square, with 'doubles' measuring 60 by 30 cm. In the first section opened at the northern defences, the rampart attained a height of 2.25 m. A single layer of strapping or 'corduroy' was observed at the base: timber found slightly higher was thought to be odd pieces accidentally embedded in the rampart.[45] Further west at Abbey Green,[46] a sector of the defences was stripped: not only was the basal corduroy found, as in the Deanery Field, but there were further layers of strapping at 0.75 m. and 1.5 m. above the base. Both excavations between the north-east angle and the Northgate showed a marked concentration of turf at the inner face of the rampart. At Abbey Green there was a turf cheek 2 m. thick, with 2 m. of sand and rubble core, and an equal width of turf at the front of the rampart. It appears that the greater part of the rampart width survived there, by contrast with the section in the Deanery Field where roughly half had been destroyed by rebuilding of the city wall in 1887.

Between the Northgate and the north-west angle, excavations on the site of the Northgate Brewery revealed a turf feature which had a sharp edge to the south, and sloped upwards to the east, attaining a height of 1 m.,[47] perhaps a turf-built *ascensus* giving access to the rampart walk near the north gate.[48]

At the north-west angle the rampart stood 2.43 m. high.[49] Neither the medieval defences nor the present city walls follow the west and south Roman defences, and on those sides opportunities arise to observe the full width of the turf rampart and to examine its relationship to the stone wall. Excavation north of Princess Street[50] found the reduced clay and turf bank 3.8 m. wide immediately behind the stone wall, a relationship later confirmed again on the same site[51] and also further south. Between Nicholas Street and Weaver Street[52] a rampart *c*. 5.8 m. across stood at least 1.9 m. high. Several features seen elsewhere recurred, such as the near-vertical inner face and the concentration of turf at the front and rear. Clear remains of the timber strapping at the base of the rampart were revealed.[53] On an extensive site north of the fortress west gate[54] the rampart was *c*. 5.8 m. or more wide, with turf cheeks roughly 1.5 m. thick front and rear, and at least 2 m. high. At the south-west angle and on the southern defences between south gate and south-east angle the wall and turf rampart shared the same line. In Newgate Street only the tail of the rampart was seen, but the distance from wall-back to rampart-tail appears to have been *c*. 6 m. Strapping was noted at the base; the surviving height was 1.2 m., and the inner face was very nearly vertical.[55]

It seems unlikely that a turf-built wall would long survive at (or near) its original height, and estimates depend on other factors and in particular its basal width. The width cannot have been much less than *c*. 6 m.; only a narrow berm separated it from the inner lip of the ditch, and while *c*. 1.2 m. of the rampart front

---

[44] *Britannia*, iii. 313; *J.C.A.S.* lviii. 134; *Ches. Arch. Bull.* i. 12.

[45] G. Webster, 'Excavations on Legionary Defences at Chester, 1949–52 (Pt. 2)', *J.C.A.S.* xl. 17–23.

[46] *Britannia*, vii. 320–1; viii. 385–7; ix. 429–30; J. C. McPeake, M. Bulmer, and J. A. Rutter, 'Excavations in Garden of No. 1 Abbey Green, Chester, 1975–77: Interim Rep.' *J.C.A.S.* lxiii. 15–37.

[47] P. J. Davey, *Chester Northgate Brewery, Phase I: Interim Rep.* 8–9.

[48] *Britannia*, iv. 284.

[49] *J.R.S.* lv. 204.

[50] Ibid. xxxvi. 136–40.

[51] Ibid. lvi. 200.

[52] G. Webster, 'A Section through Legionary Defences on W. Side of Fortress', *J.C.A.S.* xlii. 45–7; F. H. Thompson, 'Excavations in Nicholas Street, 1957', ibid. xlix. 5–8.

[53] Ibid. xlix, fig. 2 and pl. 2b.

[54] Ibid. xl. 1–6; F. H. Thompson, 'Excavations at Linenhall St., Chester, 1961–2', ibid. lvi. 1–21; *J.R.S.* liv. 156.

[55] F. H. Thompson and F. W. Tobias, 'Excavations in Newgate Street, Chester, 1955', *J.C.A.S.* xliv. 29–40. The rampart has been observed north of Pepper Street: ibid. xxxvi. 61.

may have been removed when the stone curtain wall was constructed,[56] sections such as that in Nicholas Street revealed a rampart which does not appear to have been pared back, and attention has been drawn to the absence of a construction trench for the wall at the south-east angle.[57] There is no clear evidence that the rampart was much wider than it is now, c. 6 m., and the siting of the timber tower discussed below appears to support that conclusion. It has been suggested that the rampart height was no more than c. 2 m., since rampart-walk paving was thought to have been found *in situ* at Abbey Green.[58] An alternative estimate of the height at c. 5.2 m.[59] was based on analogy with the turf-built western sector of Hadrian's Wall and the supposed similarity of its restored height to the known height of the north wall at Chester. The height of Hadrian's turf wall, however, was c. 3.65 m.,[60] whereas the height of the wall-walk of the stone wall at Chester is over 1 m. more. The rampart may have continued to serve a useful function as a rearward extension of the wall-walk,[61] for if the walk of the stone wall was effectively blocked by one man, some means were needed to enable men to pass, and the rampart height cannot have been greatly different from that of the wall-walk of the stone wall. The excavation at Abbey Green may cast doubt on earlier conclusions on the issue, but several published sections show a rampart height exceeding, although not greatly, the 2 m. recorded there, and the question therefore remains open.

It is generally assumed, and there seems no reason to doubt, that the 1st-century defences had timber gates and towers. Of gates there is no positive evidence: if, as has been suggested,[62] the Flavian *via principalis* lay c. 22.85 m. north of the later one, Flavian east and west gates were displaced similarly to the north. That does not, however, seem to have been the case. The only timber interval tower to have been found, at Abbey Green,[63] was clearly built before the rampart. Four posts c. 35 cm. square were set in rock-cut post-pits with ramped rear edges, making a structure 4 m. by 4.25 m. It lay c. 10 m. west of a stone-built interval tower, and it seems certain that the towers of the two periods do not coincide except, necessarily, at the angles. A calculation based on the position of the timber tower at Abbey Green suggests that three timber towers were placed between the north gate and the north-east angle at roughly 50-m. intervals, appreciably closer together than the two stone towers in the same sector. If that is so there were six towers on each of the shorter sides of the fortress. The same spacing on the longer east and west sides would give seven towers on either side of the *retentura*, as against the five stone towers assumed to have occupied that length. Whether there were two or three towers between the east and west gates and the southern angles of the fortress is not clear, one difficulty being lack of precise knowledge of the sites of those gates. The full total of timber towers, including those at the four corners, was 34 or 36. On the site of St. Martin's churchyard at the corner of White Friars and St. Martin's Ash a large rectangular post-pit of a timber tower had evidently been cut by the north-west wall of the stone angle tower: nothing similar has been seen at the south-east angle tower.

A turf rampart was accompanied by one or more ditches. Excavation at Linenhall Street[64] and Frodsham Street[65] revealed that there was only one ditch for the east and west defences. A ditch c. 3.65 m. wide and 1.5 m. deep, of

[56] Thompson, *Roman Ches.* 25–6 and fig. 5.
[57] *J.C.A.S.* xxxix. 4.
[58] Ibid. lxiii. 17; but cf. ibid. lxv. 32.
[59] Ibid. xl. 5; G. Webster, 'Defences of Roman Chester', (Manchester Univ. M.A. thesis, 1951).

[60] J. C. Bruce, *Roman Wall*, ed. C. M. Daniels, 20; D. J. Breeze and B. Dobson, *Hadrian's Wall*, 32.
[61] *J.C.A.S.* xl. 5 and fig. 4.
[62] Ibid. xxxviii. 17.
[63] Ibid. lxiii. 17.
[64] Ibid. lvi. 1–21.
[65] *J.R.S.* lvii. 179–80.

which only the bottom and inner face survived at the latter site,[66] was presumed to be the Flavian ditch, all trace of which was normally removed by a later recut. The feature may have been present at Princess Street on the west side, although not recognized. The recut ditch is substantially larger, c. 6–8 m. wide and c. 2.7–3 m. deep.[67]

Beneath the conventional Flavian turf-built rampart at Abbey Green were the scattered elements of what appeared to be an earlier rampart, consisting of parallel lines of post-pits at c. 1.55 m. spacing; its width was estimated at 3.25–3.5 m. Box construction ramparts are found rarely in Roman Britain; at the legionary fortress at Lincoln such a rampart was 3 m. wide, reasonably close to the postulated width at Abbey Green.[69] Since the feature underlies a Flavian rampart it may be pre-Flavian in date, as at Lincoln: direct evidence of its date, like that of the turf rampart, is very sparse.

It has been calculated that the fortress's turf rampart could have been completed in 12–14 days.[70] The measurements used do not agree with those at Chester, but the volume of turf required for a rampart some 25 per cent narrower surrounding an enclosure 20 per cent larger than those cited was probably similar.

The Stone Defences

A stone curtain wall surrounded the fortress, defining an enclosure c. 590 m. by c. 410 m.,[71] the longer axis lying roughly north–south; the area contained was 24.33 ha. (59.8 a.). Although the line of the fortress wall on its north and east sides is broadly followed by the present city wall, the surviving lengths in the Kaleyards and near the cathedral bell tower demonstrate that the two walls do not share a common line in detail, nor does the later wall consistently base itself on the earlier. Immediately north and south of the Eastgate the lines of city wall and fortress wall coincide, but behind no. 6 St. John Street the fortress wall was some distance in advance of the later one, as earlier excavations had proved in the sector adjoining the south-east angle.[72] Stukeley refers to the Roman wall in that sector 'between Eastgate and the river' as 'pretty perfect for 100 yards together'.[73] From extant walling, and from excavations on the east and west defences, the fortress wall can be seen to have a base course, placed on a foundation which varies in width and character but always coincides at the rear with the inner face of the wall; at the front the foundation is usually oversailed by the base course. Above the base course the wall narrows by an offset of 30 cm. to a chamfered plinth, and narrows again above the plinth to a width of 1.36 m. The face of the wall consists of large and carefully laid blocks of sandstone, with courses 22 cm. or more in depth.[74] Probably the most cunning masons' work was seen at the north-west angle, where very careful joggling of courses took place. At that point an exceptionally preserved fragment of wall, no less than 4.5 m. high, was embedded in the later city wall.[75] Recent examination of the north wall east of the Northgate has revealed important

[66] Below, plate.

[67] The sections of the ditch recorded are St. John Street (c. 6.7 × 2.7 m.), the south-east angle (7 × c. 2.5 m.), Frodsham Street (6 × 2.9 m.), Linenhall Street (c. 7.9 × 3.2 m.), Princess Street (8.2 × 3 m.), St. Martin's Fields (c. 8.5 × 2.9 m.), St. Martin's Ash (6.4 × 2.3 m.), Pepper Street (more than 7.6 × 3.1 m.), and Linenhall Street again (c. 7.5 × 2.75 m.). The last four are unpublished; for the remainder see *J.C.A.S.* xvi. 17–19; xxix. 47–8 and pl. 17; lvi. 6 and fig. 3; *J.R.S.* xxxvi. 136–40; lvii. 179–80.

[68] *New Evidence*, 13; *J.C.A.S.* lxiii. 15–17.

[69] M. J. Jones, *Roman Fort-Defences to A.D. 117* (Brit. Arch. Rep. xxi), 82; *Arch. Jnl.* cxvii. 48–50.

[70] *Roman Frontier Studies 1967*, ed. S. Applebaum, 31.

[71] Nash-Williams, *Roman Frontier in Wales*, 35.

[72] *Jnl. Brit. Arch. Assoc.* v. 212; *J.C.A.S.* N.S. i. 190–1; ii. 60–1; v. 118; xvi. 5–24; xxix. 41–8; xxxvi. 53–5; xxxix. 21–8; Lawson, 'Schedule', nos. XLVI, XLVIII, XCIV; *J.R.S.* lvii. 179–80; *Britannia*, v. 418–19.

[73] W. Stukeley, *Iter Boreale*, 33.

[74] Fig. 24.

[75] *J.R.S.* lv. 204.

evidence of the form of the curtain wall. Above the chamfered plinth the outer face of the wall rose vertically to cornice level at 4.5 m. above ground level. It was formed of 13 courses, excluding the plinth, cornice, and parapet, the sandstone blocks being *c.* 1.2–1.6 m. long and 30–34 cm. high. The width of the wall was *c.* 1.3–1.5 m., and its height to the wall-walk was *c.* 5.2 m. above the base of the wall, *c.* 7 m. being suggested as the total height including the parapet. There was a moulding over the cornice with a rebate 36–40 cm. back from its front edge designed to take the stones of the parapet. The parapet is estimated at 37 cm. thick, and perhaps 1.6 m. high. Behind it the much worn surfacing of the wall-walk was detected.[76]

Wherever the point can be examined, principally on the west, the stone wall is found to share closely the alignment of the turf rampart. Indeed, at the south-east angle it was thought that 'the wall and rampart were evidently laid down at the same time, and as part of the same job', a conclusion based on the overlapping of projecting masonry by the turf work of the 'clay' rampart.[77] Later investigation confirmed the filling of clean sand and small stones in immediate contact with the turf construction observed earlier,[78] and the absence of a clear construction trench for the wall was noted. The case for a Trajanic rather than a Flavian date rested largely on analogy: since the excavation of Inchtuthil, however, a Flavian fortress with a stone curtain wall is no longer an anomaly,[79] and a stone wall need not necessarily imply stone gates or towers. The sandstone wall at Inchtuthil was 1.4–1.5 m. thick, and fronted a turf rampart; each gate consisted of massive timber towers flanking double portals, but no timber interval towers have been located. Thus there may be some justification for the term 'rampart wall', and in the absence of direct evidence from the wall itself it is reasonable to retain the option of a Flavian date. A wall only 1.36 m. thick and reduced by breastworks to probably under 1 m. required ancillary space behind it to provide a fighting platform; therefore either the wall and rampart were built as part of one scheme, or the curtain wall when it was added was built so that the two wall-walks coincided in height.[80] It has been suggested that the Flavian defences continued in use throughout the 2nd century until radical rebuilding took place under Severus.[81] Nevertheless, while the enlargement of the rampart recognized at several sites could have taken place at the same time as the building of the curtain wall, at least one stone interval tower was demolished *c.* A.D. 200, and it seems unlikely that stone towers existed when a curtain wall was absent.[82]

At each angle of the fortress there was a tower: the most completely known is the south-eastern, although something is known about each of the other three. The front wall of the tower is formed by the fortress wall: at the south-east angle the width of the wall was reduced by as much as 30 cm.; the side walls were 1.23 m. and 1.31 m. thick respectively at the base, barely less than the curtain wall. The depth of the tower, including the width of the rear wall, was 8.5 m. from the outer face of the fortress wall; it was 9.5 m. wide at the front and 7.9 m. wide at the rear, as the side walls converged. The other tower whose plan is known is at the

[76] T. J. Strickland, 'Defences of Roman Chester: Note on Discoveries made on the North Wall, 1982', *J.C.A.S.* lxv. 25–35; inf. from Mr. T. J. Strickland. The wall contains no re-used masonry.

[77] *J.C.A.S.* xxix. 44, figs. 1,14; plate 20.

[78] Ibid. xxxix. 24 and fig. 15.

[79] L. F. Pitts and J. K. St. Joseph, *Inchtuthil: The Roman Legionary Fortress* (*Britannia* monograph ser. vi), 61–71;

J.R.S. xlii. 104; xliv. 84 and fig. 8. A stone wall was virtually contemporary with the turf rampart in view of the very short period of occupation at Inchtuthil.

[80] *J.C.A.S.* xl. 4, fig. 4.

[81] Ibid. lxv. 34–5.

[82] Although stone gates predated the curtain wall at several towns in Roman Britain, that would not necessarily have been acceptable on a military site.

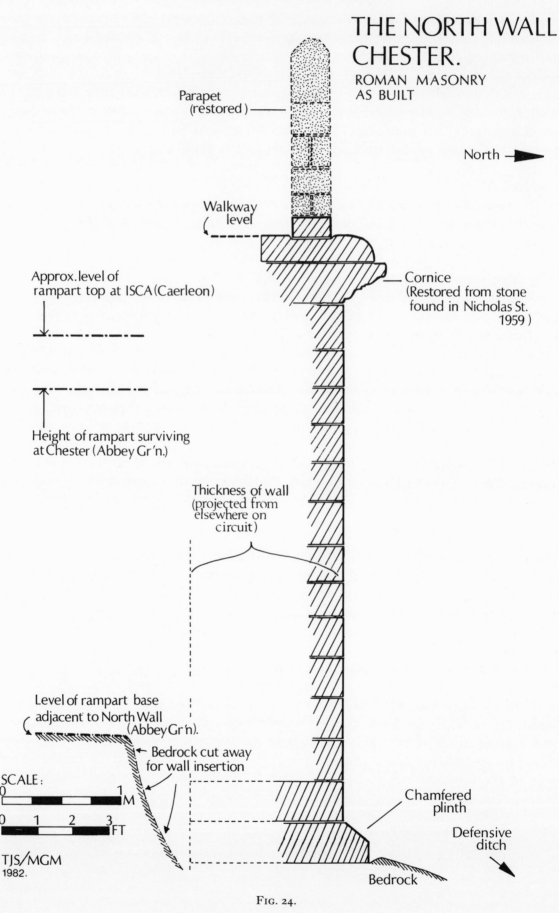

THE NORTH WALL CHESTER.
ROMAN MASONRY AS BUILT

North →

Parapet (restored)

Walkway level

Cornice (Restored from stone found in Nicholas St. 1959)

Approx. level of rampart top at ISCA (Caerleon)

Height of rampart surviving at Chester (Abbey Gr'n.)

Thickness of wall (projected from elsewhere on circuit)

Level of rampart base adjacent to North Wall (Abbey Gr'n).

Bedrock cut away for wall insertion

Chamfered plinth

Defensive ditch

Bedrock

SCALE:
0   1 M

0   1   2   3 FT

TJS/MGM
1982.

FIG. 24.

north-west angle. Demolition of part of the city wall for a new road revealed the north-east side wall of the tower standing up to 3 m. high. The tower was 9.74 m. wide at the front, but narrowed to 9 m. at the back; the depth from the curtain wall front to the outer face of the back wall was a little over 9.5 m. Its walls were 1.06 m. thick above offsets. By contrast, the south-west angle tower was found to be very badly damaged, as its site coincided with the small graveyard attached to the former St. Martin's church. The fortress wall had been completely robbed at that point, but the lowest part of the north-west wall of the tower survived. All that is known of the north-east tower is that during the levelling of the Deanery Field soil was taken from that corner of the field, laying bare a very short section of a substantial wall identified as being the back wall of the tower. The indications are that the Roman tower underlies the medieval tower, which itself acts as the substructure for the King Charles or Phoenix Tower.[83]

In addition to the relatively large angle towers, smaller regularly spaced turrets or 'interval towers' were provided. There were two between the north gate and the north-east corner, and the westernmost of the pair, revealed at Abbey Green, was c. 6.7 m. square, its rear wall trench-built within the rampart; it is thought to have had a tiled roof. The dimensions of the other tower were very similar, and in each case the walls narrowed by offsets to an effective thickness of 90 cm. or a little less. Each of the shorter sides of the fortress had four interval towers, and the longer east and west sides presumably seven each, two south and five north of the gates. The towers on the east and west walls in the *retentura* were apparently at a somewhat greater interval than elsewhere in the circuit, perhaps the result of a revised plan.[84] The total number of stone interval towers was therefore at first twenty-two. The only tower to have been found on the southern defences, the first west of the south-east angle tower, appears to have been demolished at the end of the 2nd century or in the early 3rd, and other towers may have been removed at the same time. The width of 6.7 m. and depth of c. 5.2 m. are close to those of the other towers explored, and the distance between the tower and the south-east angle tower, c. 58 m., corresponds to the spacing of the towers on the north wall. The only other tower to have been substantially excavated lay between the west gate and the south-west angle tower, being the northernmost of two in that sector. The width of the tower was 6.54 m., and its internal projection of nearly 5.2 m. indicates, given the thickness of the fortress wall, that the towers were planned as square. The walls were 90 cm. thick above offsets and at one point stood 1.5 m. high. The survival of timber strapping under the tower confirms that the tower walls were inserted through the rampart.

North of the west gate the sites of two towers have been recorded, but relatively little is known about them. One had been completely robbed to its footings, and so was not initially recognized. Later investigation revealed the robber trench of the rear corners of the tower, and its south wall. The tower immediately north of the west gate was partially revealed during its destruction by building work. No interval towers belonging to the eastern defences have been identified.[85]

The angle and interval towers, which clearly belonged to the same system of defence, were certainly all of one date. Nevertheless it is not so clear that they are of one date with the curtain wall, although there must be a strong presumption that

[83] SE. angle tower: *J.C.A.S.* xxix. 41–8; xxxvi. 56–8; xxxix. 21–7; NW. angle tower: *J.R.S.* lv. 204; lvi. 200; SW. angle tower: ibid. lv. 204; NE. angle tower: *Liverpool Annals*, xxiii. 11.

[84] *J.C.A.S.* lx. 36.

[85] *Liverpool Annals*, xxii. 19–20; xxiii. 10–11; *Britannia*, vii. 320–1; viii. 387; *J.C.A.S.* xliv. 29–40; xlix. 5–8; lvi. 1–21; lxiii. 19; *J.R.S.* xxxvi. 136–40; lvi. 200.

wall, towers, and gates belong to a single scheme, and it is usual to date the rebuilding of the defences in stone to the Trajanic period. Only one tower, at Newgate Street, has produced evidence of date: it post-dated an early Trajanic rampart building, and had been demolished at the end of the 2nd century. On Abbey Green, by contrast, the tower's west and south walls were rebuilt *c.* 200: a raising and extending of the rampart effectively sealed the Newgate Street tower.

Although relatively little is known about internal features, neither angle nor interval towers were entered at ground level. At Abbey Green the interior was made up with alternating layers of turf and sandstone rubble, and at the south-east angle the interior of the tower contained turf belonging to the rampart. It seems clear, therefore, that they were watch towers, entered at wall-walk level.

What little has been recorded about the gates of the fortress poses problems of interpretation. There were four gates, one to each side, the north and south gates being placed in the centre of their respective sides, and the east and west gates being offset towards the south end.[86] The sites of the north and east gates were later occupied by gates belonging to the medieval defences, which were in turn demolished to make way for the present arches. On the west and south sides of the fortress, where the line of the Roman wall was superseded by medieval defences overlooking the river, the sites of the gates are marked by churches, Holy Trinity and St. Michael's respectively.

The east gate (*porta principalis sinistra*) has received most attention,[87] though opinions of what has been observed vary. The earliest known drawing of the medieval gate, done before the siege of Chester in the 1640s, shows no sign of Roman construction.[88] Stukeley in 1725 recorded what he believed were the arches of a Roman gate. Despite doubts expressed since then, his account carries conviction.[89] He depicted and described front and rear arches, with the remains of flanking arches, and seems to have been influenced by knowledge of Newport Arch at Lincoln in postulating one large portal with flanking footways. An alternative interpretation is a larger gate with two carriageways flanked by footways; the northern arch may well have been as large as that surviving, judging by Stukeley's drawing, while the springing shown for the southern arch would better suit a smaller footway. The rear arch was 5.0–5.5 m. across.

After the medieval gate was taken down in 1768[90] it was noted that 'two regular Roman arches on the same extended line were found secreted in the body of this structure'.[91] It is not clear whether those arches were the ones visible to Stukeley or whether they were additional. A drawing made in the early 18th century before the demolition[92] confirms the front and rear arches as drawn by Stukeley. The drawings and reconstructions made after 1768[93] while appearing highly speculative may well have had some basis in fact for showing a gate consisting of two main portals,[94] and it does not seem excessive to restore arched footways on either side of them, since this was a principal gateway of the fortress. Presumably the gate was

[86] Nash-Williams, *Roman Frontier in Wales*, figs. 80–2; P. Carrington, 'Planning and Date of Legionary Fortress at Chester', *J.C.A.S.* lx. 35–42.
[87] W. Stukeley, *Iter Boreale*, 31; T. Pennant, *Tour of Wales* (1784 edn.), i. 114–15; D. and S. Lysons, *Magna Britannia*, ii. 427; Ormerod, *Hist. Ches.* i. 295; P. Broster, *Chester Guide* (1781 edn.), 20; J. Hemingway, *Hist. Chester*, i. 340; Watkin, *Roman Ches.* 106–13; *T.H.S.L.C.* i. 82; *J.C.A.S.* [1st ser.] iii. 44; xl. 23; P. H. Alebon, P. J. Davey, and D. J. Robinson, 'The Eastgate, Chester, 1972', ibid. lix. 37–49; Lawson, 'Schedule', no. xxix; Webster, 'Defences', 44–8.

[88] *J.C.A.S.* lix. fig. 22.
[89] 'I observed . . . two arches of Roman work. It was a square of 20 feet . . . in the same manner as at Lincoln.' The drawing, dated 2 Aug. 1725, strongly confirms the resemblance to Newport Arch: below, plate.
[90] Chester City R.O., AB/4, ff. 256–256v.
[91] Watkin, *Roman Ches.* 107.
[92] *J.C.A.S.* lix. fig. 23.
[93] Watkin, *Roman Ches.* 108, 110.
[94] The southern portal may have been blocked later: *J.C.A.S.* lxvii. 20.

flanked by towers, the ground floor of one or both serving as a guard-chamber. Walling belonging to the south guard-chamber of the gate may have survived *in situ* on the south side of the street.[95] A stone relief said to have been revealed in the spandrel between the main arches on the outer (east) face of the gate when it was demolished gave rise to speculation, and doubt has been cast on the authenticity of the report: the stone, preserved at the time, has since been lost.[96] Such a relief would not normally be found on a Roman gate: when the structure was taken down part of a legionary tombstone showing a relief of the deceased, perhaps a standard-bearer, may have come to light;[97] the stone, although Roman, may have formed part of the medieval gate. Masonry said to have extended to about 18 m. east of the present gate was almost certainly medieval.[98] It is possible that the lower of two pavements noted was Roman, though the putative depth may be excessive at 2.75 m.; the upper has since been dated to the 17th century.[99] In Foregate Street adjoining the Eastgate what might be the Roman road was 1.5 m. below ground level.[1] Two distinct surfaces were identified, the under side of the lower being at a depth of 2.9 m.: it sealed a line of pipes running towards the Eastgate thought to form part of the Roman water supply. A ditch 6.7 m. wide was presumably that of the Roman fortress. A Corinthian capital is said to have been found several feet under ground when the east gate was pulled down.[2]

Of the north gate (*porta decumana*) very little can be said. When Thomas Harrison pulled down the Northgate in 1808 to build the new one he found the substructure to be Roman,[3] as the inscription on the new gate confirms, but no details were apparently recorded. Nothing of the Roman gate is visible, though Harrison may have left the Roman foundations mostly undisturbed.

The site of the south gate (*porta praetoria*) is thought to be covered in part by St. Michael's church, and in part by the adjacent Bridge Street. A foundation covering an area of 4.26 m. under the steps of the church is described as being so unyielding that it was not possible to procure a specimen.[4] It was assumed that the south gate of the fortress had been discovered,[5] and the foundation formed part of the east tower. A further part of what may well be the same structure was found in excavating a drain from no. 63 Bridge Street, immediately north of the church. As before, the concrete was formed of small boulder stones and very hard mortar, softer on the west side. The foundation was said to have extended along the Bridge Street frontage of the church. A further 1.75 m. of foundation was found to the south.[6] It seems likely that the outer and undoubtedly substantial element was part of the structure of the gate. Whether it was originally one with the foundation running under the shop is not so clear, and other interpretations are possible. It may be that the two foundations ran parallel, and were the side walls of the eastern footway of a gate with two large and two small portals, such as has been postulated for the east gate.[7] A massive structure also found on the east side of the street is more likely to belong to the baths.[8]

[95] Lawson, 'Schedule', no. XXIX; Webster, 'Defences', 47; *J.C.A.S.* xl. 23.

[96] Pennant, *Tour in Wales*, 119 refers to the stone as in the garden of Mr. Lawton, and it passed through other hands. Exposure to weather may have completed the destruction of the relief, which was damaged when found.

[97] Webster, 'Defences', 48.

[98] *T.H.S.L.C.* l. 82; Watkin, *Roman Ches.* 112–13.

[99] *J.C.A.S.* lix. 43.

[1] Ibid. v. 325–30.

[2] *Jnl. Brit. Arch. Assoc.* v. 215.

[3] Ibid. 214; *Antiquary*, xvii. 44.

[4] *J.C.A.S.* N.S. i. 213. The foundations of the nearby bath building similarly consisted of 'small boulder stones' in very hard concrete.

[5] *J.C.A.S.* N.S. i. 213; iii. 79. The foundations extended for 14 ft.

[6] Ibid. xvi. 24–7; *Liverpool Annals*, ii. 67–9 and 69 n.

[7] Architectural fragments found re-used in the walls of St. Michael's church are likely to have been Romanesque rather than Roman: *J.C.A.S.* [1st ser.] i. 199.

[8] Ibid. xxvii. 109–10; Lawson, 'Schedule', no. XLI.

Like the south gate, the west gate (*porta principalis dextra*) is also thought to lie in part under a church, Holy Trinity, as well as under the adjacent Watergate Street and possibly also the buildings on its south side.[9] While no structure belonging to the gate has been recorded, the known positions of the interval towers to north and south permit a rough calculation of the width of the gate (including towers) at *c.* 25 m., not excessive by comparison with gates at other fortresses.

One of the most puzzling features of the defences is the so-called postern gate excavated in the Deanery Field.[10] The wall with a series of offsets, identified as the inner face of the fortress wall, differs from the inner face exposed elsewhere, and appears to be further west than it ought to be. While the *retentura* of the fortress at Chester was longer than normal and might justify posterns which other fortresses do not appear to have, the evidence presented need not support the conclusion drawn.[11]

There is no direct evidence of the date of construction of the stone gates, though it is often stated that a fragment of an inscription found in the Hop Pole Paddock[12] came from the east gate. Sufficient survives to permit its restoration as a building inscription of Trajanic date, *c.* A.D. 102–17. The rubbish piled against the fortress wall in the north-west corner of the paddock, which included the inscription, may have come from the Hop Pole Hotel; since the inn was just outside the east gate, it may have come from the latter. The line of argument is very tenuous, and in fact the inscription reveals only that a substantial building was completed under Trajan. It does not prove that the turf and timber defences of the 1st century were rebuilt in stone at that time; no confirmatory evidence has yet been adduced.[13]

The defences described were modified in various ways. An interval tower on the north wall was perhaps rebuilt *c.* A.D. 200; one on the south wall was dismantled at the same time.[14] The raising and widening of the rampart, which is thought to have remained more or less unaltered since its erection in the Flavian period, has been dated to the late 2nd century or the early 3rd. At Abbey Green and the Deanery Field it extended over the remains of ovens and rampart buildings; the rampart was also widened on the western defences.[15]

THE NORTH WALL. The north wall of the city incorporates substantial remains of the Roman curtain wall, principally between the north gate and north-east angle. The large number of Roman inscribed and sculptured stones recovered from it indicates building using re-used stone no earlier than the Severan period. The earliest recorded discoveries were made in 1883–4, when part of the wall near Morgan's Mount, west of the Northgate, required repair. Architectural fragments and one tombstone were found.[16] It was concluded that none of the walling was Roman.[17] The discovery may have prompted closer observation of wall repairs; in 1887 more inscribed stones were recovered near the Phoenix Tower.[18] Between 1890 and 1892 the wall west of Northgate was extensively examined: 63 tombstones from the north wall were placed in the Grosvenor Museum during the year 1891–

---

[9] The churches may at first have been housed in the remains of Roman gate towers.

[10] *Liverpool Annals*, xxiii. 12–14 and plates 4, 25.

[11] *J.R.S.* xxvi. 247.

[12] *J.C.A.S.* xxxviii. 19–20; *R.I.B.* i, no. 464; *R.I.S.S.* no. 15; F. H. Williams, *Synopsis of Roman Inscriptions of Chester*, 59, 63; *Arch. Jnl.* xlv. 180.

[13] Cf. G. Lloyd-Morgan and D. J. Robinson, *Roman Inscrips. in Grosvenor Mus., Chester*, addenda.

[14] Above; *Ches. Arch. Bull.* ix. 32–3.

[15] *J.C.A.S.* xl. 6 and figs. 2, 14, 15.

[16] Ibid. N.S. i. 98; Watkin, *Roman Ches.* 211–12; *Academy*, 5 May 1883, 318; *Arch. Jnl.* xli. 174–5; *R.I.S.S.* no. 63; *R.I.B.* i, no. 519.

[17] *J.C.A.S.* N.S. i. 177–84.

[18] I. M. Jones, 'Official Rep. on Discoveries of Roman Remains at Chester during First Repairs to North Wall, 1887', ibid. N.S. ii. 1–24; *Arch. Jnl.* xlv. 172–81, erroneously attributing the Hop Pole Paddock inscription to the north wall.

2, and the work of 1887 and 1890-2 is said to have added some 150 tombstones or the like, and many other moulded stones.[19]

Although the collection of inscribed and sculptured stones is very important in its own right, from the outset it was appreciated that it provided evidence for understanding the defences of Roman Chester. Despite controversy[20] it was eventually accepted that the north wall was rebuilt during the Roman period, and that it incorporated a large number of re-used stones taken mainly from one of the cemeteries.[21] The recording of the discovery of the stones was not detailed, and has left problems of interpretation. The section exposed in 1883 was thought to show a wall of two distinct periods of construction, an inner and older wall, and a newer and outer one which by contrast was faced with good ashlar: the inscribed and other stones came from the latter.[22] The discoveries of 1887 near King Charles's Tower were described in some detail with a section of the north wall, together with a plan showing the location of the stones course by course over a length of some 27 m.:[23] the schematic drawings indicate that Roman stones were recovered throughout the fabric of the wall to cornice level, coming mainly but perhaps not exclusively from the wall-core. It was, however, affirmed[24] that the stones came from the lower courses of the wall, which were faced with massive blocks of evident Roman masonry; they were 'ranged with considerable regularity' and were exclusively Roman. The lower part of the structure, at least, could be taken as Roman work. The width at the base of the wall was c. 2.75 m., so that one feature of the rebuilt wall was its greater width; another was the curious 'tumble-home' profile in the upper part below the cornice.[25] Recent careful examination of the north wall during further repairs, during which no re-used Roman inscribed or sculptured stones were seen, showed that its shape was caused by gradual collapse of the upper courses of Roman masonry rearwards, the movement at cornice level being nearly 1 m.[26] The north wall does not appear to have been faced on the inner side, and reduction of the rampart height would therefore have had serious consequences for the stability of the upper part of the wall.[27] It can be assumed that, wherever the cornice moulding survives, the Roman work is complete to that height.[28]

That the north wall was rebuilt to repair damage sustained during Albinus's usurpation (A.D. 196), as was formerly believed,[29] is no longer tenable: there is abundant evidence that the repairs are no earlier than the early 3rd century. The late 3rd century has been suggested,[30] and they were probably undertaken during the Roman period. A tombstone from the north wall, west of the north gate, can be dated to A.D. 213-22.[31] Other tombstones from the north wall can be dated to the 3rd century, for example that of M. Aurelius Alexander, who cannot have been given citizenship before A.D. 161, which suggests that his death at the age of 72 cannot have occurred before the reign of Caracalla.[32] The tombstone of a cavalryman[33] cannot be earlier

[19] W. de G. Birch, 'Inscribed Roman Stones recently found at Chester', J.C.A.S. N.S. ii. 98-131; ibid. 210, 212; iii. 273; iv. 199, 208-9, 214, 223-4; v. 116, 120; vii. 6-7. Cornice and other fragments must derive from several buildings: ibid. N.S. ii. 128; iii. 84.

[20] G. W. Shrubsole, 'Walls of Chester: Are they Roman or Edwardian?' ibid. N.S. iii. 71-113; Watkin, Roman Ches. 95-101; R.I.S.S. no. 120; Proc. Soc. Antiq. [2nd ser.], xii. 44-5.

[21] J.C.A.S. vii. 6, 8; Liverpool Annals, ii. 53.

[22] J.C.A.S. N.S. i. 177-8; vii, frontispiece.

[23] Ibid. N.S. ii, facing pp. 1, 4.

[24] Ibid. vii. 6.

[25] Ibid. N.S. ii, facing p. 46; cf. ibid. xl. 23.

[26] Ibid. lxv. 25-36. Thanks are due to Mr. T. J. Strickland

for discussing his findings before publication.

[27] Ibid. N.S. ii. 46. Curiously, no inner facing was introduced in the late Roman repairs.

[28] The wall exposed in 1982 lacked a base course.

[29] R. G. Collingwood and J. N. L. Myres, Roman Brit. and Eng. Settlements, 156.

[30] J.C.A.S. xxxviii. 20; Thompson, Roman Ches. 28-9; Frere, Britannia, 383, 385.

[31] J.R.S. xxxix. 114; R.I.S.S. no. 77; R.I.B. i, no. 488. The legionary titles on the stone include Antoniniana, assignable to the time of Caracalla or Elagabalus; the presence of a soldier of Legio II Augusta has not been explained.

[32] R.I.B. i, no. 490; R.I.S.S. no. 36.

[33] R.I.B. i, no. 557.

than the 3rd century if the man was a legionary *eques*, since it was not until then that the 120 mounted men of the legion were divided into *turmae*. Two other tombstones from the north wall[34] refer to the wives of serving soldiers and therefore presumably post-date relaxation by Severus of the rule forbidding serving soldiers to marry. Another stone[35] may also be 3rd century and later than the *constitutio Antoniniana*. A small coin of Constantius II as Caesar (A.D. 324–37) was said to have come from 'one of the unmortared joints of the lower wall', a point of some importance if the evidence can be accepted, but the genuineness of the find was strongly contested. Its value as dating evidence is clearly limited, although the account of the coin's discovery seems circumstantial enough.[36] It serves as a reminder that the 4th century provides several possible occasions for the rebuilding or strengthening of defences.

Much of the argument and conjecture surrounding the rebuilding of the north wall proceeds from the assumption that it was unique in containing Roman inscribed and sculptured stones. The evidence suggests otherwise, for such stones have also come from the wall or its immediate vicinity on the east and west sides and probably from the south side too. Whether the repairs using stones from a cemetery all took place at the same time cannot be proved, although it seems *prima facie* likely; conversely it seems unlikely that those were the only repairs required over two centuries or more, and perhaps they represent the latest in a succession.

THE WEST WALL. The western defences were in part rebuilt from the ground up, incorporating re-used stones.[37] The curtain wall between the west gate and the interval tower to the north had a footing 1.5–1.8 m. wider than usual, the width over all being *c*. 3.35 m.;[38] it incorporated the upper corner of a 'banquet' type tombstone, and an uninscribed tombstone came from the fill of the ditch nearby.[39] The ditch fill in Nicholas Street south of the west gate contained massive dressed stones at a depth of 2.4 m., and two fragments evidently from the cornice of the fortress wall.[40] A re-used cornice moulding in the wall footing, thought to be from the Trajanic wall, proved that the wall there was rebuilt from its foundations.[41] On the site of St. Martin's House there may also have been a rebuilding of the wall to a wider gauge, but the outer portion appeared to be founded on an apron of masonry in front of the earlier foundation rather than behind it.[42] The width of the rebuilt wall seems to have been *c*. 3.2–3.3 m., presumably narrowing by an offset and chamfered plinth as in the fortress wall elsewhere, to *c*. 2.85 m.

THE SOUTH AND EAST WALLS. The reliefs from White Friars may come from the south wall. Unlike the wall at the north-west angle, which yielded architectural fragments from its core when exposed as a result of building works, the south-east angle wall shows no sign of rebuilding, nor does the length of wall immediately north of it. Immediately north of the east gate part of a tombstone was recovered from the city wall, which was thought to have included Roman masonry at that point.[43] The supposed relief from the east gate might convincingly be identified as a fragmentary tomb relief, built into a repaired gate,[44] and the tombstone found on the site of the Corn Exchange may also have been destined for a wall repair.[45] Repairs incorporating re-used stones may therefore have been undertaken on the east as well as the north and west walls. A site examined north of the Kaleyard Gate showed that the masonry of the wall resembled that of the north wall, and the

[34] *R.I.B.* i, nos. 505, 507.
[35] Ibid. no. 523. Ibid. no. 491 may also be 3rd-cent.
[36] *J.C.A.S.* n.s. ii. 66, 84, 97.
[37] *J.R.S.* liv. 156; lv. 204; Nash-Williams, *Roman Frontier in Wales*, 41.
[38] *J.C.A.S.* lvi. 2 and fig. 3.
[39] Ibid. plate 1b.
[40] Ibid. xlix. 8.
[41] Ibid. xlii. 45, fig. 2.
[42] *J.R.S.* xxxvi, fig. 12; lvi. 200.
[43] *J.C.A.S.* liv. 14–15 and plate 3a.
[44] Above.
[45] *J.C.A.S*, n.s. ii. 82.

berm associated with it contained weathered dressed masonry which could have derived from an earlier curtain wall. The upstanding wall may be later than the mid 2nd century, and the masonry must derive from the earlier wall to which a Trajanic date is customarily attached.[46] A centurial stone may have been found in this length of wall.[47]

There has been a tendency to assume that the features described above represent a scheme of demolition and reconstruction of part or perhaps all of the defences. The picture presented by the western defences, and seemingly by the north wall also, is patchy rather than consistent, as would be expected if the repairs were carried out in precisely the same piecemeal way as repairs to the city wall today, producing variations in measurement, detail of construction, and possibly appearance above ground level. None of the features of late Roman defences such as bastions have been incorporated, which argues against a unified reconstruction in the later 3rd or 4th century.[48]

The Fortress Ditch. A single large ditch surrounded the stone defences. There is no direct evidence of the date at which it superseded the earlier and smaller ditch, although it might well have been dug at the time when the stone defences were being built; it was recut more than once. Where the sides had been cut through the solid rock they dipped more steeply to a narrow slot at the bottom: layers of clean silt at the bottom of one section[49] had been only partially removed by a later cleaning. A brown loam fill above was thought to represent an accumulated fill during the late 2nd century and the 3rd; the fill appeared to have been cut away to form a ditch which was smaller and had a more rounded profile. That ditch was assigned a date of c. A.D. 300, and may belong to a general refurbishment of the defences at the time.[50] A section at the west end of Hunter Street was similar.[51] The lower fill of clean sand and clay silt had been cleaned out to a rather shallower profile, and rubble had accumulated in the bottom. In both sections subsequent fills obliterated the ditch. One section on the eastern defences has also produced evidence of successive recutting.[52] It resembled the western ditch in showing silty fills at the bottom, cut by a shallower ditch which in turn silted up before being cut by a ditch with a rounded profile containing a fill of rubble and sand.

The ditch has not been revealed north of the fortress, where the berm may be wider than normal,[53] although recent observations suggest that the ditch was in its usual position.

Immediately outside the western ditch, there was a road of sandstone rubble with traces of gravel surfacing, and a stone-lined drain at or near its western edge. Initially the road was some 6 m. wide, but resurfacing extended it almost to the outer lip of the ditch. There appeared to have been a fence between road and ditch in the first period.[54]

The Interior of the Fortress

The foundation date of the fortress is not precisely known. The site has produced pre-Flavian samian,[55] but the quantity is no greater than would be expected from a Flavian site. All the evidence points to a date in Vespasian's reign, either during

[46] *Ches. Arch. Bull.* ix. 49–50.
[47] *R.I.B.* i, no. 474.
[48] *J.C.A.S.* lxv. 34.
[49] Ibid. lvi, fig. 3.
[50] The ditch fill produced black-burnished pottery dating from the Antonine period to the 3rd cent.
[51] Unpublished. There were no finds.

[52] *J.R.S.* lvii. 179–80.
[53] Thompson, *Roman Ches.* 29; *J.C.A.S.* xl. 21.
[54] *J.R.S.* xxxvi. 138; *J.C.A.S.* lvi. 5–6 and fig. 3.
[55] *Britannia*, iii. 11; *J.C.A.S.* lxii. 49 and fig. 3. South Gaulish samian from the site resembles that from Agricolan forts in Scotland. See also *Roman Pottery Research in Brit. and NW. Europe* (Brit. Arch. Rep. Internat. Ser. cxxiii), 243.

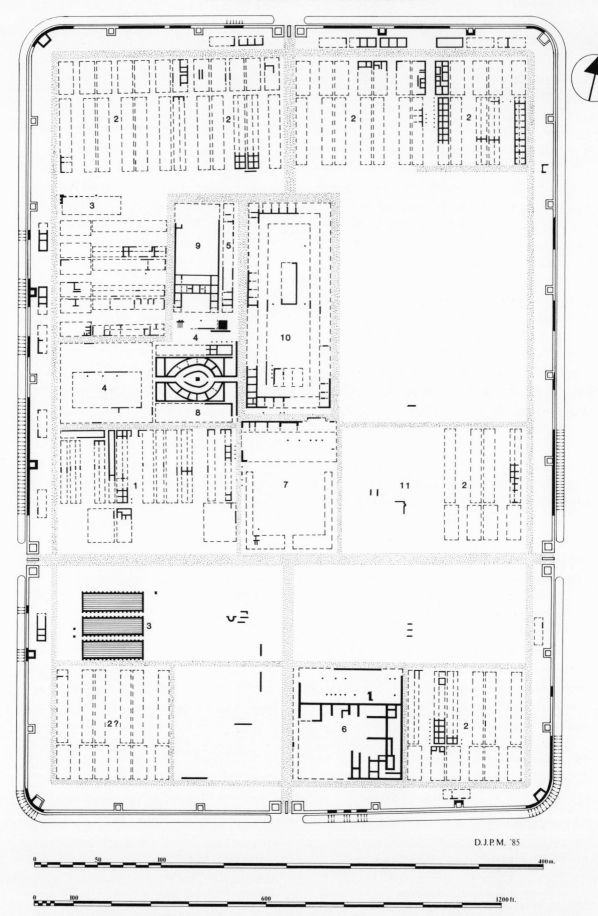

D.J.P.M. '85

FIG. 25. Chester: Legionary Fortress in the Early 3rd Century: 1. Barracks of the First Cohort; 2. Barracks of the other cohorts; 3. Granaries (*horrea*); 4. Workshops (*fabricae*); 5. Stores building; 6. Main bath-house (*thermae*); 7. Headquarters building (*principia*); 8. Minor bath-house (*balneum*); 9. Building with walled compound; 10. Possible hospital, formerly supposed *praetorium*; 11. Possible *praetorium*.

the governorship of Frontinus or early in that of his successor, Agricola.[56] The inscription from Bridge Street is evidence for the completion of a major stone building in the first half of A.D. 79; the Agricolan lead water pipes similarly record work on the water supply, possibly one of the last construction tasks. Work cannot have begun later than A.D. 78 in view of the inclusion of more than one large stone building in the Flavian plan; when the smaller fortress at Inchtuthil was abandoned after about three years of construction it still lacked major internal buildings.[57] In the circumstances a date A.D. 76–8 seems reasonable.

Whether there was Roman occupation of the site before the establishment of the Flavian fortress is uncertain.[58] Evidence of military occupation resulting from the campaigns of Scapula or Paullinus is not strong. Apart from historical and strategic considerations, the case[59] rests almost completely on the reported discovery of cremation burials within the area covered by the Flavian fortress. Because burials were not permitted within the defences of a military or a civil site, the cemetery from which they came lay outside the fort or fortress to which it belonged, which therefore pre-dated that founded by Frontinus or Agricola. The only evidence of the date of the cemetery stems from the two-handled jar known as Stevens's Urn, which is claimed to be Claudio–Neronian in date,[60] although that dating has been questioned.[61] It was found in a yard behind a house on the east side of Northgate Street between Abbey Square and Abbey Green and is said to have contained burnt bones, but no cremated bone is now associated with it. Indeed, a contemporary letter about the discovery says nothing about a cremation burial, although it refers to 'some portions of annular brass money, much corroded'.[62] A few years afterwards two urns filled with burnt bones were discovered close by in the Deanery Field.[63] There have been no finds of cremation burials since the mid 19th century, and extensive excavations in the area have not revealed the supposed cemetery, so that the evidence for its existence is not strong.

The case for a pre-fortress military site would be strengthened if features associated with one were to be consistently identified underlying the fortress: such features would not accord in layout with the buildings of the fortress. The only site to have produced such evidence is Abbey Green, where a rampart of box construction may have been found immediately behind the Flavian rampart, and on a slightly different alignment to it; the orientation of a timber building to the south was completely different.[64] The box-rampart, distinguished from the later turf rampart by having post-pits at front and rear for the revetments, has never been identified in previous excavations of the defences: nevertheless the relatively narrow trenches excavated across the defences in the past may have failed to reveal such a feature. Whether the box-construction rampart shared the same line as the turf rampart is unknown; where a site was reoccupied in this fashion the forts need not be on precisely the same site. In material finds little of unquestionably pre-Flavian date has been discovered. While the site may have been occupied before the fortress was built, such occupation was not necessarily pre-Flavian. If the fortress itself was not

[56] *J.C.A.S.* xxxviii. 18; lx. 38; *Culture and Environment*, 256; Nash-Williams, *Roman Frontier in Wales*, 35; Thompson, *Roman Ches.* 9.

[57] Pitts and St. Joseph, *Inchtuthil*, 54. Legio II Adiutrix was still at Lincoln in A.D. 76: *R.I.B.* i, no. 258.

[58] Perhaps an auxiliary fort; a vexillation fortress of c. 25–30 a. is not out of the question: below.

[59] Argued e.g. in Frere, *Britannia*, 104.

[60] *J.C.A.S.* xxxviii. 18 and fig. 14 (2).

[61] Ibid. lx. 38. Similar pottery has come from early occupation levels in the fortress.

[62] Ibid. [1st ser.], iii. 28, 260–1; *T.H.S.L.C.* i. 83; Lawson, 'Schedule', no. VI. The urn was covered with a stone slab: Watkin, *Roman Ches.* 88, 214.

[63] Watkin, *Roman Ches.* 214. The discoveries were apparently not noted by any other writer; the urns have not survived.

[64] *J.C.A.S.* lxiii. 15–17 and fig. 2.

founded until Frontinus's governorship, an earlier military site may have been established by Cerialis to support his campaigns in the north from A.D. 71 onwards.[65]

Until 1948 it was generally supposed that the fortress had always been entirely of stone construction, but by excavation it was first shown that even major buildings like the *principia* might be built initially of timber, a discovery which led to a belief that all 1st-century buildings in the fortress were of timber. The main phases of building activity in the fortress thereafter were thought to have been first, its rebuilding in stone soon after the beginning of the 2nd century;[66] second, after further building in the Antonine period, major reconstruction under Severus or a little later; and third, continued occupation until the late Roman period, although the absence of *Deva* from the British section of the *Notitia Dignitatum* implied that the fortress had been abandoned before the end of the 4th century.[67] That chronology can now be modified. Of the major buildings known to have been of timber initially the *principia* is the most significant, while the earliest barracks with their accompanying centurions' houses were also consistently built of timber. Nevertheless many of the fortress buildings have failed to reveal precursors in timber, or do not cover timber buildings of any sort: examples include the internal bath building, for which a Vespasianic date is likely, the '*praetorium*', the stone granaries, and the 'elliptical building'. Clearly the distinction once made between the timber fortress of the 1st century and the stone fortress of the 2nd and successive centuries has become meaningless.

Substantial building in stone began early in the 2nd century, encompassing the *principia*, '*praetorium*', granaries, a workshop or smithy west of the '*praetorium*', and one of the tribunes' houses, as well as barracks at Abbey Green, Folliott House, Goss Street, Princess Street, and Crook Street. Rampart buildings also seem to belong to that period, sometimes covering earlier timber structures. Completion of a major building in the early 2nd century is indicated by the Hop Pole Paddock inscription,[68] but it is not known how long the extensive rebuilding took. Some barracks may not indeed have been rebuilt in stone before the legion turned its energies to construction and fighting on the northern frontiers under Hadrian and Antoninus Pius: the barrack excavated at the Northgate Brewery, for example, was partially rebuilt in timber and lasted in that form until *c.* A.D. 120, when it was abandoned until rebuilt in stone *c.* A.D. 160. An Antonine phase of repair or alteration was recognized at Goss Street, and probably also at Trinity Street and Folliott House, as well as in one of the rampart buildings at Abbey Green; it may have been made necessary by the return of part of the legion from the north.[69]

The Severan period saw much building activity,[70] which appears to have affected the *principia*, '*praetorium*', and barracks. The 'elliptical building' seems to have been completed, and a vacant site in the *retentura* was provided with a large courtyard building. Modification of the internal plan noted in several barracks probably reflects changes in conditions of service. Whether the colonnaded buildings lying

[65] *J.C.A.S.* xxxv. 50, xxxviii. 18. Legio II Adiutrix may have provided the garrison for a Cerialian vexillation fortress: *Roman Pottery Research*, 243.

[66] Nash-Williams, *Roman Frontier in Wales*, 37.

[67] Resulting from either the *barbarica conspiratio* of A.D. 367-8 or the legion's withdrawal by Magnus Maximus in A.D. 383: Thompson, *Roman Ches.* 13; Frere, *Britannia*, 267. The *Notitia* omits other fortresses in the NW.

[68] *R.I.B.* i, no. 464; above.

[69] Legionary vexillations were detached for considerable periods, like that of two cohorts of Legio xx known to have been stationed at Newstead in the Antonine period: R.C.A.M. (Scot.), *Roxburgh*, 314-15; *Proc. Soc. Antiq. Scot.* lxxxiv. 21.

[70] Building work was in progress A.D. 194-6: *R.I.B.* i, no. 465.

west of Bridge Street were built at the same time is uncertain, but the southernmost was apparently Severan or later.

Only one timber structure can be assigned to the Severan period,[71] and apparently by the early 3rd century the fortress was wholly of stone and complete in all material respects. Maintenance of buildings by Legio xx continued into the mid 3rd century, as is proved by the occurrence of stamped legionary tiles which can be dated A.D. 249-51,[72] and by the Shoemakers' Row inscription[73] which is apparently of the same date.

Evidence has accumulated of the demolition or dismantling of fortress buildings, and in particular barracks, well before the end of the Roman period.[74] At Abbey Green centurions' houses were demolished at the end of the 3rd century, while the barrack on the site of the Northgate Brewery may have been dismantled slightly earlier. Evidence of demolition has also come from the barracks in Goss Street and Crook Street, while the granaries and a water tank are thought to have been demolished at about the same time. Systematic removal of the buildings most closely associated with the garrison's accommodation and supply indicates either reduction or complete withdrawal of the garrison. Evacuation of *Isca* by Legio ii Augusta is thought to have taken place early in Carausius's usurpation,[75] and while it does not necessarily follow that Chester ceased to be a legionary base at precisely the same date, events at the two fortresses may have been linked. The latest inscriptions naming Legio xx are no later than the mid 3rd century. The stamped tiles and inscription referred to above attest the presence of the Twentieth at Chester until A.D. 249-51. The legion is also named on an altar from Milecastle 52 on Hadrian's Wall[76] which is datable to A.D. 262-6, while the inclusion of the Twentieth in the legionary coinage of Carausius[77] indicates that it was still in existence then, and probably still in Britain, though not necessarily at Chester. It was either disbanded after the recovery of Britain by Constantius Chlorus in A.D. 296, withdrawn from the province, or destroyed during the usurpation of Carausius and Allectus.

There is a significant difference between the fortresses at Caerleon and Chester. At the former demolition included such buildings as the *principia*, *praetorium*, and *thermae*, as well as barracks; by contrast the major buildings at Chester appear to have been spared, and continued to be used well into the 4th century.[78] The sites of a number of demolished buildings were afterwards paved, and in several instances further occupation followed,[79] associated with timber buildings which in one instance echoed the plan of the underlying stone building. Withdrawal of Legio xx did not deprive Chester of its strategic significance, and it may have had a role to play in the defence of the western coast, though the evidence is not strong.[80] Occupation and use of some major fortress buildings continued well into, and possibly throughout, the 4th century, perhaps serving as the public buildings of a town.[81]

The essentials of the internal plan show clearly in the street plan of Chester. Of the principal streets which meet at the Cross, Bridge Street represents the *via*

---

[71] Unidentified: *J.C.A.S.* lxv. 11–12. Late Roman timber buildings have been identified on several sites: *New Evidence*, 42–3. Some 'timber' buildings may have had stone sill walls.

[72] The inscription on the tiles ends in DE, formerly expanded *De[vensis]* but more convincingly restored as *De[ciana]*, a title bestowed by the emperor Decius (249–51): *J.R.S.* xlv. 146; *Y Cymmrodor*, xli. 140–1.

[73] *R.I.B.* i, no. 449.

[74] *Liverpool Annals*, xxiii. 5–6.

[75] Boon, *Isca*, 65.

[76] *R.I.B.* i, no. 1956; *Arch. Camb.* cxvii. 88.

[77] *Roman Imperial Coinage*, v (2), 470 (nos. 82–3), 488 (no. 275). The third reads LEG XX AUG.

[78] Present evidence from the *principia* is inconclusive.

[79] *New Evidence*, 41.

[80] A. Dornier, 'Coastal *Limes* of W. Brit.' *Roman Frontier Studies 1967*, 18; Frere, *Britannia*, 380.

[81] There is a fair scatter of 4th-cent. coins from the fortress.

praetoria[82] and Eastgate Street and Watergate Street the *via principalis*, while Northgate Street is for part of its length on the line of the *via decumana*. Some of the minor Roman streets can also be restored, particularly the rampart or 'intervallum' road represented by White Friars, Weaver Street, and Trinity Street; Commonhall Street possibly preserves the line of a minor street,[83] and other instances may be found.

The internal layout of the fortress and its size have been analysed comparatively.[84] While the plan at Chester is not yet complete enough to permit grouping of the internal buildings into *insulae*, as at Caerleon,[85] nevertheless with growing knowledge of the legionary fortresses in Britain[86] it has become increasingly clear that Chester is abnormal in both size and shape. The area of the fortress is 24.33 ha. (very nearly 60 a.), compared with Inchtuthil 21.5 ha., Caerleon 20.5 ha., York 20.24 ha., and Colchester *c.* 20.6 ha., which may all be categorized as '50-acre' fortresses. At 15.6 ha. Lincoln is as unusually small as Chester is large.[87]

Whereas Chester closely resembles York and Caerleon in breadth[88] it differs from other fortresses in being longer in relation to its breadth. While the gates on the longer sides of a fortress are always offset to some extent towards one end of the enclosure, the tendency is for *praetentura* and *retentura* to equate more nearly in size in the instances named than at Chester, where the proportion is more nearly one third south of the *via principalis* to two thirds north of it. Since the defensive circuit remained the same throughout the period the factor which dictated a different arrangement at Chester operated from the beginning, and was probably still operating later, since a reduction in size, fairly common in auxiliary forts, never took place. Less is known of the internal plan of the 1st century, when buildings were of timber, than of the 2nd century. Nevertheless it seems that the extra space was not provided to accommodate a greater number of buildings. Possibly Chester was intended at first to be of regular size, but during planning or construction it was decided that extra space was needed, and in effect another *retentura* was added to its plan.[89] Three theories have been put forward to account for the unusually large size of the fortress. First, because tombstones of the men of two legions were found at Chester it was suggested that it might have been a double fortress,[90] but increasing knowledge of the internal layout discounts that theory. The possibility that a naval squadron was based at Chester has also been suggested, but it is doubtful whether a legion would have shared a fortress with sailors unless the fortress was divided internally.[91] The relatively small area of the fortress at Lincoln is attributed to absence of part of the garrison elsewhere;[92] it has therefore been proposed that the reverse might apply at Chester, and that an auxiliary unit, presumably a cavalry *ala*, was present. One tombstone from the north wall is generally accepted as representing a Sarmatian;[93] another similarly represents a trooper wearing mailed tunic and breeches, and his mount appears to wear armour also.[94] Nothing of the text on the former stone, and very little on the latter, survives. Of the six other tombstones from Chester which belong to *equites* but do not state the

[82] For the relationship of Roman and present building lines in Bridge Street see *J.C.A.S.* xlv. 26.

[83] Below.

[84] *J.C.A.S.* lx. 35–7.

[85] G. C. Boon and C. Williams, *Plan of Caerleon*; plan of fortress in Boon, *Isca*.

[86] e.g. Lincoln, Gloucester, and Colchester.

[87] Cf. Nash-Williams, *Roman Frontier in Wales*, 150.

[88] Chester 413 m., Caerleon 416 m., York 400 m., Inchtuthil 460 m.

[89] *J.C.A.S.* lx. 36.

[90] F. Haverfield, 'Origins of *Deva*', ibid. v. 99–103; ibid. 354.

[91] One inscription from Chester may refer to a sailor: *R.I.B.* i, no. 544; C. G. Starr, *Roman Imperial Navy 31 B.C.–A.D. 324*, 165, n. 105. That L. Annius Marcellus (*R.I.B.* i, no. 487) may have initially been a sailor can no longer be accepted: *Britannia*, xiv. 252.

[92] *Arch. Jnl.* cxvii. 48 and n. 3.

[93] *R.I.S.S.* no. 137.

[94] *R.I.B.* i, no. 550; *R.I.S.S.* no. 98.

name of their unit or have lost the relevant part of the inscription, one looks like an auxiliary trooper's. Its inscription refers to a *turma*, a word usually translated as 'troop', the subdivision of a cavalry *ala*.[95] Conversely three of the ambiguous stones are almost certainly legionary.[96] The remaining stones are so fragmentary that the evidence is inconclusive.[97]

What is known of the fortress within the defences is here described from the centre outwards, moving from the greater buildings to the lesser, and ending with the buildings and features found immediately within the defences.

THE PRINCIPIA was the repository for the eagle and other standards (*signa*), the pay-chest, and the legionary archives, as well as the centre for much of the day-to-day administration of the unit; the central location of the building reflects its function. Excavations in Goss Street and on the site of the Old Market Hall can be taken with earlier discovery of part of the cross-hall (*basilica principiorum*) to give a fair impression of the building.[98]

In Goss Street the west façade of the stone *principia* was found to consist of a succession of large columns, of which the plinths and bases alone survived, with at the north end of the excavation the south-west corner of the *basilica principiorum*, alongside which was postulated a subsidiary entrance to the courtyard with an internal colonnade to match the external one. Beneath the flooring of the external colonnade was a north–south timber slot interpreted as the west wall of an earlier timber *principia* of similar size. Later excavation in the same area[99] revealed a short stretch of the west wall of the stone *principia* with three construction phases. A line of substantial post-pits more than a metre square and containing posts at 3-m. intervals formed the western colonnade of the Flavian *principia* west of the later one of stone.[1] At no. 23 Northgate Street (Shoemakers' Row) five large column-bases still in position, with spaces for two others, belong to the north colonnade of the aisled hall at the northern end of the *principia*. One capital of the Corinthian order was found, and the top end of a fallen shaft from the south colonnade projected into the cellar. A line of five rectangular pits, also running east–west south of the stone bases and, being similar in size and spacing, formerly thought to be abortive foundation holes for a colonnade which was not erected, were the post-pits for the north arcade of the timber *principia*.[2] The stone colonnade covered the remains of the north wall of the timber basilica, of which the north aisle was a little over 4 m. wide. The west wall of the basilica contained a worn coin of A.D. 77-8, suggesting construction in the late 1st century or early 2nd. The south front of the *principia* was impressive, as its base stood a metre or more above the level of the adjacent *via principalis*.[3] It was described as a building of 'massive proportions . . . of some stateliness', and it is therefore surprising that part of the west wall of the Trajanic basilica above the lowest courses was rebuilt in the Severan period, not only as a slighter wall but also poorer in quality.

On the site of the Market Hall work at the north end of the *principia*[4] showed the post-pits of an external colonnade on the north side of the timber building at

95 *R.I.B.* i, no. 557. *R.I.S.S.* no. 93.
96 *R.I.B.* i, nos. 522, 538, 541.
97 Ibid. no. 551; *R.I.S.S.* no. 136.
98 *J.C.A.S.* vi. 139, 277–81; *Proc. Soc. Antiq.* (2nd ser.) xviii. 91–3; Lawson, 'Schedule', no. xvi; I. A. Richmond and G. Webster, 'Excavations in Goss Street, Chester, 1948–9', *J.C.A.S.* xxxviii. 1–38; *New Evidence*, 9–10 (Goss Street); D. F. Petch, 'Excavations on Site of Old Market Hall, Chester, 2nd Summary Rep. 1968–70', *J.C.A.S.* lvii. 3–26.
99 *Britannia*, vi. 240; *Ches. Arch. Bull.* ii. 15–16; *New*

Evidence, passim.
1 *New Evidence*, figs. on pp. 10, 26.
2 The stone columns are based on the living rock without any substructure, and timber features can still be identified: *J.C.A.S.* xxxviii, plate 7 (2). The usual form of construction places the column on a plinth which in turn is based on a substantial concrete foundation.
3 *J.C.A.S.* xxxviii. 14.
4 Ibid. lvii. 11–20; *New Evidence*, 17, 18 (plan).

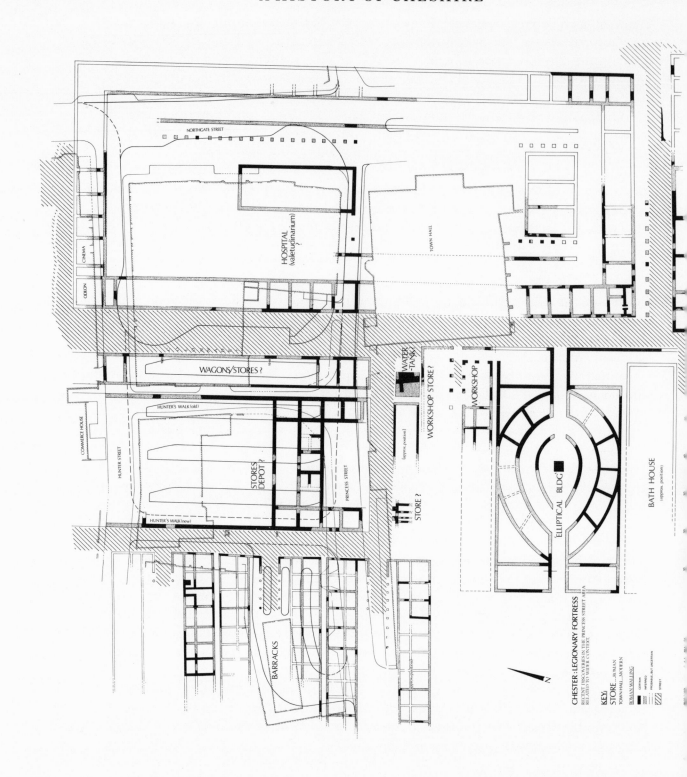

CHESTER : LEGIONARY FORTRESS

RECENT DISCOVERIES IN THE PRINCESS STREET AREA
RELATED TO WIDER CONTEXT

KEY:
STORE .... ROMAN
TOWN HALL ...MODERN

ROMAN WALLING
CERTAIN
INFERRED
PROBABLE, BUT UNCERTAIN
STREET

least 2 m. wide, containing 20–25-cm. posts. No floor levels of that period survived. The timber *principia* was at least 73 m. long[5] and at most as long as the stone *principia*, probably *c.* 100 m. The timber colonnade lay under the range of rooms on the north side of the cross-hall or basilica of the stone *principia*. The easternmost room exposed was the *sacellum* or *aedes*, the shrine in which the standards of the legion were kept, recognizable not only from its position on the main axis of the building but also in having a rock-cut strongroom below its floor. The room was *c.* 12 m. wide, while the two rooms west of it were virtually identical in width at nearly 9 m. The remaining two rooms in the range were 3.7 m. and almost 5 m. wide. Given the known position of the north arcade of the basilica, and of its south-west corner, it is possible to estimate the size of that part of the building as 73 m. long by *c.* 24 m. wide, the nave and aisles measuring *c.* 12 m. and *c.* 6 m. respectively. The north range of rooms was consistently *c.* 9 m. across from north to south. Little useful dating material was recovered from the excavation; flooring no earlier than the 3rd century was noted. Recent work in Watergate Street has revealed walls belonging to the range on the south side of the forecourt.[6]

An inscribed stone found lying near the bases of the columns of the basilica[7] is a moulded fragment from the jamb of a door or niche, only the left margin being intact. The dedication *Genio legionis XX VV* is followed by a title whose first letter is D, presumably to be expanded *Deciana*, and the inscription therefore attests to continuing use of the *principia* by Legio XX when that title was current in the mid 3rd century. From the same excavations came a fragment of a millstone with an inscription translated as 'The century of Naevius . . .'.[8]

THE SUPPOSED PRAETORIUM. North of the *principia* lay a street 6 m. wide, with eaves-drip gutters on both sides. On the north side was a building with a colonnade along the south front, and, it is inferred, a central entrance.[9] On the south and west sides lay ranges of rooms of regular size, typically on the west side 8.5 m. by 5.2 m. At the south-west corner there was a smaller heated room with unheated ante-chamber and stokehole adjoining. Wide doorways (*c.* 3 m.) for most of the rooms facing the courtyard suggest use for storage, but subsequent narrowing and even blocking of the wide openings made other uses possible. Within the area enclosed by the south and west ranges were other traces of buildings, the most clearly defined being a colonnade running north–south some 6 m. east of the inner wall of the west range. Immediately east of that lay a wall with a return to the east. The building was of stone and had no timber precursor, but it covered and partly re-used the foundations of an uncompleted building, apparently Flavian, the completed building being of the late Trajanic or early Hadrianic period. Subsequent use continued well into the 4th century, with various alterations and repairs, including the paving of the courtyard, probably early in the 4th century. From that context came an altar dedicated to Aesculapius, Hygeia, and Panacea by a physician, Antiochus.[10] An altar found on the site of the Saracen's Head inn was dedicated to 'the mighty saviour gods' by another physician, Hermogenes.[11] Only *c.* 20 m. separate the find spots of the altars.[12] The text is in Greek on both, and their dedicators

[5] An estimate based on the doubtful premise that the inscribed lead pipes found in 1899–1900 mark the north side of the Flavian *via principalis*; the siting of timber barracks west of the *principia* does not bear it out.

[6] Inf. from Mr. T. J. Strickland.

[7] *J.C.A.S.* vi. 139–40; *J.R.S.* xlv. 146; *R.I.B.* i, no. 449.

[8] *J.C.A.S.* vii. 89, no. 204.

[9] D. F. Petch, 'The Praetorium at Deva', ibid. lv. 1–5; ibid. lvii. 11–12, 16–20, and fig. 5; *New Evidence*, 18–20.

[10] V. Nutton, 'A Greek Doctor at Chester', *J.C.A.S.* lv. 7–13; *J.R.S.* lix. 235, no. 3 and plate 18 (2); R. W. Davies, *Epigraphische Studien*, ix. 1–11.

[11] *R.I.B.* i, no. 461; Watkin, *Roman Ches.* 179–80; *J.C.A.S.* [1st ser.], i. 359–61, where the find is reported as made during excavation of a deep sewer behind the Exchange.

[12] *J.C.A.S.* lvii, fig. 5.

bear Greek names. Their connexion with the army is uncertain,[13] but the legion's doctor may have been quartered in the *praetorium*: the legate's health was an important charge on him, and the *praetorium* and *valetudinarium* were often close together. Hospitals whose complete plans are known had no accommodation for the medical staff, who were therefore quartered elsewhere in the fortress. Both altars are presumed to have been removed from their original contexts. Under and north of Princess Street the west side of a range of at least six rooms with partition walls consistently *c.* 5 m. apart[14] may be a continuation of the west range of the same building, for the similarities are striking. The northern extent of the building, revealed in Hunter Street, appears to be marked by a further range of rooms aligned east–west, varying in width between *c.* 2 m. and *c.* 6.5 m.; three rooms were approximately as wide as those to the south. On that site the earliest building was possibly of timber; the first stone building, which had footings of cobbles in clay, may not have been completed. After the mid 2nd century the building was either completed or rebuilt, new foundations of sandstone rubble capped with puddled clay being laid then. Early in the 3rd century there was a systematic rebuilding in the same form: both that and the previous building are thought to have had a timber-framed superstructure. Alterations early in the 4th century included provision of new roofs and floors, and occupation continued thereafter well into the century.[15] If the structures found in Princess Street and Hunter Street belong to the building excavated on the site of the Market Hall its length from north to south is close to 150 m.,[16] too large to be the *praetorium*. An alternative identification is the hospital, since the length of such buildings ranges up to 125 m., but the plan is not particularly close to that found elsewhere of a double range of wards with corridor between, and the wide openings referred to above do not fit well into the plan of a hospital. The discovery of altars with medical associations has been taken as reinforcing the identification as a *valetudinarium*, but in fact one, and probably both, were found out of context. Alternatively a parallel with a great store-building at Corbridge has been suggested.[17]

Earlier finds have been recorded from the area. Stukeley recorded 'a hypocaust of the Romans, made of bricks all marked with the twentieth legion', and commented on 'many fragments, seemingly of pillars and capitals . . . particularly in Parson's Lane'.[18] The hypocaust was apparently at Cholmondeley House at the corner of Parson's Lane, later occupied by a carriage manufactory.[19] It was apparently believed that the architectural fragments found in the north wall of the city derived from excavation of the foundations of Cholmondeley House in 1700, and were used during the wall repairs of 1701–8, but there is no supporting evidence.[20] References by early writers to a tile kiln at or near the spot all evidently issue from discovery of a hypocaust, as described by Stukeley. A fragment of an inscription on a moulding from the top of an altar or an architectural feature reading NVMINI]B.AVGG.ET.[DEO . . . was possibly found on the west side of Northgate Street between the old Shambles and the Northgate.[21]

THE 'ELLIPTICAL BUILDING'. Immediately west of the building just described

---

[13] It has been suggested that both were servile, since they give only *cognomina*: *Britannia*, xiv. 7, n. 36.

[14] Ibid. xii. 332–3; xiv. 297; *Roman West in 3rd Cent.* 425–6.

[15] T. J. Strickland, 'Chester: Excavations in Princess Street/Hunter Street Area, 1978–82: First Rep. on Discoveries of Roman Period', *J.C.A.S.* lxv. 16–22; inf. from Mr. Strickland.

[16] Probably *c.* 157 m. long and *c.* 65 m. wide: *Ches. Arch.*

Bull. ix. 54.

[17] For problems of identifying the larger buildings within fortresses, cf. Boon, *Isca, passim*.

[18] W. Stukeley, *Iter Boreale*, 33. Parson's Lane is now Princess Street.

[19] Lawson, 'Schedule', no. x.

[20] Watkin, *Roman Ches.* 129.

[21] *R.I.B.* i, no. 459. Watkin, *Roman Ches.* 190; *Arch. Jnl.* xxxvi. 163–4.

lies another of the principal buildings of the fortress, excavated in 1939.[22] Initial construction was dated to the end of the 1st century, and it has been suggested that traces of earlier occupation belonged to timber buildings.[23] Substantial paving 15–23 cm. thick was assigned an early 3rd-century date, as a coin of Elagabalus was securely sealed by the flagging: a similar context produced a coin of Tetricus.[24] Later finds and features were thought to be associated with an unrelated building post-dating the first. Two tiles bearing the *Deciana* title were found over the flagged floor, and there were hints of the walls of 'a late building'. Of forty identifiable coins, thirteen were of the period of Constantine I or later.

Further excavations (1963–9) have shown that the building was *c.* 67 m. long and 34 m. wide.[25] At its centre was an elliptical courtyard, around which was a colonnade. Behind that lay two concentric elliptical walls marking the inner and outer walls of rooms presumably entered from the colonnade; they were delimited by radial party walls.[26] There were two openings on the long axis by which the courtyard was entered from outside. The southern axial room was entered by a monumental archway and an opening in a screen which ran across its width. The outer elliptical wall was contained within a rectangular perimeter wall, and at the east and west ends were further ranges of rooms, each range fronted by a colonnade. Initial assessment of the evidence suggested a period of dereliction between the laying of the foundations and the completion of the building, probably in the 3rd century. The completed building did not quite match the original layout, and was marked by inferior workmanship. The period between initial work and completion was sufficient for a layer of humus to accumulate, and clearly the foundation trenches of the completed building had been cut from above that layer.[27] Thereafter occupation continued well into the 4th century.[28] In the centre of the courtyard a concrete foundation marked the position of a monument,[29] close to which was a length of inscribed lead water pipe almost identical with those from Eastgate Street.[30] Immediately south of the 'elliptical building' lay a bath building.

The building was clearly part of the original plan of the fortress, although its construction probably began only after more essential work on the defences and accommodation had been completed. The Agricolan water pipe proves that work was in progress in A.D. 79: the pits and trenches for the foundations of columns had been dug, and the foundations largely completed, when work was discontinued soon afterwards. Thereafter the site remained open and unused until building began again at the end of the 2nd century or the beginning of the 3rd. Occupation of the elliptical part of the building extended at least to the early 4th century, while the east range of rooms was rebuilt under Theodosius and joined to the bath building to the south. A further phase of construction takes the history of the building down to the end of the 4th century or later. The unusual plan presents problems of identification, for convincing parallels do not seem to exist. It is difficult to believe that such a distinctive and, from a constructional viewpoint, difficult plan was

[22] R. Newstead and J. P. Droop, 'Excavations at Chester, 1939: Princess Street Clearance Area', *J.C.A.S.* xxxiv. 5–45.

[23] R. Newstead, *Roman Occupation of Chester (Deva)*, 13.

[24] The date may therefore be later 3rd cent., but see *J.C.A.S.* xxxiv. 14 and pl. 5.

[25] *J.R.S.* liv. 156, lviii. 183; Nash-Williams, *Roman Frontier in Wales*, 39; *Arch. News Letter*, vii. 12. The director of the excavation, Mr. J. V. H. Eames, circulated a summary of conclusions in Sept. 1969.

[26] Fig. 26.

[27] The humus layer was so deep that no trace could have

been seen of the original layout. The building was therefore completed from an architect's draft, a point confirmed by variation of the ellipses of the two phases.

[28] Theodosian coins were sealed by reflooring: inf. from Mr. Eames.

[29] A large rectangular hole cut into the rock may have been some form of *mundus*, and the concrete foundation which formed the greater part of its fill supported an object of altar size: inf. from Mr. Eames.

[30] *Britannia*, ii. 292–3, no. 17.

adopted for such mundane purposes as stores, workshops, or stables. For that reason various unusual proposals have been put forward, such as a theatre,[31] the palace of a deposed and exiled queen, Cartimandua, the *praesidium* of the *praeses Britanniae Secundae*, and the headquarters of the *Dux Britanniarum*.[32] Whatever function required such a building in the early Flavian period must have existed in the early 3rd century: perhaps a need foreseen under Agricola re-emerged under Severus, for virtually the same plan was adopted in both periods.[33]

In the western half of the central *insulae* of the fortress, north of the 'elliptical building' and west of the '*praetorium*', lay smaller buildings. Initially a timber barrack lay immediately north of the 'elliptical building', the two being only 1 m. apart. A second timber building *c.* 12 m. wide further north cannot have been a barrack, but is unidentified. From the 2nd century a stone building 8 m. wide and at least 30 m. long replaced the barrack. At its east end a smithy occupied its full width: it had a centrally placed and much used hearth, and its east and north walls were arcaded. Further west the building was divided into smaller rooms. The date assigned to it was the early 2nd century, and its use continued into the 3rd. Alterations to it included provision of a portico on the east front which narrowed the street on that side from 11 m. to 8 m.; the arcading in the eastern room was blocked up, and an *opus signinum* floor provided. At the northern end a stone base nearly 6.5 m. across and at least 5 m. east–west was identified as the base for a water tank on the analogy of those at Corbridge (Northumb.), built by Legio XX, and at Lincoln.[34] It was demolished, perhaps in the late 3rd century, and a lead water pipe was laid through the demolition fill.

A pitched foundation between the water tank and the smithy and workshop, also cut through by the water pipe, may have supported the north wall of a simple building whose south side was represented by a succession of bases; its floor was nothing more than rubble. An alternative interpretation is that the bases, which were clearly renewed at least once, represent a veranda on the north side of the workshop.[35] If so the pitched foundation may have been no more than a wall bounding an area of hard standing. Exploration of the ground north of the 'elliptical building' in 1939 appeared to reveal a granary, but more recent work casts some doubt on the interpretation.[36] Excavation of the site of the present market located three buildings on an east–west orientation.[37] If a granary existed it was exceptionally small for such a building,[38] and not of the same massive construction as the granaries of the *praetentura*.[39]

THE LEGIONARY WORKSHOP. West of the 'elliptical building' and the group of structures just described lay an area occupied by what is thought, from the abundant deposits of slag and other industrial waste, to be the legionary *fabrica*.[40] The area lay immediately north of a row of barracks, separated from them by a narrow 5-m. alley with a culvert. The plan conjectured from rather slight evidence was of large sheds surrounding a central court. The south range was 12 m. wide, and the court behind it 25.5 m.; the north range, at 23 m., may have had some form of basilican layout. The building as a whole therefore measured *c.* 60 m. from north to south,

[31] Proposed by Newstead and Droop, only to be dismissed: *J.C.A.S.* xxxiv. 13.

[32] P. Salway, *Roman Brit.* 133 n. 3; *Britannia*, xiii. 257–8; xv. 5–6; *Studien zu den Militargrenzen Roms: Vortrage des 10 Internationalen Limeskongresses in der Germania Inferior*, 41–3; *Roman West in 3rd Cent.* 416–17.

[33] Thanks are due to Mr. Eames for inf. and discussions in advance of publication.

[34] *Arch. Aeliana*, 3rd ser. iv. 272–81; *J.R.S.* xlvi. 32–6. A recent find may confirm this: inf. from Mr. Strickland.

[35] Plan in *New Evidence*, 21; *J.C.A.S.* lvii. 7–11.

[36] *J.C.A.S.* xxxiv. 6–8.

[37] From S. to N. 8 m., 6.25 m., and 7 m. wide.

[38] *c.* 25 m. by 27 m. The wall thought to be buttressed agreed in position with the N. wall of the northernmost building found a little to the E. in 1965; probably the excavators were mistaken.

[39] Below.

[40] *J.R.S.* lv. 204.

and its width was *c.* 70 m. Its dimensions can be compared with the timber *fabrica* at Inchtuthil which was nearly 60 m. square.[41] The west, north, and south ranges at Inchtuthil were all *c.* 14 m. wide.[42] It is likely that the walls found immediately north of the *fabrica* belong to the southernmost barrack of a cohort group arranged *per scamna*.[43]

THE GRANARIES. Three granaries (*horrea*) lay east–west in the *praetentura*, close to the *porta principalis dextra* and to the harbour.[44] The southernmost was 48.5 m. long, and the others were probably similar in length, as their widths (13.7 m. for the outermost granaries, and 13.4 m. for that in the centre) and other details of construction closely coincided. Chester's granaries are exceptionally large; the only other stone-built examples to approach them in size are Benwell (Northumb.) at 45.72 m. long and Newstead at 40 m.[45] Their massive outer walls were 1 m. thick, with buttresses nearly 1 m. square at 2-m. intervals, laid on good foundations of the concrete type found elsewhere in the fortress. Among a thick spread of broken tiles between the granaries were some with the *Deciana* stamp, showing that their roofs were still being maintained in the mid 3rd century. Some tile debris was also found within the granaries, between the sleeper walls, and can have reached that position only after the flooring was removed. That suggests that the granaries were robbed of roof tiles and floor slabs and partly or wholly demolished. It is possible that at least one of the granaries was converted to another use.[46] Evidence of the date of dismantling was provided by two coins of the later 3rd century from the layer of tiles, and three 4th-century coins from disturbed levels above it. From slight evidence the granaries appear to have been built early in the 2nd century, perhaps as late as Hadrian's reign. Since no clear traces of earlier structures of timber were found it is uncertain where the 1st-century granaries were in the fortress. The Flavian layout may have resembled that at Inchtuthil,[47] in which granaries were dispersed among the barracks to reduce the risk of loss by fire. The timber granaries at Inchtuthil were not much smaller than the stone ones at Chester, measuring 41.5 m. long and 12.8 m. wide. Six were found there, suggesting that there may be more at Chester; indeed, at the west end of Hunter Street part of the west end of a possible granary orientated east–west has been found.[48] Unlike the granaries in the *praetentura*, which were set back from the intervallum road, the presumed granary had its loading bay immediately alongside the rampart road.

THE LEGIONARY BATHS. The internal bath-building (*thermae*) lay on the east side of the *via praetoria*, just within the south gate. The earliest discovery was in 1746 when a hypocaust was seen on the south side of Feathers Stairs,[49] but the building was not identified with certainty until 1964, when much of it was destroyed during building work.[50] In the mid 19th century the remains of a large basilica were revealed,[51] and on the south side of it heated rooms with fragmentary pavements.[52] A fragment of an inscription in Purbeck marble, found roughly half way along the

---

[41] Ibid. li. 160, fig. 10.

[42] The *fabrica* occupies a similar place in Chester and Inchtuthil: Pitts and St. Joseph, *Inchtuthil*, 107.

[43] *J.C.A.S.* lxv. 9 n. 4; ibid., plan facing p. 24. Thanks are due to Mr. Strickland for discussing his findings.

[44] D. F. Petch and F. H. Thompson, 'Excavations in Commonhall Street, Chester, 1954–6: Granaries of Legionary Fortress of *Deva*', *J.C.A.S.* xlvi. 33–60.

[45] A. P. Gentry, *Roman Military Stone-built Granaries in Brit.* (Brit. Arch. Rep. xxxii), 59, 85.

[46] D. A. Welsby, *Roman Military Defence of Brit. Provinces in its Latest Phases* (Brit. Arch. Rep. ci), 25.

[47] *J.R.S.* li. 158, fig. 9.

[48] *Britannia*, xiv. 297; *Ches. Arch. Bull.* ix. 53. The north wall foundation incorporated re-used column bases and capitals.

[49] J. Horsley, *Britannia Romana*, ii. 318; Watkin, *Roman Ches.* 131.

[50] *J.R.S.* lv. 204; *New Evidence*, 22–4 and plan. Brushfield suggested that it was a bath-building in his report of the 1863 discoveries, and Haverfield came to the same conclusion: *J.C.A.S.* xvi. 118.

[51] *J.C.A.S.* [1st ser.], i. 355–6; iii. 1–106. Columns and capitals are preserved in the 'Roman Garden' outside the Newgate.

[52] Ibid. iii. 38–9.

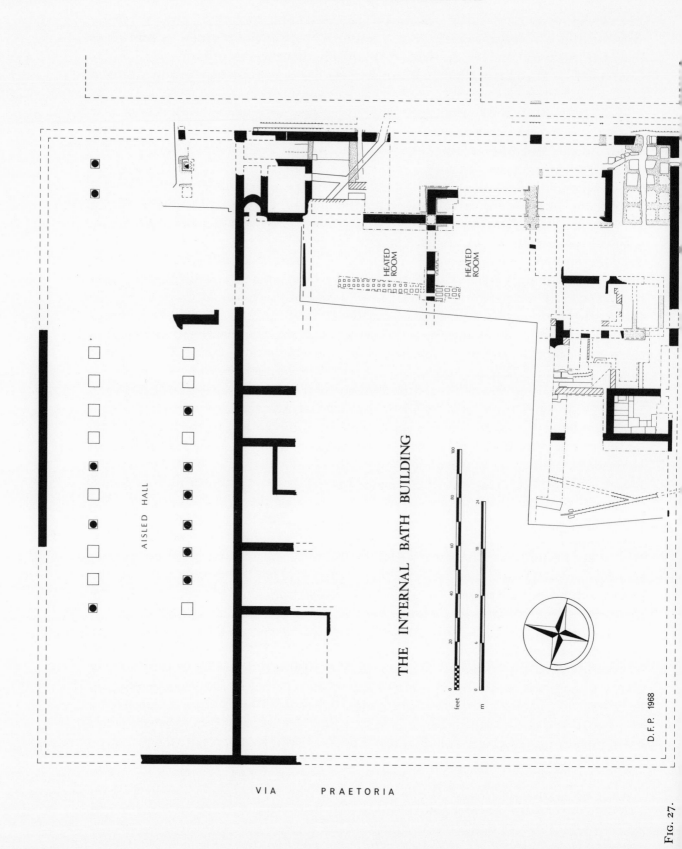

THE INTERNAL BATH BUILDING

AISLED HALL

HEATED ROOM

HEATED ROOM

VIA PRAETORIA

D.F.P. 1968

FIG. 27.

south aisle of the basilica, can be dated to the first half of A.D. 79; it probably derives from the building in which it was found, and dates its initial construction.[53] Further details of the plan were added in St. Michael's Arcade, and finds included the remains of more pavements.[54] The basilica is *c*. 78 m. long, and *c*. 24 m. across, with 20 columns in each colonnade: there may also have been an external colonnade on the west side, facing the *via praetoria*.[55] Discoveries made near Pepper Street[56] hinted at the possible size of the complex, and in 1963–4 more information on the layout was obtained; less than a third of the site was occupied by the basilica, the remainder being taken up with the baths proper. The basilica was in fact a covered *palaestra*, perhaps an early concession to the vagaries of the British climate.[57] The complex measured *c*. 83.5 m. north–south and *c*. 80.5 m. east–west.[58] A lead water main found east of the bath-building presumably supplied the baths.[59]

The bath-building at Caerleon has been found to be in a similar location. The imperial inscription of A.D. 79 probably dates the construction of the building at Chester, and it therefore seems that large and elaborate baths were provided very early in the fortress's history; the Caerleon baths, apparently a little later, are nevertheless comparable.[60] Those at Chester were enlarged and modified over a long period, and hypocausts, floors, drains, and other features repaired and renewed. It was usually possible to identify the Flavian work because of its exceptional quality; an excellent instance of the high standard of work of that period was seen in the north wall of the basilica revealed during excavation of a cellar behind the *Chester Chronicle* office. The wall, 1 m. thick, was laid in a trench cut into solid rock 1.7 m. deep, the lower 52 cm. being the cobble concrete foundation characteristic of the early work. It is difficult to estimate how long use of the building continued: the evidence of the 3rd- and 4th-century coins is far from conclusive.

THE TRIBUNES' HOUSES normally front the *via principalis* and face the *principia*, and finds on the south side of Eastgate Street and Watergate Street may be assigned to them, although very little is known about their plans or arrangement. There were six military tribunes, one of senatorial rank and five equestrians: the house of the former can often be identified by its larger size, as at Inchtuthil. The space available at Chester was adequate for the six houses required for the *tribuni*. The form of each is likely to have been of a courtyard house of simple plan: those at Inchtuthil measured 42 m. by 30 m., and those at Caerleon *c*. 40 m. by 30 m. The largest house at Inchtuthil was *c*. 50 m. by 30 m.

Extension of a cellar behind Quellyn Roberts's in Watergate Street produced what appears to have been part of a baths suite, presumably from the first house west of the *via praetoria*: comparison of size with the space available suggests that, as at Inchtuthil, the *tribunus laticlavius* may have had his house there. Evidently the structure was of more than one period: one 4th-century coin was recovered.[61] Also west of Bridge Street, excavation of a cellar on the south side of Watergate Street produced part of a slate dedication slab,[62] which apparently survived until

[53] *R.I.B.* i, no. 463; *R.I.S.S.* no. 14; Nash-Williams, *Roman Frontier in Wales*, 35. The fragments were seen by chance by Peacock; others may well have been lost unrecorded. See also *Jnl. Brit. Arch. Assoc.* N.S. i. 70; Watkin, *Roman Ches.* 142.

[54] *J.C.A.S.* xvi. 115–16, 118; xxi. 191; xxvii. 114–25, 126–39 (with plan), pl. 18.

[55] Ibid. xxvii. 109–10; Lawson, 'Schedule', no. XLI; *Ches. Arch. Bull.* vii. 37–9; *Britannia*, xii. 331–2.

[56] *J.C.A.S.* xxxvi. 62–4; xliii. 48; li. 80.

[57] Frere, *Britannia*, 277.

[58] *J.R.S.* liv. 156; *Ches. Arch. Bull.* ix. 52.

[59] *J.C.A.S.* v. 32; Lawson, 'Schedule', no. XXXIII. The pipe line probably followed the street at the north end of the barracks.

[60] Boon, *Isca*, 77–82.

[61] *Jnl. Brit. Arch. Assoc.* N.S. i. 69–80; Lawson, 'Schedule', no. XXVI.

[62] Horsley, *Britannia Romana*, 316–18, Cheshire vi; *R.I.B.* i, no. 458.

1771. The dedication is to the divinity of the emperor, perhaps coupled with another dedication unknown; the last line records that some unidentified person had the inscription set up in accordance with a vow. The penultimate line was deliberately erased, and presumably named, perhaps as part of the title of a unit, an emperor whose memory was later condemned. The second and third lines have so far resisted attempts to construe them. The dedication is appropriate to a senior officer of the legion.[63] The lower part of the slab was apparently decorated.[64] A large column base and capital, the former remaining *in situ*, was found behind a building on the east side of Old Hall Place.[65] The base lies 9–12 m. north-east of the northern granary, and relates to no known building. Samian and other pottery, not necessarily Roman, was found at the rear of God's Providence House.[66]

East of Bridge Street finds have been recorded from several sites on the south side of Eastgate Street. An altar found on the site of the first putative Roman building east of the *via praetoria* is dedicated to Minerva by Furius Fortunatus, who describes himself as '*magister*'; the word following has been interpreted as *primus*.[67] Alterations behind no. 27 Bridge Street revealed a quantity of Roman pottery, but nothing of structural significance: the findspot lies immediately north of the legionary baths.[68] On another site 60 m. east of Bridge Street and 52 m. south of Eastgate Street part of a black and white tessellated pavement was found.[69] A layer of broken tile on sandstone rubble on the same site was probably the surfacing of a courtyard or alley.[70] A number of sherds of Roman pottery came from the site. A masonry building of two periods was found and recorded during extension of cellars at Browns'. A wall running east–west had a hypocaust on its south side, and an *opus signinum* floor on the other; a second wall lay 3.6 m. north of the first, and there was the robber trench of a third 3.9 m. further north again. The building was no later than the Trajanic period, and the plan was later modified, with new walls. The coins from the site had a bias towards the 4th century; pottery was mainly 2nd-century, but one of the brooches found is likely to be 3rd-century.[71] The quality of the finds supports identification of the site as a *domus tribuni*. An altar dedicated by a military tribune of Legio xx, Flavius Longus, evidently came from the house nearest the east gate, as it was found at the corner of Newgate Street. The dedication is for the welfare of jointly reigning emperors, indicating a date no earlier than the Severan period, coupled with the genius of the place.[72] A second altar found between the Grosvenor Hotel and the steps to the city walls was re-used as a building stone and damaged, only the dedication to Jupiter Best and Greatest surviving.[73] A gold coin of Vitellius was found during building of an extension to the Grosvenor Hotel.[74]

BARRACK BUILDINGS. The legionaries were housed in buildings of a characteristic plan found, *mutatis mutandis*, in fortresses elsewhere. The full plan of the men's accommodation has been revealed in the Deanery Field where barracks at the northern end of the fortress have been excavated (fig. 28).

[63] A similar dedication by a centurion comes from Bath: *R.I.B.* i, no. 152.

[64] 'Mr. Dyson's house' cannot now be traced. For the location of the cellar see Watkin, *Roman Ches.* 188.

[65] *J.C.A.S.* iv. 205–6; *Jnl. Brit. Arch. Assoc.* N.S. i. 305; Lawson, 'Schedule', no. xxv.

[66] *J.C.A.S.* [1st ser.], ii. 414.

[67] *R.I.B.* i, no. 457; *J.C.A.S.* [1st ser.] ii. 406–7 and fig.; Watkin, *Roman Ches.* 181–3; Lawson, 'Schedule', no. xxxi; R. H. Morris, *Chester in Plantagenet and Tudor Reigns*, 249. The altar may have been erected for a *collegium Minervae*; it is possibly re-used.

[68] *J.C.A.S.* xlix. 59.

[69] Ibid. viii. 104; ix. 141; Lawson, 'Schedule', no. xxxii.

[70] Street surfacing of crushed tile has been found at several sites.

[71] *J.C.A.S.* xlviii. 48; liv. 21–2.

[72] *R.I.B.* i, no. 450; Watkin, *Roman Ches.* 169–73; Lawson, 'Schedule', no. xxvii, mistakenly gives the dedication as *genio loci* alone.

[73] *Arch. Jnl.* xlii. 147–8; Watkin, *Roman Ches.* 185–6; *R.I.B.* i, no. 453; Lawson, 'Schedule', no. xxviii.

[74] Grosvenor Mus. 30.C.1965.

The length of the men's quarters at Chester was *c.* 50 m., and the breadth 8.5 m.: an internal wall ran the length of the building, and partition walls at 4-m. intervals divided it into *contubernia* consisting of a larger inner room with a hearth, and a smaller outer room: each pair of rooms thus defined was occupied by a 'section' of eight men. The men's quarters were entered from a veranda *c.* 3 m. wide with posts at 3-m. intervals. Although 10 *contubernia* were sufficient to house the 80 men of a century, at Chester 11 were consistently provided.[75] At one end of the barrack, and possibly integrally roofed with it, was a centurion's house 26.5 m. long, and 11.5 m. wide: a corridor or alley 1.5 m. wide separated the officer's quarters from the men's. Once again, the only complete plan comes from the Deanery Field, where the house was divided internally into 10 rooms with linking corridor, the most likely position for the entrance being almost half way along the side fronting the lane *c.* 5.5 m. wide which each pair of barracks faced. Each barrack stood closely back-to-back with a neighbour facing in the opposite direction. A group of six was assigned to each cohort from II to X; the first cohort required more. Thus the apparently uninterrupted run of barracks across the north end of the *retentura* of the fortress held four of the ten cohorts of the legion.[76] From the more fragmentary remains of barracks excavated elsewhere in the fortress it is known where the barracks for a further four cohorts were placed, including the first cohort; the sites of the remaining two can be suggested. The form of the barracks described above is that of the 2nd century; in the 1st the mode of construction differed. On the site of the Old Market Hall a timber barrack lay immediately north of the 'elliptical building'.[77] Slots were excavated through the sand and soft rock 38–53 cm. wide and *c.* 76 cm. deep: into those the uprights for the framework of the building were put, and the spoil then replaced and consolidated to hold posts *c.* 12.5 cm. square at intervals of 60–80 cm. The wattle and daub infill of the wall panels was rendered with plaster. As in the later barracks, hearths were provided in the inner rooms. Although the building was narrower than the later barracks, the internal dimensions of the rooms were not significantly different save that the spacing of the partition walls between *contubernia* was a little closer. Either the wall spacing had been miscalculated or additional space had deliberately been provided at the east end, perhaps for the N.C.O.s of the century. The barrack faced north, and the veranda lay on that side; in the space between the barrack and the 'elliptical building' a urinal and its soakaway were provided. The 1st-century barrack appeared to stand in isolation from others, as the building to the north did not resemble a barrack in plan. The stone building which replaced it, occupying the same site, differed in function.[78]

The Deanery Field was not only the first site in Chester to be subjected to exploratory excavation but also the scene of the first steps towards scientific excavation.[79] Of the cohort allocation of barracks in the north-east corner of the fortress only one produced no evidence; two were sectioned, while two others were substantially stripped and between them provided the evidence for a restored plan. Relatively little was seen of the western barrack block apart from the centurion's house, where a complex building history was indicated.

There were thought to be two clearly defined phases in the occupation of the

[75] At Caerleon there were 12 and at Inchtuthil 14.

[76] Thompson, *Roman Ches.* 34–6 and plan; Nash-Williams, *Roman Frontier in Wales*, 163–5 and fig. 88.

[77] *J.C.A.S.* lvii. 5–7 and fig. 2; *New Evidence*, 22, plan.

[78] Above.

[79] The exploratory excavation was undertaken by W. T.

Watkin in 1884: *T.L.C.A.S.* ii. 33–8; *T.H.S.L.C.* xxxvi. 8–10; *Roman Ches.* 158–60. Excavation between 1922 and 1935 was carried out by R. Newstead, latterly in collaboration with J. P. Droop: *Liverpool Annals*, xi. 59–86; xv. 3–32; xviii. 6–18, 113–47; xxii. 14–30; xxiii. 3–50.

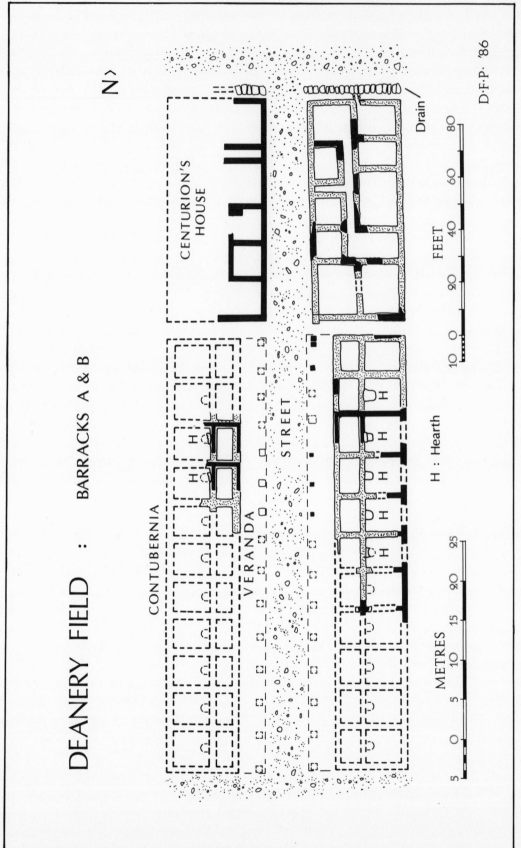

DEANERY FIELD : BARRACKS A & B

FIG. 28.

barracks. The first, termed the 'establishment phase', was shown by coins and pottery to have begun *c.* A.D. 70–85; the association of that phase with timber structures was not recognized. Intensive occupation followed until the end of the 1st or the early 2nd century, and 'no evidence of a later occupation of [the barracks] was discoverable'. No radical change in layout occurred before the second, or 'dismantling', phase, represented by a uniform layer overspreading the foundations and floors of the first: it was dated to the close of the 2nd century or the beginning of the 3rd. It was recognized that some 3rd- and 4th-century material came from what was termed 'the upper Roman stratum': the earliest investigation produced a small 4th-century hoard with coins of Magnentius, Valentinian I, and Valens, and at least a quarter of the other coin finds in the first season were 4th-century from Constantine I to Gratian.[80] Extensive structural alterations to the barracks were noted, including areas of paving which incorporated re-used architectural fragments.[81] Two inscriptions were found. Of the first, part of a slate-cut inscription, it could only be said that 'of the remains of two lines . . . VI . . . is legible'.[82] The second is on a white marble base with the back rounded for a niche: the top has an iron dowel as for a statuette.[83] It came from the angle formed by the front wall and partition wall in one of the *contubernia* in Block A.

An area explored more recently in the garden of no. 1 Abbey Green[84] extended from the defences through the intervallum to the northern ends of three centurions' houses; initially the latter were a pair of timber houses 2 m. apart, with the northwest corner of a third 4–5 m. to the east. The timber houses were apparently rebuilt at least twice before being replaced in stone *c.* A.D. 100. They were rebuilt again about a century later, but evidence of the work had been obscured by widespread demolition, followed by paving of parts of the site, datable to the end of the 3rd century. Between the intervallum road and the barracks was a drain 1.3 m. wide and *c.* 90 cm. deep, originally timber-lined, but rebuilt in stone in the mid 2nd century.

That barracks lay west of the *via decumana* was first suspected when excavation for a lift well on the site of the Northgate Brewery revealed two walls.[85] Subsequently the southern ends of two further barracks were found standing back-to-back at Folliott House.[86] Investigation of the site of the Northgate Brewery revealed further evidence of the layout and history of the barracks on that side of the *retentura*.[87] The earliest signs of occupation were a few pits and stake-holes which were presumed to represent activity immediately before the erection of a timber barrack *c.* A.D. 80. After partial demolition it was rebuilt to much the same plan, with resited partition walls. The timber building was used, possibly with further repair or adaptation, until dismantled *c.* A.D. 120. After its vacation many rubbish pits were dug, and a layer of soil accumulated: the abandonment presumably reflects the deployment of legionary vexillations on the northern frontiers until Scotland was abandoned. The site remained open until *c.* A.D. 160 when the centurion's house and adjoining barrack were rebuilt in stone. With subsequent repair and rebuilding, including blocking of the passage between the centurion's quarters and the barrack, the stone buildings stood until demolished *c.* A.D. 270–85. Traces were

[80] Another hoard found in the same season ran to Severus: *Liverpool Annals*, xi. 64. The work of 1923–4 uncovered structures which did not relate to the barracks subsequently excavated: ibid. plate 2; xv. plate 1.

[81] Substantial rebuilding of the barracks is proved: ibid. xv. 13.   [82] Ibid. xi. 85; *R.I.B.* i, no. 573.

[83] *R.I.B.* i, no. 451. The dedication is to the standards, or (less likely) to their bearers.

[84] *J.C.A.S.* lxiii. 14–37; *Britannia*, vii. 320–1 and fig. 12; viii. 385–7; ix. 429–30; *New Evidence, passim.*

[85] *J.C.A.S.* xxxviii. 174–5 and figs. 21–2.

[86] *J.R.S.* xlvi. 125, fig. 25.

[87] S. Ward and T. J. Strickland, *Excavations on Site of Northgate Brewery 1974–5.*

seen of later occupation in the form of timber structures lasting for an indefinite period after the stone buildings were demolished, a phenomenon seen elsewhere in the fortress. In position and layout the timber and stone buildings agreed: the barrack was the westernmost of the first cohort group west of the *via decumana*.[88]

The cohort-group of barracks at the west end of the range was probably orientated north–south like all the others. By contrast, a barrack in Hunter Street was orientated the other way, *per scamna*.[89] Six *contubernia* included what was thought to be the west end of the men's quarters. The barrack faced north, and 1.3 m. south of it lay the back wall of its neighbour. There were signs of modifications to the plan at the east end. An unusual number of stamped tiles included one of the ANTONINIANA type, of A.D. 213–22. Conversely no coins were found between Commodus and Victorinus. A hoard of iron work included a plough share. Analysis of the bones found on the site revealed plentiful ox bones, with those of pigs almost as abundant; red deer, sheep or goat, and horse bones were also represented. On the site of the Odeon Cinema at the junction of Hunter Street and Northgate Street a suggested barrack revealed no sign of the characteristic plan; the site is 60 m. east of the Masonic Lodge, where the earlier discoveries were made. The features recorded included a wall traced for 15.25 m., a large stone-lined drain, and *opus signinum* floors, and may be related to recent discoveries immediately to the south.[90]

Two centurions' houses belonging to the same cohort as the Hunter Street barrack stood back-to-back on the site of St. Martin's House Combined Health Clinic. The earliest timber buildings were repaired before being replaced in stone on a similar plan.[91] Subsequent investigation nearby revealed more of those barracks and provided a framework for their dating. The timber structures were replaced early in the 2nd century, and although the barracks which replaced them had footings and sill walls of masonry they were probably otherwise of timber. Between the mid 3rd century and the mid 4th the barracks became derelict. Whether they were later systematically dismantled is not clear. Some 4th-century activity on the site was noted. The southern barrack of the group appears to lie south of Princess Street.[92]

Between the *principia* and the western defences lay barracks and related buildings which are likely to have been the quarters of the first cohort.[93]

In Goss Street[94] a structure interpreted as a stone barrack facing the *principia* diverged from the normal plan: its 'spine' wall appeared to be missing, and no doorways giving access to the veranda were found. Beneath lay the remains of a timber barrack facing west, and from a grey spread associated with its construction came a *sestertius* of A.D. 72–3 in fresh condition. The early 2nd-century building which succeeded it was apparently timber-framed, based on a rubble footing brought to a level finish with a 5-cm. spread of mortar. Later in the 2nd century it was dismantled, and a building either of masonry or of timber based upon low sill walls was erected. An internal change of plan took place no earlier than the early twenties of the 3rd century, but how long thereafter occupation continued is unknown. That the adjacent street continued in use is proved by the sealing of a jar of 3rd-century or later date beneath its uppermost surface.[95] A centurion's house

[88] Inf. from Mr. Strickland.

[89] *J.C.A.S.* xvi. 114; R. Newstead, 'Rec. of Arch. Finds at Chester: Hunter Street', ibid. xxvii (2), 61–79.

[90] R. Newstead, 'Rec. of Arch. finds at Chester: Hunter Street—Site of the Odeon Theatre', ibid. xxxiii. 49–63.

[91] *J.R.S.* lvi. 200.

[92] *Britannia*, xiv. 297; *J.C.A.S.* lxv, fig. 1 and plan facing p. 24. The recent work has shown that the Hunter Street barrack was incorrectly sited on previous plans of the fortress.

[93] *Britannia*, xi. 51–60.

[94] *J.C.A.S.* xxxviii. 1–38.

[95] Ibid. fig. 10, no. 34. The black burnished jar is comparable to Gillam's Forms 145–8 which date from *c.* 270 to the later 4th century: *Arch. Aeliana*, 4th ser. xxxv. 16, 57.

lay 3 m. south of the barrack, but little of its plan was revealed. The floor of one room lay 83 cm. below normal floor level. A site at the corner of Goss Street and Watergate Street[96] revealed timber walls running north–south and east–west, which were repaired or rebuilt before the erection of a stone centurion's house. The latter was represented by a north–south wall which aligned with a wall found earlier, and may be the east wall of the house. Three successive *opus signinum* floors were seen, and the building had painted wall-plaster. It was demolished presumably in the late Roman period. Further work[97] on the supposed barrack has shown that the early 2nd-century building with stone footings was only 5.5 m. wide, with internal partition walls *c.* 4 m. apart. The veranda had post-footings at 2.5 m. intervals, giving a spacing for the posts of 3 m. The Flavian building was similar in plan, although the partition walls were not as regularly spaced. The early 2nd-century building was interpreted as a stable converted to living accommodation or offices during reconstruction in the early 3rd century.[98] It was taken down, *c.* A.D. 280–300, and its site paved with the resulting rubble. A timber building similar in plan was erected in the mid 4th century.[99] On the Old Market Hall site what appeared to be the northern end of a conventional barrack facing west was found, with a second building 6 m. wide lying 4.5 m. west of it.[1] On the site of Goldsmith House on the west side of Goss Street the western building was found to face a veranda almost 3 m. wide, beyond which lay a barrack of normal plan facing east, the men's quarters and the centurion's house being separated by an alley 3.6 m. wide. A second east-facing building fronting a 2.7 m. veranda lay west of the barrack. There were signs that the verandas of some of the buildings had been walled in.[2]

A second group of buildings in the western half of the range was exposed on five sites between Trinity Street and Crook Street. Immediately east of Trinity Street was what appeared to be a barrack facing east.[3] The earliest building was completely of timber, and it was suggested that the 'stone' barrack which followed was perhaps timber-framed in both of the phases recognized. A floor of stone slabs was thought to belong to a Severan reconstruction, though there was no conclusive evidence of its date. Further walls were found whose spacing did not fit the expected pattern, and it was concluded that a building with a central courtyard or road had perhaps been discovered, for the fragmentary remains of Roman walling could not be fitted into a coherent plan.[4] Later work west of Crook Street[5] showed that barracks of normal plan were interspersed with narrower buildings 5–5.5 m. wide, with a veranda *c.* 2.5 m. wide. The latter were provisionally identified as barracks without provision for equipment, although little of their plan was revealed apart from one internal wall. It is suggested, therefore, that the earlier investigation found a pair of barracks of normal plan facing each other, with a 'narrow' building lying between the western of the pair and the intervallum. The more recent work revealed the full width of the eastern barrack, and to the east a second narrow building facing west, standing back-to-back with a normal barrack facing east. A building 5 m. wide, and probably *c.* 70 m. long, lay transversely across the northern ends of the first three buildings, curtailing their length by 6 or 7 m.; how it was subdivided internally is unknown. Three *contubernia* at the south end of the eastern barrack were explored, together with the north end of the adjacent centurion's house, in

[96] T. E. Ward, 'Excavations in Goss Street, Chester, 1971', *J.C.A.S.* lviii. 47–51.

[97] *Ches. Arch. Bull.* ii. 15–16; *Britannia*, vi. 240; *New Evidence, passim.*

[98] *New Evidence*, 26–8.

[99] Ibid. 42.

[1] Ibid. 25, plan.

[2] *Britannia*, i. 282; ii. 255.

[3] *J.C.A.S.* xl. 6–7 and fig. 1.

[4] Ibid. xliii. 27–33.

[5] *J.R.S.* liv. 156.

1974.[6] Built initially in timber, the barrack was rebuilt with stone footings in the early 2nd century, and was afterwards extensively reconstructed before being demolished in the later 3rd. Areas of paving post-dated that demolition. The site was left open until possibly the mid 4th century, when there was a final phase of timber construction. A notable feature of the centurion's house was the elaborately decorated wall-plaster it yielded. Partial enclosure of the veranda, and the movement of internal partition walls also noted in the barracks east of the internal baths, may represent an attempt to improve the standard of accommodation, to which a Severan date has been assigned.[7]

Thus while barracks of standard size and layout existed between the *principia* and the western defences, other buildings of the same length but some 3 m. narrower are also found there. At Caerleon at least two blocks of single rooms in the range assigned to the first cohort appear to be regularly arranged in relation to the normal barracks.[8] Such a pattern may equally have held good at Chester, where the space allotted to barracks of the first cohort was very similar, *c.* 140 m. compared to the *c.* 145 m. at Caerleon. At Inchtuthil, if the two buildings immediately behind the senior centurion's house are included, the equivalent measurement would be *c.* 150 m. The layout at the western end of the range seems to follow a logical pattern. Whatever the position nearer the *principia*, it seems that the sequence, from west to east, is narrow–normal–normal–narrow–normal–?normal.

No more than six conventional barracks were needed for the first cohort in the 2nd century;[9] since four and possibly five have already been found at Chester there is no difficulty in finding space for the one or two remaining. The narrow or 'single-cell' blocks found not only at Chester but also at Caerleon and Nijmegen (Netherlands) must presumably be related to the unusually high establishment of the first cohort, but the suggestion that the first cohort had on its strength many men with duties outside those of an ordinary soldier will not bear detailed examination.[10] It is not known whether the Flavian timber barracks of the first cohort at Chester were arranged similarly to those described above, but their layout may have resembled that of the fortress at Inchtuthil, where five manipular pairs of conventional barracks housed a milliary cohort.

There were five centurions in the first cohort, the *primi ordines*. Their houses are roughly twice the size of those allotted to centurions in the other nine cohorts, reflecting their higher rank. At Caerleon those of the senior centurions measured *c.* 25 m. by 20 m., the ordinary centurions' *c.* 22 m. by 10 m. A similar difference occurred at Inchtuthil, where the houses at the opposing ends of the row belonging to the first cohort are larger than the rest. At Chester *primus pilus*, the senior centurion, had a house approximately a third larger than the rest of the *primi ordines*, whose house-plans are likely to have resembled those at Caerleon and Inchtuthil. The slight traces excavated in Goss Street evidently belong to the senior centurion's house, but define little more than its east side. More substantial details of the centurion's quarters in Crook Street appear to show that the house was no larger than that belonging to a centurion of the ordinary grade, but the house may have extended further west than was thought.[11] That another centurion's house lay on the east side of Crook Street is indicated by the discovery of an *opus signinum*

---

[6] *Britannia*, vi. 240; *New Evidence*, 12 and plan on p. 25.

[7] *Roman West in 3rd Cent.* 424; Nash-Williams, *Roman Frontier in Wales*, 39 and fig. 15; *J.R.S.* lv. 204.

[8] Boon, *Isca*, 89. One single (narrow) block may have been assigned to each manipular pair.

[9] *Britannia*, xi. 58.

[10] *J.R.S.* lix. 53. Men serving their last 5 years as *veterani sub vexillo* may have been allotted to the 1st cohort.

[11] *New Evidence*, plan on p. 25. This would leave sufficient space for three further houses.

floor 18–35 cm. thick resting on dirty sand. Nine coins ranging in date from Severus to the house of Constantine were found.[12]

A building inscription built into the wall of a cellar at no. 64 Watergate Street[13] may have come from either the last centurion's house in the row or from a building intervening, as some did at Caerleon, between it and the *via principalis*. The text refers to 'the work which had been restored after falling into ruin', and is thought to refer to a Mother Goddess, so that the stone's origin within the fortress seems doubtful, the 'work' in question being presumably some sort of shrine or temple.[14]

East of the *principia* a site north of Eastgate Street between the city walls and St. Werburgh Street[15] revealed parts of five *contubernia* of a barrack facing west; nothing of the earlier timber plan was recovered. Tiled, flagged, and mortar floors were recorded, and there were signs of reconstruction and possible changes of plan affecting the veranda areas of that and the other barrack of the pair. Two column bases bore no relation to the barrack plan. Six barracks may be postulated there, possibly assigned to the second cohort or conceivably to the third; a cohort was quartered in a similar position at Caerleon, and clearly neither fortress could have fitted a further cohort into the remaining space.

A Roman hypocaust was found on the site of the Mitre tavern at the east end of Eastgate Row North, now occupied by the National Westminster Bank.[16] From its position it belonged to one of the centurion's houses. A building stone naming a centurion of the third cohort came from the site of the shop immediately west of the bank.[17] Massive foundations and a spear-head were found.[18] A fine altar found on the east side of Godstall Lane from 'a bed of solid soil some 13 feet below the surface'[19] was dedicated to the genius of the century by an *optio*; the findspot, *c.* 21.5 m. north of Eastgate Street, was presumably in or near a centurion's house. Another altar with the same dedication was found on the east side of St. Werburgh Street *c.* 36.5 m. north of Eastgate Street, well within the area covered by the barracks: although brief, the inscription appears complete.[20] A third altar, like the second, does not give the name of the donor: its dedication is to the Mother Goddesses. It appears to have come from the eastern barrack of the group, or from the intervallum space on its east side.[21] Antiquities, including samian and 1st–3rd-century coins, were collected by F. H. Williams from the site of Douglas's buildings on the east side of St. Werburgh Street. A tombstone of the 'banquet' type dedicated to Fesonia Severiana was found close by during excavation of the foundations of the Corn Exchange.[22] Since it cannot have been found *in situ* the most likely explanation for its appearance within the fortress is that it was robbed from a Roman cemetery for re-use as building stone. Part of another tombstone from the city wall a little further south was dedicated to a nonagenarian Roman citizen,

[12] *J.C.A.S.* xxxvi. 64–5. Rebuilding of a warehouse east of Crook Street in 1923 apparently revealed 'a line of columns': inf. from Mr. H. Cordery.

[13] *R.I.B.* i, no. 455; *J.R.S.* xxix. 225; xl. 115; *J.C.A.S.* xxxviii. 176 and plate 9 (2); *R.I.S.S.* no. 7a. Only the bottom right corner has survived.

[14] If the inscription is correctly restored. The name of the deity to whom the work is dedicated should appear above the penultimate line, and the form of the inscription is otherwise entirely suitable for the restoration of a military building after a period of neglect.

[15] *J.C.A.S.* liv. 9–19.

[16] Ibid. xxvii (2), 190; Lawson, 'Schedule', no. xxiv.

[17] *R.I.B.* i, no. 468. The centurion's name is probably Ferronius; he may be the centurion of the third cohort, Ferronius Vegetus, known from building stones found near Walltown and Willowford on Hadrian's Wall: ibid. nos. 1769, 1867.

[18] *J.C.A.S.* n.s. iii. 47, 212.

[19] Ibid. [1st ser.], ii. 406 and fig. facing; Watkin, *Roman Ches.* 180–1; Lawson, 'Schedule', no. xxiii; *R.I.B.* i, no. 448.

[20] *J.C.A.S.* vi. 76–8; *R.I.B.* i, no. 446; Lawson, 'Schedule', no. xxi.

[21] *R.I.B.* i, no. 456; *J.C.A.S.* [1st ser.], ii. 422–3; *Arch. Jnl.* xxxiv. 142; Watkin, *Roman Ches.* 183–4; Lawson, 'Schedule', no. xix. DEAE in the first line should read DEAB[VS].

[22] *J.C.A.S.* [1st ser.], ii. 410; iii. 257; Watkin, *Roman Ches.* 209–11; Lawson, 'Schedule', no. xix; *R.I.B.* i, no. 563. There is some uncertainty as to the date of the find: *J.C.A.S.* [1st ser.], ii. 422.

Aurelius Timotheus, and his wife.[23] Such stray finds suggest repairs, incorporating tombstones, to the eastern defences.[24]

Barracks have also been located in the *praetentura*. On the west side of Newgate Street two barracks orientated north–south have been investigated, and the space between the *thermae* and the east wall is precisely that required for a cohort group. Timber barracks initially erected on a similar plan, but extending slightly further south, were replaced by barracks of stone in which three distinct periods were recognized, involving such changes in plan as movement of doors and internal walls, as well as renewal of veranda posts.[25] Two stamped tiles found nearby of the ANTONINIANA type indicated repairs in the period A.D. 213–22.[26] The northern ends of the western pair of barracks were recorded during extension of Browns' store in St. Michael's Street.[27] The first lay 9 m. east of the *basilica* of the baths, and a layer of gravel found east of it presumably marks the alley separating it from the next barrack. The position of the internal wall indicates a modification of the internal plan as seen elsewhere in the group. Enclosure of the veranda may have taken place, as at Crook Street. A coin of Constantius II was found with many broken roof-tiles, and five other 4th-century coins.

A relief found in 1737 or 1738 'in digging the foundations of a house belonging to John Philpot in Fleshmongers' Lane', later Newgate Street, represents a gladiatorial contest, in which only the *retiarius* is clearly represented.[28] It forms part of a slate-cut frieze 18.7 cm. deep, original length unknown: the surviving fragment is 26.2 cm. long. The relief disappeared in the mid 18th century,[29] and has only recently come to light.[30] It may be Antonine in date;[31] the findspot is 200 m. or less from the amphitheatre.[32]

Not far away a centurial stone of the first cohort found in digging 'very deep' in a garden on the east side of Newgate Street[33] possibly originated in the east wall of the fortress; the letters LMP at the end of the inscription may be the *tria nomina* of the soldier who cut it.[34] The upper part of an altar dedicated to Mars the Preserver was found to the south of and behind the last house in Newgate Street (east side) just within the city walls.[35]

Sufficient barracks are known to accommodate eight of the ten cohorts of the legion, and it therefore remains to consider where the other two would have been placed. One likely site is in the south-west corner, a conjecture possibly confirmed in Weaver Street, where an east-west wall of two periods was found.[36] A likely location for the remaining cohort is in the *retentura*, south of the Deanery Field barracks, and in all probability orientated *per scamna* like the matching group on the west side.

RAMPART BUILDINGS AND OVENS. The space 9–11 m. wide between the rampart

[23] *J.C.A.S.* liv. 14–15; lvi. 10; *J.R.S.* l. 236–7.
[24] Above.
[25] *J.R.S.* liv. 156; lv. 204; *J.C.A.S.* lii. 50; Nash-Williams, *Roman Frontier in Wales*, 39.
[26] *Arch. Jnl.* xliii. 289; *T.H.S.L.C.* xxxix. 53.
[27] *J.C.A.S.* xxvii. 126–30.
[28] Soc. of Antiq. minute bk., 25 Nov. 1742; *R.I.S.S.*, p. 57 and pl. 49; *J.C.A.S.* [1st ser.], i. 332; Watkin, *Roman Ches.* 201–2; Lawson, 'Schedule', no. xliv. D. and S. Lysons, *Magna Britannia*, ii (2), 431, give the findspot as the market place.
[29] An illustration was published in 1743: *Vetusta Monumenta*, i, pl. lxv. Two plaster casts were made, one of which is in the Grosvenor Mus.
[30] *Britannia*, xiv. 87–95; below, plate. Thanks are due to Dr. G. Lloyd-Morgan for informing the author of the redis-covery of the original, and to Mr. R. Jackson for allowing him to see his article before publication.
[31] Cf. the Bridgeness distance slab from the Antonine Wall: *R.I.B.* i, no. 2139.
[32] Mr. Philpot owned two houses in Fleshmongers' Lane, but neither can be identified. The relief may derive from a funerary monument, in which case it was looted from a cemetery in the late- or post-Roman period.
[33] Watkin, *Roman Ches.* 120–1; Lawson, 'Schedule', no. xlv; *R.I.B.* i, no. 467; *J.C.A.S.* [1st ser.], iii. 125.
[34] Cf. a stone from Llanio: *R.I.B.* i, no. 409.
[35] Watkin, *Roman Ches.* 184–5; Lawson, 'Schedule', no. xlv; *Arch. Jnl.* xli. 175; *R.I.B.* i, no. 454.
[36] F. H. Thompson, 'Excavations in Weaver Street, 1956', *J.C.A.S.* xlvi. 69–72.

and the intervallum road was occupied by two readily recognizable types of structures. One, consistently some 20–21 m. long and 7.3 m. wide, and normally divided into three rooms, is termed, for lack of knowledge of its function, a 'rampart building'. Such buildings are supposed to have been stores and armouries, although some seem to have served as cook-houses or workshops. The second type consists of ovens.

Knowledge of rampart buildings is mainly confined to the north and west sides of the fortress. One was discovered in the Deanery Field lying parallel to, and immediately south of, the north wall. It was 21.3 m. long and 7.3 m. wide.[37] A second rampart building was immediately south of an interval tower in Abbey Green.[38] Its length was 19.8 m. and it was divided into three rooms, those at the east and west ends measuring 6.2 m. and 7.3 m., and that in the centre 4.9 m. The width was not established, but cannot vary much from those measured elsewhere.[39] It was uncovered again in 1975–7, with another rampart building 2 m. to the west.[40] The stone buildings were built shortly before the end of the 1st century; they covered earlier timber buildings, latrines, and ovens. Various internal alterations or repairs were carried out in the eastern of the two between c. A.D. 100 and 150, and afterwards the building was partially dismantled, and bread ovens built within the remains. The walls in the southern part of the building were rebuilt, and a roof was added to the stoking area in front of the ovens. Extension of the rampart c. A.D. 200 obliterated all those features. A fourth rampart building revealed in the Deanery Field[41] was of normal width. One internal partition wall was found. It appears to have been demolished and ultimately concealed beneath the extended rampart.[42] A rampart building west of the *porta decumana* on the site of the Northgate Brewery was 19 m. long, and its three rooms were 6 m., 5.2 m., and 6.3 m. wide. The eastern room had a clay floor, and the western contained a hearth perhaps used for metal-working. Its dismantling at the end of the 2nd century was followed by the laying of sandstone paving.[43] The badly robbed remains of the east and south walls of another building immediately to the west were presumed to be those of another rampart building.[44]

Six rampart buildings have been found on the west side of the fortress. North of Princess Street two rampart buildings 28.3 m. apart were found.[45] Stripping of the northernmost revealed the bedding trench for a timber wall parallel to, and immediately east of, the back wall of the stone building. The wall ran for more than 15.5 m., and probably belonged to a rampart building of timber. One internal wall was found. The building was 4–6 m. wide. The south room of the stone building measured 6.8 m. north–south, and the central room nearly 4 m. The southern rampart building also covered a timber structure. Its north room measured 7.2 m., and the centre room 4.3 m. The width of both buildings was the same, c. 7.3 m.

In the space between the rampart buildings there were at least two ovens, and probably more, one of which was examined in some detail, together with a timber-lined stoke-hole immediately to the east of it, which contained many spreads of ash representing the rakings of the oven. The posts of the board revetment were at 1-m. intervals set in the usual trench: it seems likely that they also supported a roof for the stoke-hole. Stages in the fill of the stoke-hole could be associated with

[37] Watkin, *Roman Ches.* 158–9; *T.H.S.L.C.* xxxvi. 9–10; *T.L.C.A.S.* ii. 33–8.
[38] *Liverpool Annals*, xxii. 24–5, fig. 1.
[39] Ibid. xxiii, plate 26.
[40] *J.C.A.S.* lxiii. 15–35.
[41] Ibid. xl. 17–22.
[42] Ibid. figs. 14–15.
[43] P. J. Davey, *Chester Northgate Brewery: Interim Report, Phase I*, 7–8 and figs. 5, 9.
[44] *New Evidence*, plan on p. 27. The intervening space was c. 2.5 m. The eastern building covered traces of an earlier timber structure.
[45] *J.R.S.* xxxvi. 136–40; lvi. 200.

repairs to the oven floor, of which there were two or three. Beneath the oven lay the traces of an earlier one with which earliest use of the stoke-hole was associated, and a sooty fill which predated the earliest use of the stoke-hole was tentatively associated with a still earlier oven. Traces of a second oven were seen, and the space available was sufficient for four. The excavated oven measured more than 3 m. long by c. 2.2 m. across, and its stoke-hole was c. 2.5 m. long: the oven's shape was that of a horse-shoe.

On an extensive site south of Princess Street[46] lay a third rampart building in that sector. It measured 21 m. by 7.3 m.: no internal partition walls were found. A stone-slabbed floor was level with an internal offset on the wall, and an accumulation of rubbish over it dated from the Hadrianic to Antonine period. The building may have been abandoned subsequently. At least one other rampart building lay between that and the buildings revealed 70 m. away north of Princess Street. The walls of a rampart building of normal width were found, but no floor levels were recognized. As with the buildings to the north, an earlier timber building was sealed by the later stone one. Its west wall lay immediately east of the rampart building's back wall, and showed two phases of construction: a timber internal wall was traced for more than 2 m. eastwards.

Between the rampart building south of Princess Street and the next to the south lay ovens. The first was immediately north of an interval tower. It had its floor renewed once, and its lower floor sealed layers of ash which presumably belonged to an earlier oven. The diameter of the oven was estimated at c. 3–3.5 m. The sandy and ashy layers above the oven did not extend beyond c. A.D. 120 in date. Two further ovens lay close together immediately south of the tower, and some 10 m. from the oven first excavated. There were probably other ovens in the space which was 40–50 m. or more in extent. A fifth rampart building north of the west gate appeared to have been demolished, and an oven or cookhouse placed over it: several superimposed refloorings of the oven took place. The two internal cross-walls of the rampart building were found to be 4.4 m. apart.[47]

The remaining rampart building on the west side of the fortress was south of the west gate.[48] Its west wall was standing to a height of 1.3 m., with a thick deposit of clean rubble internally, but no trace of flooring survived. A large sherd of Trajanic samian from the fill between the back of the rampart and the west wall provided a *terminus ante quem* for its construction. The building was traced for the full width of the site, 15 m., and two internal walls were seen, the northerly of which made a butt-joint with the west wall. It appears that the internal walls were not arranged in the same way as in the other rampart buildings on the west and north sides of the fortress. When the east and south walls of the building were discovered no further internal walls were seen. The width was the same as that found elsewhere.[49]

Only one rampart building has been found on the south side of the fortress. In Newgate Street 12 m. of the south wall, one of the internal cross-walls, and a mortar floor, belonging to a rampart building, were found. The building was dated to the early Trajanic period, and was found to predate an interval tower. It was apparently demolished at the end of the 2nd century and its remains covered by an extension of the rampart.

No rampart buildings have been identified on the east side of the fortress. Immediately north of the east gate two ovens roughly 3 m. apart were found immedi-

[46] *J.C.A.S.* lvi. 1–21.
[47] The change in function is comparable to that observed at Abbey Green.
[48] *J.C.A.S.* xlii. 45–7.
[49] Ibid. xlix. 5–6, fig. 1.

ately within the rampart. They had an internal diameter of *c.* 3 m., were of the usual sandstone-with-clay construction, and had a stoke-hole or ash-pit on the west side, the fill of which produced pottery of the Flavian–Trajanic period. Traces of earlier ovens were seen, and a third oven was suspected to lie to the south. A low wall or kerb separated the ovens from the intervallum road: it lay 9 m. west of the rampart back.[50]

OTHER BUILDINGS. A number of discoveries cannot be assigned to known fortress buildings. In the south-west quadrant of the *praetentura*, for example, traces of buildings of some size have been seen on the west side of the *via praetoria*. Just within the southern defences at White Friars Cottage, at the corner of White Friars and Bolland's Court, at a depth of between 1.2 and 2.1 m., several fragments of columns 40 cm. in diameter, and three (one 2.75 m. long) of 60 cm. diameter were found by chance in 1884.[51] A stylobate foundation resting on 62 cm. of concrete ran east–west with an eaves-drip on its south side. Two large stone blocks, one measuring 1.14 m. by 1.39 m. and the other possibly 1.8 m. north–south, rested on the stylobate, but there were no column bases. At a depth of 2.1 m. the surface of the intervallum road, composed of broken tile, sandstone, and pebbles, was found south of the building: it was claimed that 7.3 m. of the frontage was revealed, but the plan shows *c.* 6 m. It was apparently traced for a further 4.26 m. under the adjoining house to the west,[52] when fragments of cornice and capitals were found. In the street outside the same house (no. 12) were found four large ashlar sandstone blocks at a depth of *c.* 3.5 m. laid on natural sands and clay.[53] A layer of wood charcoal in places just above the stylobate indicated the possibility that the building was destroyed by fire. Of 35 coins found, 11 were illegible, although probably compatible in date with the remainder which ran from Gallienus to Constantine I. Other finds included stamped tiles and a quantity of pottery.[54] The stylobate continued on the east side of Bolland's Court, bringing the frontage of the building to at least 16.45 m. A tile was found with the stamp IVLIVS,[55] and a fragment of a sculptured stone.[56] In Bolland's Court some 34 m. to the north the earliest buildings were shown to be of timber, and apparently orientated east–west.[57] Make-up sealing the last timber phase contained late 2nd- or 3rd-century pottery, and a coin of Severus Alexander, and was capped by massive paving stones, one a re-used pilaster base or capital.

Approximately 40 m. east of the flagging described above, rebuilding at no. 40 Bridge Street brought to light the north front of a colonnaded building. A stylobate foundation was found *c.* 15 m. west of Bridge Street, and running along the south side of Pierpoint Lane for 16.75 m. It shared with an eaves-drip gulley on its north side a foundation of concrete possibly *c.* 30 cm. thick, beneath which a layer of clay overlay the natural rock. The bases of three columns were found in position: the first is said to have been well cut, its diameter being 66 cm.; the other two were simpler with square bases, and the diameter of their shafts was only 45 cm. The base and mouldings of the larger column resembled those found on the east side of Bridge Street in 1863. The interval between the bases was consistent at 3.65 m.,

[50] Ibid. liv. 12, fig. 1.

[51] Watkin, *Roman Ches.* 147–50.

[52] Ibid. 149: the author mistakenly wrote 'south'. It seems that the culvert on the south side of the rampart road was also found: ibid. 150.

[53] *Ches. Arch. Bull.* i. 20–1.

[54] A list of 52 coins in the Grosvenor Mus. from the site includes no less than 42 from Gordian III to the Tetrici,

perhaps a hoard. The mus. has in its collections a fused mass of coins, mainly radiate types, from White Friars and Bollands Court: inf. from Dr. G. Lloyd-Morgan.

[55] *Y Cymmrodor*, xli. 141, fig. 59 (16).

[56] Watkin, *Roman Ches.* 150.

[57] F. H. Thompson, 'Excavations at Bolland's Court, Chester, 1954 and 1959', *J.C.A.S.* liv. 1–3. The buildings are unlikely to have been barracks, as initially suggested.

and from the first and largest base to Bridge Street was 20.78 m.[58] Another base thought to belong to the same colonnade, although square, with part of a square pillar on it, was found on the south side of Pierpoint Lane.[59] The Pierpoint Lane and White Friars discoveries may represent the north and south sides of the same building fronting on the *via praetoria*. If so, its dimensions were *c*. 45.75 m. north–south and *c*. 85 m. east–west.[60] Part of a centurial stone apparently named the same centurion, Abucinus, as another stone from Commonhall Street,[61] and a bronze *phalera* was also discovered.[62]

In the next premises to the south a hoard of coins was found[63] *c*. 24 m. west of the street frontage and *c*. 3 m. from the surface. A mass of coins was fused together inside the hoard pot which was covered by a flat stone slab. Lumps of the hoard were broken off and divided amongst the workmen; one small lump when examined consisted of 83 *antoniniani* extending in date from Gordian III to Claudius II. The hoard probably numbered several hundred coins.[64] Pottery and coins were also found at Richard Jones's (now Owen Owen), and coins came from the shop at the corner of Bridge Street and White Friars.[65] A stone relief of Cautopates found built into the wall of a cellar in White Friars, together with another stone from the north wall of the fortress, is evidence of a mithraeum at Chester, although not necessarily near the findspot; like another relief from the same street identified as Atys it may have been built into, and later robbed from, the south wall of the fortress close by.[66] Another damaged figure of Cautopates[67] is variously said to have been found 'near the river', 'by the scite of the Roman warrior', by which Edgar's Field was apparently intended, and 'under a niche of the wall between the East gate and the river'. It was perhaps re-used, either in a Roman wall repair or later. Other structural remains have been found west of Bridge Street. On the site of the Grotto, formerly the Harp and Crown inn, at the corner of Commonhall Street and Bridge Street, building revealed two column bases *c*. 2.43 m. apart aligned north–south *c*. 14.5 m. west of Bridge Street: they were on a stylobate, with an eaves-drip on its west side.[68] A slighter return wall opposite the northern column implied alteration of the original plan. As at White Friars, charcoal and charred timber occurred in an almost continuous layer, suggesting that the building had burned down: most of the finds came from that layer. The only coins recorded are of 4th-century date, 'many common types of the Constantines, and one of Crispus', perhaps comprising a small hoard. The colonnade was thought to belong to a large Roman building; clearly the limited space between the colonnade and the *via praetoria* requires a court plan, in which rooms were fronted by a portico.[69]

That find may be linked with a row of four foundations for columns which ran east–west in the centre of Commonhall Street, each consisting of broken cobbles in hard mortar. A stone plinth 1.25 m. square and 40 cm. deep was placed on each foundation to receive the column base, a style of construction employed in the

[58] *J.C.A.S.* [1st ser.], iii. 76 and plan, 106.
[59] Watkin, *Roman Ches.* 151.
[60] Ibid. The east–west dimension is governed by the space covered by the barrack group postulated above.
[61] There has been confusion in the past concerning these identical inscriptions. The stone from Welsby's is *R.I.B.* i, no. 470. The other (ibid. no. 469) is lost.
[62] Watkin, *Roman Ches.* 151, 205.
[63] *Gent. Mag.* ccv (2), 609–11; Watkin, *Roman Ches.* 151, 237–8; *Coin Hoards*, v. 54, no. 157.
[64] Some of the hoard found its way to the Grosvenor Mus.: J. T. Davies and F. W. Longbottom, 'Cat. of Roman Coins in Chester Mus.' *J.C.A.S.* xxiv. 156. The coins run from

Gordian III to the Tetrici.
[65] Watkin, *Roman Ches.* 152.
[66] *J.C.A.S.* [1st ser.], i. 202–3, 431; *R.I.S.S.* nos. 169–70; Watkin, *Roman Ches.* 191–2.
[67] Horsley, *Britannia Romana*, Ches. v. 316. It was thought to have been lost, but may have been rediscovered at Upholland (Lancs.): B. J. N. Edwards, 'A Chester Mithraic Figure Recovered?', *J.C.A.S.* lx. 56–60.
[68] *J.C.A.S.* vi. 395–9; xiv. 251; *Proc. Soc. Antiq.* xviii. 96–7.
[69] The feature remained until 1906: *J.C.A.S.* xiii. 139–42. It was believed that the bases had been re-used.

basilica of the baths.[70] The columns were *c.* 2.75 m. apart. Other finds included an antefix, a column capital, and nearby a moulded stone marked ƆABVCINI.[71] 'Embedded in a thick wall at the same place' was a lead pig reading CAESARIS [　] NI[ ]VADON.[72] The meaning of the inscription is unknown.

The finds in Commonhall Street belong to a second building incorporating colonnades at least 40 m. north–south, a little less than the southern building. Two finds apparently associated with the same building were the drum of a column found nearly 55 m. west of Bridge Street, and a capital revealed by building behind no. 34. Both finds reinforce the impression of the building's monumental scale;[73] the capital, however, initially assigned to the composite order, was unfinished.[74] The colonnade at the Grotto has never been seen further south; a Roman colonnade shown on a plan of no. 36 Bridge Street,[75] *c.* 13.7 m. west of the street frontage, was apparently an extrapolation from the Grotto find.

Rebuilding at Messrs. Woods (no. 38 Bridge Street) is said to have revealed many Roman tiles with legionary stamps, one of the two-line type, brick *pilae*, and walls.[76] North of Commonhall Street a wall 1.06 m. thick with a step-like stylobate finish along the top was found facing east slightly above street level behind nos. 24 and 26 Bridge Street, *c.* 12 m. west of the frontage.[77] Whether that wall relates to the finds under Commonhall Street and the Grotto is uncertain. It is sometimes supposed that Commonhall Street represents a minor street in the fortress plan,[78] but there is no supporting evidence and it seems very likely that the independent column foundations found in Commonhall Street came from the internal arcading of a basilica. Clearly at least one and probably two buildings of some architectural presence[79] occupied much the same space on the west side of the *via praetoria* as the baths on the east, roughly 80 m. square. There is evidence of a widespread fire, but no sign of subsequent repair or rebuilding. Since there has been so little excavation no firm conclusions are possible, although the work in Bolland's Court suggests that the southern building was built in the early 3rd century. Until then that part of the fortress may have been occupied by timber buildings, perhaps latterly lying vacant.

Between the *principia* and the range of barracks east of it lay structures about which little is known. Part of a tile floor of herringbone pattern and a fragment of a black and white tessellated pavement were found *c.* 30 m. east of Northgate Street and *c.* 55 m. north of Eastgate Street.[80] In the next building to the south a hypocaust with sandstone *pilae* and fragments of its floor was found, associated with a wall 70 cm. wide with a course of tile *c.* 60 cm. above its base.[81] Recent investigation revealed only slight traces of Roman levels.[82] An apse *c.* 15 m. to the east was built of masonry and tile, resting on a floor of thick concrete and large tiles, the inner surface being covered with three grades of plaster;[83] it presumably formed part of a baths suite. A concrete floor, over which a number of finds were made, was traced

[70] *Jnl. Brit. Arch. Assoc.* v. 230; *J.C.A.S.* [1st ser.], iii. 51, 58; Watkin, *Roman Ches.* 147.

[71] *R.I.B.* i, no. 469; *J.C.A.S.* [1st ser.], iii. 125. It is not a conventional centurial stone and was initially identified as a cornice moulding. It was lost in a fire in 1862. *R.I.B.* i, no. 470 names the same centurion: *J.C.A.S.* vii. 25.

[72] *Jnl. Brit. Arch. Assoc.* v. 225–6, 230; ibid. N.S. iv. 274–5; *Arch. Jnl.* xvi. 31; xxxiv. 145; *R.I.S.S.* no. 198; Watkin, *Roman Ches.* 161; *J.R.S.* xxi. 258 n. 1; *Flints. Hist. Soc. Trans.* xiii. 22–3.

[73] *J.C.A.S.* xxxviii. 176; xli. 85; *R.I.S.S.* p. 57 and plate 47 (c).

[74] *J.C.A.S.* lvii. 14 n. 21.

[75] Ibid. xlv. 3.

[76] Watkin, *Roman Ches.* 119, 152; *Jnl. Brit. Arch. Assoc.* N.S. i. 75.

[77] Lawson, 'Schedule', no. xxx.

[78] e.g. Nash-Williams, *Roman Frontier in Wales*, fig. 15.

[79] Described by Foote Gower as 'grand and public edifices'.

[80] *J.C.A.S.* [1st ser.], iii. 32, 39; Watkin, *Roman Ches.* 157; Lawson, 'Schedule', no. XVIII.

[81] *J.C.A.S.* v. 105–8, 130; *Jnl. Brit. Arch. Assoc.* xlix. 298–303 and plan.

[82] *Ches. Arch. Bull.* iv. 26.

[83] *Reliquary and Illustrated Archaeologist*, N.S. vi. 111–14.

from the apse to Godstall Lane.[84] A hypocaust with radiating flues lay at the south-west part of the site, in the angle of Northgate Street and Eastgate Street.[85] All those discoveries probably belong to the same building, whose east–west extent was c. 50 m.; its north–south measurement is unknown but the equivalent building at Caerleon, tentatively identified as stables, occupied a site c. 43 m. by 73 m. over all.[86] The building at Chester was probably residential, perhaps the legate's quarters; it has yielded inscribed lead water pipes[87] similar to that from the 'elliptical building',[88] and originally forming an east–west main. The length uncovered was 5 m., with joints between 2.1 and 2.5 m. apart. Each pipe bore an identical inscription on a slightly raised panel: naming Vespasian and Titus, and Agricola as *legatus Augusti*, it dates the pipes to the first half of A.D. 79.[89] Chester is unique in possessing inscribed water pipes: it is not clear whether the text is a building inscription or, if so, whether it was intended to be seen.[90] It is likely that the pipes lay within the building discussed above, for the find spot lay c. 50 m. east of Northgate Street and c. 23 m. north of Eastgate Street.[91]

Roman buildings north of the range between the *principia* and the east defences are largely overlain by the cathedral and related structures. A coin hoard estimated as 'a bucket full' in quantity, found in the cellar of no. 40 or 42 Northgate Street, may belong to the building described above.[92] During excavation of the foundations for the war memorial in St. Werburgh Street an ashlar wall 1.2 m. thick was found 11 m. south of the cathedral, with another 1.5 m. south of it. The walls lay roughly east–west; architectural fragments were also found, not necessarily Roman.[93] Excavation of a tree hole outside Barclay's Bank revealed a sandstone wall on the same alignment c. 60 cm. wide, which resembled Roman structures encountered elsewhere in the city.[94] A gold coin of Valentinian I was found near the cathedral.[95]

Restoration of the Lady Chapel revealed concrete foundations which may have been Roman, one of which ran under the south-east buttress of the chapel. A drain, also thought to be Roman, ran under the east wall.[96] A coin of Domitian and a centurial stone reading 'Century of Quintus Maximus' were found in it.[97] The only other find within the cathedral was of fragments of pottery discovered in excavating through the floor of the crypt; all were Flavian.[98] East of the Chapter House a drain tall enough for a man to stand in ran east and then south-east from the remains of the abbey and may be Roman but more probably was associated with the monastic buildings.[99] A fragment of an inscription found behind the King's School read MIIC or probably MEC.[1]

A large site between Princess Street and Hunter Street, extending c. 75 m. east-west from the Masonic Hall towards Northgate Street, was investigated before development as a bus exchange point and library. In the 1st century and for much

[84] *J.C.A.S.* vii. 188, 205; viii. 82–7; *Proc. Soc. Antiq.* xviii. 93–6. The apse is described as having alternating courses of tiles and masonry: Lawson, 'Schedule', no. xx.

[85] *J.C.A.S.* xxvii. 190.

[86] Boon, *Isca*, 15 and plan.

[87] *J.C.A.S.* vii. 86, no. 199; viii. 87–93; *Reliquary and Illustrated Archaeologist*, N.S. vi. 111–14; vii. 45–8; *Proc. Soc. Antiq.* xviii. 97–8; Lawson, 'Schedule', no. XXII.

[88] *Britannia*, ii. 292–3, no. 17; above.

[89] *R.I.S.S.*, pp. 48–9, no. 199.

[90] The pipe from the 'elliptical building' showed signs of weathering.

[91] The suggestion (*J.C.A.S.* xxxviii. 17) that the piping originally lay under or near the Flavian *via principalis* seems unlikely.

[92] Lawson, 'Schedule', no. XVII. It is said to have contained

both small and large bronze coins. One coin of Antoninus Pius survives: *J.C.A.S.* xxvii. 169.

[93] *J.R.S.* xi. 204–5; Lawson, 'Schedule', no. xv. The latter mentions cobble foundations.

[94] *Ches. Arch. Bull.* ii. 18.

[95] *T.H.S.L.C.* i. 68; Watkin, *Roman Ches.* 239.

[96] *J.C.A.S.* [1st ser.], iii. 254; N.S. iii. 90; Watkin, *Roman Ches.* 116, 124; Lawson, 'Schedule', no. XIV. The description of 'large pebbles firmly set in a bed of cement' makes a Roman date seem likely.

[97] *R.I.B.* i, no. 473; *Arch. Jnl.* xli. 175–6. It was doubted whether this was the stone found in 1868.

[98] *J.C.A.S.* xxxvi. 68–9.

[99] Watkin, *Roman Ches.* 115–16 and refs. cited therein; Lawson, 'Schedule', no. XI.

[1] *Arch. Jnl.* xlv. 181; *R.I.B.* i, no. 570. The stone is lost.

of the 2nd the space was unoccupied, and rubbish accumulated until in the later 2nd century a timber structure 15 m. by 5 m., and 2 m. deep, was built and soon afterwards dismantled again. Early in the 3rd century a large building with foundations 1 m. wide and nearly 2 m. deep was erected on a site measuring c. 35 m. east–west and at least 72 m. north–south. About a century later the building was repaired or modified, and some parts remained in use until the end of the 4th century: among the finds was a gold solidus of Magnentius. Immediately to the east lay a long narrow building c. 8 m. wide and at least 85 m. long, which had partition walls at c. 5 m. intervals.[2]

On the site of the Odeon Cinema a wall running east–west was traced for 15.25 m.; with it was associated an *opus signinum* floor. A substantially built drain was traced for 7.3 m.[3] Some pottery was 3rd- or 4th-century in date,[4] and three out of six coins found were 4th-century. Close by in Hunter Street a small hoard of eleven 4th-century bronze coins and a bronze finger-ring were found.[5] On the adjacent Folliott House site north of the Odeon an east–west wall, presumably belonging to the building revealed on the Odeon site, was found c. 2 m. south of the barracks.[6]

STREETS. The general disposition of the major streets of the fortress is better known than their size and construction. At Caerleon, where such details can better be tested, the *via principalis* and *via praetoria* were c. 7.5 m. wide. As at Inchtuthil, they were probably lined with *tabernae*.[7] The *via principalis* at Caerleon had a central sewer 0.5 m. wide and 1.3 m. deep, in addition to side drains,[8] and in Chester the discovery of a sewer under the Eastgate 'as high as a common man, and wide enough to drive a wheelbarrow in', suggests similar provision there. Best known is the intervallum road, alternatively called the rampart road or *via sagularis*, of which lengths have been examined at Abbey Green and on the site of the Northgate Brewery. At the latter the road was found to be up to 5.5 m. wide. A kerb marked its outer edge, and three surfaces were apparent.[9] East of the north gate at Abbey Green the street was bounded by a kerb on the north and a stone-lined drain on the south, the latter initially of timber. The street was c. 6 m. wide, and was resurfaced more than once.[10] At St. Martin's Fields the rampart road was c. 4 m. wide, with a kerb on the west side, and on the east side a stone-lined drain with capstones still in position. Both features appeared on the Woolworth's (Eastgate Street) site and the kerb also at Newgate Street on the south side of the fortress. At Newgate Street and Northgate Street three surfaces were apparent; at St. Martin's Fields four, the kerb having been resited more than once; the earliest surface was offset c. 3 m. to the west. Sandstone, cobbles, and gravel were all used as road material.

Of the minor streets those bounding the *principia* to north and west were typical. The former was 6.4 m. wide; between the eaves-drip gutters which lined it, the ground was completely occupied by the street surfacing which was built up as a layer of sandstone with sand above clean natural sand. The number of surfaces varied, no doubt resulting from patching, but there were always at least three, and crushed tile was used as well as more conventional materials.[11] The street west of

[2] *J.C.A.S.* lxv. 5–24; *Britannia*, xiv. 297.

[3] *J.C.A.S.* xxxiii. 49–63.   [4] e.g. ibid. fig. 10 (11).

[5] Ibid. 61. Only 10 coins were identified: Constantine I, Constantinian (2), Valentinian I, and Valens (6).

[6] *J.R.S.* xlvi. 125, fig. 25.

[7] At Chester a width of c. 18.3 m. was postulated for the *via praetoria*: P. H. Lawson and J. T. Smith, 'The Rows of Chester: Two Interpretations', *J.C.A.S.* xlv. 1–31. For Caerleon *see* Boon, *Isca*, 25.   [8] Boon, *Isca*, fig. 10.

[9] Davey, *Chester Northgate Brewery Phase I*, 4–6.

[10] *Britannia*, vii. 321; *New Evidence*, plan on end paper; *J.C.A.S.* lxiii. 17–19.

[11] *J.C.A.S.* lvii. 17. Tile surfacing has also been noted at Caerleon: Boon, *Isca*, 25.

the *principia* also had at least three surfaces. The earliest was a 7.5 cm. spread of gravel laid directly on the natural surface: it was completely covered by a second road 10–20 cm. thick formed of gravel on cobbles or crushed sandstone rammed hard, which showed cart ruts. A third surface of tightly-packed fine gravel on a massive bottoming 15.25–17.75 cm. deep seemed to be confined to the east side, and was sealed by a layer of sand associated with reconstruction in the early 3rd century.[12]

THE STATUS OF ROMAN CHESTER

Early antiquaries made no clear distinction between civil and military aspects of Roman Chester, although recognizing its connexion with the army and particularly with Legio xx. The statement that '*Deva* was from first to last a fortress' without 'organized civic life and municipal institutions' while providing a necessary corrective at the time now appears over-simplified.[13] That two altars give *Deva* as the place of origin of the dedicator[14] seems to imply that at some time later but before A.D. 212 the civil settlement was raised to the status of either a *colonia* or a *municipium*.[15] Such a chartered town could have coexisted with the fortress, as at York.[16] In practice the evidence from Chester does not indicate a large or prosperous civil settlement,[17] and there is no known instance of the promotion of *canabae* to fully independent communities before the time of Severus.[18] The name *Deva* is by no means unique to Chester,[19] and it seems likely that the inscriptions, from Germania Superior and Gallia Belgica, refer to another place of the same name.[20] It has also been suggested that an inscription from Chester may represent a public record of a legislative transaction or imperial edict relating to the *canabae*, perhaps put up at the creation of a chartered town.[21] The style and scale of the inscription lend it an 'official' air, while it resembles none of the stereotyped military inscriptions, yet it must be admitted that too little of the text survives to confirm the theory. The lettering is 2nd-century, perhaps as early as the Hadrianic period; links with the 'elliptical building'[22] or with a short-lived 'demilitarization' of the fortress[23] cannot be sustained.

When the province of Britain was divided under Severus, *Deva* apparently lay in Britannia Superior. A further subdivision into four provinces took place a century later, with a fifth, Valentia, being subsequently added.[24] If Valentia comprised north Wales, much of central Wales, and northern England west of the Pennines, Chester was very suitable as its administrative centre,[25] though there is no direct evidence of such a change in function other than the abandonment of some barracks and granaries in the later 3rd century and the continued existence of major buildings which could be used by the civil authorities. If the site was thus vacated by the

---

[12] *J.C.A.S.* xxxviii. 8–9.
[13] Ibid. v. 353.
[14] From Worms (*C.I.L.* xiii. 6221) and Trier (*Revue Archéologique*, 5th ser. i. 370, no. 70).
[15] *J.C.A.S.* xxxvi. 175. An alternative suggestion is that *Deva* became the *civitas* capital of the Cornovii: *Britannia*, xiii. 255.
[16] The *canabae* at York became a *colonia*, possibly under Severus. The *coloniae* of Colchester, Lincoln, and Gloucester occupied the sites of abandoned fortresses.
[17] Nash-Williams, *Roman Frontier in Wales*, 40.
[18] D. J. P. Mason, '*Canabae* and *Vici* of Roman Brit.' (Liverpool Univ. Ph.D. thesis, 1985), 489.

[19] Rivet and Smith, *Place Names of Roman Brit.* 337.
[20] The writer owes this suggestion to Professor Frere.
[21] *J.C.A.S.* lvii. 24–6; *R.I.B.* i, no. 462.
[22] N. Reed, 'Cartimandua in Chester?' *Studien zu den Militärgrenzen Roms*, 41–3.
[23] *Roman West in 3rd Cent.* 416.
[24] Frere, *Britannia*, 240–3; P. Salway, *Roman Brit.* 316–17, 392–3.
[25] *Britannia*, xiii. 253–60. Valentia, under an earlier and unknown name, was apparently established after compilation of the Verona List (A.D. 312–14) but before 367. The change in name took place in 369.

army to provide a new provincial capital, any military garrison restored later did not necessarily displace the civilian administrators, for in the late Roman world distinctions between military and civil sites became increasingly blurred.[26]

THE EXTRA-MURAL AREA

The civil settlement which grew up outside the walls of the fortress was doubtless inhabited mainly by merchants and others attracted by the ready market provided by five thousand relatively well paid soldiers. The dependents of soldiers probably formed an increasing proportion of the civilian population, particularly after soldiers were permitted to marry on service and the pool of possible brides was increased by the *constitutio Antoniniana*. Not all extramural buildings necessarily belonged to the civil settlement, and those which were military or official will be described first.

The Amphitheatre

The amphitheatre was placed between the south-east corner of the fortress and the steep slope to the river bank. Its site remained unknown until 1929, when a chance discovery led to its recognition and eventually to the excavation and conservation of its northern half.[27]

In form the amphitheatre consisted of an elliptical arena surrounded by banks of seating: the two major entrances to the arena were at the 'narrow' north and south ends, and smaller entrances gave access to the seating. The earliest amphitheatre was of timber, and the bank of seating was only 13.2 m. wide, much narrower than that of the later stone amphitheatre. The arena, however, remained the same size throughout, measuring 57.91 m. by 48.76 m.

The change of garrison from Legio II Adiutrix to Legio XX was followed by reconstruction *c*. A.D. 90–110. Although the new building was mainly of stone its seating was probably placed partly on timber staging. Its size was nearly 100 m. by 84 m., and it held *c*. 7,000 spectators.[28] It is much larger than the only other known from a British fortress, at Caerleon. Since the minimum number of seats was presumably determined by the establishment of the legion, any excess capacity may imply that civilians or veterans from the *canabae* were allowed to attend some of the entertainments, the surplus of seats indicating the likely civilian audience. Military amphitheatres are thought to have been intended primarily for the garrison although their supposed use for training is doubtful.[29] A wooden platform in the arena, measuring 6 m. by 3 m., probably formed part of the staging for ceremonial and religious occasions which took place there.

With maintenance including a re-flooring of the east entrance, the amphitheatre continued in use throughout the 2nd century. It lay neglected during much of the 3rd: dark loam which accumulated in the arena contained pottery of Antonine to 3rd-century date, with coins to the 270s. The building was restored in the last quarter of the 3rd century, when the loam in the arena was sealed by flagging;

[26] It has been surmised that Chester was the headquarters of the *Dux Britanniarum*, and also the seat of an ecclesiastical metropolitan in the late or post-Roman period: *Britannia*, xiii. 253–60; *Current Arch.* viii (1), no. 84.6.

[27] *J.C.A.S.* xxviii. 218–19; R. Newstead and J. P. Droop, 'Roman Amphitheatre at Chester', ibid. xxix. 5–40; ibid. 66–8; F. H. Thompson, 'Excavation of Roman Amphi-

theatre at Chester', *Archaeologia*, cv. 127–239.

[28] Probably a conservative estimate. It is based on an allocation of 60 cm. per spectator; the estimated capacity of the amphitheatre at Caerleon (*c*. 83 m. by 69 m.) of *c*. 6,000 was based on 45 cm. per place, and at that ratio Chester's capacity was more than 9,000 spectators.

[29] *Archaeologia*, cv. 142–3.

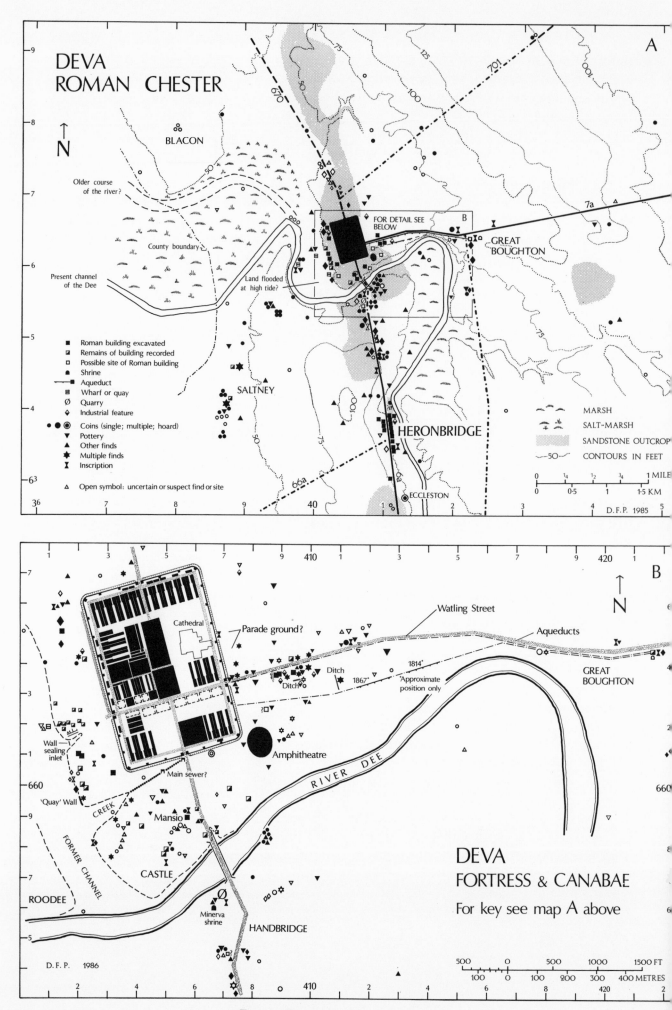

A

DEVA ROMAN CHESTER

↑ N

BLACON

Older course
of the river?

County boundary

Present channel
of the Dee

FOR DETAIL SEE
BELOW

B

GREAT
BOUGHTON

7a

Land flooded
at high tide?

■ Roman building excavated
▣ Remains of building recorded
□ Possible site of Roman building
▪ Shrine
— Aqueduct
▣ Wharf or quay
Ø Quarry
◇ Industrial feature
● ◉ Coins (single; multiple; hoard)
▼ Pottery
▲ Other finds
✦ Multiple finds
Ⅰ Inscription

△ Open symbol: uncertain or suspect find or site

SALTNEY

HERONBRIDGE

◉ ECCLESTON

⌇⌇ MARSH
🌿 SALT-MARSH
▨ SANDSTONE OUTCROP
⋯50⋯ CONTOURS IN FEET

0   ¼   ½   ¾   1 MILE
0   0.5   1   1.5 K.M

D.F.P. 1985

B

↑ N

Watling Street

Aqueducts

Cathedral

Parade ground?

Ditch
1867'

Ditch

1814'
'Approximate
position only

GREAT
BOUGHTON

Amphitheatre

RIVER DEE

Wall
sealing
inlet

Main sewer?

660   660

'Quay' Wall

CREEK

Mansio

FORMER CHANNEL

CASTLE

ROODEE

Ø
Minerva
shrine

HANDBRIDGE

DEVA
FORTRESS & CANABAE

For key see map A above

D.F.P.   1986

500   0   500   1000   1500 FT
100   0   100   200   300   400 METRES

FIG. 29. Roman Chester and its Environs.

thereafter use is thought to have continued until *c*. A.D. 350. The periods of the amphitheatre's use and neglect do not coincide with those of the fortress.[30]

The Supposed Mansio

An important Roman building was situated in Castle Street, south of the fortress.[31] It was at first built of timber, with external verandas and probably a courtyard. Erected between A.D. 75 and 80, it was soon destroyed by fire and replaced by a second somewhat larger building which was demolished at the end of the 1st century. A third timber building replaced it, to be demolished in its turn *c*. A.D. 120; the site lay vacant, and only *c*. A.D. 180 was a stone building completed on the site. A fire about a century later destroyed much or all of the building; the site was cleared and levelled for new structures, and occupation continued until at least the mid 4th century, when a well was back-filled, and the upper fills of a second well topped up with masonry from demolished walls. The similarity between the timber buildings found on the site and contemporary buildings within the fortress suggests that they were erected and maintained by the army. Significantly, a road led to the building from the south gate of the fortress. The suggested identification as a *mansio* or lodging house for officials using the *cursus publicus* rests mainly on the similarity of its plan to other *mansiones*. Its size, estimated at 65 m. or more east–west by 40–50 m. north–south, is larger than the *mansio* at Caerleon, where the longer side is not more than *c*. 30 m. An altar dedicated to the *numina* of the emperors erected in the 3rd-century building was re-used, broken, in its fourth stone phase. Such a dedication was appropriate for use by an imperial official.[32] Another type of building provided by the army outside fortresses, the market, was similar in layout, consisting of a courtyard surrounded by porticos, but most examples are at least twice the estimated size of the Chester building, and the painted wall-plaster and glazed windows with which it was provided in the third stone phase were far more appropriate to a residence than to a market. Nevertheless if the building was a *mansio* it is puzzling that at times it lay empty and derelict, and presumably unrequired. The approximate coincidence of its dereliction between *c*. A.D. 130 and *c*. A.D. 180 with the army's preoccupation with Scotland suggests a closer association with the legion and its activities than was usual for a *mansio*.

A *mansio* had its own suite of baths. A 'vault, wherein were many Roman tiles', found in the 17th century at Gamul House, was probably a hypocaust, and discovery at the same time of stamped legionary tiles with the *Deciana* suffix indicates repair in the mid 3rd century.[33] That date agrees with the major period of use of the *mansio*, although no repairs of that time were found in the part excavated. The use of legionary stamped tiles confirms that the building was official.[34] Another discovery related to the building was a 'great wall' against the north wall of St. Mary's rectory.[35] Part of the *mansio* courtyard was probably revealed at the corner of Castle Street and St. Mary's Hill. Four surfaces broadly corresponded to the known sequence; if the identification is correct it gives evidence of the size of the *mansio*

[30] In particular, the abandonment of the fortress in the late 3rd or early 4th cent. Coins of Victorinus and Carausius, however, came from fill which was later than the building's abandonment, and the only 4th-century coin was found in an unstratified context.

[31] D. J. P. Mason, *Excavations at Chester: 11–15 Castle Street and Neighbouring Sites, 1974–8*.

[32] *Britannia*, viii. 429, no. 16; xiii. 302–3.

[33] Watkin, *Roman Ches*. 117. Lawson, 'Schedule', no. XCI,

identifies the site, Mr. Recorder Whitby's house, as Gamul House.

[34] If Lawson was mistaken, an alternative site is the internal bath building, which yielded *Deciana*-type tile in 1942: *J.C.A.S.* xxxvi. 62–4. Tiles made by the army were, however, sometimes sold to civilians.

[35] Watkin, *Roman Ches*. 197; Lawson, 'Schedule', no. LIX; Mason, *Castle Street*.

from east to west.[36] At no. 76 Lower Bridge Street pottery of the late 1st and early 2nd century was found, together with a lead water pipe with graffiti.[37]

DEVA: CIVIL SETTLEMENT

Despite relatively little study of the civil settlement (*canabae*) at Chester there is sufficient evidence to permit some conclusions to be drawn.[38] Occupation east of the fortress seems predominantly domestic, with hints of industrial activity. While finds have been made over an extensive area, known structural remains are virtually confined to either side of Watling Street, and in the main consist of strip buildings similar to those found in other towns and settlements of Roman Britain. There is no evidence of public buildings such as a chartered town required. Occupation was most intensive in the Flavian–Antonine period, but the widespread destruction once postulated at the end of the 2nd century can probably be discounted. It has been suggested that the civil settlement was defended, but ditches found south of Foregate Street were not necessarily defensive and may not even be Roman. Even if they were both, they may belong to a construction camp or annexe associated with the Flavian fortress. The supposed *mansio*, the only building examined south of the fortress, more nearly approaches the larger dwellings of chartered towns of the province in size and sophistication, but is an official rather than a private residence. The ribbon development found east of the fortress did not recur on the road between its south gate and the river crossing, but another Roman building may lie beneath the castle. Roman buildings have been identified between the western defences of the fortress and the river. How many were privately owned is unknown, although it has been suggested that those immediately south of Watergate Street were used by the army. In addition to a large bath building extending from Watergate Street to Stanley Place there may have been another near Black Friars. A clay and turf bank at Greyfriars Court apparently erected *c.* A.D. 200 may have been an extension of the defences to protect the *canabae* west of the fortress; alternatively, it was perhaps designed to protect military extra-mural buildings. North of the fortress there have been relatively few finds and no buildings have been identified.

The Area East of the Fortress

The civil settlement is usually thought to have lain mainly east of the fortress. The line of Foregate Street coincides with that of the Roman road issuing from the east gate and proceeding eastwards towards Northwich and Manchester.[39] How far eastward the settlement extended is not clear: construction of the eastern section of the Inner Ring Road revealed pottery and an auxiliary cavalry bronze pendant, and on the east side of Dee Lane at the Bars much 2nd- and 3rd-century pottery was found.[40] In the latter instance, however, the material was thought to result from rubbish tipping, and in the former no structural finds were recorded. Those finds excluded, Roman buildings appear to extend no more than *c.* 250 m. east of the fortress defences. How far occupation spread north and south of Watling Street is difficult to estimate.

---

[36] *Britannia*, viii. 387.
[37] Ibid. 435, nos. 39, 41, 45; ix. 430; *Ches. Arch. Bull.* v. 28; *Roman Pottery Research*, 25.
[38] *New Evidence*, 29–40.
[39] Ibid. 31, fig. 1.
[40] *J.C.A.S.* xli. 85–8; *J.R.S.* xlvi. 151, no. 35 (a–b).

THE ROMAN PERIOD

At nos. 62–6 Foregate Street[41] traces of timber and masonry structures were revealed. The earlier of two floors associated with the former sealed scraps of Flavian samian, while clay and cobble wall footings were inserted through layers of make-up running into the Hadrianic–Antonine period.[42] No 3rd- or 4th-century material was found, and it is not clear to what period the masonry building belonged, though it was presumably Antonine or later. Its length north–south was at least 9 m.; its width was presumably much more than the 3 m. exposed.

On a second site in Foregate Street, west of the first,[43] the earliest timber structures were associated with Flavian–Trajanic pottery. Two stone buildings with clay floors, one also having *opus signinum* flooring, were in use *c.* A.D. 120–200. Towards the end of the 3rd century heavy stone make-up was laid, associated with the wall footings of a large but crudely constructed building which continued in use until at least the mid 4th century. Immediately west of those buildings lay a cobbled lane running north–south, with on its west side a branch of the aqueduct, consisting of clay water pipes. The 3rd-century hiatus in building does not mark a break in occupation: a small furnace for making nails was still operating then, and most of the coins from the site are 3rd-century. The two buildings were orientated north–south with their narrow ends facing Watling Street in a manner familiar from many Roman civil sites;[44] the strip buildings were probably 9–12 m. wide, and 30 m. or more long. On the site of C & A Modes, previously occupied by the Tatler cinema, no clear conclusions could be drawn;[45] trial holes on a site north of Foregate Street also proved largely negative except near the street frontage.[46]

Some sites on the south side of Foregate Street were prolific of finds. At the Chester Co-operative Society's store at the corner of Foregate Street and Love Street,[47] discoveries included a ditch 5.2 m. wide at the top and more than 1.8 m. deep, running north–south over 9 m. east of Love Street; *c.* 24.5 m. further east was a line of oak stakes similarly aligned.[48] Roman fills averaging 76 cm. in thickness contained much burnt wood and fine charcoal. The finds included nearly 800 samian sherds, but only one coin, of Domitian. The fill of the ditch contained samian and coarse pottery, as well as six large netting-needles.[49] Misgivings were later expressed about the interpretation and dating of what was seen.[50] A further extension to the store north of Forest Street revealed a heavily burnt area, apparently Roman, measuring *c.* 4.57 m. by 2.74 m., and much pottery was found dating from the Flavian period to the later 2nd century.[51]

The site of the ABC cinema west of Love Street[52] also contained a ditch, running nearly parallel to Foregate Street and *c.* 40 m. south of it. Cut into the natural boulder clay, it had a V-shaped profile with perhaps the hint of a cleaning-out slot at one point. The ditch was 2.2–2.6 m. wide and 1.36–1.43 m. deep. A second ditch was apparently cut parallel to and immediately south of the first; only one side of it was seen. The primary ditch-filling was a thin layer of discoloured clay with scraps of charcoal and pottery, with at the bottom a section of lead water pipe no less than 30 cm. in diameter; the remaining fill contained much charcoal, mussel shells, bones, and masses of broken pottery. The fill apparently dated from the first decade of the 2nd century and was certainly no earlier than the late Flavian period. It is

[41] F. H. Thompson, 'Excavation at 62–66 Foregate Street, 1956', *J.C.A.S.* xlvi. 62–8.
[42] Ibid. fig. 3, section B–C.
[43] J. B. Whitwell and S. M. McNamee, 'Excavations in Foregate Street', ibid. li. 1–19.
[44] Thompson, *Roman Ches.* 46.
[45] *J.C.A.S.* lviii. 134.
[46] *Ches. Arch. Bull.* vi. 61–2; *Britannia*, ix. 430.
[47] *J.C.A.S.* xxvii. 93–5.
[48] Ibid. xxix. 69.
[49] Ibid. xii. 91.
[50] Ibid. xxxiii. 113.
[51] Ibid. 114.
[52] Ibid. xxxiii. 83–5; *J.R.S.* xxvii. 231.

doubtful whether the ditch was associated with that found earlier east of Love Street. If it was military it may define an annexe attached to the Flavian fortress. Much pottery dating from the late 1st century to the Antonine period was found in the 'undisturbed strata' on both sides of the ditch, and construed as representing occupation. A feature paralleled in the earlier discoveries was a line of six stakes running east–west, associated with sherds of late 1st- and early 2nd-century pottery. In the south-eastern part of the site was a continuous layer composed largely of clay, burnt to a brick-red colour, and irregularly streaked and capped with much charcoal. Within that general spread, which may originally have been much more extensive, a burnt floor was defined measuring 4.57 m. north–south and 3.35 m. east–west, consisting of a sandstone rubble base capped by a spread of clay 7.6–12.7 cm. thick burnt to a brick-red colour, from which came an Antonine sherd.

A similar burnt floor was found on the site of the Tatler cinema.[53] The narrow frontage to Foregate Street was occupied by a spread of sandstone c. 30 cm. thick, resting on natural clay, set in and capped by clay fired to a brick-red colour: it was c. 6 m. wide north–south. The rubble base sealed a Trajanic–Hadrianic samian potter's stamp, and much pottery was found, mainly 1st- and 2nd-century. In contrast, the coins found included Postumus, Tetricus I, and Crispus, as well as Vespasian, Domitian, and Hadrian.[54]

The site of Marks and Spencer's store yielded 'a fair amount' of Roman pottery dating from the late 1st to the late 2nd century, but no structural remains of Roman buildings were observed.[55]

North of Foregate Street at Littlewoods' store finds included a 35 cm. layer 'heavily charged with pottery' ranging in date from the Flavian period to the late 3rd or 4th century.[56] Again there was no sign of structure. Another site north of Foregate Street, however, revealed roughly constructed walls; two black layers producing Flavian and Flavian–Trajanic pottery respectively were separated by clean sand.[57] The site was c. 230 m. east of the east gate, roughly opposite the ABC cinema.

The sites described present a limited but reasonably coherent and consistent picture. The working floors of roughly similar size imply industrial activity, a conclusion reinforced by the quantity of ash and burnt material on each site. What the industrial processes were remains conjectural, as no slag or other waste products were found, although evidence of iron-working was discovered later. If wooden structures existed on the sites recorded before the Second World War, they were not detected, and there were no masonry buildings.

Behind the main frontages south of Foregate Street, building at the telephone exchange west of St. John Street[58] produced few Roman finds apart from a possible side road serving the amphitheatre, with which was associated a small group of Flavian–Trajanic pottery. A later attempt to intercept the Roman road, however, revealed no Roman remains other than a pit.[59] Recent excavations[60] revealed a north–south road towards the east side of the site, below which was a ditch similarly aligned. West of the road lay a deep drain, probably at first stone-lined, on a different alignment. A clay spread on its east side may have been a floor, but there was no sign of structure. The drain may have been abandoned incomplete; pottery

[53] *J.C.A.S.* xxxiii. 64–5.
[54] The writer has not attempted to revise Newstead's dating of samian and coarse pottery in his reports, other than in a few instances where a published piece would now be dated differently; the reappraisal of the material finds from those sites would be most interesting and valuable.
[55] *J.C.A.S.* xxxvi. 75–8.
[56] Ibid. 78–81; *J.R.S.* xxviii. 180.
[57] *J.R.S.* xlvii. 208.
[58] *J.C.A.S.* xxxiii. 9–11.
[59] Ibid. xli. 89.
[60] Ibid. lviii. 41–6.

of the late 1st century came from high in the fill. A number of stake- and post-holes of that period formed no clear pattern, and while there were hints of industrial activity nearby the general impression was of a low level of occupation. Stratified material from the build-up of Roman levels ranged from the last quarter of the 1st century to the mid 2nd, and the unstratified material was almost entirely earlier than the 3rd century. The simple and short-lived occupation may suggest that the site was reserved for a major extra-mural building which was not built. The size of the drain suggests a bath-building, which a branch of the aqueduct[61] may have been intended to serve. A spread of sandstone fragments often over 1 ft. (30 cm.) thick towards the western part of the site may be debris from construction of, or repairs to, the fortress wall. The road perhaps marked the eastern edge of an area outside the defences in which building was not permitted, in order to preserve a clear field of fire for the garrison. On a site between Frodsham Street and the city walls, a zone 9 m. wide beyond the fortress ditch was defined on the east by a low bank 6 m. wide. East of that lay successive spreads of sandstone metalling covering an area at least 28 m. north–south, and possibly more than 24.5 m. east–west, interpreted as surfacing of the parade-ground. Nowhere within the area was there any sign of encroachment by civilian buildings of the *canabae*.[62] Building nearby appears to have revealed the same surfacing, with finds of the Roman period.[63]

The remaining evidence for the area immediately outside the eastern defences of the fortress is derived from finds made by chance. On the site of the City Baths, Union Street, Roman material, including a quantity of samian, was found; a ditch[64] ran approximately north–south for 65.5 m., and was described as roughly U-shaped, 2.1 m. wide at the top narrowing to 91 cm., and on average 3.35 m. deep. There is no evidence that the ditch was defensive. The same ditch, seen again 56 m. south of Foregate Street, and *c.* 365 m. east of the fortress,[65] produced 1st- and 2nd-century samian, and some oak paddles came from a dark peaty fill towards the bottom.

A cobbled pavement was observed in advance of the present building line north of Foregate Street, and close to it a length of lead water pipe. The finds were not certainly Roman, though samian sherds were found under the paving.[66] More samian came from the same site, and from the shop to the west, together with a 'cinerary urn' and bronze objects. In the same area was found a fragment of an inscription cut on a slate slab apparently used as paving.[67] The findspot lay between the junctions of Seller Street and City Road with Foregate Street. Several coins of Vespasian, possibly a small hoard, were found at the junction of Foregate Street and Seller Street during the excavation of a cellar, together with a cream-coloured 'lachrymatory', perhaps the container of the hoard.[68] Apart from the fragment mentioned above the only inscription from the area east of the fortress is a sandstone altar.[69] It has an unusual dedication, in which Jupiter is linked with a Celtic god probably to be equated with Taranis.[70] The dedicator was *princeps*, second senior centurion, of Legio xx; his senior rank, the first element of the dedication, and the dating of the inscription to A.D. 154, combine to give it a quasi-official air. The findspot was approximately at the junction of Foregate Street and St. John Street.[71]

[61] Below.

[62] *Arch. Newsletter*, ix. 14; *J.R.S.* lvii. 179–80.

[63] *J.C.A.S.* xxvii. 191; Lawson, 'Schedule', no. LXXXIX.

[64] *J.C.A.S.* viii. 93–100; *Reliquary and Illustrated Archaeologist*, N.S. vii. 48.

[65] *J.R.S.* xxviii. 180–1.

[66] Lawson, 'Schedule', no. LXVIII.

[67] Ibid. no. LXXXII; *R.I.B.* i, no. 462; above.

[68] Hemingway, *Hist. Chester*, ii. 353. It is difficult to accept the interpretation of the find as a burial: Watkin, *Roman Ches.* 219.

[69] *R.I.B.* i, no. 452; *J.R.S.* lvi. 229. 1648 was suggested as the date of discovery: Watkin, *Roman Ches.* 165–6.

[70] R. G. Collingwood, 'Jupiter Tanarus', *J.C.A.S.* xxvi. 154–61; M. J. Green, 'Tanarus, Taranis, and the Chester Altar', ibid. lxv. 37–44.

[71] Lawson, 'Schedule', no. XLIX.

Some finds from Foregate Street were made at inns: the Brewers' Arms,[72] the Old Queen's Head[73] (1st–4th-century coins), the Hop Pole hotel,[74] and the Ring o' Bells (late 1st- and early 2nd-century pottery).[75] Smaller casual finds in and near Foregate Street include an *aureus* of Titus from the corner of Love Street,[76] and others of Titus and Nero.[77] Although the finds tend to be 1st- or 2nd-century, with little of the 3rd or 4th, later items include a coin of Tetricus I from the Little Dolphin,[78] one of Victorinus,[79] and two of Constantinopolis.[80] A 'knee' brooch of Collingwood's Group V, of the later 2nd or 3rd century, was found at Lloyds Bank.[81] Finds other than pottery and coins include querns,[82] a spindle whorl from Love Street,[83] a seal-box from the site of the Old Brewers' Arms,[84] and a lamp found west of Frodsham Street.[85] The site of the Lord Raglan hotel in the same street 'proved rich in material finds';[86] many fragments of 1st- and 2nd-century pottery came from the site of the Gaumont Picture Palace, Brook Street, a little further south.[87] Other finds away from the main cluster along Foregate Street include Roman pottery of the late 1st and early 2nd century from a site in Queen Street, mostly unstratified because of later disturbance,[88] and an *aureus* of Domitian from the north end of Queen Street.[89] Finds are recorded from the southern end of City Road including samian and a coin of Trajan,[90] and a sherd of an amphora bearing a stamp of the mid 2nd century was found at Parker's Buildings.[91] At Thomas Street, near the former cattle market, *c.* 150 m. east of the north-east angle of the fortress,[92] signs of iron working were discovered; Roman pottery from the area was not necessarily associated with the industrial activity. A samian bowl of form Dr. 29, possibly pre-Flavian, was found in St. Anne Street in 1914.[93]

South of Foregate Street finds near St. John's church include a *denarius* of Gordian III found in digging a grave on the north side of the churchyard,[94] a box tile,[95] a lamp,[96] amphora sherds with graffiti,[97] and from the former bishop's palace (Y.M.C.A. hostel) pottery dating from *c.* A.D. 140 to the later 3rd century.[98] A sewer trench in Vicar's Lane near the church revealed stones with mouldings, including the base of a small altar, as well as coins and samian.[99] Pottery, an antefix, stamped tiles, marble, glass, and samian were found near Vicar's Lane,[1] and a lead lamp-holder[2] and Roman pottery including samian of the Domitianic–Hadrianic period in the Grosvenor Park.[3] A quantity of samian was recovered from a site at the corner of Love Street and Vicar's Lane in 1892,[4] and a samian cup (Dr. 33) seems to have come from that general area in 1900.[5] A sherd of decorated samian from St. John's churchyard was in F. H. Williams's collection.

The Roman road eastward from the east gate of the fortress was exposed in

---

[72] Lawson, 'Schedule', no. LXVIII; *J.C.A.S.* xxxvi. 138; 22 coins and a quantity of samian were in the F. H. Williams Colln. in the Grosvenor Mus.

[73] *J.C.A.S.* xxvi. 16; xxxvi. 87–94.

[74] Finds included a small fragment of a mosaic floor, as well as 1st- and 2nd-century pottery: ibid. xxxvi. 81–7; xlvii. 35.

[75] Ibid. xxxvi. 95–9.

[76] Ibid. xlix. 60.

[77] Watkin, *Roman Ches.* 238–9; 1 *Sheaf*, ii. 89.

[78] *J.C.A.S.* xxiv. 151.

[79] Ibid. xxxvi. 150.

[80] Not precisely located: ibid. xxiv. 153.

[81] Ibid. xlv. 72.

[82] Ibid. iii. 200; xvii. 150.

[83] Ibid. xvi. 136.

[84] Nos. 61–3 Foregate Street: ibid. lxi. 31.

[85] Ibid. viii. 105; xii. 93. A samian vessel with stamp from Parry's Entry was in the F. H. Williams Colln.

[86] *J.C.A.S.* xxxvi. 59–61.

[87] Ibid. 72–3.

[88] Ibid. 70–2.

[89] Inf. from Dr. G. Lloyd-Morgan.

[90] *J.C.A.S.* xxvi. 13 (no. 3), 18 (no. 53), 24 (no. 111), 30 (no. 163); xxxvi. 148; *Ches. Arch. Bull.* ix. 101.

[91] *J.C.A.S.* xxx. 59; xxxi. 76.

[92] Ibid. xxxvi. 74–5. The street no longer exists.

[93] Ibid. xxvi. 11, no. 8.

[94] Ibid. N.S. i. 137; Watkin, *Roman Ches.* 240.

[95] *J.C.A.S.* [1st ser.], iii. 30.

[96] Watkin, *Roman Ches.* 207, 224.

[97] Ibid. 225–6; *Arch. Jnl.* xli. 176.

[98] *Ches. Arch. Bull.* v. 33–5.

[99] Watkin, *Roman Ches.* 186–7.

[1] *J.C.A.S.* N.S. ii. 5.

[2] Ibid. vi. 160–1.

[3] Ibid. xxxvi. 73. The F. H. Williams Colln. included a large pot found in laying out the park, *c.* 1867.

[4] In the F. H. Williams Colln.

[5] *J.C.A.S.* xxvi. 27, no. 139.

Foregate Street near the Eastgate.[6] At a depth of *c.* 1.5 m. a road described as 'roughly formed' of boulders, pebbles, and gravel about 12.7 cm. thick, was laid on a well consolidated sandstone rubble foundation *c.* 53 cm. thick. Immediately below it was another surface of gravel, flints, and boulders, laid upon a foundation of sandstone roach which was more compacted than the upper. The latter was thought to be Roman and produced an amphora sherd and a piece of Roman tile: possibly both surfaces were Roman. The lower was *c.* 2 m. below street level, and its foundation rested on natural clay at *c.* 2.2 m. Two surfaces were found earlier just outside the Eastgate, but their depths do not agree with those above.[7] At nos. 46–50 Foregate Street the southern edge of Watling Street was found *c.* 6 m. south of the modern kerb; two cobbled layers were seen and a side alley of which little survived.[8]

The Area South of the Fortress

The amphitheatre largely fills the gap between the south-east corner of the fortress and the bluffs overlooking the river; the finds described above lie roughly north-east of it, while a second and apparently distinct group of sites lies south of the fortress, and mainly west of Lower Bridge Street.[9] One of the few finds from its east side is a massive wall in Duke Street;[10] Roman pottery was recovered in the same street, and a samian cup (Dr. 27) with stamp has also been found.[11] A stone 'cupid' from Duke Street is not Roman.[12] First century 'urn-burials' said to have been found near St. Olave Street[13] may belong to a cemetery perhaps pre-dating the Flavian fortress. On the nearby site of St. Olave's school fragments of pottery and two coins, of Elagabalus and Constans, were found.[14] Recent excavations on the site of the Drill Hall, Duke Street, have shown traces of timber features, and evidence of a substantial Roman building nearby, with finds running in date at least to the end of the 4th century.[15] Occupation in the Lower Bridge Street area seems from the few recorded finds to have been slight[16] and it is unlikely that Watling Street south of the fortress was lined with buildings.[17] The only known Roman building occupied a sizeable site, bounded on the east by Watling Street and on the south by steeper ground.[18] The surfacing of a courtyard thought to belong to it was revealed at no. 25 Castle Street, at the corner with St. Mary's Hill.[19] Other finds from Castle Street are a coin of Claudius II[20] and a fragment of a Roman mirror.[21] The lower half of a figurine of Venus in white clay from St. Mary's Hill[22] and coins of Severus, Gratian,[23] Trajan, Hadrian, and Sabina have also been found.[24] A bronze bracelet from the north porch of the church was in the F. H. Williams Collection. A 'great wall' containing very large stones against the north wall of St. Mary's rectory was probably part of the *mansio*;[25] the top of a well was revealed at the same time.

Recent building in Shipgate Street has revealed a junction of Roman culverts of

[6] Ibid. v. 327–8.
[7] Ibid. [1st ser.], iii. 475; *T.H.S.L.C.* i. 82.
[8] *J.C.A.S.* li. 1.
[9] D. J. P. Mason, *Excavations in Chester: 11–15 Castle Street and Neighbouring Sites, 1974–8*, 85–7.
[10] Watkin, *Roman Ches.* 197; *J.C.A.S.* N.S. i. 185. The wall is thought to have resembled Roman work but there is no positive evidence of its date.
[11] *J.C.A.S.* xxvi. 22, no. 96.
[12] Ibid. [1st ser.], i. 198; Watkin, *Roman Ches.* 192; Lawson, 'Schedule', no. LXII.
[13] Ibid. no. XC, citing *Sheaf*: the ref. has not been verified.
[14] *J.C.A.S.* xxxvi. 118–19.

[15] *Ches. Arch. Bull.* ix. 50.
[16] Mason, *Castle Street*, 75–9.
[17] Ibid. 85; *Ches. Arch. Bull.* iii. 40.
[18] Above, the supposed *mansio*.
[19] Mason, *Castle Street*, 65–8; *Britannia*, viii. 387. Alternatively it may be a road on the W. side of the *mansio*.
[20] *Ches. Arch. Bull.* vi. 76.
[21] *J.C.A.S.* lxiii. 39.
[22] Watkin, *Roman Ches.* 220.
[23] *J.C.A.S.* xlv. 74.
[24] Watkin, *Roman Ches.* 240.
[25] *J.C.A.S.* [1st ser.], iii. 483; Watkin, *Roman Ches.* 197; Lawson, 'Schedule', no. LIX; Mason, *Castle Street*, 3.

the late 1st to early 2nd century and traces of a substantial Roman building of unknown function and plan. It occupied a riverside site, since it is believed that the river level may have been up to 2 m. higher in the Roman period than at present. The building was abandoned and demolished before the end of the Roman period.[26]

Between the *mansio* and the southern defences of the fortress a 'vase' and a flanged bowl were found on the site of the savings bank at the corner of Grosvenor Street and Castle Street.[27] A coin of Trajan came from the site of the Grosvenor Museum,[28] and from its extension a lead weight,[29] while an Antonine samian cup is recorded from the site of the Saddle inn at the corner of Bunce Street and Grosvenor Street.[30] Much pottery is said to have come from a cut for a water main near the museum, dating from the late 1st to late 2nd century.[31] A coin of Vespasian is recorded from Cuppin Street,[32] and six coins, possibly a small hoard, from Pepper Street include one of Constantine I and another of Valens.[33] A deep rock-cut channel reported from Pepper Street, continuing under Lamb Row and along Grosvenor Street and Cuppin Street,[34] is thought to have been the main sewer of the fortress, which presumably lay under the *via praetoria* and left the fortress by the south gate. Another such channel was apparently seen in St. John Street. The length found in Pepper Street may have carried waste water from the internal bath-building. Its outfall was presumably in the creek under Nuns' Field, which is known to have been an open sewer or watercourse in 1817.[35] The channel is said to have been *c.* 3-4 m. below the surface and wide enough for two men to walk abreast, with apertures at intervals presumably for the man-holes provided in Roman sewers for cleaning out.

WATLING STREET AND THE DEE CROSSING. Watling Street is generally thought to have followed the line of Lower Bridge Street between the south gate (*porta praetoria*) and a crossing place at or near the Old Dee Bridge, the best site for a ford or bridge.[36] A massive stone wall in Lower Bridge Street has been identified as the east edge of a causeway leading to a Roman bridge.[37] There is evidence of the filling of an inlet at that point during the Roman period,[38] and traces of the bridge are thought to have been found in 1984.[39] While the river can be forded, the inconvenience and delay caused by tide and weather probably prompted the building of a bridge, whose remains may have been incorporated into the earliest medieval bridge.[40]

The Area South-West of the Fortress

Finds made while preparing approaches for the Grosvenor Bridge included an ivory stylus, a denarius of Severus, 'a piece of Roman pottery, being the half of a female face in relief', perhaps part of a face jar,[41] a lead lamp-holder,[42] a lachrymatory, and several Roman coins and vessels found near the castle.[43] Near the new St. Bridget's church at the junction of Grosvenor Street and Castle Esplanade,

---

[26] *Ches. Arch. Bull.* ix. 57.

[27] *Arch. Camb.* 3rd ser. iv. 464; Watkin, *Roman Ches.* 216; Lawson, 'Schedule', no. LVIII; *J.C.A.S.* xxxvi. 108.

[28] *J.C.A.S.* xxiv. 122.

[29] Ibid. vii. 89, no. 207.

[30] With other finds: ibid. viii. 102; xxvi. 13, no. 9; Lawson, 'Schedule', no. LVIII.

[31] *J.C.A.S.* xxxvi. 107-8.

[32] Ibid. [1st ser], i. 199.

[33] Ibid. xliv. 54.

[34] Hemingway, *Hist. Chester*, ii. 356; *J.C.A.S.* [1st ser.], i. 461-2; N.S. i. 210-11; v. 33; *T.H.S.L.C.* i. 79-82; Watkin, *Roman Ches.* 115; Lawson, 'Schedule', no. L; *New Evidence*, 34, fig. 2; Mason, *Castle Street*, fig. 47.

[35] *J.C.A.S.* N.S. i. 77; Watkin, *Roman Ches.* 102.

[36] *J.C.A.S.* lix. 15-19.

[37] Ibid. xlvii. 34-5.

[38] *Ches. Arch. Bull.* v. 19-27.

[39] T. J. Strickland, 'Roman Heritage of Chester', *J.C.A.S.* lxvii. 25, 27, and plate 1.

[40] If the level of the river rose by as much as 2 m. during the Roman period (*Ches. Arch. Bull.* ix. 57) the crossing became increasingly difficult.

[41] *Gent. Mag.* xcix (1), 70; Lawson, 'Schedule', no. LVIII; Watkin, *Roman Ches.* 224.

[42] Watkin, *Roman Ches.* 207.

[43] Ibid. 216; *T.H.S.L.C.* xxviii. 71.

since demolished, an uninscribed altar was found among loose stones, with roofing tiles (some with legionary stamps), Roman coins, pottery, a brooch, a lead lamp, and the lid of a seal-box with enamelled decoration.[44] Part of a jet bracelet was found in Castle Esplanade,[45] and a coin of Maximian I near Grosvenor Bridge.[46]

At Chester castle part of a tessellated pavement was recorded before 1780.[47] Clearance of the outer bailey to make way for Thomas Harrison's new buildings revealed pottery, including several samian potters' stamps;[48] coins, mutilated inscriptions, and a tessellated pavement were said to have been discovered 'in the recent alterations at the castle',[49] and apparently some concrete foundations were revealed.[50] An *aureus* of Vespasian was found 'in making the foundations of the castle'.[51] Near the Julius Caesar or Agricola Tower part of a tombstone was revealed.[52] A legionary antefix was found at the castle[53] and a *denarius* of Severus and one of Elagabalus from the site of County Hall.[54] Second-century samian was found in or near County Hall.[55] An arch incorporated into the Agricola Tower, thought by some antiquaries to be Roman, is medieval.[56]

Close to the castle, in the Nuns' Field, Roman finds include coins of Trajan[57] and an *aureus* of Faustina.[58] A vase and terracotta lamp were found in a grave in the Nuns' Garden, and fragments of legionary stamped tiles, samian ware, and other pottery and glass have also been discovered.[59] Roman material has been recovered during recording of burials at the Benedictine nunnery of St. Mary, when traces of an *opus signinum* floor were seen, and a Roman 'stratum' 45.7 cm. thick underlying the nuns' graves produced samian and coarse pottery, chiefly of the 2nd century.[60] On the site of the county police headquarters much 2nd- and 3rd-century pottery was found, as well as an incomplete lead cover for a glass mirror, and fragments of a bronze mirror of 1st-century type.[61] No structures of the Roman period were seen, and the finds probably came from rubbish deposits.[62] An *aureus* of Nero is said to have been found in a field near Smith's Walk, Nicholas Street, near Captain Wrench's house.[63] As a Mr. Wrench owned Nuns' Field in 1803[64] that may have been the findspot of the coin.

The Area West of the Fortress

In Nicholas Street between Grey Friars and Black Friars a building *c.* 66 m. west of the fortress displayed several constructional phases, including two of timber.[65] Further west substantial traces of buildings include a hypocaust with brick *pilae* at the west end of Black Friars.[66] The walls were *c.* 90 cm. thick, and apparently the floor of the room was partially intact; the room was nearly 6 m. long, and had an

[44] Hemingway, *Hist. Chester*, ii. 351–2; Watkin, *Roman Ches.* 177, 207; *J.C.A.S.* lxi. 31.

[45] *J.C.A.S.* lxiv. 44, no. 11.

[46] Ibid. xlv. 74.

[47] Watkin, *Roman Ches.* 192. The find was made before Foote Gower's death in 1780. The record cannot be unreservedly accepted.

[48] *Jnl. Brit. Arch. Assoc.* v. 229–30; D. and S. Lysons, *Magna Britannia*, ii. 431; Watkin, *Roman Ches.* 225; Lawson, 'Schedule', no. LXXVIII.

[49] Ormerod, *Hist. Ches.* i. 295; Hemingway, *Hist. Chester*, ii. 351.

[50] The foundations are said to have been difficult to remove: Watkin, *Roman Ches.* 194–5. The discovery is dated *c.* 1790: Lawson, 'Schedule', no. LXXVIII.

[51] Hemingway, *Hist. Chester*, ii. 354; Watkin, *Roman Ches.* 239.

[52] *R.I.B.* i, no. 569; *Arch. Jnl.* xxxv. 73; xli. 188; xlv. 181; *Jnl. Brit. Arch. Assoc.* v. 214; Watkin, *Roman Ches.* 212.

[53] *J.C.A.S.* [1st ser.], i. 423 and fig.

[54] Ibid. xxxvi. 150; xliv. 53.

[55] Ibid. xliv. 53.

[56] Watkin, *Roman Ches.* 195.

[57] *J.C.A.S.* xlv. 74.

[58] Hemingway, *Hist. Chester*, ii. 354; Watkin, *Roman Ches.* 239.

[59] *Arch. Camb.* 3rd ser. iv. 464.

[60] *J.C.A.S.* xxxvi. 162–6.

[61] Ibid. lx. 49 and pl. 5.

[62] The record of discovery of a tessellated pavement in 1803 seems best disregarded: Watkin, *Roman Ches.* 192–4; *J.C.A.S.* vii. 90.

[63] Hemingway, *Hist. Chester*, ii. 355; Watkin, *Roman Ches.* 238.

[64] Watkin, *Roman Ches.* 192.

[65] *New Evidence*, 37, fig. 3; *Britannia*, vi. 240; *Ches. Arch. Bull.* iii. 41–2.

[66] Watkin, *Roman Ches.* 319–20; *T.H.S.L.C.* xxxix. 53–5; Lawson, 'Schedule', no. LXXVII.

apse at the west end. More than one major period of construction was probably seen, and stone *pilae* were found as well as hypocaust tiles; a coin of Constantine, with another unidentified, was found between the pillars of the hypocaust. The site is one of the few known to have produced a tile of Legio xx with a two-line stamp.[67] A section of wall possibly belonging to the same building was found *c.* 11 m. to the north, on the east side of City Walls Road. Repairs to the city walls *c.* 27 m. south of Black Friars revealed 1st- and 4th-century coins, Roman wall-plaster painted in various colours, Flavian–Trajanic samian, and a bronze strigil blade.[68] Nevertheless from observation at the west end of Black Friars the building evidently extended no further south.[69] Excavations at Grey Friars House revealed traces of a substantial building 30 m. north of the earlier finds.[70] At the west end of Grey Friars an *opus signinum* floor 15.25 m. wide, patched towards the east end with roofing tiles, was exposed in the road.[71] A site 25 m. north of Grey Friars revealed several phases of buildings, with occupation continuing into the 4th century;[72] buildings which may have been warehouses were demolished to make way for a clay and turf bank before the end of the 2nd century. To the east lay timber buildings replaced in stone in the 2nd century. Further north a timber building of the early 2nd century had a veranda on its south side, and some of its rooms were plastered and painted in imitation marble designs. Its life was short, as the rubbish and silt over it contained early 2nd-century material. Later the southern half of the site was covered with dumped clay which formed two terraces, on the lower of which was a stone building with projecting wings; it had been extensively robbed in the medieval period, but small patches of internal fills showed that occupation continued until at least the late 3rd century and possibly a century longer.[73] A lead ownership-tag inscribed COH I > ATTII ANTONI on both sides was found in Grey Friars.[74]

North of the buildings in Grey Friars lay an inlet which was blocked off and filled during the early 2nd century before the construction of a building on its north side.[75] Traces of timber construction, confined to the west side of the site, were dated to the late 1st century. The earliest stone building, dated to the early 2nd, consisted of a simple corridor or room *c.* 6 m. wide with no apparent internal divisions. In the easternmost section a succession of surfaces was noted immediately north of the building. Further west a tile-lined drain pre-dated a range of rooms added just before the mid 2nd century: they did not extend to the eastern end of the site. The building apparently fell out of use towards the end of the 2nd century. The first stone phase was probably Antonine and the second may have been short-lived.[76] The purpose of the building cannot be established with confidence. It may have been a storehouse, or perhaps a stable.

A building north of Watergate Street, possibly residential in character but usually identified as a bath-building perhaps for the use of the officers of the garrison, has been revealed on several occasions since the 18th century. House building in Watergate Flags revealed a hypocaust, tessellated pavement, and other finds, including an altar naming a legionary legate, T. Pomponius Mamilianus.[77] The tesserae of the pavement were blue, red, and white, unusual for Chester, where

[67] *Arch. Jnl.* xliv. 125.
[68] Lawson, 'Schedule', no. LXXVII.
[69] *Ches. Arch. Bull.* i. 21.   [70] Ibid. ix. 52.
[71] *J.C.A.S.* xxvii. 113; Lawson, 'Schedule', no. LV.
[72] *Britannia,* ix. 430; x. 292; *New Evidence,* 37; *Ches. Arch. Bull.* vi. 60–1; vii. 43.
[73] *Ches. Arch. Bull.* viii. 36–7; *Britannia,* xiii. 353.
[74] *Arch. Jnl.* xliv. 125–6.
[75] D. B. Kelly, 'Excavations at Watergate House, Chester,

1959', *J.C.A.S.* lii. 1–21.
[76] In Trench G what was thought to be the earliest floor sealed fill containing black-burnished pottery, and the same context in Trench H/J yielded Hadrianic–Antonine pottery.
[77] *R.I.B.* i, no. 445. He was probably the Mamilianus who was a friend of the younger Pliny. He was suffect consul in A.D. 100, and his appointment as commander of Legio xx was probably in the early 90s: A. Birley, *Fasti of Roman Brit.* 234–5. Another Mamilianus was suffect consul in A.D. 120.

simple black and white geometric patterns were the norm. Several stamped legionary tiles were found, and other roof tiles, one with a legionary stamp, were apparently found nearby during construction of the Linenhall, as well as more than 20 coins, one of Nero.[78] The find has been linked with the later discovery of a mortar floor about 15 cm. thick.[79] A hypocaust furnace arch and portions of floors are preserved in the cellar of the house at the corner of Watergate Street and City Walls.[80] A sewer from Stanley Place across City Walls Road and through the city wall cut into a Roman wall with tile coursing, presumably belonging to a hypocaust.[81] Fragments of wall plaster and *opus signinum* came from the city walls opposite the north-west end of Stanley Place,[82] and repairs to the city walls immediately north of the Watergate led to the recovery of tiles. A large quantity of tiles and Roman bricks came from the site of the Royal Infirmary *c.* 1759.[83] Extension of offices at the corner of Stanley Place and Stanley Street revealed further parts of the bath-building, which measured at least 90 m. north–south; its size east–west appears to be at least as much. Its south frontage was colonnaded: two column bases *c.* 4.5 m. apart were found under Stanley Street.[84] A square pillar was said to have been found in a Roman building on the site of Stanley Place.[85] Other discoveries nearby may belong to the building. In Watergate Street the massive foundations of a Roman wall about 1.8 m. thick were said to have been found near the last house on the north side.[86] A massive foundation of cobble and mortar 5.18 m. wide 11.57 m. east of the Watergate ran north–south, and was interpreted as the foundation of a retaining wall. A second wall was observed 9 m. west of the north-east corner of Watergate House.[87] A length of wall was found in Watergate Street in 1882, but its position is not known.[88] Some 7.5 m. south of the westernmost of those walls the foundation of what appeared to be the north-west corner of a Roman building, seen when the corner of the garden of Watergate House was removed,[89] consisted of glacial boulders set in very hard mortar,[90] and measured at least 2.28 m. by 1.83 m., the depth being at least 75 cm. It appears to stand in isolation, as nothing matching it was found in the garden.[91] It was perhaps Flavian: the base was sealed by a black layer containing charcoal, possibly derived from a hypocaust furnace, which produced a small group of late 2nd-century pottery. The location of another 3.65–4.26 m. of wall found in Watergate Street is unknown.[92] The bath-building was no later in date than the late 1st century, and from the description of the foundations may be as early as the internal baths; it presumably continued in use until at least the late 3rd century, as a coin of Diocletian is said to have been found.[93]

The discovery of Roman walls under Watergate Street indicates that the road assumed to link the west gate of the fortress with the harbour did not coincide with the present street, although a cobbled road was discovered *c.* 12 m. south-east of the Watergate.[94]

[78] Hemingway, *Hist. Chester*, ii. 352.

[79] Lawson, 'Schedule', no. LIII; *J.C.A.S.* xxiv. 68.

[80] *J.C.A.S.* v. 324; xxvii. 110. A stamped tile found in lowering the road between Watergate Flags and the city walls was in F. H. Williams's colln.; 'foundations of a Roman structure' were said to have been unearthed.

[81] Watkin, *Roman Ches.* 104.

[82] Lawson, 'Schedule', no. LII.

[83] Watkin, *Roman Ches.* 94 n.

[84] Lawson, 'Schedule', no. LIII; *J.C.A.S.* [1st ser.], i. 199; Watkin, *Roman Ches.* 156, where a parallel is drawn with the bases found in the internal baths in 1863. A contemporary drawing is in the Grosvenor Mus.

[85] *J.C.A.S.* vii. 84.

[86] Watkin, *Roman Ches.* 156 and plan facing p. 86. The wall ran diagonally across the road; its foundation was so hard that it was removed by blasting.

[87] Inf. from Mr. F. H. Thompson.

[88] *J.C.A.S.* n.s. iii. 81.

[89] Ibid. xxxvi. 109–18.

[90] A pneumatic drill made little impression on the foundation, which was compared with those of the legionary baths.

[91] The position of the base, which clearly cannot have extended much further E. or S., is shown in *J.C.A.S.* lii. 3, fig. 2.

[92] Ibid. n.s. iii. 81–2. It may be identical with the foundations noted near the Watergate: ibid. ii. 63.

[93] G. Cuitt, *Hist. Chester*, 322.

[94] *J.R.S.* xxiii. 195.

A building found beneath a new wing of the Royal Infirmary[95] measured 15.24 m. east–west by 12.2 m., with one large room at the west end and six smaller rooms. The wall footings were of poor construction, consisting of rough sandstone blocks set in stiff clay, perhaps the substructure for a timber-framed building. The natural clay was covered by a sand make-up, but no floors survived, possibly because they too were wooden. A dark occupation spread found over the sand contained material of c. A.D. 90–125, and the building therefore predates the cemetery in the Infirmary Field; its function is unknown.[96] The area later exposed by construction revealed only a line of post-holes north of the building, perhaps a fence marking the limit of the property. A ditch was seen west of the building. Features revealed earlier and described as 'paved footways' may have been footings. One which had two courses of sandstone blocks set in clay 58.4 cm. wide was traced north–south for 4.57 m., and another had a small portion of a column base and many fragments of roofing tiles associated with it.

North of Bedward Row a 'furnace' 1–1.06 m. in diameter had a floor and sides of burnt clay; the entrance on the east was paved with blocks of sandstone and fragments of tiles, and its fill consisted of the caved-in roof, with sherds of Roman pottery and fragments of tile. The structure was sealed by a burnt layer which predated two Roman inhumation burials. The hearth may have been used for metalworking; the burnt layer was perhaps produced by nearby industrial activity.[97] In Bedward Row four phases of Roman occupation have been revealed. In the early 2nd century irregularly spaced stake holes delimited by drainage gullies were covered by a thick rubbish layer rich in finds running in date to the end of the 2nd century. Early in the 3rd the rubbish was sealed by clay and soil, and a light timber structure was built. A drainage ditch belonging to the same phase silted up by the late 3rd century, when the building was demolished and areas of sandstone paving were laid.[98] The only casual find from Bedward Row is a coin of Valentinian I,[99] and few finds have been made from the area at large. A samian cup (Dr. 27), from the Infirmary Field is said not to have been associated with a burial.[1] A quantity of pottery came from Stanley Place in 1940,[2] and two coins from Nicholas Street, an *aureus* of Nero[3] and a coin of Valentinian I.[4] A brooch from Nicholas Street Mews was in F. H. Williams's collection. A coin of Valerian was found in repairs to the city wall near the infirmary,[5] and a silver coin near Stanley Place.[6] Finds from the Roodee include two samian vessels with stamps,[7] and a coin of Domitian.[8]

THE HARBOUR. The harbour was downstream of the Grosvenor Bridge below the narrow gorge where the river cut through the sandstone ridge on which the fortress was built. Excavations for a gas-holder revealed oak timbers identified as belonging to a Roman wharf placed alongside a deep channel: associated with the wharf was a clay bank. Each pile was terminated by an iron shoe 38 cm. long. Finds included a lead pig datable to A.D. 74, three coins of Vespasian and one of Titus as well as others unidentified, fragments of Roman pottery including samian, animal bones, and two or four human skulls.[9] The finds were apparently recovered from river gravel at a depth of 6 m. or more. Coal was also found, the quantity being

---

[95] *J.R.S.* xlii. 94; *Ches. Historian*, no. 2, p. 33; no. 3, p. 24; *J.C.A.S.* xlix. 1–3.
[96] *J.R.S.* xlviii. 136; below.
[97] The date of the burnt layer is not clear: *Liverpool Annals*, vi. 159; viii. 50.
[98] *Britannia*, ix. 430; *Ches. Arch. Bull.* vi. 62.
[99] *J.C.A.S.* xxxvi. 151.
[1] Ibid. xxvi. 13, no. 11.
[2] Ibid. xxxvi. 109.

[3] Watkin, *Roman Ches.* 238; above.
[4] *J.C.A.S.* xl. 64.
[5] Ibid. xxxi. 77.
[6] Hemingway, *Hist. Chester*, ii. 354.
[7] *J.C.A.S.* xxvi. 17 (no. 41), 22 (no. 98).
[8] Ibid. xxiv. 150.
[9] Ibid. n.s. i, 77, 79–80, 84–5, 106–8; iv. 68–9; *T.H.S.L.C.* xxxix. 52–3; *Arch. Jnl.* xliv. 124–5; Watkin, *Roman Ches.* 163; *R.I.S.S.* no. 197; Lawson, 'Schedule', no. LXXXVII.

described as little less than a ton; it was believed that the source was local outcrops, but there was less agreement over when it was mined. Other finds were pieces of lime and a fragment of concrete. It has been suggested that the wharf was on the west bank of the river,[10] whereas the findspot now lies some 50 m. east of it; a wharf on the opposite bank of the river to the fortress was hardly convenient. The datable finds are Flavian, and the wharf was already in use when occupation of the fortress began. A second timber wharf or pier, revealed during construction of a sewer outside the Watergate on the Roodee, consisted of oak piles; large quantities of Roman tiles and pottery were dumped not far away.[11]

The so-called quay wall has long been in dispute. Antiquarian attention was first drawn to it in 1850.[12] It is situated in advance of the city wall near Black Friars, where the creek below Nuns' Field joined the river. Subsequent excavation of its face revealed more than 4.5 m. of massive masonry, but water prevented examination of the footings.[13] Masonry 2.47 m. high showed above ground level, with an offset at the base. Further excavation showed that the masonry was 2.44 m. thick, backed with hard concrete on the city side, the whole forming a solid mass nearly 4 m. thick.[14] The wall could be traced for nearly 45 m. and was curved in plan: its outer face is said to have had pilaster-like buttresses. The present height is 7.7 m. Some of the masonry appeared to have been re-used. Erection of the Dee Stands revealed more of it, and the line could be followed from the exposed portion to the Roodee keeper's lodge near the Watergate. A lead pipe was found apparently *in situ* on massive blocks of masonry.[15] Although a Roman date is widely accepted for the wall its purpose remains uncertain, and a suggested link with the massive wall found in Watergate Street is unproved.[16]

The Area North of the Fortress

Roman occupation north of the fortress appears to have been slight. A stamped tile of the two-line type was found near Pemberton's Parlour,[17] and a samian vessel with stamp was found during repairs to the city wall immediately west of Morgan's Mount.[18] At the Bluecoat Hospital just outside the north gate various Roman objects recovered when foundations were dug for almshouses included an antefix, much samian and other pottery, and some bronze objects including a brooch and a spoon.[19] Another similar brooch was found nearby.[20] Two samian vessels and 2nd–4th-century pottery were found in Delamere Street,[21] and construction of a new road north of the George and Dragon produced a small quantity of Roman pottery and fragments of skeletons thought to be from the graveyard of St. Thomas's chapel.[22] A bronze finger-ring found in the garden of a house near Chester College in Parkgate Road has traces of gilding, and contains an intaglio of glass paste depicting a Victory: it is probably later 2nd-century.[23] Sepulchral urns are said to have been found near Abbot's Grange and Chester College;[24] samian and bronze

---

[10] *J.C.A.S.* lix. 14–15.
[11] Watkin, *Roman Ches.* 114, 223; *J.C.A.S.* N.S. i. 80; iii, plan facing p. 71. The date of the wharf is uncertain.
[12] *Jnl. Brit. Arch. Assoc.* v. 214.
[13] *J.C.A.S.* N.S. i. 190. The face of the wall was battered: Watkin, *Roman Ches.* 101.
[14] *J.C.A.S.* N.S. ii. 61–4.
[15] Ibid. xvi. 115, 117.
[16] Watkin, *Roman Ches.* 101–2, was sceptical about the date, and Lawson, 'Schedule', nos. LVI, LXXXVIII referred to the feature as 'presumed Roman quay'. Recent calculations suggest that it is unlikely to have been a quay wall: Mason, 'Canabae'.

[17] *Jnl. Brit. Arch. Assoc.* N.S. i. 75; *J.C.A.S.* v. 130–1; vii. 88.
[18] *J.C.A.S.* xxix. 71; Lawson, 'Schedule', no. C.
[19] *J.C.A.S.* [1st ser.], i. 153, 356, 423–4, and facing 153; Lawson, 'Schedule', no. LXXXI.
[20] *J.C.A.S.* [1st ser.], ii. 127.
[21] Ibid. xxvi. 20 (no. 80), 21 (no. 90), both of form Dr. 18; *Ches. Arch. Bull.* ix. 59.
[22] *J.C.A.S.* xlix. 59.
[23] Ibid. [1st ser.], i. 168 and drawing facing p. 149; lx. 43–4; Watkin, *Roman Ches.* 205.
[24] Watkin, *Roman Ches.* 220.

objects have also been found.[25] A bronze brooch with enamelled decoration, perhaps 3rd-century, was found in a field on Parkgate Road.[26] Other finds nearby were coins: a *denarius* of Faustina II and possibly a broken *denarius* of Domitian in Parkgate Road,[27] and an *as* of Severus in a garden in Woodlands Avenue.[28] Not far from Chester College, in Cambrian View, a lead weight was found;[29] a coin of Antoninus Pius was found in Canal Street,[30] and samian, coarse pottery, and broken roof tiles were reported from the junction of Canal Street and Raymond Street.[31] Two coins of Constantine I and a third of Constantine II as Caesar were found in Sealand Road; another of similar date is known.[32] Samian and a bronze bell from Crane Street were purchased by the Grosvenor Museum.[33] The few finds in Upton, Newton, and Hoole are scattered, and probably represent casual loss rather than occupation. The coins range in date from the Republic to the 4th century, and samian of the late 1st to the late 2nd century came from Christ Church school.[34]

The Cemeteries

The tombstones built into the north wall are supposed to have come from a cemetery on the north side of the fortress.[35] Apart, however, from a report of 'sepulchral urns',[36] and the recent discovery of a lead coffin with inhumation, possibly 2nd-century,[37] evidence from the Liverpool Road and Parkgate Road area is thin. The use of tombstones for repairs elsewhere in the circuit of the fortress wall also weakens the argument, and the existence of a cemetery outside the north wall is doubtful.[38] By far the greatest concentration of burials is found south of the river in Handbridge, where the major cemetery lay.[39]

The only cemetery explored systematically lies in the Infirmary Field,[40] to the west of the fortress. Burials were recorded in 1858. An interment of a young girl was accompanied by a pair of gold ear-rings; the grave was covered by three roof-tiles on each side, and contained a small lamp and two pots, one with a coin of Domitian in it.[41] A deep drain dug across the field five years later cut through an inhumation grave with a tile cover,[42] and a fragment of a military tombstone found *c.* 30 m. west of Pemberton's Parlour presumably derives from the cemetery.[43] Its northern extent may be indicated by five inhumation burials found alongside the canal.[44] Forty inhumation burials were recorded on the site of an extension to Chester Royal Infirmary.[45] Two graves each contained two burials, and three cists showed no sign of interment, two of which from their size were intended for child burials. Child burials formed a very small proportion of the total; of the adult burials, many were of people in their twenties. Roughly a third of the bodies were of undetermined sex, but among the rest males predominated. At least fourteen of

[25] In F. H. Williams's colln.: Lawson, 'Schedule', no. LXXXIII.

[26] *T.H.S.L.C.* i. 28; *Arch. Jnl.* vi. 198; Watkin, *Roman Ches.* 202–3. Once in the Mechanics' Inst. mus., now lost.

[27] *J.C.A.S.* xxxvi. 138–9.

[28] *Ches. Arch. Bull.* vi. 75.

[29] *J.C.A.S.* xxxix. 110–11 and fig. 20; *J.R.S.* xlii. 106, no. 15.

[30] *J.C.A.S.* xxxvi. 149.

[31] Ibid. 72.

[32] Ibid. xlvi. 80; *Ches. Arch. Bull.* vii. 61.

[33] *J.C.A.S.* xiii. 162; xv. 158. For an antefix from Crane Street see Watkin, *Roman Ches.* 320.

[34] *J.C.A.S.* viii. 105; ix. 140–1; xxxvi. 70, 149, 151; *Ches. Arch. Bull.* i. 5; vi. 76; Watkin, *Roman Ches.* 240; Hemingway, *Hist. Chester*, ii. 354.

[35] *J.C.A.S.* vii. 8.

[36] Watkin, *Roman Ches.* 220; Thompson, *Roman Ches.* 49. Watkin doubted the report.

[37] Inf. from Dr. P. Carrington.

[38] Two of the inscribed stones from the N. wall are not tombstones: *R.I.B.* i, nos. 466, possibly the dedication of a shrine or temple, and 471, a centurial stone.

[39] Thompson, *Roman Ches.*, fig. 11.

[40] Also known as Barrow Field, perhaps because of earlier discoveries.

[41] *J.C.A.S.* [1st ser.], ii. 408, 425; iii. 17, 28, 161–2; *Gent. Mag.* N.S. xii. 321; Watkin, *Roman Ches.* 212–13.

[42] *J.C.A.S.* [1st ser.], ii. 320.

[43] *R.I.B.* i, no. 531; *J.C.A.S.* vii, no. 74. The stone is lost.

[44] *J.C.A.S.* viii. 100–1; no dating material was found, but a Roman date seems likely.

[45] *Liverpool Annals*, vi. 121–67; viii. 49–60. Clearance for a further extension in 1956 revealed no burials.

the graves had roof-tiles in their construction, the whole grave sometimes being built of tiles; nine of the tiles bore stamps of Legio xx. Sandals placed at the feet of the deceased in five or six graves were presumably for the journey to come, and a coin either in the mouth or on the body found in seven was for Charon's fee. Of twelve graves which yielded datable finds, seven produced coins, all but one of Antoninus Pius, and the seventh of Commodus. The main period of use of the cemetery was therefore in the Antonine period, but other finds show clearly that some of the burials were 3rd-century, while at least one may be as late as the 4th.[46] Ritual destruction or damage of the grave goods was noted, for instance in Grave 19 where a mirror was broken before being placed in a pot, and in Grave 23 where each of three pots had a hole punched in its base, the fragments being found under the interment, although the pots were deposited outside the tiles forming the grave. Iron nails, presumably used to make wooden coffins, were found in nearly all the graves. The most common interments were in a simple grave dug into the clay subsoil or, in three cases, a pocket of made ground. Tiles used in constructing graves took the form of a pitched roof (seven graves)[47] or a horizontal covering (three graves), while vertically placed tiles at sides and ends occurred in two graves, and one grave had a combination of vertical side tiles and a tile floor; three graves had a tile floor. The presence of fragments of tile on the floor of a number of other graves suggests that they also shared the same tradition. Apart from the graves incorporating tiles two inhumation burials were contained in cists formed of rough-hewn sandstone blocks covered with tiles and rubble, and two burials were covered with pieces of sandstone in line over the centre of the burial. Of the remainder, which cannot be easily classified, two graves stand out. Grave 1 was a rectangular chamber with a roughly corbelled roof, for which the term 'tomb' is appropriate. The young woman buried there was accompanied by a glass vessel and a Rhenish beaker which is late Antonine at earliest, and may well date from the first half of the 3rd century.[48] The second was a simple earth-dug grave, again with a female interment, over which had been placed a thick sheet of lead. Few items were placed in the grave, and its date is uncertain.

No cremation burials have been found. The rite of inhumation, introduced in Britain in the later 2nd century, had completely supplanted cremation by the end of the 3rd. Chester therefore possesses a notably early inhumation cemetery, although not as early as was once thought,[49] as its use continued into the 3rd century and perhaps even longer. Though a fragment of an inscription reading XVIII may be part of a tombstone,[50] in general tombstones are absent and may have been robbed for re-use as building stone in the Roman period.[51] Two mirrors were found, one possibly a hand mirror, and if so an extremely rare find,[52] the other of a type believed to have been made in Lower Germany in the 2nd or 3rd century. Nine skeletons, only three of which were intact, found near Bedward Row are believed to have been Roman.

Another inhumation cemetery lay south of Watergate Street. Most finds have been made immediately west of the city wall, and its full extent is unknown. The first burial noted lay in a tile-built grave resembling those in the Infirmary Field;

[46] A latticed grey jar from Grave 38 is closely comparable to late 3rd- or 4th-cent. types: J. P. Gillam, *Types of Roman Coarse Pottery in North Britain*, types 147–8; *Liverpool Annals*, viii, plate 7 (1).

[47] An eighth was found later: *J.C.A.S.* xxxvi. 119.

[48] Lawson, 'Schedule', no. LI.

[49] R. G. Collingwood and I. A. Richmond, *Arch. of Roman Brit.* 166.

[50] R.I.B. i, no. 572, now lost.

[51] *Brit. Academy Supplemental Papers*, ii. 14 (ix). It is possible that many of the graves in the cemetery were not marked by tombstones.

[52] *J.C.A.S.* lx. 49.

denarii of Otho and Nerva were believed to have been associated with it.[53] Other inhumation burials were later described:[54] one under the south end of the Dee Stands was accompanied by a samian vessel, and another found 'in repairing the steps' yielded an unidentified Roman coin. A third burial was in a sandstone cist: no grave goods are mentioned. Two further inhumations were found. A gem found near one of them, originally believed to be 4th-century, is thought to be more probably of the late 1st or 2nd.[55] A Roman tombstone was found apparently *in situ* 12 m. west of the city wall,[56] and in association with it two skulls and some of the bones of the upper body. The dedication was to Flavius Callimorphus aged 42, and Serapion aged three and a half: the stone was put up by Thesaeus to brother and son. From their Greek names the family probably belonged to the *canabae* rather than the legion. Two associated finds were a gold ring and a coin of Domitian; the poor condition of the coin implied that it had been in circulation for some time before being deposited. An inhumation burial seen in a garden in or near Grey Friars had a *denarius* of Vespasian with it. A tombstone of the 'banquet' type with a long inscription was apparently found when the Dee Stands were enlarged.[57] The finds from the cemetery are generally earlier than those from the Infirmary Field, despite some similarities between the two.[58]

HANDBRIDGE CEMETERY. Finds from Handbridge clearly belong to a Roman cemetery which follows Watling Street (Eaton Road) southward; by the mid 19th century it was recognized as the principal cemetery of the fortress. The earliest recorded discovery was at Netherleigh, where a possible *columbarium*, in which the tomb was provided with 'pigeon-holes' for urns containing cremations, was found.[59] A 'demi-figure habited in a sacerdotal costume' was probably a Roman tomb relief. One complete pot and a number of fragments are recorded, but the number of urns or burials is unknown.[60] Also at Netherleigh a coping stone surmounted by a crouching lion discovered *c.* 20 m. from the road is thought to be part of a tomb surround: no associated finds were reported.[61]

The growth of Handbridge as a suburb from the mid 19th century resulted in discoveries along Eaton Road. Pots containing ashes and burnt bones, with coins, are said to have been plentiful, the coins ranging in date from Vespasian to Constantine I. A fragment of the relief of a 'banquet' type tombstone, a lead canister containing ashes and burnt bones, and a leaden *ossuarium* were also found.[62] A stone coffin with a lead lining was discovered in Queen's Park, together with two accessory vessels, one probably colour-coated and the other possibly in black-burnished ware. The coffin contained the body of a child.[63] The site of the church of St. Mary-without-the-Walls yielded about seven supposed interments, which may alternatively have been rubbish pits.[64] The northern extent of the cemetery was indicated by a cremation burial in a pot, accompanied by a latticed jar, discovered at the tobacco mill. The pots were thought to be late 2nd-century, but one of them is later.[65] A pottery figurine of an unknown goddess was found nearby. In Eccleston

[53] *J.C.A.S.* [1st ser.], ii. 320, 425; iii. 28, 250, and facing p. 256; Watkin, *Roman Ches.* 214.

[54] 1 *Sheaf*, ii, pp. 389–90, 394.

[55] *J.C.A.S.* lix. 35–6; Lawson, 'Schedule', no. LVI. There were at least seven burials.

[56] *Arch. Camb.* 4th ser. v. 260–1; *Arch. Jnl.* xxxiii. 359; *R.I.B.* i, no. 558; Watkin, *Roman Ches.* 214–16; Lawson, 'Schedule', no. LXI.

[57] *J.C.A.S.* xlvi. 75–6.

[58] The 'vase' and lamp recorded from Nuns' Garden possibly came from a Roman grave: *Arch. Camb.* 3rd ser. iv. 464.

[59] Watkin, *Roman Ches.* 217.

[60] Hemingway, *Hist. Chester*, ii. 352.

[61] Watkin, *Roman Ches.* 217; *R.I.S.S.* no. 168.

[62] *J.C.A.S.* [1st ser.], i. 425, 460; ii. 432; iii. 255, 307; vii. 157; Watkin, *Roman Ches.* 217–18; Lawson, 'Schedule', no. LXVI.

[63] *J.C.A.S.* [1st ser.], i. 424 and fig. facing, 425; ibid. xxxvi. 127; Lawson, 'Schedule', no. LXIV.

[64] Watkin, *Roman Ches.* 219; Lawson, 'Schedule', no. LXV.

[65] *J.C.A.S.* xxxvi. 121–2; Gillam, *Roman Coarse Pottery*, no. 145 (*c.* 270–340).

Avenue, 7.6 m. east of Eaton Road, a large jar was found embedded in, and containing, calcined bones, charcoal, and stiff clay. Other pottery found nearby included an Oxford ware mortar, but the cremation pot was late 1st- or early 2nd-century. Masonry was found which was thought to be part of the moulded plinth of a tomb: one piece came from the new road, and another lay immediately north of it.[66] Another cremation c. 100 m. north of Eccleston Avenue was found in a 1st-century pot, and parts of two other urns were found. Two rubble foundations c. 5 m. apart were noted.[67] A stone pine cone found in Appleyards Lane was probably from a tomb.[68] At Ebury Place the lower part of a large jar was found with a cremation and a coin of the late 1st or early 2nd century. A black burnished jar with obtuse and narrow latticing, 3rd-century at the earliest, was perhaps associated with a burial, although no skeletal material was found.[69] A cremation contained in a flagon of the late 1st or early 2nd century was found recently in Eaton Road.[70]

Two slate-cut inscriptions have been found. The first lay face down on a paved surface of sandstone and cobbles over 50 m. east of Eaton Road, and proved to be the major part of a tombstone to a standard-bearer of Legio xx.[71] The second, found opposite Greenbank House,[72] was part of an inscription detailing the career of an officer who served in Legio xxii Deiotariana, probably as *primus pilus*, before promotion to the rank of *praefectus* in Legio xx. With that information the inscription apparently ends, but it may have continued on a second slab. The inscription probably came from a tomb, but had been re-used. Its date is 2nd-century, no later than c. A.D. 170.[73]

Although often considered solely as a cemetery, Handbridge may also have been a suburb. In addition to the finds at the church which may be rubbish pits and the occurrence of sherds of pottery,[74] a sandstone hypocaust *pila* is thought to have come from the site of the church institute close by,[75] and a large Corinthian capital is known from Handbridge, possibly from the vicinity of the church.[76] Pottery has been found without association with burials, for example in Queen's Park Road.[77] Casual finds of coins include two of Theodosius I,[78] and an *aureus* of Titus.[79] Coins of Nero, Gallienus, Maxentius, and the house of Constantine have also been found.[80] In few instances have structures been revealed: when found they appear to belong to tombs.[81]

The antiquity for which Handbridge has been best known since Stukeley's time is the Minerva Shrine in Edgar's Field. Little of what early antiquarians described and drew of it can be discerned, though certain features were said to be easily recognizable as late as 1870.[82] What could once be seen, perhaps with the eye of

[66] *J.C.A.S.* xxviii. 216-17; xxxvi. 124-6; *J.R.S.* xix. 192; Lawson, 'Schedule', nos. xcv, xcvi.

[67] *J.C.A.S.* xxviii. 217.

[68] Ibid. xxxvi. 132-3; *R.I.S.S.* no. 186c.

[69] *J.C.A.S.* xxxvi. 123-4; Gillam, *Roman Coarse Pottery*, no. 146 (c. 280-350).

[70] *Ches. Arch. Bull.* vii. 46.

[71] *J.C.A.S.* xxx. 56-8; *J.R.S.* xxiv. 219, no. 3; *R.I.B.* i, no. 510. The stone was in poor condition when found, and probably disintegrated when allowed to dry out in the museum: *J.C.A.S.* xlvi. 77. It may have been part of a built tomb rather than a free-standing tombstone.

[72] *J.C.A.S.* lix. 31-4; *J.R.S.* lv. 221 and plate 18 (1).

[73] Legio xxii Deiotariana was in Alexandria in A.D. 119. At some time thereafter it ceased to exist, perhaps annihilated during the Jewish revolt in Hadrian's reign. Alternatively it may be the legion lost in A.D. 161. Most scholars prefer the earlier date (cf. *Cambridge Ancient Hist.* xi. 314; Frere, *Britannia*, 161), which makes the date of the inscription cor-

respondingly early. Use of the title *praefectus legionis* without qualification at so early a date is noteworthy.

[74] Watkin, *Roman Ches.* 226.

[75] Lawson, 'Schedule', no. lxv.

[76] *J.C.A.S.* [1st ser.], i. 199, 460; *R.I.S.S.* no. 174; Lawson, 'Schedule', no. lxv; Watkin, *Roman Ches.* 200.

[77] *J.C.A.S.* xxxvi. 123-4, 126-33. Ebury Place yielded many Roman sherds and a bronze brooch.

[78] *J.C.A.S.* xxxiii. 117; *J.R.S.* xxvii. 232.

[79] Watkin, *Roman Ches.* 239; Lawson, 'Schedule', no. xciii; *J.C.A.S.* x. 140. Struck in A.D. 75 under Vespasian.

[80] *Ches. Arch. Bull.* iii. 60; vii. 61.

[81] *J.C.A.S.* xxviii. 216. A footing of rubble and cobbles 60 cm. or more in thickness, inserted into the clay in Eccleston Avenue. A similar feature c. 50 m. to the north produced a mortar rim of the early 2nd cent. For an earlier find of coins from Queen's Park Road see Watkin, *Roman Ches.* 240.

[82] Horsley, *Britannia Romana*, 316, Ches. IV.

faith, was the goddess Pallas Athene (Minerva), standing in an *aedicula*, with an owl, the bird associated with her, on her shoulder. The goddess held spear and shield, and to her right was an altar. Edgar's Field is a disused quarry which was certainly worked in the Roman period.[83] Quarrying apparently began in the closing years of the 1st century, and had ceased by the later 2nd, the waste being sealed by dumped rubbish of the Roman period.[84] The principal find was part of a Severan inscription, presumably derived from a demolished building inside the fortress.[85] The relief was probably carved by legionary quarrymen.

Boughton

The suburb of Boughton, 1.5 km. east of the fortress, was the source of the aqueduct. The principal evidence is an altar dedicated to the Nymphs and Fountains, whose inscription appears on both front and back, unusual but suitable if the altar was meant to be seen in the round. It was found in a garden or field called the Daniels during digging in a sand pit. An almost contemporary letter describes the altar as having been found in a 'reclining posture' detached from the pedestal, a square stone 15 cm. thick, with building debris probably derived from the structure which originally accompanied it, and covered with stones and rubbish.[86] A second altar, also said to have been found during sand digging, came from near the junction of Tarvin Road and Bulkeley Street, either north or south of Tarvin Road.[87] The dedication is to the genius of the century of Aulus Verinus. A samian vessel was found at the same time.

A lead pig almost identical with that from the gas works on the Roodee was found during construction of the Crewe–Chester railway near Tarvin Road bridge, not far north of the garden where the first altar was found. The find may relate to the aqueduct, as lead was freely used in making water pipes and for lining cisterns and water tanks. Like the ingot from the Roodee, the lead was derived from Deceanglian mines in the nearer part of Wales; it was cast in A.D. 74.[88]

Several cremation burials have been found at Boughton, at least two from the Cherry Orchard sand pit, two flagons and two jars with cremations being noted.[89] An urn reportedly found near the road junction at the centre of Boughton was thought to contain burnt bones, although no mention is made of an associated cremation in the earliest account.[90] In Stocks Lane, 300 m. or more to the south, a Flavian–Trajanic jar containing a cremation was found; with the burial was a small glass flask, and the jar is said to have been covered with a glass sheet. Another complete jar filled with earth and bones was found 'a few yards' away. Fragments of four other pots were recovered, but the cremation was said to have been associated solely with the complete vessel.[91] A cremation contained in a jar of the period *c*. A.D. 80–120 was found in the garden of no. 21 Stocks Lane.[92] The only burial to have been examined *in situ* came to light during the building of a new school in Bachelor's Lane. A cremation was contained in a 1st-century jar placed at a depth

[83] *J.C.A.S.* xxvii. 103–8.

[84] Ibid. 146–9.

[85] *R.I.B.* i, no. 465, dated A.D. 194–6; but see also *J.R.S.* lvi. 230.

[86] *Gent. Mag.* xciii (2), 388; *R.I.B.* i, no. 460; Watkin, *Roman Ches.* 175–7; *J.C.A.S.* [1st ser.], iii. 262–3; v. 31. The accepted date of the find is 1821; a sketch in Lancs. R. O. captioned 'Sketch of a Roman altar discovered in an orchard in Further Boughton near Chester taken by Will. Latham June 16, 1816' is probably mistaken: Latham is known to have been in Chester in 1822 when he drew *R.I.B.* i, no. 467.

[87] *R.I.B.* i, no. 447; Lawson, 'Schedule', no. LXXII; *Jnl.*

Brit. Arch. Assoc. v. 225; *J.C.A.S.* [1st ser.], iii. 264–5; vi. 77–8; Watkin, *Roman Ches.* 177–8. It probably originated inside the fortress.

[88] *Arch. Jnl.* xvi. 27–8; *J.C.A.S.* [1st ser.], iii. 265–6; N.S. i. 84; Watkin, *Roman Ches.* 162–3; *C.I.L.* vii. 1204; above.

[89] *J.C.A.S.* [1st ser.], iii. 264.

[90] Hemingway, *Hist. Chester*, ii. 353; Watkin, *Roman Ches.* 219–20.

[91] *J.C.A.S.* vi. 156–8; viii. 101. Little of the cremation found in 1900 survived; examination of the bones found in 1897 suggested that they belonged to an adult.

[92] *Ches. Arch. Bull.* viii. 43–5.

of *c.* 1.2 m. in sand. Coarse pottery of Flavian–Trajanic date and a badly corroded *as* of Vespasian were also found.[93] Although *c.* 500 m. south of the Stocks Lane burials the find presumably belongs to the same cemetery.

While apparently no more than six in number, the cremation burials from Boughton have been found over an area not far short of 1 km. from north to south, and many more may await discovery. The apparent lack of inhumation burials accords with the generally early date of the finds from the area, although a suggestion that the burials belong to a pre-fortress military site cannot be supported.[94] As the fortress with its *canabae* is nearly 2 km. away Boughton may have been a distinct settlement, although forming part of the *canabae*. Boughton has yielded Roman pottery in abundance, including samian,[95] some of which presumably derives from occupation rather than burials. A Roman 'water bottle' was given to the Grosvenor Museum in 1910.[96] An *aureus* and two *denarii* of Trajan, one from Dee Lane, are also recorded.[97] Nevertheless no traces of buildings have been found, other than the remains associated with the altar dedicated to the Nymphs and Fountains, which may well represent a shrine or temple. A suggestion that Boughton was a religious site, its existence presumably linked with the local springs, has much to recommend it.[98] The linear scatter of the burials there has also prompted speculation that an alternative course to the supposed line of Watling Street through the legionary fortress may have lain from Boughton along the east bank of the Dee, but supporting evidence is lacking.[99] What may have been the surface of Watling Street west of Boughton Cross has, however, been recorded.[1]

THE AQUEDUCT. The altar dedicated to the Nymphs and Fountains indicates the source of the piped water supply with which the fortress was provided, for there are abundant springs of good water nearby. An aqueduct followed the line of Watling Street from Boughton 1.5 km. west to the fortress. A long line of earthenware water pipes running east–west was found near Dee Hills, Boughton, and in Foregate Street a similar line of pipes sealed by the surfacing and substructure of Watling Street was revealed running towards the fortress east gate. A similar east–west line of pipes was observed in Grosvenor Park, possibly connected with the lead water pipe found in Newgate Street, since the latter presumably fed the internal baths. Another smaller branch was found at nos. 46–50 Foregate Street crossing the western part of the site from north to south; it is surprising that the aqueduct was thus tapped for a private outlet.[2]

That the supply dates from the earliest years of the fortress is shown by the inscribed lead water pipes which record completion in the first half of A.D. 79. Among the buildings supplied were the 'elliptical building' and the internal baths; a water tank has been identified in the *retentura*. A lead water pipe 20 cm. in diameter, found on the site of the Odeon cinema, suggests that more than one pipeline existed.

[93] Ibid. iv. 22–5.

[94] *New Evidence*, 40; *Ches. Arch. Bull.* iv. 23; Watkin, *Roman Ches.* 300.

[95] *J.C.A.S.* v. 31, 36; *Arch. Jnl.* xxxiv. 137; *Ches. Arch. Bull.* vii. 63.

[96] *J.C.A.S.* xviii. 248.

[97] Hemingway, *Hist. Chester*, ii. 354; Watkin, *Roman Ches.* 239–40; *J.C.A.S.* xxxvi. 148.

[98] *Ches. Arch. Bull.* iv. 23.

[99] *New Evidence*, 40; inf. from Dr. D. J. P. Mason.

[1] *Ches. Arch. Bull.* vii. 37.

[2] *J.C.A.S.* v. 29–30, 329; Lawson, 'Schedule', no. LXXIX.

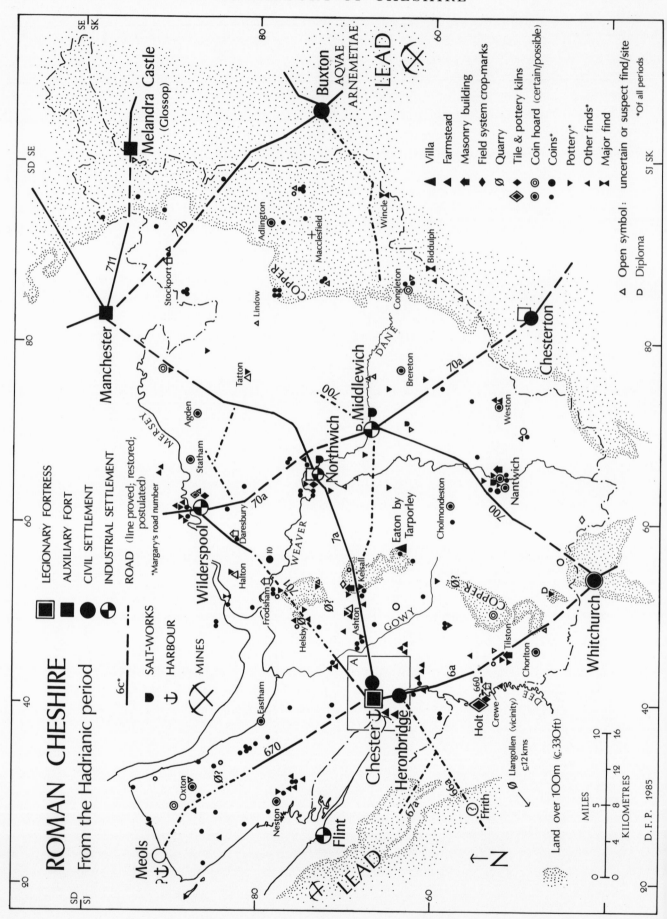

SETTLEMENTS OUTSIDE CHESTER

Examination of the settlements of Roman Cheshire reveals great variety. Northwich cannot now be accepted as a settlement, except in the limited sense that a fort normally had attached to it a *vicus* or civil settlement. There is only slight evidence of occupation at Northwich after the mid 2nd century, indicating that such a permanent settlement did not materialize. The evidence from Saltney may represent two farms, and Nantwich cannot certainly be classed as a settlement for lack of evidence. Heronbridge, Wilderspool, and Middlewich all came into existence at about the same time, in the late 1st century, and Meols also probably dates from the Flavian period. Apart from Northwich, where military occupation was paramount, there is no clear evidence that any other settlement began as a military site, and at both Wilderspool and Middlewich the trend of the evidence is otherwise. At Wilderspool the 'defences' have been disproved, and excavations in the interior of the supposed fort have revealed no traces of military buildings; at Middlewich the Harbutt's Field site has been discredited, although it remains possible that a fortlet was established to oversee the production of salt.

Although salt was also made at Northwich and Nantwich, only at Middlewich is there sufficient evidence to indicate its production over a lengthy period, and in quantity, thereby justifying its identification as an industrial settlement. Of the other Cheshire sites, only Wilderspool has produced unequivocal evidence, in the form of metalworking and pottery production, for industrial status. At Wilderspool industrial activity did not extend much beyond the end of the 2nd century; whatever caused the cessation dealt the settlement its death blow, while Middlewich by contrast apparently expanded in the 3rd century and was occupied well into the 4th. Heronbridge, where industrial activity was no greater than at any other rural settlement, similarly survived through the 3rd century and into the 4th, as did the site, whatever it was, at Nantwich, which may even have reached its apogee in the 3rd century.[3] The list of coins found at Meols suggests that occupation there continued into the late 4th century.

At both Middlewich and Heronbridge the linear nature of the settlement emerges very clearly, and *mutatis mutandis* Wilderspool is similar: both the Stockton Heath and Lousher's Lane sites display a straggle of buildings along the main road. None of those sites demonstrates a formal plan or indeed the other niceties of urban life such as public buildings. The single exception may be at Wilderspool, where sufficient architectural fragments have been found to suggest at least one building of classical form. Not one of the settlements has so far yielded signs of a bathbuilding, although all are likely to have had one.

The settlements at Heronbridge, Wilderspool, and Middlewich presumably had the status of *vici* of the canton of the Cornovii. The *vicus* represents the lowest level of self-government within the *civitas*, and the *vicani* were responsible to the *ordo* or council and its magistrates. It was not uncommon within large tribal areas to use the *pagus* or district as a convenient subdivision, with one settlement as the *caput* of each. If the tribal area of the Cornovii was thus subdivided then a northern district taking in much of the Cheshire plain with its *caput* at Whitchurch (*Mediolanum*) is conceivable. In contrast to the Cheshire sites, Whitchurch has yielded evidence of masonry buildings, including what appears to be a public market, and

---

[3] With the exception of those concerning Heronbridge, the comments above are based largely on unpublished evidence.

indications of town walls.[4] Apparently none of the Cheshire sites was defended: if the earthwork at Heronbridge was a late Roman defence for the settlement, it is odd that the buildings are not enclosed within it. The Cheshire settlements are small, but the same is true of sites like Great Casterton, Horncastle, and Caistor (all Lincs.), which were given walls and bastions in the 4th century.

The Roman occupation of the Cheshire countryside may be summarized as follows. Sediment samples and pollen records from Cheshire suggest that agricultural activity was intensified during the Roman period, and that there had earlier been considerable clearance in the Peckforton area. The evidence of many agricultural settlements may have been destroyed by later farming or buried deeply under sediments transported by erosion. The site at Chester, fortress and *canabae*, had far the biggest influence on rural occupation. Only near Chester did occupation attain a level of intensity general in other parts of the province. An extension of that influence as far as the Mid-Cheshire Ridge and the Helsby–Frodsham–Halton cliffs suggests a special reason, possibly forest clearance, and some native occupation; improved Roman methods of farming permitted colonization of some of the intervening lower ground. Occupation in Wirral was probably low-key, and largely self-contained.

Identification of one simple villa at Eaton-by-Tarporley suggests the likelihood that others existed. A probable site is Ashton, on the basis of the material finds, but as yet no sign of structure has come to light. Kelsall is more likely in that Roman tiles are recorded as having been found; two other sites which have yielded apparently Roman structure are Daresbury and Frodsham. Nevertheless early identifications of 'Roman' structure may be in error, just as vague terms like 'tessellated pavement' may indicate a medieval tiled floor. The hypocaust *pilae* located at Oakmere were taken there from Chester. The settlements of central Cheshire seem to have had relatively little influence on their hinterland, judging by the scarcity of finds except in their immediate vicinity. The strange empty area roughly centred on Knutsford, and traversed by Watling Street, is perhaps the clearest indication of a large expanse of uncleared and uninhabitable forest on which the fuel requirements of the industries at Wilderspool and Middlewich made only very limited impact. The sites of east Cheshire are probably more closely related to the Pennines than to sites elsewhere in the county, and modest both in their prosperity and their degree of romanization. It is therefore surprising that from near Congleton have come two important hoards unequalled elsewhere in the county.

The extent of the territory annexed to the fortress is unknown. If agricultural activity was stimulated by being in the *prata legionis*, then the land from the fortress eastward to the Mid-Cheshire Ridge was included. The sites at Middlewich and, to a lesser extent, Northwich owed their position to the availability of brine for salt-working. It seems likely that the industrial settlement at Wilderspool and the villa at Eaton-by-Tarporley were both outside the *prata legionis*.

Heronbridge

Only 2.5 km. south of the fortress, the settlement at Heronbridge remained undiscovered until 1929; before then few finds were made. The 'considerable deposit of sepulchral urns' found at Primrose Hill may represent a cemetery at the southern end of the settlement or may be prehistoric.[5] That find and the discovery

---

[4] *Arch. Jnl.* cxxv. 193–254; *Britannia*, ix. 436–7.
[5] Ormerod, *Hist. Ches.* i. 295; *Jnl. Brit. Arch. Assoc.* v.

228; Lawson, 'Schedule', no. LXVII; Watkin, *Roman Ches.* 217. None of the urns survive.

at the same time of the Roman road were perhaps associated with the making of the present road to Eccleston.[6] Antonine samian was found *c.* 100 m. west of Eaton Road.[7] A hoard of 43 *denarii* deposited in the Antonine period was probably concealed by an inhabitant of the settlement; it was found either at Eccleston, *c.* 1 km. south, or more likely at Heronbridge.[8]

The one visible feature at Heronbridge, an earthwork, attracted little attention,[9] but a tradition that its bank marked the line of the Roman road prompted excavations in 1929 to investigate Watling Street. Occupation debris was incidentally revealed ranging from the 1st to the 4th century together with foundations, surfaces, and roads.[10]

During excavations in 1930–1 the north wall of one building was traced for 25.6 m. east–west.[11] A pitched stone surface *c.* 8 m. north–south and *c.* 9 m. east–west bounded by the wall and by a return southwards 6 m. long may indicate its use as a workshop or shed. Its south side was possibly open. How ovens or furnaces to north and south related to it in time or function remains uncertain, as does their purpose; no waste products were detected. Nearly 5 m. north of the first lay a second stone building; 6.7 m. of its south wall was revealed, and its east wall, pierced by a doorway 3 m. wide, was traced for *c.* 8.2 m. On either side of the opening the wall overlay earlier 'industrial' features, and it may have been later in date than the longer building to the south. The buildings were thought to show two distinct periods of occupation, the first *c.* A.D. 100–60 and the second ending in the mid 3rd century. Human remains are said to have been found over an extensive area; attention was concentrated, however, on a number of complete or nearly complete skeletons, 14 of which were examined. All were adult males: 6 were classified as young, 5 as middle-aged, and 3 as old. All the long bones showed well marked muscular attachments. Almost half had injuries to the head apparently inflicted by a long sword wielded by a cavalryman, from which they presumably died. In the absence of grave-goods or other associated objects it is impossible to date the burials. The action which resulted in the death of the men and their unceremonious interment took place when the southern building was no longer standing or even visible, although perhaps the northern building was still standing, as no burials are recorded from it. A date late in the Roman period is possible: the slight evidence is consistent with the deaths having occurred during civil disorder. Alternatively, the burials may be later than the Roman period.[12]

The earthwork had a substantial ditch on its west side. Near its northern end the ditch was 5.8 m. wide, and its depth was estimated at 2.9 m., the profile being V-shaped. Pottery from its fill ran to the 3rd century. The bank consisted of dark occupation material capped with clay; both bank and ditch were affected by later levelling, so that there is no surface indication of the ditch. Some 230 m. to the south[13] the ditch was 4.5 m. wide and 2.7 m. deep, the profile of the outer face suggesting that it was recut. The pottery from the silt fill again ran to the 3rd

[6] *J.C.A.S.* xxxix. 3; for the relationship of Roman and modern roads, ibid. lviii. 31.

[7] Ibid. xxxi. 76–7.

[8] It is said to have been found at Eccleston at the beginning of the 19th cent. It was owned by G. Cuitt and then by W. F. Ayrton, in whose family it remained until given to the Grosvenor Mus. in 1917. A list published in 1921, however, gives the findspot as 'Heron Bridge . . . in 1855'; despite the discrepancy in date the same hoard is clearly being described. As the Roman settlement had not been discovered at that time there seems no reason to doubt the attribution: *T.H.S.L.C.* xxxix. 55–6; W. T. Ready, 'Hoard of 43 Roman Denarii found at Eccleston, near Chester', *J.C.A.S.* N.S. i. 91–7; xxiv. 157–61; *Archaeologia*, liv. 493.

[9] Ormerod, *Hist. Ches.* ii. 583–4; *T.L.C.A.S.* xxv. 150.

[10] *J.R.S.* xix. 192–3; W. J. Williams, 'Watling Street at Heronbridge', *J.C.A.S.* xxx. 50–5; Lawson, 'Schedule', no. xcix.

[11] J. A. Petch, 'Excavations at Heronbridge, 1930–1', *J.C.A.S.* xxx. 5–49.

[12] Perhaps as late as the Civil War: L. and J. Laing, *Dark Ages of W. Ches.* 4, 16–19.

[13] W. J. Williams, 'Roman Ditch at Heronbridge', *J.C.A.S.* xxx. 111–17.

century: both ditch and rampart were sealed by clay. Masonry concentrated towards the front of the bank was wrongly construed as the foundation of a defensive wall. The ditch and bank covered the remains of Roman buildings, to which the masonry belonged,[14] and the defensive feature post-dates the buildings' use and abandonment. A Roman building c. 16 m. wide east–west, facing Watling Street on one side and perhaps a courtyard on the other, was partly covered by the bank and partly removed when the ditch was dug.[15] A thick occupation layer beneath the bank contained 3rd-century pottery and a coin of Claudius II,[16] and the bank itself was no earlier than the late 3rd century.[17]

About 150 m. further north six or seven stone buildings fronted Watling Street.[18] They were of a type well known in Romano-British settlements and towns, long and narrow in plan, the shorter side facing the street.[19] Beneath lay the floors and walls of earlier buildings, wholly or mainly of timber and perhaps similar in plan, which belonged to an initial phase of occupation which began c. A.D. 90 and was intense for the last decade of the 1st century, although perhaps less so in the period A.D. 100-30. The character of the site changed c. A.D. 130-40 with the construction of strip buildings in a comprehensive development. They were arranged in groups separated by side streets up to 6 m. wide, a pattern similar to that at the southern end of the site.[20] The buildings were apparently of uniform length, perhaps as much as 35 m., and 9–11.5 m. wide, but their internal layout differed. Two substantial walls 7 m. apart towards the south end of the range were interpreted as the sides of a dock. Beyond it was a somewhat narrower (7.3 m.) building, and to the south isolated walls perhaps indicated lean-to sheds.[21] Occupation of the buildings north of the 'dock' did not outlast the Antonine period, but the building south of it was rebuilt in the late 2nd or early 3rd century, and subsequently extended westwards. No stratified material was associated with the final phase but there was much 3rd-century pottery in the topsoil. Further north the back wall of a shed open to the north was found, and a base which may be for a water tank; northwards rough sandstone paving eventually thinned out. The shed was perhaps rebuilt at the end of the 2nd century, and occupation may extend into the 3rd.[22]

The supposed dock is difficult to accept, particularly in view of the effort and cost of building the necessary locks from the river: it is at least 6 m. higher than the river, and the difference was greater in the Roman period when there was no weir at Chester. The north wall of the 'dock' 7.6 m. east of the main section was traced down for 2.13 m. and showed no sign of the stepped profile found to the west. Sheet lead found in quantity was thought to be sheathing for the stepped bottom. Two alternative interpretations suggested are the tail-race of a mill,[23] and a catchment or tank for water, possibly for industrial activity. The feature is thought to have fallen out of use by the beginning of the 3rd century.

West of Eaton Road within the north angle of a side street two stone buildings separated by a courtyard were built in, and occupied throughout, the 3rd century.[24] A late 3rd- or 4th-century building with hypocausts also lay west of Watling Street.[25] Further south timber strip buildings were built c. A.D. 90 and later in stone

[14] Cf. *J.C.A.S.* xxx,. plate 46, which shows an eaves-drip gutter.

[15] Ibid. plate 45.

[16] *J.C.A.S.* xlii. 50; *J.R.S.* xlv. 129-30.

[17] *J.R.S.* xlvi. 125-6; *J.C.A.S.* xliii. 55. It may be post-Roman: Laing and Laing, *Dark Ages of W. Ches.* 12-15.

[18] B. R. Hartley, 'Excavations at Heronbridge, 1947-8', *J.C.A.S.* xxxix. 1-20; B. R. Hartley and K. F. Kaine, 'Roman Dock and Buildings', ibid. xli. 15-37. The in-

vestigations were prompted by discovery of an uninscribed altar: *J.R.S.* xxxii. 110; xxxvii. 170.

[19] Collingwood and Richmond, *Arch. of Roman Brit.* 125-6.

[20] *J.R.S.* xix. 192-3.

[21] *J.C.A.S.* xli. 22.   [22] Thompson, *Roman Ches.* 64.

[23] Inf. from the late Sir Ian Richmond.

[24] *J.R.S.* xxvii. 232; *J.C.A.S.* xxxix, fig. 1. A plan prepared at the time shows features, including a column.

[25] *J.C.A.S.* xxxix. 10 n. 7.

c. 140. The stone walls were inserted through a thick layer of burnt daub; occupation did not outlast the 2nd century. Another timber building *c*. 4.5 m. wide was late 1st- or early 2nd-century; after repairs it was replaced by a stone building 6 m. wide, apparently no earlier than the late 3rd century. A side street immediately to the north was remade more than once; in its 4th-century form it was 4.5 m. wide with a substantial kerb on the north. There were no buildings adjacent to the road on its north side.[26] As on the east side of the Roman road, there were apparently groups of buildings on the west bounded on either side by side-roads or alleys.

The settlement extends *c*. 300 m. on the east side of Watling Street, and at least 60 m. on the west side. Roman pottery and tiles have been found *c*. 0.3 km. to the north;[27] how far south the settlement extended is uncertain, but a building discovered on the line of the Chester southerly by-pass, *c*. 0.5 km. south of the southernmost site,[28] measured 29.2 m. east–west by 11.4 m., a size comparable to that of the strip buildings. No internal walls were found; two large openings 3 m. and 2 m. wide in the east wall gave access to a surfaced area alongside Watling Street. Foundations 70 cm. wide supported a superstructure partially of stone. No floor levels, rubbish deposits, or pits were found, but the footing yielded a little coarse pottery, and a Roman date seems *prima facie* likely in view of the relationship with the Roman road and the proximity of the settlement. The building was probably a barn. Investigation of an extensive area east of the Roman road at the same point revealed no features other than a ditch.[29]

The extent to which buildings were confined to the Watling Street frontage is unknown. Smaller structures are recorded behind the strip buildings, and the side streets which separated the groups may have served further buildings behind the main frontage.[30]

Industrial activity in the first phase of occupation at Heronbridge, *c*. A.D. 90–140, is suggested by discovery of a bronze-smith's hearth with moulds and by slags from pits.[31] A possible corn-drier dates from the same period. In the second phase, from *c*. 140 onwards, there is no reliable evidence of industrial activity apart from lead-working at the northern end of the site. The ovens or furnaces give no clue as to their product, and may be corn-drying kilns.[32] Heronbridge had a short-lived industrial phase and cannot be compared with Wilderspool or Middlewich. The proximity of the road to the Dee, the likely use of the river for transporting goods to the fortress, and the obstacle to navigation presented by the narrow gorge between Chester and Handbridge have combined to suggest that Heronbridge was a suitable transhipment point where water-borne supplies, such as pottery and tiles from the works at Holt, could be stored before onward transmission by road. The quantity of Holt pottery from the site appeared to substantiate the theory, but the major period of pottery production at Holt ended before the stone 'store buildings' at Heronbridge were built.[33] Furthermore, transhipment could have been effected much nearer the fortress. Whatever the character of its early occupation, Heronbridge was a civil settlement from the Antonine period onwards, probably linked with the rural economy as much as with the fortress. The site is so close to the

[26] Thompson, *Roman Ches.* 64; *J.R.S.* lvii. 180–1; *J.C.A.S.* lv. 92–3; *Arch. Newsletter*, ix. 14.

[27] *Ches. Arch. Bull.* i. 20, vi. 75.

[28] *Britannia*, vii. 321; *Ches. Arch. Bull.* iv. 26–7.

[29] D. F. Petch, 'Excavations in Eaton Road, Eccleston, Chester, 1972', *J.C.A.S.* lviii. 15–39.

[30] Few notes or drawings supplement *J.C.A.S.* xxx. 111–17. A building *c*. 11.5 m. by 6 m. lay *c*. 36 m. west of the road: *J.R.S.* xxxvii. 171.

[31] B. R. Hartley, 'Heronbridge Excavations: Bronze-Worker's Hearth', *J.C.A.S.* xli. 1–14. It is uncertain whether enamelling of bronzes took place: J. D. Bateson, *Enamel-Working in Iron Age, Roman, and Sub-Roman Brit.* (Brit. Arch. Rep. xciii), 106.

[32] One may have been a malting kiln.

[33] *Arch. Camb.* cxv. 52. Civilian potters made pottery similar to Holt ware: below.

fortress that it must be considered as part of its *canabae*, and its buildings represent the same miscellany of houses, shops, workshops, and stores as found in any similar settlement. A mercantile element in the population is indicated by an altar dedicated to the Mother Goddesses Ollototae.[34] The cult of the *matres* Ollototae, sometimes alternatively Transmarinae, is centred on the Rhineland, and the altar, put up by Julius Secundus and Aelia Augustina (?), both evidently civilians, may indicate trade links with Lower Germany.[35] A number of Roman lead weights have been found at Heronbridge or nearby.[36]

It has been suggested that Heronbridge was a settlement of veterans,[37] or alternatively that the postulated 'citizens of *Deva*' originated from Heronbridge rather than from the community closer to the fortress, for on the Danube the status of *municipium* was conferred on the more distant of two civil settlements outside fortresses at *Carnuntum*, *Aquincum*, and *Viminacium*.[38] Nevertheless on present evidence it is difficult to believe that the modest straggling settlement at Heronbridge was distinguished enough to enjoy the status of either a *municipium* or a *colonia*.[39]

Heronbridge has been thought to be the *Bovium* of the Antonine Itinerary: if the distance from *Deva* to *Bovium* is amended from x to 11 miles that would restore the correct distance to *Mediolanum* (Whitchurch, Salop.).[40] *Bovium* is usually identified as Holt.[41]

Saltney

Finds are recorded from Cliveden Road, mainly in the service trenches for new houses;[42] two concentrations were noted *c.* 300 m. apart. The northern produced more finds and structures. Two linear ditches or drainage gulleys ran roughly east–west 64 m. apart, and a third approximately at right angles to them was traced for 36–90 m. The junction of two walls was seen 1.5 m. east of the third ditch, and another wall lay 39.6 m. north of it: the alignment of walls and ditches corresponded. The footings of the walls consisted of sandstone and cobbles, with some broken tile and amphora sherds, in puddled clay. No upstanding wall apparently survived. Many of the finds seem to have come from the ditches, although an occupation spread was also traced. The finds and features were contained in an area *c.* 120 m. from north to south but of unknown east–west measurement.

A length of foundation in the southern area running roughly north-west to south-east was similar in character. Much Roman pottery was found in a waterlogged deposit and on both sides of Cliveden Road for up to 100 m. to the south. Two querns were also found.

Although Saltney may have been a settlement the features could equally well represent two independent farmsteads with slightly different histories. The northern, higher, and more attractive site was occupied from the late 1st century, whereas the southern appears to date from the mid 2nd. Occupation, at its most intensive during the later 2nd century, apparently continued to the end of the 3rd or later.

[34] *R.I.B.* i, no. 574; *J.C.A.S.* xxx. 40–1 and plate 8 (2). A column capital found nearby may come from the shrine or temple in which the altar was placed. An uninscribed altar has also been found: *J.R.S.* xxxii. 110.
[35] M. Hassall, 'Epigraphic Evidence for Roman Trade', *Roman Shipping and Trade: Britain and the Rhine Provinces*, ed. J. du Plat Taylor and H. Cleere, 42. The altar is likely to be 2nd-cent. There are three dedications to the *matres* Ollototae from Binchester: *R.I.B.* i, nos. 1030–2.
[36] *Ches. Arch. Bull.* vii. 63; *J.R.S.* xlv. 147, no. 14.

[37] Thompson, *Roman Ches.* 65. Officially sponsored settlement is unlikely.
[38] *New Evidence*, 40.
[39] Mason, '*Canabae*'.
[40] *J.C.A.S.* xxx. 118–19.
[41] Rivet and Smith, *Place Names of Roman Brit.* 274; *Y Cymmrodor*, xli. 6; O.S. Map, Roman Brit. (4th edn.).
[42] *Liverpool Annals*, xxii. 3–18; Thompson, *Roman Ches.* 16, 65.

1. THE MID-CHESHIRE RIDGE

View southwards, from Willington across the Gowy valley, of the west-facing sandstone escarpment extending from Beeston Castle to Maiden Castle, with the barely undulating glacial till of the Dee-Gowy lowland in the foreground and Beeston Gap on the left.

2. THE CHESHIRE PENNINES

View south-eastwards from Tegg's Nose Country Park, near Macclesfield, across the upper Bollin valley towards Shutlingsloe (506 m.), showing the stepped profile of the summit resulting from alternating beds of grit and shales

4. TEGG'S NOSE NEAR MACCLESFIELD

Disused Millstone Grit quarry with a stone-cutting frame in the foreground

3. BICKERTON

Boiler-house chimney of the old copper mine

5. THE DEE ESTUARY

Aerial view from the south of Parkgate showing the sea-front and salt marsh resulting from
the progressive silting of the estuary

6. THURSTASTON CLIFFS

View from the west of cliffs of till (boulder clay) exposed along the Dee shoreline of Wirral

7. CHURTON
Aerial view of cropmark

8. BRIDESTONES
The chambered cairn

9. BICKERTON HILLFORT

10. EDDISBURY HILLFORT

11. HELSBY HILLFORT

12. BEESTON CASTLE

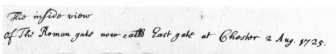

13. CHESTER
The east wall of the legionary fortress

14. CHESTER
Stukeley's drawing of the Roman east gate

15. CHESTER
Relief depicting a *retiarius*

16. NORTHWICH

Cavalry parade helmet

17. CHESTER

Altar from the supposed *mansio*

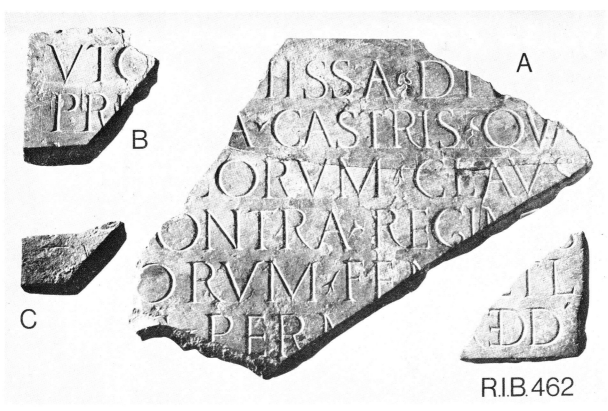

18. CHESTER

Inscriptions from the site of the Old Market Hall and (bottom right) Foregate Street

19. ECCLESTON

The curvilinear churchyard with the ancient site of the church at the centre of the half ellipse marked by a
fragment of wall and rows of graves

20. SANDBACH

The crosses from north-west

21. Sandbach
Lower portions of the north side of the smaller cross and the east side of the larger cross

22. Sandbach
Upper portion of the east side of the
larger cross

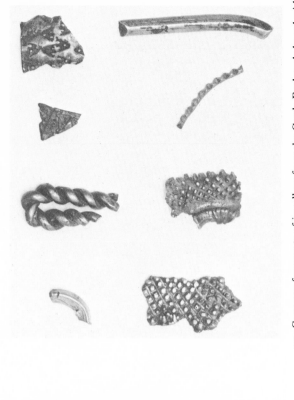

23. CHESTER: Chester ware pot from the Princess Street and Hunter's Walk excavations

24. CHESTER: open-work disc brooch from the Princess Street and Hunter's Walk excavations

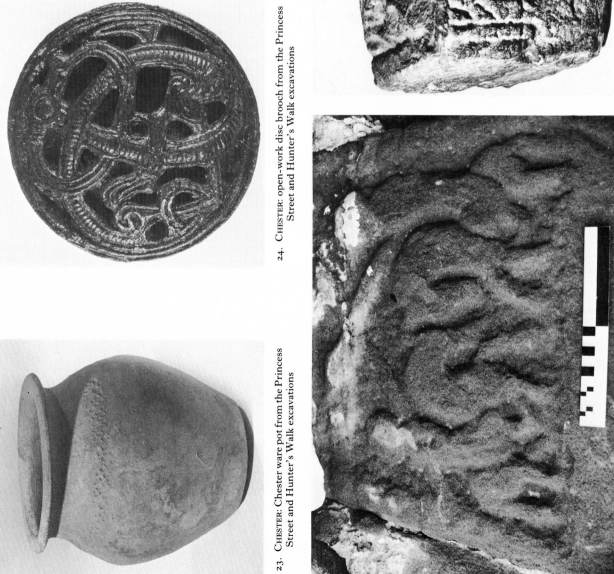

25. CHESTER: fragments of jewellery from the Castle Esplanade hoard with Hiberno-Norse decoration

26. NESTON: sculpture on a grave cross of two mounted men bearing spears

27. OVERCHURCH: stone with runic inscription

Only three coins were recovered, of Vespasian, Trajan, and Marcus Aurelius. The buildings were rectilinear in plan, and may have resembled that found south of Heronbridge. Division of the land on which they stood into plots by means of ditches is reminiscent of arrangements at Middlewich and Wilderspool; the clay subsoil necessitated surface drainage. The farm roofs were probably tiled, as broken Roman roof tiles were scattered over the area. Presumably the owners or tenants of the farms depended on the market provided by the legion; farms so near the fortress may indeed have been leased out annually by one of the senior centurions acting as the legion's agent.

Two finds recorded nearby are a burial with Roman pottery from St. Mark's Road *c.* 250 m. north-west of the northern site, and a gem found in Lache Lane near its junction with Cliveden Road 350 m. to the south-east.[43] Other finds suggest 4th-century occupation. Two coins of Constantine I and one of Constantine II as Caesar were found in the Cliveden Road area, near Circular Drive, a *follis* of Constantine I and a coin of Valens south of Lache Hall,[44] and an *ae* of Constantine I in Lache Lane.[45]

Other finds from that neighbourhood south-west of the fortress include a lead weight from Lache Lane, a *sestertius* of Antoninus Pius or M. Aurelius,[46] and a small cluster of finds, mainly of coins, from Curzon Park. The last are mainly of the later Roman period.[47] Slightly to the north, at Brewers Hall, a coin of Trajan has been found.[48]

Meols

Meols, the only coastal site of consequence in Cheshire in the Roman period,[49] raises problems of interpretation and of location. Archaeological material began to be collected on the foreshore in the early 19th century, although only a relatively small proportion was Roman. Sixty-three identifiable coins are said to have been found, and a number of brooches; other metalwork was scanty and pottery virtually absent apart from 'a few small fragments of plain samian' and 'black Upchurch ware'.

Most finds of the Roman period are said to have been made east of Dove Point, whereas later material lay up to 800 m. south-west, and it was thought that the Roman settlement probably lay more than 1 km. seaward of high water mark, though it was also observed that finds were washed out by the highest tides, especially those accompanied by strong northerly gales. It was evidently believed that finds were made *in situ*: the Roman material was associated with a peat layer 90 cm. thick. What were believed to be sections of the foundations or floors of houses became visible after an unusually high tide. They were described as puddled clay floors, and walls 23–38 cm. high made of wood framework, filled with clay similar to the floor. Other features noted were possibly the bases for roof supports. The relationship of finds to structures is uncertain.

Among coins recorded from Meols are some of the pre-Roman Iron Age;[50] the earliest Roman coin is Claudian, and the latest of Magnus Maximus. The brooches which can be dated are from the 1st to the 3rd century. The site was therefore

[43] *Liverpool Annals*, xxii. 3, 16.
[44] *Ches. Arch. Bull.* vii. 62–3.
[45] *J.C.A.S.* xxxvi. 151.   [46] *Ches. Arch. Bull.* vii. 62.
[47] Coins of Vespasian, Trajan, Hadrian, Probus, Diocletian (2), Maximian I, Constantine II, and Constantius II: *J.C.A.S.* xlvi. 80; xlvii. 37; xlviii. 45. A white glass bead of the 1st cent. was found, with pottery of unknown date: *Ches.*

Arch. Bull. iv. 38.
[48] *J.C.A.S.* vi. 410.
[49] A. Hume, *Ancient Meols*; Watkin, *Roman Ches.* 274–85; *T.H.S.L.C.* xxviii. 128 sqq.; G. Lloyd-Morgan, *Roman Finds from Meols* (forthcoming).
[50] Not necessarily proof of pre-Roman occupation, as Iron Age coins are found on 1st-cent. Roman sites.

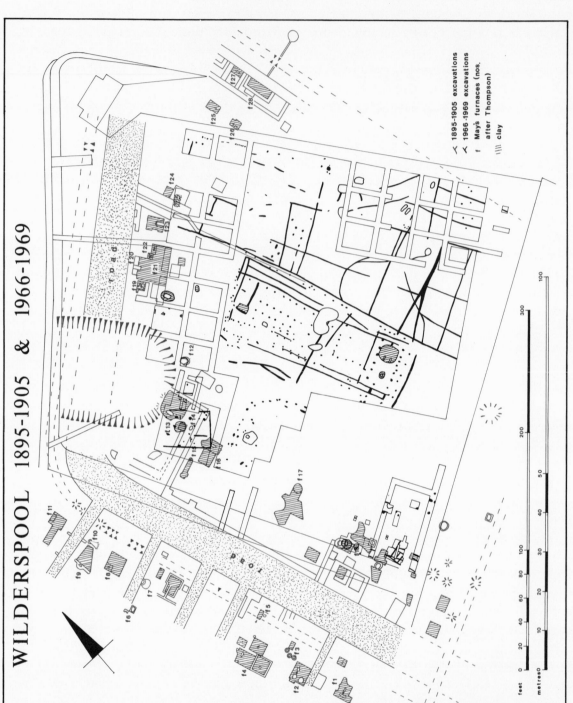

WILDERSPOOL 1895-1905 & 1966-1969

1895-1905 excavations
1966-1969 excavations
May's furnaces (nos. after Thompson)
clay

FIG. 31.

probably occupied throughout the Roman period.[51] Certainly more than a simple fishing village, Meols was possibly a major harbour.[52]

Wilderspool

A Roman industrial settlement lay on the south bank of the Mersey where the river was crossed by King Street.[53] The earliest finds were reported in 1770 during construction of the Bridgewater canal c. 800 m. south of the apparent core of the settlement near the Greenall Whitley brewery. Further canal cutting in 1801–3, for the Old Quay canal, yielded coins of Vespasian and Domitian with other Roman material, including the bases, shafts, and capitals of Roman columns, ashlar masonry blocks, and possibly foundations. What may have been industrial hearths were found in the Town Field. Excavation for the foundations of Mr. Greenall's house yielded Roman finds, as did building of the brewery,[54] in the field behind which pottery and coins were found; excavations in 1849 yielded samian and coarse pottery and foundations.[55] Coins and pottery were found when a row of cottages was built;[56] removal of spoil and sand from the field in the angle between canal and river yielded much pottery and other material but no structural remains.[57] Other finds included a column base and capital and a pottery face mask.[58] The finds came mainly from large ditches 'which traversed the site of the station in various directions', appearing on both sides of the Old Quay canal,[59] and it was estimated that Roman material was found over an area of 14.5 ha. Shallow pits or hollows filled with clay, the upper part partially burnt or baked, were clearly associated with industrial activity on the site, although at the time construed as the result of an extensive fire. The industrial basis of the site was not at first recognized, although by the 1870s it was believed that much of the pottery found was made locally.[60] On the evidence of the coins occupation was relatively short-lived.[61] Archaeological investigation between 1895 and 1905 made assessment of the character of the site possible.[62] Roman Wilderspool was strongly industrial in character, yielding a variety of clay working floors, hearths, ovens, and furnaces. Some were evidently associated with buildings, one of which measured no less than c. 45 m. by c. 24 m. Such remains were not confined to the principal site explored, immediately west of the brewery, but also appeared on a second site 250 m. south in Stockton Heath, where similar floors and furnaces were seen on either side of King Street. The only building which could be confidently described lay west of the road: it was 18.3 m. long and 8.5 m. wide, with a veranda on the south side, and contained working hearths. Most of the industrial remains on the site cannot be expressly related to a process, but among those which can be identified are shaft and bowl furnaces for iron smelting and smithing respectively, and two furnaces for producing bronze,

[51] The evenness of the coin list is unusual. Among Cheshire sites only Chester and Wilderspool have produced more coins.

[52] *Arch. and Coastal Change*, ed. F. H. Thompson, 93–7. The mean high water mark at spring tides may have been 1 m. higher in the late 3rd cent. than at present.

[53] Watkin, *Roman Ches.* 260–73; T. May, *Warrington's Roman Remains*. Thompson, *Roman Ches.* 18–19, 67–87, reconsiders the early discoveries and May's excavations, and analyses the industrial aspects of the site.

[54] Watkin, *Roman Ches.* 260–1; W. Beamont, *Account of Roman Station at Wilderspool*, 9, 16–19; Watkin, *Roman Ches.* 260–1; Kendrick, *Guide Book to Colln. of Roman Remains from Wilderspool, near Warrington*, 4. The hearths, both circular and square, were lined with clay and were full of ash. They were concentrated in one part of the field.

[55] *T.H.S.L.C.* ii. 29–31. Several trenches were opened in the same field in 1831.

[56] Watkin, *Roman Ches.* 263. They were probably the cottages between the river and Big Cress Brook Field.

[57] *Reliquary*, x. 88–90. Large-scale sand digging began in 1863, and in 1871 extraction was proceeding so rapidly that it was impossible to continue to record the finds: *J.C.A.S.* [1st ser.], iii. 194, 199.

[58] Watkin, *Roman Ches.* 268–9; Thompson, *Roman Ches.* 86 and fig. 21 (1); Kendrick, *Guide Book*, 14; Warrington Mus. RA 1224.

[59] *J.C.A.S.* [1st ser.], iii, facing p. 194.

[60] *Jnl. Brit. Arch. Assoc.* xxvii. 430–7.

[61] Watkin, *Roman Ches.* 272; *J.C.A.S.* [1st ser.], iii. 197.

[62] *T.H.S.L.C.* xlviii. 1–28; l. 1–40; lii. 1–52; lv–lvi. 209–37; lviii. 15–40; May, *Warrington's Roman remains, passim.*

with associated crucibles.[63] The large number of pieces of lead suggested that lead working was carried out. Glass making was attested by a small crucible containing a black glass paste, and by glass slag and cullet. Pairs of furnaces were tentatively identified as for glass working, one for fritting and melting, and the other for annealing: beads may have been the main product. Pottery was also produced, including *mortaria*, and the stokehole of one of the three pottery kilns located yielded a *denarius* of Antoninus Pius.

An area of *c.* 1.2 ha. between the Ship Canal and the Mersey was believed to have been defended with a stone-faced rampart and multiple ditches. The suggested defences were not, however, in commission at the same time as the industrial features:[64] on the west, side roads at intervals of 15 m. or less nullified the rampart and ditch, and to the east the rampart apparently coincided with the back wall of a building. It was later suggested that the rampart and ditches belonged to an Agrico-lan fort on the important river crossing, the industrial site being developed after its abandonment,[65] but it is easy to overstate the importance of the river crossing at that early date, for the road following the edge of the Pennines was probably more important initially.[66] Investigation has failed to find the 'defences' at the north-west corner and on the north side,[67] and it seems that the settlement was open from the beginning, and at no time military or under army control.[68] Industrial activity is thought to have begun as early as *c.* A.D. 85–90, and to have been intense during the earlier 2nd century.[69] Subsequently there seems to be a progressive reduction of occupation until the end of the 2nd century, and perhaps abandonment by the early 3rd. The 3rd- and 4th-century pottery from the site represents very slight occupation in the later Roman period.[70]

In 1930 pipe-laying 500 m. east of the main Greenall Whitley brewery site in Lousher's Lane yielded quantities of Roman material, indicating the likely extent of the settlement in that direction.[71] Substantial traces of structure included a hypocaust, unique on the site. More than 12 m. west lay a smaller structure 6 m. by 3.6 m. built of sandstone with a puddled clay floor. Painted wall plaster was found, and the building was therefore residential as well as industrial. The pottery from the site runs from the 2nd to the 4th century; in addition to the hypocaust tiles there are roof and flue tiles, some of which appear to be wasters, while others appear unfinished or unused, indicating the presence of a tile kiln nearby.[72]

Excavation between 1966 and 1969 on the site of an extension to the brewery[73] revealed large timber buildings which contained many clay working floors.[74] Occu-pation began either late in the 1st century or early in the 2nd. There were at least two phases of timber buildings, and the character of the occupation appeared to

[63] Cf. Thompson, *Roman Ches.* fig. 19. Unusually large shaft furnaces and bowl hearths were identified: R. Tylecote, *Metallurgy in Archaeology*, 222–4, 236. It is possible that enamelling of bronze took place: Bateson, *Enamel Working*, 103.

[64] May's description of the rampart and ditches is not compelling. He suggested that the features west of the 'defences' were placed in annexes.

[65] There is little dating evidence to support Agricolan occupation, and the irregular area proposed for the fort was very unusual in the Flavian period: Thompson, *Roman Ches.* 19, 70; *Northern Hist.* i. 3.

[66] *Northern Hist.* iii. 17. The road crossing the Mersey at Wilderspool and going to Lancaster by Wigan and Walton-le-Dale (both Lancs.) became important later.

[67] *J.R.S.* lvii. 179; *Britannia*, i. 281.

[68] The suggestion that Wilderspool was a works depot of Legio xx in the same manner as Holt is not borne out by

recent investigation.

[69] Thompson, *Roman Ches.* 81.

[70] P. V. Webster, 'Later Roman Occupation at Wilders-pool', *J.C.A.S.* lviii. 91–2.

[71] *J.R.S.* xxi. 223; xxiii. 196; Thompson, *Roman Ches.* 79–80. Plan in S. Grealey and others, *Arch. of Warrington's Past*, plate 2: the scale should read 0–50 ft.

[72] Thompson, *Roman Ches.* 80. A coin of Florian from the site is lost, and there is doubt as to its genuineness as a find.

[73] *J.R.S.* lvii. 179; lviii. 182 and plan, fig. 10; *Britannia*, i. 281–2; viii. 385; *Northern Hist.* iii. 12–16; Grealey, *Arch. of Warrington's Past*, 27–36. Thanks are due to Mr. J. H. Williams and Mr. J. Hinchcliffe for access to their reports before publication.

[74] The closest analogy to these great timber sheds is the *fabricae* of legionary fortresses; that at Inchtuthil was almost 60 m. square over all: *J.R.S.* li. 160 and fig. 10.

change *c.* A.D. 150. Thereafter the site declined, occupation ending late in the 2nd century.[75]

In 1973–6 work in Lousher's Lane revealed new features.[76] Ditches excavated into the natural sand defined rectangular enclosures on either side of a trackway; timber buildings 17 m. by 8.5 m. and 11 m. by 3 m. were found. Circular buildings 8.5 m. and 10.5 m. in diameter presumably indicate survival into the Romano-British period of an older tradition of building. Although industrial remains were found, activity was not on a large scale: iron, lead, and bronze working were all traced, but not all the features could be identified. The buildings were both domestic and industrial, and possibly linked with agriculture. Occupation of that part of the settlement did not begin until the Hadrianic period at the earliest, and the decline which set in on the brewery site from *c.* A.D. 160 did not begin until the late 2nd or early 3rd century when there was a marked decline.[77] Architectural fragments, which include three fragments of column shafts and a Corinthian capital, hint at masonry buildings. The settlement has yielded no inscriptions other than graffiti[78] and lead weights;[79] an uninscribed altar has been found.[80]

In its heyday under Hadrian and Antoninus Pius the settlement may have covered as much as 10 ha. Nonetheless while occupation may have persisted into the 3rd century, Wilderspool's appearance from the Severan period onwards resembled a ghost town. The settlement's rise and fall over a period of less than a century presumably resulted from economic forces now difficult to perceive. A market was offered for many of the products of Wilderspool by the forts of Lancashire and the Pennines and their *vici*, and by the fortress of Chester and its *canabae*:[81] studies of the *mortaria* and other coarse ware may indicate what happened in other industries at Wilderspool.[82] It has proved possible to identify the products of Wilderspool kilns fairly confidently. One is the rough-cast beaker long identified as a local ware;[83] a variation is a rouletted beaker. A very much larger range of pottery was produced in a fabric more nearly comparable with that from the legionary potteries at Holt. Most of the forms produced seem to have been localized in distribution, but one unusual type, the Triple Vase, was marketed over a radius of *c.* 80 km. extending as far as the forts at Melandra and Ribchester, as well as Chester, Northwich, and Manchester. Pottery was therefore supplied to the army, but only to the forts in the immediate region. *Mortaria*, however, were an exception. At least nine potters can be assigned to Wilderspool, and three or four others may also have worked there.[84] The distribution of their products extended north from Cheshire through Lancashire and Cumbria to the western and central parts of Hadrian's Wall; in certain forts a particularly high proportion of Wilderspool *mortaria* is found, reaching almost half in one instance.[85] Nevertheless the distribution of stamped *mortaria*

[75] The kilns making *mortaria* were at peak production *c.* A.D. 110–70: below.

[76] Following work in the early 1930s, further excavation began in 1973. The Central Excavation Unit completed the programme in 1976. Work before 1976 is discussed in Grealey, *Arch. of Warrington's Past*; see also *Britannia*, vi. 240; viii. 385.

[77] Dr. D. Shotter has studied the coins and concludes that there was occupation from the 90s of the 1st cent., a burst of activity under Trajan and Hadrian, and a decline in the Antonine period; 3rd-cent. coins are virtually absent and 4th-cent. coins form an abnormally small proportion. The fact that few sites in the region have yielded as many coins is a measure of the intensity of 2nd-cent. occupation.

[78] *Britannia*, viii. 430 (no. 17), 436–7 (no. 49).

[79] *J.R.S.* xliii. 130, nos. 10a, 10b; Thompson, *Roman Ches.*, fig. 21 (16).

[80] *T.H.S.L.C.* xlviii. 10–13 and plate 1b; May, *Warrington's Roman Remains*, 70. [81] Thompson, *Roman Ches.* 86.

[82] *Arch. Jnl.* cxxx. 77–103.

[83] *Jnl. Brit. Arch. Assoc.* xxvii. 430–7.

[84] Analysis confirmed that potters assigned to Wilderspool did work there, and suggested a link between Wilderspool and a source near Carlisle: *Inst. of Arch. Bull.* v. 25–43; V. G. Swan, *Pottery Kilns of Roman Brit.* (R. C. H. M. suppl. ser. v), 104–5.

[85] Their markets for pottery were the forts and *vici* at Ambleside, Hardknott, Lancaster, Melandra Castle, Middlewich, Northwich, Ribchester, Walton-le-Dale, Watercrook, and elsewhere in Cheshire, Lancashire, the Peak District, and the southern half of Cumbria. Smaller quantities are found outside the area, in north Wales, the western sector of Hadrian's Wall, and even the Antonine Wall. The pottery is also found at Chester.

attributable to the Wilderspool kilns is noticeably slighter in Scotland.[86] Pottery was produced at Wilderspool mainly *c.* A.D. 100–65; the kilns were thus in production until the Roman withdrawal from Scotland. Potters migrated to the site, particularly from the Midlands, partly because of its position in relation to potential markets, and because raw materials were accessible. For a time they successfully marketed their products in the north-west; the decline of the industry apparently began when Scotland was reoccupied as far as the Tay. The uprooting of a large proportion of the army, and its movement northwards, distanced the potters from much of their market: their reaction was to migrate north, perhaps to the valley of the river Petteril near Carlisle; so simple was their plant that such a move was quite easy.[87]

In other industries the investment in buildings and fittings was higher, and the owners were probably more reluctant to write them off by moving elsewhere. The structure of industry at Wilderspool is unknown, but evidence of sizeable stone buildings may imply men of substance comparable to the villa-dwellers who owned the potteries in the Nene valley rather than small manufacturers, in which case the workers may have been slaves. The eventual demise of the settlement can probably be put down to the flight of capital, rather than migration of the workers or manufacturers.

Considering the intensity of occupation at Wilderspool, surprisingly few indications of its cemeteries have appeared. An oak coffin lined with lead inside and out was found on the north bank of the Ship Canal; nearby was an 'Upchurch' cinerary urn with cremation.[88] A second coffin much like the first was found at about the same spot *c.* 250 m. east of the site near the Greenall Whitley brewery, and *c.* 400 m. or more from the site most recently excavated. Two infant cremations have been reported from a site in the same area. The cemetery therefore appears to be close to the settlement on its south and east sides. Interments are said to have been found during sand-quarrying.[89]

A scatter of Roman finds on the Warrington side of the river suggests a minor settlement on the north bank. From the centre of the town have come bronze coins of Vespasian and Marius, and a Republican *denarius*.[90] Pottery has also come from two sites.[91] A little further east is a cluster of finds near the site of the castle, including a *patera* handle, a penannular brooch, and coarse pottery.[92]

Northwich

Northwich long remained largely unknown as a Roman site. Chance discoveries[93] lay principally on the elevated ground west of the river Weaver, known locally as Castle, traversed by Watling Street as it approaches the river crossing. A reference in 1850 to 'large remains of foundations . . . having been dug up, and . . . antiquities which have come to light',[94] was followed from *c.* 1852 by more Roman finds:

[86] 45 per cent of AVSTINVS's stamps are from Antonine sites in Scotland, a quite abnormal distribution for a Wilderspool potter, and it is likely that this potter moved to the Eden valley. DIS/LDB is another potter who may have migrated.

[87] Reoccupation of Scot. diverted pottery supply to the army from the W. coast to the E., reflected in the declining supply of Wilderspool *mortaria* from *c.* A.D. 140. It has been pointed out that there seems to be a general decline in settlements in Ches. in the later 2nd cent., another possible reason for the demise of the pottery industry.

[88] *T.H.S.L.C.* xlviii, plate 1; l. 19–20.

[89] Kendrick, *Guide Book*, 6.

[90] W. Beamont, *Hist. Latchford*, 1; Grealey, *Arch. of Warrington's Past*, gazetteer, nos. 27–8.

[91] Grealey, *Arch. of Warrington's Past*, gazetteer, nos. 21–2.

[92] Ibid. nos. 19–20; *J.C.A.S.* lx. 113.

[93] Watkin, *Roman Ches.* 251–9; Thompson, *Roman Ches.* 18, 88–91.

[94] *J.C.A.S.* [1st ser.], i. 46. Cf. Baines, *Lancs. and Ches. Past and Present*, i. 262, referring to 'urns containing calcined bones, large quantities of Roman pottery, and a *mortarium* inscribed MARIVS [? MARINVS] FECIT'.

Mr. Rothwell's house, barely 50 m. south of the church, yielded three coins, the latest of Vespasian, 'red pottery', part of an amphora, and a bead; Highfield, the adjacent house to the south, yielded Roman tiles and pottery including samian, glass, and a lead 'lamp', probably a lamp-holder. When New End Cottages were built c. 200 m. south of the church and c. 100 m. from Highfield much pottery is said to have been found, though the only certain Roman piece was the rim of a *mortarium* with the stamp of Similis.[95] Perhaps 100 m. or less from New End Cottages at Castle Dockyard lead brine pans were found.

Finds have also been made near Winnington Hill, c. 500 m. north of Castle. Two urns of the early 2nd century containing cremations were found when the foundations of Oakleigh were being dug, together with bronze objects and coins, one of Vespasian.[96] Evidently the cemetery lies in that direction, though not all finds derive from it. Querns found at the bottom of Winnington Hill are occupation debris; a small beaker of 3rd-century date and a bronze spoon were found at the same time.[97] Pottery has been found at Winnington.[98]

Until the mid 1960s it was possible only to speculate that initial occupation was military, succeeded by a settlement possibly linked with salt production.[99] Investigation during clearance south-west of the church from 1966 revealed an auxiliary fort.[1] The defences consisted of a rampart and at least one ditch. A ditch c. 5.5 m. wide had been partly removed by a later one 6 m. wide; both were 1.5 m. deep. To the south of the ditch traces were found of a rampart more than 3.6 m. wide, placed on a raft of packed cobble and gravel. Its front was removed by later insertion of a stone curtain wall up to 1.5 m. thick. The fill of the earlier ditch contained turf from the first rampart. Nothing remained of the wall *in situ*, but the fill of the later ditch yielded ashlar blocks presumably derived from it. Post-holes in the outer lip of the ditch may represent additional obstacles in the defensive system, and beyond the ditch a patrol track surfaced with sandstone and cobbles was noted. Within the fort one of the streets and small parts of several timber buildings were found. Two distinct road surfaces were separated by a layer of earth, each road having its own drain: the width of the street was not determined. Timber buildings were defined by post alignments and clay floors, in every instance of two periods, the earlier being Flavian at the earliest; the second period began soon after A.D. 100. Little of the plan could be recovered, although the buildings agreed in orientation with the street and rampart. One building over 26 m. long was tentatively identified as a barrack.

The defences of the fort have been found only on its north-east side, and little is known of its internal layout. It is not possible to describe its position and size, even conjecturally.[2] The Roman road, which is supposed to equate in position and alignment with the present Chester Road,[3] does not lead to or proceed from the gates of the fort, but rather seems to cross the site without paying any regard to it.

Further investigation north of Chester Road suggests that there were in fact two forts at Northwich on distinct axes, each having timber buildings of two periods. In its final phase the later fort was reduced in size, and provided with a rampart at least 8 m. wide on a sandstone foundation, accompanied by double ditches. Both

[95] Mrs. Hartley has kindly identified the stamp from the illustration in Watkin, *Roman Ches.* 255.

[96] Watkin appears to describe the same find twice.

[97] Watkin, *Roman Ches.* 256.

[98] *Arch. Newsletter*, xvi. 8.

[99] Thompson, *Roman Ches.* 18, 90.

[1] For investigations to 1972 see *Arch. Jnl.* cxxviii. 31–

77 and summary reports in *J.R.S.* lviii. 183; lix. 209–10; *Britannia*, i. 282–3; ii. 255–6.

[2] Prof. G. D. B. Jones refers to the line of the western defences being found: *Arch. Jnl.* cxxviii. 76. Survival of the southern defences is thought doubtful.

[3] Confirmed in 1973 with exposure of the *agger*: *Ches. Arch. Bull.* ii. 31.

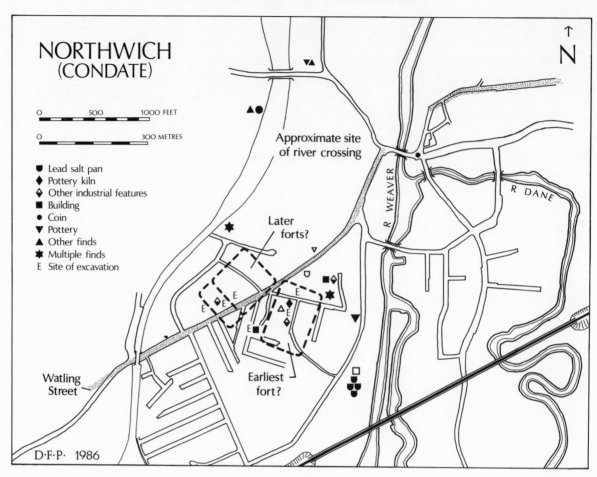

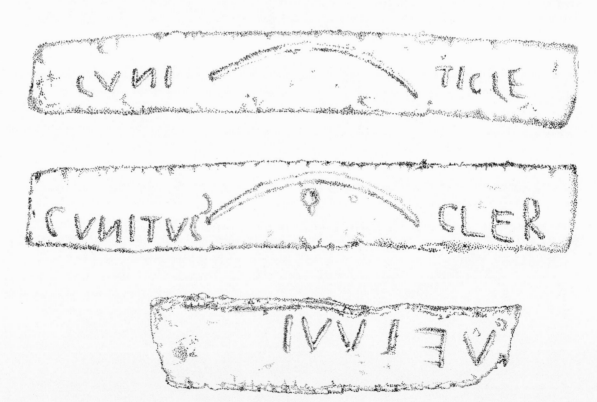

FIG. 32. Roman saltworks: 1. Northwich; 2. Inscriptions on saltpans from Nantwich (top and middle) and Northwich (bottom), scale approx. 2:9.

were rather larger than the single ditch of the previous fort. Internal buildings may have been barracks or stables.[4]

The fort commanded an important river crossing on the direct route between Chester and York, almost midway between the former and Manchester. The sandy plateau raises the fort site above flood level. The scanty evidence and historical probability suggest foundation in the Flavian period, at latest under Agricola. Soon after the turn of the 2nd century the defences and internal buildings were rebuilt, albeit on substantially the same lines as before, following abandonment and possibly a change of garrison. Evidence for the break was found in the garden of Highfield at the supposed north-east corner of the fort.[5] As no inscriptions survive the size and type of garrison cannot be identified in either period, although discovery of an iron cavalry parade helmet similar to an example from Newstead[6] makes it likely that a cavalry *ala*, probably a quingenary unit, formed the garrison at one time.[7]

A timber slot dug through debris resulting from demolition of the fort buildings, and on a different orientation from them, may hint at civilian occupation after the fort's abandonment. A pottery kiln found *c.* 42.5 m. within the fort defences yielded pottery of late Flavian to early Hadrianic date. Because civilian potters did not work inside an occupied fort, the kiln belongs to the hiatus between the two periods of military occupation. The potter's repertoire consisted in the main of jars, flagons, and bowls in a soft orange-buff fabric. Production was apparently modest in quantity and short-lived. Six iron-reducing furnaces just outside the fort on the north-east side were associated with much late Flavian to Trajanic pottery, and they too probably belonged to a short interlude of civilian occupation.[8] North of Chester Road further evidence of industrial activity has been found.

The only building of the *vicus* to have been excavated lay west of the fort; its size exceeded 18 m. by 16 m. The slots for its timbers yielded pottery of the early 2nd century: there was a subsequent rebuild, and it seems likely that the building was occupied during the second period of the fort and perhaps outlived it. Its orientation differed from those of the fort and Watling Street.[9] Another find presumably associated with the *vicus* was made in Queen's Gate, also west of the fort, where much pottery datable to *c.* A.D. 100 was found, with Republican *denarii*, a *denarius* of Domitian, and a *sestertius* of Vespasian. The finds also included two iron spears.[10] Building work in Zion Street yielded samian and coarse pottery.[11]

Occupation of the site was connected with exploitation of the springs of natural brine for making salt. Four lead pans were found when a dock at Castle Dockyard was being extended, of which all but one had been broken up before their significance was realized.[12] The complete pan is uninscribed, but two others bore apparently meaningless inscriptions, one reading IIICCCIII, and the other EVE preceded by a reversed C:[13] it is unknown whether the latter is complete, but the former (still extant) certainly is. Though they were at first identified as Roman, knowledge that lead pans were used in the Middle Ages and uncertainty concerning the inscriptions

[4] Thanks are due to Prof. G. D. B. Jones for supplying inf. before publication. The newly discovered fort is 2nd-cent., but more precise dating awaits analysis of the finds.

[5] Indicated by the ditch system: *Arch. Jnl.* cxxviii. 77.

[6] H. Russell Robinson, *Armour of Imperial Rome*, 94–5, 115–16 and plates 247–9, 318–23; above, plate. Bronzes found on Winnington Hill may have been correctly identified as horse trappings: Watkin, *Roman Ches.* 254.

[7] In view of the discovery of a diploma at Middlewich issued to a trooper in the *ala Classiana*, that unit may have been at Northwich before A.D. 205. Presumably there was a change in garrison when the later fort was reduced in size.

[8] *Britannia*, iv. 284. They are said to have resembled furnaces at Manchester: G. D. B. Jones and others, *Roman Manchester*, 67–74, 143–55. For the pottery kiln see below.

[9] *Britannia*, vi. 242; *Ches. Arch. Bull.* iii. 53–4 and plan.

[10] *Ches. Arch. Bull.* iii. 60; vii. 65.

[11] Inf. from Mr. S. R. Williams.

[12] *T.H.S.L.C.* xviii. 199–203; *Arch. Jnl.* xxii. 77–8; Watkin, *Roman Ches.* 258; 1 *Sheaf*, ii, p. 80. The complete pan is in the Salt Mus., Northwich.

[13] The proposed reading DEVAE is unacceptable.

led to later doubts about their date. Recent discovery, during building on Castle *c.* 70 m. north of the church, of a fragment from the side of a lead pan with the inscription VELVVI retrograde confirms that some lead pans were Roman.[14] Two complete lead pans found near Nantwich,[15] also unquestionably Roman, agree well in size, appearance, and form of construction with the complete pan found at Northwich. Uncertainty remains only about a pan found at Ashton's works, a little under 1 km. east of the river,[16] which is markedly smaller than those known to be Roman.

From the quite detailed description of the dockyard discovery it seems likely that the salt pans were found *in situ.* They lay side by side embedded in charcoal or burnt wood, half-consumed timber being found under one when it was lifted.[17] Strong wooden posts found may have been a suspension system or a shed containing the pans. No sign of a flue or furnace was seen. The findspot is on the west bank of the Weaver 500 m. upstream from the crossing, and some 200 m. south-east of the fort. A feature interpreted as a brine kiln was reported in 1968.[18]

It might be expected that the fort was followed by a settlement largely concerned with making or trading salt, benefiting from its position on a trunk road at the crossing of a navigable river. Samian and coarse pottery from the site need be no later than *c.* A.D. 150,[19] and few finds are later.[20] There is no evidence that such a settlement existed at Northwich, and the salt workings did not long outlive the fort. While the settlement may have moved to another site nearby, possibly on the east bank of the river, the only find known from that area, apart from a lead pan, is a much-corroded 'first brass' coin found in an old salt working at the Bull Ring.[21] A curiosity of the road system near Northwich is that King Street crosses Watling Street 2.5 km. east of the fort, and a later settlement might reasonably be sought there.

The extent of the *vicus* during occupation of the fort is unknown, though the greatest concentration of relevant finds lies south of the church. Cremation burials in urns found near Hartford station are usually associated with Northwich, although over 2.5 km. to the west.[22] Two coins, of Hadrian and Maximinus, were reported from Wallerscote *c.* 2 km. north-west of the fort, and a possible coin hoard is said to have been found at Barnton, a little further north; two silver coins were identified as of Constantine I.[23]

The name of Roman Northwich is believed to have been *Condate*, derived from the Celtic word for a confluence of rivers, in this instance the Weaver and Dane.[24]

Middlewich

In the late 19th century it was thought that among Cheshire sites Middlewich[25] was second only to *Deva.* Casual finds and archaeological excavations have since

[14] A Romano-Celtic personal name in the genitive case, the word understood presumably 'salt pan'. see fig. 32.2.

[15] Below.

[16] Watkin, *Roman Ches.* 258; O.S. Arch. Rec. 67 SE. Now in the Salt Mus.

[17] One pan is described as partially melted by direct contact with heat, and it is possible that at least four pans were found, since the workmen may already have disposed of others. The weight of a complete pan, more than 100 kg., would make it difficult to carry far in one piece.

[18] *J.R.S.* lviii. 183.

[19] A small amount of samian could be early Flavian, but most of the 1st-cent. samian was Flavian-Trajanic; latest occupation is attested by a group of Central Gaulish bowls of Hadrianic to early Antonine date. The coarse pottery suggested occupation between the late 1st and early to mid 2nd cent., with parallels in Pennine forts thought to have been

abandoned *c.* A.D. 140. The *mortaria* included Hadrianic-Antonine products, the latest a piece dated *c.* A.D. 130-70. Casual finds from the site at large in no case differed from material recovered during excavations.

[20] Watkin's coin list includes a bronze coin of Aurelian.

[21] 2 *Sheaf,* ii, pp. 87-8; Watkin, *Roman Ches.* 258.

[22] *T.H.S.L.C.* iii. 1; Watkin, *Roman Ches.* 257. Two surviving urns of the late 1st or early 2nd cent. are in Warrington Mus.: Thompson, *Roman Ches.* 89-90 and fig. 24.

[23] 4 *Sheaf,* v. 32.

[24] *Archaeologia,* xciii. 29; Rivet and Smith, *Place Names of Roman Brit.* 315-16. An alternative, *Salinae,* is no longer entertained.

[25] A number of finds from the Roman site are in the library. Many of those mentioned by Watkin have been lost; some material is in private hands, but the bulk of the recently excavated finds is in the Ches. Mus.

defined a settlement estimated at 20–30 ha., comparable in area to some of the chartered towns of Roman Britain,[26] though comparison with sites defined by a town wall is difficult. Occupation is believed to have begun in the mid Flavian period and to have continued without serious fluctuation until at least the mid 4th century.[27]

Middlewich, like Northwich, is at the confluence of two rivers, the Dane and the Croco, and some writers have identified it as *Condate*.[28] The theory appeared to gain authority from a superficial resemblance between the place-names *Condate* and Kinderton, under which the site was long known, but they are in no way related. The site has also been identified as *Mediolanum*, since it lies in the middle of the Cheshire plain. It is now generally agreed that Middlewich was *Salinae*, meaning 'salt works':[29] of the three sites in Cheshire to which the name might reasonably apply Middlewich has the strongest claim in terms of evidence of salt working in the Roman period.

Early attention was concentrated on the supposed earthworks in Harbutt's Field at the northern end of the settlement.[30] Excavations in 1921–2 cast doubt on the conjectured military site and revealed three clay patches with signs of burning and slag, perhaps iron-working hearths. Finds included three coins, one of Hostilian, A.D. 250–1, and pottery of 1st–3rd-century date.[31] In 1854 excavations for a gas-holder yielded, reputedly in association with Roman pottery, basket work made of hazel rods and well preserved oak, some sawn and morticed, as well as birch used in the round, some again morticed.[32] 'Hand-made potters' bricks' resembled the briquetage found at coastal saltern sites, and it was concluded that a Roman salt works had been found. Two lead brine pans had been found on the nearby river bank 'many years' earlier, and small lead pans 'at a spot rich in Roman remains'.[33] The latter are said to have been marked S:V:T, and are the more readily acceptable as Roman.

Further evidence of Roman salt working at Middlewich emerged in 1960. On a site west of King Street and close to the findspot of a military diploma, a hearth or kiln was revealed where brine was boiled to make salt.[34] It was 3.05 m. long, 61 cm. wide, and 50 cm. deep, and on the longer sides a ledge some 30 cm. above the floor provided a seating for fire bars. The clay fill above the ledge produced a complete fire bar which was found to fit the ledge; other briquetage included a second fire bar, 8 wedge-shaped bricks, 9 cylindrical supports, and at least 5 rectangular plates. Some of the items bore salt glaze caused by spillage of brine, confirming the purpose of the kiln beyond doubt. Pottery from the excavation dated from the end of the 1st century to *c.* A.D. 180. The brine kiln was the only Roman inland salting known at that time.

Investigation arising from the discovery took place between 1964 and 1975.[35] A major site *c.* 150 m. north of the kiln found in 1960 yielded evidence of the relationship of the kilns to other features at a salt works.[36] The beginning of salt

[26] e.g. Caistor-by-Norwich (14 ha.), Caerwent (17.6 ha.).

[27] *Princeton Encyclopaedia of Classical Sites*, ed. R. Stilwell, s.v. *Salinae*.

[28] e.g. Watkin, *Roman Ches.* 243.

[29] The nominative form is *Salinis*: Rivet and Smith, *Place Names of Roman Brit.* 451. Nantwich was suggested as a candidate for the name, but Middlewich has more usually been preferred: *Archaeologia*, xciii. 44; I. A. Richmond, *Roman Brit.* 170. A second place in Britain of the same name is probably Droitwich.

[30] Watkin, *Roman Ches.* 244–5.   [31] *J.R.S.* xi. 205–6.

[32] *J.C.A.S.* [1st ser.], i. 464–5; Watkin, *Roman Ches.* 247.

[33] The find is said to have been made 'many years ago': C. F. Lawrence, *Glimpses of Bygone Middlewich*, 10.

[34] Unpublished. The account which follows is a conflation of summaries by F. H. Thompson, *Roman Ches.* 94–5, and by J. D. Bestwick in *Salt: The Study of an Ancient Industry*, ed. K. W. de Brisay and K. A. Evans, 66.

[35] Directed by J. D. Bestwick. What follows is based on summaries published at the time. The evidence is reviewed in *Salt*, 66–70.

[36] Site C, excavated 1964–9: *Salt*, 66–8; *J.R.S.* lvii. 181; lix. 210–11; *Britannia*, i. 282, 313. The key to the letters used to identify sites is in *Salt*, fig. 41a.

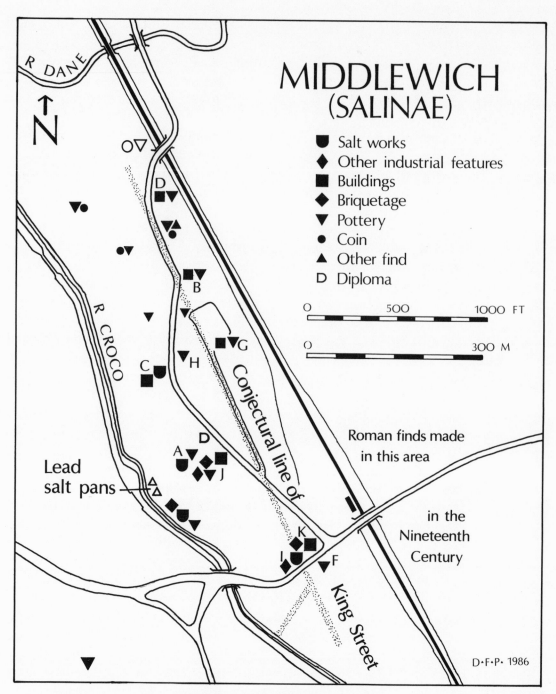

FIG. 33. Roman Middlewich.

production was dated as early as *c.* A.D. 80; timber buildings and other features belonging to a salt works of the 2nd century were sealed by domestic buildings of the 3rd and 4th. A brine pit 3.6 m. in diameter and 2.75 m. deep may have been opened in the 1st century, and yielded, in addition to coins, brooches, and pottery of the late 1st to early 2nd century, a thick deposit of hazel branches. The filling also produced many fragments of sandals discarded by a shoemaker, and at some time after 130, and certainly by the mid 2nd century, the pit was sealed beneath the floor of a timber building which formed the south side of a yard 8–9 m. across. The yard contained salt-working features, including a second brine pit 2.75 m. in diameter, but little more than half the depth of the first, with hazel branches at the bottom.[37] No more than 2 m. separated the pit from a brine kiln resembling that found in 1960 which was abandoned by the mid 2nd century. It overlay a circular hearth 1 m. in diameter. A unique rectangular kiln was also found. Salt glazing found on its floor does not seem compatible with the suggested use for stoving the salt. No briquetage was found. At least two, and perhaps as many as five, amphorae placed in the yard were probably used in salt making. One bore a graffito reading AMVRCA, a word normally translated as the lees remaining after crushing olives to extract the oil, but perhaps by extension applicable to waste resulting from the evaporation of brine. *Amurca* was used in a variety of ways and the by-products of salt making were also worth retaining.[38] An alternative reading of the inscription as MVRIA ('brine') has been dismissed, although *prima facie* highly likely in the context:[39] the graffito may equally be coincidental to re-use of the amphora in the salt works. The building on the south side of the yard was built *c.* A.D. 130–50, but the date of that on the north side is unknown. A third building linking them, and closing the west side of the yard, was added towards the mid 2nd century,[40] and may be of the same date as the building to the north, since the two structures shared identical wall lines and orientation.

A site 600 m. from the first, near the southern end of the settlement, also produced evidence of salt working.[41] Five circular furnaces or kilns, four of them in pairs, were provisionally identified as stoving furnaces. The entire area, including the infill of the furnaces, was covered with large pieces of briquetage including many firebars, and one furnace had firebars in its foundation. A turf and timber leat carried water or possibly brine. Pits containing pottery of *c.* A.D. 80 or earlier also yielded briquetage, as did the fill of Flavian ditches, thus confirming the beginning of salt working in the 1st century.[42] Timber strip buildings were dated from the early 2nd century to the 3rd, and the possibility of later occupation nearby was indicated by scattered 4th-century pottery found in disturbed contexts. Another site immediately to the east yielded an extensive spread of briquetage 10–60 cm. thick. Deep pits, perhaps originally brine pits, containing briquetage were dated *c.* A.D. 70–80. In the early to mid 2nd century a timber building at least 6 m. wide and 27.75 m. long occupied part of the site, but was apparently demolished, after being twice rebuilt, to make way for a ditch of the 3rd or 4th century.[43]

It is natural to assume that salt production, having begun in the Flavian period,

[37] The vertical sides of the brine pits were evidently revetted, as they were dug in sand. Both held 1 m. of water, and the Roman water table was presumably higher.

[38] During the evaporation of brine a scum was formed which in more recent times was skimmed off and retained for use. Thanks are due to Lady Rochester and Mr. G. Twigg for discussing the technology with the author.

[39] *Britannia*, i. 313 (no. 37), n. 47. It is possible that a semi-literate salt worker with an uncertain command of

Latin could have confused the two words.

[40] *Salt*, fig. 41b.

[41] Site I, excavated 1969–72: *Salt*, 68; *Ches. Arch. Bull.* iii. 49; *Britannia*, ii. 255.

[42] *Arch. Newsletter*, xx. 8–9.

[43] Site K, excavated 1973–4: *Salt*, 68; *Ches. Arch. Bull.* iii. 49–51; *Britannia*, iii. 314; v. 419; vi. 242; *Arch. Newsletter*, xxiv. 10–11.

continued thereafter until at least the mid 4th century: indeed, it might seem strange if that were not so. Nevertheless one salt works assigned to the 2nd century is said to have been sealed by 'a series of buildings of the 3rd and 4th centuries of a domestic type'.[44] Similarly, on two other sites 'the volume of salt-working evidence prior to the Antonine period suggests considerable industrial activity in the late 1st and early 2nd centuries',[45] and apparently none of the sites so far explored has produced clear evidence of salt production later than the 2nd century, and in some instances it continued no later than the mid 2nd. A site lying south-east of the 1960 kiln, on the western fringe of the settlement,[46] appeared to be divided into plots perhaps *c*. 7.6 m. wide and 40 m. long by ditches *c*. 1 m. wide. In those plots iron was worked during the late 2nd century and throughout the 3rd, attested not only by heaps of slag resulting from smelting, scaling, and smithing, but also by five furnaces of three distinct types. They are evidently not the only furnaces at Middlewich.[47] Only one could be attributed to smithing: two other bowl furnaces located within 1.5 m. of the first were similar but produced no smithing slag. None of the furnaces found were for smelting, although two pieces of smelting slag with fragments of the furnace hearth still attached indicate a smelting furnace nearby.[48] Forging blocks and scaling hearths were also suspected. Salt working was carried out earlier, since briquetage was found, but no associated structures survived. All the industrial features lay west of timber buildings of the 2nd and 3rd century: on the site itself there were only slight traces of post-built structures. Fourth-century pottery and a coin attested late occupation. In addition to salt making and iron working other industrial activities recorded included bronze working, lead casting and working, window glass making, weaving, fulling, and shoemaking. It would be reasonable to expect pottery to be made locally,[49] as the briquetage and furniture for brine kilns certainly was.[50] Since salt is used in tanning it seems likely that that was also a local industry, although no tanneries have been identified; leather working is attested by a mass of leather offcuts, apparently derived from sandal making, dumped in a disused brine pit. The army provided a ready market for sandals and for other leather equipment; it also required the salt meat which Middlewich may have supplied. It is suggested that the settlement developed a close relationship with its rural hinterland, and its early almost exclusive reliance on salt production was reduced. It apparently grew in size during the 2nd and 3rd centuries, for one 2nd-century salt works was covered by later buildings, and the sites at the southern end of the settlement, initially open and covered with much briquetage, were occupied by buildings from the mid 2nd century. How extensive the settlement was on that side is not known, but even in the late 1st century it may have extended beyond the junction of King Street and Kinderton Street.[51] On one site the iron working seems to have eventually given way to agriculture, although it is uncertain whether that was late or post-Roman in date.[52]

No masonry structures have as yet been recorded at Middlewich, but timber strip buildings have been found on at least six sites.[53] They were from 6.4–7.3 m. wide, and over 15 m. long, with the narrow ends facing the street: one 2nd-century

[44] *Salt*, 66–7.
[45] Ibid. 68.
[46] Site J, excavated 1972–5: *Britannia*, iv. 284; v. 419; vi. 242; vii. 321; *Ches. Arch. Bull.* ii. 29–30; iii. 49.
[47] Ten have been found: J. D. Bestwick and J. H. Cleland, 'Metal Working in the North West', *Roman Manchester*, ed. G. D. B. Jones and others, 147.
[48] *Ches. Arch. Bull.* ii. 30.

[49] Watkin, *Roman Ches.* 250.
[50] *Arch. Newsletter*, xiv–xv. 8; *Britannia*, ii. 255; Swan, *Pottery Kilns of Roman Brit.*, gazetteer, 1.239.
[51] *Arch. Newsletter*, ix. 15.
[52] *Britannia*, vii. 321.
[53] Ibid. i. 282. Three sites revealed such buildings: *Arch. Newsletter*, xiv–xv. 8.

building exceeded 27.75 m.[54] Such buildings, well known on the urban sites of Roman Britain, served any or all of the functions of house, shop, workshop, and store, as at Heronbridge. Not all were necessarily of that form, for a corridor house possibly of 3rd-century date, 13 m. wide, overlay earlier strip buildings. One estimate of the area of the settlement is as much as 40 acres (16 ha.), and possibly twice that if all traces of industrial activity are included.[55]

An old sandpit in Fountain's Field, Queen Street, c. 0.5 km. south-west of the southern end of the settlement, revealed plain samian cups and bowls stacked inside what appeared to be a clay oven.[56] The oven can hardly have been a pottery kiln, but may have been some other industrial feature. The foundations of a supposedly Roman building were found on the Newton side of the Croco opposite Harbutt's Field.[57] East of the settlement a 2nd-century brooch was found.[58] Handmade bricks were found near Tetton Hall Farm c. 3.5 km. south of Middlewich.[59] The briquetage was probably found in association with a brine kiln, and the area over which salt works of the Roman period might be sought near Middlewich is probably greater than generally supposed. Conversely excavations in the centre of the town may produce no Roman occupation material.[60]

No cemeteries have been found. A 'probably funereal' urn was found near the southern end of the settlement, but there is no evidence that it contained a cremation or accompanied an inhumation.[61] The field in which it was found yielded much archaeological material; a largely complete samian bowl of Dragendorff Form 37 by Cinnamus was described as found 'in a sort of hole filled with dried black mud', possibly a filled brine pit.[62] A pit c. 1.2 m. deep contained charcoal and burnt bones, and part of a skull and shin bone were seen. Immediately adjacent was a shaft c. 4.25 m. deep lined with timber, which yielded a copper coin thought to be Roman. The deeper shaft was probably a brine pit; a similar feature was noted c. 100 m. further north. The field apparently yielded briquetage, described as 'a heap of pot sherds . . . of the coarsest kinds'.[63] The account of excavations in 1921-2 at the north end of the settlement refers to finds possibly from a cemetery.[64]

One of the two auxiliary *diplomata* from Cheshire was found at Middlewich, together with fragments of samian and coarse pottery, when a house was built on the west side of King Street.[65] It comprises most of the second sheet of a diploma issued in A.D. 105 to a cavalryman discharged in Britain.[66] The trooper, whose name cannot be read, served with a unit called the *Ala Classiana C[ivium] R[omanorum]*.[67] His father was Rammus, and his wife Amabilis. Because it could be used to prove citizenship, and to legitimize and enfranchise the issue of a previously illegal union, such a document was carefully preserved. It indicates that one element in the early population of the settlement may have consisted of discharged soldiers. The diploma is almost the only inscription from the site, the others being the graffito on an amphora discussed above and one on a grey latticed cooking pot found near the centre of the settlement which reads MERCVRI.[68]

[54] *J.R.S.* lix. 210-11; *Princeton Encyc. Class. Sites*, 798.
[55] Inf. from Mr. J. D. Bestwick.
[56] O. S. Arch. Rec. 76 NW; *J.R.S.* xxii. 205; *J.C.A.S.* xli. 88-9; Thompson, *Roman Ches.* 97. All were Antonine in date.
[57] Watkin, *Roman Ches.* 250.
[58] Form R iv, a type which reached a peak of production in the earlier 2nd cent.
[59] Watkin, *Roman Ches.* 313; *Proc. Soc. Antiq.* iv. 245; *J.C.A.S.* [1st ser.], i. 48; *T.H.S.L.C.* i. 41.
[60] Inf. from Mr. D. J. Freke.
[61] Watkin, *Roman Ches.* 246.
[62] Ibid. 247-8.
[63] Ibid. 248.
[64] *J.R.S.* xi. 205-6.
[65] Ibid. l. 238 (no. 14) and fig. 35; *J.C.A.S.* xlvii. 33-4; Thompson, *Roman Ches.* 94 and figs. 25-6.
[66] M. M. Roxan, *Roman Military Diplomas, 1974-7*, 39. Two *alae* and eleven cohorts discharged men in A.D. 105.
[67] The title *Civium Romanorum* was an honorific one, recording past distinction; it did not imply that any of the serving soldiers were Roman citizens, which would have been unlikely at that date. The full title of the unit was *Gallorum et Thracorum Classiana Civium Romanorum*: *C.I.L.* xvi. 69.
[68] *J.R.S.* lviii. 213, no. 73.

Although it might be thought likely that exploitation of the brine springs began in the pre-Roman period, no Iron Age finds have yet been made at or near Middlewich. Some hillforts in the Marches, for example the Breiddin and Moel y Gaer (Rhosesmor), have yielded very coarse pottery (V.C.P.) one type of which is thought to have originated in south Cheshire,[69] and may have been related to the briquetage recovered at Middlewich. No link can yet be proved, and it seems that the Roman army initiated salt production for its own use. The supposed military site at Harbutt's Field is no longer accepted, but a fortlet may await discovery. A ditch 4 m. wide and 1.2 m. deep on the west side of the site, from the silt at the bottom of which came Flavian pottery, may be military.[70] Direct military control may have been exercised from Northwich, and extended no longer than the early Antonine period. Even so, the salt works may have been leased to private contractors before then, the strongest piece of evidence being the diploma of A.D. 105 which could indicate investment by a veteran of his savings and gratuity in a new industry. Leasing of the salt works to private contractors may have taken place when the garrison at Northwich was temporarily withdrawn, possibly towards the end of the 1st century.

As no 1st-century brine kilns or related structures have yet been found at Middlewich the details of early salt working are unknown. The 2nd-century kilns and associated features and buildings indicate that by then the industry was in the hands of small contractors operating on relatively small plots, and employing simple methods of production. Clearly salt was at first the staple, and possibly the only, product of the settlement, and the later diversification of activity can be variously interpreted. Some industries, such as leather working or perhaps cheese making, needed salt, and their growth perhaps resulted from opening the primary industry to private capital. In other instances, such as metal working, the new industry may mark a decline in the old. Industrial activity at Middlewich developed when Wilderspool and Heronbridge were also gaining prominence, but Middlewich avoided the collapse at Wilderspool, and its apparent growth in the 2nd and 3rd centuries may result from a *rapport* with the immediate hinterland which Wilderspool did not achieve.

The unplanned ribbon development along both sides of King Street for a distance of at least 1.2 km.[71] closely resembled that at Heronbridge. The settlement's width east–west has been estimated as *c.* 300 m.; it had no formal layout and may have lacked even a bath building. That its population was partly immigrant is shown by the diploma, whose owner may have come from Germany.[72] Nevertheless the extent to which the salt workers were imported or indigenous, slave or free, remains unknown.

Nantwich

The name of Nantwich in the Roman period is unknown. At one time it was thought to be the *Salinis* of the Ravenna Cosmography,[73] but there seems no doubt that *Salinis* was Middlewich.[74] Evidence of Roman occupation at Nantwich long amounted to no more than a scatter of coins.[75] Wall Field was identified as the

[69] E. Morris, 'Salt and Ceramic Exchange in Western Brit. during 1st Millennium B.C.' (Southampton Univ. Ph.D. thesis, 1983).

[70] *Arch. Newsletter*, xx. 9.

[71] *Britannia*, i. 282.

[72] His father's name may be German, and the *ala Classiana* may have been in Germania Inferior as late as the Flavian period: Roxan, *Roman Military Diplomas*, 39 n. 6.

[73] *Archaeologia*, xciii. 44–5.

[74] Rivet and Smith, *Place Names of Roman Brit.* 451; *Culture and Environment*, 254.

[75] Watkin, *Roman Ches.* 291–2; Thompson, *Roman Ches.* 102–4, 106.

position of the site, apparently because of the supposed junction of two Roman roads there and the 'significant' name, but the only recorded finds were 15 coins from a tanyard in nearby Wall Lane,[76] found together 'in a hard lump of earth' and perhaps forming a small hoard of the early 4th century.[77] A third group of 12 coins was found in Marsh Lane, *c.* 500 m. west of the river Weaver.[78] A *follis* of Constantine was found in Barony Road,[79] and of four coins from west of the river Weaver, three found north of Welsh Row were Antonine, consisting of a *denarius* of Antoninus Pius, a *sestertius* of M. Aurelius, and another *sestertius*, perhaps of Commodus. The fourth coin, a *sestertius* of Domitian, was found in the adjacent parish of Henhull.[80]

The relatively abundant coin finds from Nantwich indicate a Roman site in the town, but there are few other material finds. An old and somewhat dubious tradition mentions Roman finds near the castle, and in 1964 roof tiles were found during building in Mount Drive.[81] A quantity of pottery was found in 1978 near the Crown Hotel.[82] Since little of the samian was 1st-century and Flavian coarse pottery was absent, occupation is unlikely to have begun before *c.* A.D. 100. Most of the samian was Hadrianic or later, and the coarse pottery indicated that the most intensive occupation of the site lay between the early 3rd century and the mid 4th. The only coin recovered was a *denarius* of Julia Domna.[83] It was deduced that the material came from a Roman site nearby, for there were no structural features. An excavation on the west bank of the Weaver in Wood Street (1979–80) yielded only a few sherds of pottery;[84] 1st- or 2nd-century pottery including samian has come from the river bed near the east bank opposite the excavation site.[85] The site of the National Westminster Bank yielded *c.* 29 Roman sherds similar in date to those from the Crown car park.[86]

The location of the Roman site thus remains unknown, although the evidence suggests a position near the centre of the present town overlooking the river crossing.[87] Past speculation that salt making at Nantwich began in the Roman period[88] was corroborated by the discovery in 1981 of two lead brine pans close to the west bank of the Weaver in Henhull parish, *c.* 500 m. downstream of the Town Bridge.[89] Both are complete, measuring *c.* 1 m. square and nearly 12 cm. deep.[90] Each carries an inscription on one end, one reading CVNI-TICLER, and the other CVNITVS-CLER.[91] The first element is clearly a personal name of Celtic origin, Cunitus,[92] while the second part can be expanded *Ti[berii] Cl[audii]) Er[. . .].*[93] Since there were no associated features or finds it is unknown whether a Roman saltworks existed nearby, though the findspot is not far from a known brine spring on Snow Hill. The only other evidence of salt making comprises a few sherds of briquetage from the Wood Street excavations.[94]

[76] J. Hall, *Hist. of Town and Par. of Nantwich*, 8.

[77] Of the possible options, a small hoard of the types of VICTORIAE LAETAE PRINC PERP and/or VIRTVS EXERCIT is the most likely, as a hoard of that species could easily have been all helmeted. Such coins belong to the period A.D. 317-20. Inf. from Dr. J. P. C. Kent.

[78] *Palatine Note Bk.* i. 199; Hall, *Hist. Nantwich*, 8. In 1667 Lord Brereton related to the Royal Soc. that when digging a salt pit near the Weaver he found a 'pavement' and some Roman coins at a depth of *c.* 2 m.: ibid.

[79] *J.C.A.S.* xlv. 74.

[80] *Ches. Arch. Bull.* iii. 60. A glass rim has also been found: ibid. ix. 101.

[81] Watkin, *Roman Ches.* 291; O. S. Arch. Rec. 65 SE.

[82] R. McNeil Sale and others, *Crown Car Park Excavations*, 18.

[83] Inf. from Miss McNeil and Mrs. P. E. Hutchings.

[84] R. McNeil Sale and others, *Wood Street Salt Works*, 24.

[85] *Ches. Arch. Bull.* vii. 31; inf. from Mr. J. Ray.

[86] Inf. from Mrs. P. E. Hutchings.

[87] Perhaps Snow Hill: *Ches. Arch. Bull.* vii. 31.

[88] Hall, *Hist. Nantwich*, 7-8; T. Pennant, *Tour from Chester to London*, 27-8.

[89] The pans are in the Salt Mus., Northwich.

[90] The pans were found inverted, one above the other: inf. from Mr. Myott of Kingsley Farm. Both are distorted, making precise measurement difficult.

[91] *Britannia*, xv. 342, nos. 18-19; fig. 32.2.

[92] Recorded at Leintwardine on a lead sheet: *J.R.S.* lix. 241, no. 31.

[93] Tiberius Claudius Er . . . was perhaps an imperial freedman, and the lessee, while Cunitus was the salter.

[94] Sale, *Wood Street Salt Works*, fig. 13.

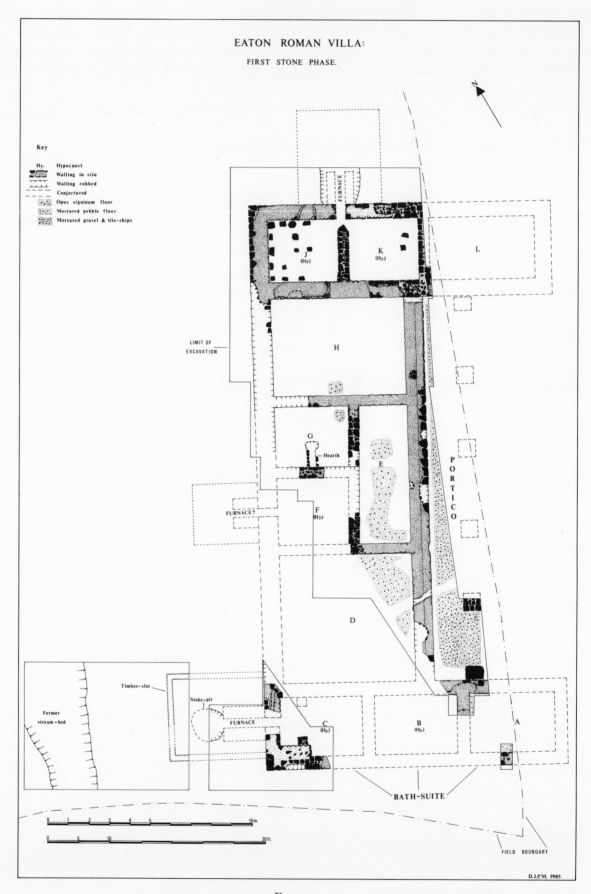

EATON ROMAN VILLA:

FIRST STONE PHASE.

Key

Hy.　Hypocaust

Walling in situ

Walling robbed

Conjectured

Opus signinum floor

Mortared pebble floor

Mortared gravel & tile-chips

LIMIT OF
EXCAVATION

J
(Hy.)

K
(Hy.)

L

FURNACE

H

G

Hearth

E

F
(Hy.)

FURNACE?

D

PORTICO

Timber-slot

Former
stream-bed

Stoke-pit

FURNACE

C
(Hy.)

B
(Hy.)

A

BATH-SUITE

FIELD BOUNDARY

0　1　2　3　4　5　　　　　　　　　10m.

0　　5　　10　　　　　　　35ft.

D.J.P.M. 1985

FIG. 34.

An initial period of Roman military occupation at Nantwich is possible but unlikely, as the line of the road linking Whitchurch and Middlewich passed to the north, and the site itself has yielded little if any Flavian material. A fragment of a stamped tile of Legio xx and a sherd from a pot thought to have been made at Holt found at Reaseheath Hall are unlikely to have come from a military site.[95] Such pottery as has been found, together with the coin evidence, indicates that occupation at Nantwich began in the 2nd century, perhaps late in Trajan's reign, and reached its highest intensity from the early 3rd century to the mid 4th. While salt making is undoubtedly attested at Nantwich it is not clear that it was a major activity, and Nantwich cannot be included in the same category of industrial settlements as Middlewich or Wilderspool.

Discovery of a jar containing a cremation burial in Welsh Row during excavation for the foundations of a new building suggests that the cemetery may lie west of the river.[96]

A Romano-British Farmhouse at Eaton-by-Tarporley

In 1886 a coin of Marcus Aurelius was found, with fragments of Roman tiles and mortar, during excavations for the Vyrnwy aqueduct at Eaton-by-Tarporley.[97] Roman tile and *opus signinum* were noted during recent field work, and subsequent excavation in 1980–2 revealed the only villa known in Cheshire.[98]

The earliest occupation was represented by two post-holes sealed by a clay floor. A second timber building measured *c.* 9 m. by at least 22 m. and may have had an aisled plan. After a fire it was replaced by a single-storeyed stone house of the winged corridor type facing south-east, whose dimensions were 26.3 m. by *c.* 14.4 m. The plan[99] was symmetrical, with heated rooms in both wings, those in the south wing belonging to a small suite of baths. One room in the central range was also heated. In the early 4th century the house was substantially reconstructed, using existing wall-lines. The former veranda was enclosed, and an upper storey added, thus increasing the accommodation. The baths suite continued in use, but other hypocausts were dismantled. Occupation continued until at least the mid 4th century, on the evidence of coins of the house of Constantine and Magnentius. Two of the rooms contained what appeared to be corn-drying ovens.

The standard of workmanship of the second stone house was markedly inferior to that of the first, which was solidly constructed. There was evidence of at least three refloorings during the first stone phase, which began *c.* A.D. 170–200. Occupation of the site may have begun earlier than the Antonine period; the initial timber buildings were relatively short-lived. The extent or form of the other farm buildings is unknown. Although modest by the standards of many elsewhere in Britain, the Eaton villa demonstrates a degree of solid comfort, and the presence of painted wall-plaster shows an attempt at refinement in the first stone building at least. The nearest known villas are in Shropshire,[1] and some seem to resemble Eaton in their relative simplicity.

[95] *J.C.A.S.* xl. 64–6. The finds are lost. They were in the possession of a building contractor at Chester; there is no reliable corroboration of the find, and in any case, on present views of the date of tile and pottery making at Holt the finds cannot be earlier than the late Flavian period.

[96] In Nantwich Mus.

[97] Watkin, *Roman Ches.* 296; *T.H.S.L.C.* xxxix. 57. The coin cannot be identified from *Roman Imperial Coinage*, iii.

[98] *Britannia*, xii. 333; xiii. 353 and fig. 11; *Ches. Arch. Bull.* viii. 49–52; ix. 67–73. Thanks are due to Dr. D. J. P. Mason for giving details in advance of publication.

[99] Fig. 34.

[1] G. Webster, *The Cornovii*, 83–9.

The Countryside

Other finds from Roman Cheshire consist almost exclusively of scattered items without associated structure. In the absence of evidence from settlements it cannot be said whether the countryside in Cheshire is comparable with other parts of the Midland Plain, to which most of it belongs physically, or with the upland areas east or west, or with the region north of the Mersey. The Eaton villa may suggest ties with lowland rather than upland Britain, but it appears that the presence of a military garrison in northern England and Wales had a depressing effect on the countryside, except near the forts or fortresses of the garrison, a low level of romanization being attained by the native population.[2] The extent of the *prata legionis*, the land attributed to the fortress, cannot be precisely defined. The quarrying of stone near Llangollen for use by the army has prompted the suggestion that the *prata legionis* extended that far, some 30 km.; perhaps lead mining and salt making also first took place under army control, and if so the sites at Ffrith and Pentre may have been in the *prata legionis*, and presumably Northwich and Middlewich also.[3] The area thus defined, while apparently extensive, accords with what is known about the *territoria* of fortresses elsewhere in the Roman Empire.[4]

Finds of Roman date[5] which come neither from the fortress nor from one or other of the civil settlements initially present an impression of a rather thin and fairly even scatter.[6] On closer investigation, however, it is possible to discern zones within the county, some productive of finds, while from others come few or none. Very few sites which have yielded finds of the Roman period can be identified by character or precise location, and it is impossible to say whether a site like Ashton by Tarvin represents a romanized farm-house or a 'native' village. In contrast to other parts of lowland Britain where arable farming and more responsive subsoils provide more suitable conditions, observation from the air has not provided significant information about the distribution and character of occupation of the Romano-British countryside. It has been conjectured that much of Cheshire was covered by dense woodland at the Roman conquest, and that relatively little clearance for agriculture took place during the Roman period; if so, evidence of settlement will be scanty and concentrated only in the cleared areas. In practice the only published evidence appears to contradict that view.[7]

Notable in the distribution of Roman finds in Cheshire is the pre-eminence of the fortress at Chester, with its satellites which comprise not only the *canabae* in the immediate vicinity and at Heronbridge, but also sites in the suburbs of the Lache (Saltney) and Blacon. The buildings at the Lache[8] may have been farms; coins from the area show a distinct bias towards the 4th century. Blacon is less certain, as it has yielded five coins, three of the 3rd century, but no pottery or signs of buildings. A gold coin of Tiberius was found on the edge of the reclaimed land on the Sealand side. Much of the land west of Chester was marsh and therefore unlikely to yield much Roman material. Both north and south of the fortress finds also thin out rapidly, but on the east in an area between the roads to Wilderspool and Northwich, and extending as far as the Mid-Cheshire Ridge, there is by far the densest scatter of finds outside the vicinity of Chester. A cluster of Iron Age hillforts indicates that it was an attractive area for settlement in the pre-Roman

---

[2] The same is true where imperial control was exercised by the procurator rather than the army, e.g. in Cranbourne Chase or the Roman Fenland.

[3] For a lead ingot with stamp reading LEG XX B F L I DOC see *Flints. Hist. Soc. Publications*, xiii. 11-12.

[4] Dr. Mason kindly advised on this point.

[5] Fig. 31.

[6] Cf. Thompson, *Roman Ches.* fig. 3.

[7] *J.C.A.S.* lviii. 9-11; *Ches. Arch. Bull.* viii. 10-11.

[8] Above, Saltney.

period. A well drained soil and lighter tree cover were equally favourable in the Roman period, but it should be noted that the lower and less well drained Gowy valley was also occupied to much the same density. Within the wedge-shaped area, concentrations of finds have been noted at Kelsall, Ashton, Helsby (including the nearby villages of Alvanley and Dunham), Aston, and Frodsham. The first and last of those sites have produced some evidence of structure, as has Daresbury where a *denarius* of Hadrian was found; it is, however, difficult to be certain whether all the early finds can be accepted as Roman. The discovery of the villa at Eaton-by-Tarporley[9] where previously recorded finds amounted only to a coin and fragments of tile and mortar makes it seem likely that other similar buildings exist at some of the sites named above. Cropmarks of a field system apparently of Iron Age or Roman date have been observed north of Kelsall, and other possible field systems have been recorded from the air, notably near Alvanley and Frodsham, although their date is not known.

South of the villa at Eaton-by-Tarporley few finds have been made on or near the line of the Mid-Cheshire Ridge except at Beeston Castle, where excavations have yielded pottery of the 2nd and 3rd centuries.[10] A coin hoard is said to have been found at Bickerton Hill. The site at Halton was at first thought to be military and of the 3rd century, but doubt has been cast on the interpretation, and it seems more likely that the pentagonal ditched enclosure was part of a farming settlement.[11] Nevertheless no signs of structure within the enclosure were noted. Finds run to the outskirts of Chester, a number having been made at Littleton, Christleton, Rowton, and Waverton.

There have been relatively few finds in south-western Cheshire, between the Mid-Cheshire Ridge and the Dee. Despite speculation about a Roman site at Malpas, the lack of finds of the period since those originally reported makes it unlikely.[12] The so-called Malpas diploma came from Bickley, 4 km. east of Malpas. Both that and the 3rd-century coin hoard from Chorlton may derive from the nearby town of *Mediolanum* (Whitchurch, Salop.). Evidence of Roman occupation with signs of buildings has been seen at Grafton, near Tilston. The finds date from the mid 2nd century to the late 4th, and include a small altar inscribed GENIO LOCI. Roman coins are said to have been found at Stretton, and at Tattenhall two coins and a little pottery. A few sherds of pottery have been found at Tushingham.

Finds from Wirral have mostly been made near the coast. Most are single coins ranging in date from the 1st to the 4th century, but three coin hoards have been found, one (Arno Hill, Oxton) of apparently the 3rd century and two (Neston and Eastham), of the 4th. Finds of pottery are less common. A miniature cauldron found at Woodchurch may resemble those from Ancaster (Lincs.) and Waulkmill, Tarland (Aberdeen).[13] Inscribed stones from West Kirby have been assigned to the Roman period, but great doubt exists about their authenticity.[14] Other finds include brooches at Thurstaston and Leasowe Castle, the latter of the Aucissa type. No clear indications of Roman buildings have been recorded in Wirral. A timber bridge on stone piers revealed by railway works at Birkenhead was thought to be Roman, but without supporting evidence. Occupation of Wirral seems to be concentrated at the northern end of the peninsula, where the only settlement of

[9] Above.

[10] *Ches. Arch. Bull.* viii. 28.

[11] *Liverpool Annals*, xxiv. 165–8; *J.R.S.* xxvii. 232; lviii. 183; *J.C.A.S.* lviii. 85–8.

[12] Watkin, *Roman Ches.* 286–7. The account, derived from Foote Gower, referred to 'Roman implements . . . with coins and tessellated pavements' near the castle.

[13] *Lincs. Arch. and Archit. Soc. Rep. and Papers*, vii (2), 99–101, fig. 2, plate 2; *Proc. Soc. Antiq. Scot.* xlix. 204–5; lxvi. 390–1.

[14] Haverfield thought both were post-Roman: *R.I.B.* i, nos. 2369, 2386.

consequence, Meols, is situated: at its base there is a zone virtually devoid of finds from Ellesmere Port to Neston, which divides Wirral from the immediate hinterland of the fortress of Chester.

Thus in the western third of the shire, where the influence of the fortress and of the two estuaries of Dee and Mersey were most clearly felt, the only semblance of urban life, apart from that in the *canabae* of the fortress, is the settlement, if such it was, at Meols. By contrast, an arc of settlements lies 25–30 km. east of the fortress, from Wilderspool in the north to Whitchurch in the south. Each has a cluster of finds in its immediate vicinity, beyond which the hinterland appears largely deserted. Among the scatter of finds are four or five coin hoards, two in the Crewe–Nantwich area, and two, possibly three, from the Mersey valley. The latter comprise the Statham and Agden hoards, one of up to 1,200 coins, and the other twice that size; both are later 3rd-century,[15] as is a hoard from Brereton *c.* 7 km. south-east of Middlewich. A Hadrianic hoard comes from Weston, while the Cholmondeston hoard, often linked with Nantwich but in fact almost as far north of that site (*c.* 7 km.) as Weston is to the east, can be dated A.D. 348 or later. None of the hoards can be associated with a nearby site of the period, but they appear at a relatively uniform distance from their nearest settlement.[16] The only site which does not have a coin hoard nearby, Northwich, appears to have been unlike the remainder in other respects also. Recent excavations at Tatton Park have revealed slight evidence of Roman occupation.[17]

Traces of such occupation are absent from an area defined by a line running east of Northwich and Wilderspool to Bowdon, Bramhall, Alderley Edge, Congleton, and Holmes Chapel. A sterile zone *c.* 16 km. east–west and *c.* 30 km. north-west to south-east clearly separates the central Cheshire sites from those to the east, and accentuates the Pennine orientation of the latter. Congleton, close under the Cloud and Congleton Edge, has yielded six or seven coins including one of Commodus, possibly a hoard, as well as isolated finds of 3rd- and 4th-century coins. A find made just outside the county boundary at Whitemore Farm, Biddulph (Staffs.),[18] consisted of four silver spoons of the 4th century, one of which bears a graffito *chi-rho* monogram. A second important hoard was found in a field at Wincle, 9.5 km. north-east of the Biddulph hoard. The contents, all of gold, consist mainly of jewellery, including a crossbow brooch of the 3rd century. A fragment of a human mask in repoussé sheet gold may have been votive and was perhaps lost from a temple. The fragmentary and damaged nature of many of the items argues against the possibility that the hoard was either personal or votive, and there is therefore no reason to suspect a house or temple nearby.[19]

Macclesfield has yielded no finds unequivocally Roman, but lies roughly at the centre of a scatter extending from Alderley Edge to beyond Rainow and from Bollington to Henbury. The finds are in the main coins of the 3rd and 4th centuries, but a hoard of twenty 1st- and 2nd-century coins has been found at Whiteley Green.

The almost wholly built-up north-east of the county has yielded another scatter of finds, again mainly of coins, but strikingly little evidence of settlement. Demolition of the castle at Stockport between 1750 and 1775 is said to have revealed

---

[15] Hoards which have the appearance of relating to Wilderspool post-date its decline.

[16] The term is used loosely to cover sites like Nantwich.

[17] *Ches. Arch. Bull.* ix. 90.

[18] *Antiquaries Jnl.* li. 323–4; lv. 62–9; *Britannia*, iii. 361;

vii. 392. The findspot lies c. 3 km. SE. of Congleton.

[19] Watkin and others associated the find with a 'square mound', but that is a natural feature: Thompson, *Roman Ches.* 108.

FIG. 35. Wincle: Fragment of Human Mask (Restored). Scale 1:1.

Roman material, but the only undoubtedly Roman item is a coin of Honorius. The road thought to have connected Manchester with Buxton crossed the Mersey there, but there is no clear evidence of a Roman site.

COMMUNICATIONS

While Roman roads inevitably command the greater share of attention when communications are considered, Cheshire is neither land-locked nor without navigable rivers.[20] It is generally thought that the choice of Chester as the site for a legionary fortress was influenced by its accessibility from the sea, and the site has produced evidence of harbour works. The industrial settlement at Wilderspool doubtless owes its siting to easy access to the Mersey, and thence to the sea. Vessels carried pottery from Wilderspool to forts in the north and in north Wales, and the discovery of twenty lead pigs on the foreshore near Runcorn indicates another cargo, possibly bound for Wilderspool, where lead working is believed to have taken place. Some of the ingots certainly, and the remainder probably, consisted of Deceanglian lead. Some can be dated to A.D. 76, others to the period A.D. 84–96.[21] The Dee was the most likely means of transporting the products of the works at

[20] The advantages of water carriage are stated in Thompson, *Roman Ches.* 22.

[21] Watkin, *Roman Ches.* 294–6 and sources therein cited; *Arch. Jnl.* xvi. 28–9; *J.C.A.S.* n.s. iv. 72; *Jnl. Brit. Arch.* *Assoc.* iv. 274–5; *Flints. Hist. Soc. Pubs.* xiii. 22; Thompson, *Roman Ches.* 20. It seems likely that the find came from a shipwreck.

Holt to the fortress,[22] and salt from Middlewich may have been carried down the river Weaver to the Mersey, and thence by sea to further destinations.[23] Meols, a harbour in the Roman period, may have been a transhipment port where goods carried by river craft in the Dee and Mersey estuaries were transferred to sea-going vessels. A link with trade in Deceanglian lead has been suggested.[24]

In the Antonine Itinerary, dating, so far as Britain is concerned, from the reign of Trajan to that of Diocletian,[25] the routes which mention places in Cheshire are II, X, and XI. The first is by far the longest, from Birrens, an outpost fort of Hadrian's Wall near Ecclefechan, to Richborough (Kent), the principal port for traffic to and from Gaul. Named Watling Street in Cheshire, it proceeds from the fort at Manchester by *Condate* (Northwich) to *Deva*, and thence to *Mediolanum* (Whitchurch). *Bovium*, placed between *Deva* and *Mediolanum* on the route, is thought to be Holt (Clwyd).[26] Route X provided an alternative way for which confirmatory evidence was long absent from *Condate* to *Mediolanum* avoiding *Deva*. The third route, XI, links *Segontium* (Caernarfon) with *Deva*. The British section of the Ravenna Cosmography, which also is thought to be derived from a Roman itinerary, in Cheshire names an otherwise unknown place, *Sandonio*, apparently between Chester and Whitchurch or on a western branch road.[27] It is now doubted whether *Sandonio* existed.[28]

Roman roads in Cheshire[29] have been said to be 'as elusive and as unsatisfactory as a will of the wisp';[30] while progress has been made in defining the principal roads, problems still exist. Six or seven can be taken as fully proven,[31] all but two radiating from the fortress at Chester. Most were probably at first strategic, built to permit the ready passage of men and material from one part of the province to another. Chester occupied a key position, for traffic between one concentration of military garrisons in Wales and the Marches and another in the north would go through it. Watling Street south of Chester is the northern end of a strategic road linking the two fortresses of Wales, while the forts in north Wales were served by two roads, a northerly route through St. Asaph to Caerhun and Caernarfon and a second running to Caer Gai and Brithdir. Units or supplies destined for the northern frontier were probably funnelled into Chester along those roads, proceeding thence by the extension of Watling Street to Northwich and Manchester. The provision later of a crossing of the Mersey at Wilderspool, with a road through mid Lancashire by Walton-le-Dale and Lancaster, implies a direct road link between Chester and Wilderspool. Another route from the fortress served Wirral: by comparison with the others it was minor and the need for it remains uncertain. A road crossing central Cheshire from Wilderspool passed Northwich, and may therefore be relatively late in date. It divides at Middlewich, one part proceeding southeastwards and the other south-westwards.

Watling Street: Chester–Whitchurch (route 6a)[32]

The Roman road which linked Chester with London, Caerleon, and the nearest centre of civil administration at Wroxeter has been extensively studied. Presumably

---

[22] *Y Cymmrodor*, xli. 11.

[23] The river Weaver was important to the salt trade in later times, after its improvement as a waterway.

[24] *Arch. and Coastal Change*, 95–7; *Ches. Arch. Bull.* ix. 6.

[25] *Britannia*, i. 34–68; Rivet and Smith, *Place Names of Roman Brit.* 150–80.

[26] Rivet and Smith, *Place Names of Roman Brit.* 274.

[27] *Archaeologia*, xciii. 45; see also map of proposed *iter* VI, p. 8.

[28] Rivet and Smith, *Place Names of Roman Brit.* 415–16. Derivation from the second element of *Mediolanum Santonum* (Saintes, Charente-Maritime) is suggested.

[29] The most comprehensive study of the roads of the province is I. D. Margary, *Roman Roads in Brit.* (3rd edn.). Margary's system of numbering the routes is used here.

[30] *Arch. Camb.* 6th ser. x. 439.

[31] Cf. O.S. Map, Roman Brit. (3rd edn.).

[32] Margary, *Roman Roads in Brit.* 296–8.

Flavian in date at the latest, it continued to be important throughout the Roman period. Issuing from the south gate of the fortress, and crossing the Dee at approximately the same point as the Old Dee Bridge, the road thereafter underlies Eaton Road.[33] Despite a suggestion to the contrary[34] the two roads appear to share the same line as far as Heronbridge[35] where they diverge, the Roman road running somewhat eastward of the present road. In trenches excavated in a field south of Heronbridge House its position was defined, and details of its construction provided.[36] In the southern trench a road 9.36 m. wide was made of cobbles, gravel, and sandstone, with a kerb on one side only. Another trench revealed a narrower 7.5 m. road, the metalling of cobbles and gravel laid on natural clay: there was a kerb on the west side, and on the east an eaves-drip was buried beneath a resurfacing of gravel which ran up to a kerb.[37] Excavations on the site of the southerly bypass, south of the settlement at Heronbridge, demonstrated that the supposed *agger* of the Roman road, a linear bank on the east side of the present one, was later.[38] The eastern edge of the Roman road was found *c.* 11 m. east of the present one; slight evidence suggested construction no earlier than the early 2nd century. The full width of the road was recorded as 12.3 m., and a top surface of sandstone over cobbles was noted.[39] The unusual width may result from the presence of a large stone building on the west side of the road.[40] The road was seen earlier, near Primrose Hill.[41] It appears to have changed direction slightly *c.* 1.6 km. south of the centre of Eccleston,[42] and two sections were excavated in the parkland of Eaton Hall south of Garden Lodge.[43] In the southern section 4 m. of road survived, consisting of rammed gravel in grey sand, with a second surface of gravel with some larger cobbles. The full width of 7.6 m. survived in the northern section, where again two periods were visible, and possibly a further resurfacing. There was no *agger*, the road being terraced into the sloping ground on the west side. In neither section did the road have an obvious camber, and no side ditches were seen. On the alignment of the road towards the ford at Aldford a foundation of piles was discovered in front of Eaton Hall.[44] When the Dee was low the paved causeway of the ford at Aldford, formed of large stones, was reputedly visible in the river bed,[45] but it has not been observed in more recent times. In 1960 sandstone flagging *c.* 3.6 m. wide with gravel shoulders was found *c.* 16.5 m. downstream from Iron Bridge.[46] The depth of 1.67 m. recorded at the centre is unusual for a ford, but the weir at Chester has raised the water level for some distance upstream.[47]

The line of the road seems clear south of the river, and excavation 1.6 km. south of Aldford revealed road surface and kerb stones. A trench 800 m. to the south in Churton also exposed part of the road.[48] Further excavations there revealed a well built road 13.7 m. wide with a sandstone foundation, capped by gravel surfacing.[49] East of it lay an earlier and less substantial road.[50] The road then proceeds through Barton to Stretton: somewhere in that sector a short branch road probably led to

[33] Watkin, *Roman Ches.* 47–8; *J.C.A.S.* N.S. i. 206; xxvii. 150; xxviii. 216; xxx. 56.

[34] *J.C.A.S.* xxx. 51.

[35] Excavations at the north end of the settlement revealed the line clearly: *J.C.A.S.* xxxix. 6; xli. 15–24.

[36] Ibid. xxx. 50–2.

[37] From the eaves-drip it appears that a building lay immediately east of the road.

[38] *J.C.A.S.* lviii. 15–39.

[39] Ibid. lix. 24–6.   [40] Above.

[41] *Jnl. Brit. Arch. Assoc.* v. 228.

[42] *J.C.A.S.* lviii. 28, fig. 6.

[43] M. Buchanan, K. E. Jermy, and D. F. Petch, 'Watling Street in Grounds of Eaton Hall: Excavations North of Garden Lodge, 1970–1', ibid. 1–13.

[44] Watkin, *Roman Ches.* 49.

[45] Ormerod, *Hist. Ches.* ii. 320; *Arch. Camb.* [3rd ser.], i. 238; 6th ser. x. 192; Watkin, *Roman Ches.* 49.

[46] *J.C.A.S.* xlviii. 25.

[47] The depth was in any event subject to fluctuation.

[48] M. St. J. Way, 'Watling South of Aldford', *J.C.A.S.* xlviii. 17–23.

[49] A. C. and E. Waddelove, 'Watling Street South of Chester', ibid. lxvi. 13–21.

[50] The apparent duplication may not be unique: ibid. 19–21; *Ches. Arch. Bull.* ix. 62.

the site at Holt,[51] perhaps on a similar course to the A 534.[52] Watling Street has been seen from the air near Stretton,[53] and fieldwork and excavation have clarified the line near Tilston; at Grafton it was at least 4 m. wide.[54] From Tilston its straight alignment is followed closely by the present road to Malpas, but in the final sector to Whitchurch the Roman road line has not been determined.

It has been argued[55] that the distribution of finds at Boughton suggests a branch road leaving Watling Street at that point. Such a route bypassing the military and civil sites at Chester, and avoiding two river crossings, one of them a ford, may well have existed from Boughton to Aldford, but is unproven.

Watling Street: Chester–Northwich–Manchester (route 7a)[56]

The name Watling Street is given locally to the road from the fortress to the forts at Northwich and Manchester, and thence over the Pennines to York. From the east gate of the fortress it is followed by present-day roads to Vicar's Cross, where the Roman road runs a little south of the present one. A machine-cut section across it revealed a scatter of cobbles 36.5 m. south of the modern road, but no recognizable *agger*.[57] At the crossing of the Gowy at Stamford Bridge[58] the road changes direction slightly and crosses fields to rejoin the modern road near Street Farm;[59] the latter soon swerves right, while the Roman road seems to hold straight. Observation suggests that it ascended the escarpment at Kelsall on a terrace.[60] At the top of the hill the road again changes direction and takes a line at the west edge of Nettleford Wood, where it was found to be 5.8 m. wide with ditches on either side.[61] East of the wood the line joined Stoney Lane, passing close to the hillfort at Eddisbury.[62] Where the Vyrnwy aqueduct cut through it, it was noted as a thick layer of gravel and broken stones *c*. 60 cm. below the surface.[63] It is visible in a field east of the B 5152, and was recorded as a well marked feature 9–10 m. across consisting of an *agger* with shallow ditches on either side *c*. 2.3 km. east of Eddisbury;[64] excavation revealed that the road was nearly 10 m. wide, although initially only half that width, and consisted of tightly packed gravel on a water-worn cobble foundation, with a ditch on the north side.[65] Thereafter the modern and Roman lines merge at Crabtree Cottages, where there was a slight shift in alignment. The road line has been confirmed in that sector,[66] but the course becomes less distinct from the junction with Cockpit Lane: it must turn to the northeast and generally follow the present road through Hartford, where it was exposed a little east of Greenbank station,[67] to Northwich. The site of the crossing of the Weaver is unknown, but seems likely, from the alignment of the road on either bank, to have been near Town Bridge.[68] The line then follows High Street and Witton Street to Wadebrook House where the alignment changes; after a short distance the present Manchester Road takes up the line. Roughly 2 km. east of the river crossing is the junction with King Street, the latter not represented by a modern road at that point. From there Watling Street turns northwards, followed

[51] Margary, *Roman Roads in Brit.* route 66o. The road may have continued and linked Holt with other sites in north Wales: *Arch. Camb.* 6th ser. x. 444.

[52] Margary, *Roman Roads in Brit.* 348.

[53] *Ches. Arch. Bull.* vi. 9.

[54] *Britannia*, xi. 365; xii. 333; *Arch. Newsletter*, xli. 9.

[55] Watkin, *Roman Ches.* 55; *New Evidence*, 38–40 and fig. 4.

[56] Margary, *Roman Roads in Brit.* 300–2.

[57] *J.C.A.S.* xlviii. 25.

[58] Recent fieldwork near Stamford Bridge is described in *Britannia*, xv. 288.

[59] The road was found near Tarvin bridge: *Arch. Camb.* 6th ser. x. 445.

[60] *Britannia*, xiv. 297.

[61] *Ibid.* xiii. 353. [62] *Ibid.* xv. 288.

[63] Watkin, *Roman Ches.* 39; *T.L.C.A.S.* iii. 119.

[64] *T.H.S.L.C.* iii. 70.

[65] *Britannia*, iii. 313; *Ches. Arch. Bull.* i. 8–10 and fig. 3. The Roman road was under a railway embankment.

[66] *Britannia*, xiv. 299.

[67] *T.L.C.A.S.* iii. 122–3.

[68] The discovery of the road at Castle Dockyard is recorded in *Arch. Camb.* 6th ser. x. 445.

by the present road, and at a point near Tabley House heads a little east of north. That alignment continues through Mere and Bucklow Hill; after a further change, to the east, the road adopts a line which it retains with only slight modification into Manchester. At the Altrincham boundary the present road leaves the Roman line, but they rejoin after *c.* 1.75 km.: two trenches excavated roughly half way through that sector found the Roman road to be *c.* 6.7 m. wide and at most 45 cm. thick.[69]

Chester–North Wales (routes 66 and 67)[70]

Chester was provided with two routes into Wales, the first serving the forts of northern Snowdonia by a route a little inland of the coast, and the second going to southern Snowdonia by Caer Gai. Since any such roads had to skirt the marshy ground to the south-west of Chester, both probably shared a common course for the first few miles. The line may have been from Handbridge along Lache Lane to Balderton; alternatively, if Watling Street was followed for the first part of the route, they probably forked off at, or near, Heronbridge. The latter suggestion is perhaps more likely in view of the discovery of the road at Broughton (Flints.),[71] and the Roman road near Ffrith (Flints.) appears, from its alignment, to have left Watling Street near Heronbridge.[72] When the piled causeway was observed in the grounds of Eaton Hall another was seen to run westward at right angles to it, and a general alignment on Belgrave Drive has alternatively been proposed.[73] It has also been suggested that the southern road left Watling Street to cross the Dee at Farndon.

Chester–Wirral (route 670)[74]

A Roman road running the length of Wirral has long been suspected, and its line has been confirmed in central Wirral.[75] A cobbled surface was found near Willaston, and further investigation showed that the cobbling was capped by a gravel surface; kerb stones were found on one side, but the full width was not determined. The alignment of the road indicates that it issued from the north gate of the fortress and followed a line through Mollington and Ledsham, where it has been recorded,[76] to the attested sector at Street Hey Lane. The most northerly point at which it has been seen is Raby,[77] beyond which its course is uncertain. Extension of the line would not take the road to any known Roman site, and it seems that its destination was Meols.[78] Whether the Mersey was crossed between Birkenhead and Liverpool, with a link to the Wirral road, remains speculative.[79]

Wilderspool–Middlewich–Sandbach (route 70a)[80]

King or Kind Street connects the settlements at Wilderspool and Middlewich; it does not include the fort at Northwich in its route, but crosses Watling Street east of it. It seems that King Street did not originate as a military road linking Northwich with the river crossing, as might be supposed, but came into existence after the fort

[69] *Arch. Newsletter*, vii. 9; viii. 12. The road was sealed by 30.5 cm. of peat in one section.
[70] Margary, *Roman Roads in Brit.* 346, 348.
[71] *Britannia*, xiv. 280.
[72] *Ches. Arch. Bull.* ix. 62.
[73] *Arch. Camb.* 3rd ser. i. 240; 6th ser. x. 439.
[74] Margary, *Roman Roads in Brit.* 299–300.
[75] K. E. Jermy, 'Roman Road in Wirral', *J.C.A.S.* xlviii. 1–13; l. 1–2; *Ches. Historian*, iii. 15–18.
[76] *Britannia*, iii. 314; xii. 333.

[77] *Arch. Newsletter*, vi. 11.
[78] *J.C.A.S.* xlviii. 1; Thompson, *Roman Ches.* 22. In view of the changes in the coastline at the northern end of Wirral it is possible that the road was initially intended to serve a site long since eroded by the sea.
[79] A timber structure at Birkenhead is thought to have been a Roman bridge, but a wharf seems more likely and there was no dating evidence: *J.C.A.S.* [1st ser.], i. 55–60, 68–76.
[80] Margary, *Roman Roads in Brit.* 302–3.

had been abandoned. Beyond Middlewich the road proceeds to Sandbach and thence to the settlement at Chesterton (Staffs.), thereafter through Rocester to Littlechester (Derb.).

The line is well known between Wilderspool and the higher ground overlooking the Mersey. Early discoveries indicate a line running west of London Road and converging with it. The line was exposed near Hillcliffe Hydro, where thick metalling of compact sand and gravel was recorded over a width of at least 10.35 m. during building.[81] The road, observed in the face of Hillcliffe quarry, merges immediately beyond with the line of the modern road. A section exposed near Appleton Hall was nearly 6 m. wide.[82] Near Stark House the present and Roman roads diverge, and c. 300 m. north of Stretton church a section of King Street was revealed in excavations for a pipeline.[83] It was 5.5 m. wide, and consisted of a gently cambered surface of pebbles and sandstone chips on a layer of brown sand; on its east side was a ditch. The road was again exposed near the north-west corner of the churchyard, where a 15–25 cm. layer of stones was recorded. The *agger* has been noted a little further south in the vicarage garden and the adjacent field.[84] Road works in Lower Stretton revealed a partial section, including the east edge of the road, and the crown of the cambered *agger* was seen. The road was made of cobbles set in sand, and probably capped with a gravelled surface. The *agger* was c. 13 m. wide.[85] There appear to have been two shifts in direction, one near Spark Hall and the other near Stretton House. Beyond that point discoveries are said to have been made during road widening in the 19th century between Antrobus and Frandley. There is no doubt as to the general course of the road, since its line south of Watling Street is accurately known, and there was evidently yet another change in alignment, probably between Wincham and Marston Hall.

King Street and Watling Street cross 2.25 km. east of the crossing of the Weaver at Northwich, and c. 2.75 km. from the site of the fort. The reason for the evasion of a more obvious junction near the fort could be topographical: as it proceeds south-west from Frandley and past Great Budworth King Street keeps to slightly higher ground, now overlooking flashes and meres resulting from subsidence. After obliteration by past and present industry the road emerges again at Broken Cross, and from that point for a distance of nearly 7 km. an impressively straight section of Roman road is still in use, which Camden referred to as 'a noble way from Middlewich to Northwich, which has been raised so high with gravel, that one may easily discern it to be Roman'.[86] Only as the road enters the Roman settlement at Middlewich does its alignment falter. There it divides, King Street turning somewhat to the east; the *agger* has been identified at Elworth, where the road was twice seen: on the second occasion the gravel surface was found to lie on a bed of sand dumped on top of the original turf. The primary surface 5.9 m. wide had been remade three times, and was flanked by a side-ditch on the east side. A cobbled area c. 8 m. wide was then added on the west, and itself subsequently resurfaced, after which a side-ditch was provided on the west side of the enlarged road and the east ditch was recut.[87] From Elworth the alignment is clearly aimed for Chesterton, but no confirmation of the line has been achieved on the ground.

[81] *J.C.A.S.* lii. 24. In earlier work the width was 12 yd., and 12 or 14 yd. (11–12.8 m.) near the Bridgewater Canal: Watkin, *Roman Ches.* 65–6.
[82] *T.H.S.L.C.* iii. 77.
[83] *J.C.A.S.* xlviii. 26.
[84] *T.L.C.A.S.* lxxvii. 28–9.
[85] *Ches. Arch. Bull.* iii. 57.
[86] *Britannia*, i. 485.
[87] *Arch. Newsletter*, viii. 12; ix. 16; 4 *Sheaf*, ii. pp. 28–9; *Britannia*, iii. 313–14.

Middlewich–Whitchurch (route 700)[88]

There was a road from Middlewich to Nantwich, thereafter continuing to join Watling Street at or near Whitchurch. The first part has a clear line, and at Occlestone Green a length of *agger* 6.3 m. wide and 90 cm. high runs for *c.* 40 m. From that alignment it might be assumed that the road led to the Roman site at Nantwich, but fieldwork has indicated a new line between Reaseheath Old Hall and Burland, and apparently somewhere near Woolstanwood a new alignment was adopted which bypassed Nantwich, a clear indication of the unimportance of that site when the road was laid out. Fieldwork and excavation in the Baddiley–Wrenbury area and at Henhull has confirmed a road of rammed gravel *c.* 3.6 m. wide on an *agger* 11.5 m. wide.[89] It is uncertain whether the road was intended to proceed to Whitchurch, as seems most likely, or joined Watling Street at Prees Heath a little south of the Roman town.

At its northern end continuation of the line north-eastwards from Middlewich to Lower Peover has been suggested,[90] but is not generally accepted.[91] Similarly, a road from Middlewich through Astbury to Buxton (*Aquae Arnemetiae*) has been proposed[92] but there is no evidence of its existence. A road on Biddulph Moor initially seen from the air,[93] and subsequently traced on the ground,[94] cannot be the road at issue, as its course is approximately NNE.–SSW.; its date is uncertain.

Chester–Wilderspool (route 701)[95]

It seems likely that a road linked the legionary fortress with Wilderspool and the river crossing there. While there are convincing road lines as far as Bridge Trafford, and from Preston on the Hill to Wilderspool, the intervening terrain is such that straight alignments were hardly possible, and the road line has not been identified; that it existed is suggested by the cluster of finds in the Frodsham area.

Other Roads

A road is conjectured as running east from the north end of King Street to Watling Street. Finds have been reported east of King Street and north of Watling Street.[96] From a point 250 m. east of Stretton church a road traced to a point immediately west of Junction 20 on the M 6 is 14.5 m. wide, between ditches 15–18 m. apart. It consisted of glacial pebbles, surfaced with rammed gravel and marl. Thereafter it is thought to have changed direction, and broadly to follow the course of the A 50. Elsewhere, on a line from Redbank Bridge through Primrose Hill to High Legh and Hoo Green,[97] it was found to be 19.2 m. wide, and consisted of a 20 cm. layer of glacial pebbles. It was aligned to join Watling Street between Mere and Bucklow Hill, *c.* 9 km. north-east of the crossing with King Street. Whether the minor route originated at King Street or further west, as has been suggested,[98] is uncertain.

Another proposed road linking Wilderspool and Manchester excavated west of Lymm was traced for a width of *c.* 7.3 m., and consisted of gravel, pebbles, and sandstone chippings mixed with sand. The average thickness was 28 cm.[99]

[88] Margary, *Roman Roads in Brit.* 303–4.
[89] *T.L.C.A.S.* lxxvii. 23–6. Further fieldwork is described in *Ches. Arch. Bull.* viii. 91 and *Britannia*, xv. 288–9.
[90] Margary, *Roman Roads in Brit.* 304.
[91] *T.L.C.A.S.* lxxvii. 20.
[92] *Antiq. Jnl.* lv. 66.
[93] *Ches. Arch. Bull.* vi. 8.
[94] Ibid. viii. 30–3.

[95] Margary, *Roman Roads in Brit.* 304–5.
[96] *J.R.S.* lix. 210; *Arch. Newsletter*, xviii. 8; xix. 5–6; *Britannia*, iii. 314; *Ches. Arch. Bull.* i. 10–11.
[97] *Britannia*, i. 282; iv. 284; *Arch. Newsletter*, xiv–xv. 10; xxi. 8–9; *Ches. Arch. Bull.* ii. 19–20; *Ches. Hist.* xiii. 13–18.
[98] *Ches. Arch. Bull.* i. 11.
[99] *Arch. Newsletter*, xiv–xv. 10; *Britannia*, iii. 314.

At Nettleford, a short distance east of Kelsall, is an apparent road junction, with a road leaving Watling Street towards Middlewich.[1] A very straight road alignment exists for *c.* 6 km. towards Over, and although writers have tended to be cautious in their assessment of it, the suggestion is that it linked Chester via Middlewich with Buxton (*Aquae Arnemitiae*); confirmation of the junction, and of the Middlewich road for 4.5 km., is reported,[2] as is an apparent Roman road near Sandiford Lodge.

Two further roads require mention, although they serve sites outside the county, and their course within Cheshire is only generally known, being untested by excavation. A road which links the forts at Manchester and Melandra Castle, Glossop (route 711), crosses Cheshire's north-east corner but its line is not determined. A second runs from Manchester to Buxton (route 71b); its course has been traced as far as Disley, but is not known with any precision thereafter.[3]

Perhaps more than any other aspect of antiquity Roman roads have prompted speculation, much of it unacceptable. Among proposed Roman roads which cannot be substantiated are Blake Street near Saighton[4] and Watfield Pavement.[5]

INDUSTRIES

Salt

The three Cheshire towns which produced salt in post-Roman times also had salt works in the Roman period, although each differs from the others in its history. Whether Middlewich, Northwich, and Nantwich were the only centres of production is unknown: the brine kiln at Tetton is perhaps near enough to Middlewich to form part of that straggling settlement, but it may be more than chance that there is a cluster of Roman finds near Lymm where there was a salt works in more recent times.[6] Although there is inferential evidence of pre-Roman salt making in Cheshire, no Iron Age sites or finds have been discovered at Middlewich, Northwich, or Nantwich.[7] Production at Northwich and Middlewich seems to have begun very soon after the establishment of the legionary fortress and its dependent forts.

The salt works at Northwich was near the fort, whose garrison could also conveniently supervise the works at Middlewich 9 km. away. Extraction of salt had been a state monopoly since the Republic; some salt works were run as part of the imperial estates, using convict or slave labour, while others were leased out to private contractors. A parallel can be drawn between salt making and lead mining in Deceanglian territory where lead ingots initially bore the names of Vespasian and then Domitian, but thereafter the mines seem to have been managed by private lessees.[8] The appearance of lead brine pans at Nantwich, Northwich, and perhaps Middlewich, bearing the names of such lessees, marks the change from direct production for the emperor to leasing. Evidence of the period at which that was happening comes from Middlewich, where the site was divided into plots containing small salt works which were under civilian management at the end of the 1st century

---

[1] *T.L.C.A.S.* iii. 124-6.

[2] Margary, *Roman Roads in Brit.* 300; Thompson, *Roman Ches.* 22; *Britannia*, xiii. 353-4; xiv. 297-9; *Ches. Arch. Bull.* ix. 63-6.

[3] Margary, *Roman Roads in Brit.* 363-5.

[4] 3 *Sheaf*, liv, pp. 25-6; lv, pp. 90-1.

[5] Watkin, *Roman Ches.* 59.

[6] There is a large hoard from Statham: below, Gazetteer.

[7] Salt was made at Droitwich (Worcs.) in the pre-Roman period, and study of the Very Coarse Pottery (V.C.P.) in which the salt was marketed indicates that salt was made in south Ches. at the same time and distributed over a wide area in the Marches. Dr. E. Morris kindly informed the writer of her research ('Salt and Ceramic Exchange'). See also *Current Arch.* lxxxvi. 89.

[8] *Flints. Hist. Soc. Pubs.* xiii. 5-17.

or early in the 2nd. The appearance of civilian contractors may be linked with the withdrawal of the garrison from Northwich for a few years at about that time. In any event the change at Northwich cannot have taken place much later than the mid 2nd century, as there is little evidence of occupation thereafter, and the period of production was relatively short.[9] By contrast, it has been suggested that salt working at Middlewich continued to be a major industrial activity until after A.D. 350.[10] Little is known about the site at Nantwich, but it seems that production was modest in scale, and perhaps short-lived.

Only at Middlewich have the details of salt making been examined in controlled excavations, the major elements being the brine pits and kilns, stoving furnaces, and work sheds. The salt works produced abundant 'briquetage', the broken and discarded brine evaporation pans and kiln furniture which seems to have been the normal stock-in-trade of the Middlewich salt worker.[11] It may represent a 'native' tradition of salt making, for similar briquetage is found on coastal saltern sites of the late Iron Age and early Roman period. The only other site to have produced it in Cheshire is Nantwich, where a few scraps have been found. Neither Northwich nor Nantwich has produced evidence of the type of brine kiln used with lead pans, although it seems likely that one was destroyed at the former site when the lead pans were found. It may well have been more durable, and perhaps larger, than the brine kilns at Middlewich. The raw material for the process was available at all sites as 'wild' brine, either from a surface spring, or in a shallow pit. Although rock salt was certainly mined elsewhere in the empire,[12] it was never necessary to mine it in Cheshire in the Roman period. Whether access to the brine was controlled, and how it was allotted to the different lessees, are equally uncertain. Since the lead pans appear to have been marked to indicate ownership it is reasonable to infer either a control on output, or possibly the levying of a toll on each pan of salt produced.[13] The scale of salt production is unknown, but the only site to produce it in quantity was probably Middlewich.

When the Romans arrived in Britain salt was produced almost exclusively in coastal salterns on the east and south coasts, like the 'Red Hills' of Essex.[14] The characteristic briquetage produced can be likened to that from a number of sites occupied for the first time during the later 1st century in the Fens. The seasonal production at such estuarine and fenland sites dwindled or ceased in the early 2nd century, as it probably did also at the salterns of the south coast from Sussex to Hampshire. While the decline in the fenland salterns may partly have resulted from exhaustion of the only fuel available, peat, and from fresh-water flooding, the rise in production at the inland sites may also have been influential. Extraction of salt from brine is simpler, as there are fewer undesirable products to exclude than in sea water; it could also be carried out throughout the year. The improvement of communications generally facilitated the marketing of the salt over greater distances, and the *negotiatores salarii* named on inscriptions from the Rhineland[15] may

---

[9] Unless it is supposed that salt making shifted its ground, perhaps to the east side of the river. There is no evidence for such a movement.

[10] *Salt*, 70. The claim does not seem entirely substantiated by the evidence: above.

[11] All briquetage examined for temperatures of firing has been fired to over 500 °C, and temperatures of 800–1100 °C were sometimes reached. Such high temperatures were certainly not required to boil the brine.

[12] e.g. in Dacia: *C.I.L.* iii, nos. 1209, 1363.

[13] The process of evaporation is simple, but there was

probably some fundamental difference between the processes using briquetage and those using lead pans: the high temperatures postulated for the former would have melted the latter.

[14] B. C. Burnham and H. B. Johnson, *Invasion and Response* (Brit. Arch. Rep. lxxiii), 158. Temperatures in the range 800–1000 °C were also produced by the brine kilns at those sites.

[15] *Année Épigraphique, 1973*, nos. 362, 364, 378 and another unpublished: inf. from Prof. J. E. Bogaers.

have been engaged in the salt trade with Britain.[16] They were perhaps lessees of the state monopoly, or employed by the lessees.

While there is evidence from Middlewich of the origins of one possible lessee, the unknown cavalryman whose diploma has been found, there is nothing to indicate whether the salt workers were slave, convict, or free. Some salt works in Britain may have used convict labour.[17]

Pottery

The pottery industry in the region is by no means fully understood, and study of coarse pottery from sites in Cheshire may reveal new sources and centres of production. Pottery was made at Wilderspool, Middlewich, Chester, and Northwich; there was also the legionary tile and pottery works at Holt (Denb.).

Cheshire has yielded little pottery of the pre-Roman Iron Age and understanding of the native wares current at the time of the Roman conquest is consequently very poor. As there were no native potters producing wares acceptable to the Roman army, military requirements were at first satisfied from outside the region. Potteries were set up under military control, and later immigrant potters arrived. Despite local production external sources of pottery, always significant, in time became completely dominant again. The Cheshire potters' relative lack of success may partly be attributed to the absence of an urban market within a reasonable distance; other factors may have been the rather sparse population of the Cheshire countryside, and the apparent fact that most communities north of the Mersey in the Roman period used pottery rather sparingly by comparison with those in the south and east of Britain.

The only known centre of production in the pre-Flavian period was at Trent Vale.[18] The pottery produced there shows a break with native traditions, and is thought to have been made under military auspices. *Mortaria* in that period came mainly from military sources, supplemented by the products of the Radlett and Brockley Hill kilns. Raetian *mortaria*, a very distinctive type with red slip over the rim, were also imported in the Flavian–Trajanic period, and are common in the Cheshire plain and north Wales. Production of Raetian *mortaria* was in time begun at Wilderspool.[19] North Gaulish fine wares, mainly beakers with rough-cast decoration, are largely found in north-west Britain, including Wales, and influenced the products of Wilderspool and also of Holt.[20] Rough-cast decoration declined in popularity from *c*. A.D. 160, and similar wares from the Nene Valley kilns captured the market by *c*. A.D. 170.

The only pottery kiln recorded in Cheshire in recent times, at Northwich,[21] was of the conventional simple updraught type. After use it was backfilled with tightly packed fragments of the dome mixed with clay and charcoal, together with fragments of the products. The latter consisted mainly of jars and cooking pots, and also flagons and *mortaria*, with a few bowls. The normal fabric was orange to buff in colour, and resembled the products of Holt, where parallels for the forms are also found. The potter, named MACO on a single stamp, was working *c*. A.D. 90–125. Although the kiln appeared within the fort it is thought that the potter established himself in the brief intermission between two periods of occupation.[22]

[16] An altar from Heronbridge implies trading links between Cheshire and the Rhineland: above.

[17] E. Birley, *Roman Brit. and Roman Army*, 51–2.

[18] *N. Staffs. Jnl. of Field Studies*, viii. 19–38.

[19] Swan, *Pottery Kilns of Roman Brit.* 104; above.

[20] For painted fine wares made at Wilderspool see A. C. and A. S. Anderson, *Roman Pottery Research in Brit. and NW. Eur.* 471–9.

[21] *Arch. Jnl.* cxxviii. 48; Swan, *Pottery Kilns of Roman Brit.* 87.

[22] The kiln may have been set up in the annexe to the fort; other industrial activity was also noted: *J.R.S.* lix. 209–10.

Wilderspool was a much more significant centre of pottery production than Northwich, supplying Lancashire, southern Cumbria, and, to a lesser extent, Cheshire with coarse wares including *mortaria*. Three pottery kilns have been recorded, the first being a chance find in a sandpit; presumably others await discovery. The known kilns were not all in operation at the same time, but it is impossible to associate pottery with specific kilns. The pottery is generally orange or pink in colour and soft in texture, like that from Northwich;[23] many of the pots had a cream-coloured slip. It belongs to the Trajanic–Antonine period, agreeing with the dates assigned to the production of *mortaria*.[24] Production of pottery at Wilderspool was never large-scale, and a surprisingly common source of *mortaria* at Wilderspool even in the 2nd century was the Hartshill kilns.

Kilns at other centres, for example Middlewich, served only local needs for a limited period before being supplanted by larger centres outside the region.[24] The discovery in the *canabae* at Chester of kiln wasters, mainly of flagons and *mortaria* resembling the products of Holt, implies the production of pottery nearby in the late 1st and early 2nd century.[25] *Mortaria* with distinctive forms and fabrics have recently been identified among the finds from Chester, and it is thought that they came from kilns in the Cheshire Plain, possibly within 16 km. of the fortress.

HOLT: THE LEGIONARY TILERIES AND POTTERIES.[26] *Bovium*,[27] the only military tile and pottery works known in detail from the Roman world, lies 12 km. south of the fortress, on the west bank of the Dee. Although just outside the county boundary, the site is closely related to the fortress. The known structures cover *c.* 8 ha.[28] Industrial buildings lie on the east of the site, close to the river bank; the river was evidently used for carrying the heavy and bulky products of the tileries downstream to the fortress. Two stone-built workshops were identified, one of which may have been the pottery throwing shed, and the other a drying shed and store. A large double-flued kiln close to the second shed may have been used for firing pottery; it was apparently abandoned during the early 2nd century, and its period of use agrees with current beliefs about the period when pottery was made at Holt. The main group of kilns, 25 m. away, consisted of six rectangular kilns sharing a common stokehole and covered fuel store. Two more kilns, one circular, were added later.

The workers were housed in a compound surrounded by a wall over 2 m. thick; that thickness indicates a considerable height. The compound measured 54.5–57.5 m. in width and *c.* 107–110 m. in length. The compound contained barracks, two smaller buildings which resemble the rampart buildings in the fortress, and a latrine. East of it lay a simple bath-building, and adjacent on the river bank a small house with six rooms, three heated, and a veranda facing the river. It is thought to have housed the officer in charge.

Holt was founded when the army was still producing a proportion of its requirements of pottery, and that aspect of the so-called 'works depot' has received particular attention, especially the fine wares.[29] Imports of samian were limited in the early 2nd century, and Holt produced plain and decorated pottery to fill the gap.[30]

[23] Thompson, *Roman Ches.* 79.

[24] Swan, *Pottery Kilns of Roman Brit.*, gazetteer, 1.239.

[25] Ibid.; A. C. and A. S. Anderson, *Roman Pottery Research*, 34.

[26] W. F. Grimes, 'Holt, Denbs.: The Works Depot of the Twentieth Legion at Castle Lyons', *Y Cymmrodor*, xli. 1–235; Nash-Williams, *Roman Frontier in Wales*, 42–4; Thompson, *Roman Ches.* 13–15, 53–9.

[27] Rivet and Smith, *Place Names of Roman Brit.* 274.

[28] The extent of the site, and its intensity of occupation at various periods, are uncertain. The excavator's records do not permit close dating of structures or periods, and it is doubtful whether timber features were recognized. Structures may await discovery outside the area explored.

[29] J. Dore and K. Greene, *Roman Pottery Studies in Brit. and Beyond* (Brit. Arch. Rep. Supp. Ser. xxx), 113–32.

[30] *J.C.A.S.* lxii. 24.

Study of the coarse wares has been hampered by uncertainty about the range of wares produced. Pottery production does not predate the Flavian period, and is unlikely to have begun much before A.D. 100.[31] It has been doubted whether pottery was made after c. 140,[32] and its manufacture may have ceased c. 125–30; from the Antonine period the needs of the garrison were supplied by civilian contractors.[33] Tile production presumably commenced in quantity when timber buildings in the fortress began to be replaced in stone.[34] Roofing tiles, hypocaust bricks, and water pipes were all made, and *tegulae* continued to be made until at least the early 3rd century, and probably until c. A.D. 250.[35] Production is unlikely to have continued for long after the mid 3rd century, as there is little later 3rd- or 4th-century material from Holt. The tileries were the dominant element, for the battery of rectangular kilns form plant unequalled in scale in Britain.[36] Tiles were supplied to military sites at Caernarfon, Caersws, and Caerhun;[37] Holt, Ffrith, and Prestatyn have also yielded Holt tiles.[38] It cannot be coincidental that most of those sites were accessible by water. Production of tiles for civilian use cannot be entirely ruled out.[39] Auxiliary soldiers are known to have been posted to Holt,[40] and the workforce may not have consisted entirely of soldiers.[41]

Quarrying

The legionary fortress at Chester is on a sandstone ridge, and the accessibility of the stone for building probably helped to determine the choice of site. Sandstone was quarried on the south bank of the river in Edgar's Field, Handbridge,[42] resulting in an accumulation of up to 2.4 m. of quarry waste, including dressed blocks. Pottery found in small pockets of rubbish among the debris suggested that quarrying began in the late 1st century, as might be expected; nevertheless from the late 2nd century or probably a little later, dumping of soil began over the thick layer of debris, and apparently quarrying ceased long before the end of the Roman period. The fill yielded part of a Severan building inscription of A.D. 194–6,[43] presumably derived with other material from the fortress. Possibly the quarry continued to be used up to the well attested rebuilding under Severus,[44] but thereafter its use declined and ceased and it was used as a rubbish tip, on the evidence of pottery found there, until the late 4th century. The only other nearby source of sandstone which may have been exploited in the Roman period is on the west bank of the river immediately downstream of Heronbridge.[45]

The sandstone near the fortress is generally rather friable, and does not make particularly good building stone. Better stone is available at Helsby, Manley, and Peckforton, which lie in an arc 12–15 km. east of the fortress. Storeton, in Wirral, c. 20 km. north-west of Chester, offers another possible source of more durable stone which was certainly much used later.[46] The only site to have produced proof

[31] *Arch. Jnl.* cxxx. 100.

[32] Dore and Greene, *Roman Pottery Studies*, 147, 158.

[33] A. C. and A. S. Anderson, *Roman Pottery Research*, 33.

[34] It cannot yet be said whether production began early enough to supply the vast quantity of tiles required for the internal bath-building.

[35] Some *tegulae* bear stamps with the suffixes ANTO[NIN-IANA] and DE[CIANA]. For tiles dated to A.D. 167 see *Britannia*, ix. 476.

[36] *World Arch.* xv. 249; A. C. and A. S. Anderson, *Roman Pottery Research*, 435–6.

[37] *Arch. Camb.* lxxx. 313, 315; 3rd ser. iii. 159; *Bull. Bd. Celtic Stud.* xx. 439; *Montgom. Collns.* xlvi. 82.

[38] *Arch. Camb.* xcii. 208–32; xciii. 175–91; *Flints. Hist.*

Soc. Pubs. ix. 72–80; xxiii. 82–5; E. Davies, *Prehist. and Roman Remains of Flints.* 226–7, 237–8.

[39] Dore and Greene, *Roman Pottery Studies*, 159.

[40] There is a graffito naming a soldier of the Third Cohort of Sunici, the 3rd-cent. garrison at Segontium: *Y Cymmrodor*, xli. 133.

[41] Dore and Greene, *Roman Pottery Studies*, 125–6.

[42] *J.C.A.S.* xxvii. 103–8, 146–9.

[43] *R.I.B.* i, no. 465; *J.R.S.* xvii. 194, 212.

[44] Above.

[45] *J.C.A.S.* xxxix. 3.

[46] Stone from those sources has been identified in the collection of inscribed and sculptured stones in the Grosvenor Mus.: *R.I.S.S.* p. 8; *T.H.S.L.C.* xlix. 56–7.

of Roman quarrying, however, is Helsby where an unfinished altar was found.[47] Presumably the rough-outs for inscribed stones were produced in a workshop close to the quarry face, and then transported to the fortress for completion. A Roman road links the quarry and fortress, and its principal purpose may have been to carry quarry traffic.

Another type of stone to be carried to the fortress was slate. While it can appear in quite humble circumstances, for example as roofing material, it was also used as a particularly fine stone for inscriptions.[48] The relatively rare use of slate for tomb inscriptions may reflect its greater cost, since it had to travel further from the quarry, but the tombstone[49] from Eaton Road, Handbridge, shows that it was used for that purpose by officers at least; the inscription found at Green Bank, Eaton Road,[50] less certainly from a tomb, is also cut on slate. The *retiarius* relief[51] was cut in slate from near Llangollen, where a quarry for milestones is also suspected.[52] Where water transport was available stone could travel a long way, and it has been suggested that sandstone from Cheshire was used for rebuilding at Caernarfon,[53] Prestatyn,[54] and Caerhun.[55]

Copper

The known history of copper mining in relatively recent times at Alderley Edge and Mottram St. Andrew in east Cheshire, and also near Bickerton,[56] has given rise to a persistent belief that those deposits were exploited in the Roman period, in particular at Alderley.[57] Old mine workings are identified at five sites there, nearly all disturbed by later mines. Many stone hammers from either the pits or their tips have been variously dated to the Bronze Age and the Roman period. Evidence of early workings at Alderley Edge is inconclusive, as the stone hammers cannot be dated, and may belong to any period up to the Middle Ages. The only certain finds of the Roman period are four coins of the 3rd and 4th centuries said to have been found at Alderley Edge;[58] a Roman date has been claimed for an iron pick-head, but the identification is suspect.[59] On the evidence available at present it seems unlikely that copper or lead mining took place in the Roman period in Cheshire.[60]

Lead

Small veins of lead ore exist in east Cheshire, but much more important deposits are found in north-east Wales not far from the fortress. Four lead pigs are extant with the letters DECEANGL (for *plumbum Deceanglicum*) moulded on their side, indicating their origin in the lead mines of Flintshire, or rather in the territory of the Deceangli. Two from Chester[61] are datable to A.D. 74, and two from Hints Common, near Tamworth (Staffs.), to A.D. 76.[62] They show that imperial mining was taking place by A.D. 74, if not earlier, for all four bear Vespasian's name and titles. An ingot found at Carmel, near Holywell has the name of a private lessee or *conductor*, C. Nipius Ascanius, presumably the same man as is named on an ingot from

[47] *J.C.A.S.* xlvi. 79; *J.R.S.* xlix. 108.
[48] cf. *R.I.B.* i, nos. 458, 462 (especially the recently found part), 464, 465. [49] Ibid. no. 510.
[50] *J.C.A.S.* lix. 31–4. [51] Above.
[52] The milestones from Rhiwiau-uchaf (*R.I.B.* i, nos. 2265–6), one Hadrianic, the other Severan: J. P. Sedgley, *Roman Milestones of Brit.* (Brit. Arch. Rep. xviii), 8, 33.
[53] *Y Cymmrodor*, xxxiii. 103; Nash-Williams, *Roman Frontier in Wales*, 62.
[54] *Arch. Camb.* xcii. 231.
[55] Ibid. lxxxiv. 77–8.

[56] *J.C.A.S.* lxiv. 47; *T.L.C.A.S.* xix. 77–118; xxiii. 17–29.
[57] *Bull. Bd. Celtic Stud.* xxvii. 132–3.
[58] *Ches. Arch. Bull.* vi. 79; *T.L.C.A.S.* xix. 95.
[59] *T.L.C.A.S.* xxiii. 23.
[60] O. Davies, *Roman Mines in Europe*, 35, 140, 160. It is equally uncertain that the iron ores associated with the copper deposits at Alderley Edge were exploited: Jones and others, *Roman Manchester*, 153.
[61] *R.I.S.S.* nos. 196–7 (*C.I.L.* vii, no. 1204 and *E.E.* vii, no. 1121).
[62] *C.I.L.* vii, no. 1205; *E.E.* ix. 1264.

Bossington (Hants) which can be dated to A.D. 60.[63] Although the latter is thought to have come from the Mendips, it is possible that Ascanius was allowed to begin lead mining in the territory of the Deceangli before its formal incorporation into the province.[64]

How long exploitation of Deceanglian lead continued is unknown, but sites at Pentre, Ffrith, and Prestatyn which may be linked with the lead industry were active in the 2nd century,[65] and possibly later.

Despite doubts[66] it is possible that Legio xx was concerned with mining and processing lead in Deceanglian territory. Mining communities controlled by procurators on behalf of the emperor, using slave or convict labour, needed military supervision; the datable lead pigs belong to the period when closer imperial control was being formulated,[67] and stamped tiles of the legion have been found at Prestatyn and Ffrith. The legion's participation was, however, indirect, and the absence of ingots naming it is not necessarily significant.

Perhaps because the silver content of lead from Flintshire is below the level at which it was profitable to mine it, interest in the exploitation of the lead mines by the state waned, and in the 2nd century mining was possibly in the hands of *conductores*.[68] If, in view of the poor silver yield, the ore was extracted for building, the volume of production was perhaps related to the needs of the fortress at Chester and its dependent forts for lead for water pipes and for lining for water tanks and cisterns. The activity apparent in the Flintshire field in the Flavian period and its subsequent decline in the 2nd century accord with what is known of building at Chester and in the forts of north Wales.[69]

GAZETTEER OF ROMANO-BRITISH FINDS ON MINOR SITES

Since major sites are discussed in the text above, only the finds from minor sites are here listed.

ACTON

CHOLMONDESTON (*c.* SJ 62 58). Hoard of 26 coins found in a sandpit before 1881. Most of those identified were of Constantius II and Constans; the latter were of the FEL TEMP REPARATIO type and therefore A.D. 348 or later.[70]

HENHULL. (a) SJ 634 538. Roman road sectioned, 1965.[71] (b) SJ 648 528. *Sestertius* of Domitian (?), found 1974.[72] (c) SJ 648 530. Two lead brine pans with inscriptions, found 1981.[73] (d) SJ 641 538. Rim of glass vessel.[74]

WORLESTON. (a) *c.* SJ 652 549. Line of Roman road confirmed by fieldwork and excavation.[75] (b) Reaseheath Hall (SJ 646 543). Stamped legionary tile and Holt ware imitation Dr. 18, probably found at Chester.[76]

ALDERLEY

Alderley Edge. (a) SJ 855 773–861 778. Copper mining of prehistoric and/or Romano-British period reported.[77] (b) *c.* SJ 85 77 or 86 77. Four coins (Elagabalus, Postumus, Crispus, and Valentinian I) said to have been found *c.* 1900.[78]

ALDERLEY, OVER. Stone head of a maenad said to have been found.[79]

---

[63] *C.I.L.* vii, no. 1203.   [64] *Britannia*, xiii. 119–22.

[65] *Flints. Hist. Soc. Pubs.* ix. 72–80; x. 3–28; *Arch. Camb.* xci. 74; xcii. 208–32; xciii. 175–91; *Bull. Bd. Celtic Stud.* xxvii. 134–5.   [66] *Flints. Hist. Soc. Pubs.* xiii. 10–14.

[67] J. P. Healy, *Mining and Metallurgy in Greek and Roman World*, 129.

[68] R. F. Tylecote, *Metallurgy in Arch.* 75. The inscription on a lead pig from Commonhall Street, Chester (*R.I.S.S.* no. 198) may conceal in a garbled form the name of a 2nd-cent. lessee.

[69] Unpublished research by the Clwyd-Powys Arch.

Trust at Flint and Prestatyn may define more clearly the details of those industrial sites.

[70] *Palatine Note Bk.* i. 199; Watkin, *Roman Ches.* 291–2.

[71] *Arch. Newsletter*, vii. 8; *T.L.C.A.S.* lxxvii. 23–4.

[72] *Ches. Arch. Bull.* iii. 60.   [73] *Britannia*, xv. 342.

[74] *Ches. Arch. Bull.* ix. 101.   [75] Inf. from Mr. J. Ray.

[76] *J.C.A.S.* xl. 64–6; O.S. Arch. Rec. 65 SW.

[77] Sainter, *Scientific Rambles*, 65; *T.L.C.A.S.* xix. 77–118; xxiii. 17–29; O.S. Arch. Rec. 87 NE.; above.

[78] *Ches. Arch. Bull.* vi. 79; *T.L.C.A.S.* xix. 95.

[79] In West Park Mus., Macclesfield.

THE ROMAN PERIOD
ALDFORD

Aldford. (a) SJ 418 602. Roman ford.[80] (b) SJ 427 576. Watling Street excavated, 1960.[81] (c) *c.* SJ 419 595. Supposed site of Roman camp.[82]

Buerton (SJ 423 613). *Denarius* of Octavian.[83]

Churton by Aldford (SJ 430 569). Watling Street excavated, 1960.[84]

ASHTON UPON MERSEY

Sale. (a) 46 coins, from Nerva to Valens, shown at a meeting of the Lancs. and Ches. Antiquarian Soc.[85] (b) SJ 771 901. Two sherds, one of a samian bowl Dr. 37, found before 1910.[86]

ASTBURY

Congleton. (a) *c.* SJ 859 626. six or seven small *ae* coins, and a large *ae* of Commodus, found *c.* 1859. A hoard?[87] (b) *c.* SJ 866 634. Coin of Constantine I, found *c.* 1910–15.[88] (c) SJ 868 626. *Follis* of Diocletian, found 1959.[89]

Newbold Astbury. (a) Bent Farm (*c.* SJ 837 620). Earthworks of Roman military site noted 1725, and said to have been destroyed by 1744. Site rediscovered 1967, when defences sectioned. Further work in 1970 revealed traces of timber buildings internally.[90] (b) *c.* SJ 850 570. 'Roman' lamp, found *c.* 1909, in a limestone quarry.[91] (c) Three sandstone querns, period unknown, since lost.[92]

AUDLEM AND WRENBURY

Newhall. Burleydam (*c.* SJ 603 430). Crop-marks, perhaps of a field system, found 1934.[93]

BACKFORD

Backford (SJ 398 713). Coin of Maximian (?), found *c.* 1920.[94]

Mollington (SJ 385 715). *As* of Domitian, found *c.* 1940.[95]

BARROW

(a) SJ 465 684. 2 *asses*, one of Vespasian.[96] (b) SJ 472 675. *As* of Trajan, rim of samian bowl of form Dr. 30, sherd of black-burnished pottery.[97] (c) SJ 480 700. Lead weight, found *c.* 1962.[98]

BARTHOMLEY

Barthomley. Mound partly composed of stones associated with the Wincle hoard (see Prestbury). Almost certainly a natural feature.[99]

Haslington (SJ 737 555). *Follis* of Constantine II as Caesar, found *c.* 1950.[1]

BEBINGTON

(a) SJ 330 848. *Antoninianus* of Postumus, found 1971.[2] (b) SJ 327 838–332 839. Supposed Roman road.[3] (c) *c.* SJ 334 840. *Antoninianus* of Valerian (pierced), found 1876.[4] (d) Storeton (*c.* SJ 316 843). Stone quarries thought to have been used in Roman period.[5]

BIDDULPH (STAFFS.)

SJ 92 61. Road line (?Roman) seen on air photo. of Biddulph Moor.[6]

[80] *Arch. Camb.* 3rd ser. i. 238; 6th ser. x. 192; Watkin, *Roman Ches.* 49; *J.C.A.S.* xlviii. 25.

[81] *J.C.A.S.* xlviii. 17–19.

[82] Watkin, *Roman Ches.* 299; O.S. Arch. Rec. 45 NW.

[83] *Ches. Arch. Bull.* vi. 76.

[84] *J.C.A.S.* xlviii. 20–1.

[85] *T.L.C.A.S.* xxvii. 194.

[86] 4 *Sheaf,* v. 30.

[87] Watkin, *Roman Ches.* 311.

[88] J. E. Gordon Cartlidge, *Newbold Astbury and its Hist.* 10.

[89] *J.C.A.S.* xlvii. 37.

[90] *T.H.S.L.C.* xxix. 84–5; Watkin, *Roman Ches.* 74; *Ches. Historian,* ix. 24; *Northern Hist.* iii. 3–4, 26; *Britannia,* ii. 255; O.S. Arch. Rec. 86 SW.

[91] *Ches. Historian,* ix. 23–4; the find is also attributed to Mow Cop.

[92] Ibid.; *Trans. N. Staffs. Field Club* (1935–6), 86.

[93] O.S. Arch. Rec. 64 SW.

[94] Ibid. 37 SE.

[95] *Ches. Arch. Bull.* i. 6.

[96] Ibid. vii. 61.

[97] Ibid.

[98] O.S. Arch. Rec. 47 SE.

[99] *T.H.S.L.C.* xxix. 88–9; *T.L.C.A.S.* xxv. 150.

[1] *Ches. Arch. Bull.* vi. 77.

[2] Ibid. i. 5.

[3] Watkin, *Roman Ches.* 59; O.S. Arch. Rec. 38 SW.

[4] *T.H.S.L.C.* xxxi. 116; Watkin, *Roman Ches.* 312.

[5] *T.H.S.L.C.* xlix. 56–8; above.

[6] *Ches. Arch. Bull.* vi. 8.

BIDSTON

BIRKENHEAD. (a) SJ 322 894. Wooden structure, interpreted as a Roman bridge, found during construction of railway, 1850.[7] (b) SJ 334 865. Coin, possibly of Hadrian, found 1952.[8] (c) SJ 312 875. Grey Roman jar 'like an amphora', found 1922.[9] (d) SJ 297 865. Roman coin given to Lady Lever Gallery.[10] (e) SJ 285 893. Coin hoard said to have been found *c.* 1900 (report doubtful).[11]

BOWDON

ALTRINCHAM (SJ 761 886). Watling Street sectioned.[12]
HALE (SJ 788 860). Sherd of decorated samian.[13]

BOWDON AND ROSTHERNE

AGDEN. (a) SJ 722 872. Hoard of *c.* 2,500 *antoniniani* from Valerian to Probus, found 1957.[14] (b) SJ 724 871. Two *antoniniani*, of Gallienus and Salonina, thought to be from the Agden hoard.[15] (c) SJ 668 881. 27 more *antoniniani* from the Agden hoard reported.[16]

BRERETON CUM SMETHWICK

c. SJ 769 637. *c.* 1,000 coins found in a fused mass, with the remains of a box, 1820. The hoard included *antoniniani* of Gallienus, Claudius II, the Tetrici, Victorinus, and Diocletian.[17]

BROMBOROUGH

(a) SJ 351 812. Coin of Domitian, found 1900.[18] (b) SJ 351 811. Coin of 4th-century type.[19] (c) SJ 351 810. Coin of Vespasian, found *c.* 1936.[20] (d) SJ 346 820. *Sestertius* of M. Aurelius as Caesar, found 1969.[21]

BUDWORTH, GREAT

ANTROBUS (SJ 641 815). Coin of Gallienus, found 1948.[22]
APPLETON. (a) SJ 617 840. Stone marking course of Roman road.[23] (b) SJ 618 836. *Sestertius* of Claudius I, found 1939–40.[24] (c) King Street recorded in drain trench.[25]
Stockton Heath. (a) Roman road, found 1928.[26] (b) SJ 628 867. Quern found, period uncertain.[27] (c) *c.* SJ 614 865. Roman (?) cemetery associated with settlement at Wilderspool.[28]
BARNTON. Two silver coins of Constantine I found with others unknown in a pot. Possibly a hoard?[29]
HARTFORD (*c.* SJ 632 718). Urns found near Hartford station.[30]
MARSTON (*c.* SJ 666 766). Two coins, one of Nero, found *c.* 1925.[31]
STRETTON. (a) King Street in Big Town Field, etc.[32] (b) King Street.[33] (c) SJ 619 831. King Street cut by pipeline, 1960.[34] (d) Branch road traced.[35] (e) SJ 6215 8197, 6215 8220. Recording and fieldwork, King Street.[36] (f) King Street and branch road.[37]

BUNBURY

ALPRAHAM. Two 'Celtic' stone heads, said to date from the 'early 1st millennium A.D.'[38]
BEESTON (SJ 540 592). 2nd- and 3rd-century Roman pottery found during excavations.[39]
PECKFORTON (SJ 543 577). Crop-mark of sub-rectangular enclosure noted by Ordnance Survey, date unknown.[40]
WARDLE (SJ 602 578). *Ae* of Constantine I.[41]

[7] *J.C.A.S.* [1st ser.], i. 55–60, 68–76.
[8] O.S. Arch. Rec. 38 NW.
[9] *J.R.S.* xii. 249.
[10] O.S. Arch. Rec. 28 NE.   [11] Ibid.
[12] *Arch. Newsletter*, vii. 9; viii. 12.
[13] Watkin, *Roman Ches.* 306–7.
[14] *J.C.A.S.* xlv. 72–3; *J.R.S.* xlviii. 136; *Num. Chron.* ii. 143–55.
[15] *Ches. Arch. Bull.* i. 5.
[16] *Britannia*, vii. 319.
[17] *Arch. Camb.* [1st ser.], ii. 182; *T.H.S.L.C.* ii. 40, 212; xxix. 86; Watkin, *Roman Ches.* 310–11.
[18] O.S. Arch. Rec. 38 SE.
[19] Ibid.
[20] A. Anderson, *Story of Bebington*, 14.
[21] Merseyside Arch. Survey.
[22] *J.C.A.S.* xxxix. 110; O.S. Arch. Rec. 68 SW.
[23] O.S. Arch. Rec. 68 SW.   [24] Ibid.
[25] *J.R.S.* xiv. 223–4.

[26] Ibid. xviii.198.
[27] O.S. Arch. Rec. 68 NW.   [28] Ibid.
[29] 4 *Sheaf*, v. 32.
[30] Baines, *Lancs. and Ches. Past and Present*, i. 262; *T.H.S.L.C.* iii. 1; Thompson, *Roman Ches.* 89–90, fig. 24.
[31] O.S. Arch. Rec. 67 NE.
[32] *T.H.S.L.C.* ii. 34.
[33] *J.C.A.S.* [1st ser.], i. 190.
[34] Ibid. xlviii. 26.   [35] *J.R.S.* lix. 210.
[36] *T.L.C.A.S.* lxxvii. 28–9; *Ches. Arch. Bull.* iii. 57.
[37] *Britannia*, iii. 314; v. 419.
[38] The stone heads were seen by the writer at Alpraham and subsequently by Mr. F. H. Thompson at Christies', London, where they were sold on 16 Dec. 1982; both were of the opinion that the heads were not Romano-British but more recent.
[39] *Ches. Arch. Bull.* viii. 28; inf. from Mr. P. Hough.
[40] O.S. Arch. Rec. 55 NW.
[41] *Ches. Arch. Bull.* vi. 77.

THE ROMAN PERIOD
CHEADLE

SJ 857 886. Three coins: *antoniniani* of Postumus and Claudius II, *ae* of Constantine I, found 1939.[42]

CHESTER: HOLY TRINITY

BLACON. (a) Three coins (Geta, Gordian III, Victorinus), found 1934.[43] (b) *Denarius* of Nerva, found 1953.[44] (c) SJ 379 671. Crop-mark (? Roman) seen.[45]

Sealand (c. SJ 375 673). Gold coin of Tiberius, found 1952.[46]

CHESTER: ST. MARY ON THE HILL

CLAVERTON (a) SJ 403 641. Brooch of 3rd-century type.[47] (b) SJ 413 654. Enamelled brooch.[48] (c) Lead weights, I *uncia* and VIII *unciae*.[49]

Heronbridge. (a) Hoard of 43 *denarii*, latest coin of M. Aurelius. The hoard, previously associated with Eccleston, seems to have been found in the immediate vicinity of the Roman settlement.[50] (b) c. SJ 411 639. Uninscribed altar, found 1941; lead weight from 1954 excavations; amphora sherds with graffiti, found 1948.[51] (c) Antonine samian, found 1897.[52] (d) c. SJ 411 643. Roman tiles and pottery found south of Green Bank.[53] (e) SJ 408 642. *Denarius* of Trajan. (f) SJ 404 638. Lead weight, I *uncia*. (g) SJ 407 642. Top of Roman key. (h) SJ 411 641. *Denarius* of Nero. (j) SJ 413 634. Lead weight, ?VII *unciae*. (k) SJ 409 642. *Sestertius* of Hadrian. (l) Lead weight, VIII *unciae*, found 300 m. N. of Green Bank.[54] (m) Quarry, possibly Roman.[55] (n) SJ 403 641. Third-cent. brooch.[56] (o) SJ 413 654. Enamelled brooch of form Collingwood and Richmond 109.[57]

Primrose Hill (SJ 411 634). Sepulchral urns, date uncertain, found 1848.[58]

MARLSTON CUM LACHE. Saltney. (a) SJ 388 649. Pottery including samian, found 1899; inhumation, period unknown.[59] (b) SJ 389 646. Settlement (northern). (c) SJ 387 641. Settlement (southern).[60] (d) *As* of Domitian, 1944; coin of Tragan, 1934; *sestertius* of Hadrian, 1937; *denarius* of Septimius Severus; coin of Constantine I, Lache Lane, 1946.[61] (e) Worn *dupondius* of Vespasian, no. 50 Curzon Street.[62] (f) *Dupondius* of Hadrian; coin of Constans.[63] (g) SJ 387 642. Three coins: Constantine I (2), Constantine II as Caesar, found c. 100 m. from Saltney (S.) site.[64] (h) SJ 387 637. Coin of Valens found c. 400 m. S. of Saltney (S.) site.[65] (j) SJ 387 636. *Sestertius* of Antoninus Pius or M. Aurelius, *follis* of Constantine I.[66] (k) SJ 393 644. Lead weight, VIII *unciae*, found c. 400 m. E. of Saltney (N.) site. Lead die, date uncertain.[67]

Curzon Park. (a) SJ 395 653. *Tetradrachms* of Probus, Diocletian (2), and Maximian I, found 1959.[68] (b) SJ 394 654. Coins of Constantius II and Constantine II, found 1958 and 1963; glass bead, found 1963.[69] (c) c. SJ 397 656. *Sestertius* of Hadrian found on river bank.[70] (d) SJ 399 653. Coin of Vespasian, no. 6 Curzon Park N.[71] (e) c. SJ 396 663. Coin of Trajan, Brewers Hall.[72]

UPTON-BY-CHESTER. Republican *denarius*, found 1901.[73]

CHESTER: ST. OSWALD

HUNTINGTON. (a) SJ 415 633. *Denarius* of Hadrian.[74] (b) SJ 428 615. Hinged lid from a Roman vessel (?).[75]

SAIGHTON. (a) SJ 427 640. Coin of Constantine II, found 1939.[76] (b) SJ 449 610. Lead weight, I *uncia*.[77] (c) SJ 449 609. Bronze figurine.[78] (d) SJ 428 637-457 624. Blakestrete, old road supposed to be Roman.[79]

[42] O.S. Arch. Rec. 88 NE.
[43] *J.C.A.S.* xxxi. 77.
[44] Ibid. xl. 64.
[45] *Ches. Arch. Bull.* vii. 11.
[46] *J.C.A.S.* xlviii. 45.
[47] Noted below: Heronbridge (n).
[48] Noted below: Heronbridge (o).
[49] Noted below: Heronbridge (f) and (l).
[50] *T.H.S.L.C.* xxxix. 55-6; *J.C.A.S.* n.s. i. 91-7; xxiv. 157-61; *Archaeologia*, liv. 493.
[51] *J.R.S.* xxxii. 110; xxxvii. 170; xlv. 147; xlviii. 155, no. 44.
[52] *J.C.A.S.* xxxi. 76-7.
[53] *Ches. Arch. Bull.* i. 20; vi. 75.
[54] Ibid. vii. 63-4.
[55] *J.C.A.S.* xxxix. 3.
[56] *Ches. Arch. Bull.* viii. 76.
[57] Ibid.
[58] *Jnl. Brit. Arch. Assoc.* v. 228; Watkin, *Roman Ches.* 48, 217; O.S. Arch. Rec. 46 SW.
[59] *29th Annual Rep. Chester Natural Science Soc.* 26-9; *J.R.S.* xxiii. 195; *Liverpool Annals*, xxii. 3.

[60] *J.R.S.* xxiii. 195; *Liverpool Annals* xxii. 3-18.
[61] *J.C.A.S.* xxxvi. 148, 150-1.
[62] Ibid. xl. 64.
[63] Ibid. xlv. 74.
[64] *Ches. Arch. Bull.* vii. 62.
[65] Ibid. 63.
[66] Ibid. 62.
[67] Ibid.
[68] *J.C.A.S.* xlvii. 37.
[69] Ibid. xlvi. 80; *Ches. Arch. Bull.* iv. 38; O.S. Arch. Rec. 36 NE.
[70] Grosvenor Mus. rec.
[71] *J.C.A.S.* xlviii. 45.
[72] Ibid. vi. 410.
[73] Ibid. viii. 105.
[74] *Ches. Arch. Bull.* vii. 65.
[75] Ibid.
[76] *J.C.A.S.* xli. 88.
[77] *Ches. Arch. Bull.* vi. 77.
[78] Ibid.
[79] 3 *Sheaf*, liv. pp. 25-6; lv. pp. 90-1; O.S. Arch. Rec. 46 SW.

CHRISTLETON

CHRISTLETON. (a) SJ 444 653. Lead weight, II *unciae*, found 1958.[80] (b) SJ 442 652. Coin of Constantine I, found 1958.[81] (c) SJ 458 672. Section across Watling Street.[82] (d) SJ 451 652. Lead weight, IIII *unciae*.[83]

LITTLETON. (a) SJ 442 666. *Dupondius* of Vespasian.[84] (b) SJ 450 669–491 678. *Agger* of Watling Street.[85] (c) SJ 440 666. Amphora sherd with stamp.[86]

Vicars Cross. Lead weight, VIII *unciae*, found *c.* 1885–6.[87]

ROWTON. *Denarius* of Verus.[88]

CODDINGTON

SJ 453 554. Lead weight, IIII *unciae*.[89]

DAVENHAM

MOULTON (SJ 651 687). Roman objects said to have been found during construction of New Bridge over the Weaver.[90]

DELAMERE

DELAMERE (SJ 568 695). Excavation of Watling Street, 1971.[91]

EDDISBURY. (a) Coins and urns said to have been found.[92] (b) Ramparts of hillfort slighted towards end of 1st cent.[93] (c) SJ 568 695. Line of Watling Street confirmed.[94] (d) Watling Street visible east of B 5152.[95]

OAKMERE. (a) SJ 572 682. Sandstone hypocaust *pilae*, probably derived from Chester.[96] (b) SJ 577 700. Junction of Watling Street and road to Middlewich located.[97]

EASTHAM

EASTHAM. (a) SJ 381 795. Coin hoard, mainly coins of Constantine I, found *c.* 1889. Number unknown; hoard subsequently dispersed.[98] (b) SJ 363 802. Coin of Constantius Gallus, found 1956.[99]

HOOTON (SJ 36 78). *Sestertius*, possibly late Antonine, found 1971.[1]

EASTHAM AND STOKE

WHITBY (SJ 396 758). Coin of Elagabalus.[2]

ECCLESTON

EATON (SJ 416 613). Eaton Hall. Watling Street excavated, 1970–1.[3]

ECCLESTON. (a) Hoard of 43 *denarii*.[4] (b) *c.* SJ 410 620. *Denarius* and *sestertius*, both of Hadrian, found before 1868.[5] (c) SJ 411 631. Watling Street excavated, Chester bypass, 1972 and 1975.[6] (d) SJ 411 633. Building thought to be Roman excavated, 1975.[7] (e) SJ 415 621. *Denarius* of Severan period.[8]

FARNDON

CREWE. (a) Hypocaust found *temp*. Charles I, tiles with stamp of Legio xx.[9] (b) SJ 420 522. Brooch found near river Dee.[10]

FRODSHAM

ALVANLEY. (a) *c.* SJ 483 731. Gold coin of Nero, found 1886, since lost; possible association with a ring.[11] (b) SJ 499 740. Lead weight, IIII *unciae*, found 1955.[12] (c) SJ 502 749. Handle of coarse ware flagon, 1st- or 2nd-cent.[13]

[80] *J.C.A.S.* xlvi. 80.
[81] Ibid.
[82] Ibid. xlviii. 25–6.
[83] *Ches. Arch. Bull.* vii. 63.
[84] Ibid. 65.
[85] O.S. Arch. Rec. 46 NE.
[86] *Ches. Arch. Bull.* i. 5.
[87] *Arch. Jnl.* xliii. 283; *J.C.A.S.* vii. 89 (no. 206); ix. 130; *Arch. Camb.* xv. 423–4.
[88] *J.C.A.S.* xxiv. 151.
[89] *Ches. Arch. Bull.* vi. 77.
[90] *J.C.A.S.* [1st ser.], i. 48.
[91] *Ches. Arch. Bull.* vi. 8–10; *Britannia*, iii. 313.
[92] Watkin, *Roman Ches.* 300–1.
[93] *J.R.S.* xxix. 206.
[94] *Ches. Arch. Bull.* i. 8.
[95] Ibid.
[96] *Britannia*, xii. 333; *Ches. Arch. Bull.* viii. 6–9.
[97] *Britannia*, xiv. 297–9; *Ches. Arch. Bull.* ix. 63–6.
[98] P. Sulley, *Hund. of Wirral*, app. II.
[99] *J.C.A.S.* xliv. 54.
[1] *Ches. Arch. Bull.* i. 5.
[2] Ibid.
[3] *J.C.A.S.* lviii. 1–13.
[4] See Chester: St. Mary on the Hill (Heronbridge).
[5] *Ches. Arch. Bull.* i. 5.
[6] *J.C.A.S.* lviii. 15–39; *Britannia*, vii. 321.
[7] *Britannia*, vii. 321; *Ches. Arch. Bull.* iv. 26–7.
[8] *Ches. Arch. Bull.* vii. 65.
[9] Watkin, *Roman Ches.* 305–6; *T.H.S.L.C.* xxxix. 56.
[10] *Ches. Arch. Bull.* vi. 77.
[11] *T.H.S.L.C.* xxxix. 57; *J.C.A.S.* n.s. iii. 268–9; Watkin, *Roman Ches.* 312.
[12] *J.C.A.S.* xliii. 47.
[13] *Ches. Arch. Bull.* vii. 61.

THE ROMAN PERIOD

FRODSHAM. (a) SJ 535 789. Roman masonry and a pavement said to have been found, 1808.[14] (b) *c.* SJ 51 77. Samian (2 fragments of form Dr. 37) formerly in a collection at Prestatyn.[15] (c) *Denarius* of Antoninus Pius.[16] (d) SJ 521 781. Two coins found.[17]

HELSBY. (a) SJ 493 757. Uninscribed altar, found 1958.[18] (b) *c.* SJ 487 753. Coin said to have been found.[19]

MANLEY. (a) *c.* SJ 527 732. Quern, sherds of 'red ware', and an amphora handle found at Crossley Hosp. *c.* 1906.[20] (b) *c.* SJ 524 734. Crop-mark, possibly Roman, on air photo.[21]

GRAPPENHALL

LATCHFORD. Fragment of quern found, possibly Roman.[22]

HESWALL

c. SJ 264 813. Coin of Antoninus Pius(?).[23]

HILBRE ISLAND

SJ 184 880. 23 sherds of 3rd- and 4th-century pottery.[24]

KIRBY, WEST

(a) Two inscribed fragments identified as Roman, one said to be part of a tombstone; since lost(?). Not Roman.[25] (b) SJ 222 860. Coin of Constantius Chlorus, found in Mount Road, 1937.[26]

KIRBY, WEST, AND THURSTASTON

GREASBY. (a) SJ 256 865. Roman road excavated.[27] (b) SJ 257 862. *As* of Domitian, found 1973.[28]

LYMM

SJ 666 867. Roman road sectioned, 1969.[29]

Statham (*c.* SJ 668 880). Coin hoard, *c.* 1,200 coins, including Valerian, Gallienus, Postumus, Marius, Victorinus, and the Tetrici, found 1778 in 'the Green Hey'. Since lost.[30]

MALPAS

BICKERTON. A number of Roman coins (? a hoard) said to have been found.[31]

BICKLEY (SJ 527 472). Auxiliary *diploma* found 1812 (the 'Malpas Diploma').[32]

CHORLTON (*c.* SJ 461 485). Hoard found in a marl pit, 1818: size unknown. Coins of Valerian and Postumus identified.[33]

MALPAS (*c.* SJ 486 472). Roman objects, coins, and pavements said to have been found *c.* 1730 near the castle.[34]

TUSHINGHAM CUM GRINDLEY (SJ 523 463). Sherds of Roman pottery.[35]

MARBURY-CUM-QUOISLEY

Roman coins said to have been found.[36]

MIDDLEWICH

SPROSTON (SJ 750 652). Samian found.[37]

NESTON

LEDSHAM (SJ 358 746). Roman road cut by service trench.[38]

NESS. (a) SJ 317 757. Trumpet brooch.[39] (b) SJ 317 758. *Sestertius* of M. Aurelius(?).[40]

[14] Watkin, *Roman Ches.* 57.
[15] *Ches. Arch. Bull.* i. 6.   [16] *J.C.A.S.* xxxvi. 149.
[17] *Ches. Arch. Bull.* iii. 60.
[18] *J.C.A.S.* xlvi. 79; *J.R.S.* xlix. 108.
[19] O.S. Arch. Rec. 47 NE.
[20] *T.L.C.A.S.* xxiv. 121–2.
[21] O.S. Arch. Rec. 57 SW.
[22] Watkin, *Roman Ches.* 266.
[23] *Ches. Arch. Bull.* vi. 77.
[24] O.S. Arch. Rec. 18 NE.
[25] *Arch. Jnl.* xlv. 181–2; *T.H.S.L.C.* xxxvii. 40; *The Antiquary*, iv, no. 70, 6–7.
[26] *T.L.C.A.S.* lxi. 193.   [27] *Arch. Newsletter*, v. 7.
[28] Merseyside Arch. Survey.
[29] *Britannia*, iii. 314.

[30] *Jnl. Brit. Arch. Assoc.* vii. 12–14; *T.H.S.L.C.* xxix. 90; Watkin, *Roman Ches.* 308.
[31] Watkin, *Roman Ches.* 310.
[32] Ibid. 287–91; Thompson, *Roman Ches.* 103, 106–8; *C.I.L.* vii. 1193; O.S. Arch. Rec. 54 NW.
[33] Ormerod, *Hist. Ches.* iii. 448; Watkin, *Roman Ches.* 309; *Chester Chron.* 27 Mar. 1818.
[34] Watkin, *Roman Ches.* 286–7; Thompson, *Roman Ches.* 104.
[35] *Ches. Arch. Bull.* ix. 97.
[36] Horsley, *Britannia Romana*, iii. 417; *V.C.H. Salop.* i. 275.
[37] Watkin, *Roman Ches.* 316.
[38] *Britannia*, xii. 333.
[39] *Ches. Arch. Bull.* viii. 77.   [40] Ibid.

NESTON. (a) Hoard of 4th-century coins including Constantine I, found 1866. Size unknown.[41] (b) SJ 300 767. Coin of Diocletian, found *c.* 1930.[42] (c) SJ 302 773. Rim sherds of two grey jars, found *c.* 1971.[43] (d) Parkgate. *Ae* of Claudius I, found 1867.[44]

WILLASTON. (a) SJ 346 768 etc. Fieldwork and excavation on Roman road.[45] (b) SJ 340 780. Roman road cut by pipe-trench, 1971.[46]

OVER

WHITEGATE (*c.* SJ 639 699). Bronze tile or brick stamp, probably an imported antiquity.[47]

WINSFORD (SJ 642 650). Rim of large grey jar thought to be Roman.[48]

PLEMSTALL

HOOLE (SJ 431 692). Coin of Constantine I.[49]

TRAFFORD, BRIDGE (*c.* SJ 445 713). *Sestertius* of Hadrian and two lead weights, both VIII *unciae*.[50]

PRESTBURY

ADLINGTON (SJ 922 787). Hoard of 20 coins, Titus to Antoninus Pius, found 1925.[51]

BOLLINGTON (SJ 933 773). Coin of Augustus, found 1952 or 1953.[52]

HURDSFIELD (SJ 938 747). Coin of Constantine I(?), found 1961.[53]

MACCLESFIELD FOREST (SJ 972 720). Toot Hill rectangular earthwork, probably medieval.[54]

MOTTRAM ST. ANDREW (SJ 875 783). Supposed site of copper mine worked in Roman period.[55]

RAINOW. (a) Lamaload Reservoir (SJ 970 753). Three coins, 2nd- and 3rd-cent., found 1961.[56] (b) Yearnslow (*c.* SJ 965 760). Roman coins, glass beads, and bones said to have been found before 1878.[57]

WINCLE. Roman gold hoard found 1877–9; in private possession.[58]

PULFORD

SJ 388 590. 2 coins, Constantine I and Constantius II.[59]

ROSTHERNE

LEGH, HIGH (SJ 711 832, 702 838, etc.). Fieldwork and excavation of Roman road, to 1968, and 1969–72.[60]

RUNCORN

ASTON BY SUTTON or ASTON GRANGE (findspot unknown). Ten coins ranging in date from Augustus to Constantine II.[61]

DARESBURY. (a) SJ 581 828. Roman concrete or mortar revealed during alteration to the church, 1872.[62] (b) SJ 578 829. *Denarius* of Hadrian.[63]

HALTON. (a) Halton Brow (SJ 534 824). Supposed late Roman military site, found 1936.[64] Further work, 1967, showed that a single ditch enclosed an irregular enclosure *c.* 106 m. by 73 m., perhaps belonging to a farm.[65] (b) Halton Castle thought to occupy one corner of a Roman site of some 40 a.[66]

NORTON. Norton Priory. 2 sherds of samian.[67]

RUNCORN. (a) *c.* SJ 518 834. Twenty lead ingots, some datable to A.D. 76 and others to 84–96, found on the foreshore.[68] (b) SJ 509 835. Coin of Domitian.[69]

SUTTON. (SJ 535 789) Roman masonry and pavement reported.[70]

THELWALL. Four incomplete Roman(?) querns bought by Grosvenor Mus.[71]

[41] *T.H.S.L.C.* vii. 170; Watkin, *Roman Ches.* 312.
[42] O.S. Arch. Rec. 37 NW.
[43] *Ches. Arch. Bull.* ii. 36.
[44] *T.H.S.L.C.* xxi. 199; Watkin, *Roman Ches.* 312.
[45] *J.C.A.S.* xlviii. 1–4; l. 2.
[46] *Britannia*, iii. 314.
[47] *Ches. Arch. Bull.* (forthcoming).
[48] Ibid. viii. 80.
[49] O.S. Arch. Rec. 46 NW.
[50] *Ches. Arch. Bull.* vii. 87.
[51] O.S. Arch. Rec. 97 NW.
[52] Ibid.
[53] Ibid. 97 SW.
[54] *T.H.S.L.C.* xxix. 87–8; J. P. Earwaker, *East Ches.* ii. 437–8; Sainter, *Scientific Rambles*, 17–18; *T.L.C.A.S.* lxx. 84–7.
[55] *T.L.C.A.S.* xix. 83, 87.
[56] O.S. Arch. Rec. 97 NE.
[57] Sainter, *Scientific Rambles*, 16.

[58] *T.H.S.L.C.* xxix. 88–9; Watkin, *Roman Ches.* 303–5; Thompson, *Roman Ches.* 108; *Antiq. Jnl.* lx. 48–58.
[59] Grosvenor Mus. record.
[60] *J.R.S.* lix. 210; *Britannia*, i. 282; iv. 284; *Ches. Arch. Bull.* i. 20; ii. 19–20.
[61] *T.H.S.L.C.* xxxix. 57.
[62] *J.C.A.S.* [1st ser.], iii. 214; Watkin, *Roman Ches.* 307.
[63] *Ches. Arch. Bull.* viii. 77.
[64] *J.R.S.* xxvii. 232; *Liverpool Annals*, xxiv. 165–8.
[65] *J.R.S.* lviii. 183; *J.C.A.S.* lviii. 85–8.
[66] Watkin, *Roman Ches.* 295.
[67] Inf. from Dr. J. P. Greene.
[68] Camden, *Brit.* (1590), 487–8; *Arch. Jnl.* xvi. 28–9; Watkin, *Roman Ches.* 294–6; *J.C.A.S.* iv. 72; *Jnl. Brit. Arch. Assoc.* iv. 274–5.
[69] *T.L.C.A.S.* xxiv. 181.
[70] See Frodsham.
[71] *J.C.A.S.* xvii. 150.

THE ROMAN PERIOD
SANDBACH

Bradwall. See Brereton cum Smethwick.

Bradwall, Elton, and Sandbach. Elworth. (a) SJ 743 611. King Street sectioned.[72] (b) SJ 743 612. *Agger* of King Street revealed.[73]

Hulme, Church. (a) SJ 760 675. Spearhead, found 1930.[74] (b) SJ 763 669. Penannular brooch, possibly Roman.[75]

Sandbach. (a) SJ 749 592. Coin of Otacilia Severa, found 1958.[76] (b) SJ 758 610. Two sherds of late 2nd–early 3rd-century pottery.[77]

STOCKPORT

Bredbury (SJ 928 919). *As* of Trajan, found 1930.[78]

Disley (SJ 980 842). Coin of Valentinian I, found *c.* 1965.[79]

Dukinfield (*c.* SJ 936 983). Coin of Tetricus I, found 1963.[80]

Hyde. Coin of Maximus, found 1905.[81]

Romiley (SJ 944 09). *Dupondius* of Augustus, found 1952.[82]

Stockport. (a) *c.* SJ 896 906. Coin of Honorius recorded by Stukeley, probably from Castle Yard.[83] (b) Roman objects found.[84] (c) *c.* SJ 897 906. Roman(?) tiles reported.[85]

SUTTON, GUILDEN

SJ 449 680. *Ae* coin of Licinius, found 1947.[86]

TARPORLEY

Eaton by Tarporley. (a) Coin of M. Aurelius, with fragments of Roman tile and *opus signinum*, found 1886 during construction of Vyrnwy aqueduct.[87] (b) SJ 572 634. Roman farmhouse, excavated 1980–3.[88]

Rushton. Cotebrook (SJ 575 662). Roman road cut by pipe-line, 1982.[89]

Tarporley (SJ 559 623). Coin commemorating Claudius II.[90]

TARVIN

Ashton. (a) *c.* SJ 500 690. Samian, coarse pottery, glass, and beads found in and near village.[91] (b) Jet ring, not certainly from Ashton.[92]

Burton (*c.* SJ 512 638). Roman coins said to have been found.[93]

Kelsall. (a) SJ 524 683. Mass of pottery and tiles found when foundations of Wesleyan chapel were dug, 1883.[94] (b) *c.* SJ 526 676. A small gold coin found *c.* 1932.[95] (c) Lead weight, VIII *unciae*, found 1950.[96] (d) *c.* SJ 530 700. Field system of prehistoric or Roman date north of Longley Farm.[97] (e) *Denarius* of Titus, found 1965.[98] (f) SJ 526 686. Sherd of colour-coated pottery.[99]

Tarvin (*c.* SJ 488 666). Coin of Constantine I as Caesar, found 1966.[1]

TATTENHALL

(a) SJ 488 587. *Denarius* of Aurelius and/or Verus, and *denarius* of Galba, found 1977.[2] (b) SJ 487 586. Roman pottery, 2nd- to 4th-cent.[3]

THORNTON LE MOORS

Dunham on the Hill. See Frodsham: Alvanley.

[72] *Britannia*, iii. 313–14.
[73] *Arch. Newsletter*, viii. 12; 4 *Sheaf*, ii. 28–9.
[74] O.S. Arch. Rec. 76 NE.   [75] Ibid.
[76] *J.C.A.S.* xlvi. 80.
[77] City Mus., Stoke on Trent.
[78] *J.C.A.S.* xliv. 54.
[79] O.S. Arch. Rec. 98 SE.
[80] Ibid. 99 NW.
[81] *T.L.C.A.S.* l. 190.
[82] *J.C.A.S.* xl. 64.
[83] *T.H.S.L.C.* xxxix. 56; Watkin, *Roman Ches.* 293–4.
[84] Watkin, *Roman Ches.* 293–4.
[85] *Ches. N. & Q.* i. 143.
[86] *J.C.A.S.* xliv. 54.
[87] *T.H.S.L.C.* xxxix. 57; Watkin, *Roman Ches.* 296, 321. Watkin gives the reverse of the coin as PRIMI DECENNALES S C, with a standing figure, a reverse legend used by Antoninus Pius (A.D. 147–8) and M. Aurelius (A.D. 170–1)

but without a standing figure.
[88] *Britannia*, xii. 333; xiii. 353.
[89] Ibid. xiv. 299.
[90] *Ches. Arch. Bull.* iv. 38.
[91] *J.C.A.S.* xxxv. 53–9; xxxvi. 152–3.
[92] Ibid. lxiv. 45.
[93] Watkin, *Roman Ches.* 59–60, 300; Horsley, *Britannia Romana*, iii. 417.
[94] Watkin, *Roman Ches.* 32.
[95] O.S. Arch. Rec. 56 NW.
[96] *J.R.S.* xli. 143; *J.C.A.S.* xxxviii. 176–7; *Ches. Historian*, i. 45.
[97] *T.L.C.A.S.* lxiv. 24–6; O.S. Arch. Rec. 57 SW.
[98] O.S. Arch. Rec. 56 NW.
[99] *Ches. Arch. Bull.* v. 51.
[1] O.S. Arch. Rec. 46 NE.
[2] *Ches. Arch. Bull.* viii. 60.
[3] Ibid. 58.

THURSTASTON

SJ 252 841. Enamelled head-stud brooch, found 1981.[4]

TILSTON

CARDEN. Roman (?prehistoric) urns said to have been found in a barrow.[5]
GRAFTON (SJ 452 519). Roman pottery found in vicinity of earthworks seen from the air.[6]
STRETTON. (a) Roman coins found.[7] (b) c. SJ 430 520. North-south road seen from the air, possibly Watling Street.[8]
TILSTON. (a) SJ 436 547. Fieldwork and excavation, Watling Street.[9] (b) SJ 453 517. Building located and excavated, 1981.[10]

WALLASEY

(a) Alexandrian *tetradrachm*, found 1958.[11] (b) SJ 269 922. *Denarius* of Trajan, found 1979.[12] (c) SJ 267 922. Brooch of Aucissa type, found 1981(?).[13] (d) SJ 314 914. *Antoninianus* of Gordian III.[14]

WARMINGHAM

(a) c. SJ 714 632. Brine kiln and briquetage, found at Tetton Hall Farm, 1841.[15] (b) SJ 705 624. Roman urn said to have been found in levelling a mound.[16]

WAVERTON

HUXLEY (c. SJ 521 612). Gold coin of Galba, found at Huxley Gorse, 1870.[17]
WAVERTON. (a) SJ 459 632. Fragment of a trumpet brooch.[18] (b) SJ 466 631. Lead weight, VIII *unciae*.[19]

WILMSLOW

Lindow Moss (c. SJ 820 805). Human head, found 1983 in a peat bog. Radiocarbon date 1740±80 B.P., i.e. A.D. 210±80. Iron pin or awl possibly associated. Late Iron Age?[20]

WISTASTON

c. SJ 674 550. 3rd-cent. coin, found c. 1951.[21]

WOODCHURCH

OXTON. Arno Hill (SJ 304 872). Hoard of (?3rd-cent.) coins.[22]
THINGWALL (SJ 281 844). *Sestertius* of Antoninus Pius.[23]
WOODCHURCH. Spearhead 'thought to be Roman' and a miniature bronze cauldron 3.8 cm. in diameter, found 1923.[24]

WRENBURY

SJ 596 488. Roman road sectioned, 1963.[25]

WYBUNBURY

WESTON (c. SJ 728 524). Hoard of 12 *denarii* from Domitian to Hadrian (latest of A.D. 134-8), and two brooches, one Collingwood Type H, found 1982.[26]
WYBUNBURY. (a) SJ 704 499. *Denarius* of Faustina II, with unidentifiable coins and a dolphin brooch.[27] (b) SJ 698 493. *Denarius* of Julia Domna.[28]

[4] Merseyside Arch. Survey.
[5] Ormerod, *Hist. Ches.* ii. 320; Watkin, *Roman Ches.* 316.
[6] Inf. from Prof. G. D. B. Jones.
[7] Stukeley, *It. Cur.* 56.
[8] *Ches. Arch. Bull.* vi. 9.
[9] *Britannia*, xi. 365.
[10] Ibid. xii. 333; xiv. 299.
[11] *J.C.A.S.* xlviii. 45.
[12] Merseyside Arch. Survey.
[13] Ibid.
[14] *Ches. Arch. Bull.* vii. 66.
[15] *T.H.S.L.C.* i. 41.
[16] *J.C.A.S.* [1st ser.], i. 48; Watkin, *Roman Ches.* 71.
[17] Watkin, *Roman Ches.* 296.
[18] Grosvenor Mus. record.
[19] *Ches. Arch. Bull.* vii. 66.
[20] Inf. from Dr. J. A. J. Gowlett, Research Lab. for Arch. and Hist. of Art, Oxford. The head may, however, be more recent than suggested by the radiocarbon date: inf. from Mr. R. C. Connolly, Liverpool Univ. Dept. of Anatomy. See also *Antiquity*, lix. 25-9, and above, Prehistory, for another bog burial found in Lindow Moss in 1984.
[21] *Ches. Arch. Bull.* vi. 80; inf. from Miss D. Sylvester.
[22] Watkin, *Roman Ches.* 309-10; Thompson, *Roman Ches.* 105.
[23] Merseyside Arch. Survey.
[24] *J.R.S.* xii. 249.
[25] Ibid. lv. 205; *T.L.C.A.S.* lxxvii. 25-6.
[26] *Ches. Arch. Bull.* viii. 79.
[27] Ibid. vii. 66.
[28] Ibid. viii. 80.

ANGLO-SAXON CHESHIRE

CHESHIRE,[1] the district dependent on Chester, is first recorded as *Legeceaster scir* in the *Anglo-Saxon Chronicle* ('C') under the year 980.[2] In 1086 it was referred to as *Cestrescir*.[3] The extent of the area so designated seems to have fluctuated considerably, and its origins are difficult to determine, though it almost certainly goes back at least to the reign of Edward the Elder (899–924). In the 10th and 11th centuries Chester was the centre of an administrative unit considerably larger than modern Cheshire with territories in north-east Wales and, perhaps, beyond the Mersey; certainly the north-west Mercian diocese extended north to the river Ribble in the 10th century.[4] Before that, however, its extent is much more problematic. The northern and eastern boundaries of the pre-1974 shire are certainly very old: the name Mersey itself implies a boundary, and indeed the river marks a zone of linguistic overlap, where Mercian and Anglian dialects mingled.[5] Moreover, until 919 Manchester lay in Northumbria, so any northern expansion of shire and diocese occurred after that, presumably with Edward the Elder's conquest of south Lancashire.[6] The eastern boundary again seems ancient, formed from the physical limits imposed by the Lyme or the Pennine scarp, but neither the southern nor the western boundary is so well defined. In the west it is clear that the boundary fluctuated, reaching Wat's Dyke and beyond, while in the south the shire boundary, after following the Dee and the Wych brook, cuts through the parish and estate of Whitchurch (Salop.), an indication that there in 1086 it was relatively recent.[7]

The evidence for the history of the region throughout the period is scanty. Even the Domesday record has its limitations,[8] and earlier sources are still more difficult to interpret. There were no great churches and so no early collections of material; only two charters are known.[9] Otherwise there are only incidental references in Welsh and Irish annals and Bede's *Ecclesiastical History*. The archaeological evidence is slight and there are no early church buildings, the only significant surviving physical remains being some early circular or oval churchyards and a considerable number of stone crosses. To the west Wat's Dyke is an important

[1] Thanks are offered to Mr. P. H. Sawyer, who was originally to have written this chapter, for much information and advice, and Dr. P. Carrington, Dr. W. Davies, Mr. J. McN. Dodgson, Dr. N. J. Higham, Dr. D. Kenyon, Dr. L. Laing, and Dr. D. J. P. Mason for helpful comments on earlier drafts and in many instances for generously making available work in advance of publication. Thanks are also due to Prof. R. Cramp for making available an unpublished research index of Cheshire sculpture, to Mrs. J. A. Rutter for much help with the pottery, and to Dr. G. Lloyd-Morgan, Mr. R. Philpott, Mr. R. C. Turner, and Mr. S. Ward for help with the gazetteer.

[2] *Two Saxon Chrons.* ed. C. Plummer and J. Earle, i. 124.

[3] Unless obscure, references to the Domesday translation have been omitted.

[4] Below, 'Impact of Scandinavians'.

[5] J. McN. Dodgson, 'Eng. Arrival in Ches.' *T.H.S.L.C.* cxix, 13–14; *P.N. Ches.* i. 31–2. Interestingly, the Mersey is one of the few major rivers in Cheshire to bear an English name.

[6] *Two Saxon Chrons.* i. 104; *V.C.H. Lancs.* i. 270.

[7] *P.N. Ches.* i. 2–3, 21–2, 39; iii. 105, 112; inf. from Dr. Kenyon.

[8] e.g. the occasional omission of the hundredal rubrics. For a discussion of the limitations of the Domesday evidence in general see P. H. Sawyer, 'A.-S. Settlement: Doc. Evidence', *A.-S. Settlement and Landscape* (Brit. Arch. Rep., Brit. ser. vi), 108–19.

[9] *A.-S. Charts.* ed. P. H. Sawyer, nos. 667, 1536; C. Hart, *Early Charts. of Northern Eng. and N. Midlands*, 119; *A.-S. Charts. II: Burton Abbey*, pp. xv–xliii, 53–6; *Chartulary of St. Werburgh's Abbey, Chester*, i (Chetham Soc. [2nd ser.] lxxix), pp. xvii–xviii, 8–13.

early feature, but its date remains the subject of debate. Much weight has therefore to be placed on the place-name evidence, despite the many problems which it poses.[10]

SUB-ROMAN CHESHIRE

The effect of the breaking of formal ties with Rome in the early 5th century was probably felt only gradually in Cheshire. How the area was then governed is unknown, but it seems likely that the late Roman administration survived in some form, since the region remained undisturbed under British control until the 7th century. Chester itself was probably the administrative centre, a function which it seems already to have been fulfilling in late Roman times. Certainly the fortress had undergone changes in the 4th century, a reduction of the garrison altering the balance between the soldiery and the civilian settlements which had grown up to the west and south, and it has recently been suggested that it became the capital of the *civitas* of the Deceangli.[11] That Chester was recognized as a significant place in early Anglo-Saxon times is indicated by the fact that it was termed a *civitas* by Bede,[12] and it has even been argued that the 6th-century British historian Gildas may have lived in the neighbourhood of the city.[13] It is also clear that the major public buildings long survived, some of them indeed at least until the 10th century.[14] Nevertheless, there remains the problem of the scarcity of the archaeological evidence, which up to 1985 had yielded no certain indication of sub-Roman habitation. The only site to suggest such a possibility is Abbey Green, inside the north wall of the legionary fortress, where a large timber-framed building on stone foundations was altered in the late Roman period and remained in use for some time thereafter.[15] The site also yielded sherds of 'B' ware amphorae, a type of imported pottery produced in the eastern Mediterranean which has been found elsewhere inside and outside the fortress. Though that pottery has a wide date range, from the 2nd to the 6th century, it is possible that at Chester it may reflect sub-Roman rather than earlier activity.[16]

In Cheshire as a whole increasing evidence of rural activity in Roman times raises the possibility of continuity of habitation thereafter. Many settlements in west Cheshire have yielded Roman finds,[17] and the villa at Eaton-by-Tarporley, which was occupied until well after 350, points to the presence of prosperous rural proprietors.[18] There is some evidence of late or post-Roman agricultural activity at Middlewich, where slots cut by a mattock and a mattock blade have been excavated, and similar work was probably going on elsewhere. In the north-east of the county, for example, pollen diagrams from Lindow Moss indicate that

---

[10] For general surveys see M. Gelling, *Signposts to the Past*, esp. 11–17; 'Chronology of Eng. Place Names', *A.-S. Settlement and Landscape* (Brit. Arch. Rep., Brit. ser. vi), 93–101; Sawyer, in *A.-S. Settlement and Landscape*, 113–16; C. Taylor, *Village and Farmstead: Hist. of Rural Settlement in Eng.* esp. 109–10; *Jnl. Eng. P.N. Soc.* xi. 54–74.

[11] *Britannia*, xiii. 253–60. Against such a suggestion, however, must be set the failure of the coin series *c.* 370, an odd circumstance if the city still contained a salaried official class: T. J. Strickland, *Roman Chester*, 34–5; J. C. McPeake, 'The End of the Affair', *New Evidence for Roman Chester*, ed. T. J. Strickland and P. J. Davey, 43.

[12] Bede, *Hist. Eccl.* ed. R. A. B. Mynors and B. Colgrave, ii. 2 (p. 140); J. Campbell, 'Bede's Names for Places', *Names,*

Words, and Graves: Early Medieval Settlement, ed. P. H. Sawyer, 34–42.

[13] *Britannia*, x. 225; but cf. *Cambridge Medieval Studies*, vi. 1–30.

[14] *Medieval Arch.* xxvii. 170; T. J. Strickland, 'Roman Heritage of Chester', *J.C.A.S.* lxvii. 17–34; *Roman Chester*, 38–42; *New Evidence for Roman Chester*, 41–4.

[15] J. C. McPeake, M. Bulmer, and J. A. Rutter, 'Excavations in the Garden of No. 1 Abbey Green, Chester, 1975–7: Interim Rep.' *J.C.A.S.* lxiii. 15–17; inf. from Mr. Ward.

[16] *J.C.A.S.* lxiii. 29–30; inf. from Dr. Carrington.

[17] For lists of stray finds in the area see *Ches. Arch. Bull.* i–ix; L. and J. Laing, *Dark Ages of W. Ches.* 33–9.

[18] *Ches. Arch. Bull.* viii. 51–2; ix. 67–73.

woodland areas had been cleared by late Roman times and that by then the region was mixed arable and pasture.[19]

By the 7th century the Chester area seems to have been linked with the Welsh kingdom of Powys. About 616 was fought the battle of Chester in which the Northumbrian king Aethelfrith (c. 592–616), raiding south of his own territory, defeated British forces which according to Bede included the monks of the great monastery of Bangor-is-y-coed (Flints.) and their *defensor* Brocmail.[20] Brocmail, who may be identified with Brochfael, a member of the royal dynasty of Powys, was said in other sources to have been accompanied by another member of the family, Selyf, son of Cynan, perhaps his grandson. It seems likely that they belonged to the Cadelling, a dynasty which almost certainly was still ruling Powys in the 9th century, and that they ruled over territories around Chester and north-east Wales. Another royal dynasty of Powys, the family of Cynddylan, was active in Shropshire in the 7th century and fought with the Mercian king Penda against the Northumbrians at Maserfelth (642), but seems to have been overthrown by the Mercian-ruled *Magonsaetan* before the century ended. The family active at Chester in the early 7th century must therefore have been restricted to north-eastern Powys and the Chester area, and perhaps ruled from Chester itself. With the extinction of the family of Cynddylan they probably expanded into the western, Welsh, territories of south Powys; by then, however, it is likely that Mercian influence was growing in Cheshire as well as Shropshire and that British rule in Chester had ended or was nearing its end.[21]

Ecclesiastically too the Chester area was significant in the 6th and 7th century. It contained the important monastery of Bangor-is-y-coed, a training ground for leaders of the British church, and probably it was the scene of a synod shortly after 600, perhaps the well known conference of c. 603 attended by seven British bishops and learned men from Bangor.[22] There are, too, considerable indications of British Christianity in the area. In particular, it seems increasingly likely that British churches preceded Anglo-Saxon ones on many west Cheshire sites, that there was continuity in ecclesiastical arrangements as in settlement patterns. Thus Eccleston, which stood on the Roman road south from Chester and clearly had some importance in Roman times, has a significant Romano-British place name, a combination of the British *egles* (from the Latin *ecclesia*—'church' or 'Christian community') and the Anglo-Saxon *tun* ('village' or 'estate'). It probably indicates a sub-Roman community with an important church surviving into the period when Anglo-Saxon replaced British as the dominant language in Cheshire. Though later a small ancient parish of only two townships, by the 6th century it may have been the *matrix ecclesia* for the fortress and its environs.[23] It is significant that the medieval church stood within an oval enclosure. Though such a feature is not identified exclusively with British sites, it is often ancient; in the north-west, for example, the curvilinear churchyard at Dacre (Cumb.) marks a monastic site in being by the early 8th century.[24]

[19] D. Kenyon, 'Arch., Place Names, and Settlement in Lancs. and Ches.' (Manchester Univ. Ph.D. thesis, 1984), chap. vi; *Britannia*, vii. 321.

[20] Bede, *Hist. Eccl.* ii. 2 (p. 140).

[21] W. Davies, *Wales in the Early Middle Ages*, 94; D. Kirby, 'Welsh Bards and the Border', in *Mercian Studies*, ed. A. Dornier, 35–8.

[22] Bede, *Hist. Eccl.* ii. 2 (pp. 136–40); E. Phillimore, *Annales Cambriae*, Y Cymmrodor, ix. 156; A. T. Thacker, 'Chester and Gloucester: Early Ecclesiastical Organization in Two Mercian Burhs', *Northern Hist.* xviii. 200; J. D.

Bu'Lock, *Pre-Conquest Ches.* 21.

[23] *Northern Hist.* xviii. 199–200; Bu'Lock, *Pre-Conquest Ches.* 5–8; A. C. Thomas, *Christianity in Roman Britain*, 262–5.

[24] The early church seems to have been on the medieval site, not at Heronbridge, where the earthworks and burials are probably 17th-cent.: *Ches. Arch. Bull.* ix. 62; Laing and Laing, *Dark Ages of W. Ches.* 4–5, 8–19. On Dacre see Bede, *Hist. Eccl.* iv. 32 (pp. 446–8); *Bull. C.B.A. Churches Arch. Cttee.* xiii. 3–5.

Other sites which suggest the presence of British Christianity in the area include Christleton, which has a curvilinear churchyard and a place name meaning 'Christians' enclosure or village'.[25] There too there are strong indications of Roman occupation.[26] Nearby at Great Barrow, where there have also been Roman finds, the church again stands in a curvilinear enclosure.[27] Further south at Farndon and Dodleston there are traces of other such churchyards, that at Farndon being especially significant because it occurs in a place which was the centre of an important estate in Anglo-Saxon times and near the major Roman site of Holt.[28] Other places where there were Roman finds and possibly early churches include Tarvin, which had a British place name and was the centre of an ancient episcopal estate, and Tattenhall with its dedication to St. Alban.[29] At Tarporley, near the Roman villa, the church was dedicated to St. Helen.[30]

There is also important evidence for sub-Roman activity in Wirral. Landican was probably the ecclesiastical centre for the area which became the large parish of Woodchurch.[31] It had a church in 1086, and its name derives from a combination of the Old Welsh *lann*, 'enclosure' or 'churchyard', and the Old Welsh personal name Tegan. The form *Llantegan* may indicate that Tegan was revered there, or, since there is no known Welsh saint of that name, that he was the original benefactor of the church. Significantly, the church stood in a curvilinear churchyard, presumably the sacred enclosure which gave the place its name.[32] Another indication of British presence in the parish is the hybrid place name of the township Pensby, whose first element is formed from the Old Welsh *penn*, 'hill'.[33]

Wallasey, whose place name is formed from the Old English *walh* and *eg*, meaning 'Welshman's' or 'Britons' island', presumably remained a British centre long after the arrival of the Anglo-Saxons, a view supported by the fact that it contains a township with the old Welsh place name of Liscard ('hall at the rock').[34] Despite its small parish containing only three townships, the church, which stood within a circular enclosure or green, may well have been ancient. Indeed, it has been suggested that the unusual dedication to St. Hilary of Poitiers could be of Romano-British origin.[35] Other curvilinear enclosures in Wirral include Overchurch and West Kirby, both at church sites which have produced fragments of pre-Norman sculpture. At Bromborough, too, the churchyard has been regarded as curvilinear and a considerable number of pre-Norman sculptural fragments has been identified;[36] clearly a mother church of some importance, by the 12th century it had a chapelry at Eastham where there is another curvilinear enclosure.[37]

Meols on the north shore of Wirral has yielded evidence of trading activity over a long period, including sub-Roman times, when it was perhaps connected with the lead and silver mines in north Wales.[38] Among finds indicating continuity from the Roman into the sub-Roman period were several penannular brooches, probably dating from before the 7th century, and two buckle plates with decoration based on late Roman types.[39] There are also a number of zoomorphic buckles, perhaps

[25] *P.N. Ches.* iv. 107–8; Kenyon, 'Arch., P.N., and Settlement', chap. i, table 4. For the cross there see below.

[26] *Ches. Arch. Bull.* vii. 61.

[27] Inf. from Dr. Laing; above, Roman Ches. gazetteer.

[28] Inf. from Dr. Laing; Kenyon, 'Arch., P.N., and Settlement', chap. i, table 4; below, 'Early Estate Organization'.

[29] *P.N. Ches.* iii. 281; above, Roman Ches. gazetteer.

[30] *Ches. Arch. Bull.* viii. 56–63.

[31] Woodchurch, where the church was located, seems originally to have been included within Landican: *P.N. Ches.* iv. 267.

[32] W. Davies, *An Early Welsh Microcosm*, 140–3; *P.N.*

Ches. iv. 266–7; G. Chitty, *Wirral Rural Fringes Survey Rep.* 8, 11.

[33] *P.N. Ches.* iv. 271.   [34] Ibid. 325, 332.

[35] Bu'Lock, *Pre-Conquest Ches.* 8, 80; Chitty, *Wirral Rural Fringes*, 8–9.

[36] Chitty, *Wirral Rural Fringes*, 6–9, 11; below, 'Early Estate Organization'; gazetteer.

[37] Kenyon, 'Arch., P.N., and Settlement', chap. i, table 4; *Chart. Chester Abbey*. i. 114, 129–30.

[38] J. D. Bu'Lock, 'Celtic, Saxon, and Scandinavian Settlement at Meols in Wirral', *T.H.S.L.C.* cxii. 1–2.

[39] Ibid. 3–5; *Medieval Arch.* xxvi. 41–68.

of similar date though probably later, and some lost bowls recalling those found in a late Roman or sub-Roman hoard at Halkyn (Flints.).[40] One possible indication of the cosmopolitan nature of the site at that time is a pottery flask of Mediterranean origin, from the shrine of St. Menas near Alexandria, destroyed in the 7th century.[41]

Other sites where there may have been continuous activity from Roman into Anglo-Saxon times are the brine springs or wiches, in particular Middlewich (Roman *Salinae*) and Northwich (*Condate*), both of which produced salt under the Romans and later.[42] At Droitwich (Worcs.) the salt trade can be traced back at least to the 9th century, and it has been suggested that the Mercian king inherited there rights which may well have gone back to Roman imperial tolls. A similar development perhaps occurred in Cheshire: the use of the term 'wich' (Old English *wic*—'trading settlement', from the Latin *vicus*) points in that direction.[43] Certainly there are indications of long-standing royal involvement in Cheshire salt production. The salt-wiches were the subject of a separate account in 1086, and the Survey's elaborate description of the customs by which they were regulated and of the tolls due to king and earl suggests that they were of great antiquity, perhaps the focus of an ancient network of saltways for the distribution of their product. Royal and comital officials were based there, and in two instances, at Middlewich and Nantwich, the renders also included the royal pleas for the appropriate hundred. Nantwich, which was originally a dependency of the great manor of Acton, probably attained importance only late in Anglo-Saxon times, but Middlewich had long been a significant place. A Roman settlement of some size, it was later a major parochial and hundredal centre. Such administrative functions in all three wiches were carried out in an adjacent 'wich-tun', and it is significant that at Middlewich in the late 10th century that tun, 'Newton by the wich', was an estate of the rich and royally descended thegn Wulfric Spot.[44] Probably the Weaver valley as a whole was an economically important area throughout the period. Certainly it was the scene of a good deal of Roman activity, and the concentration there of place names in *-ham* and *-tun* suggests that it remained significant under the Anglo-Saxons.[45] Curvilinear churchyards at Over, Warmingham, and Holmes Chapel are perhaps evidence of early churches in the area; significantly, Warmingham represents an early stratum in Anglo-Saxon place names in Cheshire, and Over, which is dedicated to St. Chad and has produced a fragment of sculpture, may be an early Mercian foundation, like Farndon.[46]

Elsewhere in Cheshire the only indications of sub-Roman activity are very slight, though there are curvilinear churchyards in the north-east of the county, at Bowdon, Lymm, Warburton, and Wilmslow.[47] The only other evidence is provided by place names.[48] As always the names of rivers and natural features are especially stable and many bear British names, including the rivers Dee, Dane, Wheelock, and Peover.[49] Predictably, the Celtic element increases westwards: it has been

[40] Bu'Lock, *Pre-Conquest Ches.* 21-6; A. Hume, *Ancient Meols*, 357; *Antiq. Jnl.* xxxvi. 181-99, esp. 194-5, 197.

[41] F. H. Thompson, 'Pilgrim Flask from Meols', *J.C.A.S.* xliii. 48-9; *T.H.S.L.C.* cxii. 6. Another flask has been found near Norton Priory: inf. from Mrs. B. Noake.

[42] J. B. Curzon, 'Condate, Roman Northwich', *Ches. Hist. News Letter*, xi. 10-11; J. D. Bestwick, 'Excavations at the Roman Settlement of Middlewich', ibid. viii. 8-9; *Britannia*, iv. 284; v. 419; vi. 242; Thompson, *Roman Ches.* 95-6.

[43] P. H. Sawyer, 'Kings and Merchants', *Early Medieval Kingship*, ed. P. H. Sawyer, 147-8; P. H. Sawyer, *From Roman Britain to Norman Eng.* 87, 225; Gelling, *Signposts*, 67-74.

[44] Bu'Lock, *Pre-Conquest Ches.* 66-7; J. Oxley, 'Nantwich: An 11th-Cent. Salt Town and Its Origins', *T.H.S.L.C.* cxxxi. 9-16; Hart, *Early Charts. of N. Eng.* 373-4; Sawyer, *Burton Abbey Charts.* pp. xix, xxix.

[45] Kenyon, 'Arch., P.N., and Settlement', chap. vi, viii.

[46] Ibid. chap. i, table 4; Ormerod, *Hist. Ches.* ii. 185.

[47] Kenyon, 'Arch., P.N., and Settlement', chap. i, table 4.

[48] For summaries see S. Potter, 'Ches. Place Names', *T.H.S.L.C.* cvi. 1-7; cxix. 23-32.

[49] *P.N. Ches.* i. 13-39.

shown that the extreme west of the county, including the Dee valley, has a particularly high proportion of British river names, while the rest has rather fewer.[50] Even so the smaller streams have not as a whole preserved their British names, and generally there are fewer settlement names than might be expected, fewer for example than in Herefordshire, Shropshire, and Lancashire. South of the Mersey, on the borders of Wirral, is Ince, from Old Welsh *inis*, 'the island', and a few miles to the east in Weaverham parish, there occur Brynn, from Old Welsh *brinn*, 'a hill', and Crewood, a hybrid name which includes the Old Welsh element *cryw*, 'a wickerwork fishweir'.[51] Further south is the ancient parish and township name Tarvin, meaning 'at the boundary river', and derived from the river on which the settlement stands (the Gowy, anciently the Terfyn). It has been connected with the township name Macefen, which derives from the later Welsh *maes y ffin*, 'boundary field', and is located in the ancient parish of Malpas in the south-west of the county. The line connecting Tarvin and Macefen along the river Gowy and the Broxton Hills has been viewed as the dividing line between the British or Welsh and their English neighbours in the 6th or 7th century,[52] but the two names need not refer to the same boundary, and even if they do it is possible that it was a purely internal one, alluded to in the local (Welsh) language.

British place names are most numerous along the south-western border of Cheshire, both west and east of Macefen, and include names such as Crewe, in Farndon, from *cryw*, and Welsh-English hybrids such as Barhill, in Tushingham (Malpas), and Chathull, a lost place name in Malpas.[53] An especially interesting group occurs round Combermere in Dodcott cum Wilkesley, including Combermere itself (from *Cumbre*, the Old English version of the Welsh *Cymry*), the lost name Dintesmere (probably from the Old Welsh personal name *Dunod*), and Brankelow, which seems to include the Old Welsh element *bron-coed*, 'hill-wood'.[54] In the east place names indicative of British occupation occur less often. Except for Werneth, 'a place growing with alders', in Stockport parish, no townships bear purely British names, and the few other names which do occur are of natural features, such as the rivers Wheelock and Peover, and of districts, such as the Lyme, an upland area on the east and south-east borders of Cheshire and the north borders of Staffordshire, which gave its name to Lyme Handley and Audlem.[55] It seems likely therefore that as in later periods British settlement was concentrated more in the western lowlands and the Dee and Weaver valleys than in the woods and uplands of the north and east.[56] The British elements in Cheshire place names were adopted into English speech in forms which suggest that they had been subject to Welsh language changes until, but not generally after, the 7th century. A few indeed may have been adopted as early as the late 6th century. It has proved possible to detect a 'progressive borrowing of Welsh place names' by English speakers from the late 6th to the late 7th century, and that, together with the high proportion of hybrid names, has led to the conclusion that there was a considerable period of co-existence, with a mixed population, during which there survived 'a living and active Welsh vernacular'. Gradually, however, areas in which British speech was dominant seem to have become more and more restricted. In some, such as that already noticed around Combermere, the relatively polite term *Cumbre* was used to designate the enclave. Elsewhere, the use of derogatory terms such as

[50] K. Jackson, *Language and Hist. in Early Britain*, 220-3; D. Sylvester, 'Ches. in the Dark Ages: A Map Study of Celtic and Anglian Settlement', *T.H.S.L.C.* cxiv. 8-9.

[51] *P.N. Ches.* iii. 195-6, 198, 251.

[52] *T.H.S.L.C.* cxix. 32.

[53] Ibid. 24-6; *P.N. Ches.* iv. 48, 53, 73.

[54] *T.H.S.L.C.* cxix. 26-7, 30-1; *P.N. Ches.* iii. 93-5.

[55] *P.N. Ches.* i. 2-6.

[56] *T.H.S.L.C.* cxiv. 8-9.

Walas, 'foreigners or inferiors', in place names such as Walton and Wallasey, has been adduced as evidence that Welsh speakers increasingly lost status. The process has been seen as a 'progressive infiltration' by the English from the late 6th century until a 'takeover' some time in the 7th.[57] Such views have much to commend them: they present a coherent picture of a period which is otherwise singularly obscure. Nevertheless, some doubts remain, not least because of the limitations of the place-name evidence. Place names, after all, provide evidence primarily of linguistic change, and the rise to dominance of a dialect of Old English in the late 6th and early 7th century is not necessarily evidence of an English conquest, though it does suggest increasing English influence over the political élite. There are, too, difficulties over the precise nature of the communities designated by early place names, many of which refer to a district embracing a large number of settlements rather than a single place.[58] It is likely that in the Roman period Cheshire was more densely populated than once was thought, and that its habitation sites then and under the Anglo-Saxons were often fluid, even where territorial boundaries were ancient and stable.[59] In such circumstances place names need not be an accurate guide to patterns or density of settlement, or even to ethnic distribution. They could well hide a large element of continuity. It seems, in fact, that the rise of the English to cultural dominance in Cheshire was gradual and relatively undramatic, involving no cataclysm, and causing little disturbance to settlement patterns and religious sites.

EARLY ANGLO-SAXON CHESHIRE

Though the battle of Chester probably represents nothing more than a successful raid in an era of highly mobile conflicts, it may have inaugurated a brief period of Northumbrian dominance in the area. King Cadfan of Gwynedd's protection of Aethelfrith's rival and eventual successor, Edwin of Deira (616–32), is perhaps to be viewed as a response to alarm at Northumbrian expansion. Such fears appear to have been justified, for later when he was established in Northumbria Edwin himself attacked Anglesey and Man, driving Cadfan's son and successor, his own foster-brother Cadwallon, into temporary exile. It has been suggested that Chester formed the naval base for that raid, and at the very least the episode indicates that British princes in the area were losing their independence.[60]

The era of Northumbrian dominance, if such there was, seems to have been very brief, and perhaps ended with Edwin's destruction at Hatfield (Yorks. W.R. or Notts.) in 633 by the forces of Cadwallon of Gwynedd and Penda of Mercia.[61] Though a later Northumbrian ruler, Oswald, died while raiding as far south, it seems, as Oswestry (Salop.) in 642, and though in 655 the whole of Mercia passed temporarily under Northumbrian control, there is no indication that those events left any mark upon Cheshire.[62] By the late 7th century the area was probably, like Shropshire, firmly within the Mercian sphere of influence. Certainly by then a

[57] *T.H.S.L.C.* cxix. 25–37.

[58] e.g. names in *-ham*: *P.N. Ches.* v (1: ii), 213–14; below, 'Early A.-S. Ches.' Cf. Taylor, *Village and Farmstead*, 121–2; Sawyer, in *A.-S. Settlement and Landscape* (Brit. Arch. Rep., Brit. ser. vi), 115.

[59] Taylor, *Village and Farmstead*, 63–106, 109–24. One possible Ches. example of such fluidity is Eccleston parish, which contains several early settlement sites, especially in

Eaton township: inf. from Dr. Laing.

[60] *Mercian Studies*, 33; J. E. Lloyd, *Hist. Wales*, i. 183–5; N. K. Chadwick, 'The Conversion of Northumbria', *Celt and Saxon*, ed. N. K. Chadwick, 147–56; Bede, *Hist. Eccl.* ii. 5, 9 (pp. 148, 162).

[61] Bede, *Hist. Eccl.* ii. 20 (p. 202); *Trans. Thoroton Soc. of Notts.* lxxix. 40–9.

[62] Bede, *Hist. Eccl.* iii. 9, 24 (pp. 240–2, 288–94).

Mercian dialect of Old English was becoming dominant in Cheshire, and indeed probably extending northwards beyond the Mersey.[63]

Archaeological evidence of an early Anglo-Saxon presence in Cheshire is minimal.[64] A bead of a type found in 7th-century Anglo-Saxon cemeteries has been discovered at Hilbre Island, and an early quoit brooch is recorded at Meols.[65] A small trefoil-headed cruciform brooch of an early Anglian, Trent valley, type, said to have been found with three beads 'in Deeside', has been held to represent a 6th-century Anglian burial; the find, however, is unprovenanced, and the absence of any comparable material suggests that it may indicate no more than casual contact with the Mercians. Otherwise there is only a rim sherd of an urn, possibly Anglo-Saxon, from Heronbridge near Chester.[66] From a somewhat later period come a number of small coins, 'sceattas' and 'stycas', from Meols, to indicate that trading continued there from sub-Roman into Anglo-Saxon times.[67] Though there have probably been some losses, such as the weapons found at Saxfield in the north-east of the county,[68] generally the sparseness of early Anglo-Saxon material is suggestive. It looks as if the newcomers were few and entered Cheshire comparatively late.

The lack of other substantial evidence makes place names particularly important for reconstructing the early Anglian period in Cheshire, and despite the reservations already voiced they offer the basis for some important generalizations.[69] One name-type which it has been suggested 'belongs to the earliest stratum of English place names in Cheshire' is that in -*ham* ('village or estate'), often found in simple constructions consisting of the element combined with a personal or river name.[70] Significantly, *ham* names occur in a number of important settlements which were later the centres of comital estates and large ancient parishes, such as Frodsham ('Frod's village or estate'), Weaverham ('village or estate by the Weaver'), and Eastham ('east [of Wirral] village or estate'). Moreover, in Cheshire names in -*ham* occur in geographically favoured locations, often at or near Roman roads, suggesting that they were the product of a phase of settlement which took place while the Roman infrastructure still survived.[71] It is clear then that such names are early, but even so there are problems which suggest the need for caution. It is difficult to distinguish place names in -*ham* from those in -*hamm*, 'land in a river-bend, a water-meadow, a hemmed-in place'. *Hamm* has a very different significance from *ham*; strongly topographical in meaning, it was used in name-forming throughout the Old English period, and could indicate places of late origin and dependent status.[72] The problem of distinguishing *ham* from *hamm* is particularly crucial in Cheshire, where two of the most significant *ham* names, Eastham and Frodsham, exhibit spelling variations which raise the possibility that they may have been names in -*hamm*. The topography of Frodsham is also compatible with its being a *hamm* name.[73] Possibly confusion had arisen because a *ham* settlement had been sited in a *hamm* topography.[74] Another reason for caution over names in -*ham* is that though in some regions, such as the south-east, they coincide with the areas

[63] *T.H.S.L.C.* cxix. 14-15.

[64] For a summary see L. Laing, 'Some Pagan Anglian Finds from Deeside', *J.C.A.S.* lix. 50-1.

[65] Bu'Lock, *Pre-Conquest Ches.* 35; *T.H.S.L.C.* cxii. 6, fig. 2e, pl. 1; *Archaeologia*, xci. 1-106.

[66] *J.C.A.S.* lix. 50-1.

[67] R. H. M. Dolley, 'Anglo-Saxon Coins from Meols Sands', *T.H.S.L.C.* cxiii. 197-8; *Brit. Numismatic Jnl.* xxx. 88-123.

[68] *P.N. Ches.* i. 236; Ormerod, *Hist. Ches.* iii. 611.

[69] *T.H.S.L.C.* cvi. 7-17; cxix. 9-23; G. Barnes, 'Early

Eng. Settlement and Soc. in Ches. from the Evidence of Place-Names', *T.L.C.A.S.* lxxi. 43-57.

[70] *T.H.S.L.C.* cxix. 15; *P.N. Ches.* v (1: ii), 213-14.

[71] *T.H.S.L.C.* cxix. 10, 15, 23.

[72] *P.N. Ches.* v (1: ii), 214; M. Gelling, *Place-Names in the Landscape*, 41-50; *Signposts*, 112; *Nam och Bygd*, xlviii. 148-62; *A.-S. Eng.* ii. 1-50.

[73] *P.N. Ches.* v (1: i), pp. xxxvii-xlii; Gelling, *P.N. in the Landscape*, 48. There is also a late variant of Weaverham in -*hamm*: inf. from Dr. Kenyon.

[74] *A.-S. Eng.* ii. 6.

which archaeology has shown to be those of earliest settlement, in others, such as Berkshire, they do not.[75] Hitherto, in Cheshire, despite the evidence of location, archaeological confirmation of the correspondence of *ham* names with early settlement has been lacking. It remains possible that those which are combined with an Old English personal name in the genitive, such as Frodsham and Swettenham, commemorate a thegn in receipt of a royal grant rather than an early eponymous founder.[76]

Linked with the *ham* names are those in *-ingas* or *-ingaham*, meaning 'the people of', or 'the village of the people of', and generally supposed to be indicators of early secondary settlement.[77] Those elements are lacking in Cheshire, where instead there appears a specialized form of the singular *-ing*, 'district of', which occurs in names such as Altrincham, Kermincham, Tushingham, Warmingham, and Wincham, where the *-ing* element is palatalized and assibilated to give the pronunciation *-indge* or *-inch*. Such names had been regarded as early genitive plural compounds, but in 1967 it was suggested that they represent a more archaic locative-inflected singular form.[78] Probably they are to be interpreted as formed by the later 8th century; like the names in *-ham* they occur along the cleared zones associated with Roman roads, though they occupy less favoured locations and, except for Warmingham, do not belong to ancient parishes.[79]

Cheshire also has some examples of early topographical names endowed with 'quasi-habitative significance'.[80] In particular, there are several names in *-dun*, of which Bowdon, from *boga dun*, 'curved hill', and Farndon, from *fearn dun*, 'fern hill', are especially likely to have been early. Elsewhere, at Dunham, in Thornton le Moors, and Dunham Massey, the element *dun* is combined with *ham*, to mean 'hill village'.[81] In almost all the Cheshire examples the hills so designated are prominent landmarks in low-lying areas, suitable for human habitation, and it has been suggested that they may have been the sites of existing settlements re-named by the English. It may therefore be significant that in two instances, Farndon and Bowdon, the name is borne by the church township of an extensive ancient parish and in a third, Dunham Massey, by a township which was later the focus of an important manor.[82]

Another significant class of place names, some of which may be early, are those in *-hlaw*, 'mound or hill'. In the south *-hlaw* is used almost exclusively to denote artificial mounds, and when combined with the genitive of an Old English personal name may be taken to indicate a contemporary burial mound and hence most probably an early pagan burial. Further north there is more likelihood that *hlaw* may refer to hills or mountains, and it is not always possible to distinguish names which allude to purely natural features from those which designate burial mounds on the top of a hill. In Cheshire it has been argued that some *hlaw* names at least seem likely to represent aristocratic pagan burials; Wilmslow, *Wighelmes-hlaw*, and *Hunwaldeslowe*, an obsolete name for Gorse Stacks in Chester, seem particularly promising examples.[83] Such burials could have considerable local significance and in some cases appear to have been the sites of local assemblies: it has been suggested

[75] *P.N. Berks.* iii. 812–22.

[76] Gelling, *Signposts*, 183; *P.N. Ches.* ii. 283–4; iii. 221–2. Cf. Ledsham and Alpraham, both late forms: *P.N. Ches.* iii. 300; iv. 217 (references supplied by Dr. Kenyon).

[77] *Medieval Arch.* x. 1–29; *Eng. Place-Name Soc. Jnl.* v. 15–73; Gelling, *Signposts*, 106–12.

[78] *T.H.S.L.C.* cxix. 9, 15–20; E. Ekwall, *English Place-Names in -ing* (2nd edn. 1962), 172–3. Doubt has been cast on whether Iddinshall belongs to the group: *P.N.*

Ches. iii. 288.

[79] Gelling, *P.N. in Landscape*, 119–21; *T.H.S.L.C.* cxix. 10, 23; Kenyon, 'Arch., P.N., and Settlement', chap. vii.

[80] Gelling, *P.N. in Landscape*, 140.

[81] *P.N. Ches.* ii. 15, 19; iii. 253; iv. 73–4.

[82] Gelling, *P.N. in Landscape*, 140–58.

[83] *T.H.S.L.C.* cxix. 11–12; *P.N. Ches.* i. 219–20; v (1: i), 68–9; Gelling, *Signposts*, 134–7, 154–7; *P.N. in Landscape*, 162–3.

with some plausibility, for example, that the meeting-place of Wilaveston hundred was Hadlow, 'Eada's mound', in Willaston township.[84] It is also possible that *Bochelau*, 'Bucca's mound', the meeting place of Bochelau hundred, is another example, though it may simply refer to a natural feature, Bucklow Hill.[85] All such interpretations, however, remain very tentative without archaeological confirmation, and none of the sites has as yet been excavated.[86]

Cheshire, as is to be expected, has its quota of names in -*bury*, from *burh*, 'a stronghold, a fortified manor house', one of the commonest of English place-name elements.[87] Among them is an important and perhaps early group, associated with significant ecclesiastical centres, the sites of the mother churches of a number of large ancient parishes, including Astbury, Bromborough, Bunbury, Wybunbury, and above all Prestbury, 'priests' burh'.[88] They were all probably early administrative and ecclesiastical centres and have parallels elsewhere in the north-west Midlands at for example Hanbury (Staffs.) and Alberbury, Chirbury, Maesbury, and Lydbury (Salop.).[89]

Such early names form a relatively small proportion of Anglo-Saxon settlement names in Cheshire. Nevertheless, one important general point emerges: the fact that the great majority are in the centre and east of the county behind the barrier formed by the Mid-Cheshire Ridge and the woodland to the south of it suggests that the earliest Anglo-Saxon settlers came from the Midlands and rose to dominance in the sparsely inhabited eastern regions before moving on to the more densely populated Dee valley, the heart of sub-Roman Cheshire.[90] Further clarification of the settlement pattern can be obtained from an examination of two of the commonest classes of Anglo-Saxon place names in the county, those in -*tun*, 'an enclosure, farmstead, estate, or village', and those in -*leah*, 'a wood or clearing in a wood'.[91] Such names, which may be regarded as neither especially early nor late, do not occur randomly: an analysis simply of township names shows that names in -*tun* are common in Wirral and in the Weaver valley, and especially numerous in the Dee valley and in the lowlands south of the Mersey estuary, while names in -*leah* are common in the upland areas of the north and east and the Mid-Cheshire Ridge. In sum, -*tun* occurs in the open lands where there was densest Romano-British settlement, and -*leah* in areas of woodland and waste. That accords with the pattern in other marcher counties, and it suggests, predictably enough, that names in -*tun* occupy territories previously cleared and kept clear by Romano-British farming communities.[92] On the other hand names in -*leah*, indicative of lightly wooded areas, are often interpreted as later sites, the product of progressive Anglo-Saxon colonization of virgin woodland.[93] Increasingly, however, that seems too simple a model. Though it is true that minor names in -*leah* form an especially numerous class, far more numerous than minor names in -*tun*, nevertheless there are many township names and even some ancient parish names with the -*ley* ending. A few, such as Barthomley, seem to be very early indeed.[94] It would therefore be unwise to exclude the possibility that, as has been suggested for

[84] *P.N. Ches.* iv. 232; W. Fergusson Irvine, 'Notes on Dom. Surv. in so far as it Relates to Hundred of Wirral', *J.C.A.S.* N.S. v. 72–84.

[85] *P.N. Ches.* ii. 1, 51.

[86] Gelling, *Signposts*, 132, 134–8, 154–7.

[87] *P.N. Ches.* v (1: i), 122; Gelling, *Signposts*, 143–4.

[88] *T.H.S.L.C.* cxiv. 15, 17; *P.N. Ches.* i. 212; ii. 286; iii. 80–1, 305; iv. 237–8.

[89] *V.C.H. Salop.* ii. 3, 18, 59; viii. 213–14; R. W. Eyton, *Antiquities of Salop.* vii. 86; x. 335; xi. 58, 64–5, 94; *Trans.*

Salop. Antiq. Soc. 4th ser. xi. 294; S. Shaw, *Hist. and Antiquities of Staffs.* i. 71.

[90] *T.H.S.L.C.* cxiv. 6–7.

[91] *P.N. Ches.* v (1: ii), 265–8, 371–2; Gelling, *P.N. in Landscape*, 198–207.

[92] *Trans. Birmingham and Warws. Arch. Soc.* lxxxvi. 59–79; M. Lloyd Jones, *Soc. and Settlement in Wales and the Marches 500 B.C.–1100 A.D.* (Brit. Arch. Rep., Brit. ser. cxxi: i), 160–1.

[93] e.g. *T.H.S.L.C.* cxiv. 4, 18.

[94] *P.N. Ches.* iii. 5; *T.H.S.L.C.* cxix. 12–13.

Warwickshire, some at least of the sites now bearing -*leah* names already existed in the Romano-British period, and that they acquired their English names from 'a recognition of the woodland nature of their setting'. Possibly, too, many of the woodland sites colonized by the English were clearings in the Roman period which had reverted to waste and woodland in some period of recession after the Roman departure.[95]

Probably then the Anglo-Saxon penetration of Cheshire as elsewhere did not have a particularly dramatic effect on settlement patterns. Often the newcomers both in open land and in woodland may simply have taken over and renamed Romano-British settlements. The numerous 'hamletted and dispersed townships' that came to characterize Cheshire, the denser settlement of the Dee valley, the north-west of the county, and the Weaver valley, and the relatively sparse habitation of the north-east all probably had their origin in periods long before the English arrival.[96] How far within that framework particular habitation sites were stable is difficult to say. In several instances the surviving early Anglo-Saxon place names designated the administrative centres of large districts containing many unnamed settlements. Within those districts the chief place was probably static, but the components may well have been less so, moving with the settlers with whom they were associated and perhaps receiving fresh names.

CHESHIRE AND NORTH-EAST WALES UNDER THE MERCIAN KINGS

There is no express mention of Cheshire in the Tribal Hidage, a list of regional names which dates perhaps from the late 7th century and provides the earliest evidence for the divisions of Mercia. If the first items in the list may be trusted, however, the area was within the territories of Mercia or the Wrekin dwellers, and in any case it was clearly within the Mercians' sphere of influence by the mid 8th century, since by then they had begun to expand into north Wales.[97] There had probably been some English settlement west of the Dee from relatively early times; it is perhaps significant that Bede refers to Bangor-is-y-coed as 'the monastery called in the *lingua Anglorum* Bancornaburg'.[98] A number of the place names in the area, such as Basingwerk and Killings (Flints.), look early, though, as has already been stressed, it is necessary to treat such evidence with circumspection.[99] The crucial evidence, however, is provided by the dykes, great earthworks designed, it seems, as frontiers. It was formerly believed that Wat's Dyke, which runs north from the river Morda (a tributary of the river Vyrnwy) to the Dee estuary near Holywell, was an 8th-century earthwork pre-dating a later frontier established by Offa further west and running north from the Vyrnwy to Prestatyn (Flints.).[1] Excavation in the 1970s, however, raised doubt as to whether there was a later western dyke as was once supposed and it now seems more likely that in the north-west Offa's great frontier was simply linked with a large part of the pre-existing Wat's Dyke by means of a convenient river valley somewhere near Treuddyn

[95] Taylor, *Village and Farmstead*, 121; Lloyd Jones, *Soc. and Settlement*, 160; Kenyon, 'Arch., P.N., and Settlement', chap. vi.   [96] *T.H.S.L.C.* cxiv. 1–21.
[97] Sawyer, *Roman Britain to Norman Eng.* 110–13; *Frühmittelalterliche Studien*, viii. 223–93.

[98] Bede, *Hist. Eccl.* ii. 2 (p. 138); Bu'Lock, *Pre-Conquest Ches.* 37.
[99] Bu'Lock, *Pre-Conquest Ches.* 38–9; B. G. Charles, *Non-Celtic Place-Names in Wales*, 192–236.
[1] C. Fox, *Offa's Dyke*, 1–28.

(Flints.).[2] Possibly too Offa was responsible for an enlargement of the area behind the dykes beside the Dee estuary, where the frontier turns north-west from its original termination at Flint to extend along the coast to Holywell and Basingwerk (all Flints.).[3]

Behind the late 8th-century frontier lay the greatest part of the land described as in English hands in 1066: the hidated portions of what was by then Atiscros hundred in Flintshire and the eastern part of the Welsh district of Maelor, the Domesday hundred of Exestan, in Denbighshire. Beyond lay the territory known as Englefield, later the great Domesday manor of Rhuddlan, and the manor of Bistre, probably largely coterminous with the important ancient parish of Mold, areas which were certainly English for long periods but not as securely as the territory behind the dyke. The place-name evidence further refines the picture, though it is complicated by linguistic changes in or after the 12th century when much of the area passed into Welsh hands and many English names acquired a heavy Welsh disguise. In 1086 English place names were largely concentrated behind the dyke, except in two areas, north along the Dee estuary from Holywell to Prestatyn, and in the Alun valley, among the berewicks of Bistre manor. The density of English names in such districts, especially between the dyke and the Dee, is an important indicator of the extent of Anglicization in the long period of English rule.[4]

The English were first recorded in north-east Wales in the late 8th century, though by then they had probably been active there for some time. In 796 a battle was fought at Rhuddlan, perhaps already a fortified settlement,[5] and in 816 Coenwulf, king of Mercia (796–821), harried the region west of Clwyd as far as Snowdonia. The king died at Basingwerk on a later expedition in 821. Further expansion took place after his death, and in 822 or 823 the Welsh fortress of Degannwy (Caern.) was destroyed and Powys overrun.[6] In the 9th century therefore English authority may have extended to the river Conway, well to the west of Rhuddlan. Renewed Welsh and Viking attacks had probably led to some contraction by the early 10th century, but even so English kings seem to have continued to dominate the area until the reign of Ethelred II (978–1016).[7]

THE IMPACT OF THE SCANDINAVIANS ON CHESHIRE

The Mercian kingship collapsed in the face of the Danes' advance in 874, and the Danes set up a short-lived puppet monarchy.[8] After the settlement between the English and the Danes in the 880s Cheshire's position is obscure. Probably, however, it remained primarily in the Mercian sphere of influence: that is suggested by the Mercian ealdorman Aethelred's conducting a campaign against the sons of Rhodri the Great in Gwynedd, which ended in his defeat at the river Conway in

[2] D. Hill, 'Offa's and Wat's Dykes: Some Exploratory Work on the Frontier between Celt and Saxon', *A.-S. Settlement and Landscape* (Brit. Arch. Rep., Brit. ser. vi), 102–7; 'Interrelation of Offa's and Wat's Dykes', *Antiquity*, xlviii. 309–12. The question of the date of Wat's Dyke itself has not been resolved.

[3] S. C. Stanford, *Arch. of Welsh Marches*, 188.

[4] Charles, *Non-Celtic P.N.* 210–34; inf. from Dr. C. P. Lewis.

[5] Lloyd, *Hist. Wales*, i. 201. Traces of ditches found be-

neath the supposedly 10th-century earthwork may represent that phase: J. C. Manley, 'The Late A.-S. Settlement of Cledemutha', *Studies in Late A.-S. Settlement*, ed. M. Faull, 57–8; *Current Arch.* vii. 304–7.

[6] Lloyd, *Hist. Wales*, i. 201–2; *Brut y Tywysogyon*, ed. T. Jones (Univ. of Wales, Bd. of Celtic Studs., Hist. and Law ser.), xi. 4; xvi. 7.

[7] W. Davies, *Wales in Early Middle Ages*, 113–15; *Current Arch.* vii. 304–7; *Welsh Hist. Rev.* x. 283–301.

[8] F. M. Stenton, *A.-S. Eng.* (3rd edn. 1971), 251–2.

881, and by his and his wife Aethelflaed's buying lands in Derbyshire from the Danes about 906-10.[9] Nevertheless, whoever was in control seems to have been unable to prevent the area's becoming something of a border region. Scandinavians are first recorded there in 893, on an expedition organized from the base in Essex whither the Danes had retreated after their defeat at the battle of Buttington earlier in that year. After collecting reinforcements from East Anglia and Northumbria, the Danes left 'their fortress and their ships' in Essex and 'went continuously by day and night till they reached a deserted city in Wirral, which was called Chester'. They occupied the site and were besieged there for two days, while the English seized cattle and ravaged the surrounding districts. The Danes, however, were not dislodged. Having spent the winter of 893-4 at Chester, in 894 they went into Wales whence they returned across Northumbria into East Anglia.[10]

The Danes' attack on Chester was perhaps prompted by an awareness of its enhanced strategic importance, with the establishment of Viking bases around the Irish Sea. Chester itself lay close to a direct route between Scandinavian Dublin and York, kingdoms which had already been briefly linked under a single ruler, Ivar the Boneless (d. 873), and which were soon to be so again. At first, however, and indeed later whenever possible, Vikings from the two cities preferred the much longer route far to the north across the narrow isthmus between the firths of Clyde and Forth and thence south to the Humber, a route which was very largely by sea, and therefore safer.[11] Later, however, Chester acquired greater strategic significance with the temporary expulsion of the Norsemen from Dublin in 902 and the establishment of a Hiberno-Norse community in Wirral. Though the Cheshire community had no royal leaders and was not the most important of the groups which fled in 902, the restoration of the Viking kingship to Dublin in 917 and the recovery of York in 919 made Wirral a significant bridging point between the two cities.[12]

The story of the Norse invasion of Wirral is preserved in some detail in an Irish text, which although late in its present form is apparently reliable in substance. A party of 'Lachlanns' (Norsemen), led by a certain Ingimund (Hingamund), left Dublin to seek refuge first on Anglesey, whence they were expelled by the Welsh king Clydog, and thereafter in Wirral. When Ingimund and his followers arrived the local ruler 'Edelfrid' was—as is stressed with curious emphasis—'in a disease', and negotiations were therefore conducted by his wife, 'Queen Edelfrida'. In response to their demands Edelfrida gave the newcomers lands near Chester where they remained 'for some time'. Then, seeing that 'the city was very wealthy and the land around it choice', Ingimund and his followers, who at that point were said to include Danes as well as Norsemen, decided on its appropriation. Edelfrida assembled a great host at Chester and defended it against the Vikings' attack. There follows a long account, full of folklore elements, in which the chronicler alleges that Edelfrida repulsed Ingimund by playing on divisions among his followers and obtaining the help of Christian Irish and Danes against the pagan Norsemen.[13] Despite its many curiosities, the story has been shown to be founded in fact. The 'Edelfrid' and 'Edelfrida' of the Irish chronicler are clearly the Mercian subking or ealdorman Aethelred and his wife, Alfred's daughter Aethelflaed. Aethelflaed is known to have refortified Chester in 907, an event most plausibly connected with

[9] D. Hill, *Atlas of A.-S. Eng.* 46; Lloyd, *Hist. Wales*, i. 329-30.

[10] F. T. Wainwright, *Scandinavian Eng.* 63-71, 73-6; *Two Saxon Chrons.* i. 87-8; Stenton, *A.-S. Eng.* 267-8.

[11] A. P. Smyth, *Scandinavian York and Dublin*, i. 15-40.

[12] Ibid. 60-3; Wainwright, *Scandinavian Eng.* 77-87, 131-61.

[13] *Annals of Ireland: Three Fragments by Dubhaltach mac Firbisigh*, ed. J. O'Donovan, 224-37.

Norse settlement in Wirral after the expulsion from Dublin.[14] Aethelred, who died in 911, could already by then have been suffering from his fatal illness. Above all, there is place-name and other evidence for a substantial Norse and Irish presence in Wirral.[15]

The refortification of Chester was only one step in a long process of burh-building accompanying the gradual reconquest of the Danelaw by Aethelflaed and her brother Edward the Elder (899–924). Forts were built by Aethelflaed at Eddisbury in 914 and Runcorn in 915, and by Edward the Elder at Thelwall and Manchester in 919 and at *Cledemutha* (Rhuddlan) in 921.[16] Chester, however, was presumably the major military and administrative centre, and the origins of the later shire may lie in arrangements made for its maintenance in the early 10th century. Probably it had already been significant in the recent past. Though described as a 'waste city' in 893, its desertion can have been only temporary: excavation has revealed that in the late 9th century a timber hut was built south of the fortress to the west of Lower Bridge Street, on land that had previously been ploughed, and the same area also produced a silver brooch of similar date and sherds of an 8th–9th-century Carolingian vessel. Indeed, it has been suggested that Roger of Wendover's account of the events of 893 may be taken to imply that defences already existed before the Viking raid.[17]

Elaborate arrangements for garrisoning the fortress existed by the mid 11th century and presumably from the early 10th. In 1086 it was recorded that for the repair of the city walls and bridge the reeve used to call up one man from each hide in the county. Enforcement was the responsibility of the local lord, who was fined 40s. for every man by which he fell short of his assessment.[18] The arrangement was clearly related to the provisions of the Burghal Hidage, a late 9th- or 10th-century document which assigned hidages to the territories supporting the burhs of Wessex and concluded with a formula for calculating garrisons on the basis of those hidages: each hide assigned to a burh would support one man, every pole (5½ yards) of fortress wall requiring four men to defend it. Where known, West Saxon burh defences appear to be of a length consonant with the operation of the Burghal Hidage formula, but in west Mercia the position is much less clear, both the extent of the burh walls and the hidage of the shires assigned to their support in the 10th century being uncertain. The County Hidage, a document probably dating from the 11th century, but not certainly pre-Conquest,[19] assessed the territory attached to Chester at 1,200 hides, a figure which, on the basis of the Burghal Hidage formula, would indicate defences *c.* 5,000 ft. in length.[20] That, however, does not tally with the length of the Roman walls, and has led to suggestions that the Aethelflaedan defences in part at least followed different lines.

Aethelflaed's walls have proved difficult to detect. Timber palisading discovered on the west wall of the legionary fortress was tentatively ascribed to the early 10th century, but that remains doubtful.[21] If that evidence is discounted the two main possibilities are that Aethelflaed's defences followed the Roman fortress walls, or that they adapted them in some way. In favour of the first is the survival of much

---

[14] *Two Saxon Chrons.* i. 94.

[15] Below.

[16] Wainwright, *Scandinavian Eng.* 89–91; F. T. Wainwright, 'Cledemutha', *E.H.R.* lxv. 203–12; *Two Saxon Chrons.* i. 98–9, 104–5.

[17] *Two Saxon Chrons.* i. 88; Mat. Paris, *Chron. Majora* (Rolls Ser.), i. 432; *Ches. Arch. Bull.* iii. 40; D. J. P. Mason, *Excavations at Lower Bridge St., Chester* (forthcoming).

[18] Below, Domesday translation, no. 1d.

[19] Hill, *Atlas of A.-S. Eng.* 97. Cf. below, 300.

[20] *Medieval Arch.* xiii. 84–92, esp. 92; Sawyer, *Roman Britain to Norman Eng.* 226–30; N. J. Alldridge, 'Aspects of Topog. of Early Medieval Chester', *J.C.A.S.* lxiv. 10–11; *V.C.H. Ches.* v (forthcoming).

[21] F. H. Thompson, 'Excavations at Linenhall St., Chester', *J.C.A.S.* lvi. 10–11.

Roman building within the fortress until the 10th century and beyond, and the discovery that a gravel road was then laid parallel to the inner side of the Roman north and east walls and perhaps also the south. It is clear too that the south and west walls survived long enough to influence the city's street pattern and the location of several churches.[22] On the other hand, the Roman defences were considerably longer than the figure suggested by the Burghal Hidage formula, and such evidence as there is for the period before the refortification suggests that activity was concentrated outside and to the south of the Roman fortress. One possible solution of the problem is that Aethelflaed's defences were L-shaped, and consisted of the north and east walls of the Roman fortress extended to the river. The Dee itself would thus have constituted the main defence to the south and west, an arrangement similar to that in Aethelflaed's important burh of Gloucester, and one which would have included the inhabited extramural area around Lower Bridge Street within the fortified area. Such defences would be some 4,530 ft. in length, leaving a surplus on the figure derived from the Burghal Hidage formula which could plausibly be accounted for by assigning men to the defence of the bridge.[23] The arrangement would not have been inconsistent with maintenance of the entire Roman enceinte, and it is indeed likely that it was that which protected the Danes in 893–4, and perhaps at first Aethelflaed herself.

The refortification was presumably accompanied by some replanning of the city's internal layout, but if so it does not seem to have been so radical as that which is known to have taken place for example at Winchester.[24] Within the fortress itself major public buildings, such as the *principia* and the legionary bath-house, were still standing, albeit in a ruinous condition, and their survival determined the later street pattern, which was closely related to the Roman one.[25] So far, however, few traces of Anglo-Saxon activity have been discovered in the area, except on a single site north of Princess Street, in the centre of the fortress, where a small sunken-featured building was built within the walled compound of a surviving Roman structure, perhaps in the earlier 10th century. Some distance east of that a long timber building was erected over Roman foundations and perhaps a street. Here then are signs of the adaptation of relatively intact buildings and the re-use of derelict sites; robbing of upstanding structures seems to have begun rather later.[26] The clearest evidence of organized settlement, however, comes from outside the legionary fortress, on a site to the south, in the angle between Castle Street and Lower Bridge Street. There excavation has revealed what appear to be traces of a rectilinear arrangement similar to that known in other early burhs, in the form of five sunken-featured, timber structures, set back from the two street frontages and probably dating from the earlier 10th century.[27]

New ecclesiastical arrangements are further evidence of Chester's enhanced importance in the early 10th century. Almost certainly it was through Aethelflaed that Chester became a centre of the cult of St. Werburgh. By 1066 the city housed two important minsters, St. Werburgh's and St. John's, the former seemingly linked closely with Aethelflaed. A late and not entirely consistent tradition ascribes to her the refoundation of a minster in Chester, formerly dedicated to St. Peter and St. Paul, in honour of St. Werburgh, a daughter of the 7th-century Mercian king,

[22] *J.C.A.S.* lxvii. 17–34, esp. 22.
[23] Mason, *Excavations at Lower Bridge St.*
[24] *Antiq. Jnl.* li. 70–85; *Winchester in the Early Middle Ages*, ed. M. Biddle (Winchester Studies, i), 449–53.
[25] *J.C.A.S.* lxvii. 17–34.
[26] Ibid. 29; inf. from Grosvenor Mus. Excavations Section.
[27] *Ches. Arch. Bull.* iii. 40–1; Mason, *Excavations at Lower Bridge St.*

Wulfred, whose relics had been brought to Chester following the Danish occupation of her original resting-place at Hanbury (Staffs.).[28] The translation of St. Werburgh is paralleled by Aethelflaed's translation in 909 of the remains of St. Oswald from their shrine at Bardney (Lincs.) to a new minster founded in their honour at the important burh of Gloucester. Indeed, it seems likely that the cult of St. Oswald, which from the 13th century at the latest was associated at Chester with that of St. Werburgh, was introduced there by Aethelflaed, since she was occupied with the refortification of the city at much the same time that she was engaged in the recovery of Oswald's bones. The importance of the relics, and of the minster which housed them (by 1066 it was the best endowed institution of its type in Cheshire), points to the significance attached to Chester in the early 10th century.[29]

Chester, then, was probably from the 10th century the centre of complex garrisoning dispositions resembling those for contemporary Wessex. The area focused upon it appears to have differed from the medieval shire, embracing territory in north-east Wales and, perhaps, north of the Mersey: it seems to have been as a result of Edward the Elder's burh-building in 919 that Manchester first came to be in some way attached to Cheshire. Probably it was soon afterwards that the whole of south Lancashire, the land between the Ribble and the Mersey, came to be associated with the shire and incorporated in the diocese of Lichfield.[30] Certainly there were links between Cheshire and south Lancashire before 1000, when Wulfric Spot held lands in both territories.[31] Wulfric's estates remained grouped together after his death, when they were left to his brother Aelfhelm, and indeed there still seems to have been some kind of connexion in 1086, when south Lancashire was surveyed together with Cheshire by the Domesday commissioners. Nevertheless, the two territories do seem to have been distinguished from one another in some way and it is not certain that the shire-moot and the reeves referred to in the south Lancashire section of Domesday were the Cheshire ones.[32]

It was probably in connexion with the military dispositions that the shire was organized into hundreds. Though there are signs of later rearrangement, it is likely that in the 10th century as in 1066 Cheshire, including the Welsh territories but excluding those between the Ribble and the Mersey, was divided into twelve hundreds: Chester itself, Dudestan, Riseton, Wilaveston (Willaston), Roelau, Bochelau (Bucklow), Tunendune, Hamestan, Mildestvic (Middlewich), Warmundestrou, Exestan, and Atiscros. Such an arrangement is consistent with the shire's assessment of 1,200 hides, recorded in the County Hidage. It need not, however, have been based entirely on new units, and indeed there are some indications that it may have been linked with earlier administrative divisions.[33]

The network of subsidiary fortresses built by Aethelflaed and her brother in Cheshire and south Lancashire reflects a response to the continuing threat posed by the Irish Sea Vikings. Burh-building took place especially after the Danes' defeat at Tettenhall (Staffs.) in 910, with Edward active in the south Midlands and Aethelflaed in west Mercia. The new Cheshire fortresses, at Eddisbury and Runcorn, were built at a period when the Irish of Ulster were fighting a Norse fleet in

[28] *Northern Hist.* xviii. 203–4; H. Bradshaw, *Life of St. Werburgh of Chester* (E.E.T.S. orig. ser. 88), 139–53. Two other versions of the origins of St. Werburgh's ignore Aethelflaed's role: R. Higden, *Polychronicon* (Rolls Ser.), vi. 126–8, 176–8, 366, says that St. Werburgh's relics were taken from Hanbury to Chester after the Danes had taken Repton (Derb.) in 874 and eventually honoured in a collegiate church from the time of King Athelstan; Bradshaw, *Life*, 151, that King Edmund (939–46) founded a college of canons.

[29] *Northern Hist.* xviii. 203–6, 209.

[30] *Two Saxon Chrons.* i. 104.

[31] *Burton Abbey Charts.* pp. xviii–xix, xxiv, xxix.

[32] *V.C.H. Lancs.* i. 269, 285, 287.

[33] *Dom. Surv. Ches.* 13–18; below, 'Early Estate Organization'.

the Irish Sea and the Norse had been victorious off the Isle of Man. With Chester they protected the vulnerable low-lying land of the Mersey estuary from attack from the Irish Sea and formed a barrier to inland penetration by the Norse settlement in Wirral. After the Norse recapture of Dublin in 917 and Dublin's reunion with York under Ragnall in 919 the area acquired even greater importance, and it is probably no coincidence that Edward the Elder built additional fortresses at Thelwall and Manchester in 919.[34] The new arrangements, which established a defensive zone on both sides of the Mersey and incorporated areas formerly regarded as part of Northumbria, seem to have endured: as late as 1066, landowners such as Uhtred and Dot had important tenancies on either side of the river.[35]

Particularly revealing of the manner in which the new fortifications were organized are the arrangements at Runcorn and Thelwall. Both came to be included within what was by 1066 the important estate of Halton and the large ancient parish of Runcorn, with its 20 townships. It might be thought that estate and parish were created to serve the spiritual and temporal needs of the new burhs but the place-name evidence suggests otherwise: the fact that the parish contains the townships of Norton, Sutton, Aston, and Weston, that is, north, south, east, and west *tun*s, indicates that the whole area may once have been organized as a single administrative unit, even though it is not clear whether in 1066 Norton, Aston, and Weston were still members of the Halton estate.[36] Such arrangements were probably of considerable antiquity and could well have pre-dated the establishment of the new burhs. A further pointer is the fact that Thelwall is detached from the rest of Runcorn parish, an indication that the parish was an older unit which had been altered in order to include both burhs within the same ecclesiastical jurisdiction.[37]

It seems likely then that the early 10th-century arrangements at Halton and Runcorn represent the remodelling of an ancient estate, comprising the western half of the Domesday hundred of Tunendune, in conjunction with the establishment of the new burhs. The remodelling was probably accompanied by new ecclesiastical dispositions. Runcorn, which still had two priests in 1086,[38] was almost certainly an Anglo-Saxon minster: significantly, like so many other similar institutions it became the site of an Augustinian priory, founded in the early 12th century and dedicated to St. Bertelin and the Virgin. The priory soon moved but St. Bertelin remained the patron of Runcorn parish church, presumably because he had been the patron of the earlier minster. Bertelin is an obscure saint, reputed to have been a Mercian prince and enshrined in a large and important minster at Stafford. Since Aethelflaed is known to have refortified Stafford in 913, just before she built the burh at Runcorn, it looks as if the dedication of the Runcorn minster was her responsibility. Like Chester, if on a smaller scale, Runcorn was to combine the roles of fortress and Mercian royal cult centre.[39]

The nature of the estate and parish which preceded the remodelling remains obscure. It is likely, however, that Halton and Runcorn were not the original manorial and ecclesiastical foci, partly because, located as they were on a heath or amid marshy land beside the Mersey estuary, they were not the most suitable sites for primary settlement within the area. The evidence points rather to Daresbury, 'Deor's stronghold', and Preston, 'priest's *tun*', as the original foci of the estate.

[34] Smyth, *Scandinavian York and Dublin*, i. 76–7; Wainwright, *Scandinavian Eng.* 88–91.

[35] Below, Domesday introduction; a point made by Mr. Sawyer.

[36] They were held by free men, probably tenants of Orme, the lord of Halton.

[37] *P.N. Ches.* ii. 137–8, 159–60, 173, 180, 182; below, fig. 37.

[38] They are listed under Halton.

[39] *Foundation Chart. of Runcorn Priory* (Chetham Soc. N.S. c), 3, 9; *V.C.H. Ches.* iii. 165; *V.C.H. Staffs.* iii. 303; iv. 44; vi. 238–9, 241; A. Oswald, *Ch. of St. Bertelin at Stafford*, 6–10; *Midland Hist.* x (forthcoming).

Both occur on land eminently suitable for primary settlement in the zone around the Roman road which runs from Chester to Wilderspool. Moreover, both are within the ancient chapelry of Daresbury, first mentioned in the 12th century. None of the chapelry's ten townships was mentioned in Domesday, and it looks as if by then it had become a dependency of the new estate centre created at Halton to serve the burhs.[40]

The Norse threat was emphasized when the new king of York, Sihtric, raided into Cheshire as far as Davenport in 920, the year of his accession, but Aethelflaed's and Edward's dispositions seem to have held.[41] In Cheshire the West Saxon king was to have more trouble with the local inhabitants than with the Vikings. Aethelflaed, who had ruled the Mercians in her own right since her husband's death in 911, herself died in 918 leaving only a daughter Aelfwyn, and Edward was thereupon chosen as the Mercian king. He initiated his rule by taking the submission of Idwal of Gwynedd and the rulers of Dyfed and shortly afterwards secured his position by placing Aelfwyn in a West Saxon nunnery. The move, however, was not popular and it is possible that Edward's visit to Cheshire with the fyrd in 919 was connected with local unrest as much as with anxiety over the Vikings.[42] In 921 Edward was in the north-west again, this time to build a burh at *Cledemutha*, the mouth of the Clwyd, now identified as Rhuddlan. Recent excavations have uncovered the remains of late Saxon defensive earthworks at Rhuddlan, enclosing some 80 acres beside the river, and it seems likely that Edward intended to establish a fortified town there on the site of what was probably already a small settlement.[43] If such measures were intended to overawe the local inhabitants they were unsuccessful, for in 924 Edward was faced with a revolt by the men of Chester in alliance with the Welsh. The king suppressed the rebellion, but it proved his last campaign, for he died immediately afterwards at the nearby royal vill of Farndon.[44] His successor, his son Athelstan, who had been brought up at the court of Ethelred and Aethelflaed, was to have less trouble with Mercian separatism. Even so he was careful to make concessions: most unusually, his royal style in his coronation *ordo* expressly includes mention of the Mercians alongside the West Saxons and Northumbrians.[45] His successors were to continue to have to take account of such sentiments, which seem to have been particularly potent in west Mercian areas like Cheshire.

SCANDINAVIAN SETTLEMENT
IN CHESHIRE

Wirral

The impact of Scandinavian settlement is most apparent in Wirral, where the place-name evidence is both copious and complex. There are some entirely Scandinavian names, including Meols (Old Norse *melr*, 'sandbank'), Tranmere (Old Norse *trani* and *melr*, 'the crane-frequented sandbank'), and Thingwall (Old

---

[40] *P.N. Ches.* ii. 146, 148–9, 156–7, 166–7; Ormerod, *Hist. Ches.* i. 732; fig. 37. The argument and much of the information in this paragraph were supplied by Dr. Higham.

[41] Smyth, *Scandinavian York and Dublin*, ii. 1–2; Wainwright, *Scandinavian Eng.* 95. The place name Davenport suggests a market town, but there is no evidence of one: *P.N. Ches.* ii. 301.

[42] *Two Saxon Chrons.* i. 96, 103–5; Wainwright, *Scandinavian Eng.* 93, 127–9.

[43] *E.H.R.* lxv. 203–12; Manley, in *Studies in Late A.-S. Settlement*, 55–64; *Current Arch.* vii. 304–7.

[44] *Two Saxon Chrons.* i. 105; *P.N. Ches.* iv. 74.

[45] C. Hohler, 'Some A.-S. Service Books', *Tenth Cent. Studies*, 68; Wainwright, *Scandinavian Eng.* 309–10, 323.

Norse, 'field where an assembly meets'), as well as the majority of the county's meagre supply of names in -*by* (Old Danish *by*, Old Norse *byr*, 'a farmstead or village').[46] The *by* names include a few wholly Scandinavian township names such as Kirby, *kirkju-byr*, 'the church hamlet', which occurs in both West Kirby and Wallasey,[47] and Raby, *ra-byr*, 'the boundary farmstead'. Others are of mixed origin: Pensby township, for example, includes the Welsh element *pen*, 'a hill'. Elsewhere, as at Greasby and Whitby, the Scandinavian *by* or *byr* element replaces an original Old English element, *byrig*, dative singular of *burh*. Such examples, and others like Gayton, where the element combined with Old English *tun* is probably Old Norse *geit*, 'a goat', suggest a mixed Anglo-Scandinavian community, the dating of the emergence of which is, however, complicated by the fact that a Scandinavian dialect was still being spoken, and place names therefore being coined, as late as the early 13th century in Cheshire.[48] The Ingimund story clearly suggests that an important element was composed of immigrants from Ireland in the early 10th century, and that those immigrants included not only Norsemen, but also Irishmen and some Danes. The place-name evidence bears that out, for Irish-speaking settlers are indicated by one township name, Noctorum, from Old Irish *cnocc* and *tirim*, 'the dry hillock', while another, Irby, 'farmstead of the Irish', points to local recognition of a community of people from Ireland, whether Irish or Norse.[49] The place name Denhall (*Danewell*) in Ness suggests that there were Danes in the region, sufficiently rare to be distinguished from other inhabitants.[50] Recently, however, it has been argued that the Ingimund episode should not be taken as furnishing the whole context for the Scandinavian immigration into Cheshire.[51] Most notably, the *by* names have been taken to point elsewhere, to the Irish Sea area as a whole and to the Isle of Man in particular. Names in -*by* were not used by the Vikings in Ireland, nor by those in north Britain and the Isles, but they were common in the Danelaw and in Man. Those in the Danelaw are far to the east, and the most probable immediate source for the names in Wirral and south Lancashire is Man. Indeed, the *by* names in those areas occur in forms closely related, sometimes identical, to the forms on Man. That the transmission was from Man to north-west England rather than vice versa is indicated by the occurrence of other names apparently imported from Man in the latter area. In particular, there are those incorporating *aergi*, a Scandinavian element derived ultimately from the Gaelic *airigh*, a shieling, which appears in Wirral at Arrowe, and is also to be found in south Lancashire. Such names have been regarded as an additional indicator of Hiberno-Norse settlement,[52] but it is perhaps more likely that they derive from another context. It has been shown that *aergi* is rare in Irish place names, but that it occurs frequently in Scotland in regions heavily colonized by Norsemen.[53] Nevertheless, it is unlikely that those areas were the immediate source of the names in Wirral and south Lancashire, where other forms of place name common in Cumbria and Galloway, in particular 'inversion compounds', are very rare.[54] A

[46] See *T.H.S.L.C.* cvi. 16–20; cxix. 1–6; J. McN. Dodgson, 'Background to the Battle of Brunanburh', *Saga Bk.* (Viking Soc. for Northern Research), xiv. 303–16; G. Barnes, 'Evidence of Place-Names for Scandinavian Settlements in Ches.' *T.L.C.A.S.* lxiii. 131–55.

[47] In Wallasey the township in which the church is located was originally known as Kirby in Waley: *P.N. Ches.* iv. 332.

[48] *P.N. Ches.* iv. 198, 229, 257–8, 271–3, 275, 291, 294–5, 297–8, 332; v (1: i), 124; *Saga Bk.* xiv. 307–8; *T.L.C.A.S.* lxiii. 143–4.

[49] *Saga Bk.* xiv. 306–7; *P.N. Ches.* iv. 264, 268.

[50] *P.N. Ches.* iv. 220.

[51] For what follows see G. Fellows Jensen, 'Scandinavian Settlement in the Isle of Man: the Place-Name Evidence', *Viking Age in the Isle of Man: Select Papers from the 9th Viking Congress*, ed. C. Fell and others, 37–52.

[52] *Saga Bk.* xiv. 308–9; *P.N. Ches.* iv. 261–3.

[53] Smyth, *Scandinavian York and Dublin*, i. 79–80; *Viking Age in Man*, 45.

[54] In such names the generic precedes the specific in the order common in the younger Celtic place names: *Viking Age in Man*, 50. Cf. Smyth, *Scandinavian York and Dublin*, i. 80–1.

better context is provided by Man where the element *eary*, derived from *airigh*, probably survived in the Norse period, and where inversion compounds appear also then to have been absent. Other place names which strengthen the case for such a link include Thingwall, found in both Wirral and south Lancashire and evidence of an institution familiar to settlers in Man and the Isles, and Frankby, probably a reference to the rare west Scandinavian name Frakki, first recorded on Man.[55]

It has been emphasized that many of the Norse place names in Wirral are minor in character. Only Meols, Thingwall, Raby, and Helsby (which, though in Eddisbury, was probably an outlier of the Norse community in Wirral) can be regarded as decisive indicators of Norse settlement, and of those only Raby and Helsby are habitative names. The Kirby names, though wholly Scandinavian, may have been descriptive of existing Anglian churches and hence merely replacements of Anglian *cirice-tun* ('church-town') names. Otherwise there are only the numerous field names and the mixed Anglo-Scandinavian names. Such evidence makes it likely that generally 'Norse village-names begin as the names of minor and insignificant farmsteads that are subsidiary settlements . . . within the framework of English townships and parishes' and that there was 'a deliberate and non-disruptive integration of Norse and English people into one Anglo-Norse community'.[56] That community seems to have preserved a strong sense of its own identity and its own institutions. Particularly significant is the place name Thingwall, with its allusion to the *Thing*, presumably the Wirral Norsemen's version of the Icelandic *Thing* or governing assembly; it corresponds to an identical place name near Liverpool on the opposite side of the Mersey, apparently the site of a similar centre for the Norse community in south-west Lancashire.[57] The southern limit of the self-governing community in Wirral may be traced at Raby and nearby at Hargrave in Little Neston, both place names containing a reference to a boundary.[58] Also perhaps connected is the area which later became known as the hundred of Caldy. In the Middle Ages it comprised Thornton Hough, Leighton, Gayton, Heswall, Thurstaston, West Kirby, Great and Little Meols, Hoose, Newton cum Larton, and Poulton cum Seacombe, but it was perhaps originally of much greater extent. In 1086 the lands of the 'hundred' were part of a compact estate held by Robert of Rhuddlan, which also included Wallasey, Neston, and Hargrave. Other territory in north Wirral was also held in compact blocks, by the barons of Dunham Massey, Halton, and Mold, and it has been suggested that such tenures originated in the area's being originally a distinct self-governing Anglo-Scandinavian enclave and later an Anglo-Saxon administrative district.[59]

Church dedications provide further evidence of the Hiberno-Norse community in Wirral. In particular, the church of West Kirby, a large parish of some nine townships, including Meols, Frankby, Caldy, and part of Greasby, is dedicated to St. Bridget, a saint particularly associated with Ireland. Though it was not mentioned in 1086, it certainly existed in 1081, when among the lands given by Robert of Rhuddlan, lord of Caldy, to the church of St. Evroul was the township of *Cherchebi*, with its church and presbytery and the attached chapel of Hilbre Island. The church may at one time have been of some importance since in the late 12th century it was described as a minster (*monasterium*). That it was probably by

[55] An alternative derivation of Frankby is from O.E. *Franca*, 'a Frenchman': *P.N. Ches.* iv. 287.

[56] *Saga Bk.* xiv. 309. Cf. G. Fellows Jensen, *Scandinavian Settlement Names in Yorks.* 227–8.

[57] *P.N. Ches.* iv. 273; Smyth, *Scandinavian York and Dublin*, i. 79–80.

[58] *P.N. Ches.* iv. 228–9.

[59] *Saga Bk.* xiv. 309–12; J. Brownbill and W. G. Collingwood, *W. Kirby and Hilbre: a Parochial Hist.* 158–63.

then of considerable antiquity is indicated by finds of 10th- or 11th-century cross fragments both at West Kirby and Hilbre.[60]

Evidence for the trading activities of the Norsemen comes from Meols, where finds suggest that the settlement, though never a Norse colony, had links with Hiberno-Norse milieux over a long period. Though the material is difficult to analyse, since much has been lost and no stratigraphical contexts recorded, it points to Viking connexions over a long period, perhaps even before the early 10th century: a bronze drinking-horn mount, similar to others found in 9th-century graves in Scandinavia and Scotland, may pre-date the arrival of Ingimund. In general, the bulk of the finds reflect mixed Hiberno-Norse trading links, one ring-headed pin having east Scandinavian parallels from the cemetery at Birka (Sweden). It seems safe to assume that Meols, on the coast and near what was probably the Hiberno-Norse church of St. Bridget, was the earliest port of the Scandinavian community.[61]

Scandinavian Chester

The Hiberno-Norse community appears quickly to have become involved in coining in the Chester area, probably at Chester itself.[62] As early as the reign of Edward the Elder one of the moneyers from the region bore the significant Scandinavian name of *Irfara*, 'the Ireland journeyer', while other noteworthy names included the Gaelic Maeldomen[63] and the Scandinavian Oslac.[64] During the reign of Edward's successor, Athelstan, Chester's moneyers appear to have been especially cosmopolitan and to have included not only significant groups of Scandinavians and Celts but also Germans or Franks. Scandinavian influence also seems to have been strong there in the late 10th and early 11th century and indeed to have remained fairly constant throughout the later Saxon period: of some hundred moneyers' names known between 910 and 1066 at least one fifth was Scandinavian, a proportion higher than at many mints in the Danelaw itself.[65]

Other indications of the Scandinavian community in Chester are to be found in the city's administration. The twelve *iudices* of the city, mentioned in 1086 as chosen from the men of the king, bishop, and earl, and obliged to attend the Chester hundred court, may resemble the lawmen of the Scandinavian boroughs.[66] Scandinavian influence is also detectable in the assessment of Handbridge, the southern suburb of Chester, in carucates rather than hides, the normal basis of assessment in Cheshire.[67] Indeed, there is some evidence that the whole area south of the Roman fortress was an area of Scandinavian settlement: it has been argued that the lost names of two gates in that part of the city, Clippe Gate (near Bridge Gate) and Wolfeld's Gate (the old name for Newgate), ultimately go back to the Old Norse personal names of *Klyppr* and *Ulfhildr*, and it also seems likely that the dedications of two churches there were Hiberno-Norse in origin. St. Olave's, in the area south of the legionary fortress and certainly in being by the early 12th century, was dedicated to the Norwegian king, Olaf Haraldsson (d. 1030), a saint

[60] Brownbill and Collingwood, *W. Kirby and Hilbre*, 14–26, 87; *P.N. Ches.* iv. 284, 294, 303; *Saga Bk.* xiv. 310; *Chart. Chester Abbey*, ii. 291; below, gazetteer.

[61] *T.H.S.L.C.* cxii. 14–20; G. Chitty and M. Warhurst, 'Ancient Meols', *Jnl. Merseyside Arch. Soc.* i. 19–42; below, gazetteer; fig. 42.

[62] R. H. M. Dolley, 'Mint at Chester, I', *J.C.A.S.* xlii. 1–6; below.

[63] Smyth suggests that the name may be Scottish: *Scandinavian York and Dublin*, i. 81–2. For another possible Scottish name among Cheshire moneyers see V. J. Smart,

'Moneyers of Late A.-S. Coinage', *Commentationes de Nummis Saeculorum IX–XI in Sueca Repertis*, ii (Kungl. Vitterhets Historie Och Antikvitets Akademien Antikvariska Serien xix), 225–6.

[64] *J.C.A.S.* xlii. 6; O. von Feilitzen, *Pre-Conquest Personal Names of Dom. Bk.* 340.

[65] *J.C.A.S.* xlii. 8, 10–11, 17 n. 40.

[66] Wainwright, *Scandinavian Eng.* 97, 99; *Dom. Surv. Ches.* 32–3; below, Domesday introduction.

[67] Wainwright, *Scandinavian Eng.* 98–9; *Dom. Surv. Ches.* 9–10; below, Domesday introduction.

much favoured by Anglo-Scandinavian communities from the mid 11th century. St. Bridget's, on the site of the south gate of the Roman fortress, has a common Hiberno-Norse dedication, which appears also at West Kirby. Though first mentioned only in the mid 13th century that reference shows it to have existed from the 12th, and it was probably much older. Its parish was once much larger and included parts of the parishes of St. Mary's and St. Olave's, and it may be presumed therefore that the church pre-dated those foundations.[68]

Further traces of the Hiberno-Norse in Chester include several ring-headed pins. Though Irish in origin, such pins were adopted by the Hiberno-Norse, and polyhedral-headed examples, particularly analogous to those at Chester, have been found on Man.[69] Fragments of arm rings and brooches from a hoard found at Castle Esplanade and deposited c. 970 or 980 also show links with Man; the jewellery resembles in character that in a hoard from Ballaquayle, and some of it may have been made on the island.[70] Other evidence suggests connexions with Dublin. The cellared timber structures to the south of the Roman fortress are similar to buildings excavated in Dublin and York, and even more significantly, a brooch, discovered at Princess Street in the middle of Chester, is identical to a brooch found in Dublin, apparently from the same mould. The copper alloy brooch, which dates from the earlier 10th century, has openwork ornament in the Borre-Jellinge style. It was found within a Roman building still standing when it was lost and was near an early sunken-featured hut, a context which perhaps suggests a Hiberno-Norse presence inside as well as outside the fortress.[71]

It seems, then, that there was an important Hiberno-Norse community in Chester and Handbridge, much concerned with minting and trade and with links with both Dublin and Man. It probably formed a distinctive element within the city from the 10th century at least until the 13th; certainly Norse names occur there throughout that period, and in 1066 indeed the bearer of one such, Gunnor, held one third of the important episcopal manor of Redcliff.[72]

Scandinavian Settlement Elsewhere in Cheshire

Throughout the rest of Cheshire there is a sprinkling of Scandinavian names, with an especial concentration in the north-east of the county. In the far east, in Macclesfield hundred, there is a number of names containing the elements *both*, 'a booth, a temporary shelter', and *hulm*, a term which relates to water meadows and marsh. Such names were not used for permanent settlements, and only two of them, Kettleshulme and Somerford Booths, belong to townships, the rest being minor names, many of them lost.[73] Both elements are generally interpreted as indicators of Old Danish rather than Old Norse settlement, but, because they have been adopted into Old and Middle English, they cannot be relied upon as such. *Hulm* is especially problematic. Place names in -*hulm* do not occur elsewhere, even in Scandinavia, and it is now thought that the element represents a late Old English or early Middle English confusion of late Old English *holm* (from the Old Norse *holmr*, 'dry ground in a marsh') with *humm*, a north-west Midlands

[68] *P.N. Ches.* v (1: i), 25-6; J. McN. Dodgson, 'Place-Names and Street Names at Chester', *J.C.A.S.* lv. 50-3; *Saga Bk.* xii. 53-80; *V.C.H. Ches.* v (forthcoming).

[69] Bu'Lock, *Pre-Conquest Ches.* 67-8, pl. 14; *Medieval Arch.* xix. 220, pl. xvi C; T. Fanning, 'Hiberno-Norse Pins from the Isle of Man', *Viking Age in Man*, 27-36, esp. 32-3; below, fig. 42.

[70] G. Webster, R. H. M. Dolley, and G. C. Dunning, 'A Saxon Treasure Hoard found at Chester', *Antiq. Jnl.* xxxiii.

26-9; J. Graham-Campbell, 'Viking Age Silver Hoards in Man', *Viking Age in Man*, 69-70 (reference supplied by Dr. Kenyon); above, plates.

[71] *Medieval Arch.* xv. 73, 79; xxvii. 170, pl. 14 A; Mason, *Excavations at Lower Bridge St.*; above, plates.

[72] He may be the Gunner who with Ulf held Mollington.

[73] *P.N. Ches.* v (1: i), 110; v (1: ii), 237-9; G. Fellows Jensen, review of *P.N. Ches.* i-ii, *Saga Bk.* xviii. 203-5.

variant of Old English *homm* or *hamm*, 'a water meadow, an enclosure (of meadow-land)'.[74]

The hundreds of Bucklow and Northwich in north and central east Cheshire contain rather more Scandinavian names, many of them again including the elements *both* and *holmr* or *hulm*. In Northwich hundred there are several township names with Scandinavian elements, including Church Hulme and Hulme Walfield, in Astbury, and a number of hybrids such as Moulton, in Davenham, Congleton, Croxton, in Middlewich, and Arclid, in Sandbach.[75] In Bucklow hundred there are again several township names, many of them concentrated in a group in the parish of Rostherne, which itself contains the Scandinavian personal name *Rauthr* or *Roth*. The chapelry of Knutsford is a focus of names which are clearly Old Danish in character, with Knutsford itself incorporating the Old Danish personal name Knut, Knutsford Booths including the Old Danish element *both*, and Toft, derived from the Old Danish or Old Norse word for a curtilage. Here the place names are corroborated by other forms of evidence: of Domesday Cheshire's 15 geldable bovates (such bovates being subdivisions of the hide, Scandinavian in origin) 7 were in the neighbourhood of Knutsford, in the Peovers and Tableys. Knutsford itself was held in 1066 by a man with an Old German name while the holder of one of the manors of Over Tabley bore the Scandinavian name of Segrid.[76] Other Scandinavian names include Keckwick, in Daresbury chapelry in Runcorn, a place which, though it does not itself appear in Domesday, was presumably part of the manor of Halton, and hence in 1066 held by a lord with the Scandinavian name of Orme.[77]

Further west, Eddisbury hundred contains relatively few Scandinavian names. The most significant, Helsby, was almost certainly an outlier of the Norse settlements in Wirral, as were also perhaps some Norse minor names in Ince ancient parish. In the south and west of the county, in Broxton and Nantwich hundreds, Scandinavian names are again rare and generally hybrids. Broxton contains the hybrid township name of Agden, in Malpas, which incorporates the Old Danish personal name of *Aggi*, and Nantwich contains Basford, in Wybunbury, which may incorporate an Old Norse personal name.[78] Further west still, in the Welsh marches, Vikings continue to be difficult to trace, though there is a cluster of Scandinavian place names on the Flintshire coast, in the parish of Llanasa.[79]

It is difficult to draw any firm conclusions from the rather puzzling evidence for the Scandinavian presence in Cheshire outside Wirral. It would seem that in the north and east of the county especially there was some Danish penetration, presumably from across the Pennines, but there are also scattered traces of Norsemen throughout the county. Such men may represent part of the general settlement in north-west England of Norse from Galloway and the Isles, as well as from Ireland and Man, and some could have been comparative late-comers, arrivals after Cnut's conquest.[80] The appearance of hybrid names and their distribution among English place names suggests very considerable intermingling and the emergence of 'an English society and language with a Scandinavian complexion'.[81]

[74] Inf. from Mr. Dodgson; Gelling, *P.N. in Landscape*, 50–2.

[75] *P.N. Ches.* ii. 207, 236, 264, 278–9, 294, 302; inf. from Dr. G. Fellows Jensen.

[76] *P.N. Ches.* ii. 56–7, 73–4, 76–7, 81; *Dom. Surv. Ches.* 10–13. For an alternative derivation for Knutsford, from Old English *cnottan ford*, see G. Fellows Jensen, 'Scandinavian Settlement in the Danelaw', *Proc. of 8th Viking Congress*, 142–3 (reference supplied by Dr. Kenyon).

[77] *P.N. Ches.* ii. 151.

[78] Ibid. iii. 48, 235–6, 251–2; iv. 3.

[79] Charles, *Non-Celtic P.N.* p. xxxiv.

[80] Smyth, *Scandinavian York and Dublin*, i. 75–92; Wainwright, *Scandinavian Eng.* 181–227; inf. from Mr. Sawyer.

[81] *T.H.S.L.C.* cxix. 6–7.

LATE ANGLO-SAXON CHESHIRE

By 924, when Edward the Elder died, Cheshire had become an area of considerable military and strategic importance, and hence a centre of royal interest. The factors contributing to that military significance were illustrated especially clearly in the important campaign which culminated in 937 in the great battle of Brunanburh, between Edward's successor, Athelstan, and the Dublin king, Olaf Gothfrithsson, and his British allies from Scotland and Strathclyde. Though the site of the battle is debated, and recently it has been placed in the forest of Bromswold in the Mercian heartland between Northampton and Bedford, a good case can still be made for Bromborough in Wirral, an important vill in the 10th century and the only known place name in England which matches Old English *Brunanburh*.[82] Whatever its location, however, the battle, with its conclusive English victory, must have made an impact on Cheshire, situated as it was between Dublin and York and next to Wales. Edward's suppression of the Welsh revolt in 924 had ushered in a period of comparative peace during the reign of Athelstan (924–39), who brought the Welsh princes, including Idwal and Iago, the rulers of Gwynedd, into attendance at his court to attest his charters under the title of *subreguli*. That peace, however, was always fragile, especially at the time of Brunanburh when some at least of the Welsh princes were tempted to join the British of Strathclyde as allies of the Norsemen. In 942 it was finally fractured. By then Athelstan's successor, Edmund (939–46), was campaigning against Olaf Cuaran, the then ruler of the restored kingdom of York, and Idwal of Gwynedd seized the opportunity to revolt. He was defeated and slain, but the threat of collusion between Welsh and Scandinavians remained while the kingdom of York survived.[83]

With the expulsion of the last Scandinavian king from York in 954, despite occasional ravagings, such as those in Gwynedd in 967 and 978, there was a long period of peaceful English domination, effectively demonstrated by the well known episode of the submission of the British princes to Edgar at Chester in 973, when the king was rowed on the river by rulers from Gwynedd, Strathclyde, Scotland, Man, and the Isles.[84] The choice of Chester as the scene for that event is significant, and illustrates the extent to which the city retained its importance for the West Saxon kings in their dealings with the Welsh and their allies. Royal interest is above all demonstrated by the rise of Chester as a centre for the production of coins. A mint which existed in north-west Mercia in the 890s seems by the reign of Edward the Elder to have been sited at Chester: at least two of Edward's Mercian moneyers were later to strike in the city, and it has been suggested that one, Snel, could have been working there from 907. By the end of the reign there may have been as many as 16 moneyers at work in Chester.[85] The impetus behind the development seems to have lain partly in the bullion obtained in Aethelflaed's conquests, especially her victories between 916 and 918 in Wales and the Midlands, and partly in proximity to the silver mines of north Wales. With the emergence of coins with an unequivocal Chester mint-signature in the reign of Athelstan it becomes clear that the mint was

[82] *Saga Bk.* xiv. 303–16. Cf. Smyth, *Scandinavian York and Dublin*, ii. 31–61; *Battle of Brunanburh*, ed. A. Campbell, 80.

[83] Smyth, *Scandinavian York and Dublin*, ii. 62–88; Davies, *Wales in Early Middle Ages*, 114, 116–17; *Welsh Hist. Rev.* x. 283–301.

[84] *Florentii Wigorniensis, Chron. ex Chron.* ed. B. Thorpe, i. 142–3; J. Nelson, 'Inauguration Rituals', *Early Medieval Kingship*, ed. P. H. Sawyer, 69–70; Stenton, *A.-S. Eng.* 369.

[85] *J.C.A.S.* xlii. 1–6.

then the most important in England. At least 28 moneyers are known to have worked at Chester between 924 and 939 and probably there were as many as 20 striking in the city at any one time, as compared with 10 at London and 7 at Winchester. That is perhaps attributable to Athelstan's close connexions with Mercia and to bullion and tribute brought in by his military victories. Thereafter the importance of the mint at Chester declined: in the reigns of Edmund and Edred (939–55) there were some 17 moneyers and in the unsettled reign of Edwy as few as 11. Under Edgar the mint recovered some of its old significance and by 970 there were once more 17 moneyers; except for a brief period at the end of the 10th century, it was to remain an important provincial mint until the Conquest, but it was never again to rival the great centres of London, York, Winchester, and Lincoln.[86]

Royal interest was accompanied by economic expansion. Chester's rise as a trading centre may be dated from the earlier 10th century, and stemmed above all from its position on the chief trading route for Ireland and the Irish Sea. The Vikings had established themselves not only in Wirral but generally on the coasts of north-west England and on the Isle of Man, all of which facilitated an Anglo-Hibernian trade focused on Chester. In addition, however, they also attempted to set up staging posts along the north Welsh coast, in particular on Anglesey, to ease the journey from Dublin to Chester. Though permanent settlement, except in Flintshire, was probably rare, fortified quaysides, harbours, and navigation points were established at Holyhead (Anglesey), and perhaps at Bangor (Caern.) and elsewhere.[87] That the Chester mint was especially involved in the trade which passed along such routes is clear from the kind of coin it produced, which in accordance with Hiberno-Norse prejudices entirely eschewed portrait heads during the period up to 973. Even after Edgar's great recoinage in that year Chester seems to have continued to strike the type II coins lacking a portrait head which are found exclusively in hoards from Ireland, Man, and Scotland.[88]

The long spell of comparatively peaceful relations with Gwynedd also promoted trade: it is likely, for example, that a coin of Hywel Dda (d. 949 or 950) was struck by Gillys, a moneyer connected with Chester who had what seems to have been a Hiberno-Norse name.[89] Later, a coin of the mid 11th-century Chester moneyer, Farngrim, was found at Caerwent (Mon.).[90] It was perhaps because of such connexions that in the 10th century Chester became for a while 'the gateway through which great quantities of silver flowed in and out of England'.[91] Nor was it the only port in the area: at Meols a handful of coins dating from the later 10th and earlier 11th century suggest that some kind of trading activity continued there throughout the later Saxon period, though oddly there are none for the years 900–73.[92]

The hoard deposited at Castle Esplanade in Chester c. 970 or 980 illustrates the activities of one who seems to have been a moneyer of the period. It included enough bullion, largely composed of ingots and fragments of jewellery, for the manufacture of about 750 pennies and 522 coins ranging from the reign of Alfred to that of Edgar. Such a large mixed silver hoard was exceptional in north-west England and Ireland by the 970s, and it has recently been suggested that it formed

[86] Ibid. 3–4.
[87] H. R. Loyn, *Vikings in Wales*, 18–21.
[88] *Jnl. of the Royal Soc. of Antiq. of Ireland*, xci. 1–18.
[89] The attribution is no longer certain: Loyn, *Vikings in Wales*, 5–6; *J.C.A.S.* xlii. 8, 17.
[90] *Arch. Camb.* cxix. 77.
[91] D. Metcalf, 'Ranking of Boroughs: Numismatic Evidence from the Reign of Aethelred II', *Ethelred the Unready* (Brit. Arch. Rep., Brit. ser. lix), 184.
[92] *T.H.S.L.C.* cxiii. 197–201.

the property of a Norseman from Man or, less probably, from Scotland. A further hoard deposited at much the same time in Eastgate Street contained 43 coins from the reigns of Edred, Edwy, and Edgar, all of a non-portrait type, and it seems likely that they and the coins from Castle Esplanade were not actually current at the time they were concealed but formed a demonetized reserve stock.[93] Additional illustration of Chester's trading links is provided by a third hoard of 122 coins deposited *c.* 980 at Pemberton's Parlour in the north-west corner of the city: the earliest coins were no more than six years old, yet the hoard includes the products of a wide variety of mints, especially from the east Midlands but also from places as remote as Totnes (Devon).[94]

The three Chester hoards were deposited at a time of renewed Viking activity, one of the earliest manifestations of which was a naval raid on Cheshire in 980.[95] It seems likely that during that raid Chester itself was sacked, since the output of the mint and the number of moneyers fell dramatically at that time. Probably too the end of occupation on the Lower Bridge Street site dates from the same period.[96] The effects of what must have been a temporarily devastating raid continued to be felt at least until the end of the reign of Ethelred II, and it is possible that they were prolonged by Ethelred's and his advisers' actions against the Anglo-Scandinavians; certainly in 1016 Ethelred's son Edmund and Earl Uhtred of Northumbria marched through north-west Mercia to Chester, ravaging because men would not come out against the Danes.[97] Moreover, though Chester had certainly recovered sufficiently by the millennium to become the base for English ships successfully harrying Vikings in and around the Irish Sea, and though the mint had certainly regained something of its former importance by the reign of Cnut, it seems gradually to have been supplanted as the principal port for Irish trade with the opening of the south route from Dublin to Bristol and the English Channel at about that time.[98]

One factor in the process may have been events in north Wales. English dominance in north Wales probably weakened with the intensification of the Viking attacks in the late 10th century, and it is unlikely that *Cledemutha* long survived as an English burh.[99] The English position further declined with the rise of Gruffudd ap Llywelyn, king of Gwynedd 1039–63. Gruffudd came to power in 1039 after he had heavily defeated a Mercian force near Welshpool (Mont.), killing the brother of Earl Leofric. In 1055 he became the ruler of the whole of Wales, and in alliance with the exiled English earl, Aelfgar, son of Leofric, he defeated King Edward's nephew, Earl Ralph, and sacked his stronghold of Hereford. The king sent Earl Harold Godwinsson to restore the situation, and in the peace which he concluded Aelfgar regained his earldom and Gruffudd was left in possession of some at least of his conquests.[1] In 1056 after defeating and killing the new and warlike bishop of Hereford Gruffudd was confirmed in his position as underking of Edward the Confessor, and it was almost certainly then that he received 'all the land which lay beyond the river Dee', a grant which may have included all the Welsh territories

[93] *Antiq. Jnl.* xxxiii. 22–33; Graham-Campbell, in *Viking Age in Man,* 69–70; R. H. M. Dolley, 'Repercussions on Chester's Prosperity of the Viking Descent on Ches. in 980', *Brit. Numismatic Jnl.* xxxiii. 44; 'A Find of Coins of Eadred, Eadwig, and Eadgar at Chester', *Brit. Numismatic Jnl.* xxiv. 47–9.
[94] Hill, *Atlas of A.-S. Eng.* 212; G. Hill, 'A Find of Coins of Eadgar, Eadweard II, and Aethelred II at Chester', *Numismatic Chron.* 4th ser. xx. 141–65.
[95] *Two Saxon Chrons.* i. 123–4.
[96] Mason, *Excavations at Lower Bridge St.*

[97] *Brit. Numismatic Jnl.* xxxiii. 39–44; Loyn, *Vikings in Wales,* 10; Bu'Lock, *Pre-Conquest Ches.* 55–6; *Two Saxon Chrons.* ii. 147.
[98] R. H. M. Dolley, 'An Unpublished Chester Penny of Harthacnut', *Num. Chron.* 1960, 191–3. For the state of Chester in 1066 see below, Domesday introduction.
[99] Manley, in *Studies in Late A.-S. Settlement,* 59–60.
[1] F. Barlow, *Edward the Confessor,* 204–11; Lloyd, *Hist. Wales,* ii. 358–69; *Dom. Surv. Ches.* 22–3, 25; C. P. Lewis, 'Eng. and Norman Govt. and Ldship. in the Welsh Borders, 1039–87' (Oxf. Univ. D.Phil. thesis, 1985), 119–24.

assigned to Cheshire in 1086, but is perhaps more likely to have referred primarily to the Domesday hundreds of Exestan and hidated Atiscros. Other territories, such as the manor of Rhuddlan, where Gruffudd was living in 1063, and that of Bistre, from which he then received the food rents, may well have been in the king's possession already. Soon after that grant, perhaps in 1057, he married the daughter of his old ally Aelfgar, by then the newly installed earl of Mercia, an event which probably contributed to Aelfgar's deprivation and exile in that year. After Aelfgar's restoration with Gruffudd's help in 1058 until his final disappearance in 1062 little is known of Welsh affairs, but his ally's removal seems to have undermined Gruffudd's position at the English court and soon after it was decided to make an end of him. Earl Harold was sent with a cavalry force to surprise the Welsh king at his residence at Rhuddlan, and though Gruffudd escaped by ship his hall was burnt. A second campaign was mounted in 1063 by Harold and his brother Tostig; Harold sailed up from Bristol ravaging the Welsh coastline, and Tostig invaded north Wales, presumably from Chester. The expedition was a success. The Welsh submitted and Gruffudd was eventually slain by his own followers.[2]

The defeat of Gruffudd led to a redistribution of his holdings on the English border. In an ambiguous passage Domesday records that the bishop of Lichfield and 'all his men' recovered all their lands in Exestan hundred, and elsewhere the most important manors were granted to Aelfgar's son Edwin, earl of Mercia, who received Hawarden, Rhuddlan, and Bistre. The new arrangements seem to have been controversial. In 1086 the bishop was still claiming that he had been wrongfully deprived of certain territories, but his rights though acknowledged were not made good.[3]

EARLY ESTATE ORGANIZATION AND THE HUNDRED IN CHESHIRE

There are some indications that there were large estates, each administered from a *caput* manor and containing many settlements, in Cheshire as in many places elsewhere.[4] The link between Wirral and the lands between the Ribble and Mersey is significant, for in south Lancashire such early 'shires' are easy to detect. The area was originally divided into five hundreds, each of which was focused on a royal *tun* and divided into royal demesne and dependent lordships. The royal *tun* formed the centre from which the demesne was administered and at which the tenants made their customary renders. Accompanying such secular administrative arrangements there were parallel ecclesiastical ones: each hundred had one or two relatively rich and important churches, often probably of the secular minster type, staffed by a body of secular priests and having very large parishes coinciding with the hundred. As the mother churches of the area such foundations were entitled to various dues, including in their fullest form a tax known as church scot, tithe and other crop renders, payments for the chrism used in baptism, and fees payable before the burial of a corpse. Ecclesiastical and secular renders were thus organized on the same units. The hundred of Salford, for example, was administered for secular

[2] Barlow, *Edw. the Conf.* 207–8, 211–12; Lloyd, *Hist. Wales*, ii. 369–71; *Flor. Wig. Chron. ex Chron.* i. 221.
[3] Below, Domesday text, no. 7; *Dom. Surv. Ches.* 25.
[4] For surveys of such estates in general see Sawyer, in *A.-S. Settlement and Landscape*, 108–19; G. R. J. Jones, 'Multiple Estates and Early Settlement', *Medieval Settlement*, ed. P. H. Sawyer, 15–40; G. W. S. Barrow, *Kingdom of Scots*, 7–68.

purposes from the royal estate centre at Salford, and for ecclesiastical purposes from the important church of St. Mary, probably in the adjacent township of Manchester; the hundred of Blackburn was focused on the royal administrative centre at Blackburn and divided into two parishes, those of Blackburn and Whalley, of which Whalley was almost certainly a minster.[5] A similar organization into districts focused on royal vills and associated with important minster churches may be reconstructed for Shropshire, in for example the hundreds of Maesbury, Alberbury, and Chirbury, though there by 1086 it had been somewhat eroded.[6]

In Cheshire the existence of such districts may be deduced from the ancient parochial structure in being by the 13th century. The many large parishes embracing numerous townships and settlements almost certainly represent the remnants of large estates, perhaps as elsewhere originally royal, though the king held no land in Cheshire in 1066. A further indicator is the fact that many large parishes constitute coherent geographical units. Since early estates are thought to have contained sufficient resources to be self-supporting, it seems likely that they formed varied territories with areas of arable, pasture, meadow, and water. In several Cheshire parishes it is possible to discern the elements of such necessary variety, with intensively cultivated and settled foci, distinguished by relatively ancient place names, interspersed with belts of poorer quality land perhaps characterized by place names in -leah. Often such barren land marks the periphery of an ancient estate or parish, dividing it from its neighbour.[7] Elements of earlier territories may also be traced in the late Anglo-Saxon system of tax assessment, which in Cheshire as elsewhere seems to have been based on a 5-hide unit. In Cheshire, where the vills were often too poor to receive a round 5-, 10-, or 15-hide assessment, larger groupings instead often served as the 'subpartitional area'. Some ancient parishes with many townships produce total assessments of 25 or 30 hides, and elsewhere it is possible to trace smaller units of 10 or 15 hides.[8] Early districts may most plausibly be detected at a number of important estates focused on vills with place names including the early element *ham*, among which perhaps the greatest was that centred on Eastham. In 1086 Eastham, then held by Earl Hugh, was a large district assessed at 22 hides comprising most of the Mersey shore of Wirral. It belonged to Earl Edwin in 1066, but it had probably once been royal: in the later 10th century it was almost certainly the main element in lands *on Wirhalum* held by Wulfric Spot, who seems to have been of royal descent on his mother's side and whose brother Aelfhelm was ealdorman of Deira.[9] Moreover the parish structure is also significant; Eastham was a large chapelry of the mother church of Bromborough, which, though much decayed by 1086, still preserved some traces of its original importance, with its detached township of Brimstage indicating that it probably once comprehended all or part of the later parish of Bebington.[10] It seems likely that as elsewhere the ancient parish was coterminous with the estate, and that Eastham was therefore originally the royal administrative centre for much of the eastern side of Wirral, if not for the whole hundred of Wilaveston.

[5] Sawyer, *Roman Britain to Norman Eng.* 175-6, 244-5; *V.C.H. Lancs.* i. 283-90.

[6] *V.C.H. Salop.* ii. 18, 59; viii. 213-14; Eyton, *Antiq. Salop.* vii. 86; x. 335; xi. 64-5.

[7] N. J. Higham, 'Estates, Par., and the Crown: Pre-Conquest Estate Structure in NW. Eng.' (unpublished paper); below, fig. 37.

[8] *Dom. Surv. Ches.* 19-21.

[9] Hart, *Early Charts. in the N. Midlands*, 373-4; *A.-S. Wills*, ed. D. Whitelock, 46-50. Aelfhelm died in 1006 and his sons were disinherited by King Ethelred, so it was perhaps then that some of Wulfric's former territories, including south Lancashire, became royal demesne. The king may also have acquired the Eastham estate at that time, but if so he later granted it to the earl of Mercia. Possibly, however, Earl Edwin inherited it from his mother, who was probably a relative of Wulfric's: *Burton Abbey Charts.* pp. xviii, xxiv, xli, xliii.

[10] *P.N. Ches.* iv. 234, 245; below, fig. 37. The township of Poulton Lancelyn in Bebington had a priest in 1086.

Frodsham is probably another example of an early royal estate. Though the manor was assessed at only 3 hides, its 9 ploughlands and pre-Conquest value of £8 suggest that it was underrated. Before the Conquest it had belonged to Earl Edwin, and attached to it was the third penny of the pleas of Roelau hundred, an indication that it was the local hundredal centre for the collection of royal revenues.[11] It, too, was an ecclesiastical centre of some importance, the focus of a large ancient parish of 8 townships.[12] Similar features can be observed at Weaverham, also in Roelau hundred, where in 1066 Earl Edwin held another manor, assessed at 13 hides. Indications of its status include the fact that 10 burgesses in Chester and 7 salthouses in *Wich* (probably Northwich) were attached to it, and that it was the centre of an ancient parish of some 8 townships.[13] It looks therefore as if the Domesday hundred of Roelau was composed of two important estates, Frodsham in the west and Weaverham in the east.

Acton is another example of such a district, probably the centre for the Domesday hundred of Warmundestrou. In the Middle Ages the parish comprised 17 townships and 3 parochial chapelries with a further 14 townships.[14] The church was almost certainly a minster; in 1086 there were two priests holding one ploughteam, and in 1291 the rectory, then valued at £53, was still one of the richest in Cheshire.[15] The manor of Acton was also important. Held by Earl Edwin or his brother Morcar in 1066, it was assessed at 8 hides, but was probably undervalued since it was said to contain enough land for 30 ploughteams.[16]

In the east of the county a further example is provided by Prestbury. The name, meaning 'priests' burh', is significant, for it suggests the presence of a group of priests, presumably serving an early minster, and it links Prestbury with other place names in *-bury*, such as Alberbury, Chirbury, and Maesbury (Salop.) with their royal hundredal churches, or Lydbury (Salop.), with its great episcopal estate and minster.[17] Prestbury was a very large ancient parish eventually composed of 31 townships and considerably larger in the early Middle Ages, when it also included the subsequently independent parishes of Gawsworth, Taxall, and Nether Alderley.[18] Among the members of that vast district, over half of the Domesday hundred of Hamestan, was the large chapelry of Macclesfield, where Earl Edwin had an important manor to which pertained the hundredal third penny.[19] Both it and the other major chapelry of Chelford were almost certainly ancient, for when the church was first mentioned in the late 12th century it was 'with chapels and all other appurtenances';[20] there is thus the same nexus of indicators as has been observed at other putative early estate centres.

In the south and west there are the examples of Farndon and Malpas. Farndon was almost certainly a royal estate in the early 10th century since Edward the Elder died there in 924.[21] By 1066 it was divided between Earl Edwin and the bishop of Chester, each of whom had a 4-hide manor there. The ancient estate seems originally to have been very large, as may be deduced from the pattern of the Domesday assessments. The core of the early district focused on Farndon was clearly the eight townships of the two later parishes of Farndon and Aldford, which comprised a neat 10-hide unit, but it seems likely that it also embraced other

[11] On the earl's third penny see Sawyer, *Roman Britain to Norman Eng.* 201, 207.
[12] *P.N. Ches.* iii. 219.
[13] Ibid. iii. 193.
[14] Ibid. iii. 28, 101, 113, 121, 124, 126, 154; Dugdale, *Mon.* v. 323–4.
[15] *Tax. Eccl.* (Rec. Com.), 248.
[16] *Dom. Surv. Ches.* 6, 151.
[17] Above, 'Early A.-S. Ches.'; *P.N. Ches.* i. 212; v (1: i), 122–3.
[18] *P.N. Ches.* i. 54, 66, 72, 94, 106, 172, 181; Ormerod, *Hist. Ches.* ii. 399, 536, 565, 782; *Chart. Chester Abbey,* i. 7; ii. 437.
[19] Ormerod, *Hist. Ches.* iii. 739.
[20] *Chart. Chester Abbey,* i. 79–80, 130–1.
[21] Above.

territories, in particular the chapelry of Holt (Denb.), which included the episcopal estate of Sutton, in Is-y-coed (Denb.), assessed at 1 hide. In 1352 Holt chapelry was linked with the mother church at Farndon, both being annexed time out of mind to the upkeep of the deanery of St. John's, Chester. The chapelry was eventually transferred to Gresford (Denb.) parish, but even as late as 1379, when the rector of Gresford and the dean of St. John's were in dispute over it, the rector did not deny the dean's claim that Holt was a 'parcel' of Farndon.[22] Moreover, throughout the Middle Ages Holt and Is-y-coed were the only parts of Gresford parish, and indeed of the whole hundred of Exestan, to be in the Lichfield diocese.[23] Also grouped with Farndon and Holt as part of the dean of St. John's emoluments was the contiguous small parish of Shocklach, in 1352 described as a chapelry. Probably it too was originally part of the ancient estate of Farndon; significantly it was assessed at 4 hides in 1066 and so with Farndon and Holt made up a 15-hide unit.[24] Possibly the district was originally even larger, and included the adjacent small parishes of Tilston, Coddington, and Handley, which together were assessed at $9\frac{1}{2}$ hides. That would give the territory once focused on Farndon a Domesday assessment of some 25 hides, comparable with other similar units still existing in 1086. Farndon church had clearly once been important, relatively well endowed and closely connected with the bishop. The dedication to St. Chad indicates an episcopal link, perhaps long-standing, and it was presumably the bishop who was responsible for its downgrading by annexation to St. John's.[25] In 1086 there were two priests with the substantial holding of $1\frac{1}{2}$ hides, and a 'priest of the vill' with $\frac{1}{2}$ ploughteam. Interestingly, too, an estate of 1 hide in Caldecot, a township of Shocklach, was in 1066 held by Wulfgar the priest with three other thegns. Wulfgar was presumably a cleric of some status, and may well have been a canon or even dean or warden of the neighbouring minster. Farndon thus has several of the characteristics that have been identified elsewhere as indicators of a multiple estate, and in the 10th century was also probably royal. It looks therefore as if the king had originally held estates in Cheshire as in Shropshire and south Lancashire and that the bishop and the earl were his successors.

The other major parish of the Domesday hundred of Dudestan was Malpas (in 1066 *Depenbech*), a parish of 25 townships, whose Domesday assessments totalled $29\frac{1}{2}$ hides. *Depenbech* itself was the focus of an 8-hide manor, but, rather oddly, no church or priest was mentioned.[26] Other factors, however, attest to the church's importance and antiquity. The church, which is next to the castle of the barons of Malpas, was certainly there in the early 13th century when David of Malpas obtained that half of it which belonged to Gilbert the clerk.[27] From the later 13th century when their names are first known there were co-rectors, that of the upper mediety also serving the chapelry of Tushingham, that of the lower the chapelry of Whitwell. Such arrangements could represent the remains of an ancient minster, as they appear to have done in nearby Prees (Salop.).[28] The dedication of the parish church to St. Oswald and of a chapel to St. Chad may point to a division between comital and episcopal interests similar to that in Farndon,

[22] *Dom. Surv. Ches.* 20; *Blk. Prince's Reg.* iii. 54; *Cal. Inq. Misc.* iv. 46.

[23] D. R. Thomas, *Hist. of Dioc. of St. Asaph*, 796, 815, 819.

[24] *Blk. Prince's Reg.* iii. 54. If Eyton was also in Holt, the total would be 16 hides: below.

[25] Below. Whether the annexation to St. John's represents a late 11th-century attempt by the bishops to augment the endowments of the new cathedral church at Chester or whether it was earlier cannot now be determined.

[26] *P.N. Ches.* iv. 3; Ormerod, *Hist. Ches.* ii. 592. There are parallels for the omission elsewhere, e.g. Alberbury (Salop.), a church with a very large ancient parish sited at a royal estate which formed the *caput* of Ruesset hundred, yet entirely omitted in Domesday.

[27] 3 *Sheaf*, xx, p. 6; Ches. R.O., DCH/D/31-7.

[28] Ormerod, *Hist. Ches.* ii. 619-20; Eyton, *Antiq. Salop.* ix. 244.

especially as the bishop is known to have had important interests elsewhere in the area.[29]

Two or three such estate centres can be postulated for each of the rural Domesday hundreds closely linked with the principal ancient parishes, and almost all were held by the earl or the bishop in 1066, the only exception being unhidated Atiscros where the large early parishes seem to have broken up and an exceptional number of undoubtedly minor churches are mentioned in the Survey.[30] Clearly, however, there were changes, even before the Conquest. In several instances hundredal and ancient parish boundaries do not coincide; Great Budworth, for example, though largely in Tunendune also included townships in Roelau and Middlewich hundreds.[31] In such circumstances it seems likely that the boundaries of the great ancient parishes are earlier and therefore a safer guide to ancient territorial arrangements. Despite such discrepancies it is clear that in general there is some link between hundredal organization and early estates as represented by the larger ancient parishes. Information relating to Domesday churches (which in Cheshire are mainly significant mother churches) was almost certainly supplied on a hundredal basis, since the terminology is generally consistent within each hundred but may vary between one hundred and another. Moreover one hundred, Hamestan, seems to have neglected to make any ecclesiastical returns, since none of its entries in Domesday Book contains a reference either to priests or churches.[32]

The age and origin of the estates is uncertain. It seems likely that in Shropshire at least the hundredal and district organization date only from the 10th century.[33] In south Lancashire, however, it has been suggested that the arrangements recorded in Domesday may have been of considerable antiquity,[34] and it is possible that in Cheshire too their counterparts may have been early, even if it is clear that in many areas there had been considerable reorganization in the late Saxon period. The place names in *-ham*, *-dun*, and *-bury* and the association of several of them with episcopal estates suggest antiquity; Farndon and Bowdon, with their ancient topographical place names and their curvilinear churchyards, indicative of British ecclesiastical centres, are especially likely to have been early.[35] Above all, there are the signs of archaic arrangements, pre-dating the burh, on the great estate of Halton, with its grouping of north, south, east, and west *tuns* and its associated townships bearing names indicative of an early stronghold and a priest's *tun*.[36] There are signs too that some at least of the hundreds may have originated in older units: the hundredal meeting places of Bochelau and Roelau, for example, were probably very ancient places of assembly at prominent local topographical features and were near the important estate centre of Weaverham and the ancient parochial centre of Rostherne.[37] Similarly, the meeting-place for the hundred of Wilaveston, which seems to have been at Hadlow ('Eada's mound') in Willaston, was held by Earl Edwin before the Conquest and, though in a township of Neston parish, was apparently connected with the neighbouring great estate of Eastham.[38]

One indication that the 10th-century reorganization of the West Saxon kings was not as thorough in Cheshire as in the south and much of the Midlands is the absence

[29] Ormerod, *Hist. Ches.* ii. 614, 619. The earliest recorded reference to the dedication to St. Chad at Tushingham appears to be 1349: *P.N. Ches.* iv. 68. See also below.

[30] Below, Domesday introduction.

[31] Ormerod, *Hist. Ches.* i. 606–7; ii. 196; iii. 140.

[32] Below, Domesday introduction; fig. 36.

[33] *V.C.H. Salop.* iii. 6.

[34] Sawyer, *Roman Britain to Norman Eng.* 175–6.

[35] Above, 'Sub-Roman Ches.', 'Early A.S.-Ches.'; below, gazetteer.

[36] Above, 'Impact of Scandinavians'.

[37] *P.N. Ches.* ii. 1; iii. 196.

[38] Ibid. iv. 167, 232.

there as in the rest of northern England of the tithing, a local grouping of 10 or 12 men mutually responsible for one another's good behaviour.[39] Instead, as in Wales, Shropshire and the Marches, Lancashire, Westmorland, Cumberland, Galloway, and elsewhere in Britain, there were serjeants of the peace, officials with wide powers of attachment and indictment entitled to free maintenance from the locality. Such officials are only recorded after the Conquest, but it seems likely that they existed long before that, and that they were Celtic in origin. In Shropshire and in Lancashire between the Mersey and the Ribble they were based on the royal hundreds, and that may originally have been the case in Cheshire, though by Norman times they were organized on a county basis with a master serjeant and 20 county serjeants complemented by special serjeanties for Macclesfield and the royal forests and for the major Cheshire baronies.[40]

Despite the sparseness of the documentary sources, there is, then, circumstantial evidence that the hundreds of the Cheshire Domesday had their origins in archaic territorial units, rearranged in the 10th century and perhaps again thereafter. It seems likely that in the 10th century there were 12 hundreds originally assessed at 1,200 hides, but if so by 1086 they had been subjected to a radical reassessment, for the county was then valued at only 512 hides. Another indication of an 11th-century rearrangement is the regularity of the assessment in several hundreds such as Exestan (20 hides), Warmundestrou (40 hides), Atiscros ($19\frac{1}{2}$ hides), and Wilaveston ($97\frac{1}{2}$ hides).[41]

THE CHURCH IN CHESHIRE

The beginnings of the church in Cheshire are obscure. The Domesday Survey included few churches, probably mainly those which had been mother churches of the large estates, but the presence of curvilinear churchyards and fragments of pre-Norman sculpture at many otherwise undocumented sites suggests that by then there were many others.[42] Almost certainly there were Christian communities in the area in late Roman or sub-Roman times, often at sites which were occupied by later churches. Continuity, however, is difficult to establish. St. John's, Chester, has the best claim to antiquity, for by the 12th century it was believed to have been established by King Ethelred of Mercia in 689. Its extramural site near the Roman amphitheatre points to the possibility of Roman antecedents, and the fact that by 1066 it was an important secular college belonging to the bishop of Lichfield, with a dean and seven canons, is a further indicator that it was early.[43] Little else is recorded of the church in Cheshire before the 10th century, when late and conflicting traditions tell of the establishment of St. Werburgh's cult in Chester.[44] The minster of St. Werburgh's was undoubtedly in existence by 958, when it received extensive grants from King Edgar, and it remained the richest ecclesiastical foundation in Cheshire throughout the later Anglo-Saxon period, staffed by a warden and 12 canons and endowed with 21 manors assessed at 28 hides in 1086.[45]

[39] Sawyer, *Roman Britain to Norman Eng.* 197–200; H. R. Loyn, *Governance of A.-S. Eng.* 140–2.

[40] *Jnl. Med. Hist.* i. 117–38, esp. 123–4, 129–30; R. Stewart-Brown, *Serjeants of the Peace in Med. Eng. and Wales; Scottish Hist. Rev.* xxxix. 170–5; W. Davies, in *Chas. the Bald: Court and Kingdom* (Brit. Arch. Rep., Internat. ser. ci), 93–9, esp. 98. Dr. Davies raises the possibility that serjeants of the peace had links with the Breton *machtierns*, local rulers with civil functions whose authority was ex-ploited by the principal early medieval rulers of Brittany but was probably independent in origin.

[41] Below, Domesday introduction; *Dom. Surv. Ches.* 13–18.

[42] Below, gazetteer; fig. 36.

[43] *Northern Hist.* xviii. 200–2; *V.C.H. Ches.* v (forthcoming).

[44] Above, 'Impact of Scandinavians'.

[45] *V.C.H. Ches.* iii. 132–3; *Northern Hist.* xviii. 204; fig. 37.

As the city's two collegiate foundations, St. John's and St. Werburgh's enjoyed considerable local prestige in the late Anglo-Saxon period. Both were repaired and enriched with ornaments and grants of privileges by Earl Leofric of Mercia (d. 1057).[46] They also shared a joint monopoly of the burial rights of the Chester area from an early period, and in a succession of agreements made in the late 12th and early 13th century sought to preserve their fees from that source in the face of competition from later foundations in the town. St. Werburgh's indeed obtained a papal bull expressly forbidding any church within the ancient limits of its parish or within the walls of Chester to disturb the *antiquum ius sepulturae* of the locality. Such actions suggest that the two churches are to be regarded as the joint mother churches of an ancient parish focused on Chester, perhaps indeed as the heirs of a sub-Roman *matrix ecclesia* based at Eccleston.[47]

Though the two Chester foundations are the only early minsters which can be traced with certainty in Cheshire, a number of the mother churches associated with early estate centres were very probably of like status. They include Runcorn, Farndon, and Acton, all of which had two priests in Domesday, and perhaps Malpas and Prestbury. Some, such as Farndon, were relatively well endowed in 1066 and most were still among the richest churches in Cheshire in 1291.[48] A few were probably cult centres; the likely establishment at Runcorn of the cult of St. Bertelin has been discussed above, and other probable early dedications include St. Boniface at Bunbury, St. Wilfrid at Davenham and Northenden, and St. Oswald at Malpas and across the Mersey at the rich and important hundredal church of Winwick (Lancs.).[49] Two other supposed cults perhaps relate to local anchorites. Plemstall, 'Plegmund's holy place', according to Gervase of Canterbury, was the site of a hermitage occupied by Archbishop Plegmund of Canterbury (890–914), while Hilbre, 'the island of Hildeburgh', may be evidence of an otherwise unknown Anglo-Saxon saint of that name. At Hilbre Anglo-Saxons were present from an early period and there was a pre-Conquest chapel annexed to West Kirby but with its own burial ground. Somewhat later the island became the focus of a devotion to the Virgin attracting pilgrims from Mercia and even the Continent.[50]

Perhaps the most significant cult in Cheshire was that of St. Chad. Cheshire was in the diocese of north-west Mercia, whose cathedral was at Lichfield, the see of St. Chad, and the cult was closely associated with the bishop's holdings in the area. Before 1066 those were extensive, albeit not as great as his long-held estates in Staffordshire. In Chester itself the bishop was possessed of considerable rights and property, far more than in the other shire towns of Stafford and Shrewsbury. In particular, he had 56 houses paying geld there in 1066, and the important customary right to exact fines from the city's traders and inhabitants for violations of the ban on working on Sundays and other holy days. The centre of his holding was the 'bishop's borough' in Redcliff, where he had a manor of $\frac{2}{3}$ hide which was said to belong to the church of St. John. St. John's, which seems to have been the focus of a whole group of ecclesiastical buildings, was in status perhaps only a little below the cathedral itself, and the bishop may have set up his *cathedra* or episcopal chair there when visiting the distant north-west corner of his large diocese. Though in Domesday its only recorded endowments are the bishop's manor and the eight

---

[46] *Flor. Wig. Chron. ex Chron.* i. 216.

[47] *Northern Hist.* xviii. 199, 204–5; *Chart. Chester Abbey,* i. 113–14; ii. 299–301; below, fig. 36.

[48] *Tax. Eccl.* (Rec. Com.), 248; below, fig. 36.

[49] Ormerod, *Hist. Ches.* ii. 256, 614; iii. 239, 615; Bu'Lock, *Pre-Conquest Ches.* 34; *V.C.H. Lancs.* i. 286. The Winwick

dedication is mentioned in Dom. Bk. There are also churches dedicated to St. Wilfrid at Grappenhall and Mobberley.

[50] Bu'Lock, *Pre-Conquest Ches.* 34, 81; Ormerod, *Hist. Ches.* ii. 501–2, 808; *P.N. Ches.* iv. 135–6, 302–3; Hume, *Ancient Meols,* 283–5, plate 27.

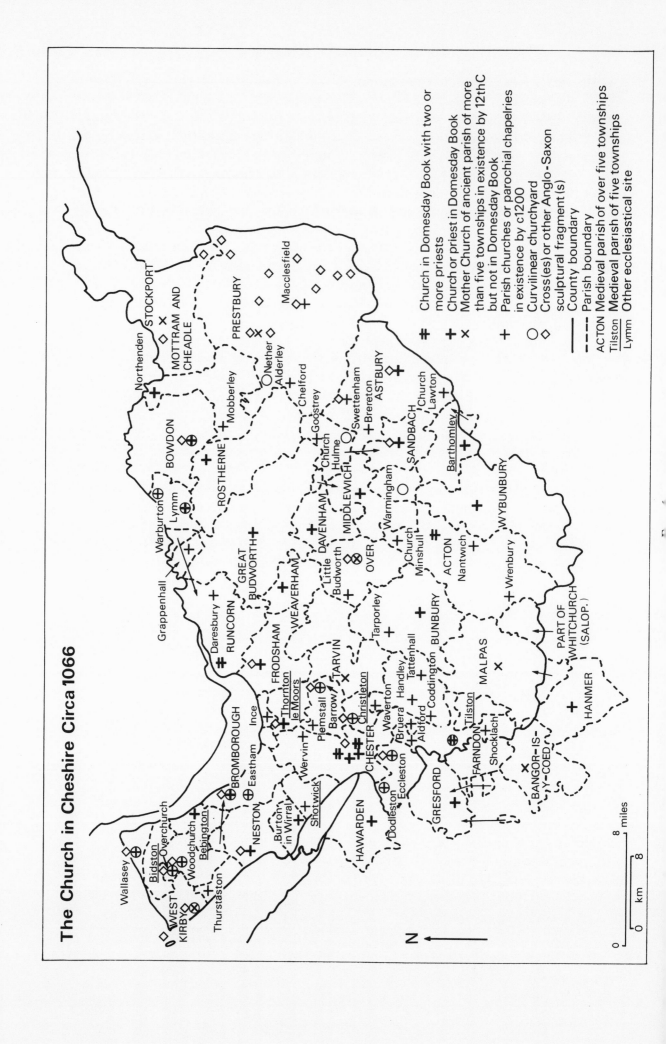

The Church in Cheshire Circa 1066

Church in Domesday Book with two or more priests

Church or priest in Domesday Book

Mother Church of ancient parish of more than five townships in existence by 12thC but not in Domesday Book

Parish churches or parochial chapelries in existence by c1200

Curvilinear churchyard

Cross(es) or other Anglo-Saxon sculptural fragment(s)

ACTON Medieval parish of over five townships

Tilston Medieval parish of five townships

Lymm Other ecclesiastical site

County boundary

Parish boundary

houses provided for the clergy, that may be simply because the bulk of its possessions were included with those of the bishop, whose principal Cheshire church it
evidently was.[51]

Elsewhere in Cheshire the bishop held a number of important estates in 1066,
and there are signs that in earlier times his holdings had been larger still. At most
major episcopal estate centres there were ancient mother churches, some of which
were almost certainly minsters and several of which seem to have been under the
patronage of St. Chad. Farndon, as has already been shown, was one. Wybunbury
was another: though in 1066 the bishop's manor there was assessed at only ½ hide,
it may well once have been larger. Certainly the church of St. Chad with its ancient
parish of 18 townships had probably once been of considerable importance, and it
looks as if the bishop's estate originally combined with the earl's manor of Acton
to form the hundred of Warmundestrou.[52] Such arrangements may once have been
widespread and certainly were not confined to Cheshire; at Prees just across the
border in Shropshire, for example, the bishop had an important manor assessed in
1066 at 8 hides and a church with an extensive parish dedicated to St. Chad
and probably collegiate.[53] In Shrewsbury itself he held a well endowed minster,
originally of 16 canonries though decayed by the Conquest, and also under the
patronage of St. Chad.[54]

There are signs that there may once have been other episcopal churches dedicated
to St. Chad in Cheshire itself. At Bettisfield and 'Burwardestone' in Dudestan
hundred the bishop had formerly held estates, lost to him by the Conquest. At
Bettisfield, a manor of 7 hides held by Earl Edwin in 1066, he claimed 2 hides
'which were the bishopric's in King Canute's time' and in 1086 the shire testified
that 'St. Chad had lost them wrongfully'. Bettisfield is one of the six townships of
the ancient parish of Hanmer (Flints.), a church dedicated to St. Chad and possibly
therefore originally held by the bishop. It may be that there as at Farndon a royal
estate had been divided between the bishop and the earl, the church being retained
by the bishop.[55] Similarly 'Burwardestone', an estate now lost but probably within
the township of Iscoed (Flints.), was the centre of a 5-hide manor held by Earl
Edwin in 1066, in which the bishop claimed 1½ hides and a salthouse. Iscoed is in
the ancient parish of Malpas, which again contains an early dedication to St. Chad,
not, it is true, the mother church but the adjacent chapelry of Tushingham. It is
possible that in that instance the earl retained the principal church with the greater
part of the estate and the bishop had a chapel to serve his much smaller manor.[56]

In Cheshire the bishop held one other important manor, Tarvin, assessed at 6
hides in 1066. Domesday mentions no church, though Tarvin was later the centre
of a large ancient parish of eleven townships, and possibly it was represented by
the priest mentioned at the episcopal estate of Burton.[57] The bishop had another
holding in the area, a small estate of 1 hide at Guilden Sutton. The interest of
those estates lies in their association with the holdings of another pre-Conquest
landowner, Thorth (*Toret*).[58] Thorth held the manor of the Tarvin township of
Ashton, which was assessed at 4 hides, making with the bishop's 6 a 10-hide unit

[51] *Dom. Surv. Ches.* 27–8; *V.C.H. Ches.* v (forthcoming).
[52] D. Sylvester, 'Rural Settlement in Ches.' *T.H.S.L.C.*
ci. 12–24; *P.N. Ches.* iii. 48; above, fig. 36.
[53] Eyton, *Antiq. Salop.* ix. 244, 256.
[54] *V.C.H. Salop.* ii. 114.
[55] Thomas, *Dioc. St. Asaph,* 820–9; *Parochialia (Arch. Camb.,* supplement, 1909–11), i. 141; 3 *Sheaf,* xiv, p. 28.
[56] Ormerod, *Hist. Ches.* ii. 592, 605–14, 619–20. The earliest mention of the dedication to St. Chad is 1349: *P.N.*

Ches. iv. 48.
[57] Ormerod, *Hist. Ches.* ii. 306. For the identification of episcopal Burton see below, Domesday translation, no. 9 and note.
[58] A Thored, perhaps the same man, held estates in Shropshire including the minster of Wroxeter: *V.C.H. Salop.* i. 299, 321, 324; Eyton, *Antiq. Salop.* vii. 309–10; below, fig. 37.

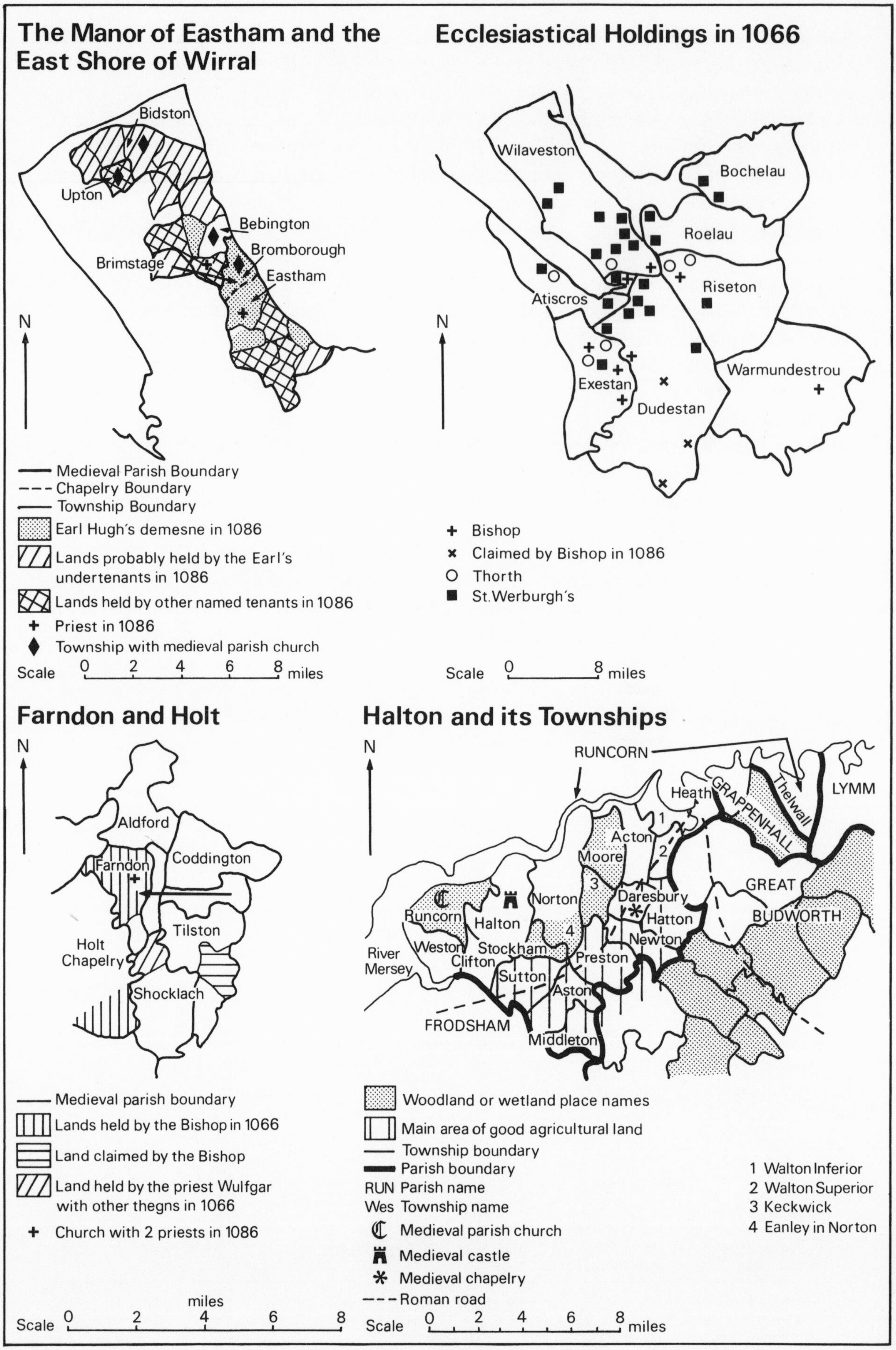

The Manor of Eastham and the East Shore of Wirral

Bidston
Upton
Brimstage
Bebington
Bromborough
Eastham

N

— Medieval Parish Boundary
– – – Chapelry Boundary
—— Township Boundary

Earl Hugh's demesne in 1086

Lands probably held by the Earl's undertenants in 1086

Lands held by other named tenants in 1086

+ Priest in 1086

◆ Township with medieval parish church

Scale 0 2 4 6 8 miles

Ecclesiastical Holdings in 1066

Wilaveston
Bochelau
Roelau
Atiscros
Riseton
Exestan
Dudestan
Warmundestrou

N

+ Bishop
× Claimed by Bishop in 1086
○ Thorth
■ St.Werburgh's

Scale 0 8 miles

Farndon and Holt

N

Aldford
Farndon
Coddington
Holt Chapelry
Tilston
Shocklach

— Medieval parish boundary

Lands held by the Bishop in 1066

Land claimed by the Bishop

Land held by the priest Wulfgar with other thegns in 1066

+ Church with 2 priests in 1086

Scale 0 2 4 6 8 miles

Halton and its Townships

RUNCORN
Heath
GRAPPENHALL
Thelwall
LYMM
Acton
Moore
Daresbury
GREAT BUDWORTH
Runcorn
Norton
Hatton
Halton
Newton
Weston
Stockham
Preston
Clifton
Sutton
Aston
FRODSHAM
Middleton
River Mersey

N

Woodland or wetland place names

Main area of good agricultural land

— Township boundary
—— Parish boundary
RUN Parish name
Wes Township name
☾ Medieval parish church
♜ Medieval castle
✳ Medieval chapelry
– – – Roman road

1 Walton Inferior
2 Walton Superior
3 Keckwick
4 Eanley in Norton

Scale 0 2 4 6 8 miles

Fig. 37.

of the kind favoured for pre-Conquest tax-assessment. He also gelded for 3 hides at Barrow, next to the bishop's small manor of Guilden Sutton, and he seems to have been closely connected with the remnants of the episcopal territories beyond the Dee.

The bishop had once had considerable lands beyond the Dee in the hundreds of Exestan and Atiscros. At Eyton, probably in Holt (Denb.),[59] and in the adjacent township of Is-y-coed (Denb.), there were two episcopal manors, each assessed at 1 hide in the reign of the Confessor but lost to the see since the Conquest. In Domesday they are grouped with Allington, in Gresford (Denb.), a manor of 3 hides held once again by Thorth. It is thus possible that the three estates though not contiguous or originally in the same parish, were treated as a single 5-hide unit for tax purposes in the mid 11th century.[60] Nearby the bishop had once had holdings valued at 1 hide at Gresford, the *caput* of a manor assessed at 13 hides in 1086 and the focus of a large medieval parish. That manor, which had a church and a priest, also belonged to Thorth in 1066 and seems to have been his largest estate, though it was then waste.[61]

The links suggest that either Thorth himself or the territories which he held had some association with the bishop. It is possible that though he is repeatedly described as a free man, he was in fact an episcopal tenant. Remarkably, the Survey records no tenants holding of the bishop in Cheshire, but that absence may be misleading and men such as Thorth were perhaps included without mention of their episcopal overlord. One possible indicator that that was so is the Domesday reference to the restoration of former holdings beyond the Dee to the bishop and all his men (*et omnibus suis hominibus*) after Gruffudd's defeat and rebellion in 1063. It has been argued that 'his men' means King Edward's but it is equally likely to mean the bishop's.[62] There are strong indications that the bishop's holdings in the area were once extensive: besides the repeated references to lost territories there is the great unhidated estate of Bistre (*Biscopestreu*), in Mold (Flints.), whose name suggests that it had once been held by a bishop, presumably the bishop of Lichfield. If so, the bishop's association with the area was probably extremely ancient.[63]

BUILDINGS, ART, AND ARTEFACTS[64]

Buildings

There are few if any traces of Anglo-Saxon structures above ground in Cheshire, except perhaps for some earthworks tentatively ascribed to the period, such as some curvilinear churchyards and the putative remains of two or three Aethelflaedan burhs.[65] Important buildings were probably made of stone, especially where it was readily available; the minsters of St. John and St. Werburgh at Chester, for example, may have been made of the friable local sandstone, already being quarried well before the Conquest for the manufacture of memorial crosses.[66] No Anglo-Saxon

[59] For the identification of Eyton see below, Domesday translation, no. 7 and note.

[60] Below, Domesday translation, nos. 7, 247–8.

[61] Thomas, *Dioc. St. Asaph*, 804–20; A. N. Palmer, 'Hist. of Old Par. of Gresford', *Arch. Cambrensis* (6th ser.), iii. 189–204; iv. 291–302.

[62] Below, Domesday translation, no. 7; *Dom. Surv. Ches.* 25.

[63] Charles, *Non-Celtic P.N.* pp. xlvi, 220; above, fig. 37.

[64] Except where otherwise indicated, references will be found under the appropriate place names in the gazetteer below.

[65] See gazetteer s.v. Alderley, Barrow, Bowdon, Bromborough, Christleton, Dodleston, Eastham, Eccleston, Farndon, Kirby, Lymm, Over, Sandbach (Hulme), Upton, Wallasey, Warburton, Warmingham, Woodchurch (churchyards); Delamere (Eddisbury), Runcorn, Thelwall (burhs).

[66] Below.

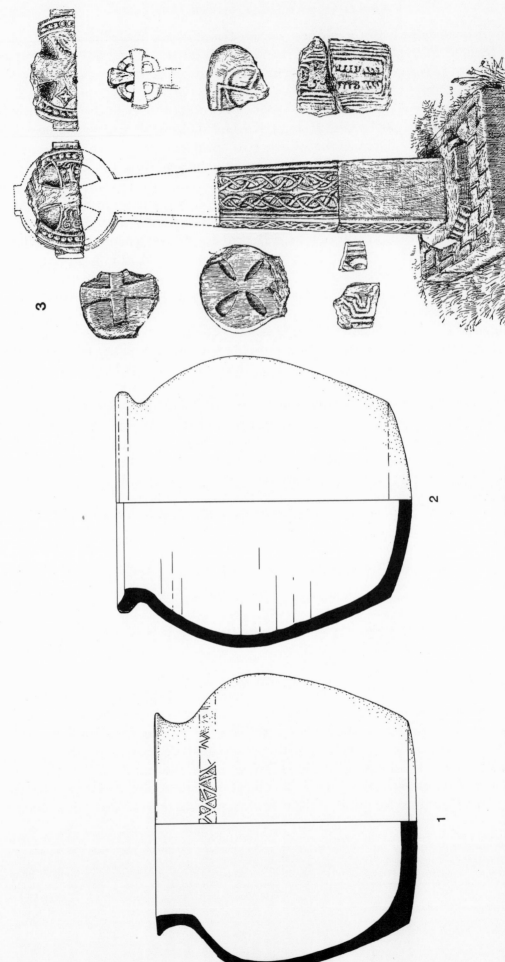

FIG. 38. 1. Chester: Castle Esplanade Hoard Pot (scale 1:2); 2. Chester: Queen's Head Hotel Pot (scale 1:2); 3. Bromborough: Cross and Fragments of Crosses and Grave Slabs, c. 1894 (scale approx. 1:20).

building masonry has been identified with certainty, however, though some may survive at Lower Bebington. Probably the most widely used material was wood, and indeed traces of several timber buildings have been discovered in the course of excavations in Chester and at one or two rural sites. The earliest structure appears to have been a large timber-framed building, dating from the late Roman or immediately post-Roman period, found in the northern part of Chester at the Abbey Green site. Another large wooden house at Tatton Park, in Knutsford, dates perhaps from the period 500-1000, though the carbon dates suggest that it is early Roman at the latest.[67] Otherwise, the remaining evidence is all from the late 9th century or after. In particular, the Lower Bridge Street site in Chester has yielded a late 9th-century sunken-featured hut and a later group of small cellared structures made of timber, wattle, and thatch, with earth and rubble ramps leading up to a first-floor entrance. The buildings, which appear to have been arranged in a rectilinear fashion were perhaps private dwellings or workshops planned when Aethelflaed refortified Chester. They resemble other Viking-age structures in Dublin and York and are probably of the 10th century.[68]

Inside the Roman fortress itself the surviving architecture was that of the main Roman public buildings, such as the *principia* and the great bath-house.[69] Some robbing had already taken place before 1066. In the centre of the city, for example, a substantial timber building, running parallel to what is now Princess Street, was constructed over the remains of a large Roman courtyard building behind the *principia*. It had rough sandstone paving made from Roman rubble in which were set several small post-holes, and seems to have survived until the Conquest.[70]

Sculpture

Sculptural remains are much more numerous, though relatively little survives from the pre-Viking period. Much of the sculpture is in the form of crosses and cross fragments, which vary from the large and monumental, adorned with numerous figured scenes, to the small and humble enriched with only the simplest abstract ornament. Often associated with significant ancient churches, many crosses were located within churchyards, which sometimes, as at Bromborough, Overchurch, and West Kirby, took the form of curvilinear enclosures. Most were presumably memorial stones from cemeteries. A few, however, were outstanding large-scale monuments, of the type which, in the early period in particular, were associated with important ecclesiastical centres, and which probably served to provide a focus of prayer and to commemorate the great and the holy. Yet others, usually simpler and plainer, were erected in remote moorlands or by ancient trackways, perhaps to serve as landmarks, wayside crosses, or boundary marks.[71]

That Anglo-Saxon Cheshire once contained a considerable number of such monuments, many of some size and grandeur, is suggested by evidence that in the Chester area alone there were until their destruction by puritan iconoclasts in the early 17th century at least seven large crosses of squared stone built 'by reverent

[67] Inf. from Dr. Higham. For further discoveries in 1985 see below, gazetteer.

[68] Above, 'Impact of Scandinavians'; Mason, *Excavations at Lower Bridge St.*

[69] *J.C.A.S.* lxvii. 17-36.

[70] Above, 'Impact of Scandinavians'; *Medieval Arch.* xxv. 167.

[71] G. F. Browne, 'Early Sculptured Stones of Ches.' *Arch. Jnl.* xliv. 146-56; J. R. Allen, 'Early Christian Monuments of Lancs. and Ches.' *T.H.S.L.C.* xlv. 1-32a; J. D. Bu'Lock,

'Pre-Norman Crosses of W. Ches. and Norse Settlements Around the Irish Sea', *T.L.C.A.S.* lxviii. 1-11; T. D. Kendrick, 'Late Saxon Sculpture in N. Eng.' *Jnl. Brit. Arch. Assoc.* 3rd ser. vi. 1-19; C. Green, 'Some Stone Monuments', *T.L.C.A.S.* lvi. 114-20; T. Pape, 'Round-Shafted Pre-Norman Crosses of N. Staffs. Area', *Trans. N. Staffs. Field Club*, lxxx. 25-49; D. Sylvester, *Hist. Atlas of Ches.* 14-15; W. G. Collingwood, *Northumbrian Crosses of Pre-Norman Age*, 5-9, 141-2; R. Cramp, *Corpus of A.-S. Sculpture*, i (1), 1-4; fig. 36.

antiquity' and reputedly some 24 ft. high. Three stood in the churchyards of Barrow, Christleton, and Eccleston and were said in 1614 to have been wrought with 'divers costly and curious marks'. The other four, which stood in Tarvin, Eccleston, Delamere Forest,[72] and at Vicar's Cross in Christleton, were simply described as stone pillars on stepped stone bases. They were not associated with churches and in 1614 were regarded as boundary marks, objects of devotion to wayfarers, or even as sites where business could be transacted. Some or even all of those monuments may have been Anglo-Saxon; with the possible exception of those at Vicar's Cross and Delamere Forest, they occur in churchyards and townships which may be plausibly credited with an Anglo-Saxon past, and in some instances they are in ancient significant places. Moreover, the 17th-century description, with its emphasis on antiquity and on curious carvings, also suggests an early date.[73]

The earliest surviving crosses in Cheshire, the great pair in the market place at Sandbach, are also the grandest, and are of a kind associated with important pre-Viking ecclesiastical enclosures. In the Middle Ages Sandbach was the centre of a large parish with dependent chapelries at Goostrey and Church Hulme, and its church may once have had rights over an even larger territory. The interweaving of Middlewich parish with Goostrey, Church Hulme, and Sandbach suggests that they were all originally part of a single unit, and the fact that the early mother church of Middlewich was located in a settlement known significantly as Newton, points to Sandbach rather than Middlewich as originally the dominant church within that unit. Sandbach church was mentioned in the Domesday Survey, and in the 12th century its patron was the earl of Chester, a further indication of its importance. It has been suggested that it was an early minster.[74]

Almost nothing is known about the scale of such important early churches or of the buildings associated with them. One thing, however, is clear: they were often associated with considerable groups of sculptured crosses.[75] While most are likely to be gravestones and memorials from the cemeteries pertaining to the churches, they might include a few large and impressive monuments, like the two principal crosses at Sandbach. Re-erected on their original site in 1816, after their dismemberment, probably by puritan iconoclasts, in the 17th century, those crosses have long stood outside the churchyard, though not far from the church. The north cross, which stands almost to its original height of c. 16 ft., was originally surmounted by a head of which only the base remains. On the east side it was adorned with scenes from the life of Christ, including the adoration of the magi (?), crucifixion, nativity, transfiguration, and Christ between two saints, possibly Peter and Paul.[76] The west face is less well preserved, but those sections which can be identified include scenes from the passion, such as Christ led away to be scourged and Simeon of Cyrene bearing the cross. The other two, narrower, faces, comprise to the south an inhabited vine-scroll and to the north many small panels with single figures, possibly a depiction of Pentecost, but more probably saints connected with Sandbach. The south cross, which is more badly damaged, is smaller and stands now to a height of 10 ft. 9 in. It is surmounted by a cross head too slight to have been part of the

[72] Ormerod marks a headless cross on the map of Delamere Forest: *Hist. Ches.* ii, opposite p. 107. The base and 2 portions, of uncertain date, are said to survive today: inf. from Mr. Turner.

[73] P.R.O., STAC 8/21/6. Thanks are due to Mr. Turner for the reference.

[74] C. R. Radford, 'Pre-Conquest Sculpture at Sandbach', *Ches. Historian*, vii. 1–6; *Sandbach Crosses* (H.M.S.O. guide, 1956); *P.N. Ches.* ii. 264; G. Ormerod, *Introductory Memoir on the Ches. Domesday Roll* (1851), 7–9; *E.H.R.* xxxviii. 497.

[75] e.g. St. Alkmund's, Derby: *Derb. Arch. Jnl.* xcvi. 26–61; Leek (Staffs.): *Trans. N. Staffs. Field Club*, lxxx. 25–49; below.

[76] It has been suggested that Peter and Paul may have been the original patrons of the minster: *Ches. Historian*, vii. 2–3.

original structure. At the bottom of the west side is a scene which may represent the final resurrection, and on the east a network of small panels containing men and beasts. The narrow north and south sides again have panels with single figures.

The two surviving crosses are very similar in style and, perhaps, iconography. Parallels have been drawn with other Mercian crosses, such as that at Wolverhampton (Staffs.), and also with crosses in Yorkshire and Lancashire. In style they are undoubtedly late Anglian and may be assigned to the 9th century. They are accompanied by other fragments, probably of the same period, including the remains of at least one other sculptured cross shaft of similar size.[77]

Another early piece of sculpture to survive in Cheshire is a fragment which belongs to a purely English context and which seems originally to have come from the now demolished church at Overchurch. The stone is inscribed in Anglo-Saxon runes with the words 'The people (or army) erected a monument; pray for Aethelmund'. Though the man so commemorated is otherwise unknown, he was probably of some importance; his monument is unique in being dedicated by a community. The stone, which may be a fragment of a shrine-shaped tomb, is decorated on the top with knot-work ending in a zoomorphic terminal regarded as 'typical of 9th-century Mercian art'.[78]

Two other carvings, made of the local red sandstone and probably from Chester, may also be pre-Viking. They are adorned with interlace and animal motifs characteristic of the west Midlands and indicative of West Saxon rather than Scandinavian influence. The stones are probably fragments of a grave slab and a recumbent tombstone and are of the mid 10th century or earlier.[79]

Evidence of a different and distinctively Anglo-Viking school of carving comes from Thornton le Moors church, where there was a cross adorned with figure sculpture, not of the best work and dating from the late 10th or early 11th century. The surviving fragment of the shaft has on one side a panel with three standing figures, perhaps representing the arrest of Christ, and on the other a single figure wearing a short flared tunic, paralleled on Viking sculptures and thought to represent contemporary Viking dress. One of the narrower sides is ornamented with interlace and the other with a fragmentary inscription, + GOD HELPE, which is placed vertically, a departure from the norm which perhaps indicates Welsh influence.[80]

Anglo-Viking figure sculpture also survives on three fragmentary crosses at Neston church. All are adorned with similar cable mouldings, key pattern, and interlace, and hence are from a single workshop, though all seem to come from separate monuments. The scenes are both sacred and secular. The smallest fragment, from the top of a shaft, bears on one side an angel and on the other two naked men, fighting with daggers. A second piece, from the lower part of a shaft, depicts a priest carrying a chalice and vested in pointed chasuble, full triangular alb, and maniple, a subject which had also been treated at Winwick (Lancs.). The third and largest fragment, which now forms the lintel of a window in the tower, consists of the base of a shaft and has two scenes on the side that is visible. The lower and larger one consists of two men on horseback, carrying large spears crossed as if they are jousting, while the upper one is of two quadrupeds, one in pursuit of the other. The whole could perhaps depict a hunt. Two further fragments of a cross

[77] Radford, *Sandbach Crosses*; *Ches. Historian*, vii. 1–6; Ormerod, *Hist. Ches.* iii. 98–9; Bu'Lock, *Pre-Conquest Ches.* 45–7; above, plates.

[78] *Vikings in Eng.* (1982 exhibition cat.), 47; Bu'Lock, *Pre-Conquest Ches.* 48–9; fig. 40.1.

[79] T. D. Kendrick, 'Two Saxon Sculptures from Ches.' *Brit. Mus. Quarterly*, xiv. 35–6.

[80] M. M. Brown, D. B. Gallagher, and J. Higgitt, 'Anglo-Viking Cross Shaft from Thornton le Moors, Ches.' *J.C.A.S.* lxvii. 23–30; fig. 40.3.

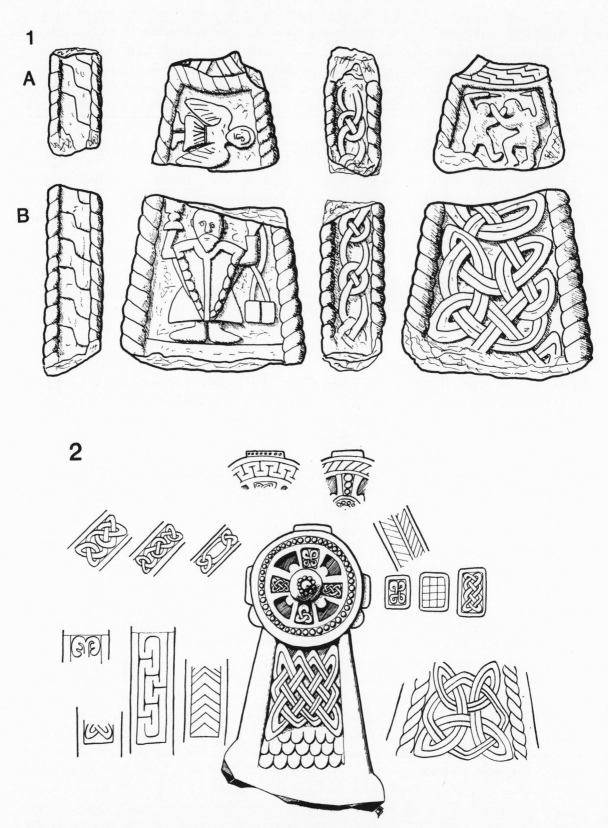

FIG. 39. Anglo-Saxon Grave Crosses: 1. Neston (scale approx. 1:15. The two fragments are not necessarily part of a single cross); 2. Chester, St. John's Church (scale 1:12).

shaft and a portion of a circle-head are again from the same workshop, though much cruder. They bear only rough interlace and cable moulding.[81]

The Neston crosses are contemporary with and related to a group of circle-headed crosses which occur in areas of Viking settlement along the western seaboard between Anglesey and Cumbria, with especially large concentrations in Cumberland, west Cheshire, and Flintshire. The group is characterized by cross heads adorned with a connecting ring forming a continuous circle superimposed over the cross arms, and may be further divided into regional subgroups. The examples from Cheshire and Flintshire make especial use of key patterns and pellets and have unpierced spandrels between the cross arms, while those from Cumbria are generally decorated with plait and have pierced spandrels. Among the Cheshire crosses a further subdivision, the product of a single workshop, has been isolated and associated with St. John's, Chester, where most exemplars of the type are preserved, including a late unfinished one. The workshop seems also to have been active in Wirral. At West Kirby and Hilbre, for example, crosses have been discovered which resemble those at St. John's closely enough to suggest that they were made there or by craftsmen from there, and other related items have been found associated with the churches of Neston, Bromborough, and Woodchurch.[82] The finest surviving example of the entire Cheshire group, is Maen Achwyfan, in Whitford (Flints.), a cross 16 ft. tall and richly adorned with interlace, crude carvings of men and animals, and Norse-style chain-pattern.[83] A fragment from Chester, probably by the same mason, suggests that there was once a similar monument there, and it is possible that the 12-ft. cross, covered with 'curious cuttings', which stood outside Wallasey church until its destruction in the 17th century, was a further related example.[84]

Most such monuments, where their location is known, are associated with a church, like the great crosses at Sandbach. In many instances, such as Thornton le Moors, Neston, Bromborough, and Woodchurch, the churches were recorded in Domesday and had extensive medieval parishes, and hence, arguably, were early ecclesiastical centres of some importance. Other similar churches elsewhere in Cheshire, including Frodsham, Prestbury, Bowdon, and Astbury, have also produced fragments of sculpture, and it looks as if they were often like St. John's associated with workshops. That was certainly so at similar churches in neighbouring parts of Staffordshire; Alstonfield and Leek, for example, both important ancient mother churches though not mentioned in Domesday,[85] were associated with considerable groups of pre-Conquest sculpture, and Alstonfield like St. John's had an unfinished piece, a clear indication that sculpture was produced there.[86]

Other churches where sculpture has been discovered were also clearly ancient, though perhaps of lesser importance. West Kirby, which has produced a hogback and some 11th-century grave covers as well as fragments of several crosses, had a church by 1081 and probably from the 10th century. It perhaps benefited from the shrine of St. Hildeburgh, located in its chapelry nearby on the island of Hilbre, where a further cross and a grave slab have been discovered.[87] Wallasey, too, though

[81] R. Bailey, *Viking Age Sculpture*, 102, 155, 231–2; Bu'Lock, *Pre-Conquest Ches.* 82–3; *T.H.S.L.C.* xlv. 31–2; fig. 39.1; above, plate.

[82] *T.L.C.A.S.* lxviii. 1–11; Bailey, *Viking Age Sculpture*, 177–82; figs. 38.3, 39.2.

[83] E. Owen, *Old Stone Crosses of the Vale of Clwyd*, 138–48; Collingwood, *Northumbrian Crosses*, 141, 143–4, 149; *Arch. Camb.*, 5th ser. viii. 74–6; lxxxi. 36–47; xcix. 333–4; *T.L.C.A.S.* lxviii. 7; R.C.H.M. Wales and Mon. ii. 95–6.

[84] *T.L.C.A.S.* lxviii. 7; 'Robinson's *Acct. of Wallasey in 1720*', ibid. xliii–xliv. 17.

[85] They were both in Totmonslow hundred, where only 1 priest was recorded and there seems to have been some defect in the ecclesiastical information provided.

[86] *Trans. N. Staffs. Field Club*, lxxx. 25–49; J. Sleigh, *Hist. of Ancient Par. of Leek* (2nd edn. 1883), 11–12, 41.

[87] W. G. Collingwood, in *W. Kirby and Hilbre*, ed. Brownbill, 14–26.

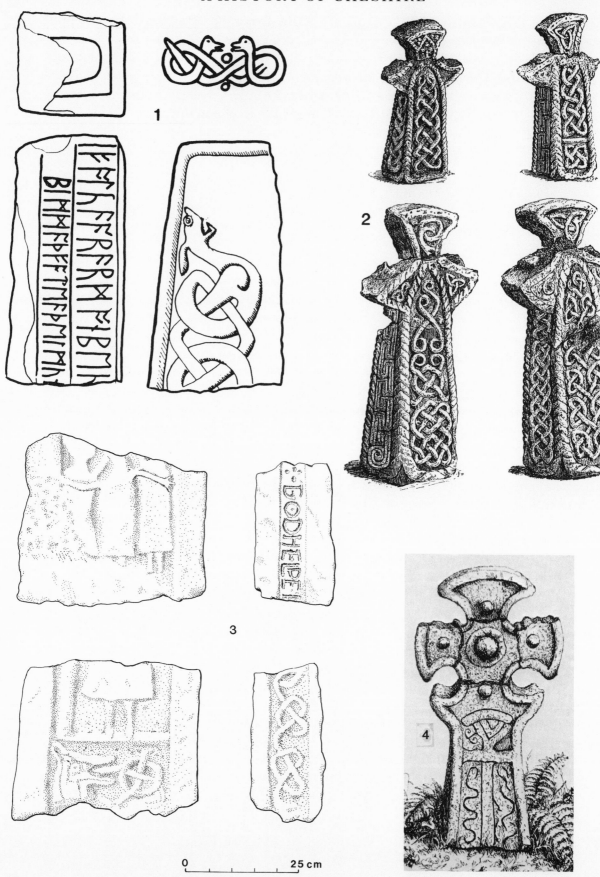

FIG. 40. Anglo-Saxon Sculptured Stones and Cross Fragments: 1. Upton in Overchurch: Pre-Viking Sculptured Stone (scale approx. 1:8); 2. Disley: Cross Heads, preserved at Lyme Hall (scale approx. 1:8); 3. Thornton-le-Moors: Cross Shaft (scale approx. 1:15); 4. Cheadle: Cross (scale approx. 1:10).

a small parish was probably an ancient one, and so may have been Over with its dedication to St. Chad and its curvilinear churchyard.[88] In such instances, as at West Kirby, the sculpture may have been imported or the work done by craftsmen from a nearby workshop.

There are some important exceptions to the pattern. The Maen Achwyfan cross is at a crossroads, not by a church, though it is within the ancient parish of Whitford, which with its eight townships and its dedication to St. Beuno, looks like an early ecclesiastical centre of some importance.[89] More exceptional is a group of round-shafted crosses found in east Cheshire, especially near Macclesfield, and elsewhere in the Peak, in Staffordshire and Derbyshire. In Staffordshire, those crosses, at Alstonfield, Leek, Ilam, Chebsey, and Stoke-on-Trent, are in churchyards, but in Cheshire they were usually erected in open moorland, beside trackways, at cross-roads, and at boundaries, often in positions of considerable prominence.[90] Cleulow cross, in Wincle (Prestbury parish), for example, was on a mound and formed a notable landmark at the head of the valley. It was also at the crossing of the Congleton–Buxton and Macclesfield–Wincle roads and near the boundary of the townships of Wincle and Sutton Downes.[91] The Greenway cross, in Oakenclough (Sutton township, Prestbury parish) was located on the edge of Wildboarclough, the valley of Clough brook. Probably such sites were typical, though many crosses have been moved from their original position. Another curious feature is the frequent occurrence of pairs of crosses: the Bow Stones in Lyme Handley (Prestbury parish), Robin Hood's Picking Rods in Ludworth (Derb.), and the paired bases at Disley church, in Stockport parish, are notable examples.[92] The crosses are of distinctive design: the main portion of the shaft, which is cylindrical, is surmounted by a smaller four-sided section, marked off by a swag or collar and sometimes adorned with interlace; in the Peak District there are also one or two raised bands between the cylindrical and squared parts. The whole originally terminated in a cross head, a feature almost always missing from the Cheshire examples. It has been suggested that such monuments were intended to serve as landmarks and aids to devotion, but their original function remains uncertain.

Pottery

Cheshire seems to have been largely aceramic from the immediate post-Roman period until the 10th century, except for a certain amount of imported ware from Gaul and the Mediterranean, found at Chester, and for exotic items such as the souvenir flask from the shrine of St. Menas found at Meols.[93] By the later 10th century, however, pottery occurs in Chester itself and in very small quantities on one or two rural sites, such as the Cistercian grange near Ellesmere Port and Tatton Park in Knutsford. Though sherds of other types of pottery, including Stamford ware, have been found, it is mostly Chester-type ware, a fine, hard, sandy-textured, unglazed fabric, generally grey at the core but varying on the surface from a reddish-brown, produced by oxidization, to a dark grey or sooty black, the result of burning after firing.[94] Sherds of such ware are ubiquitous in Chester, having been found at almost every site excavated since the early 1950s within the walls and along the line of Foregate Street.[95] Most pieces are from jars,

[88] Above, 'Sub-Roman Ches.'

[89] Thomas, *Hist. Dioc. St. Asaph*, 487; Owen, *Old Stone Crosses*, 138–48.

[90] *Trans. N. Staffs. Field Club*, lxxx. 25–49; *T.L.C.A.S.* lvi. 114–20; Collingwood, *Northumbrian Crosses*, 5–9; Bu'Lock, *Pre-Conquest Ches.* 84; *T.L.C.A.S.* xxxii. 264–9.

[91] *P.N. Ches.* i. 165–6; fig. 41.2.

[92] Earwaker, *E. Ches.* ii. 314; *Trans. N. Staffs. Field Club*,

lxxx. 39; *T.L.C.A.S.* xxxii. 266–7; fig. 41.3.

[93] Above; see gazetteer s.v. Chester (Abbey Green, Lower Bridge St.); *J.C.A.S.* xliii. 48–9.

[94] *Ches. Arch. Bull.* iii. 3; J. A. Rutter, in Mason, *Excavations at Lower Bridge St.*

[95] The most notable exception is the Northgate Brewery site.

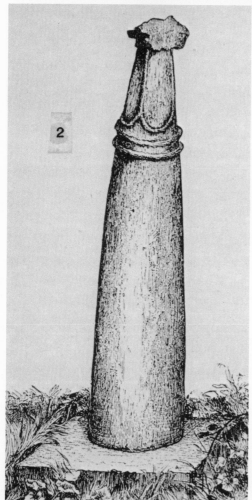

FIG. 41. Anglo-Saxon Cylindrical Shafted Crosses: 1. Macclesfield, West Park: Cross Shafts (scale approx. 1:24); 2. Cleulow Cross, Wincle (scale approx. 1:24); 3. Bow Stones, Lyme Handley (scale approx. 1:20).

often impressed with a band of characteristic lattice decoration on the shoulder, but spouted pitchers, fragments of bowls, and lamps or possibly lids have also been found.[96] Up to 1985 three impressive, largely complete vessels have been discovered. The first was in Foregate Street in 1938, but was not identified as Chester ware until the discovery in 1950 at Castle Esplanade of the broken jar which established a date for the currency of the material and from which it was named. The third remarkably undamaged jar was discovered at the Princess Street site in 1981. Particularly large assemblages of sherds were recovered from Princess Street (1979–81) and Abbey Green (1975–8), while at Crook Street an important pit group was found in 1974.[97] Chester-type ware is distributed throughout western Mercia and along the Marches, with finds in Gloucester, Worcester, Hereford, Shrewsbury, Leintwardine (Herefs.), Lichfield (Staffs.), and Stafford. It occurs as far east as Derbyshire, where sherds have been found at Barton Blount.[98] There have also been finds in Dublin, in the Fishamble Street area on the Wood Quay excavation, probably exported there from Chester.[99] It is, therefore, the only ware on the western side of the country, where smaller amounts of pottery were in circulation, to have as broad and sophisticated a distribution range as the contemporary Thetford, Torksey, and St. Neots types in the east. Up to 1985 the only centre of production to have been discovered was at Stafford, where three kilns have been excavated.[1] Chester-type ware seems to have begun to circulate in the early 10th century and to have continued in common use throughout the west Midlands at least until the mid 11th. Both in Cheshire and elsewhere the pottery seems to occur almost exclusively in urban contexts; up to 1985, the very rare finds in rural Cheshire have been matched by a total absence of the ware in rural Herefordshire, Worcestershire, and Gloucestershire.[2] The life span of Chester ware in Chester itself has not been determined. One rim-sherd not conforming to the normal types may represent an unusually late example, but as elsewhere no clear evidence of survival into the Norman period has been found.[3]

Metalwork

Relatively little sub-Roman or Anglo-Saxon metalwork has been found in Cheshire. Such as there is comes from two main locations, Chester and Meols, though stray finds have been made elsewhere. An important hoard of bronze vessels, including three cauldrons of a type produced in the Rhineland, was deposited at Halkyn (Flints.) in the late Roman or sub-Roman period.[4] A 6th-century Anglo-Saxon brooch, possibly from a burial, is said to have been found 'in Deeside' (Flints.) in the 19th century.[5] Otherwise the only stray finds outside the two major sites are the bronze mount found near Nantwich and the gold finger-ring from Middlewich. No weapons have been found, apart from a scramasax from Chester, though the Delamere Forest dagger and the Saxfield hoard may have been Anglo-Saxon.[6]

[96] *Ches. Arch. Bull.* iii. 3–4; P. Carrington, in *Medieval Pottery from Excavations in NW.* ed. P. J. Davey, 16; Mason, *Excavations at Lower Bridge St.*

[97] *Medieval Pottery from NW.* 14–17; fig. 38.1–2; above, plate.

[98] Mason, *Excavations at Lower Bridge St.*; inf. from Mr. M. O. Carver.   [99] Inf. from Mrs. Rutter.

[1] *Medieval Arch.* xx. 169–71; xxviii. 239–40; *W. Midlands Arch.* xvii. 67; xviii. 55–6; xx. 73; xxiv. 101–10; xxv. 96–105; xxvi. 49–65.

[2] The urban nature of the distribution may be more apparent than real, however, and reflect only the predominantly urban location of excavations up to 1985.

[3] *Medieval Pottery from NW.* 14; Mason, *Excavations at Lower Bridge St.*

[4] *Antiq. Jnl.* xxxvi. 194–5; *J.C.A.S.* lix. 50–1; *Archaeologia*, xiv. 275, plate XLIX; C. F. C. Hawkes, in *Aspects of Arch. in Britain and Beyond*, ed. W. F. Grimes, 172–99, esp. 188. It should be noted that the other basins associated with the bowls could be considerably earlier: inf. from Dr. Lloyd-Morgan.

[5] *J.C.A.S.* lix. 50–1.

[6] See gazetteer s.v. Chester (Abbey Green), Frodsham (Manley), Northenden (Saxfield).

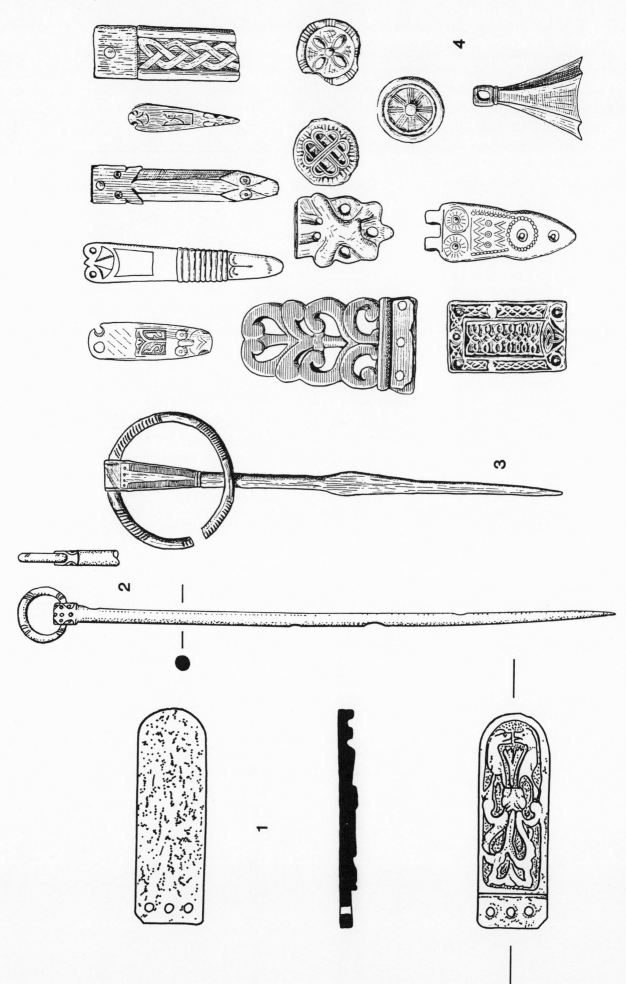

FIG. 42. Anglo-Saxon Bonework and Metalwork from Chester and Meols: 1. Chester, Whitefriars: Bone Plaque; 2. Chester, Crook St.: Ringed Pin; 3. Meols: Ringed Pin; 4. Meols: Metal Strap-Ends and Mounts (all scale 1:1).

At Chester there is evidence of metalworking at the Lower Bridge Street site, where a stone mould for casting ingots was found in association with industrial waste and a smelting hearth. Nevertheless, up to 1985 the city has yielded only a modest collection of finds. Brooches include a 9th-century roundel of silver alloy from Lower Bridge Street, and later examples showing Scandinavian influence, such as the 10th-century disc brooch from Princess Street and fragments of penannular brooches from the Castle Esplanade hoard. Pins include one related to late 6th-century Irish exemplars and an important group of four 10th- or 11th-century copper alloy ringed pins, of an Irish type much favoured by the Vikings.[7] The fragment of a silver ring found at Northgate brewery may also be from a similar pin. Other miscellaneous items include 8th- or 9th-century bronze hooked tags from Greyfriars Court and Princess Street and a Viking-age gold finger-ring from St. Werburgh's Street.

At Meols the abandoned beach market at Dove Point, though yielding little Dark Age pottery, has produced a considerable number of small pieces of metalwork ranging in date from Roman and post-Roman to late Anglo-Saxon and beyond. Finds from the early period, which include penannular and annular brooches and belt fittings, are relatively few, though coins such as the 8th-century sceattas and 9th-century Northumbrian stycas suggest that by then the market had significant trading contacts outside Mercia. Later finds are much more numerous, and indicate a more substantial trading post in the 10th and 11th centuries, though the absence of coins from the earlier 10th century when the Chester mint was at the height of its activity is very curious. By then the community may have been producing rather poor quality small metal items locally, including ringed pins showing Hiberno-Norse influence and perhaps some of the cruder zoomorphic buckles.[8]

Bone Working

There is evidence for a horn, antler, and bone working industry at Abbey Green, Chester, where there were pits, perhaps used for soaking, and an associated sluice, all containing such waste as cow horn cores and bone blanks for making combs. The same site also produced flint flakes and worked deer-antler tips, perhaps used as tools, and a bone plaque ornamented with the tree of life design.[9] Bone items from elsewhere in Chester include another plaque, a comb, and pins.[10]

Leather Working

Fragments of leather, the remains of a tanning and leather working industry flourishing throughout the 11th century, were found at Lower Bridge Street, Chester, where some of the cellars of the wooden buildings were re-used in the processing. The south-west corner of the city seems to have remained a centre of lighter leather crafts such as glove making and leather dressing throughout the Middle Ages.[11]

Glass

Very few glass items have been found, only the sherd and glass implement from Chester and beads from Hilbre Island and Deeside.[12]

[7] See gazetteer s.v. Chester (Crook St., Deanery Field, Foregate St., Linenhall St.); fig. 42.2.

[8] *T.H.S.L.C.* cxii. 1–28; cxiii. 197–201; *Jnl. Merseyside Arch. Soc.* i. 19–42; Hume, *Ancient Meols*; fig. 42.

[9] *J.C.A.S.* lxiii. 31.

[10] See gazetteer s.v. Chester (Foregate St., Lower Bridge St., Whitefriars).

[11] Mason, *Excavations at Lower Bridge St.*

[12] *J.C.A.S.* lix. 50–1.

GAZETTEER OF ANGLO-SAXON SITES AND FINDS

ALDERLEY, NETHER

St. Mary's church (SJ 841 761). Curvilinear churchyard.[13]

ASTBURY

ASTBURY. St. Mary's church (SJ 847 616). Pink sandstone fragment of cylindrical cross shaft carved with scroll; two further fragments, possibly architectural, with Anglo-Saxon foliage. In church.[14]

MORETON CUM ALCUMLOW. Great Moreton Hall (SJ 840 595). Steps of possible Anglo-Saxon cross in front of hall. Removed *c.* 1806.[15]

BARROW

St. Bartholomew's church (SJ 469 684). Curvilinear churchyard with large carved cross, now lost but possibly Anglo-Saxon.[16]

BEBINGTON

BEBINGTON, LOWER. St. Andrew's church (SJ 333 839). South wall of nave may incorporate some stones of Anglo-Saxon church.[17]

STORETON. Quarries (SJ 156 843). Produced distinctive good quality cream-white stone used locally by Romans and later by Anglo-Saxons for sculpture at Neston and West Kirby and perhaps for foundations of Bebington church. Quarries continued to be used throughout Middle Ages and beyond. Destroyed.[18]

BOWDON

St. Mary's church (SJ 759 869). (a) Fragments·of sculpture, one with interlace, another with ecclesiastic vested in chasuble and stole. In church.[19] (b) Curvilinear churchyard, where coin of King Edmund found 1853. Coin lost.[20]

BROMBOROUGH

St. Barnabas's church (SJ 349 822). Curvilinear churchyard.[21] Three 10th-11th-century fragments including circle-head and portions of shaft decorated on all sides with interlace, incorporated into cross in 1958. Found together with fragments of several other crosses and grave slab in 1863 at demolition of church, itself built of stones from earlier, probably Norman, church demolished in 1828. Most of fragments lost in 1934.[22]

BURTON

Burton Point (SJ 303 736). Earthwork, possibly Viking-age, associated with 29 male burials, discovered *c.* 1886.[23]

CHEADLE

(Findspot unknown) Late 10th- or 11th-century cross with fan-shaped arms and crude incised volutes found 1875. In Cheadle Town Hall. With it was found circular stone shaft, like those in Macclesfield Park. Lost.[24]

CHESTER

(Findspot unknown). Portion of cross shaft with interlace, related to Whitford cross and dating from 10th-11th century. Grosvenor Mus.[25]

(Findspot unknown). Red sandstone fragments of top of shaft and grave slab with animal carving, probably from Chester and dating from before *c.* 950. B.M.[26]

[13] Kenyon, 'Arch., P.N., and Settlement', chap. i, table 4.

[14] G. Cartlidge, *Newbold Astbury and its Hist.* 26-7; Cramp, Ches. index; *Hist. Congleton*, ed. W. B. Stephens, 15.

[15] Ormerod, *Hist. Ches.* iii. 46.

[16] P.R.O., STAC 8/21/6; inf. from Mr. Turner and Dr. Laing.

[17] Ches. Sites and Mon. Rec. 9/AR.082 1.

[18] *T.H.S.L.C.* xlix. 56-60; Merseyside County Mus., Sites and Mon. Rec. 3083.03

[19] Inf. from Dr. Higham and Dr. J. D. Bu'Lock; Cramp, Ches. index.

[20] M. Morris, *Medieval Manchester, Arch. of Greater Manchester*, i, ed. P. Holdsworth, 13; Kenyon, 'Arch., P.N.,

and Settlement', chap. i, table 4.

[21] G. Chitty, *Wirral Rural Fringes Survey Rep.* 8, 11.

[22] *T.H.S.L.C.* xlv. 27-8, plate xiii; xlvii. 242-3; P. Sulley, *Hundred of Wirral*, 207-8; *T.L.C.A.S.* lxviii. 10-11 (A 10, D 5, 17); fig. 38.3.

[23] Sulley, *Hundred of Wirral*, 170; Laing, *Dark Ages of W. Ches.* 55-7.

[24] Earwaker, *E. Ches.* i. 185-6; Collingwood, *Northumbrian Crosses*, 177, fig. 221; *Arch. Jnl.* xliv. 151; *T.L.C.A.S.* xxxvii. 95-109; fig. 40.4.

[25] *T.L.C.A.S.* lxviii. 11 (C 2).

[26] *B.M. Quarterly*, xiv. 35-6; Bu'Lock, *Pre-Conquest Ches.* 47-8; Cramp, Ches. index.

(Findspot unknown). Glass implement of Viking period, used for pressing seams of linen and presumed to have been found at Chester. Location unknown.[27]

Abbey Green (SJ 404 666). Timber-framed building, altered in the late Roman or sub-Roman period, metalled road with small pebbles running parallel to defences and dating from 10th century or later, and pits showing traces of horn, antler, and bone working industry, found 1975–7. Small finds include sherds of 'B' ware amphorae (2nd–6th-century) and Stamford ware (10th–11th-century), over 600 sherds of Chester ware, annular bronze brooch (possibly 5th–8th-century), bone plaque with interlace decoration, and scramasax. All in Grosvenor Mus.[28]

Amphitheatre (SJ 408 662). Portion of grave slab with incised cross, found 1936. Grosvenor Mus.[29]

Castle Esplanade (SJ 403 660). Broken Chester ware pot with roller stamped decoration on shoulder, containing over 500 coins dating from *c.* 900 to 975 and over 140 pieces of silver bullion, including hacksilver bearing Hiberno-Norse ornament, found 1950. Deposited *c.* 970 × 980. Bullion in Grosvenor Mus., coins divided between Grosvenor and British Museums, except for 50–100 dispersed, probably with other pieces of bullion.[30]

City Wall, engineering yard near Northgate (SJ 403 666). Sherd of Chester ware, found 1980. Grosvenor Mus.[31]

City Wall, near south-east angle tower (SJ 407 662). Portion of circle-head cross found in core of wall in 1937. Grosvenor Mus.[32]

Commonhall St., Crypt Court (SJ 403 661). Sherds of Chester ware representing several pots, found 1954. Grosvenor Mus.[33]

Crook St. (a) SJ 403 663. Sherds of Chester ware found 1964. Grosvenor Mus.[34] (b) SJ 404 663. Important group of sherds of Chester ware from single pit and copper alloy ringed pin of Hiberno-Norse type, found 1973–4. Grosvenor Mus.[35]

Deanery Field (SJ 405 666). Copper alloy ringed pin of Hiberno-Norse type, found 1935. Grosvenor Mus.[36]

Duke St., Drill Hall (SJ 407 660). Sherd of Chester ware, found 1983. Private ownership.[37]

Eastgate St., 97 Eastgate Row (SJ 406 663). Coin hoard of 43 silver pennies of Kings Edred, Eadwy, and Edgar, deposited *c.* 960 × 980. Found 1857. Grosvenor Mus.[38]

Foregate St., nos. 46–50 (SJ 408 663). Portion of bone comb, found 1961. Grosvenor Mus.[39]

Foregate St. (SJ 407 663). Copper alloy ringed pin of Hiberno-Norse type, found 1954. Grosvenor Mus.[40]

Foregate St., near Queen's Head Hotel (*c.* SJ 41 65). Pot, possibly Saxon, found 1938. Grosvenor Mus.[41]

Goss St. (SJ 405 663). Bronze hooked tag and a few sherds of Chester ware, found 1973. Grosvenor Mus.[42]

Greyfriars Court (SJ 402 661). Bronze hooked tag, small collection of Chester ware and coin of Edward the Confessor, found 1976–81. Grosvenor Mus.[43]

Grosvenor St. (SJ 404 660). Sherd of Chester ware found 1985. Grosvenor Mus.[44]

Linenhall St. (SJ 403 663). Sherds of Chester ware and copper alloy ringed pin of Hiberno-Norse type, found 1961–2. Grosvenor Mus.[45]

Lower Bridge St. (SJ 405 666). Late 9th-century timber hut and five 10th-century sunken-featured timber structures, excavated 1974–6. Finds include later 9th-century silver alloy brooch in form of openwork roundel, sherds of 8th–9th-century Carolingian vessel, over 180 sherds of Chester ware, ingot mould, bone pin, glass sherd, and fragments of leather indicating 11th-century tanning industry. All in Grosvenor Mus.[46]

Nicholas St. (SJ 403 661). Sherd of Chester ware found 1957 against north wall of Roman interval tower. Another sherd found on adjacent site in 1974. Grosvenor Mus.[47]

Northgate Brewery (SJ 403 667). Little if any Chester ware. Fragment of silver ring, perhaps from ring-headed pin, found 1973–5. Grosvenor Mus.[48]

Old Market Hall (SJ 404 665). Sherds of Chester ware, found 1967–70. Grosvenor Mus.[49]

Old Palace Yard (SJ 408 660). Sherds of Chester ware, found in 1976. Grosvenor Mus.[50]

[27] H. Shetelig, *Viking Antiquities of Gt. Britain and Ireland*, iv. 69–70. Though Shetelig locates it in the Grosvenor Mus. there is no trace of it there.

[28] *J.C.A.S.* lxiii. 15–31.

[29] Ibid. xxxvi. 157; *T.L.C.A.S.* lxviii. 11 (D 16, fig. 6).

[30] *T.L.C.A.S.* lxi. 190–2; *Antiq. Jnl.* xxxiii. 22–32; *Brit. Numismatic Jnl.* xxvii. 125–60; *Medieval Pottery from NW.* 12–13; *Vikings in Eng.* 76 (E 18); fig. 38.1; above, plate.

[31] *Ches. Arch. Bull.* vii. 42.

[32] *J.C.A.S.* xxxvi. 157; *T.L.C.A.S.* lxviii. 11 (B 7).

[33] *Ches. Arch. Bull.* iii. 3; *J.C.A.S.* xlvi. 58–60, fig. 14, nos. 1–8.

[34] *J.C.A.S.* lvi. 13; *Medieval Pottery from NW.* 16.

[35] *Medieval Pottery from NW.* 14–17; *Ches. Arch. Bull.* iii. 3–4; *Medieval Arch.* xix. 220, plate xvi C; *Vikings in Eng.* 75 (E 14); fig. 42.2.

[36] *Liverpool Annals*, xxiii. 37, plate 9, no. 8.

[37] Inf. from Mrs. Rutter.

[38] *Brit. Numismatic Jnl.* xxiv. 47–9; xxxvii. 126.

[39] *J.C.A.S.* li. 18, fig. 13, no. 3.

[40] Ibid. xlv. 72.

[41] Ibid. xxxvi. 88, 158–9; xlvi. 60; *Antiq. Jnl.* xxxiii. 1; *Medieval Pottery from NW.* 16–17; fig. 38.2.

[42] *Medieval Pottery from NW.* 16; *Ches. Arch. Bull.* ii. 15; inf. from Dr. Lloyd-Morgan.

[43] Inf. from Mr. Ward and Mrs. Rutter.

[44] Inf. from Mrs. Rutter.

[45] *J.C.A.S.* xlix. 59–60; *Medieval Arch.* vi–vii. 306.

[46] Mason, *Excavations in Lower Bridge St.*; *Ches. Arch. Bull.* iii. 19–21; *Vikings in Eng.* 76 (E 19).

[47] *J.C.A.S.* xlix. 8; *Medieval Pottery from NW.* 16.

[48] *Medieval Pottery from NW.* 16; inf. from Dr. Lloyd-Morgan.

[49] *J.C.A.S.* lvi. 11.

[50] Inf. from Mrs. Rutter; *Ches. Arch. Bull.* v. 33.

Pemberton's Parlour (SJ 402 666). Coin hoard of 122 silver pennies, almost all of Edgar, Edward II, and Ethelred II, deposited c. 980. Grosvenor and British Museums.[51]

Princess St./Hunter's Walk. (a) SJ 404 664. Small sunken-featured and long timber building, both 10th- or 11th-century, excavated 1978-82. Small finds include open-work disc brooch with Borre-Jellinge style animal ornament, dating from earlier 10th century, and found under patch of rubble from ruination of Roman building near sunken-featured hut; also intact Chester ware pot, large collection of Chester ware sherds, whetstone, and bronze hooked tag. All in Grosvenor Mus.[52] (b) SJ 40 66. Bronze pin, possibly late 6th-century and related to Irish exemplars, found 1939. Grosvenor Mus.[53]

St. John's church (SJ 409 366). (a) Red sandstone sculptural fragments of 10th and 11th centuries, main group comprising complete circle-headed cross in two fragments, three other cross heads, and portions of two shafts (one lost). Related material includes two further cross heads, one unfinished, a grave slab (lost), and fragments of interlace (lost). All surviving stones in church.[54] (b) Coin hoard of c. 40 coins, all of early 10th century and none later than 920, found just W. of church in 1862. Fifteen coins identified in private ownership, rest lost.[55]

St. Werburgh St. (SJ 405 664). Viking-age twisted gold finger-ring, found 1851. Grosvenor Mus.[56]

Watergate St. (SJ 404 663). Sherd of Chester ware, found 1985. Grosvenor Mus.[57]

Weaver St. (SJ 403 661). Sherd of Chester ware, found 1956. Grosvenor Mus.[58]

Whitefriars, SW. angle-tower (SJ 403 660). Decorative bone plaque with tree of life design forming tag-end for belt, found 1964. Grosvenor Mus.[59]

CHESTER, ST. MARY-ON-THE-HILL PARISH (RURAL PORTION)

CLAVERTON. Heronbridge (SJ 40 64). Rim-sherd of handmade pottery, possibly early Anglo-Saxon. Grosvenor Mus.[60]

CHESTER, ST. OSWALD'S PARISH (RURAL PORTION)

BRUERA. St. Oswald's church (SJ 438 606). Carved stones, possibly Anglo-Scandinavian, built into inside arch of south doorway.[61]

CHRISTLETON

St. James's church (SJ 441 658). Curvilinear churchyard with large sculptured cross, lost but possibly pre-Norman.[62]

DELAMERE

EDDISBURY (SJ 553 693). Rebuilding of original Iron Age rampart may be 10th-century. Occupation floor provided much pottery originally identified as Anglo-Saxon. Hut high up in silting of inner ditch was attributed to 8th century.[63] A recent re-examination of the published evidence assigns material to Iron Age.[64]

DODLESTON

St. Mary's church (SJ 362 609). Curvilinear churchyard.[65]

EASTHAM

St. Mary's church (SJ 361 800). Curvilinear churchyard.[66]

ECCLESTON

St. Mary's church (SJ 412 627). Curvilinear churchyard with large carved cross, now lost but possibly pre-Norman.[67]

FARNDON

St. Chad's church (SJ 412 545). Curvilinear churchyard.[68]

---

[51] Above, 'Late A.-S. Ches.'; *Numismatic Chron.* 4th ser. xx. 141-65; *Antiq. Jnl.* xxxiii. 25, plan.

[52] Above, 'Impact of Scandinavians', 'Scandinavian Settlement', 'Buildings, Art, and Artefacts'; *Medieval Arch.* xxv. 167; xxvii. 170, plate 14a; inf. from Mrs. Rutter, Mr. Ward; above, plates.

[53] *J.C.A.S.* xxxiv. 39, plate 10, no. 10; inf. from Dr. Lloyd-Morgan.

[54] *T.L.C.A.S.* lxviii. 10-11 (B 1-6, D 9-11, 15); fig. 39.2.

[55] *J.C.A.S.* [1st ser.], ii. 289-308; *Brit. Numismatic Jnl.* xxxvi. 36-9.

[56] Shetelig, *Viking Antiquities*, iv. 30; *Ches. Arch. Bull.* i. 6; Watkin, *Roman Ches.* 206; *Vikings in Eng.*

[57] Inf. from Mrs. Rutter and Mr. Ward.

[58] *J.C.A.S.* xlvi. 72.

[59] Inf. from Dr. Lloyd-Morgan; fig. 42.2.

[60] *J.C.A.S.* lix. 51.

[61] Inf. from Mr. S. R. Williams and Mr. O. Bott.

[62] P.R.O., STAC 8/21/6; Kenyon, 'Arch., P.N., and Settlement', chap. i, table 4.

[63] *T.H.S.L.C.* cii. 1-68, esp. 23-8, 59-63, plate 8, fig. 9; *J.C.A.S.* lvi. 14; *T.L.C.A.S.* lxxii. 23-5.

[64] Kenyon, 'Arch., P.N., and Settlement', chap. i, pp. 50 sqq.

[65] Ibid., chap. i, table 4.

[66] Ibid.

[67] Laing, *Dark Ages of W. Ches.* 20, 23-4; P.R.O., STAC 8/21/6; above, plate.

[68] Inf. from Dr. Laing.

ANGLO-SAXON CHESHIRE

FRODSHAM

FRODSHAM. St. Laurence's church (SJ 521 773). Fragments of figure sculpture and grave slab with incised circle-head set into inside wall of tower.[69]

MANLEY (SJ 51 72). Dagger, found 1825 and then supposed, probably wrongly, to be Anglo-Saxon. Formerly in custody of Scottish Society of Antiquaries, but lost in 1985.[70]

GRAPPENHALL

LATCHFORD (SJ 631 876). Dug-out canoe of Anglo-Scandinavian type, found 1930. Seven similar canoes found in river Mersey and riverbank 1893-1933, several associated with primitive fish-traps made of stakes. (Findspots: SJ 599 866, 601 865, 607 864, 610 877, 612 877, 633 866.) All in Warrington Mus.[71]

HILBRE ISLAND

SJ 184 879. (a) Bead of blue glass with yellow and green ornament, perhaps 7th-century. Found on supposed site of island cemetery in 1865. Merseyside County Museums.[72] (b) Red sandstone cross head, resembling those at St. John's, Chester, found 1852. Grosvenor Mus.[73] (c) Grave slab, late 11th-century and found on supposed site of island cemetery in 1864. Charles Dawson Brown Mus.[74]

KIRBY, WEST

KIRBY, WEST. (a) St. Bridget's church (SJ 218 864). Curvilinear churchyard.[75] Sculptured stones, including three fragments of two cross heads of St. John's type, two fragments of cross shafts, one possibly earlier than cross heads, other late. All found when early church was demolished in 1869. Charles Dawson Brown Mus. (b) Findspot unlocated. Hogback tombstone of greyish sandstone, probably 11th-century. Charles Dawson Brown Mus.[76]

MEOLS. Dove Point (c. SJ 23 90). Abandoned beach head trading post buried beneath sand-dunes and eroded in 19th century. Between 1817 and 1920 local antiquaries made large collections of finds, most of which were eventually deposited in local museums. Finds unstratified and very difficult to date, but overall they suggest trading post existing in Roman and sub-Roman times and flourishing in 10th and 11th centuries, under Hiberno-Norse influence. Market possibly connected with lead mining at Halkyn Mountain. Surprisingly no sub-Roman or Anglo-Saxon pottery, within collections of post-Roman material taken from site, except for St. Menas flask, but numerous pieces of metalwork, especially in lead, and coins. Early material includes sub-Roman bronze penannular brooches and possibly buckle-plates, and early Saxon annular brooches and belt fittings. More abundant later Anglo-Saxon (i.e. 8th-11th-century) items include faceted and disc-headed pins, usually of bronze, though one of silver, strap ends and mounts, some decorated with animals, palmettes, or interlace, and a bronze bell. Material showing Hiberno-Norse influence includes important group of bronze ringed pins, generally similar to those from Chester, though some probably pre-Viking Irish and one paralleled at cemetery at Birka (Sweden); also bronze mounts with decoration in Ringerike style. Other items include zoomorphic buckles of two types, all probably 9th-12th-century, and some 19 coins: 2 silver sceattas of c. 725, 3 Northumbrian copper stycas of c. 850, and remainder from reigns of Edgar, Ethelred II, Cnut, Harthacnut, and Edward the Confessor (i.e. 973-1066). Many finds lost, but much remaining in Grosvenor Mus. (especially in Potter and Longueville collections) and in Merseyside County Museums (chiefly in Mayer and Ecroyd Smith collections). Other finds in Warrington Mus. and Williamson Art Gallery and Mus., Birkenhead, and a few still in private ownership.[77]

KNUTSFORD

Tatton Park (SJ 756 813). Early Roman or Anglo-Saxon timber 'long-house' and associated smaller building, fences, and palisades; sherd of Chester-type ware. Further complex of early medieval buildings, including a large timber-framed structure discovered nearby in 1985.[78]

[69] *T.L.C.A.S.* lxviii. 8, 11 (D 18); P. Thompson, *Frodsham: the Arch. Potential of a Town*, 5; Pevsner and Hubbard, *Buildings of Eng.: Ches.* 221.

[70] Ormerod, *Hist. Ches.* ii. 106; *T.L.C.A.S.* xxiv. 124; inf. from Nat. Mus. of Antiquities of Scot.

[71] *Antiq. Jnl.* vi. 136 sqq.; *T.L.C.A.S.* xlvii. 16-26; *T.H.S.L.C.* xlvi. 97-106; xlviii. 1-28, esp. 9-10; *NW. Naturalist*, vi. 47-8; Ches. Sites and Mon. Rec. 1/AR.127 1-9.

[72] *Jnl. Merseyside Arch. Soc.* i. 25 (no. 14); *J.C.A.S.* lix. 50; *T.H.S.L.C.* xviii. 210-11; Bu'Lock, *Pre-Conquest Ches.* 35; Hume, *Ancient Meols*, 162.

[73] *T.H.S.L.C.* xv. 233-4; *T.L.C.A.S.* lxviii. 10 (B 8); Collingwood, in *W. Kirby and Hilbre*, 14; Hume, *Ancient Meols*, 267.

[74] *T.H.S.L.C.* xxiii. 42; xlv. 30, plate xv; *T.L.C.A.S.* lxviii. 11 (D 14); Collingwood, in *W. Kirby and Hilbre*, 22; Sulley, *Hundred of Wirral*, 245.

[75] Chitty, *Wirral Rural Fringes*, 8-9.

[76] Collingwood, in *W. Kirby and Hilbre*, 14-26; *T.L.C.A.S.* lxviii. 10-11 (B 9-10, 6-8, 13); *Arch. Jnl.* xliv. 146.

[77] *T.H.S.L.C.* cxii. 1-28; cxiii. 197-201; *Jnl. Merseyside Arch. Soc.* i. 19-42; *J.C.A.S.* xliii. 48-9; Hume, *Ancient Meols; Vikings in Eng.* 75 (E 13); G. D. B. Jones, 'Arch. and Coastal Change in NW.', *Arch. and Coastal Change*, ed. F. H. Thompson, 93, 95-7 (reference supplied by Dr. Kenyon); fig. 42.

[78] *Ches. Arch. Bull.* ix. 90; inf. from Dr. Higham.

LYMM

St. Mary's church (SJ 682 868). Curvilinear churchyard.[79]

MIDDLEWICH

Findspot unknown. Gold finger-ring, similar in construction to Viking-age rings but possibly earlier, found on site of Roman settlement in 1971. Grosvenor Mus.[80]

NANTWICH

Findspot unknown. 8th- or early 9th-century bronze mount found just outside Nantwich and probably from horse harness. Private ownership.[81]

NESTON

St. Mary's and St. Helen's church (SJ 292 774). Portions of at least three and probably five crosses, including three with figure sculpture. All 10th–11th-century. All in church or built into belfry.[82]

NORTHENDEN

Saxfield (SJ 825 900). Weapons reputedly Anglo-Saxon, found in early 19th century. Lost.[83]

OVER

St. Chad's church (SJ 634 663). Remains of curvilinear churchyard within present churchyard. Fragment of rectangular cross shaft ornamented with interlace.[84]

PRESTBURY

ADLINGTON. Adlington Hall Garden (SJ 905 803). Anglo-Scandinavian cylindrical cross shaft moved and re-used as sundial in early 18th century.[85] Another cylindrical shaft stood nearby until 1950s, when moved to the Mount, Prestbury.[86]

FALLIBROOME (SJ 897 751). Anglo-Scandinavian cylindrical cross shaft of buff sandstone, at township boundary and near junction on B 5087. Moved slightly when road was widened in 1935.[87]

LYME HANDLEY. The Bow Stones (SJ 974 813). Pair of cylindrical Anglo-Scandinavian cross shafts set in twin base standing beside old ridgeway between Disley and Macclesfield. Perhaps originally pillars belonging to Disley cross heads and socket stone and moved from Disley common.[88]

MACCLESFIELD. (a) St. Michael's church (SJ 918 737). Two fragments of rectangular cross shafts, one carved with ring-interlace similar to Disley cross. Two fragments of cylindrical cross shafts. All in church.[89] (b) West Park (SJ 911 741). Remains of three cylindrical Anglo-Danish cross shafts, two formerly at Ridge Farm, Sutton. One ornamented with interlace related to rectangular cross shafts in St. Michael's church and Disley cross heads.[90]

MACCLESFIELD FOREST (SJ 978 714). Two portions of socket stone of cylindrical shafted cross, built into field wall and moved slightly from their former position.[91]

PRESTBURY. (a) St. Peter's church (SJ 901 769). Three cross fragments, two of upright rectangular shaft and one of cross head. Shaft fragments much worn but carved with just discernible figures clothed in tunics, their arms outstretched, and various quadrupeds. Cross head with interlace. Under glass case in churchyard.[92] (b) The Mount (SJ 901 797). Anglo-Scandinavian cylindrical cross shaft of pink gritstone, formerly next to sundial in Adlington Hall gardens, but moved to present site in 1950s.[93]

RAINOW. (a) Eddisbury Hill (SJ 943 734). Bank and ditch on township boundary in defensible situation, possibly Anglo-Saxon.[94] (b) Blue Boar Farm (SJ 971 765). Fragment of cylindrical cross shaft in garden wall. Not *in situ* but near supposed site.[95]

SUTTON. (a) Greenway Cross (SJ 956 693). Rough roundish shaft slab having cross within circle at the top.[96] (b) Ridge Hall Farm (SJ 940 705). Site of cylindrical cross shafts removed to Macclesfield Park in 1857.[97]

[79] Kenyon, 'Arch., P.N., and Settlement', chap. i, table 4.

[80] Inf. from Dr. Lloyd-Morgan.

[81] *Ches. Arch. Bull.* ix. 101–2.

[82] Bailey, *Viking Age Sculpture*, 102, 155, 231–2; *T.L.C.A.S.* lxviii. 7; *T.H.S.L.C.* xxvii. 88–94; xlv. 31–2, plate xvi; R. H. White, *Pre- and Post-Norman Stones at Neston* (forthcoming); above; fig. 39.1; above, plate.

[83] Ormerod, *Hist. Ches.* iii. 611; *P.N. Ches.* i. 236.

[84] Laing, *Dark Ages of W. Ches.* 30.

[85] Ches. Sites and Mon. Rec. 5/AR.370 0.

[86] Below, Prestbury (Prestbury: the Mount).

[87] Inf. from Mr. Turner.

[88] *Antiquity*, xi. 294–9; *Trans. N. Staffs. Field Club*, lxxx. 39; *P.N. Ches.* i. 199; Earwaker, *E. Ches.* ii. 285, 314; Collingwood, *Northumbrian Crosses*, 5–8; S. Marshall, 'The Bowstones of Lyme Handley', *T.L.C.A.S.* lxxviii.

65–74; Ches. Sites and Mon. Rec. 5/AR.166 0; fig. 41.3.

[89] Ches. Sites and Mon. Rec. 5/AR.114 2; Cramp, Ches. index.

[90] *Trans. N. Staffs. Field Club*, lxxx. 38–9; *T.L.C.A.S.* xxxii. 264, 268; Ches. Sites and Mon. Rec. 5/AR.115 0; Cramp, Ches. index; fig. 41.1.

[91] Ches. Sites and Mon. Rec. 5/AR.112 1.

[92] Ibid. 5/AR.125 1; *Jnl. Brit. Arch. Assoc.* 3rd ser. vi. 9; J. S. Croston, 'A.-S. Cross at Prestbury', *Reliquary*, xxv. 1–9; Cramp, Ches. index.

[93] Ches. Sites and Mon. Rec. 5/AR.372 0.

[94] Ibid. 5/AR.379 0.

[95] Ibid. 5/AR.383 0.

[96] *P.N. Ches.* i. 153; Earwaker, *E. Ches.* ii. 449.

[97] Above, Prestbury (Macclesfield: West Park).

ANGLO-SAXON CHESHIRE

UPTON (SJ 897 751). Fragment of cylindrical cross shaft, *c.* 6 ft., built into stone wall. Similar to three shafts at Macclesfield Park.[98]

WINCLE. (a) Cleulow Cross (SJ 952 674). Well-preserved Anglo-Scandinavian cylindrical shafted cross of red sandstone, standing on mound near township boundary and crossroads.[99] (b) Wincle Grange (SJ 955 654). Site of cylindrical cross shaft until *c.* 1880. Shaft now in Swythamley (Staffs.).[1]

RUNCORN

PRESTON ON THE HILL (SJ 565 813). St. Menas flask. Stray find of early medieval flask more likely to have been brought back in post-medieval rather than Anglo-Saxon period. Norton Priory Mus.[2]

RUNCORN. Castle Rock (SJ 508 833). Earthworks and ditch, possibly remains of Aethelflaedan burh. Destroyed in 1868.[3]

THELWALL. (a) SJ 655 875. Two arms of earthen bank, possibly remains of Aethelflaedan burh. (b) SJ 655 874. Another earthen bank, also possibly remains of burh.[4]

SANDBACH

HULME, CHURCH. St. Luke's church (SJ 759 608). Curvilinear churchyard.[5]

SANDBACH. (a) Market Place (SJ 761 608). Two large pre-Viking sculptured crosses on stepped base, one bearing cross head from another smaller cross. Large headstone built into cross base. (b) St. Mary's churchyard (SJ 759 608). Three fragments from shaft of at least one other cross of similar size and date to those in Market Place, all much worn but two with figure sculpture and angle cable moulding still discernible. Two pre-Viking fragments of tomb slabs with figure and animal carving. All formerly built into cross base in Market Place but removed to churchyard in 1956.[6]

STOCKPORT

DISLEY. (a) SJ 984 835. Pair of 11th-century red sandstone cross heads, ornamented with interlace and plaits, and originally attached to cylindrical cross shafts, perhaps Bow Stones. Found at Black Farm, Disley, *c.* 1845. At Lyme Hall.[7] (b) SJ 974 844. Socket stone of twin cylindrical shafted crosses, found 1958. Probably base of Bow Stones. At Disley church.[8]

STOKE

STANNEY, GREAT. Grange Cow Worth (SJ 411 754). Sherds of Chester ware. Grosvenor Mus.[9]

SWETTENHAM

St. Peter's church (SJ 801 672). Small circular slab with wheelhead-style cross raised in relief. Found during restoration of church in 1846 and built into inside wall.[10]

THORNTON LE MOORS

St. Mary's church (SJ 441 745). Inscribed and sculptured late 10th- or early 11th-century cross fragment, found 1982. In church.[11]

UPTON IN OVERCHURCH

SJ 264 889. (a) Curvilinear churchyard, disused since 1813.[12] (b) Pre-Viking sculptured stone with runic inscription, possibly fragment of shrine-tomb. Found 1863 at demolition of church and probably from early church demolished in 1813. Grosvenor Mus., on extended loan to Williamson Art Gallery and Mus.[13]

---

[98] Earwaker, *E. Ches.* ii. 345; Collingwood, *Northumbrian Crosses*, 8; *T.L.C.A.S.* lvi. 119; *Trans. N. Staffs. Field Club*, lxxx. 38; Ches. Sites and Mon. Rec. 5/AR.038 0.

[99] Above; Earwaker, *E. Ches.* ii. 435; *P.N. Ches.* i. 165–6; Ches. Sites and Mon. Rec. 5/AR.099 0; fig. 41.2.

[1] Earwaker, *E. Ches.* ii. 433; *Trans. N. Staffs. Field Club*, lxxx. 37–8.

[2] Inf. from Mrs. B. Noake.

[3] J. H. Hanshall, *Hist. of Co. Palatine of Chester*, 418; W. Beamont, *Hist. of Castle of Halton*, 4–5; C. Nickson, *Hist. of Runcorn*, 8–13.

[4] Ches. Sites and Mon. Rec. 1/AR.141 0.

[5] Kenyon, 'Arch., P.N., and Settlement', chap. i, table 4.

[6] Above; Radford, *Sandbach Crosses*; *Ches. Historian*, vii.

1–6; above, plates.

[7] Earwaker, *E. Ches.* ii. 101, 313; *Arch. Jnl.* v. 337; *Trans. N. Staffs. Field Club*, lxxx. 39; *T.L.C.A.S.* xxix. 216–17; lxxviii. 65–74; Ches. Sites and Mon. Rec. 5/AR.164 0; above, Prestbury (Lyme Handley); fig. 40.2.

[8] *T.L.C.A.S.* lxviii. 142; lxxviii. 65–74; Ches. Sites and Mon. Rec. 5/AR.168 0; above, Prestbury (Lyme Handley).

[9] *Medieval Arch.* xi. 263; *J.C.A.S.* lviii. 79, fig. 5.1.

[10] Ches. Sites and Mon. Rec. 8/AR.072 2.

[11] Above; *J.C.A.S.* lxvi. 23–30; fig. 40.3.

[12] Chitty, *Wirral Rural Fringes*, 8, 11.

[13] Above; R. M. V. Elliot, in *Melanges de linguistique et de philologie: Fernand Mosse*, 140–7; *T.H.S.L.C.* xliii–xliv. 305–20; xlv. 26; *Vikings in Eng.* 47 (C 6); fig. 40.1.

WALLASEY

St. Hilary's church (SJ 296 921). Church stands on large curvilinear green. Churchyard had large sculptured cross, possibly Anglo-Saxon, until 17th century. Base perhaps large socket stone found when rectory enlarged.[14]

WARBURTON

St. Werburgh's church (SJ 697 896). Curvilinear churchyard.[15]

WARMINGHAM

St. Leonard's church (SJ 709 611). Curvilinear churchyard.[16]

WOODCHURCH

Holy Cross church (SJ 275 868). Curvilinear churchyard. Plain 10th- or 11th-century circle-head cross.[17]

YEARDSLEY CUM WHALEY

The Dipping Stone (SJ 996 817). On former county boundary. Stone base with two sockets for twin cylindrical cross shafts.[18]

[14] *T.L.C.A.S.* lxviii. 7; *T.H.S.L.C.* xliii–xliv. 17, 31; xlvii. 241; Chitty, *Wirral Rural Fringes*, 8–9.
[15] Kenyon, 'Arch., P.N., and Settlement', chap. i, table 4.
[16] Ibid.
[17] *P.N. Ches.* iv. 266–7; Chitty, *Wirral Rural Fringes*, 8, 11; *T.L.C.A.S.* lxviii. 11 (D 12).
[18] *Antiquity*, xi. 294–9; *Athenaeum*, 9 July 1904, 562; *T.L.C.A.S.* lvi. 114. Yeardsley cum Whaley has been in Derb. since 1936.

DOMESDAY SURVEY

COMPILATION

THE DOMESDAY Survey[1] was compiled for two main reasons: to discover what the king's own resources were, or should have been, and to find out what land was held by others and what it was worth. The decision to make the inquiry was made at the Christmas Council 1085 and the work was completed in the course of 1086. Domesday Book may in fact have been ready before William left England for the last time in the autumn of that year. Contemporary sources provide a little information about the way the inquiry was conducted but our knowledge of its methods depends largely on the internal evidence of the text itself and of the so-called Domesday satellites, that is, texts that derive from earlier stages of the inquiry.[2] Though there is no independent evidence of the preliminary stages of the inquiry in Cheshire and the account of that shire in the Survey gives few clues to the way it was compiled, there is no reason to doubt that much the same procedure was followed as in other, better documented, shires.

Each shire was surveyed and described separately. It has been argued that shires were grouped in circuits for the purposes of collecting information and that in each circuit the work was supervised by a group of royal commissioners. There is, however, no direct evidence for such circuits. Their existence and composition has been deduced from similarities and differences in the treatment of the several shires. It has, for example, been generally agreed that Cheshire, together with its appendixes dealing with Atiscros hundred and the land between Ribble and Mersey, belonged to the same west Midland circuit as Shropshire, which immediately precedes it in Domesday Book. The arrangement of the manorial entries in both shires is almost identical, but very different from that followed in neighbouring Derbyshire and other shires of the supposed northern circuit. In Cheshire and Shropshire most entries begin with the name of the current owner and then give, in order, the name of the place, the undertenant or tenants, if any, the name of the pre-Conquest owner, and the assessment. In Derbyshire, Nottinghamshire, Yorkshire, Lincolnshire, and Huntingdonshire, separate entries do not normally name the current owner; that information is given in headings before each fief. In those shires most manorial entries begin with the place name and then give the pre-Conquest tenants and the assessment, undertenants being named at the end of each entry.[3]

It has been claimed that Cheshire and Shropshire formed part of a large western circuit that also included Herefordshire, Gloucestershire, and Worcestershire, in all of which the manorial entries follow the same general pattern.[4] There are, however, significant differences between the Domesday accounts of those shires. The Shropshire Domesday never mentions meadow for which information is given

[1] Thanks are offered to Mr. P. H. W. Booth, Dr. N. J. Higham, Dr. H. M. Jewell, Dr. D. Kenyon, Mrs. J. I. Kermode, and Dr. C. P. Lewis for much helpful advice on earlier drafts of this chapter.
[2] V. H. Galbraith, *Making of Dom. Bk.*; *E.H.R.* lxxxvi.
753-73.
[3] *Dom. Rebound* (H.M.S.O. 1954).
[4] A. Ballard, *Dom. Inquest*, 12; *V.C.H. Salop.* i. 304; for an attempt to introduce Staffs. into the circuit see *Speculum*, xii. 1-15.

in many entries in Cheshire and other shires.[5] That alone suggests that the inquiry in Shropshire was not conducted by the same people as in Cheshire. Another difference is that the extent of woodland in Shropshire is often expressed in terms of the number of swine it could support, a method that is never used in Cheshire.[6] There are also differences in the way information about ploughlands is given. In Cheshire it is normally in the form 'terra est *x* carucis'. That formula is also used in Shropshire but in many manors alternatives are used, such as 'et adhuc *x* carucae plus possent esse' after the number of ploughs at work has been stated. Such a form is used once in Cheshire, twice in Gloucestershire, and more frequently in both Herefordshire and Worcestershire. The Cheshire form 'terra est *x* carucis' occurs only once in Gloucestershire, as an interlineation, twice in Worcestershire, and occasionally in Herefordshire.[7] There are further differences in the way the status of pre-Conquest tenants is described. In Cheshire the forms are 'liber homo fuit', '*N* tenuit ut liber homo', and '*N* liber homo tenuit'. The same forms also occur in Shropshire but there are also variants such as 'liber cum hac terra' and the like. In the three southern shires of the supposed western circuit such clauses are replaced by forms of the type 'poterat ire quo volebat', which is found once each in Shropshire and Cheshire.[8]

Those and other differences clearly illustrate the compilers' acceptance of variation upon which Round and others have commented.[9] They also suggest that each shire was in fact surveyed separately. The similarities between shires reflect not the process of collection but a later stage in which the information was edited in preparation for the compilation of the final text of Domesday Book. There is good evidence elsewhere for the preparation of such draft surveys covering several shires. One has survived for the south-western shires in a manuscript known as *Liber Exoniensis*, while that prepared for the eastern shires of Essex, Norfolk, and Suffolk now forms the second volume of Domesday Book.[10] It is therefore possible that the western shires of Worcestershire, Gloucestershire, Herefordshire, Shropshire, and Cheshire, and perhaps Staffordshire as well, were edited as a group. Some features of the descriptions of the boroughs of Chester, Shrewsbury, Worcester, and Hereford certainly imply that they were not dealt with separately. For example, they all include information about the payments made by moneyers when the currency was changed, which is otherwise mentioned in the descriptions only of Lewes (Suss.) and of the Dorset boroughs.[11]

There is little doubt that at the final draft Shropshire and Cheshire were edited together. While the description of most shires begins on a separate quire or gathering of the manuscript, Cheshire shares a quire with Shropshire. The arrangement of the Cheshire folios in two quires is illustrated in the diagram.

The most natural explanation of the arrangement is that the scribe wrote the account of Cheshire after finishing Shropshire, but left some space for later additions, one of many indications that the text was being written before the inquiry was complete.[12] At least one textual detail supports the suggestion that Cheshire was written after Shropshire. Though at the beginning of the description of Shropshire the scribe occasionally used the form 'terra est *x* carucis', up to f. 257 the alternative,

[5] Below; *Dom. Geog. of N. Eng.* ed. H. C. Darby and I. S. Maxwell, 359; *Dom. Geog. of Midland Eng.* ed. H. C. Darby and I. B. Terrett (2nd edn. 1971), 141–2.

[6] *Dom. Geog. of Midland Eng.* 136–7.

[7] Ibid. 15, 68–9, 124, 232–3.

[8] For Salop. see *V.C.H. Salop.* i. 309–49.

[9] J. H. Round, *Feudal Eng.* (1964 edn.), 31, 34, 77; F. W.

Maitland, *Dom. Bk. and Beyond*, 8; H. C. Darby, *Dom. Eng.* 69, 139, 176–7; R. W. Finn, *Intro. to Dom. Bk.* 41.

[10] Galbraith, *Making of Dom. Bk.* 4–7, 102–22.

[11] no. 1d and n. 10.

[12] *E.H.R.* lxvi. 561–4; *Dom. Rebound*, esp. 22–4 and appendix 1.

┌— 260, with the last part of Shropshire
├— 261, blank
│ ┌— 262, recto blank; verso has description of Chester
│ └— 263 Cheshire
├— 264 Cheshire
└— 265 Cheshire
┌— 266 Cheshire
├— 267 Cheshire
│ ┌— 268, recto has the end of Cheshire, including the salt-wiches; verso has
│ │ the first column blank, and the beginning of Atiscros hundred in the second
│ │ column
│ └— 269, recto Atiscros hundred; verso Between Ribble and Mersey
├— 270, recto end of Between Ribble and Mersey; verso blank
└— 271, blank

'x carucae plus possent esse', is more common.[13] On f. 257, however, the alternative form is used less often, and after that never. Similarly, the longer form 'liber cum hac terra' is used only twice after f. 256v. and does not occur in Cheshire.[14] Such changes imply that half way through writing out the account of Shropshire the scribe decided, or was instructed, to use the shorter forms where possible, perhaps to save both space and time. The lack of rulings in that section of Domesday Book may be yet another indication that it was one of the last parts to be written. It is certainly one of the sparsest; apart from the description of Chester and the salt-wiches there is virtually no additional information of the kind that enlivens the accounts of every other shire.

The Cheshire Domesday offers few clues to the sources of the information which it contains. Some details were presumably supplied by landholders or their agents but there are no significant differences between fiefs. The uniformity of the secular fiefs could perhaps result from the fact that they were all held under the earl, but it is remarkable that the descriptions of the manors of the bishop and St. Werburgh's have the same order, content, and forms as the others. Whatever variety there may have been in the information supplied it was all reduced to common form. For the same reason it is impossible to say what role local juries played. There are a few references to the testimony of the shire, showing that on some matters it was consulted, but there is no mention of any hundredal verdicts. It is, however, clear that the hundreds did play an important role in the inquiry. The hundreds in which manors lay are regularly indicated. There are a few mistakes: Puddington is described as in Warmundestrou hundred instead of Wilaveston in no. 226, and Burton may have been placed wrongly in Riseton hundred.[15] There are also some omissions. The most serious has led to the assumption that Dudestan hundred had two detached areas, one in Roelau hundred and the other in Riseton.[16] Those are the only examples of detached parts of other Cheshire hundreds and they seem to be simply the result of the omission of hundredal rubrics. The fact that one of the supposedly detached parts of Dudestan hundred included Rushton, the place from which Riseton hundred appears to have derived its name, is particularly indicative of such an omission, and a rubric referring to that hundred should presumably have been placed before no. 52. The same heading was elsewhere placed too low,

---

[13] Darby, *Dom. Eng.* 347.
[14] The occurrences of the longer form are as follows: Dom. Bk. ff. 254 (4), 254v. (1), 255 (3), 255v. (2), 256v. (1), 258v.
(1), 259 (1).
[15] no. 9 and n. 20.
[16] *Dom. Surv. Ches.* 13–14.

making no. 250 appear to belong to Dudestan hundred, while the other apparently detached part of Dudestan hundred, in Roelau hundred, presumably results from the omission of a hundredal rubric before no. 235. Other omissions have been generally accepted, namely Dudestan before nos. 13 and 129-30 and Chester before nos. 10 and 218. It is not clear whether no. 300 should be referred to Hamestan hundred.

The order in which the hundreds are described in each fief is generally the same, and the emendations that have been noted above are in conformity with that order, viz. Chester 1, Dudestan 2, Riseton 3, Wilaveston 4, Roelau 5, Bochelau 6, Tunendune 7, Hamestan 8, Middlewich 9, Warmundestrou 10, Exestan 11, Atiscros 12. Using those numbers, the hundredal order within fiefs that extended into two or more hundreds can be shown as follows:

Bishop of Chester: 1, 2, 3, 4, 11, 10, 3, 1, 2 (later addition)
Churches: 1, 2, 3, 4, 5, 7, 11, 2, 12
Earl Hugh: 5, 6 (intruded into 5), 2, 3, 4, 8, 9, 4, 7
Robert FitzHugh: 2, 3, 4, 8
Richard de Vernon: 3, 4, 7, 9, 10, 8 (no. 131, a later addition)
Walter de Vernon: 3, 4
William Malbank: 2, 3, 4, 9, 10
William FitzNiel (FitzNigel): 1, 2, 3, 4, 6, 7, 9, 8 (later addition), 9 (later addition)
Hugh de Mara: 1, 4
Hugh FitzNorman: 9, 8, 9 (in two parts, nos. 214-17, 222-5)
Hugh FitzOsbern: 1, 2, 3
Hamon de Massey: 4, 6, 8, 6 (later additions)
Bigot de Loges: 2, 5, 6, 8, 9
Gilbert de Venables: 2, 3, 5, 6, 11, 9, 10 (the scribe seems to have considered nos. 261-6, in the last two hundreds, as belonging to a separate Gilbert)
Joscelin: 9, 6 (? later addition)
Ranulph (de Mesnilwarin): 4, 5, 6, 7, 9
Ilbert: 2, 3
Osbern FitzTesson: 2, 4, 5, 6, 7
Niel (Nigel) de Burcy: 3, 4

It is clear that in most of the fiefs each hundred was treated separately and that in fifteen of them an identical order was initially followed, though in five of the fifteen additions to the text later disrupted that order. The earl's fief is rather less regular, partly because Roelau hundred, in which his main holdings were, was displaced and dealt with first.

The remarkable consistency in the spelling of the hundred names should also be noted. It implies that the scribe worked from a written text. That is also suggested by the fact that when two or more places within a hundred were divided between fiefs, they are described in the same order in both. Thus Raby follows Neston in the fiefs of both St. Werburgh's (26-7) and William FitzNiel (186-7), and the places in Middlewich hundred where the earl and Bigot each had holdings are described in the same order in both fiefs (168, 242-59). It appears therefore that at some stage of the inquiry the information gathered was arranged hundredally and that the fiefs were extracted in turn from the hundredally arranged material.

The only feature that suggests that some information may have been supplied hundred by hundred is the different treatment of churches in different hundreds.

In some priests only are mentioned, while in others the priests are always noted with a church. The details, excluding Chester itself, are as follows:

Dudestan: priests (nos. 4, 72)
Warmundestrou: priests (8, 151, 165)
Riseton: priests (?9,[17] 96)
Roelau: priest and church (36, 43, 235)[18]
Wilaveston: priests (?9,[19] 57, 142, 186, 290)
Tunendune: priests (197, 205)
Exestan: church and priest (314)
Bochelau: church and priest (228, 255, with 254 plus 292, a divided place). There was also a church at Northenden (312), but the manor was waste so no population was recorded.
Middlewich: 2 manors with priest and church (125, 242) and 2 with only priests (261, 267)
Atiscros: church (320, 340 plus 349, divided place, 359, 363); church and priest (347, 350, 355); waste church (360); priest only (372)
Hamestan: none

Despite the small numbers and the irregularity of Middlewich and Atiscros, the pattern does suggest that information about churches was either supplied or processed separately in each hundred. The omission of churches or priests from Hamestan hundred is probably because of the failure of that hundred to supply the information: the evidence of the pre-Norman stone crosses and of the place name Prestbury shows that there were certainly churches there.[20]

ASSESSMENTS

One of the main purposes of the inquiry was to investigate royal resources. They were very limited in Cheshire: there was no *terra regis* either before or after the Conquest, and the king's rights were apparently restricted to the city of Chester itself and the salt-wiches.[21] The only royal resource that was of general concern throughout the Survey was of course the assessment for the geld and other purposes.

Most Cheshire assessments were expressed in hides and virgates. The fractions of a hide that were mentioned include $\frac{1}{2}$, $\frac{1}{3}$, $\frac{2}{3}$, and $\frac{1}{6}$. A quarter was never used because that was expressed as a virgate. The only subdivision of a virgate mentioned was $\frac{1}{2}$. There was one use of acres, at Sutton in Middlewich, which was assessed at 3 virgates 16 acres, but it is difficult to determine what part of a virgate the acres represented (68). A small number of assessments were expressed in terms of carucates or bovates. The carucate and its eighth part, the bovate, the Domesday units of assessment in large parts of eastern and northern England, also occur in parts of England that were assessed in hides, but generally they are explicitly said not to have been geldable.[22] At least some of the Cheshire carucates and bovates are therefore unusual in being described as subject to geld.

---

[17] For the location of Burton and its priest see no. 9, n. 20.

[18] All three are mentioned among the manorial appurtenances.

[19] For the location of Burton see no. 9, n. 20.

[20] Above, 'A.-S. Ches.'.

[21] Below.

[22] i.e. they were exempt from the geld, though liable for military duties and, perhaps, other burdens.

TABLE I: ASSESSMENTS IN CARUCATES AND BOVATES

No.	Place	Assessment	Ploughlands
183	Handbridge	1 carucate of land that pays geld	not stated
211	Handbridge	1 carucate of land that pays geld	not stated
218	Handbridge	1 carucate of land that pays geld	not stated
11	St. Mary's, Chester	2 bovates of land	not stated
68	Sutton in Middlewich	4 bovates of land that pay geld	in all there is land for 7 ploughs (i.e. in 6 manors of which Sutton was one)
140	Overpool	land of 4 bovates that pays geld	not stated
195	Tabley Superior	1 bovate of land and a third part of 1 hide that pay geld	the land is for 1 plough
258	Peover	2 bovates of land that pay geld	not stated
269	Tabley Inferior	2 bovates of land that pay geld	the land is for ½ plough
275	Peover	2 bovates of land that pay geld	the land is for ½ plough

It has been pointed out that the 3 carucates at Handbridge formed part of the $1\frac{1}{2}$ hides beyond the bridge mentioned in no. 1a. The $\frac{1}{2}$ hide is accounted for by the two holdings in Netherleigh and Overleigh, each assessed at 1 virgate, leaving the 3 carucates as the equivalent of 1 hide.[23] That figure compares with the ratio of 6 carucates to 1 hide known to have been used in the district between the Ribble and the Mersey.[24] Both there and in Cheshire hides and virgates were an old assessment and carucates and bovates a newer one, the product of Scandinavian influence and perhaps applying to land not previously assessed.[25] In both territories local administrators needed a rule to bring hides and carucates into a single tax system. The most probable explanation of the Cheshire bovates is that they were each $\frac{1}{8}$ carucate, as elsewhere in England, so that in Cheshire the bovate was $\frac{1}{24}$ hide. As well as the single bovate at Tabley Superior, they occur in groups of two (i.e. $\frac{1}{12}$ hide) and four ($\frac{1}{6}$ hide, a unit expressly mentioned in no. 272). At each of the three places which had an assessment expressed in both bovates and hides or virgates, the conversion of the bovates into their equivalent hidation yields suggestive results. At Tabley Superior (195) 1 bovate and $\frac{1}{3}$ hide make $1\frac{1}{2}$ virgates, an assessment found elsewhere in the county. At Peover (258, 275) 2 bovates and 2 bovates make $\frac{1}{6}$ hide, which with $\frac{1}{2}$ hide at Peover Superior (273), makes $\frac{2}{3}$ hide, the figure at which Nether Peover (196) was also assessed. At Sutton in Middlewich (68, 243) 4 bovates and 3 virgates and 16 acres make up $\frac{11}{12}$ hide and 16 acres. The

[23] *Dom. Surv. Ches.* 9–10; below.
[24] *Dom. Surv. Ches.* 10; Dom. Bk. f. 269v.
[25] There was one such unassessed holding in Ches., in

Tunendune hundred, and there were also 5 hides at Halton not liable to geld (no. 197).

other places divided, like Sutton, between Earl Hugh and Bigot de Loges made up regular total assessments of 1 hide (Sandbach) and $\frac{1}{2}$ hide (Wimboldsley and Weaver). Possibly then Sutton was also assessed at 1 hide, divided awkwardly between the two men. If so, 16 acres were the equivalent of $\frac{1}{12}$ hide and there were 192 acres to the hide in Cheshire. Such a ratio would have a bearing on the collection of geld, since the subdivision of the fiscal hide into 192 fiscal acres, instead of the usual 120, might have facilitated accounting in a shire where two units of account were probably in use side by side, the English shilling of 12*d.* and the Scandinavian *ora* of 16*d.* For instance, when a normal Danegeld of 2*s.* on the hide was levied in Cheshire, 8*d.* ($\frac{1}{2}$ *ora*) would have been due from each carucate, and, putatively, $\frac{1}{8}$*d.* from each fiscal acre ($\frac{1}{8}$*d.* is almost certainly the forfeiture of a *minuta* mentioned in no. 319).[26]

At Handbridge, where none of the entries states the number of ploughlands, it is possible that there was some confusion between assessments and ploughlands; a ratio of 3 ploughlands to 1 hide is reported in many Cheshire manors.[27] A similar explanation may apply at Overpool but not elsewhere. The possibility that the scribe made a mistake and wrote bovates instead of virgates is not only inherently improbable but is ruled out at Sutton, where 4 virgates would have amounted to 1 hide.

The assessments are distributed very unevenly between the hundreds, as shown in Table II.

TABLE II: ASSESSMENT OF HUNDREDS

Hundred	Assessment	Ploughlands
Chester	50 hides	
Dudestan	117 hides	203
Riseton	$42\frac{1}{2}$ hides	$94\frac{1}{2}$
Wilaveston	$97\frac{1}{6}$ hides, 4 bovates	$173\frac{1}{2}$
Roelau	42 hides	80
Bochelau	$19\frac{1}{2}$ hides, 7 bovates	$45\frac{3}{4}$
Tunendune	$27\frac{1}{2}$ hides, $\frac{1}{2}$ virgate	$57\frac{1}{4}$
Hamestan	$28\frac{1}{6}$ hides	113
Middlewich	$37\frac{3}{4}$ hides, 16 acres, 4 bovates	$84\frac{3}{4}$
Warmundestrou	$39\frac{1}{4}$ hides	$106\frac{3}{4}$
Exestan	20 hides	21
Atiscros	$19\frac{1}{2}$ hides	$23\frac{1}{3}$ in hidated part; 35 in unhidated part
Totals	$540\frac{11}{24}$ hides, 15 bovates, 16 acres	$1002\frac{5}{6}$ including hidated part of Atiscros

For only two of the hundreds does the Survey give a total assessment; Chester at 50 hides and Atiscros at 20 hides. The discrepancy between the latter total and the actual number of hides recorded is a reminder of the problem posed by undetectable

[26] The above paragraphs on the relationship between the assessments in hides and carucates were contributed by Dr. Lewis. For an earlier discussion see *Dom. Surv. Ches.* 8–13.

[27] This material is being subjected to computer analysis. Preliminary results suggest that the ratio may be closer to 2:1: inf. from Dr. Kenyon.

errors in the figures given. Another is the difference between the assessment given for Antrobus in nos. 36 and 71, the former giving it as 1 virgate, the latter as $1\frac{1}{2}$ virgates. With such small errors possible, it is reasonable to see in some of the hundredal totals basic units of 20 or 50 hides. The only exceptions are Hamestan and Tunendune, and if the 5 geld-free hides are deducted from the latter the remaining total is fairly close to 20 hides. There is no reason to suppose that the Cheshire assessments had been reduced or that hundreds other than Dudestan and Wilaveston had earlier been assessed at 100 hides. It was long ago pointed out that the assessments correspond reasonably well with the distribution of recorded resources and have 'some rough relation to their agricultural capacity and population'.[28] What is more, the only places for which there are pre-Conquest assessments independent of Domesday Book, in the endowment charter of St. Werburgh's, do not lend any support to the theory of a systematic reduction. The so-called County Hidage has been cited in support of the view that Cheshire was once assessed at 1,200 hides, but the text survives only in later copies and the reasons for assigning to it a pre-Conquest date merit re-examination. Even if it is substantially from the early 11th century, there may have been some misunderstanding about Cheshire (and Shropshire). In Cheshire it could well be that the compiler or copyist assumed that 12 hundreds would amount to 1,200 hides.[29]

It appears that Cheshire's assessment of some 540 hides was distributed unevenly between the hundreds, generally in units of 20 or 50. There are five 5-hide manors, Broxton (85), 'Burwardestone' (73), Eccleston (249), Tattenhall (136), and Worthenbury (74), and one 10-hide, Halton (197), though there 5 hides were geld-free. There are also some neighbouring manors that together formed 5-hide units, for example Blakenhall (266) and Walgherton (157). More remarkably, it appears that there were larger units, some of them parishes, assessed in multiples of five hides. The list includes:[30]

Malpas, $34\frac{1}{2}$ hides (73, 75, 78–83, 85–7, 89–91)[31]
Prestbury, 20 hides (60–6, 101, 208, 222–3, 238–40, 307, 309)[32]
Bunbury, 15 hides (92, 94–9, 221, 250)
Great Budworth, $14\frac{2}{3}$ hides and 4 bovates (71, 119, 196, 202–6, 209, 256, 265, 269, 271, 279, 291, 294–5, 301–3, 311)[33]
Farndon and Aldford, 10 hides (4, 93, 184, 233)
Neston, 10 hides (26–7, 59, 105–6, 114–15, 133–4, 186–7)
Wybunbury, 10 hides (8, 153, 155, 157–8, 160, 162–3, 169, 266)[34]
Allington, Eyton, and Sutton, 5 hides (247–8)[35]
Astbury, 5 hides (215, 225, 241, 261, 264, 315)[36]
Audlem, 5 hides (127, 159, 167–8)
Heswall and Thurstaston, 5 hides (107–9)[37]
Tattenhall, 5 hides (136)[38]
Waverton, 5 hides (285–6)

---

[28] *Dom. Surv. Ches.* 17.
[29] Sawyer, *Roman Britain to Norman Eng.* 228–9.
[30] Thanks are offered to Dr. Lewis for help with the figures.
[31] The total includes 'Burwardestone' (73) and $\frac{1}{2}$ hide, imperfectly erased, at Hampton (80).
[32] The inclusion of 'Hofinchel' gives 20 hides.
[33] The total excludes an unidentified Peover estate (275) and Hartford in Great Budworth and Weaverham (253).
[34] The total excludes Wistaston (161) and Coppenhall

(177), both chapelries and later independent parishes.
[35] All in Gresford parish, they were treated as a unit in 1086 and perhaps also in 1066: above, 'A.-S. Ches.'.
[36] The total excludes estates in the chapelries of Church Lawton (214), Swettenham (224), and Brereton (262), and 1 virgate at 'Sumreford', possibly Somerford Booths (300).
[37] The total excludes Greasby in Thurstaston and West Kirby (298).
[38] The total excludes Golborne Bellow (137).

It is notable that some of those units crossed hundredal boundaries; Bunbury and Great Budworth are striking examples.[39]

The part of Atiscros hundred which lay beyond Wat's Dyke was unhidated and for those manors only ploughlands were given. The interpretation of such ploughlands is controversial. The commonsense empirical reading is that they represent estimates of potential capacity, but they could clearly also serve as an alternative basis for assessment and it is possible that it was for that purpose that the Domesday inquiry assembled information about them. The figures given in Cheshire often agree with the number of ploughteams recorded but there are also many in which the number of teams is much lower than the number of ploughlands. That was clearly sometimes the result of wasting.[40] There are also a few examples of ploughteams exceeding ploughlands in number, which have been dismissed, not necessarily correctly, as errors.[41] In other counties an excess of teams over lands is common, and sometimes resulted from recent reorganization of the manor following the creation or extension of demesne.[42] Nevertheless it seems unlikely that a surplus of teams could long be maintained, and it is more likely that in such cases ploughlands represent an alternative assessment. That assessment could often, if not always, have been based on the existing teams, and may well have included non-arable resources, where they existed.[43] It is important to emphasize that in Cheshire the ploughland figures were not based simply on the number of ploughs for either 1066 or 1086, for in many manors ploughlands were given though the manor was waste at both dates. That suggests that either such figures bear no relation to the number of teams working (i.e. they are simply assessments of potential capacity, arable and non-arable), or that they were determined at a much earlier time.[44] The latter explanation is not very convincing, for it is unlikely that Hamestan, for example, had such a large number of teams at any time. Another peculiarity of the ploughlands is that they were not given for subdivisions of manors. Thus Eastham (57) had 22 hides and 22 ploughlands. The hidation of the component parts was carefully noted, but no separate figures were given for the ploughlands. The same is true of Halton (197), Weaverham (36), and other places. There are also several composite entries for which ploughland totals are given along with separate assessments on the component parts.[45] The cancelled no. 283 appears to be an exception, for although it was only a component of the principal manor, described in no. 314, the number of ploughlands is given. Nevertheless, in the main entry the total number of ploughlands is recorded as usual, and the exceptional treatment of Rainald's share in no. 283 apparently springs from Rainald's regarding it as his own manor, when in fact he was a joint holder, or rather undertenant.

It would seem, then, that the ploughlands represent an assessment alternative to, or instead of, hidation. There may have been some attempt at reassessment during the Domesday inquiry, but the details given for manors that were waste in 1066 and 1086 suggest that they were at least partly based on old figures. That assessment was based on the number of ploughteams functioning in arable areas, but elsewhere was artificial.

[39] *Dom. Surv. Ches.* 18–19.
[40] *Dom. Geog. N. Eng.* 340–3.
[41] Ibid.; *Dom. Surv. Ches.* 73, 145, 203.
[42] The presence of numerous bordars on some of the over-stocked Cheshire manors suggests that there too overstocking could indicate expansion. Cf. S. P. J. Harvey, 'Evidence for Settlement Study: Dom. Bk.', *Medieval Settlement*, ed.

P. H. Sawyer, 197–9.
[43] Cf. Yorks. E.R.: *Dom. Geog. N. Eng.* 185–91; P. E. Dove, *Dom. Studies*, i. 149 sqq.; S. Harvey, in *Dom. Bk.: A Reassessment*, ed. P. H. Sawyer (forthcoming).
[44] For a further explanation of waste, that it means non-productive rather than totally abandoned land, see below.
[45] e.g. nos. 66, 68.

There is certainly no simple or regular relationship between hides and plough-lands. The ratios vary from 1:1 to 1:6. Different ratios also occur in a single place, for example at Lymm, where it was variously 1:2 (254) and 1:4 (292). Many other examples could be cited. A revealing one is that of Tatton, which contained 1 hide or $3\frac{1}{2}$ ploughlands (191) and $\frac{1}{8}$ hide or $\frac{1}{2}$ ploughland (272). Those figures do not produce very different ratios, 1:3.5 and 1:3 respectively, but it seems as though the whole had been treated as 4 ploughlands which were then divided between the separate manors.

TENANTS

The second main purpose of the inquiry was to discover what lands were held by tenants in chief and their undertenants. No attempt was made to record the names of all land-sitting men, only those of some account; there are many entries which show that there was a tenant but offer no identification.[46]

Ecclesiastical Tenants

Although the Survey expressly states that the bishop, Robert de Limesey, was the only tenant in chief in Cheshire beside the earl, the church of St. Werburgh was recorded separately, immediately after the bishop. All the ecclesiastical holdings (1–35) were concentrated in west Cheshire and beyond the Dee, and there are signs that that had long been so.

The diocese appears to have gained no new holdings after the Conquest, and by then to have sustained a number of losses, especially in its lands beyond the Dee. In 1086 the bishop was admitted to have lost territory, possibly demesne, which he had previously held in Gresford, Sutton, and Eyton, and it seems at least possible that he may even have been deprived of the lordship of the entire hundred of Exestan.[47] Elsewhere in Dudestan hundred he had lost land at 'Burwardestone' (73) and Bettisfield (13, 72) and perhaps, though that was disputed, at Tilston (76). While some of those holdings had been lost as long ago as Cnut's reign (1016–35), others, such as the Exestan estates, appear to have been taken away after the Conquest. Despite the findings of the county court in his favour the bishop appears to have recovered none of the lost possessions. Thus the salthouse which he claimed at 'Burwardestone' appears to have been that granted by Robert FitzHugh to St. Werburgh's before 1093.[48] Such failures are perhaps due to rivalry between the earl and the bishop, a rivalry which culminated in the refoundation of St. Werburgh's and was probably ultimately responsible for the brevity of Chester's elevation to the status of a see.[49]

In 1086, in addition to his extensive rights and properties in Chester, the bishop still possessed some six manors, assessed at over 15 hides, with 8 ploughteams in demesne. Only one tenant, William (probably William Malbank), at Tarvin and Wybunbury, was mentioned, in notable contrast with the numerous tenants recorded on the bishop's Staffordshire estates.[50] Nevertheless, the continued importance of the bishop's Cheshire holdings, above all in Chester itself, was reflected in the removal of the principal seat of the north-west Mercian diocese from Lichfield to St. John's, Chester, in 1075.[51] Though St. John's was to remain the cathedral

[46] e.g. nos. 36, 72–5, 253, 255, 304.
[47] no. 7, 248, 314; *Dom. Surv. Ches.* 27–8; above, 'A.-S. Ches.'.
[48] *Chart. Chester Abbey*, i. 18.
[49] Below.
[50] nos. 1–13; *V.C.H. Staffs.* iv. 41–3; above, 'A.-S. Ches.'.
[51] *Northern Hist.* xviii. 201–3; *V.C.H. Ches.* v (forthcoming).

for only a brief period after 1086, it was probably permanently affected by the reorganization, its lands being merged with those of the bishop. That was almost certainly the case at 'Redcliff' (10), which was listed as one of the bishop's manors in 1086, but was also said to belong to St. John's.[52]

The church of St. Werburgh had 13 houses in the city of Chester, free of all customary dues, and 21 manors assessed at nearly 28 hides (14–35). There were undertenants on 5 manors and 12 ploughteams in demesne. The church's holdings were concentrated in and near Chester, in southern Wirral, western Roelau, and northern Dudestan, with isolated estates in Riseton (Iddinshall) and Exestan (Hoseley, Flints.). Whereas the bishop's Exestan holdings seem to have been much diminished, St. Werburgh's managed to retain their $\frac{1}{2}$ hide intact, though they sustained a few losses elsewhere: at Burwardsley (92) 1 hide had been taken and sold by the reeves of earls Edwin and Morcar, and at Stanney (70) they claimed 'the fifth acre' of the earl's manor.[53]

Though the Cheshire Domesday recorded other ecclesiastical tenants, all at a much lower level than the two Cheshire minsters, it made no attempt to provide a comprehensive list of churches. In all it mentioned only 18 (excluding Chester) and 32 priests, amounting to 34 separate foundations. As was argued above, except in unhidated Atiscros most of those included were mother churches of large parishes, originally coterminous with pre-Conquest estates. That in 1066 many were still held by Earl Edwin and the bishop, or by a small group of men of high status, such as Wulfgeat, Orme, Edward, Osmaer, and Thorth, is evidence that they then retained something of their former importance, and even in 1086 the great majority remained in the hands of the bishop, Earl Hugh, and his principal tenants.[54] The fact that some similar churches, such as Prestbury, Malpas, and, perhaps, Tarvin, were omitted is evidence of the incompleteness of the Survey as an ecclesiastical record rather than an indicator of disappearance or decline, though undoubtedly by 1086 many once prosperous foundations were in decay.[55] The richest was Farndon (4) with two priests holding $1\frac{1}{2}$ hides and a 'priest of the vill' with $\frac{1}{2}$ ploughteam.[56] Other churches with some landed endowment include Burton (9), where a priest held three ploughteams, with a radman, 7 villeins, and 3 bordars,[57] Acton (151), Bettisfield (probably Hanmer) (72), and Astbury (261), each with 1 ploughteam, Bowdon (228) with $\frac{1}{2}$ hide, Hawarden (320) with $\frac{1}{2}$ carucate, Frodsham (43) with 1 virgate, and Lymm (254, 292), which was divided into two portions each of $\frac{1}{2}$ virgate, one being apparently quit of geld. In many cases priests appear to have been of low social status, often grouped with radmen and even villeins.[58] The one exception is Wulfgar, the priest who in 1066 held Caldecote (219) with three thegns; the estate was held as three manors, implying that Wulfgar himself was the lord of the thegns. Since Caldecote is near Farndon, in Shocklach parish, it is possible that Wulfgar was one of the canons, perhaps indeed the warden, there.[59]

Lay Tenants in 1086

Apart from the bishop, the earl was the only tenant in chief in Cheshire, an arrangement unique in England. Earl Hugh was a young man to receive the vast

[52] Above, 'A.-S. Ches.'; fig. 38.2.
[53] The claim seems eventually to have been vindicated: the abbey of Stanlaw, which received the estate from the earl, later rendered 2 stone of wax to St. Werburgh's: *Dom. Surv. Ches.* 119. See fig. 38.2.
[54] nos. 4, 8–9, 36, 43, 57, 72, 125, 151, 197, 205, 254–5, 261, 292, 312, 314, 320; below, 'Pre-Conquest Tenants';

figs. 36, 43.
[55] On minsters in general see J. Blair, 'Secular Minsters in Dom. Bk.', *Dom. Bk.: A Reassessment*, ed. P. H. Sawyer (forthcoming).
[56] Above, 'A.-S. Ches.'.
[57] See no. 9, n. 20.
[58] e.g. nos. 8, 142, 165, 186, 290, etc.
[59] Above, 'A.-S. Ches.'.

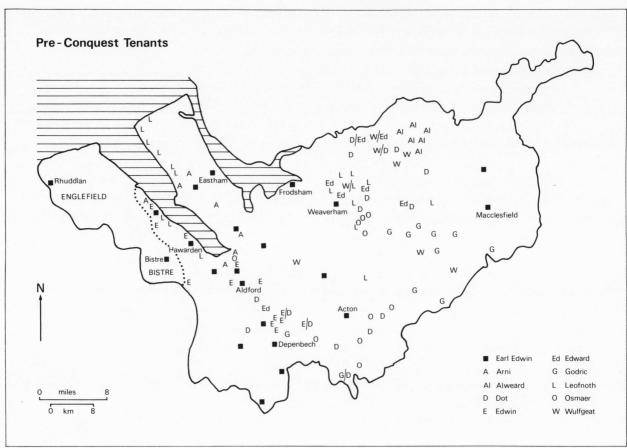

Pre-Conquest Tenants

Rhuddlan
ENGLEFIELD
Eastham
Frodsham
Weaverham
Macclesfield
Hawarden
Bistre
BISTRE
Aldford
Acton
Depenbech

N

	Earl Edwin	Ed	Edward
A	Arni	G	Godric
Al	Alweard	L	Leofnoth
D	Dot	O	Osmaer
E	Edwin	W	Wulfgeat

0 miles 8
0 km 8

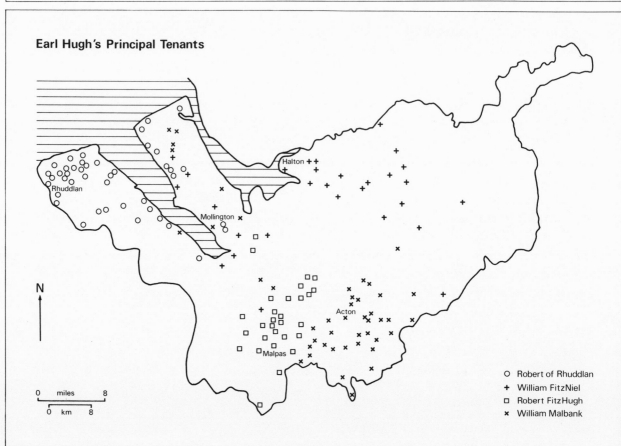

Earl Hugh's Principal Tenants

Halton
Rhuddlan
Mollington
Acton
Malpas

N

O	Robert of Rhuddlan
+	William FitzNiel
□	Robert FitzHugh
×	William Malbank

0 miles 8
0 km 8

FIG. 43.

304

honor bestowed on him, but the choice is rendered less surprising by the fact that his family had long been important in Normandy.[60] In Cheshire his demesne holdings amounted to some 50 manors, assessed at *c.* 90 hides and spread mainly over the northern half of the county, the south being dominated by the fiefs of his undertenants, Robert FitzHugh and William Malbank.[61] The earl also retained half of the great unhidated manor of Rhuddlan, including half of Rhuddlan itself, with its castle, burgesses, mint, and church, half the iron mines and woods, half the fisheries, mills, and tolls of the river Clwyd, half the vill of Bryn, and more than a third of the berewicks (340-8). The strength of his holding perhaps reflects the exceptional position in the county of his predecessor Earl Edwin, from whom came some 55½ of Earl Hugh's 90 hides, and the pattern of whose holdings largely determined that of Earl Hugh's. Particularly important was the great manor of Eastham and a group of hundredal manors, including Frodsham and Macclesfield, to which the earl's penny was expressly said to be attached.[62]

Much of the earl's Cheshire holding seems to have been at farm or exploited only indirectly. Substantial parts of the manors of Eastham (57), Weaverham (36), Upton (69), and Rhuddlan (347-8) were subinfeudated to named tenants, and at Weaverham much of the manor may have been held of the earl by an unidentified Frenchman.[63] There was demesne on only 13 manors. Discounting the estates subinfeudated to major mesne tenants such as Hamon de Massey, William Malbank, Hugh FitzNorman, and Joscelin, there were 58½ ploughteams, of which only 16½ were working directly in demesne.[64] Moreover, for some unspecified period before 1086 the earl's pleas in the county and in all the hundreds except that of Englefield (that is, the manor of Rhuddlan) had been farmed to Mundret for £50 and 1 mark of gold, and the same man had also held the city of Chester for a further £70 and 1 mark of gold (1e). Domesday, however, refers to those arrangements as in the past and it is uncertain what had superseded them.[65] Other profits also came from the salt-wiches, though they had much declined since 1066.[66] Extensive as Earl Hugh's subinfeudation was in 1086, it was probably not complete. In east Cheshire, where he held the two wasted but once important manors of Macclesfield and Adlington (60-1), there were no undertenants, and many townships, not mentioned in the Survey, were subinfeudated only in or after the 12th century. Moreover, in Middlewich hundred, in four vills largely subinfeudated to Bigot de Loges, the earl still retained small holdings, later to disappear entirely.[67]

The earl's Cheshire estates were only part of an enormous honor, which included lands in twenty other counties: Berkshire, Buckinghamshire, Derbyshire, Devon, Dorset, Gloucestershire, Hampshire, Huntingdonshire, Leicestershire, Lincolnshire, Norfolk, Northamptonshire, Nottinghamshire, Oxfordshire, Rutland, Somerset, Suffolk, Warwickshire, Wiltshire, and Yorkshire. Earl Hugh's estates in Yorkshire and Lincolnshire, which came largely from Earls Siward and Harold, were especially extensive. Some of the fief may have been acquired as early as 1067, but the bulk was obtained in the 1070s when Hugh succeeded to Earl Edwin's estates in Cheshire, and later still when there were probably important additions in Berkshire, Buckinghamshire, Devon, Dorset, Norfolk, Somerset, Suffolk, and Wiltshire.[68]

[60] C. P. Lewis, 'Eng. and Norm. Govt. and Lordship in the Welsh Borders, 1039-87' (Oxf. Univ. D. Phil. thesis, 1985), 179-80; *Complete Peerage*, iii. 164-5; *Hist.* xxviii. 146, n. 4.

[61] nos. 36-71; *Dom. Surv. Ches.* 30.

[62] nos. 36, 43, 48, 57, 59-61, 69; *Dom. Surv. Ches.* 30 n. 3.

[63] See no. 36, n. 37.

[64] nos. 36, 38-9, 43, 48-50, 57-8, 60, 69, 320, 340.

[65] no. 1e; *Dom. Surv. Ches.* 31; below.   [66] Below.

[67] Lewis, 'Eng. and Norm. Govt.' 185-8; below.

[68] W. Farrer, *Honours and Kts.' Fees*, ii. 5-6; *V.C.H. Ches.* ii. 1.

Though poor, Cheshire was strategically important, and one of the purposes of William's grants to Earl Hugh was perhaps to provide him with the means to sustain the county as a base for campaigns against the Welsh and a defence against Scandinavian attack. Hugh's potential receipts from his other estates far exceeded what he could obtain from Cheshire itself, though the farm of the city of Chester and the hundred courts considerably improved the exiguous income which he derived from his rural manors.[69] Moreover, it is clear that the earl's extensive subinfeudations were often dictated by strategic considerations, as in his creation of the compact fiefs of Robert of Rhuddlan and Robert FitzHugh, with their castles and knightly undertenants, to provide bases for operations against the Welsh.[70]

Though Earl Hugh's undertenants on his estates as a whole included some who were leading magnates of the realm, few if any of them held land in Cheshire itself. There Hugh's own men were much more numerous. Only one of those was himself a tenant in chief, and most, though they held lands outside Cheshire, did so almost invariably on other fiefs of Earl Hugh.[71] Their origins are diverse. Few came from Hugh's own district, the Avranchin, perhaps only Ilbert de Roullours and Niel de Burcy, both minor figures. Robert of Rhuddlan was a relative, and others perhaps came from the districts round Bayeux and Caen, the Seine valley in eastern Normandy, and Flanders. On the whole, then, it does not seem that Cheshire was settled primarily with Hugh's Norman tenants and servants, possibly because Hugh's father, Richard had remained in Normandy and chose to keep his men about him there. Two at least of Hugh's most prominent supporters, Robert of Rhuddlan and William FitzNiel, were, like Hugh himself, young men in the 1070s, and it has been suggested that after 1070 Cheshire was settled by 'a youthful band of warriors, in search of adventure and fortunes'.[72]

Some of the greatest Cheshire tenants, such as William Malbank and Robert FitzHugh, held exceptionally compact blocks of territory, though most also had an outlier near Chester, however distant the bulk of their estates may have been.[73] Such men seem to have been regarded by the earl as his barons, a style which was eventually restricted to the lords of certain fiefs but was probably once more fluid.[74] There were traditionally seven Cheshire baronies which were believed to have originated in the time of Earl Hugh: Dunham Massey, Halton, Kinderton, Malpas, Mold, Nantwich, and Shipbrook.[75] The reason why those particular fiefs were singled out is not entirely clear. Some, such as Malpas, Nantwich, and Halton, were among the largest Cheshire fiefs, while others, such as Mold, were comparatively small, smaller than other holdings never accorded baronial status. Some at least may have been important pre-Conquest entities. Halton, Malpas, Mold, and Nantwich were focused on estates which were of considerable administrative importance before, possibly long before, 1066; and at both Shipbrook and to a lesser extent Dunham Massey the main estates appear to have been taken over with a minimum of reorganization from a single Anglo-Saxon landowner. In all those

[69] Lewis, 'Eng. and Norm. Govt.' 182.

[70] Fig. 43.2. Another reason for the compactness of FitzHugh's fief is the fact that it was an Anglo-Saxon estate, distinguished by numerous Welsh landholders. It was perhaps retained as an entity to maintain those landholders within a single lordship: Lewis, 'Eng. and Norm. Govt.' 205-6.

[71] The exceptions are William Malbank and William Fitz-Niel: below.

[72] Lewis, 'Eng. and Norm. Govt.' 188-9.

[73] Below.

[74] *Chart. Chester Abbey*, i. 17; *V.C.H. Ches.* ii. 2.

[75] Ormerod, *Hist. Ches.* i. 51-3, 55-6, 58, 149-50, 520, 688; ii. 245, 592; iii. 187, 421. Opinions were divided about the origins of the eighth barony, Stockport, which some were inclined to assign to the later 12th century. There are signs that Stockport may have been a significant place from ancient times; it was, for instance, the focus of a large ancient parish and its place name suggests a trading centre. Nevertheless, it does not appear in the survey, and it was not later held in chief of the earl. Its history, even its existence, before the mid 12th century can only be regarded as conjectural: Ormerod, *Hist. Ches.* i. 53, 57; iii. 788; *P.N. Ches.* i. 294-5; v (1: ii), 311; inf. from Mr. Booth.

instances, what was to become the *caput* of the barony was distinguished in Domesday by being placed first among the holder's estates in the hundred, the only exception being Kinderton, which was in no way distinguished from the other Middlewich holdings of Gilbert de Venables.[76] Two omissions from the later list of baronies are notable. Robert of Rhuddlan would certainly have been regarded by Earl Hugh as one, perhaps indeed the most important, of his barons, yet his lands seem never to have been regarded as a barony. It has traditionally been argued that that was because they were dispersed after Robert's death without legitimate issue, but there is evidence to suggest that they may well have survived as an entity at least until 1120.[77] Equally odd is the case of Bigot de Loges, whose *caput* was an important, formerly royal, manor and whose fief, though considerably greater than some of the baronies, never achieved baronial status.

Earl Hugh's leading tenant was his cousin Robert of Rhuddlan, the son of Humphrey de Tilleul and Adelina de Grandmesnil.[78] Robert had been a squire to Edward the Confessor, at whose hands he was knighted. He returned to England after 1066 with Hugh of Avranches, and when Hugh was granted the county of Chester he was made 'commander of his forces and governor of the whole province' (*princeps militiae eius et totius provinciae gubernator*). He was associated with Hugh in the campaign to expand into north Wales, and they had a shared base at Rhuddlan where at the king's command Robert built a castle in the 1070s. Robert later established another castle at Degannwy (Caern.), and eventually, with the collapse of the Welsh opposition in 1081, was granted north Wales as an independent fief, building yet more castles in Snowdonia and Anglesey. Though he was a benefactor of Orderic's monastery of St. Evroul, the chronicler seems to have had reservations about the *bellicosus marchio*: he was, he says, 'driven by pride and greed to unrestrained plunder and slaughter' which eventually brought him to a terrible end.[79] Robert was formerly believed to have died in 1088 but is much more likely to have survived until 1093. Certainly he was dead by 1094, when Earl Hugh granted lands which he held in chief to his new Benedictine foundation at St. Werburgh's, where Robert himself was originally buried before his body was removed to St. Evroul.[80] Though some of his property seems thus to have been dispersed after his death, in 1120 his son William was said to have been coming over from Normandy 'to receive the estates of his father in England', when he was drowned in the White Ship, a statement which implies that most of Robert's holdings were retained as an entity until that date.[81] Certainly members of his family continued to hold his estate of Thurstaston in the time of Earl Ranulph (I) (1121–9), when Matthew of Rhuddlan granted the church there to St. Werburgh's abbey on the occasion of his brother Simon's becoming a monk.[82] Matthew's descendants retained the manor and by the mid 12th century had adopted Thurstaston as the family name.[83]

Robert's Cheshire estates consisted of a compact group of manors in north-west Wirral assessed at 13 hides and a further two manors to the south assessed at an additional 2½ hides (103–13). Another group of manors on the opposite bank of the Dee in hidated Atiscros were assessed at 4⅜ hides (322–7). The bulk of those

---

[76] Below. Mollington occupied a similar position among Robert of Rhuddlan's Wirral estates. It is placed first and contains almost all Robert's Cheshire demesne. Thanks are due to Dr. Lewis for this point.

[77] Ormerod, *Hist. Ches.* i. 55–6; ii. 472, 494, 573, etc.; below.

[78] There is no discernible general principle behind the order in the survey's treatment of the Ches. tenants, and it

is not followed here. Instead tenants are listed roughly in order of wealth and rank.

[79] Orderic Vitalis, *Hist. Eccl.*, ed. M. Chibnall, iv. 134–47; Lewis, 'Eng. and Norm. Govt.' 313–23.

[80] Orderic Vitalis, *Hist. Eccl.* iv, pp. xxxiv–xxxviii.

[81] Ibid. iv. 304–5.

[82] *Chart. Chester Abbey*, i. 48, 51.

[83] Ormerod, *Hist. Ches.* ii. 503–4.

estates almost certainly formed a single entity before the Conquest, when six manors in Wirral and three in Atiscros were held by the same man, Leofnoth.[84] They may have had a strategic function, controlling the Dee approaches, though they constituted a relatively modest holding, with some 9 of the 17 manors subinfeudated and only 1¼ ploughteams in demesne. Earlier Robert had also held land and churches in West Kirby and Hilbre and the church of St. Peter in Chester, all of which were among his grants to the abbey of St. Evroul, confirmed by William I in 1081.[85] It is also possible that he continued to have interests in Chester, where in 1086 he claimed unsuccessfully that the land on which the church of St. Peter stood was 'thegnland' belonging to a manor outside the city, and hence liable to military service rather than the customs of the borough.[86] Robert's real strength, however, seems always to have lain in his share of the great manor of Rhuddlan, which was considerably larger and more valuable than the earl's. In addition to half the castle and borough, with 10 burgesses and half the church and mint, he held half the vill of Bryn and a further 38 berewicks (as opposed to Hugh's 22). There, in marked contrast to the earl's share, he had extensive holdings in demesne, farmed by 17 ploughteams (349–66).

Robert was also Earl Hugh's undertenant on the large estate of Mentmore (Bucks.), assessed at 18 hides, and on eight of the earl's Northamptonshire manors, assessed at just under 21 hides. He perhaps also held a further 8 hides in Gloucestershire.[87]

After Robert of Rhuddlan, Robert FitzHugh was treated by Orderic as the most prominent of Earl Hugh's barons in his Welsh wars, though his origins are particularly obscure. FitzHugh's fief of 29 manors was assessed at 75 hides, more than any other Cheshire holding apart from the earl's, and it was remarkably compact.[88] Twenty-one of FitzHugh's manors lay in a block in the southern half of Dudestan hundred, and a further six lay in the adjacent hundred of Riseton. The remaining two were outliers near Chester itself, a pattern familiar in most Cheshire fiefs (72–102). Robert FitzHugh's *caput* lay at Malpas (Anglo-Saxon 'Depenbech') where Robert had a castle and 3 ploughteams in demesne and where stood a church dedicated to St. Oswald, the mother church of a large ancient parish (75). The core of his holdings was formed by a group of six manors formerly belonging to Earl Edwin and assessed at 36 hides, including the great block of 'Depenbech', 'Burwardestone', Bettisfield, and Worthenbury, comprising south-west Cheshire and the detached portion of Flintshire known as Maelor Saesneg. They contained 8 of Robert's 12 demesne ploughteams, and on them he had enfeoffed 11 *milites*, who between them held some 8 ploughteams (72–7). Such enfeoffments underscore the military and strategic elements in Robert's fief.

It is possible that the great bulk of FitzHugh's fief was taken over with a minimum of rearrangement from Edwin; a considerable number, some 14 of his estates were subinfeudated, and it is likely that in them FitzHugh succeeded Earl Edwin as lord, even though in Domesday the earl is not expressly said to have preceded him. Significantly, beside his Norman undertenants, Ranulph, Drew (*Drogo*), Roger, Picot, Humphrey, and William, there were the Englishmen Edwin and Mundret, the former of whom retained several of the estates which he held as 'a free man' before the Conquest. FitzHugh's fief was one of Cheshire's ancient baronies, though FitzHugh himself died without a male heir and his estates were divided between

---

[84] nos. 105, 107, 109–12, 322, 324–5; fig. 43.

[85] Brownbill, *W. Kirby and Hilbre*, 87–9.

[86] *Dom. Surv. Ches.* 46; no. 1e.

[87] Farrer, *Hons. and Kts.' Fees*, ii. 13–14, 51–2, 211–12, 214–16, 220, 224.

[88] Orderic Vitalis, *Hist. Eccl.* ii. 260–1; fig. 43.2.

his two daughters.[89] FitzHugh was alive when St. Werburgh's abbey was founded in 1093, but by the time of Earl Ranulph (I) (1121–9) his daughter, Letitia of Malpas, was making grants to the community, and it seems likely that by then he was dead and the barony divided.[90] On Earl Hugh's estates outside Cheshire it is difficult to distinguish FitzHugh from numerous other undifferentiated Roberts. Nevertheless, the occurrence of Drew and Ranulph among the undertenants suggests that he held from the earl the great 40-hide manor of Buscot (Berks.). He seems also to have held Tackley (Oxon.), Coppingford (Hunts.), Kegworth (Leics.), and Sutton-on-Trent and Bonnington (Notts.).[91]

William Malbank may have been related to Alfred Malbedenc or Malbenhenc, who came from the district round Caen and may, like William, have been a tenant of Earl Roger of Montgomery.[92] William's Cheshire fief was second in size of assessment to that of Robert FitzHugh, and he held considerably more manors. In addition he was the bishop's undertenant at Wybunbury and possibly at Tarvin, and St. Werburgh's at Wepre (Flints.). He was also a tenant on the earl's great manor of Eastham. In all he held some 50 manors assessed at over 60 hides.[93] William's fief was compact, concentrated mainly in Warmundestrou hundred, where lay the *caput* of his barony, Earl Edwin's[94] hundredal manor of Acton, an ancient administrative centre with an important church. Probably William's holding of the profits of Warmundestrou hundred and of all royal and comital rights in the salt-town of Nantwich (itself in Acton parish) were associated with his tenure of the manor. Besides Acton he held some 30 manors in Warmundestrou and another five nearby in Middlewich hundred. In addition he had a number of estates in Wilaveston hundred, including a compact group of four, assessed at $11\frac{1}{2}$ hides, around the important ancient parish of Landican in Woodchurch.[95]

Much of William's fief, at least 22 of his manors, was waste when he received it, and presumably rendered no return to its lord. William, however, seems to have undertaken a thorough reorganization, retaining in demesne land on 21 manors farmed by 27 ploughteams, more than any other Cheshire landholder. Particularly interesting are the oxmen, who are regularly found in the ratio of two men to one ploughteam, especially on estates in Warmundestrou hundred, probably a sign of new agricultural arrangements.[96] There is no special pattern discernible among William's pre-Conquest antecessors, and it may be that his large compact fief was created from a tract of lands that were from the lord's point of view waste and in need of the kind of reorganization that they seem to have received under William. Nevertheless, the territory came to form the Cheshire barony of Wich Malbank or Nantwich, which passed to his son Hugh Malbank before 1119 and was eventually parcelled out among coheirs by the reign of Henry III.[97] William held other lands of Earl Hugh, in Buckinghamshire, Somerset, Wiltshire, and Dorset, where he had some 10 manors assessed at 28 hides. He was also the tenant of Earl Roger of Montgomery in the extreme north-east of Shropshire, where he held four manors abutting his holdings in Warmundestrou hundred.[98]

William FitzNiel (FitzNigel), constable of Chester, had Flemish relatives with

[89] Ormerod, *Hist. Ches.* ii. 592–8.
[90] *Chart. Chester Abbey*, i. 22, 49, 51, 58, 60.
[91] Farrer, *Hons. and Kts.' Fees*, ii. 22–3, 27–8, 75–6, 79, 242–4; inf. from Dr. Lewis.
[92] Lewis, 'Eng. and Norm. Govt.' 195–6.
[93] *Dom. Surv. Ches.* 48.
[94] Rather than Morcar as in the text: below, no. 151 and n. 84.

[95] nos. 5, 8, 34, 57, 136–80, 316, 328–9; fig. 43.2.
[96] Lewis, 'Eng. and Norm. Govt.' 210–12; nos. 136, 145, 152, 154, 156, 159–61, 163–6, 169–72.
[97] Ormerod, *Hist. Ches.* iii. 422–4; *Chart. Chester Abbey*, i. 32, 42.
[98] Farrer, *Hons. and Kts.' Fees*, ii. 16, 261, 284–8; *Dom. Surv. Ches.* 48.

whom he was in close contact, and may have been first established in Cheshire by Earl Hugh's predecessor, Gherbod the Fleming.[99] In 1086 he held some 30 manors assessed at *c.* 45 hides, including 4 manors held as an undertenant of St. Werburgh.[1] His honor was also fairly compact, located largely in north Cheshire, especially in the hundred of Tunendune where lay its *caput*, the great manor of Halton, and a further 9 manors, originally rated at *c.* 19 hides, though by 1086 5 of the 10 hides of Halton did not pay geld (197–206). Another 7 manors were in Bochelau hundred, and there were also, as with other major fiefs, outliers near Chester, at Newton, Netherleigh, and Handbridge (181–3). William also held half of the manor of Odd Rode (319). In demesne there were some 9½ ploughteams working on 7 manors and on five estates, including Halton, there were ploughteams with oxmen in the ratio of one to two, perhaps the result of some reorganization. William had undertenants on *c.* 11 of his manors, including 6 at Halton, defined as *milites* and holding lands assessed at 6½ hides. One of them, Odard, was also a tenant of Earl Hugh at another manor in Tunendune (301).

William's holdings, like those of other important Cheshire tenants, formed something of a marcher fief, defending the south side of the river Mersey and hence the southern half of the Runcorn Gap. Its military significance is highlighted by the fact that William also held considerable estates of Roger the Poitevin at Widnes and elsewhere along the north side of the river, so that he had full control of the entire gap.[2] The honor of Halton formed one of the Cheshire baronies, passing to a succession of William FitzNiels in the 12th century. Its continued importance is shown by the fact that FitzNiel's holding was reconstituted after its division between coheirs in the mid 12th century, in favour of the family which eventually became the Lacy earls of Lincoln. By then too Halton appears to have received a stone-built castle, perhaps the successor to an earlier motte and bailey fortification served by the men enfeoffed with six small holdings on the manor (197).[3] The honor seems to have comprised the estates of a number of important Anglo-Saxon antecessors, including Orme at Halton and Arni on at least seven estates in the hundreds of Chester, Wilaveston, and Atiscros.[4] Elsewhere, antecessors described as free men appear after the Conquest as undertenants. Edward, for example, was William's antecessor in four manors and remained Osbern FitzTezzon's undertenant on a further three; and Erchenbrand retained one of his two manors as an undertenant of William himself. Both of those men may have been the tenants of some unnamed Anglo-Saxon lord.[5] William also had other holdings of Earl Hugh, especially in Lincolnshire, where he held two important manors, and Oxfordshire where he held the great 40-hide estate of Pyrton.[6]

Robert of Rhuddlan, Robert FitzHugh, William Malbank, and William FitzNiel were the four main tenants of Earl Hugh, both in Cheshire and elsewhere on his fief. Beneath them there was a group of tenants who were still significant and included the holders of the remaining Cheshire baronies, but who were more diverse in wealth and status.[7] One of the most important was Gilbert de Venables, possibly from east Normandy, who had a fief of 18 manors assessed at some 30 hides, listed rather curiously in Domesday after several lesser tenants.[8] The holding was a scattered one, dispersed over seven hundreds, the largest group being six

[99] Lewis, 'Eng. and Norm. Govt.' 195.
[1] nos. 26–7, 30–1, 181–209, 315, 330; fig. 43.2.
[2] *Dom. Surv. Ches.* 48; *V.C.H. Lancs.* i. 280, 285*b*, 286*b*.
[3] Ormerod, *Hist. Ches.* i. 688–97; B. M. C. Husain, *Ches. Under the Norm. Earls*, 18–19; below.
[4] nos. 181–3, 186–8, 197, 330.
[5] nos. 184, 191, 193, 196, 202–3, 205, 292, 294, 296; below.
[6] Farrer, *Hons. and Kts.' Fees*, ii. 193, 201, 204, 250–1; *Dom. Surv. Ches.* 49.
[7] Lewis, 'Eng. and Norm. Govt.' 192–4.
[8] nos. 249–66, 313.

manors in Bochelau hundred, including a moiety of Lymm and Rostherne, High Legh, and Mere, all in Rostherne (254-9). In Middlewich hundred there was a further group of four manors, perhaps focused on the ancient centre of Astbury, together with Witton next to the salt-town of Northwich (261-5). Those estates were credited to Gilbert the Hunter (*Venator*), perhaps intended to be distinguished from Gilbert de Venables, though the later history of the estates shows the two to have been the same man.[9] They include Kinderton (263), which was later to be the *caput* of the Cheshire barony of the Venables family, though there is nothing to indicate that it had special status in 1086.[10]

Despite the scattered nature of the fief, at its core was the holding of a single Anglo-Saxon, Wulfgeat, who was Gilbert's antecessor in Riseton, Bochelau, and Middlewich hundreds and who also held Gilbert's two important churches of Astbury and Rostherne and his moiety of the church at Lymm.[11] Other important antecessors include Dot, who held or shared four of Gilbert's estates, and Godwin who held three, including Kinderton.[12] Though none of Gilbert's holdings had a named undertenant in 1086, he had only five demesne ploughteams working on five manors and many of his estates seem to have been of that relatively minor kind where a few radmen and even villeins held a single ploughteam.[13] Only at Hartford was there a *miles*, with 1 ploughteam, 2 oxmen, and 3 bordars (253).

Gilbert cannot be proved to have held land elsewhere in Earl Hugh's honor, though it is possible that he was the tenant of that name at Fifehead Magdalen (Dorset).[14]

Other baronial fiefs of the second rank include that of Richard de Vernon, perhaps the son of William de Vernon, lord of Vernon (Eure, arr. d'Evreux), who held 14 manors assessed at $17\frac{1}{2}$ hides, of which 7 formed a group around Shipbrook, the *caput* of his fief, in Middlewich hundred. The manor of Picton in Wilaveston hundred formed an outlier near Chester, and there were also scattered holdings in Riseton, Tunendune, Warmundestrou, and Hamestan hundreds.[15] Richard's most important antecessor, Osmaer, preceded him on 6 manors, including Shipbrook and at least 3 other estates in Middlewich hundred and 2 in Warmundestrou.[16] The Vernon honor formed the Cheshire barony of Shipbrook, and the fact that the nucleus of seven manors in Middlewich hundred (120-6) seems to have been co-extensive with the ancient parish of Davenham and largely if not wholly held by a single Anglo-Saxon antecessor suggests that Richard took over the principal holdings of an important Anglo-Saxon landowner with relatively little reorganization. The barony remained in the hands of Richard's descendants until the reign of Henry VI.[17]

Domesday names only two undertenants on the Vernon honor, and in 1086 there were 8 ploughteams, working on demesne on 8 manors. Besides his Cheshire estates Richard also held lands of Earl Hugh in Norfolk.[18] A further 4 Cheshire manors assessed at 5 hides were held by his brother Walter de Vernon, who also held the 20-hide manor of Churchill (Oxon.) of Earl Hugh, and was a tenant in chief in Buckinghamshire.[19] Walter's Cheshire estates reverted to the earl after his death apparently without issue some time after 1093.[20]

[9] no. 261, n. 22.
[10] Ormerod, *Hist. Ches.* iii. 187.
[11] nos. 251, 254-5, 257, 259, 261-2; below.
[12] nos. 255-6, 258, 263-6.
[13] nos. 249, 251, 256, 262-3.
[14] Inf. from Mr. Sawyer.
[15] nos. 116-29; below.   [16] nos. 120, 122, 125-8.

[17] Ormerod, *Hist. Ches.* iii. 245-53. Almost all the townships in Davenham not mentioned in the Survey were later in the Shipbrook barony.
[18] Farrer, *Hons. and Kts.' Fees*, ii. 232-3.
[19] nos. 132-5; *Dom. Surv. Ches.* 47; Farrer, *Hons. and Kts.' Fees*, ii. 248; *V.C.H. Bucks.* i. 265.
[20] Ormerod, *Hist. Ches.* iii. 245.

Hamon, who came from Macey in the Avranchin or, less probably, from Massy in the Pays de Caux, held nine manors and a share in the divided manor of Sinderland cum Baguley. He was also Earl Hugh's undertenant at Upton by Chester and Eastham, where his holdings were assessed at 7 hides. His whole fief was assessed at *c.* 17 hides.[21] Hamon's principal holding was a compact group of some five manors in Bochelau hundred, on all of which he had been preceded by the same Anglo-Saxon lord, Aelfweard (227-9, 231-2). It included Dunham Massey, later if not in 1086 the *caput* of his fief, and Bowdon, with its important ancient church still in 1086 endowed with ½ hide. The Bochelau estates, however, were assessed at only a little over 4 hides, considerably less than Hamon's holdings in Wirral. Two were waste, and only at Dunham was any demesne recorded. Since Domesday gives no details of Hamon's important holdings as an undertenant, no reliable impression can be formed of the economic strength of his holdings. His family continued to hold the Cheshire barony of Dunham Massey until the reign of Edward III, and by 1172 had built a castle at Dunham.[22] Hamon himself also held lands in Wiltshire of Earl Hugh, and by the 12th century his successors held other lands in Nottinghamshire, Derbyshire, and Lancashire.[23]

The holdings of Hugh FitzNorman, ancestor of the barons of Mold, stewards of the earls of Chester, are difficult to determine because of confusion with other Hughs. The treatment of his fief in Domesday itself illustrates the uncertainty, for the main entries relating to Hugh are in two parts separated by the holdings of Hugh FitzOsbern. Hugh's Cheshire holdings consisted of 8 manors, 5 in Middlewich and 3 in Hamestan hundred, all held by the same Anglo-Saxon antecessor, Godric. Their value to their lord, however, must have been limited, since 7 of them were waste.[24] In addition Hugh held a moiety of the great but wasted manor of Bistre, with Leeswood and 'Sudfell' and 5 berewicks (367, 369). The manor included the site of Mold, later the *caput* of the barony, and seems to have been Hugh's principal possession. His only ploughteam in demesne was there, and it is only in the entry relating to that manor and in the nearby estate of 'Edritone' in hidated Atiscros (333), where he was Hugh FitzOsbern's undertenant, that he is expressly distinguished as FitzNorman. Hugh was alive in 1093, when he and his brother Ralph the Steward made joint grants to the newly founded abbey of St. Werburgh. By 1130 Hugh's son William seems to have succeeded to the estates of both Hugh and Ralph, though a charter of 1121-9 names Ralph's son Robert, ancestor of the later barons of Mold, as steward, perhaps jointly with his father.[25]

Hugh FitzNorman was also the earl's tenant in Yorkshire and Suffolk.[26] He has been identified with Hugh de Mara, who immediately precedes him in the Domesday entries, and who held four manors in or near Chester.[27] That identification depends upon a rather doubtful reference to a later interest of Mold in Overleigh, one of Hugh de Mara's manors, and is contradicted by the fact that Hugh de Mara is recorded separately from Hugh FitzNorman when making a grant of another of his manors, 'Redcliff', to St. Werburgh's in 1093.[28] It has also been suggested that the otherwise unidentified Hugh who held 5 hides at Gresford either jointly with or as a tenant of Osbern FitzTezzon was Hugh FitzNorman, but it is more likely that he was in fact Hugh FitzOsbern.[29]

[21] nos. 57, 69, 226-32, 335-6; *Dom. Surv. Ches.* 52-3; L. C. Loyd, *Origins of Some Anglo-Norman Families*, 61-2; below.

[22] Ormerod, *Hist. Ches.* i. 520-2, 533.

[23] Farrer, *Hons. and Kts.' Fees*, ii. 288-9.

[24] nos. 214-17, 222-5; *Dom. Surv. Ches.* 50.

[25] *Chart. Chester Abbey*, i. 18-19, 27, 33, 50.

[26] Farrer, *Hons. and Kts.' Fees*, ii. 236; *V.C.H. Yorks.* ii. 219.

[27] nos. 210-13; *Dom. Surv. Ches.* 50-1; Ormerod, *Hist. Ches.* i. 56-7.

[28] Ormerod, *Hist. Ches.* i. 373.

[29] *Dom. Surv. Ches.* 56, 217; below.

Besides the Cheshire baronies there were a few other fiefs of similar size which, curiously, were not accorded similar status. Bigot de Loges, for example, held a scattered fief of 13 manors assessed at *c.* 16 hides, the *caput* of which was the pre-Conquest earl's share of the important manor of Farndon, later known as Aldford (233–45). Bigot, who was possibly a relative of Earl Hugh's great East Anglian tenant, Roger Bigod, also held a moiety of Northenden manor with Ranulph Mainwaring (312). Aldford itself, a substantial estate assessed at 4 hides with 2 plough-teams in demesne (233), had a castle by the mid 12th century, when it was the seat of the family to which it gave its name.[30] The lords of Aldford were presumably descended from Bigot himself, who was alive in 1093 and was probably the father of the Robert FitzBigot who attested a charter of Earl Ranulph (I) (1121–9). The *Roes uxor Pigoti* who granted Northenden and its church to St. Werburgh's abbey in 1119 was perhaps Bigot's widow, and so Robert may have succeeded to his father's estates by then.[31]

No substantial undertenants, except a thegn with half a ploughteam at Mobberley, are named on Bigot's lands. Many other manors were occupied only by radmen or Frenchmen, or even villeins and bordars, and two were waste. Four manors contained 4 ploughteams with 4 oxmen in demesne. Bigot also held three manors of Earl Hugh in Suffolk.[32]

Osbern FitzTezzon held a fief of some 12 estates assessed at 18 hides, largely in north and west Cheshire. In the west he held manors at Dodleston (334), Handley (288), Golborne David (289), and Poulton (290) together with the major share of the great manor of Gresford (314), where Hugh (FitzOsbern?) and Rainald de Bailleul were his co-tenants, or perhaps undertenants.[33] He was also the undertenant of Hugh FitzOsbern at 'Edritone' in hidated Atiscros (333).[34] A further six manors were in north Cheshire along the Mersey and in Roelau and the southern part of Tunendune hundred (291–6).

Osbern's north Cheshire fiefs seem to have been little disturbed by their new lord. On three estates his antecessor, Edward, continued to hold of Osbern as an undertenant in 1086. One of those estates, Grappenhall (296), was held as two manors by Edward and Dot, perhaps an indication that Edward was a tenant of Dot, who may indeed have been the chief lord of several of Osbern's north Cheshire manors.[35] Osbern's principal demesne holdings were in the west, where he had four ploughteams directly in demesne, together with his share of the demesne of Gresford. His *caput* was probably Dodleston, with its castle, its 1½ ploughteams in demesne, and its 15 burgesses in Chester.[36] Osbern also held land elsewhere in Earl Hugh's honor, in particular some 9 carucates in Lincolnshire.[37]

Hugh FitzOsbern has traditionally been believed to have been the son of Osbern FitzTezzon, and there are some indications of links between the two. An Osbern FitzHugh was reputed the ancestor of the Boydells of Dodleston, and it has been assumed that his father was Hugh FitzOsbern who as heir of Osbern FitzTezzon had inherited Dodleston on FitzTezzon's death.[38] Moreover, like FitzTezzon, FitzOsbern also held of Earl Hugh lands which had belonged to the Anglo-Saxon thegn Godric in Lincolnshire.[39] In Cheshire, FitzTezzon and FitzOsbern are associated at

[30] *Dom. Surv. Ches.* 53; Ormerod, *Hist. Ches.* ii. 754–8; Lewis, 'Eng. and Norm. Govt.' 189–90.
[31] *Chart. Chester Abbey*, i. 18, 40, 44–5, 50.
[32] Farrer, *Hons. and Kts.' Fees*, ii. 238.
[33] That Osbern held Gresford hall and mill suggests that he was the principal lord there: below.
[34] A difficult entry: *Dom. Surv. Ches.* 229.

[35] Below, 'Pre-Conquest Tenants'.
[36] For the castle see Ormerod, *Hist. Ches.* ii. 847.
[37] Farrer, *Hons. and Kts.' Fees*, ii. 175–6; *Dom. Surv. Ches.* 52.
[38] Ormerod, *Hist. Ches.* ii. 844–5; *Dom. Surv. Ches.* 52.
[39] Farrer, *Hons. and Kts.' Fees*, ii. 127–8; *Lincs. Dom.* (Lincs. Rec. Soc. xix), nos. 13/24, 33, 41–2, 45.

'Edritone' (333), and perhaps also at Gresford (314). It is likely that FitzTezzon's co-tenant there was Hugh FitzOsbern rather than Hugh FitzNorman, since the Anglo-Saxon holder of Gresford, Thorth, was also FitzOsbern's antecessor in the three neighbouring manors of Allington, Sutton, and Eyton (247-8). All three manors, like Gresford, were in the small hundred of Exestan and members of the parish of Gresford; it is, therefore, at least possible that Osbern and Hugh were a father and son who were granted the holdings of Thorth in that hundred, just as they obtained a portion of Godric's estates in Lincolnshire.[40] FitzOsbern also held other estates in Chester, Dudestan, Riseton, and Atiscros hundreds, of which the most valuable was Claverton, with its ploughteam in demesne and its 12 burgesses.[41]

The remaining Norman tenants were lesser men. Ranulph, who from later evidence can be identified as the ancestor of the Mainwarings, held 12 manors assessed at *c*. 9 hides, and also had shares in the manors of Northenden and Sinderland and Baguley.[42] Seven of his manors formed a group in Bochelau hundred, but they included no demesne and were assessed at only 2 hides and 2 bovates (272-8). Three of them and another of Ranulph's estates in Middlewich hundred had belonged to a single Anglo-Saxon woman, Godgyth, a minor landowner who seems to have held no other estates (274, 276-7, 281). The only demesne manors, where there were 3 ploughteams, were Blacon (270) and Wheelock (280), both of which had belonged to important Anglo-Saxon landowners, Blacon to Thorth and Wheelock to Earl Morcar. Ranulph, whose estates included both later seats of the Mainwarings, at Warmingham (281) and Peover Superior (273), seems to have been succeeded by his sons, Richard and Roger de Mesnilwarin, shortly after 1086.[43] His estates in Norfolk which he held as a tenant of Earl Hugh were also retained by the family.[44]

Ilbert held three manors assessed at 8 hides, but had only 1 ploughteam in demesne (285-7). His principal estate was in Waverton parish where he was succeeded by Richard de Rullos (perhaps Roullours, Calvados, canton de Vire), presumed to be his son. No other holdings by Ilbert elsewhere on Earl Hugh's estates have been identified.[45]

Joscelin (*Gozelinus*) held three manors assessed at 2 hides and 2 bovates (267-9) and a further 4 hides as Earl Hugh's undertenant at Weaverham (36). He had 2 ploughteams in demesne and his holding included the important church of Middlewich. He is perhaps to be identified with the ancestor of the Tuschet (Touchet) family who were Earl Hugh's tenants in Derbyshire, Lincolnshire, and Rutland.[46]

Among the most minor of Earl Hugh's Cheshire tenants one name stands out, that of Rainald de Bailleul, who held ½ hide at Erbistock (283) and 1½ hides at Gresford (284), perhaps as the tenant of Osbern FitzTezzon. Rainald was the sheriff of Shropshire under Roger of Montgomery, and had extensive holdings in his own county and in Sussex, Staffordshire, and Warwickshire, though he appears nowhere else as a tenant of Earl Hugh. It may be significant that Thorth, the Anglo-Saxon lord of Gresford, was also Rainald's antecessor in six Shropshire manors, three of which he retained as Rainald's undertenant in 1086.[47]

Niel (*Nigellus*), identified in other sources as from Burcy (Calvados, canton de

[40] Above.
[41] nos. 218-21, 331-2.
[42] nos. 270-81, 312-13; *Dom. Surv. Ches.* 55.
[43] *Dom. Surv. Ches.* 55; Ormerod, *Hist. Ches.* iii. 226.
[44] Farrer, *Hons. and Kts.' Fees*, ii. 227.
[45] *Dom. Surv. Ches.* 58.
[46] Farrer, *Hons. and Kts.' Fees*, ii. 208-9, 254.
[47] *Dom. Surv. Ches.* 56; *V.C.H. Salop.* i. 299.

Vassy), not far from Ilbert's presumed home at Roullours, had three manors, assessed at 4½ hides and all held by Dunning before the Conquest, though not constituting the whole of Dunning's holding (297-9).[48] Ralph the Hunter (*Venator*) also held three manors, assessed at 3 hides (280-2), and was still alive in 1093, when he granted land to St. Werburgh's.[49] Baudry (*Baldricus*) held only one small manor in Cheshire (246), though he also held land of Earl Hugh in Lincolnshire, where he was known under the soubriquet de Lindsey.[50] Two other Norman tenants are worthy of note: Robert the Cook, who held two manors in Wirral (114-15), and Richard the Butler. Richard held two manors assessed at 3 hides in Dudestan hundred, of which one, Poulton by Pulford, though assessed at only 1 hide, had 3 ploughteams in demesne and a reeve and 3 bordars with a further 2 ploughteams (130-1). Richard was still alive in 1119, and his descendants retained Poulton, where in 1146 they founded an abbey.[51] The only other Norman tenants were two very minor lords holding one manor apiece (300-1) and Odin, who held half the manor of Bistre and three berewicks of Rhuddlan of Earl Hugh (347, 368).

There were also a number of English and Welshmen who held small fiefs of the earl. The most important seems to have been Mundret, who was an undertenant of the earl's at Eastham (57) and Upton by Chester (69) and of Robert FitzHugh at Chowley (84), and who also held the manor of Bartington (302), where his antecessor was Dunning, a pre-Conquest tenant who still retained one of his estates in 1086.[52] Mundret's total holding in Cheshire was assessed at 4½ hides, but he must have been a man of some substance since for a period before 1086 he had farmed the city of Chester and the earl's pleas in the county court and all but one of the hundred courts (1e). Mundret also seems to have been a tenant of Roger of Montgomery at Ellesmere (Salop.). Unlike the other tenants bearing native names, however, there is no evidence that he held lands in Cheshire before the Conquest.[53] The most substantial of those who undoubtedly retained or inherited pre-Conquest holdings were Gamel, who had succeeded his father in two manors assessed at 3½ hides (303, 309) and who may have been the Gamel FitzGrifin who held lands in Staffordshire in 1086, and Wulfric, who continued in two of his pre-Conquest manors as a tenant of Earl Hugh (307, 310) and in another as an undertenant of Richard de Vernon (129), the whole holding being assessed at *c.* 2⅔ hides. Others survived simply as undertenants. Of those the greatest was Edwin, who held four manors assessed at 5 hides and had a share in a further three assessed at 5½. All except one, which was held of Robert of Rhuddlan (327), were held of Robert FitzHugh (78-93). Another English landowner who survived as an undertenant on three of the estates which he had held before the Conquest was Edward, whose holding in 1086 was assessed at just over 2½ hides (292, 294, 296).[54] One or two Englishmen, such as Mundret and Leofric, were granted or inherited estates held by other Englishmen before the Conquest (302, 306).

After the English tenants the Survey lists manors held jointly by two or three Norman lords (312-15). Their exact status is uncertain, but it seems likely that in one case at least, that of Gresford, two of the three holders may in fact have been in some degree of subinfeudation to the third.[55]

48 *Dom. Surv. Ches.* 58.
49 *Chart. Chester Abbey,* i. 19.
50 *Dom. Surv. Ches.* 54; Farrer, *Hons. and Kts.' Fees,* ii. 117-19.
51 G. Barraclough, *Early Ches. Chart.* 1-5; Ormerod, *Hist. Ches.* ii. 862; *Dom. Surv. Ches.* 47.
52 Below, 'Pre-Conquest Tenants'.
53 *Dom. Surv. Ches.* 31; O. von Feilitzen, *Pre-Conquest Pers. Names of Dom. Bk.* 331; Farrer, *Hons. and Kts.' Fees,* ii. 237.
54 Below, 'Pre-Conquest Tenants'.
55 *Dom. Surv. Ches.* 56-7.

Pre-Conquest Lay Tenants

Earl Edwin enjoyed an exceptional position in pre-Conquest Cheshire, in which, as after 1066, the king seems to have had little interest. Probably the Survey disguises the full extent of his dominance, and many of the small, seemingly independent, Anglo-Saxon landowners whom it records were Edwin's tenants or commended to him.[56] Edwin's Cheshire holding comprised 20 manors assessed at $107\frac{1}{2}$ hides, the core of which was formed by a group of large estates focused on ancient administrative centres, including Eastham in Wilaveston hundred (57), Frodsham and Weaverham in Roelau (36, 43), Macclesfield in Hamestan (60), 'Depenbech' and Farndon in Dudestan (75, 233), and Acton in Warmundestrou (151). In some cases the earl is known to have held hundredal meeting places, notably Hadlow in Wilaveston (59) and 'Radinton' in Atiscros (321). Moreover, at least two of his manors were clearly hundredal ones on the pattern of those in Shropshire and Lancashire, for they had the earl's third penny attached to them, an indication that royal revenues were collected there.[57]

Apart from two important manors in Hamestan hundred Earl Edwin's holdings were mostly in west Cheshire, especially in Wirral and the Dee valley. The biggest concentration was in the hundred of Dudestan where he held $43\frac{1}{2}$ hides, followed by Wilaveston ($27\frac{1}{2}$) and Roelau (16). The earl had no estates at all in the hundreds of Exestan, Bochelau, and Tunendune, and in Middlewich his holdings were confined to his rights over the salt-towns of Middlewich and Northwich.[58] That distribution was to affect the pattern of Earl Hugh's Cheshire estates, though in some areas, notably Roelau, Hugh built up much larger concentrations of manors than his predecessor.[59]

Edwin also had important estates across the Dee, presumably largely obtained after the defeat of the Welsh king Gruffudd ap Llywelyn in 1063.[60] They included the great unhidated manors of Rhuddlan (340–66)and Bistre (367–73) and that of Hawarden in hidated Atiscros (320). The earl's holdings in Flintshire also included the whole of the detached portion of the county that came to be known as Maelor Saesneg (72–4). Only in Exestan, a hundred dominated by the holdings of St. Werburgh and of the bishop and his putative tenant, Thorth, did Earl Edwin have no estates. The extent to which the earl actually controlled those large territories remains, however, conjectural. Both Rhuddlan and Bistre were said to be waste both in 1066 and when Earl Hugh received them, probably an indication that seigneurial control had been greatly weakened following the death of Gruffudd and their transfer to English lordship. It is significant that the Survey records the state of Bistre and the food rents which it rendered in the Welsh king's time. That weakening was, however, only temporary, for by 1086 Edwin's successors had restored the ancient arrangements: they had 1 ploughteam in demesne, like Gruffudd, and a further $5\frac{1}{2}$ ploughteams working on the manor, hardly fewer than the 6 there in Gruffudd's time.[61]

Those holdings, together with their considerable rights over the customs, tolls, and fines of Chester itself, made Cheshire exceptionally important to the Mercian earls, an importance reflected, it has been suggested, in the style 'earl of Chester' assigned to Earl Leofric in the spurious charter founding Coventry abbey in 1043.[62]

[56] Below.
[57] *Dom. Surv. Ches.* 30–1; Sawyer, *Roman Britain to Norman Eng.* 201; fig. 43.1.   [58] Below, 'Salt-Wiches'.
[59] Lewis, 'Eng. and Norm. Govt.' 184–5.
[60] *Dom. Surv. Ches.* 22–3; above, 'A.-S. Ches.'.

[61] Below, 'Settlement and Agrarian Economy'.
[62] *Dom. Surv. Ches.* 31; *Cod. Dip.* ed. Kemble, iv. 273; P. H. Sawyer, *A.-S. Chart.* no. 1226; *Dom. Surv. Ches.* 31; but cf. *Essays Presented to R. L. Poole*, ed. H. W. C. Davis, 164.

Earl Edwin was the principal antecessor of Earl Hugh himself and of one of his greatest tenants, Robert FitzHugh, and a further four of his manors formed the *capita* of the fiefs of Robert of Rhuddlan (349), William Malbank (151), Hugh FitzNorman (367), and Bigot de Loges (233). Indeed, Earl Edwin's position may have been even stronger than suggested by the 20 manors listed in the Survey. Evidence from Lincolnshire has suggested that not all those named in Domesday as the pre-Conquest antecessor of the Norman lord were so in the fullest sense. Some may have been undertenants of an unnamed lord.[63] If, as seems likely, such arrangements also obtained in Cheshire, they would have obscured the full extent of the territories of Earl Edwin, who may have been the unnamed lord of numerous Anglo-Saxon free men holding estates there in 1066. Almost all of those manors named as Edwin's in the Survey contained demesne, though some also had undertenants, and it is probable that manors wholly in the possession of an undertenant appear under that tenant's name. Such an arrangement seems particularly likely on the fief of Robert FitzHugh, the core of whose fief was formed from six important manors formerly held by Earl Edwin (72–7). Robert's subinfeudations seem to have followed pre-Conquest dispositions especially closely; indeed two pre-Conquest free men, Edwin and Eli, survived as his undertenants, at Edge (78, 83), Duckington (82), and Crewe by Farndon (93). Elsewhere places which were held as two manors before the Conquest received two undertenants under Robert. Thus Hampton (80) and Cholmondeley (78), the one held by Edwin, the other by Edwin and Dot as two manors in 1066, were both held by Edwin and Drew as Robert's undertenants in 1086, while Broxton (85), held by Brihtmar and Raven as two manors in 1066, was held by the Norman undertenants Roger and Picot in 1086. In yet other instances an estate with a single Anglo-Saxon tenant passed to a single post-Conquest undertenant: Chowley (84), held by the free woman Wulfgifu, was subinfeudated to Mundret by 1086, Shocklach (88) had passed from Dot to Drew, Tushingham (89) from Earnwine to Humphrey, and Bickley (90) from Wudeman to Fulk. Only in a few instances were relatively small Anglo-Saxon estates grouped to form a manor with a single Norman undertenant: Bickerton (91) and Burwardsley (92), each held by three pre-Conquest tenants, were subinfeudated to the Normans Humphrey and Drew. Such evidence suggests a considerable degree of continuity in the tenurial structure of south-west Cheshire, and it may be that Robert FitzHugh's honor was constituted almost entirely from a great block of territory held by Earl Edwin, with Robert himself retaining the demesne manors and redistributing the undertenancies. If that was indeed so, Earl Edwin's position in Cheshire as a whole was perhaps even closer to that of the Norman earls in size and importance than is suggested by an initial reading of the Survey.

That hypothesis renders problematic the status of many other pre-Conquest tenants in Cheshire. No undertenancies are explicitly mentioned except at Somerford Booths (300), held as three manors by two free men and by Morfar 'who could not leave his [unnamed] lord'. Though that alone is enough to suggest the pattern observable elsewhere in the Survey, namely that pre-Conquest tenants were often undertenants, there are no clues to which of the people named were superior and which inferior. It is also difficult to determine whether the same name refers to one or several people. One reasonably safe criterion is that tenants bearing the same name whose estates passed to the same Norman successor may be identified as a single individual. An example is the Godric who was Hugh FitzNorman's

[63] P. H. Sawyer, in *Dom. Bk.: A Reassessment*, ed. Sawyer (forthcoming).

antecessor on all his manors except Bistre,[64] and whose estates formed a compact holding along the river Dane.[65] That case is unusual, for generally the bearer, or bearers, of a single pre-Conquest name became antecessors of more than one Norman lord, and clearly where the name was a common one it cannot be assumed that a single individual is in question. Where the name is rare it is much more likely that all references are to one person, though the possibility cannot be discounted that a rare name had a vogue in a particular locality and hence was borne by several people. One example of the references being to a single man seems to be Arni, who occurs only in Cheshire and once in Yorkshire, where it may be a completely different name. Most of Arni's estates passed to William FitzNiel, but two did not: Upton was retained by Earl Hugh and Bagillt (Flints.) passed to Robert of Rhuddlan.[66] Other similar instances confirm that the estates of one pre-Conquest tenant did not necessarily pass to one successor. In some cases the principle of division may have been topographical, a single pre-Conquest landholder's dispersed estates passing to the principal Norman tenant in each of the areas in which he held territory.[67] There is also the possibility that, as elsewhere, some pre-Conquest groupings were dispersed because they included not only lands held, so to speak, 'in chief' but also undertenancies of another pre-Conquest landholder, or because they represented undertenancies of several different pre-Conquest landholders. In such circumstances dispersal may, for example, have arisen from the fact that one Norman obtained the lands held 'in chief' by an English predecessor, while another obtained the lands which that same Englishman held as undertenancies. Thus the possibility that men such as Edwin and Dot may have been Earl Edwin's undertenants in south-west Cheshire but not elsewhere may help to explain the division of their holdings between Earl Edwin's successor in that area, Robert FitzHugh, and other Norman lords. It follows that it is impossible to determine the full extent of any pre-Conquest holding; the most that can be discovered is the demesne estates, held 'in chief', and even those may be confused by lands held as undertenancies.

A closely connected problem is that of the multiple manors, that is places or groups of places treated as a single unit yet held as two or more manors, generally by as many different pre-Conquest tenants. Thus, Coddington, held as a single manor by Earl Hugh and the subject of a single entry, was said to have been held before the Conquest by Earnwig, Ansgot, and Dot as three manors (50). Occasionally, a place treated as two manors is held by a single man: Hampton, for example, was held by Edwin as two manors before the Conquest and by Edwin and Drew as undertenants of Robert FitzHugh in 1086 (80). In some cases too the number of tenants does not coincide with the number of manors: Caldecote, for example, was held by the priest Wulfgar and 'three other thegns' as three manors (219), and Sinderland and Baguley, which was held by four named tenants as four manors before the Conquest, was shared between three Norman lords in 1086 (313). Such groupings are found all over Cheshire but mostly in the south, as Table III makes clear.

It is difficult to establish why multiple manors were treated as units. It might be thought that they represented groupings of separate manors that were first brought together after the Conquest, but they were given a single valuation in 1066 as in 1086. Elsewhere in the Survey marginalia mark them out in such a way as to suggest

[64] At Byley (216) he was named first among 3 A.-S. tenants. [65] nos. 214–17, 222–5; below.
[66] nos. 53, 181–4, 187–8, 326, 330; below. [67] e.g. perhaps Dot and Osmaer: below.

TABLE III: MULTIPLE MANORS IN EACH HUNDRED

Hundred	2 manors	3 manors	4 manors	6 manors	8 manors	Total
Dudestan	5	4	I	–	–	10
Wilaveston	2	I	–	–	–	3
Middlewich	6	I	–	I	–	8
Tunendune	3	–	–	–	–	3
Bochelau	2	–	I	–	–	3
Roelau	2	–	–	–	–	2
Riseton	I	–	–	–	–	I
Atiscros	3	–	–	–	–	3
Warmundestrou	11	2	–	–	–	13
Hamestan	–	I	–	–	?1	?2

that their multiple character was significant.[68] In Cheshire such marginalia are not used, but some post-Conquest multiple manors are listed separately at the end of the Survey, two of which were multiple manors before the Conquest (312-15). At Gresford, which was held by Thorth as a single large manor in 1066 and had three Norman lords in 1086, it is possible that the whole was under Osbern FitzTezzon who was noted as having a hall and a mill grinding corn for it (314). Similarly, it looks as if before the Conquest Godric was lord of all three manors at Byley (216), which passed with the rest of his holdings to Hugh FitzNorman. Archil and Godwin, the other two men named there in 1066, were presumably in some undefined way Godric's tenants. It is worth noting that although Archil is a common name in the Survey, in Cheshire it occurs only at Byley, and that there were other multiple manors whose pre-Conquest tenants included men with rare or unique names. Thus, at Sutton in Middlewich (243) the two manors were held by Alstan and Belam, the latter a unique name, the former occurring nowhere else in Cheshire or the neighbouring shires. At Broxton (85) one of the tenants, Brihtmar, had a name which, though common elsewhere, does not occur again in Cheshire and its neighbours; Bers at Shurlach (121) had a unique name; Colbert at Burwardesley (92) had a name otherwise known only in Devon and Lincolnshire, and Derch at Church Minshull (149) and Batherton (163) had a name which is again unique. All those appear to be instances of very minor landholders, who were more likely to have been undertenants of greater lords.

In sum, the evidence suggests that the multiple manors represent territories linked under some kind of lordship, whether of one of the named tenants or some other unnamed lord. In that connexion it may be significant that they are treated as units not only in respect of value but also of ploughlands.[69] The reason for the division of such lordship groups into separate manors is not clear. In some instances it seems that each manor represents a unit that was later a township, and certainly such groupings occur in areas containing townships not named in the Survey. Elsewhere, however, it is clear that multiple manors existed within what was later a single township.[70]

Besides Earl Edwin there were only two other landowners of the first importance in Cheshire in 1066. Earl Morcar held the single manor of Wheelock (280),[71] and

---

[68] Inf. from Mr. Sawyer.
[69] e.g. no. 163.
[70] Below, 'Settlement and Agrarian Economy'.

[71] He is also credited with holding Acton man. (151), but elsewhere it is said to have been held by Edwin, which seems much more probable: *Dom. Surv. Ches.* 151.

in south Cheshire Earl Harold Godwinsson had four outlying berewicks of his Shropshire manor of Whitchurch (156, 176). Otherwise the Cheshire tenants seem to have included men only of local importance. Among them the principal men, holders of at least four manors or of lands assessed at 5 hides or more, are as follows:

Aelfric (Alvric, Elric, Elvric). Though von Feilitzen distinguishes *Alric (Elric)* (164) from Aelfric (*Alvric, Elvric*) (92, 169, 174, 175), the fact that there was the same successor, William Malbank, in all but one place (92) suggests identity. All the manors were fairly close. William was also Aelfric's successor at Gravenhunger (Salop.) in an area where William had other Cheshire antecessors such as Edwin and Leofwine. Three estates were multiple manors, where Aelfric was perhaps the lord of the other tenants (92, 164, 169).

Aescwulf (Essul). An important if localized landholder, whose name is unique in Domesday. He held 7 hides and an ancient church at Landican in Wirral, where he was succeeded by William Malbank (142), and 3 hides in parage at Dunham in Roelau hundred, which in 1086 Earl Hugh retained in demesne (38).

Alweard (Elward). The six holdings in Bochelau hundred (227-9, 231-2, 313) form a compact group, and in 1086 were held by Hamon de Massey. The only one to contain demesne was Dunham (227), which became the *caput* of the Massey fief. Demesne was also recorded at two other estates (121, 164) in which Alweard had a share, and at Bowdon (228) he had a church with ½ hide. Three of the estates where Alweard held land were multiple manors. The name is recorded several times in Staffs. and south Salop., and once in north Salop. (Fig. 43.1.)

Arni (Erne, Erni). A Scandinavian name and rare; the only other possible occurrence in Domesday is in Yorks., spelt *Earne*, which may be a different name. The Ches. instances almost certainly represent one man: in seven (181-4, 187-8, 330) he was the antecessor of William FitzNiel. Those and an eighth (53) are all in south Wirral or close to Chester. The exception is 326. Demesne is recorded at two manors (163, 186), one of which contained the important ancient church of Neston. (Fig. 43.1.)

Brun. The five holdings form two compact groups, one in the middle (65, 208, 239) and one in the north part (208, 237) of Hamestan hundred. Bigot de Loges was the successor in one in each group. One (208) was a multiple manor. The name occurs elsewhere including Derb. but nowhere with the same successors.

Colbert. The name occurs elsewhere in Domesday only in Devon and Lincs. In Ches. two of the holdings (143, 145) are close; in those and a third (129) the successor was William Malbank. In one (143) Colbert himself was William's undertenant, and there was also an undertenant in 1086 in another which passed to William (145) and in one which passed to Robert FitzHugh (92), suggesting that Colbert's pre-Conquest tenure was at a lower level than William's or Robert's.

Dedol (Dedou). The name, which may derive from Old Norse *Thiodulfe* or Old German *Theodulf*, is not found elsewhere in Domesday, though it does occur in the place name Thealby (Lincs.). Two of the Ches. holdings (96-7) are close and had the same successor; Dedol's tenure of an ancient church at Bunbury, where there was demesne in 1086 (96), may indicate high status, and on a third (119), held as two manors in 1066, the presence of an undertenant in 1086 suggests that Dedol was the lord of the other tenant T.R.E. A fourth holding was no. 54.

Dot. A relatively rare name, occurring also in Berks. and in the eastern counties Beds., Cambs., Essex, and Suff., it probably represents a single man in Lancs.,

Salop., and Ches., where it occurs most frequently. Dot's holdings in Ches. fall into three groups. In Dudestan hundred (50, 78, 88, 91, 130), where his main successor was Robert FitzHugh, he was perhaps a tenant of Earl Edwin, since three holdings (78, 88, 91) passed to undertenants of Edwin's successor (see above), though another (50) was one of Earl Hugh's demesne manors in 1086. In his four holdings in Warmundestrou hundred (152, 158, 167, 169) his successor was William Malbank. In both areas Dot's holdings were largely on multiple manors (50, 78, 91, 158, 167, 169); in Warmundestrou the only exception (152) is also the only one on which demesne is recorded. A particularly compact group of holdings in Boche-lau, Middlewich, and Tunendune hundreds (255–6, 258, 265) was mostly divided between two successors, Gilbert de Venables and Osbern FitzTezzon. They in-cluded Grappenhall (296) and High Legh (255), with the church which was prob-ably the mother church of the great parish of Rostherne. Both were multiple manors, one shared with Wulfgeat, another thegn of high status, the other with Edward (see below). Since Edward was Osbern FitzTezzon's undertenant (292, 294, 296) and was followed by an undertenant in Great Budworth (205), it is likely that in Grappenhall and elsewhere Dot was his lord T.R.E. Dot had two other holdings in Bochelau hundred (192, 236). In Lancs. he held Huyton and Tarbock quit of all dues except the geld; his land straddling the Mersey may have been connected with the defence of the Runcorn gap. (See above and fig. 43.1.)

Dunning. The name occurs in Derb., Devon, Hunts., Notts., and Yorks., but is most frequent in the west Midlands, in Glos., Salop., Staffs., and Worcs. In Ches. a single Dunning was Niel de Burcy's antecessor in all three of his manors (297–9), two of which (298–9) were close together in Wirral and contained demesne. Two others (205, 302) were also close; one was retained by Dunning, the other passed to Mundret (see above). Possibly the holder of Knighton (Staffs.) T.R.E. and in 1086 was the same man. In Ches. a Dunning also held Sandbach with its ancient church (242), where he was succeeded by Bigot.

Earngeat (Erniet). The name also occurs in Derb., Herefs., Salop., Suff., and Worcs. In Ches. four manors in Wirral (132–4, 213), three of which passed to Walter de Vernon, were probably all held by the same man T.R.E. A bearer of the name also held an estate in Bochelau hundred (273).

Earnwig (Ernui). A not uncommon name, often, as perhaps in 50, confused with Earnwine. The form *Ernui* occurs four times in Ches., in apparently unrelated contexts (50, 190, 306, 329).

Earnwine (Ernuin). The thegn Earnwine who held one of Robert FitzHugh's demesne manors and who was with Dot one of three holders of a multiple manor that was granted to one of Robert's undertenants, may have been the *Ernui* who was one of Dot's co-tenants at Coddington (50). He was perhaps also William Malbank's antecessor in the 5-hide manor of Tattenhall and in Wirral (136, 140). A bearer of the name was Ilbert de Rullours' antecessor in two of his three manors (285–6).

Edward. A common name, but in Ches. all certainly one man. He held five manors in Tunendune hundred and two in Bochelau, all fairly close (196, 202–3, 205, 292, 294, 296). In three (196, 202–3) he was succeeded by William FitzNiel and in one by an undertenant of William FitzNiel. The other three he retained as an undertenant of Osbern FitzTezzon. One (296) was a multiple manor, shared with Dot, who may have been his lord there (see above). Edward also had a share in another multiple manor (184) where William FitzNiel later held demesne. His holdings of Grappenhall, Great Budworth with its ancient church, and a moiety of Lymm and its church suggest importance. (Fig. 43.1.)

Edwin. A fairly common name, but with significant concentration in Ches., especially on the Welsh border. One bearer of the name, probably the Welshman Edwin of Tegeingl,[72] held a compact group of seven manors in south-west Ches. all of which were held by undertenants of Robert FitzHugh in 1086, three by Edwin himself, three by Edwin and Drew, and one by Drew alone (78–83, 91). Three were multiple manors, on two of which the number of Anglo-Saxon manors was the same as the number of Norman undertenants (78, 80, 91; see above). An Edwin, probably the same man, also retained Coleshill (Flints.) in Atiscros hundred, in 1086, as an undertenant of Robert of Rhuddlan (327). In the same hundred he was probably the T.R.E. tenant of 335 and co-tenant of 336, perhaps under the other holder, Thorth (see above). Other T.R.E. holdings, all probably of the same man, include Gilbert de Venables's important demesne manor of Eccleston (249), and Hope (260), also held by Gilbert. Nearby, Edwin was the T.R.E. holder of manors in which Osbern FitzTezzon and Richard the Butler held demesne in 1086 (130, 289). (Fig. 43.1.)

Gamel. Gamel himself held one manor T.R.E. (290), which later passed to Osbern FitzTezzon and which included the ancient church of Bebington. His father held two manors (303, 309) which Gamel himself had inherited by 1086. The name is common in the Danelaw, but even so the Ches. Gamel is probably to be identified with the Gamel FitzGrifin who in 1086 held three manors in Staffs., formerly the estates of Wulfric and Godric and all close to the Ches. border.[73] His father held Biddulph (Staffs.) and perhaps Weston in Tunendune hundred and Wulfric Spot's manor of Newton by Middlewich with its ancient church (198, 267). Gamel may also be the privileged thegn who held Rochdale (Lancs.) T.R.E. and in 1086. If so, the family was important.

Godgyth (Godid). She held four manors, three of them close together in Bochelau hundred (274, 276–7, 281). In 1086 they were all held by Ranulph, though Godgyth retained one (274) as an undertenant. The assessments were all fairly low, and all were said to be waste T.R.E. The name is fairly rare, though one occurs in south Salop.

Godric. A very common name, but in Ches. the antecessor of Hugh FitzNorman on nine holdings forming a fairly compact group in Middlewich and Hamestan hundreds (214–17, 222–5, 315) was a single individual (see above). Of the two instances (216, 315) in which the manors were multiple, one passed solely to Hugh and was therefore presumably under Godric's lordship (see above), but the other continued to be shared between Hugh and William Malbank in 1086. Probably Hugh did not obtain all of Godric's estates; three other nearby holdings, two in the Dane valley (63, 102) and one further south in Middlewich hundred (147), which seem almost certain to be the same Godric's, passed to Earl Hugh, Robert of Rhuddlan, and William Malbank. Two others (44, 167) are more distant and therefore more doubtful. In all, therefore, Godric probably had at least 12 holdings in Ches., assessed at some 7 or 8 hides. On none of them, however, is demesne recorded and some seven were waste by 1070 and perhaps before. The name also occurs in Salop. and Staffs., where the antecessor of Gamel in Talke and Audley is perhaps the Ches. man. (Fig. 43.1.)

Godwin. A very common name, which occurs on twelve pre-Conquest holdings

---

[72] Lewis, 'Eng. and Norm. Govt.' 145.　　　[73] *V.C.H. Staffs.* iv. 57.

(47, 49, 64, 103, 158, 216, 238, 241, 263-4, 266, 268). The antecessor of Gilbert de Venables on three manors, including his demesne manor of Kinderton, was probably a single individual (263-4, 266).

Gruffudd ap Llywelyn (Rex Grifin). Gruffudd had held extensive lands beyond the Dee until his rebellion and death in 1063 or 1064, including much of Exestan, and the great manors of Rhuddlan and Bistre (7; see above). Domesday records the food rents which the king collected at Bistre (373).

Leofnoth (Levenot). The name, which occurs elsewhere especially in Salop. and Derb., is found in Ches. on 18 manors (71, 105, 107, 109-12, 116, 123, 148, 204, 206, 271, 278, 303, 322, 324-5). The holder of the nine estates in Wirral and Atiscros hundred which later passed to Robert of Rhuddlan was clearly a single important individual, with estates assessed at nearly 11 hides. He may have held a second group of some eight estates, assessed at over $5\frac{1}{2}$ hides, mostly fairly close, in or near Tunendune hundred, which were later divided between Earl Hugh, William FitzNiel, Richard de Vernon, Ranulph, and Wulfgeat (71, 116, 123, 204, 206, 271, 278, 303). Three of them also had the same undertenant (116, 204, 206). No demesne is recorded on Leofnoth's estates and only two (116, 325) were multiple manors. (Fig. 43.1.)

Leofwine (Lewin). A very common name, occurring on seven Ches. manors (170, 173, 194, 210-11, 244, 272). Two adjacent estates near Chester (210-11) which passed to Hugh de Mara were both probably held by the same man. Two others, both held as two manors with Osmaer, were later held by William Malbank, who was also the successor of Leofwine and Edric on two manors in Hodnet hundred (Salop.). All four instances were perhaps the same man.

Orme. Orme is recorded holding only one manor in Ches. T.R.E., the great manor of Halton (197), assessed at 10 hides, of which by 1086 only 5 paid geld. The name occurs elsewhere, once in Lincs. and often in Yorks. The Ches. Orme, who as antecessor of William FitzNiel was presumably an important local figure, may be the same as the important Yorks. Orme, son of Gamel, the restorer of St. Gregory's, Kirkdale, Yorks. was after all an area where Edwin and Morcar had significant estates.[74]

Osmaer (Osmer). A rare name which occurs on 10 holdings in Ches. (120, 122, 125-8, 166, 170, 173, 332). Of those, six were later held by Richard de Vernon, four in a compact group in Middlewich hundred, including Richard's *caput* of Shipbrook, Davenham with its ancient church, and another demesne manor, and two were some distance away in Warmundestrou hundred (120, 122, 125-8; see above). Three other holdings in Warmundestrou, all multiple manors in which Osmaer occurs with another tenant, passed to William Malbank. One outlier near Chester (332) was later held by Hugh FitzOsbern. Osmaer's estates were fairly widely dispersed, though they had an obvious focus in the ancient parish of Davenham, also the main component of the Norman barony of Shipbrook. (See above and fig. 43.1.)

Ravenkel (Ravechel, Ravechet, Ravecate). The name also occurs in Yorks., Herefs., Staffs., and Derb. In Ches. Ravenkel was one of the T.R.E. holders of the multiple manor of Burwardesley and may have been its lord, since Domesday records that he bought there a hide of land taken from St. Werburgh's and sold by the reeves of Earls Edwin and Morcar (92). The estate was later held by an undertenant of Robert FitzHugh. Ravenkel also held land in Warmundestrou

[74] *V.C.H. Yorks.* ii. 177; Lewis, 'Eng. and Norm. Govt.' 94-5.

and Atiscros hundreds which passed to William Malbank and Hugh FitzOsbern (179, 328, 333). No demesne is recorded on his holdings and three of the four were held by undertenants in 1086 (92, 328, 333).

Ravensward (*Ravesuar, Ravesua, Ravesue, Ravesuard*). The name occurs also in Herefs., Salop., Staffs., and Yorks. In Ches. it is found on four dispersed estates T.R.E., three of them multiple manors (189, 300, 315, 331).

Stenulf. A fairly rare name which in Ches. may refer to a single individual with three holdings, assessed at just over 5 hides (94, 245, 287). They were all quite close together in the middle of the shire, but had different post-Conquest successors.

Thorth (*Thoret, Toret, Toreth*). An important landholder with seven holdings in Ches., including the great manor of Gresford (116, 185, 247, 283, 314, 335). The name also occurs in East Anglia and Salop., where it probably represents the same man. (See above and fig. 38.2.)

Toki. A fairly common name, but the holder of three manors in southern Wirral (100, 117–18) later held by Richard de Vernon and Robert FitzHugh was probably a single individual. Two other holdings in Roelau hundred retained by Earl Hugh (39, 41) presumably also belonged to the same man. A Toki was also one of the two tenants of a multiple manor in Tunendune hundred (200), later held by an undertenant of William FitzNiel.

Wulfgeat (*Uviet, Ulviet*). An important landowner who perhaps survived the Conquest as the earl's tenant at Bartington, though he retained none of his T.R.E. estates. Wulfgeat was the principal antecessor of Gilbert de Venables, who succeeded him in seven estates (251, 254–5, 257, 259, 261–2), and he was almost certainly the antecessor of Ranulf de Mesnilwarin in another two (279, 312). His holding included an exceptionally large number of Domesday churches: High Legh and Rostherne (which he held with Dot), Astbury, a moiety of Lymm, and Northenden (254–5, 261, 312). The bulk of his estates were in Bochelau hundred, around Rostherne, and in Middlewich around Newbold Astbury, but he also had an important manor in Riseton hundred, where Gilbert de Venables later held demesne (251). In all, his estates were assessed at *c.* 10 hides. The name occurs elsewhere at manors in Wirral, Roelau, and Warmundestrou (46, 135, 153) later held by the earl, Walter de Venables, and William Malbank, but since it is very common it is uncertain whether they represent the same man. The holder of half the church of Stoke (Staffs.) may, however, be identical with the holder of the Ches. churches. (Fig. 43.1.)

Wulfheah (*Ulfac*). The name occurs mostly in Ches. but also in Salop. and Staffs. Two holdings where Wulfheah preceded William Malbank, one in Riseton the other in Warmundestrou hundred (138, 177) were presumably held by one man, who perhaps also held another manor in Riseton (246). A bearer of the name also held two other Ches. estates T.R.E. (37, 337).

Wulfric (*Ulvric*). A fairly common name, and if all referring to the same man in Ches. his estates were widespread (67, 98–9, 129, 161, 220, 226, 307, 310). The Wulfric who retained two estates in Hamestan hundred in 1086 was probably the man who continued to hold another as the undertenant of Richard de Vernon (129, 307, 310; see above). Another pre-Conquest group was perhaps the two estates in Riseton hundred which passed to Robert FitzHugh (98–9). The name also occurs in Dudestan, Middlewich, and Wirral hundreds (67, 220, 226).

The names of the remaining Anglo-Saxon tenants named in the Ches. Domesday, holders of three or fewer manors, or of under five hides, are as follows:

Almaer (*Elmar*), 150, 333; Alnoth (*Alnod*), 286; Alsige (*Alsi*), 122, 124; Alstan (*Alestan*), 243; Alweald (*Alwold*), 221; Ansgot, 50, 234; Archil, 216; Arngrim (*Haregrim, Aregrim*), 124, 149; Auti (*Outi*), 146; Beollan (*Belam*), 243; Beornwulf (*Bernulf*), 62, 240; Bers, 121; Brihtmar (*Brismer*), 85; Carle, 45, 154; Colben, 207, 311; Cypping (*Cheping*), 52; Deorc (*Derch*), 149, 163; Doda (*Dodo*), 253; Eadric (*Edric*), 135, 168, 171; Earnwig (*Ernui*) Fot, 42; Eli, 93; Erchenbrand (*Echebrant, Erchebrand*), 191, 193; Erlekin, 162; Esbern (*Sberne*), 338; Frani (*Fran*), 155; Glewin, 252; Grim, 39; Grimkel (*Grinchel*), 288; Gunnar (*Gunner*), 104, 212; Gunning (*Gunninc*), 157; Guthlac (*Gothlac*), 40; Hacon, 164, 172, 230; Hasten, 209; Healfdene (*Alden, Halden*), 157, 163, 177; Hunding (*Hundin*), 101, 291; Hundulf, 97; Ketel (*Chetel*), 300; Leofgeat (*Leviet*), 189; Leofric (*Levric*), 40, 162, 199; Loten, 137; Luvede, 135; Lyfing (*Leving*), 141; Morfar, 300; Ording (*Ordm*), 58; Osgot, 114–15; Owen (*Owine*), 162, 166; Pat, 313; Ragenald (*Ragenal*), 70; Raven (*Ravene*), 85, 293, 301; Rhys (*Rees*), 284; Saeweard (*Seward*), 159, 165; Segrid, 195; Stein, 51, 55; Steinketel (*Steinchetel*), 235; Sucga (*Suga*), 313; Uhtbrand (*Ostebrand*), 269; Uhtraed (*Uctred*), 113, 200; Ulf, 104; Ulfketel (*Ulchetel, Ulchel*), 106, 108, 160; Wicga (*Wighe*), 201; Wintrelet, 144; Wudumann (*Udeman*), 90, 313; Wulfbert (*Ulbert*), 325; Wulfgar (*Ulgar*), priest, 219; Wulfgifu (*Ulveva, Ulveve*), 84, 178, 180; Wulfmaer (*Ulmer*), 323; Wulfnoth (*Ulnod*), 218; Wulfsige (*Ulsi*), 195, 282; Wulfwig (*Ulvoi*), 86–7, 95; Wulfwine 'cild' (*Vluuinchit*), 184.

THE BOROUGHS

Chester[75]

Though Domesday provides an exceptionally detailed treatment of Chester, its account is in many ways so unusual that it is difficult to interpret. Particular problems are posed by its rare allusions to trade and to the borough court, its detailed account of offences and forfeitures, and its reticence about burgesses and burgage tenure.

Chester, like other major towns, was treated as a hundred in Domesday. With its assessment of 50 hides it belongs to the category of the half-hundred, though unlike, for example, Ipswich it was never formally designated as such.[76] The hundred had a small suburban or non-urban belt comprising what might be reckoned the four vills of 'Bruge' (Handbridge), Newton by Chester, 'Lee' (Overleigh and Netherleigh), and 'Redcliff', which were expressly said to be 'outside the city', but which gelded with it and were assessed at 3½ hides. Also included in the suburban area, and seemingly distinguished from 'Redcliff', is the 'bishop's borough' (*burgus episcopi*), which appears to have been quit of geld.[77] In 1066 the principal landowners in the city were the king, the earl, and the bishop. There were then 431 houses in demesne in the city, presumably paying *gablum* or rent to king and earl, and a further 56 held by the bishop (1a). Another 13 houses were held by the canons of St. Werburgh's and 8 by the canons of St. John's, all free from the customary dues (12, 14). The city seems to have been characterized by tenurial heterogeneity; for besides such house tenures, the Survey refers to a claim by Robert of Rhuddlan

---

[75] Full treatment of Chester in the 11th century is reserved for *V.C.H. Ches.* v.

[76] J. Tait, *Medieval Boro.* 45–8.

[77] nos. 1a and n.3, 10, 181–3, 210–12.

that his church of St. Peter was located on 'thegnland' attached to a rural manor and occupied not by burgesses but by *hospites* exempt from the dues to king and earl (1e). In the hundred outside the city itself there were also eight manors, one held by the bishop (10), three by Arni (181–3), two by Leofwine (210–11), and one each by Gunnor (212) and Wulfnoth (218). After the Conquest, the borough was mediatized and Earl Hugh acquired the rights of Anglo-Saxon king and earl (1e). By then there were other landowners besides the bishop, for the Survey tells of 37 burgesses belonging to the manors of Dodleston (334), Claverton (332), and Weaverham (36), and a further 3 burgages (*masurae, domus*) belonging to Hawarden (320) and Dunham Massey (227). There also remained the eight suburban manors, the bishop retaining his at Redcliff, those of Arni passing to William FitzNiel, those of Leofwine and Gunnor to Hugh de Mara, and that of Wulfnoth to Hugh FitzOsbern.

The dominant position of king, earl, and bishop in the life of the pre-Conquest city is indicated by the fact that the 12 'judges' (*iudices civitatis*) who presided over the Chester hundred court were drawn from their men. The judges, who were liable to fines of 10s. payable to the king and the earl for failure to attend, have been regarded as a sign of Scandinavian influence and equated with the 'lawmen' (*lagemen*) of such boroughs as Lincoln and Stamford, and the *iudices* of York. There is, however, no indication that they enjoyed the same status as their namesakes in the Danelaw towns, with their extensive properties and judicial privileges, but even so the reference is significant, since it provides a rare unambiguous allusion to a pre-Conquest borough court, which though known as the hundred court must have been rather different from those of the rural hundreds.[78]

The laws of Chester are defined in exceptional detail (1b), and demonstrate the variety of local usage, for the penalties they prescribed differ considerably from those enjoined for similar offences in other cities of the Welsh border such as Hereford and Shrewsbury. They included the great pleas of the Crown, such as 'hamfare' (housebreaking), 'forsteal', and homicide, and it is probable that in the pre-Conquest period such serious crimes came before the borough court, even though afterwards they are more likely to have been subject to the earl of Chester. The arrangements under the Norman earls are conjectural, but by the late 13th century the justiciar of the royal earls presided over a separate court of Crown pleas for the city.[79]

The Chester customs suggest that as in other western towns the burgesses' status was comparatively low; they were obliged on pain of forfeiture to pay 10s. relief on taking up land in the city, and were also liable to heavy fines for failure to pay their *gablum* or rent, for wrongful disseisin or even making wrongful claims to another's land, and for allowing fire to break out in their houses. Other fines were imposed upon ships which arrived at or left the port without a royal licence, or which came thither in defiance of a royal prohibition, and upon those responsible for false measures or bad beer. Dues were payable on each load shipped from the port, and tolls exacted on pain of a fine of 40s. if they were withheld for more than three nights (1c).[80]

All such fines and other dues were shared between king and earl mostly in the proportion of two thirds to one third, and collected by their local representatives or reeves. The whole of the borough renders were at farm in 1066 for the sum of

[78] Tait, *Medieval Boro.* 43–4; *Dom. Surv. Ches.* 32–3; S. Reynolds, *Eng. Medieval Town*, 95.

[79] Tait, *Medieval Boro.* 44–5.

[80] *Dom. Surv. Ches.* 35.

£45 and three 'timbres' of marten skins (1d), perhaps the equivalent of the £70 and a mark of gold paid by Mundret to Earl Hugh after the Conquest (1c). Presumably the principal items so farmed were tolls and the judicial profits, which probably included the Crown pleas for the shire as a whole.[81] Other dues not included in the farm were the fines levied on the lords of those who defaulted on their duty to maintain the city's bridge and defences, and the £7 payable by the seven moneyers when the coinage was changed (1d). A further render of $10\frac{1}{2}$ marks of silver, two thirds to the king, one third to the earl, perhaps represents the total amount of *gablum* payable by the demesne houses (1a).[82]

The earl's position at Chester appears to have been relatively powerful, much more so than in Shrewsbury, for example. Like the king he appointed a representative to safeguard his interests there, referred to variously as a reeve (*praepositus*) or *minister*, whose peace, like that of the king's reeve, was protected from infringement by a fine of 40s. (1c).[83] The king's reeve, significantly never referred to as sheriff, also reserved a pre-emptive right to the purchase of marten pelts imported into the city, and a reeve, presumably the same official, had the duty to summon a man from each hide of the shire to repair the city wall and bridge, under the threat of a fine (1b, 1c).

The bishop too was entitled to fines levied in Chester, in particular to those exacted for infringements of the prohibitions on working or trading on Sundays and holy days in the city and its environs (*leuua civitatis*). His position in Chester, with his extensive property in the city and in Redcliff, and his other rights, is exceptional, and considerably stronger than in the other shire towns in his diocese.[84]

In 1066 Chester had 508 houses, representing a sizable urban population by 11th-century standards (1a, 12, 14). It was still a town of some importance, with a varied economic base. Besides coining, other activities included bone, leather, and metal working, and at St. John's there was a workshop manufacturing memorial crosses. Archaeologically the contrast with the period before the later 9th century is striking. Timber structures were built both within the legionary fortress and to the south of it and Chester ware has been found at sites all over the city, though no kilns like those at Stafford have been located.[85]

The city was described as 'greatly wasted' when Earl Hugh received it, presumably in the campaign of 1069-70 (1e). It was then worth only £30, and there were, as there remained in 1086, 205 houses fewer than there had been in 1066, a depletion partly to be accounted for by the construction of the castle in the south-west corner of the city.[86] It has been estimated that in 1086 the population was not more than 1,500.[87] Nevertheless, in other ways, notably in the moving of the cathedral from Lichfield to Chester in 1075, the city had benefited from the advent of Norman rule. It remained a trading centre with strong Hiberno-Norse connexions, the only commodity expressly mentioned being martens' skins, probably from Ireland or Scandinavia.[88]

Rhuddlan

Rhuddlan is the only other borough in the Cheshire Domesday. Long an important centre, the *caput* of Englefield, in the 1070s the town was divided between Earl

[81] Ibid. 33; Tait, *Medieval Boro.* 143-4, 153.
[82] *Dom. Surv. Ches.* 36.
[83] Tait, *Medieval Boro.* 143-4.
[84] nos. 1a, 1d, 3; *Dom. Surv. Ches.* 27; *V.C.H. Ches.* v, forthcoming.
[85] Above, 'A.-S. Ches.'.
[86] *V.C.H. Ches.* ii. 1; *J.C.A.S.* lxiv. 21-7.
[87] Darby, *Dom. Eng.* 307.
[88] *Dom. Surv. Ches.* 35-6; Tait, *Medieval Boro.* 117; *V.C.H. Ches.* v, forthcoming.

Hugh and Robert of Rhuddlan, and made the focus of the Norman attack on North Wales. It received a motte and bailey castle, at a site now called Twt hill, separated from the Edwardian castle and connected with the presumed burh of *Cledemutha*. By then it also had a mint and a church, like the castle shared between the earl and Robert. Robert's moiety was probably more important, for he had 10 burgesses to the earl's 8, and was credited by Orderic with responsibility for building the castle at the king's command. Hugh and Robert modelled their new borough on customs already extant, granting the burgesses there as in so many other new boroughs the laws and customs of Hereford and Breteuil, the distinguishing characteristic of which was a fine of 1s. for all except the most serious crimes, such as homicide and 'hamfare'. By 1086 the borough's importance was probably still primarily military; its tolls were farmed for a mere 3s.[89]

THE SALT-WICHES

The Cheshire Domesday contains a uniquely detailed account of the arrangements governing the manufacture and distribution of salt in the three main wiches of Nantwich, Northwich, and Middlewich. Nantwich (316) was the most productive. In 1066 it contained a brinepit and eight demesne salthouses (*salinae*), belonging to the king and Earl Edwin, where the 'boilings' which produced the salt took place. A further salthouse belonging to the earl was attached to his manor of Acton, of which Nantwich was originally a dependency. Nantwich also contained an unspecified number of additional salthouses held by 'very many men of the country' (*patria*), presumably those held in common which were contrasted with those in demesne in the Survey. The renders or 'boilings' of the salthouses were carefully regulated, and were shared between king and earl in the usual ratio of two to one. The demesne houses yielded 16 boilings, or just over one packload of salt, each Friday after a week of work throughout the year, while the others made such renders only in the winter, from Martinmas (11 November) to Ascension Day. By 1066 Nantwich was the most valuable of the salt-wiches, at farm for £21, a sum which also included the profits from the Crown pleas of the hundred in which it lay. It suffered considerably in the devastation of 1069–70, for when William Malbank received it from Earl Hugh it was waste except for one salthouse. By 1086 it had recovered somewhat, the wich itself being at farm for £10 and the hundred which went with it for a further £2.

Middlewich (317) contained no demesne salthouses, though in 1066 as at Nantwich the renders were shared between the king and earl. It was then at farm for £8, together with the hundred in which it lay which brought in a further £2. When Earl Hugh received it, however, it was waste, and in 1086 it and the hundred were at farm for £3 5s.

At Northwich (319) no demesne was mentioned, though in 1066 the king and earl divided the renders as in the other two wiches. An unspecified number of thegns were mentioned as having salthouses there but were exempt from the render of Friday boilings throughout the year. Northwich too was then at farm for £8 but was waste when Earl Hugh received it. In 1086 it was worth 35s.

In addition to the references to salthouses under the main entries relating to the wiches there are references to others attached to various manors scattered through-

---

[89] nos. 340, 349, 366; *Dom. Surv. Ches.* 38–9.

out the Cheshire Domesday. That at Nantwich belonging to Acton manor has already been mentioned, but there were 11½ others attached to Weaverham, Frodsham, Hartford, Halton, Wincham, and Tatton, all at an unspecified 'Wich', which on grounds of proximity should probably be identified with Northwich. One other attached to Claverton manor was definitely at Northwich, and another at 'Burwardestone' was perhaps at Dirtwich, a minor salt spring south of Malpas.[90]

Salt was an important commodity in the early Middle Ages and in Cheshire as elsewhere it was regulated by an elaborate system of tolls. In the winter months, between Martinmas and Ascensiontide, tolls were paid on all salt produced but in the summer they were paid only on salt which was sold. In Nantwich and Middlewich tolls were assessed by the oxcart, according to the size of the load and the number of oxen, and by the load carried by a packhorse or a man. Distinctions were made between men of the 'home' hundred and those of other hundreds in the shire. In Northwich tolls were rather lighter, and the crucial distinction was between the men of Cheshire and those from other shires, perhaps because Northwich unlike Nantwich and Middlewich was not the *caput* of a hundred. A further regulation prescribed tolls for those who 'carted salt about the county to sell it'. The seasonal differences in the tolls were perhaps occasioned by the important extra uses to which salt was put in the summer and autumn months, in preserving herring and slaughtered beasts.[91]

In Middlewich and Nantwich penalties for various offences connected with the salt trade, such as the overloading of carts and horses, were payable to locally based officials (*ministri*) of the king or the earl. Their authority seems to have extended 1 league outside the salt-wiches. At Nantwich, too, there was a boundary within which anyone incurring a forfeiture could make amends with 2s. or 30 boilings of salt, except for theft or homicide which were punishable by death.[92]

The detailed provisions regulating the itinerant traders and the sale of salt to men from other hundreds and from outside the shire suggest that the trade extended over a wide area, and that many of the saltways in use in the Middle Ages were already in being before the Conquest. Place names suggest that there were three routes running westwards from the salt-wiches to Chester, which was evidently the principal market for Cheshire salt and which in the Middle Ages levied tolls at the Eastgate.[93] Possibly the salt was exported to Wales; certainly it crossed the Dee at Farndon to go to Holt. Other routes led east from the salt-wiches to Macclesfield and across the Pennines into Derbyshire, and a further group went north via Warrington and Manchester into Lancashire and along the valleys of the Aire and Wharfe into Yorkshire. There was also a route from Stockport through the remote regions of Longdendale and the Etherow valley.[94]

The fact that the salt-wiches were the focus of such a wide-ranging network of trade routes, and that in Domesday they were the subject of a separate and detailed section suggests that they were places of considerable importance, not simply 'little manufacturing enclaves'.[95] The association of Nantwich and Middlewich with hundredal administration and justice and the presence there of royal officials confirms that impression. Indeed, it has been suggested that they should be regarded as towns, and certainly both Nantwich and Middlewich were associated with places of ancient significance.[96]

[90] nos. 36, 43, 151, 253, 256, 272; J. Oxley, 'Nantwich: an 11th-Century Salt Town and its Origin', *T.H.S.L.C.* cxxxi. 5-6.
[91] *T.H.S.L.C.* cxxxi. 1-3.
[92] Ibid. 4-5; no. 318.
[93] On the Eastgate see *V.C.H. Ches.* v, forthcoming.
[94] W. B. Crump, 'Saltways from the Cheshire Wiches', *T.L.C.A.S.* liv. 84-142.
[95] *Dom. Surv. Ches.* 40.
[96] *T.H.S.L.C.* cxxxi. 6-9, 11-16.

THE RURAL POPULATION

At the top of the social scale and presumably generally absentees were the earl's undertenants on his largest demesne manors, such as Eastham (57), Weaverham (36), and Upton (69). They included his principal baronial tenants, men such as William Malbank, Hamon de Massey, Hugh FitzNorman, and Joscelin. Such men could also hold of one another. At 'Edritone' (Flints.), for example, there were especially complex arrangements; the estate was held of Hugh FitzOsbern by an undertenant called Richard, but both Osbern FitzTezzon and Hugh FitzNorman were also said to have lands there, assessed at the full 1½ hides assigned to the manor, and the relationship between them and Richard remains obscure (333). Other than the earl and his principal undertenants, the top stratum of rural society in Cheshire in 1086 comprised a large and fairly diverse group of named, mainly French, landholders, unnamed 'Frenchmen' (*francigenae*), and unnamed knights (*milites*) and serjeants (*servientes*), also presumably newcomers.[97] The various categories within the group overlapped to some extent, though the men distinguished by name presumably had more status than the unnamed and the knights appear to have enjoyed a higher form of tenure than the 'Frenchmen'. Only one of the latter was named, Tual, who held of Robert of Rhuddlan in unhidated Atiscros (359).

Only three serjeants are expressly recorded in Cheshire, two holding of the earl (304, 342) and one of Robert of Rhuddlan, the latter closely associated with a Frenchman at Robert's estate of Caldy (110). Probably the lesser Frenchmen who held directly of the earl also commonly held by serjeanty tenures. They included those whose holdings were listed collectively towards the end of Hugh's honor, in a position equivalent to that of the king's serjeants and king's thegns in counties where there was royal demesne (300–11). One indeed was entered simply as a 'serjeant of the earl' (304). Even some of the Englishmen so listed were probably Earl Hugh's serjeants, particularly Dunning, whose manor of Kingsley (305) was later held by a family occupying the hereditary post of master forester of Delamere. Kingsley had been put in the forest by 1086 and the manor included a hawk's eyrie and no fewer than four deer hedges.[98] Dunning may himself have been the first of the line of master foresters. Though most of the men enfeoffed with holdings on Earl Hugh's demesne were his barons, at least one seems to have been a serjeant: Herbert of Upton by Chester (69) was almost certainly Herbert the Jerkin-maker, and that surname probably identifies him as a serjeant.[99]

The presence of Odard among Earl Hugh's serjeants (301) links that group with the undertenants of the barons, since Odard was primarily a man of William FitzNiel on the fee of Halton (197–9, 206). Most of the earl's leading tenants had made enfeoffments in Cheshire to named men, and naturally the lords of the great baronial fiefs had most; Robert of Rhuddlan, for example, had at least 6, William FitzNiel 13, and Robert FitzHugh 10.[1] Named undertenants, like their lords, might have scattered holdings elsewhere on Earl Hugh's fief. It seems likely, for example, that the Drew and Ranulph who held of Robert FitzHugh at Buscot (Berks.) are to be identified with the tenants bearing the same names who held of Robert in Cheshire, and that the Humphrey who held of the same lord at Tushingham was

---

[97] The following paragraphs on the tenants were contributed by Dr. Lewis.

[98] Ormerod, *Hist. Ches.* ii. 87–9.

[99] *T.H.S.L.C.* cxxxi. 159–60.

[1] *Dom. Surv. Ches.* 62; nos. 104–9, 324, 326–7 (Rob. of Rhuddlan); 188–9, 193, 197–9, 204–7, 315, 330 (Wm. Fitz-Niel); 78–85, 88–94 (Rob. FitzHugh).

Humphrey de Costentin who held of the earl at Coppingford (Hunts.).[2] Similarly, the Pain (*Pagen*) who in Cheshire held land of Richard de Vernon and William FitzNiel may be the Pain de Vilars who was later lord of Warrington (Lancs.). If so, it is further evidence of that interweaving of landholding on either side of the Mersey apparently initiated in the 10th century.[3]

FitzNiel's named tenants at Halton (197) were referred to as knights (*milites*), and probably at least some of the undertenants of the other barons were of the same low knightly status.[4] There was also in Cheshire a group of 12 unnamed knights who overlapped with named men. Those whose holdings were given individual fiscal assessments, including the men of Halton, had between $\frac{1}{2}$ hide and 2 hides each, though some of the named baronial undertenants had rather more. The group of knights enfeoffed by Robert FitzHugh at his *caput* of Malpas and the nearby estates of Bettisfield, 'Burwardestone', and Worthenbury (72–5) compares closely with FitzNiel's named men at Halton.

The 40 'Frenchmen' of Domesday Cheshire were socially below the knights; all were listed among the rural population associated with ploughteams and none had a fiscally assessed tenement. Those whose holdings can be computed had $\frac{1}{2}$, $\frac{3}{4}$, or 1 ploughteam. Others were commonly listed before the radmen, villeins, and bordars with whom they were linked, an indication that they may have enjoyed some degree of lordship over the English peasantry.

Radmen, of whom 134 were recorded in Cheshire, were virtually confined to the counties of the Domesday west Midlands circuit.[5] Called radknights (*radchenistres*) in the southern part of the Welsh border, they were freemen whose place in society can be equated with that of the *liberi homines* and sokemen of the eastern counties. They were almost certainly identical as a class with the men subject to the *lex equitandi* on the bishop of Worcester's estates, and are generally thought to have performed honourable riding services, not necessarily military in nature, for their lords. They probably held larger agricultural tenements than the villeins. Within Cheshire they were most numerous in the southern and eastern hundreds of Hamestan, Middlewich, Riseton, and Warmundestrou, and in hidated Atiscros where they constituted some 10 per cent of the recorded rural population. They were most sparse west of Wat's Dyke and in Exestan hundred. Radmen were spread fairly evenly among 93 estates within the county, mostly singly or in twos, though there were seven on the earl's great manor of Eastham. Two thirds had holdings, usually associated with villeins and other peasants, on estates where the lord had no home farm, indicating that a radman's tenement was in some way a substitute for direct exploitation of demesne. Nearly all those radmen were listed before the other classes of the rural population. Radmen living on manors with home farms were not usually so placed and may have been of different status.

Most numerous were the labouring classes, the 677 villeins and 577 bordars. They form about the same proportion of the recorded population in Cheshire as in England as a whole. Generally, as elsewhere they were associated with men of higher status, but occasionally they appear to have held very small manors without a resident lord or radman. Though villeins formed the largest single group in the recorded population, they were absent from many holdings where cultivation was

[2] Farrer, *Hons. and Kts.' Fees*, ii. 22–3, 27; nos. 77–8, 80–1, 88–9, 91–2.

[3] nos. 119, 204–6; *V.C.H. Lancs.* i. 280; above, 'A.-S. Ches.'.

[4] For a discussion of knightly status see R. Allen Brown,

'Status of the Norman Kt.' *War and Government in the Middle Ages*, ed. J. Gillingham and J. C. Holt, 18–32.

[5] Darby, *Dom. Eng.* 83–4; P. Vinogradoff, *Eng. Soc. in 11th Cent.* 69–71.

carried on by bordars, oxmen, and serfs.[6] The term bordar could simply mean peasants of a lower economic status than villeins, but it could also be applied to those living on the margins of estates and perhaps involved in assarts.[7] In Cheshire their distribution suggests that in some areas at least they may be interpreted as agents of agricultural expansion. In west Cheshire, where there was relatively little woodland and much of what there was was probably of a managed kind, they occurred in greatest numbers on manors without recorded woodland, especially in Wirral where they were numerous. In east Cheshire, in Hamestan hundred, where there was considerably more ancient woodland, they were comparatively few. Probably in neither area were bordars involved in clearance. In central Cheshire, however, in a hundred such as Warmundestrou, they were relatively numerous, but were more densely distributed on manors with woodland than on those without. There they may have been involved in assarts. Their distribution suggests, then, that by 1086 west Cheshire had largely been cleared, while in the centre clearance was still going on, and in the east it had hardly begun.[8]

Where villeins or bordars or radmen were the sole holders of ploughteams on an estate, some indication can be gained of their relative prosperity. Assuming that eight oxen formed a team, the 95 villeins for whom such a calculation is possible had an average of 2.7 oxen. The much smaller samples of 24 bordars and 13 radmen averaged 1.9 and 5 oxen respectively. The figures conceal the likely preponderance of villeins owning 2 or 4 oxen and of bordars owning 1 or 2.[9] They also obscure differences in the peasants' economic position on the various types of manor; for instance the 33 villeins on manors where they were the only recorded inhabitants held on average 3.5 oxen each. Such variations in economic status underline the fact that the terms *villanus*, *bordarius*, etc. were applied in Domesday to what may well have been diverse groups of men.

At the very lowest level were the 205 serfs (*servi*) and bondwomen (*ancillae*), and the 163 oxmen (*bovarii*).[10] Except for a single example from Warwickshire, oxmen were confined in the Survey to Cheshire, Shropshire, Herefordshire, and Worcestershire, and it has been argued that they were virtually the same as serfs.[11] In Cheshire, however, serfs and oxmen were distinguished by rather different patterns of distribution, though both groups were connected almost exclusively with demesne farms. Oxmen were especially linked with arable cultivation, and 149 of them were distributed in Cheshire at the ratio of 2 to each demesne plough. Generally the home farm was worked by a single ploughteam with 2 oxmen, though there were instances of $\frac{1}{2}$ ploughteam worked by 1 oxman, and of $1\frac{1}{2}$, 2, 3, and 4 teams worked by 3, 4, 6, and 8 men, perhaps the result of counting together the home farms of several undertenants within a large estate. The agricultural practice thus represented was probably, as in the later Middle Ages, a ploughman guiding the plough with an assistant, perhaps a boy, to lead the team. Eighty-one of the 188 *servi* were disposed in the same way, but they seem to have performed a wider range of functions on the demesne. Oxmen were, in fact, a specialized form of serf. Some estates appear to have distinguished between the two groups; on Earl Hugh's home farm at Weaverham (36), for instance, the two ploughteams were operated by two oxmen and two serfs. Elsewhere, however, the distinction may have been purely one of nomenclature; the bishop of Chester, for example,

[6] *Dom. Surv. Ches.* 64–5; *Dom. Geog. N. Eng.* 347, 387; below, table iv; nos. 250, 253, 261.
[7] Harvey, in *Medieval Settlement*, 197–9.
[8] Inf. from Dr. Higham.
[9] *Econ. Jnl.* lv. 244–6; lxi. 342–71.
[10] *Dom. Geog. N. Eng.* 347; *Dom. Surv. Ches.* 67–70.
[11] Darby, *Dom. Eng.* 78–9.

had six oxmen and no serfs on his home farms, while St. Werburgh's had no oxmen and 23 serfs.

The handful of bondwomen evidently represented different types of servile tenants. Those at Christleton (77) were probably working the ploughs since no *servi* or oxmen were recorded, whereas those at Warford (274) were perhaps the domestic servants of Ranulph's resident female undertenant, Godgyth. The few recorded cannot have comprised the entire female servile population in 1086.

The six referred to as 'men' (*homines*) should not be regarded as a homogeneous class. The three 'other men' at Bettisfield (72) were contrasted with villeins, bordars, and *servi* and may have been Welsh. The man at Larkton (81) was contrasted with a bordar and, since he paid a lower rent, may have been of lower status.

TABLE IV: THE CLASSES OF POPULATION

Of various estimates of the Domesday population of Cheshire no two entirely agree: e.g. *Dom. Geog. N. Eng.* 347, 387; *Dom. Surv. Ches.* 62–71; *T.L.C.A.S.* li. 26. The figures below are for the area covered by the pre-1974 county of Cheshire together with the hidated and unhidated portions of Wales included in the Cheshire folios.

villeins	677	radmen	134	unnamed *milites*	12	*hospites*	3
bordars	577	Frenchmen	40	*Homines*	6	serjeants	3
serfs and bondwomen	205	priests	32	reeves	6	miller	1
oxmen	163	fishermen	14	smiths	4	thegn	1

TOTAL 1,878

SETTLEMENT AND THE AGRARIAN ECONOMY

The basic unit of the Survey[12] was the estate, which in Cheshire was occasionally fairly large, as at Eastham, Weaverham, and Halton, but more often relatively small. No neat equation can be made between estate and settlement and the Survey should not be regarded as in any way a comprehensive indicator of the latter. There were probably numerous omissions, especially on the great estates, in whose assessments many unrecorded dependent settlements were included. For that reason the density of Domesday names is relatively low around Eastham and Halton, and many later townships near those estate centres were omitted from the Survey. In some instances there is early evidence for the pre-Conquest existence of places not included in Domesday Book; Runcorn and Thelwall, the sites of 10th-century burhs and later of medieval settlements are important examples.[13]

The largest Cheshire assessment, 22 hides, was borne by Eastham, but that was exceptional. Only two other estates were assessed in double figures, and many, such as the bulk of the holdings of Gilbert de Venables, were credited with very low hidages indeed, being tenanted only by radmen or even a few villeins and bordars with half a ploughteam.[14] Such estates might be coterminous with what was to

---

[12] Full treatment of the economic and social aspects of the Domesday survey is reserved for forthcoming volumes. For the most comprehensive published account see *Dom. Geog. N. Eng.* 330–91.

[13] Above; Ormerod, *Hist. Ches.* i. 674–5, 746; *Ches. Arch. Bull.* viii. 20.

[14] nos. 57, 250, 252–3, 261, 264, 266.

become a single township or even smaller. Thus Dutton in Great Budworth contained three manors, assessed at $\frac{1}{2}$ hide, $\frac{1}{2}$ virgate, and $1\frac{1}{2}$ virgates (202, 294, 301), while the small adjacent township of Bartington, also in Great Budworth, was divided between a further two, both again $\frac{1}{2}$ hide (302–3). Norton in Runcorn contained the manor of Eanley in Norton as well as Norton itself (200–1), while the vill of Tabley Superior was expressly said to contain three small estates and was already divided from Tabley Inferior which had one (194–5, 269). At Peover there were four Domesday estates, none assessed at more than $\frac{2}{3}$ hide, and all clearly contained within the later townships of Nether Peover, Peover Inferior, and Peover Superior, though not all can be identified.[15] Probably the existence of numerous small estates helps to explain the multiple manors so common in Cheshire before the Conquest. In some instances such estates were consolidated; Norton, which had been held as two manors, is an example. Elsewhere, however, multiple manors might remain. That is particularly so on Robert FitzHugh's estates in Malpas, where Cholmondeley, for example, was held as two manors by Edwin and Dot in 1066, and continued in 1086 to be held by two undertenants (78). Probably some of the joint tenancies listed after the main tenants are further examples of similar linkings of small estates. An obvious instance is Sinderland and Baguley, which was assessed at 1 hide, but held as four manors before the Conquest and as three after (313).

The process by which what had once been a single territorial unit broke down into smaller estates, which sometimes became medieval townships, was complex. The examples of the Peovers and Tableys have already been mentioned, but there were many others. In some instances, such as the Meols (111–12), two manors bearing the same name and obviously components of a former territorial unit were held by the same lord both in 1066 and 1086. Elsewhere, as with the Mollingtons (103–4), Traffords (28, 40, 58), Tableys, and Peovers, manors held by different tenants before the Conquest continued to be treated as separate entities even though in some instances they had passed to the same post-Conquest lord.

Only a minority of the estates described in the Cheshire Domesday were organized on the lines of the manorial system as it is usually understood, with a simple division between the lord's home farm, worked by serfs and oxmen, and the holdings of his dependent peasants, mostly villeins and bordars, who had their own ploughteams. Of 325 estates in the Domesday county excluding the unhidated portion of Atiscros hundred, only 86 were manors of that type, a further 12 being complex estates which had been partially subinfeudated and so contained one or more such classical manors. In contrast 24 estates comprised simply a home farm, while a further 47 lacked one altogether, the only ploughteams belonging to villeins, bordars, and others. The figures exclude the large number of small manors which were occupied by an individual of greater status than a villein, but lower than the French and English undertenants of Earl Hugh and his barons. Most of the 69 such manors were in the hands of radmen, though a few were held by Frenchmen and one by a thegn. The group is characterized by the absence of demesne ploughteams and the listing of the radmen or their equivalents first among the tenantry. Where *servi* and oxmen were on the holding, they were commonly there in the ratio of two to each ploughteam. That suggests that the tenure of the radmen or Frenchmen was intermediate between that of the named feudal lord and the villeins and bordars.

[15] nos. 196, 258, 273, 275; *Ches. Arch. Bull.* viii. 15.

Twenty-three estates had demesne ploughteams, with *servi* or oxmen, and villeins and others without teams. It is unclear whether the latter belonged to the demesne, and hence whether the manors were of the classical or purely home farm type. A further 58 estates were recorded as waste, without population, and 6 lacked details because they were at farm.

In the hidated areas covered by the Cheshire Survey the pattern of estate organization is fairly clear. Large fiefs, some scattered but a few important ones very compact, were focused on a *caput*, which had often been an administrative centre before the Conquest.[16] In the unhidated territories in Wales, however, there were rather different arrangements. Bistre, which probably corresponded with the great ancient parish of Mold, was recorded very much as if it were still a large discrete estate with numerous berewicks divided into seven groupings, each of one ploughteam. Before 1063 one such grouping was held by the Welsh king in demesne, the other six by tenants, all of whom paid a customary food-rent when the king came thither. The arrangement seems to have persisted, with a few modifications, in 1086, when there was still said to be land enough for 7 ploughteams, though only 6½ were there in the time of Hugh FitzNorman (367–73).

More complex was the structure of the great manor of Rhuddlan, representing the Welsh district of Englefield (340–66). The manor had numerous berewicks, far more than Bistre, and they were again arranged in groups, often of three, each assessed as 1 ploughland. It is not clear why the berewicks were so grouped, since their constituent parts were not always contiguous. The arrangement was very different from that obtaining in Cheshire by 1086 and presumably as at Bistre was ordered towards the payment of the customary renders.

Beyond Rhuddlan lay the districts of Rhos and Rhufoniog (374–6), perhaps organized similarly but not recorded in the Survey beyond the bare statement that they were assessed at 20 ploughlands. They were held by Robert of Rhuddlan directly of the king, together with the rest of the lands to which he had made good his claims in the kingdom of Gwynedd ('Nortwales').

Cheshire as a whole was poor and sparsely inhabited. Throughout the shire there were many manors on which there was little or no demesne, and Cheshire villeins often had fewer oxen than their fellows in more favoured districts.[17] Undoubtedly, however, it was richer and more settled in the west, especially in Wirral and the Dee basin where Domesday records three to four inhabitants and at least one ploughteam per square mile. In the upland districts of the east and centre, the figures were much lower; on the Pennine slope, for example, the Domesday densities of population and ploughteams were respectively under one and 0.2 per square mile.[18] In the east in particular there seems to have been still much unsettled or unoccupied land in 1086, and even as late as the 14th century many settlements in Macclesfield manor forest were described as assarts.[19] Not all such territory had been distributed by the earl in 1086. An example of apparently unoccupied and unapportioned land then still in the earl's hands is the six small waste holdings in Middlewich hundred, grouped into one Domesday entry and mostly parts of vills where Bigot de Loges had the main manor. In none of them does the earl appear to have retained land and most seem soon to have been subsumed into the fiefs of

---

[16] Above, 'A.-S. Ches.'.

[17] *T.H.S.L.C.* ci. 7; *Dom. Surv. Ches.* 66–7.

[18] *Dom. Geog. N. Eng.* 344–5, 354, 380–3.

[19] P.R.O. SC 6/802/2. The assize rents of Macclesfield

manor rose sharply in the later 13th century, suggesting that the vills described as assarts were settled then: P. H. W. Booth, *Financial Administration of the Ldship. and Cty. of Chester*, 155–7. References and inf. supplied by Mr. Booth.

Aldford and Shipbrook.[20] Another similar entry groups eight waste manors in Hamestan hundred, most of which were again not long retained by the earl.[21] In Hamestan hundred the great excess of estimated capacity over actual ploughteams is a further indicator that the land was not fully exploited. Moreover, the multiplicity of small manors, especially in the north and east, where there are several instances of a number of estates to a vill, suggests sparse, scattered, non-nucleated settlement.[22]

Linked with the problem of density of settlement is that of waste, found throughout the shire both in 1086 and earlier. The Cheshire Domesday at its fullest records waste at three separate periods, in 1066, 1086, and when the Norman tenant took over (i.e. *c*. 1070). There are, however, many ambiguities and inconsistencies; in particular it is difficult to interpret the phrases *wasta fuit* ('it was waste') and *wasta fuit et est* ('it was and is waste'). Clearly the present tense refers to 1086, but it is uncertain whether the past tense refers to 1066 or the early 1070s, a matter which bears on the effectiveness of the Conqueror's harrying of Cheshire. Probably *wasta fuit* should generally be taken as referring to *c*. 1070, for in several instances where it occurs a value is assigned to the estate in 1066, implying that it was not then waste.[23]

A further problem is the interpretation of 'waste'. The traditional and still widely held view is that it means devastated, and that its widespread occurrence in both Yorkshire and Cheshire is evidence of the ferocity of William's harrying of the north. Waste cannot, however, always mean precisely that, for there are instances where an estate so described has a value assigned to it. Northenden, for example, though said to be waste in 1086 then had a church and was valued at 3*s*., though no population or ploughteams were recorded (312). Caldecote, though waste in 1066, was said then to render 2*s*. (219). A possible explanation for such anomalies is that the term waste may be a technical one simply describing the value of the land to the lord, rather than necessarily indicating a devastated estate. That interpretation seems to fit the application of the term in 1066 to large areas of the Welsh border only recently regained from King Gruffudd. It is difficult to believe that the whole of the great manors of Rhuddlan and Bistre were entirely devastated at that time, though clearly their administration was considerably disrupted, so that they yielded little of value to the new holder, Earl Edwin, in 1066. That such areas were not substantially remodelled after their recovery is indicated by the tenurial arrangements of Bistre, which in 1086 were almost identical to those under Gruffudd.[24]

Elsewhere, especially in the north and east, waste seems to have meant what it has traditionally been assumed to mean. In Bochelau hundred, for example, though there is very little reference to land being waste in 1066, many manors were waste in 1086, and far more, if not all, had been found waste or had been waste at some unspecified time in the past, presumably after 1070.[25] The record in Hamestan hundred is similar. The occurrence of waste on such a large scale over such a long period in those areas after the Conquest is almost certainly evidence of the Conqueror's harrying of the north. It is different from conditions on the Welsh borders where there was little waste in 1086, where many areas that were said to be waste *c*. 1070 were already so recorded in 1066, and where Erbistock manor,

[20] Ormerod, *Hist. Ches.* ii. 206; iii. 95–6, 209, 214, 216, 219.
[21] Ormerod, *Hist. Ches.* iii. 704, 722, 848, 850, 869, 872.
[22] *Ches. Arch. Bull.* viii. 15–17.
[23] *Dom. Geog. N. Eng.* 365–76; *Ches. Arch. Bull.* viii. 18–19.
[24] Above.
[25] *Ches. Arch. Bull.* viii. 18–19.

for example, was described as waste in 1066 but later (i.e. in the 1070s) valued at 10*s.* (284).

There are signs that even the areas which suffered most heavily from William's ravaging, in north and east Cheshire, had made a modest recovery under new landlords by 1086. In Bochelau hundred, for example, several manors described as waste in the 1070s were assigned a value in 1086, though virtually none had recovered their 1066 value. In the neighbouring hundred of Tunendune, where again there had been much waste after 1070, the recovery had been much greater, but even so in 1086 only the important manorial centre of Halton and the nearby estates of Weston and Aston by Sutton had significantly improved on their 1066 value; under William FitzNiel and his Norman tenant, Odard, the three manors had together more than doubled their earlier value despite being waste *c.* 1070. Significantly, it was only manors directly exploited by an active tenant that experienced recovery; all those still in the earl's hands remained waste, as did those largely untenanted holdings of William FitzNiel remote from Halton itself.[26]

In the west the picture was more varied. In Dudestan hundred, for example, the principal manors of the major landowner, Robert FitzHugh, all of which he was said to have found waste, were in 1086 still valued at far below the 1066 figures, though some of the lesser estates in the hands of his tenants achieved small increases. Other landowners, however, seem to have been more successful. The estates of the earl himself, of the bishop, and of St. Werburgh changed relatively little in value, while those of William Malbank, Bigot de Loges, Gilbert de Venables, Hugh FitzNorman, and Richard the Butler considerably improved. Though many estates were designated waste in 1070, a few, including the earl's relatively valuable manor of Eaton, were valued, and others belonging to the bishop and St. Werburgh seem not to have been only because they remained in the same hands.[27] In Wirral there were far fewer waste estates in 1070, though there seems to have been a fairly general decline in values between 1066 and 1086.[28]

In general, then, there seems to have been a very widespread incidence of waste throughout the shire *c.* 1070 resembling Yorkshire's in its intensity.[29] Only in Wirral were values recorded in any number for that period. In 1066 and 1086, however, there is much more variation. In the Welsh borderlands there was much waste in 1066, reflecting perhaps mainly administrative disruption after the fall of King Gruffudd, but there, in common with the rest of western Cheshire there seems to have been a considerable recovery in the 1070s and 1080s. In the north and east, by contrast, there seems to have been little waste in 1066, but far less recovery from the ravaging of 1069–70, an indication that there the harrying was especially severe.

Such a wasted and relatively unpeopled shire could be expected to have much woodland, and indeed Cheshire appears to have been fairly wooded in 1086. Woodland is generally recorded in terms of leagues and furlongs, but curiously some entries combine leagues and acres. Though the significance of such measurements is obscure it is clear that woodland was widespread throughout the county, except in the west in Wirral and the Dee valley.[30] Probably many of the vacant areas on the Domesday map were wooded; the belt of clay lands between the hundreds of Tunendune and Bochelau, for example, contains many woodland place names, only

[26] Ibid. 19.

[27] nos. 4, 13, 15–18, 48–51, 72–93, 130–1, 136–7, 184, 219–20, 233–4, 249, 285–6, 288–9.

[28] nos. 6, 20–7, 57–9, 69–70, 100, 103–15, 117–18, 133–5,

139–45, 186–9, 213, 270, 290, 298–9.

[29] *Dom. Geog. N. Eng.* 365.

[30] Ibid. 355–7, 384, 389.

one of which, Tabley, is recorded in Domesday.[31] Elsewhere, Delamere, an area of sandy soil and sparse settlement, had already been placed within the earl's forest, though little woodland is recorded there.[32] A further forest is recorded in hidated Atiscros, where the earl was said to have placed all the woods within the hundred in his forest, thereby depreciating the value of the manors (339). In the east, though the medieval forest of Macclesfield is not mentioned, exceptionally large amounts of woodland were assigned to the earl's manors of Macclesfield and Adlington; again the area, which included the infertile Pennine slope, was one in which very few settlements were recorded.[33]

The manors of Macclesfield and Adlington also contained especially large numbers of hays (enclosures) and hawk's eyries, both of which were associated with heavily wooded areas. In Delamere too there were hays and eyries, at Weaverham and Kingsley, and there the hays were expressly associated with the catching of roe deer, animals of deep woodland. In all, hays are recorded in over 50 places in Cheshire, almost all in the east of the county, though there were also two hays and two eyries at Gresford.[34]

The agricultural resources of Cheshire were relatively poor. There were altogether some 500 ploughteams working in the hidated portions and a further 35 in Rhuddlan and Atiscros. Almost everywhere there was a deficiency of ploughteams in comparison with estimated agricultural potential in the form of ploughlands, which for the whole area totalled some 1,040, almost double the number of the teams. Ploughteam densities were considerably greater in west Cheshire, in Wirral and the Dee valley. The average there of 1–1.2 per square mile is almost double the nearest figures, those for the Weaver basin and the area around Halton, and far in excess of the extremely low densities of 0.1 in the north and east. The Welsh borderlands also seem to have been thinly cultivated, especially Exestan where again there were ploughteam densities of only 0.1 per square mile. In all those areas the excess of ploughlands over ploughteams is particularly marked, indicating an artificially low level of exploitation, probably largely the result of William's or the Welsh king's devastations.[35]

Perhaps a further reflection of the undeveloped nature of the Cheshire economy is the absence of reference to meadow. Small amounts were associated with the Weaver, Dee, and Gowy rivers and their tributaries, but elsewhere there was very little.[36] Nevertheless, what there was was clearly valuable: in Hamestan hundred, for example, there is a clear correlation between the possession of meadow and the size of assessment.[37] Other resources were also limited. In the entire area only 25 mills and some 21 fisheries were recorded. It should be noted, however, that such figures were almost certainly not comprehensive. Mills, for example, seem to have been recorded especially in connexion with halls or rivers, in particular the Weaver, Dee, and Gowy, a pattern which prompts a suspicion that there were omissions elsewhere. Similarly fishermen and boats and nets were recorded at a number of places where fisheries as such were not mentioned.[38] Moreover, there were probably other fisheries in the area, besides those in the survey. There seems to be no record, for example, of the fisheries that are known to have been along the Mersey at Thelwall by the 12th century and probably long before, though they may be

[31] *Ches. Arch. Bull.* viii. 17.
[32] nos. 36–7, 45–6, 305; *V.C.H. Ches.* ii. 167, 172.
[33] *V.C.H. Ches.* ii. 178–9; *Dom. Geog. N. Eng.* 357.
[34] *Dom. Geog. N. Eng.* 359, 384.
[35] Ibid. 340–6, 384, 389; *Dom. Surv. Ches.* 5 n.; *Ches.*

Arch. Bull. viii. 20–1.
[36] *Dom. Geog. N. Eng.* 359–60, 384.
[37] Inf. from Dr. Kenyon.
[38] *Dom. Geog. N. Eng.* 361–2, 376, 384–5, 388–9.

represented by the two fishermen at Halton.[39] Fishing was especially important along the Dee and the Weaver, and at the confluence of the Weaver and the Mersey, though Earl Hugh and Robert of Rhuddlan also had plans to exploit the potential of the river Clwyd.[40] A fishery could be a major asset; some indication of scale is given by the record of that at the earl's important manor of Eaton in Eccleston, which had six fishermen and an annual render of 1,000 salmon (48).

[39] Ormerod, *Hist. Ches.* i. 747; above, Anglo-Saxon gazetteer, s.v. Grappenhall.
[40] *Dom. Geog. N. Eng.* 361–2; below, nos. 340, 349.

DOMESDAY CHESHIRE

L A N C A

(INTER RIPAM

Wallasey

Great Meols
Little Meols · Upton
Noctorum
Hilbre Island
Grange · Greasby
Landican
Caldy · Thurstaston · Thingwall
Barnston · Storeton
Poulton
Heswall · Thornton Hough
Gayton · Raby
Leighton · Hargrave · Eastham
Great Neston · Hooton · Overpool
Hadlow · III
Little Neston · Sutton · Stanney
Ness · Ledsham
Burton · Capenhurst · Puddington
Shotwick · Lea by Backford
Saughall · Great Mollington · Mickle Trafford
Little Mollington · Upton by Chester · Barrow
Blacon · Newton · Guilden Sutton
CHESTER IV · 'Redcliff' · Great Boughton · Tarvin
Handbridge · Christleton
Overleigh · Netherleigh · Clotton
Lache · Claverton · Waverton · Iddinshall
Marlston · Huntington · Saighton · Foulk Stapleford
Eccleston · Cheaveley · Eaton · Hatton
Dodleston · Eaton
Pulford · Aldford · Golborne Bellow
Poulton · Golborne David
Leahall · Tattenhall
Handley · Burwardsley
Chowley · Coddington
Farndon · Clutton · Broxton
Crewe Hall · Bickerton
Duckington · Larkton
Caldecott · Little Edge · Cholmondeley
Tilston · Edge · Bickley
Shocklach · Hampton
Overton · Malpas · Norbury
Cuddington · Tushingham · Marbury
Wirswall

Norton
Halton
Weston · Eanley
Clifton
Aston by Sutton
Frodsham · Middleton
Ince
Elton · Helsby
Thornton le Moors · Kingsley
Alvanley · 'Alderley'
Wimbolds Trafford · Dunham on the Hill · Manley
Croughton
Wervin · Bridge Trafford
Picton · Eddisbury
Ashton
Willington

Gronant · Gwesbyr
Prestatyn · Golden Grove · Kelston
Rhydorddwy · 1. · Picton
Meliden · 2. · Carnychan · Mostyn
Cwybr Bâch · Pentre · 3. · Dincolyn · Axton · Bychton
Cwybr · Bryn · Diserth · Trelawnyd · Whitford · Greenfield
Rhuddlan · Cefn Du · Hiraddug · Brynhedydd · Mertyn
Cyrchynan · Bryngwyn · Bagillt
Bodeugan · Maenefa · Gellilyfdy · Calcot · Brynford · Coleshill
St. Asaph · Blorant · 4. · Trefraith
Cilowen · Tremeirchion · Caerwys · 'Radington'
Bodfari · IA · Halkyn · Leadbrook · Golftyn
Ysgeifiog · Trellyniau · Llys Edwin · Wepre
Llystyn Hunedd · Soughton · Aston
Mechlas · Gwysaney · IB
Llys y Coed · Hawarden
Bistre · Broughton
Hendrebifa
Broncoed · Rhos Ithel · Leeswood
Hope · Allington
'Radnor'
Gresford · Hoseley
Eyton · II
Sutton
Worthenbury
Erbistock
Bettisfield
Burwardestone · Whitchurch

R. Elwy
R. Clwyd
R. Alun
R. Dee
R. Gowy

D E N B I G H S H I R E

1. Tan y Fron
2. Gwaunysgor
3. Llewerllyd
4. Trefedwen

HUNDREDS

IA	Atiscros (unhidated)	**VII**	Roelau
IB	Atiscros (hidated)	**VIII**	Riseton
II	Exestan	**IX**	Warmundestrou
III	Wilaveston	**X**	Tunendune
IV	Chester	**XI**	Middlewich
V	Dudestan	**XII**	Hamestan
VI	Bochelau		

Earl Hugh had demesne manors at places
underlined thus: _Eastham_

– – County boundaries of Cheshire, Flintshire (with
two detached parts) and adjoining counties 1880

S H R O P S H I R E

YORKSHIRE

S H I R E

ET MERSHAM)

R. Etherow

R. Tame

Tintwistle

Hollingworth

Werneth

Bredbury

Romile

R. Govt

R. Mersey

• *Sinderland*

Baguley

• *Warburton*

Northenden

• *Cheadle*

Leighton

DERBYSHIRE

Dunham Massey

'*Alretunstall*'

• *Hale*

Grappenhall

• *Lymm*

Bowdon

• *Bramhall*

• *Norbury*

• *Millington*

Ashley

XII

• *Appleton*

High Legh

• *Rostherne*

R. Bollin

Mere • *Tatton*

X

• *Adlington*

Whitley • *Antrobus*

• *Tabley Superior*

• *Mobberley*

Dutton *Aston by Budworth*

• *Knutsford*

• *Mottram St. Andrew*

Cogshall *Great Budworth*

Warford

• *Butley*

Bartington *Little Leigh*

• *Tabley Inferior*

Ollerton

• *Nether Alderley*

Winnington • *Wincham*

'*Chapmonswiche*'

Chelford

• *Over Alderley*

Weaverham *Northwich*

• *Nether Peover*

Snelson

Macclesfield

Hartford *Witton* *Shurlach*

Peover

Henbury

VII *Leftwich*

Peover Superior

Capesthorne

Shipbrook

Lach Dennis

• *Siddington*

Davenham

• *Goostrey*

'*Hungrewenitune*'

• *Gawsworth*

'*Conersley*'

Moulton

Byley

Bostock *Croxton*

• *Cranage*

Kermincham

• *Marton*

Wharton

Sproston

R. Dane

North Rode

Qver *Newton*

Middlewich

Davenport

Somerford Booths

• *Bosley*

Oulton • *Little Budworth*

Clive

Kinderton

Somerford

Rushton

Weaver

Sutton

Brereton

• *Buglawton*

Eaton

Occlestone

Tetton

XI

Congleton

VIII *Wettenhall*

Wimboldsley

Alpraham

Church Minshull

Sandbach

Newbold Astbury

Tilstone Fearnall

Minshull Vernon

• *Wheelock*

Bunbury *Cholmondeston*

• *Hassall*

Odd Rode

Wardle

• *Coppenhall*

Worleston

Alsager

• *Church Lawton*

Aston juxta Mondrum

Poole

Wistaston • *Crewe*

Acton *Wisterson*

Willaston *Basford*

Barthomley

Stoneley *Nantwich*

Shavington

Chorley

Baddiley

Batherton

Stapeley *Chorlton*

N

Frith *Wrenbury*

Austerson

Wybunbury

Aston

Broomhall

Walgherton

Hatherton

Blakenhall

IX

R. Weaver

Audlem

STAFFORDSHIRE

Wilkesley

Buerton

Tittenley

0 ___ miles ___ 10

0 ___ km ___ 10

CESTRESCIRE

[f. 262v. col. 1]

(1a) The city of CESTRE [Chester] paid geld T.R.E. for 50 hides. [There are] 3½ hides which are outside the city, that is 1½ hides beyond the bridge,[1] and 2 hides in NEUTONE [Newton by Chester in St. Oswald's] and REDECLIVE ['Redcliff' in Chester][2] and in the bishop's borough;[3] these paid geld with the city. There were in the same city T.R.E. 431 houses paying geld and besides these the bishop had 56 houses paying geld. This city then rendered 10½ marks of silver. Two parts were the king's and the third the earl's.

(1b) And these were the laws there:

If the peace given by the hand of the king or by his writ or by his agent (*per suum legatum*) were broken by anyone, the king had thence 100s. But if the (same *interlined*) peace of the king, given at his command by the earl (*pax regis iussu eius a comite data*), were broken, the earl had the third penny of the 100s. which were given for this. If, however, the same peace, given by the king's reeve or by the earl's servant (*a preposito regis aut ministro comitis*), were broken, amends were made by the payment of 40s. and the third penny was the earl's.

If any free man, breaking the king's peace that had been given, killed a man in a house, his land and all his chattels (*pecunia*) were the king's and he himself became an outlaw (*utlagh*). The earl had the same only from his own men making this forfeiture. But no-one could restore peace to any outlaw except by the will of the king (*nisi per regem*).

He who shed blood between the morning of Monday and noon on Saturday made amends with 10s. But from noon on Saturday to Monday morning amends were made for bloodshed with 20s. Similarly, he paid 20s. who did this in the twelve days of Christmas, and on Candlemas day, and on the first day of Easter, and on the first day of Whitsun, and on Ascension day, and on the [day of] the Assumption or of the Nativity of St. Mary, and on the feast day of All Saints.

He who killed a man on these holy days made amends with £4, but on other days with 40s. Similarly, he who committed hamfare or forestall (*heinfaram vel forestel*)[4] on these feast days

(and on Sunday *interlined*) paid £4, on other days 40s.

He who incurred hangwite (*Hangeuuitham faciens*)[5] in the city gave 10s., but a reeve of the king or the earl incurring this forfeiture made amends with 20s.

He who committed robbery or theft (*Revelach vel Latrocinium*)[6] or did violence to a woman (in a house *interlined*), made amends for each of these with 40s.

If a widow had unlawful intercourse with any man, she made amends with 20s., but a maiden [paid] 10s. for the same offence.

He who seized the land of another in the city or could not prove it to be his made amends with 40s. Similarly, too, he who made claim thereto, if he could not prove that it ought to be his.

He who wished to take up (*relevare*) his land or that of his kinsman gave 10s. (If he could not or would not, the reeve took his land into the king's hand. *Sentence misplaced after the next but directed here by marginal signs and superscript letters.*)

He who did not render his gafol (*gablum*) at the term it was due made amends with 10s.

If fire broke out in the city (*Si ignis civitatem comburebat*), the man from whose house it came made amends with 3 ounces of pennies (*oras denariorum*)[7] and to his next neighbour he gave 2s.

Two parts of all these forfeitures were the king's and the third [part] the earl's.

(1c) If ships arrived at or departed from the port of the city without the king's licence, the king and the earl had 40s. from each man who was on the ships. If a ship came against the king's peace and in spite of his prohibition, the king and the earl had both the ship and the men with all that was in it.

But if it came in the king's peace and with his licence, those who were on board sold what they had undisturbed. When it left, however, the king and the earl had 4d. from each load (*lesth*). If the king's reeve ordered those who had (*habentibus* corrected above the line from *habentes*) marten pelts (*martrinas pelles*) not to sell to anyone until

---

[1] The 1½ hides consisted of 2 virgates in Netherleigh and Overleigh, held by William FitzNiel and Hugh de Mara respectively (nos. 182, 210), together with the 3 geldable carucates in Handbridge held by them and Hugh FitzOsbern (nos. 183, 211, 218). See above.

[2] One hide held by William FitzNiel (no. 181), the other by the bishop and Hugh FitzNorman (nos. 10, 212). The name *Redeclive*, which refers to the red sandstone on which St. John's is built, was last used in the 13th century: *P.N. Ches.* v (1: i), 80–1.

[3] If the bishop's borough was not the same as *Redeclive* (no. 10) it appears to have been free of geld. It was probably the area around St. John's church and included St. Mary's, where there were 2 bovates that were not described as

geldable (no. 11).

[4] Hamfare or hamsocn was forcible entry into, or assault on a person in, a house; forestall was the offence of causing an obstruction or waylaying someone: F. E. Harmer, *A.-S. Writs*, 79–81.

[5] When a thief was captured 10s. hengwite was exacted from the victim if he had failed to raise the hue and cry: *Laws of Kings of Eng. from Edmund to Hen. I*, ed. A. J. Robertson, 254.

[6] *Revelach* derives from Old English *reaflac*. For the distinction between robbery and theft see F. Pollock and F. W. Maitland, *Hist. of Eng. Law* (1898 edn.), ii. 493–5.

[7] An *ora* consisted of 16 pence: *Econ. H.R.* 2nd ser. xx. 221–8.

they had first been shown to him and he had bought, whoever did not observe this made amends with 40s.[8]

A man or woman caught giving false measure in the city made amends with 4s. Similarly, the brewer of bad beer was either put in the cucking-stool (*cathedra stercoris*) or gave 4s. to the reeves.

[f. 262v. col. 2]

The servants of the king and earl took this forfeiture in the city in whosoever's land it arose, whether the bishop's or that of [any] other man. In like manner [they took] toll (*theloneum*); if anyone detained it beyond three nights he made amends with 40s.[9]

(1d) T.R.E. there were in this city 7 moneyers who paid £7 to the king and earl over and above the farm when the coinage was changed (*quando moneta vertebatur*).[10]

There were then 12 judges (*iudices*) of the city and these were [chosen or taken] from the men of the king and the bishop and the earl. If any of them absented himself without obvious excuse from the hundred [court] on a day on which it sat, he made amends with 10s. [divided] between the king and the earl.

For the repair of the city wall and bridge the reeve used to call up one man from each hide in the county. The lord of any man who failed to come made amends with 40s. to the king and the earl; this forfeiture was not included in the farm.

This city then rendered a farm of £45 and 3 timbers (*timbres*)[11] of marten pelts. The third part was the earl's and two [parts] the king's.

(1e) When (Earl *interlined*) Hugh received it, it was not worth more than £30, for it was greatly wasted. There were 205 fewer houses than there had been T.R.E. There are now as many there as he found.

Mundret held the city from the earl for £70 and 1 mark of gold. The same [man] had at farm for £50 and 1 mark of gold all the earl's pleas in the county and the hundreds except Inglefeld [Englefield].

The land on which the church of St. Peter stands, which Robert of Rhuddlan (*Rodelend*) claimed as thegn-land (*teinland*), never belonged to a manor outside the city, as the county proved, but belongs to the borough and always paid dues to the king and earl like [the land] of other burgesses.[12]

(2) In CESTRESCIRE [Cheshire] the bishop of the said city holds of the king what belongs to his bishopric. Earl Hugh with his men holds from the king all the rest of the land of the county.

Roger de Poitou (*Pictav'*) held the land between RIPE [the Ribble] and MERSHAM [the Mersey]; the king holds it now.

[f. 263 col. 1]

(3) THE BISHOP OF CHESTER has these customary dues in the same city: if any free man works on a holy day, the bishop takes 8s. for it, but from a serf or bondwoman (*ancilla*) breaking a holy day the bishop has 4s. If a merchant coming to the city with a bale of goods should break it open without licence of the bishop's official (*minister*) between Saturday noon and Monday, or on any other feast day, the bishop has for that 4s. as forfeiture. If a man of the bishop find any man loading (*carricantem*) within the territory (*leuuam*) of the city, the bishop takes for that as forfeiture 4s. or 2 oxen.

IN DUDESTAN HUNDRED

(4) The same bishop holds FERENTONE [Farndon] and held it T.R.E. There [are] 4 hides that pay geld. The land is for 5 ploughs. In demesne are 2 [ploughs] and 7 villeins with 1 plough. The wood there [is] 1 league long and ½ [league] wide. Of this land 2 priests hold 1½ hides of the bishop. There [is] 1 plough in demesne, and 2 Frenchmen and 2 villeins and 1 bordar with 1½ ploughs, and 4 serfs. The priest of the vill has ½ plough, and 5 bordars with 1 plough. The whole was worth T.R.E. 40s., now 60s. It was waste.

IN RISETONE HUNDRED

(5) The same bishop held and holds TERVE [Tarvin]. There [are] 6 hides that pay geld. The land is for 22 ploughs. In demesne are 3 ploughs and 6 oxmen, and 3 radmen (*radmans*) and 7 villeins and 7 bordars with 6 ploughs. Wood 1 league in length and ½ [league] in width. Of the land of this manor William[13] holds 2 hides of the bishop and has there ½ plough, and 4 villeins and 3 bordars with 3½ ploughs. The whole was worth T.R.E. £8, now £4 10s. It was wasted.

IN WILAVESTON HUNDRED

(6) The same bishop held and holds SUDTONE [Guilden Sutton]. There [is] 1 hide that pays geld. The land is for 3 ploughs. In demesne there is 1 [plough], and 5 villeins and 2 bordars with 1 plough. There [are] 6 acres of meadow. T.R.E. it was worth 40s., now 20s.

IN EXESTAN HUNDRED

(7) St. Chad[14] held EITUNE [Eyton, in Holt, Denb.][15] T.R.E. There [is] 1 hide.[16] In Eitune

---

[8] The right of pre-emption and the payment of part of the city farm in marten pelts (no. 1d) implies high quality pelts, which are more likely to have come from Scandinavia than Ireland.   [9] Cf. nos. 316, 319.

[10] Throughout the 11th century the coinage was changed at intervals of 2–6 years: *A.-S. Coins*, ed. R. H. M. Dolley, 136–68. Cf. *V.C.H. Dors.* iii. 61–3; *Herefs.* i. 309; *Salop.* i. 310; *Suss.* i. 435; *Worcs.* i. 282. For the Chester mint see above.

[11] A timber was a bundle of 40 pelts: *O.E.D.*

[12] Above. Rest of column left blank except for next entry, written on the last 5 lines.

[13] Possibly William Malbank. See no. 8.

[14] The dedication of Lichfield cathedral, whose bishop transferred his see to Chester in 1075: above.

[15] Possibly Eyton in Erbistock (Denb.), but more probably the lost townships of Eyton Fawr and Eyton Fechan in Holt, near Sutton and Allington: cf. nos. 247–8. If it was the *Eatuna iuxta aquam quae dicitur Dee*, granted to Coventry abbey by Earl Leofric in 1043 and later given by Abbot Leofwine II to Earl Hugh of Chester, it perhaps passed to the see under Bishop Leofwine (1054–66), earlier the first abbot of that name at Coventry. Since there were two Eytons near the Dee, possibly one was the bishop's, the other the abbot's, the second being omitted in Domesday Bk.: *Dom. Surv. Ches.* 27–8, 91; *Trans. Denb. Hist. Soc.* xxvii. 89–149, esp. 102, 110, 117; inf. from Mr. D. Pratt.

[16] Hugh FitzOsbern apparently held this hide (no. 248). That may explain the *R* in the margin, perhaps *reclamat*, 'he claimed' (*Dom. Surv. Ches.* 91) or *require*, 'inquire'.

the same saint has 1 villein and ½ fishery and ½ acre of meadow and 2 acres of wood. It was worth 5s.

King Edward gave to King Gruffudd (*Grifin*) all the land that lay beyond the water which is called De (Dee). But after the same Gruffudd wronged him (*forisfecit ei*), he took this land from him, and restored it to the bishop of Chester and to all his men[17] who had formerly held it.

IN WARMUNDESTROU HUNDRED

(8) The same bishop holds WIMEBERIE [Wybunbury] and held it T.R.E. and now William[18] holds it of him. There [is] ½ hide that pays geld. The land is for 2 ploughs. There [are] 1 priest and 2 villeins and 2 bordars with 1 plough. There [is] wood ½ league long and as much wide and there [are] 2 hays. T.R.E. it was worth 64d., now 4s. It was waste.

IN RISETON[19] HUNDRED

(9) The same bishop holds BURTONE [Burton][20] and held it T.R.E. There [are] 3 hides that pay geld. The land is for 7 ploughs. In demesne are 2 ploughs, and 7 villeins and 4 bordars and a priest and 1 radman with 3 ploughs. There [is] 1 acre of meadow. T.R.E. it was worth 40s., now as much. When he received it 15s.

[IN CESTRE HUNDRED][21]

(10) The same bishop held and holds in REDECLIVE ['Redcliff' in Chester] 2 [third] parts of 1 hide that pay geld.[22] T.R.E. it was worth 13s., now it is worth 2d. more. (It belongs *interlined*) to the church of St. John.

(11) In the minster (*monasterio*) of St. Mary which is near the church of St. John there lie 2 bovates of land which were waste and are now waste.[23]

(12) The church of St. John has in the city 8 houses free from all customary dues. One of these is [the house] of the dean (*matricularius*)[24] of the church, the others are the canons'.

[IN DUDESTAN HUNDRED][25]

(13) In a manor of Robert FitzHugh (BEDESFELD [Bettisfield in Hanmer, Flints.] *interlined*) the bishop of Chester claims 2 hides[26] which belonged to the bishopric in the time of King Cnut, and the county (*for* bishop *erased and cancelled*) testifies for him that St. Chad lost them unjustly.[27]

[f. 263 col. 2]

[IN CESTRE HUNDRED][28]

(14) In the city of Chester THE CHURCH OF ST. WERBURGH (*Wareburg*) has 13 houses free from all customary dues. One is the warden's (*custos ecclesiae*), the others (are *interlined*) the canons'.

IN DUDESTAN HUNDRED

(15) The same church holds SALTONE [Saighton in St. Oswald's] and held it T.R.E. There [are] 2 hides that pay geld. The land is for 8 ploughs. In demesne is 1 plough and 1 serf, and 9 villeins with 5 ploughs. It was and is worth 40s.

(16) The same church holds CAVELEA [Cheaveley in Huntington, St. Oswald's parish] and held it T.R.E. There [are] 3 hides that pay geld. The land is for 5 ploughs. In demesne are 2 [ploughs] and 3 serfs, and 3 villeins and 1 bordar with 2 ploughs. There [is] a small boat (*navicula*) and a net. T.R.E. it was worth 30s., now 20s.

(17) The same church holds HUNDITONE [Huntington in St. Oswald's] and held it T.R.E. There [are] 3 hides that pay geld. The land is for 6 ploughs. In demesne are 2 [ploughs] and 4 serfs, and 2 villeins and 2 bordars with 1 plough. There [is] 1 acre of meadow, and a small boat (*navicula*) and a net. T.R.E. it was waste, now it is worth 16s.

(18) The same church holds BOCSTONE [Great Boughton in St. Oswald's] and held it T.R.E. There [are] 3 hides that pay geld. The land is for 5 ploughs. In demesne are 2 [ploughs] and 4 serfs, and 5 villeins and 4 bordars with 3 ploughs. T.R.E. it was worth 20s., now 16s.

IN RISETON HUNDRED

(19) The same church holds ETINGEHALLE [Iddinshall in St. Oswald's] and held it T.R.E. There [is] 1 hide that pays geld. The land is for 1 plough. In demesne is ½ plough and 1 serf. There [is] wood ½ league long and 1 acre wide. T.R.E. it was worth 8s., now 5s.

---

[17] It is not clear whether the men were the bishop's or the king's: above, 'A.-S. Ches.'.
[18] Probably William Malbank: Ormerod, *Hist. Ches.* iii. 482.
[19] Possibly in error for Wilaveston: see following note.
[20] Traditionally Burton in Tarvin, in Riseton hundred (*Dom. Surv. Ches.* 91; Ormerod, *Hist. Ches.* ii. 327) but possibly Burton in Wirral. Both Burtons were later held by the bishop of Lichfield and Coventry; that in Tarvin may have been included in the episcopal manor there (no. 5), but that in Wirral can be accounted for by no other entry. A 13th-century survey of Burton in Wirral enumerates 7 villein holdings, the same number as in this entry: Staffs. R.O., D 1734/J2268; *Ches. Hist.* iv. 28–42; reference supplied by Mr. P. H. W. Booth. Other mistakes in the hundredal rubrics

are known: above.
[21] Hundredal rubric omitted.
[22] See note 2 above.
[23] See note 3 above.
[24] Dean rather than bishop or cathedral canon: J. F. Niermeyer, *Mediae Latinitatis Lexicon Minus*, s.v. *matricularius*, senses 5–7. Cf. no. 14. The church later had a dean and 7 canons.
[25] Hundredal rubric omitted, presumably because entry was added.
[26] Perhaps around Hanmer, whose church is dedicated to St. Chad: *Dom. Surv. Ches.* 93. The claim was mentioned again in no. 72.
[27] Entry, not rubricated, added in space at foot of column.
[28] Hundredal rubric perhaps thought unnecessary.

In Wilaveston Hundred

(20) The same church holds WIVEVRENE [Wervin in St. Oswald's] and held it T.R.E. There [is] 1 hide and 2 [third] parts of 1 hide. The land is for 3 ploughs. There 4 villeins and 2 bordars have 1½ ploughs. There [is] ½ acre of meadow. T.R.E. it was worth 30s., now 20s.

(21) The same church holds CROSTONE [Croughton in St. Oswald's] and held it T.R.E. There [is] 1 hide that pays geld. The land is for 1 plough. There 1 radman and 2 villeins and 1 bordar have 1 plough. There [is] 1 acre of meadow. It was and is worth 10s.

(22) The same church held and holds WISDELEA [Lea by Backford in Backford].[29] There [is] 1 hide that pays geld. The land is for 3 ploughs. In demesne is 1 [plough] and 2 serfs, and 2 villeins and 2 bordars with 1 plough, and 1 acre of meadow. T.R.E. it was worth 10s., now as much.

(23) The same church holds SUDTONE [Sutton in Eastham] and held it T.R.E. There [is] 1 hide that pays geld. The land is for 5 ploughs. In demesne is ½ plough, and 5 villeins and 9 bordars with 2 ploughs. T.R.E. it was worth 40s., now 30s.

(24) The same church held and holds SALHARE [Saughall in Shotwick]. There [is] 1 hide that pays geld. The land is for 1 plough. It is there in demesne and 2 serfs, and 1 villein and 1 bordar. T.R.E. it was worth 16s., now as much.

(25) The same church held and holds SOTOWICHE [Shotwick]. There [is] 1 hide that pays geld. The land is for 3 ploughs. There [are] 4 villeins and 2 bordars with 1 plough, and 1 acre of meadow. T.R.E. it was worth 16s., now 13s. 3d.

(26) The same church held and holds NESTONE [Great Neston in Neston], and William[30] [holds] of it. There [is] a third part of 2 hides that pays geld. The land is for 1 plough. It rendered and renders in farm 17s. 4d.

(27) The same church held and holds RABIE [Raby in Neston], and William[31] [holds] of it. There [is] ½ hide that pays geld. The land is for 1 plough. It rendered and renders in farm 6s. 8d.

In Roelau Hundred

(28) The same church held and holds TROSFORD [Bridge Trafford in Plemstall]. There [is] 1 hide that pays geld. The land is for [blank].[32] In demesne is 1 plough and 4 serfs, and 1 bondwoman, and 1 bordar, and 1 acre of meadow, and a man rendering 20d. T.R.E. it was worth 5s., now 8s.

(29) The same church held and holds INISE [Ince]. There [are] 3 hides that pay geld. The land is for 5 ploughs. In demesne is 1 plough and 2 serfs, and 8 villeins and 1 bordar with 1 plough. T.R.E. it was worth 30s., now 15s. There [are] 2 acres of meadow.

In Tunendune Hundred

(30) The same church held and holds MIDESTUNE [Middleton Grange in Aston by Sutton, Runcorn parish], and William[33] [holds] of it. There [is] 1 hide that pays geld. The land is for 3 ploughs. In demesne is ½ plough and 1 oxman, and 3 villeins with ½ plough and 1 bordar. There [are] 2 acres of wood. T.R.E. it rendered 16s., now it is worth 10s.

(31) (The same church held and holds CLISTUNE [Clifton in Runcorn] and William[34] [holds] of it. There [is] 1 hide that pays geld. The land is for 2 ploughs. In demesne is 1 [plough] and 2 oxmen, and 1 radman and 1 bordar with 1 [plough]. It is worth 10s. It was waste. *Whole entry added in the margin.*)

In Exestan Hundred

(32) The same church held and holds ODESLEI [Hoseley, Flints., in Gresford, Denb. and Flints.]. There [is] ½ hide that pays geld. The land is for 1 plough. There is 1 villein rendering 8d. It is worth 3s. It was waste.

[f. 263v. col. 1]

In Dudestan Hundred

(33) The same church holds PULFORD [Pulford] and held it T.R.E. There [is] ½ hide that pays geld. The land is for 1 plough. It is there with 1 villein and 1 bordar. It was worth 4s., now 5s.

In Atiscros Hundred

(34) The same church held and holds WEPRE [Wepre in Northop, Flints.]. There [are] 2 [third] parts of 1 hide that pay geld. The land is for 1 plough. It is there with 2 villeins and 2 bordars. William[35] holds [it] of the church. There is wood 1 league long and ½ league wide.

(35) The same church held LECHE [Lache in Marlston cum Lache, St. Mary on the Hill parish]. There [is] 1 virgate that pays geld. The land is for ½ plough. It was and is waste.[36]

In Roelau Hundred

(36) EARL HUGH holds WIVREHAM [Weaverham] in demesne. Earl Edwin held it. There [are] 13 hides that pay geld. The land is for 18 ploughs. In demesne are 2 [ploughs] and 2 oxmen and 2 serfs, and 10 villeins and 1 bordar, and 1 radman with 1 villein. Between them all they have 3 ploughs. There [is] a church and a priest, and a mill serving the hall (*aula*), and 1 acre of meadow. Wood 2 leagues long and 1 league wide, and there [are] 2 hays for roe deer (*haiae capreolorum*).

---

[29] Unnecessary doubts have been expressed about this identification: *Dom. Surv. Ches.* 97.
[30] Presumably William FitzNiel: cf. no. 186.
[31] Presumably William FitzNiel: cf. no. 187.
[32] Space left for number of ploughs but figure not given.

[33] Presumably William FitzNiel, who held Aston: no. 199.
[34] Probably William FitzNiel, who held most of the adjoining manors: nos. 197–201.
[35] Probably William Malbank: cf. no. 329.
[36] Nine lines left blank before next entry.

To this manor belong 10 burgesses in the city. Of these 6 render 10s. 8d. and 4 render nothing. A Frenchman holds [the render][37] of the earl.

In WICH [? Northwich][38] there were 7 salt-houses (*salinae*) belonging to this manor. One of these now supplies the hall (*aula*) with salt, the others are waste.

In another hundred 1 virgate of land called ENTREBUS [Antrobus in Great Budworth] belongs to this manor and is waste.[39]

Of the land of this manor Joscelin (*Gozelinus*)[40] holds 4 hides of the earl and has there 1 plough and 3 serfs, and 5 villeins and 1 radman with 2 ploughs and ½ fishery.

The earl has placed 3 hides of this land in the forest. The whole manor was at farm T.R.E. for £10. The earl found it waste. Now his demesne [is worth] 50s. Joscelin's [land is worth] 10s.

(37) The same earl holds KENARDESLIE ['Conersley', unidentified in Whitegate].[41] Wulfheah (*Ulfac*), a free man, held it. There [is] 1 hide (that pays geld *interlined*). The land is for 2 ploughs. It is all in the forest. Wood 1 league long and ½ league wide. T.R.E. it was worth 6s. It was waste.

(38) The same earl holds DONEHAM [Dunham on the Hill in Thornton le Moors]. Aescwulf (*Essul*) held it in parage[42] as a free man. There [are] 3 hides that pay geld. The land is for 9 ploughs. In demesne is ½ plough, and 7 villeins and a smith and 3 bordars with 1½ ploughs. There [are] 2 acres of meadow. Wood ½ league long and a fourth part [of a league] wide. T.R.E. it was worth 40s., now 16s. It was waste.

(39) The same earl holds ELTONE [Elton in Thornton le Moors]. Toki and Grim held it (as 2 manors *interlined*) as free men. There [are] 2 hides that pay geld. The land is for 7 ploughs. In demesne is 1 [plough] and 2 oxmen, and 6 villeins and 1 bordar with 1 plough. T.R.E. it was worth 38s., now 6s. It was waste.

(40) The same earl holds TROFORD [Wimbolds Trafford in Thornton le Moors]. Leofric (*Levric*) and Guthlac (*Gotlac*) held it as 2 manors as free men. There [is] 1 hide that pays geld. The land is for 1 plough. It is there with 1 radman and 2 bordars. T.R.E. it was worth 10s., now 2s. He found it waste.

(41) The same earl holds MENLIE [Manley in Frodsham]. Toki held it as a free man. There [is] ½ hide that pays geld. The land is for 1 plough. It renders in farm a mark of silver. T.R.E. it was worth 10s.

(42) The same earl holds HELESBE [Helsby in Frodsham]. Earnwig (*Ernui*) (Fot *interlined*) held it as a free man. There [is] 1 hide that pays geld. The land is for 3 ploughs. There 3 villeins with

1 bordar have 1 plough. There [is] 1 acre of meadow, and wood ½ league long and as much wide. T.R.E. it was worth 12s., now 10s.

(43) The same earl holds FROTESHAM [Frodsham]. (Earl *interlined*) Edwin held it. There [are] 3 hides that pay geld. The land is for 9 ploughs. In demesne are 2 [ploughs] and 1 serf, and 8 villeins and 3 bordars with 2 ploughs.

[f. 263v. col. 2]

There a priest and a church have 1 virgate of land, and a winter mill there, and 2½ fisheries, and 3 acres of meadow, and wood ½ league long and ½ league wide and 2 hays there, and in WICH [? Northwich] ½ salthouse serving the hall (*aula*). The third penny of the pleas of this hundred belonged to this manor T.R.E. It was then worth £8, now £4. It was waste.

[f. 263v. col. 1]

IN BOCHELAU HUNDRED

(44) The same earl holds ALRETUNE [Ollerton in Knutsford]. Godric held it. There [is] 1 virgate of land that pays geld. The land is for ½ plough. It was and is waste.[43]

[f. 263v. col. 2]

(IN ROELAU HUNDRED)[44]

(45) The same earl holds ALDREDELIE ['Alderley', unidentified in Kingsley, Frodsham parish].[45] Carle held it. There [are] 3 hides that pay geld. The land is for 6 ploughs. It was waste and is now in the earl's forest. T.R.E. it was worth 30s.

(46) The same earl holds DONE [unidentified].[46] Wulfgeat (*Uviet*) held it as a free man. There are 2 hides that pay geld. The land is for 2 ploughs. It was waste and is now in the earl's forest. T.R.E. it was worth 10s.

(47) The same earl [holds] EDESBERIE [Eddisbury in Delamere]. Godwin held it as a free man. There [are] 2 hides that pay geld. The land is for 6 ploughs. It was and is waste. This land is 1 league long and as much wide.

IN DUDESTAN HUNDRED

(48) The same earl holds ETONE [Eaton in Eccleston]. (Earl *interlined*) Edwin held it. There [are] 1½ hides that pay geld. The land is for 2 ploughs. In demesne is 1 [plough] and 2 oxmen, and 2 villeins with 1 plough. There [is] a fishery rendering 1,000 salmon, and 6 fishermen, and 1 acre of meadow. T.R.E. it was worth £10 and afterwards £8, now £10.

(49) The same earl holds LAI [Leahall in Lea Newbold, St. Oswald's parish].[47] Godwin, a free man, held it. There [are] 1½ hides that pay geld.

---

[37] More likely than the entire manor.
[38] Purely on grounds of proximity: *T.H.S.L.C.* cxxxi. 6.
[39] See no. 71.
[40] Probably the Joscelin of nos. 267–9.
[41] 'Conersley' was a grange of Vale Royal abbey, perhaps near Earnshaw Grange in Whitegate parish: *P.N. Ches.* iii. 207.
[42] For parage see *Past and Present*, lvii. 44–5.
[43] Entry and hundredal rubric added in bottom margin of

column in middle of entry no. 43.
[44] Three entries still under hundredal rubrication of Roelau: see preceding note.
[45] *P.N. Ches.* iii. 239–40; located in S. part of Kingsley township.
[46] In Delamere forest: *P.N. Ches.* iii. 161.
[47] Lea Newbold township was named from Lea and Newbold. Of three Domesday manors named Lea, one or more may have lain at Newbold.

The land is for 4 ploughs. In demesne is 1 [plough] and 2 oxmen, and 8 villeins with 1 plough. There [is] 1 acre of wood. T.R.E. it was worth 30*s.* and afterwards 5*s.*, now 10*s.*

(50) The same earl holds COTINTONE [Codding-ton]. Earnwig (*Ernui*) and Ansgot and Dot held it as 3 manors. There [are] 2 hides that pay geld. The land is for 4 ploughs. In demesne is 1 [plough] and 2 oxmen, and 5 villeins and 1 bordar and 1 radman and 1 Frenchman with 2 ploughs. There [is] a mill and 12 acres of meadow. T.R.E. it was worth 9*s.* 6*d.*, now 12*s.* He found it waste.

(51) The same earl holds LAI [Leahall in Lea Newbold, St. Oswald's parish].[48] Stein held it as a free man. There [is] ½ hide that pays geld. The land is for 1 plough. It is waste.

[IN RISEDON HUNDRED][49]

(52) The same earl holds RUSITONE [Rushton in Tarporley]. Cypping (*Chepin*) held it as a free man. There [is] ½ hide that pays geld. The land is for 2 ploughs. It is waste.

(53) The same earl holds OPETONE [uniden-tified, ? Eaton in Tarporley].[50] Arni (*Erni*), a free man, held it. There [is] 1 hide that pays geld. The land is for 2 ploughs. It is waste. There [is] wood 1 league long and 2 acres wide.

(54) The same earl holds BODEURDE [Little Bud-worth]. Dedol, a free man, held it. There is ½ hide that pays geld. The land is for 2 ploughs. It is waste. Wood 1 league long and ½ [league] wide.

(55) The same earl holds ALRETONE [uniden-tified].[51] Stein held it. He was a free man. There [is] 1 hide that pays geld. The land is for 2 ploughs. It is waste.

(56) The same earl holds OVRE [Over]. Four free men held it as 4 manors. There [is] 1 hide that pays geld. The land is for 5 ploughs. There [is] 1 radman with 1 plough. There [is] wood ½ league long and as much wide. It was worth 6*s.*, now 5*s.*

IN WILAVESTON HUNDRED

(57) The same earl holds ESTHAM [Eastham]. (Earl *interlined*) Edwin held it. There [are] 22 hides that pay geld. The land (is *interlined*) for as many ploughs. In demesne are 2 ploughs and 4 serfs, and 14 villeins and 10 bordars with 6 ploughs. There [is] a mill and 2 radmen and 1 priest.

Of the land of this manor Mundret holds 2 hides, and Hugh 2 hides, and William 1 hide, (and Walter ½ hide *added in the margin*), Hamon 7 hides, Robert 1 hide, Robert ½ hide.[52] In demesne are 4 ploughs and 8 oxmen, and 22 villeins and 11 bordars and 5 radmen and 2 Frenchmen with 9 ploughs. The whole manor T.R.E. was worth £24 and afterwards £4. Now the earl's demesne is worth £4, his men's [land] 112*s.*

(58) The same earl holds TRAFORD [Mickle Trafford in Plemstall]. Ording (*Ordm*)[53] held it. He was a free man. There [are] 2 hides that pay geld. The land is for 6 ploughs. In demesne are 2 [ploughs] and 2 serfs, and 4 villeins and 2 bordars with 1 plough. T.R.E. it was worth 100*s.*, now 40*s.* He found it waste.

(59) The same earl holds EDELAUE [Hadlow in Willaston, Neston parish].[54] (Earl *interlined*) Edwin held it. There [is] 1 hide that pays geld. The land is for 1 plough. It was waste. Now a certain man ploughs there and renders 2*s.*

IN HAMESTAN HUNDRED

(60) The same earl holds MACLESFELD [Maccles-field in Prestbury]. (Earl *interlined*) Edwin held it. There are 2 hides that pay geld. The land is for 10 ploughs. In demesne is 1 plough and 4 serfs. There [is] a mill serving the hall (*curia*). Wood 6 leagues long and 4 [leagues] wide and 7 hays were there. Meadow for the oxen. The third penny of the hundred belongs to this manor. T.R.E. it was worth £8, now 20*s.* It was waste.

[f. 264 col. 1]

(61) The same earl holds EDULVINTUNE [Adling-ton in Prestbury]. (Earl *interlined*) Edwin held it. There [are] 4 (½ *interlined*) hides that pay geld. The land is for 10 ploughs. There [are] 2 radmen and 6 villeins and 3 bordars with 3 ploughs. There [are] 21 acres of meadow. Wood 11 leagues long and 2 wide, and there [are] 7 hays and 4 eyries of hawks. T.R.E. it was worth £8, now 20*s.* He found it waste.

(62) The same earl holds GOVESURDE [Gaws-worth]. Beornwulf [*Bernulf*], a free man, held it. There [is] 1 hide that pays geld. The land is for 6 ploughs. It is waste. T.R.E. it was worth 20*s.* There [is] wood 2 leagues long and 2 leagues wide and 2 hays.

(63) The same earl holds MERUTUNE [Marton in Prestbury]. Godric held it.[55] He was a free man.

48 See preceding note.
49 Nos. 52–6, generally considered to form a detached part of Dudestan hundred, are more likely to have had the hundredal rubric omitted, an apparent space being left at the end of no. 51; see above.
50 Unlikely to be Upton by Chester: *P.N. Ches.* iii. 161. Perhaps the Domesday form represents 'Up-Eaton', referring to Eaton in Tarporley, adjacent to Rushton: 3 *Sheaf*, nos. 499, 518. Rushton and Eaton manors later descended together: Ormerod, *Hist. Ches.* ii. 238.
51 Not Oulton in Little Budworth, as in *Dom. Surv. Ches.* iii, unsupported by etymology. Cf. *P.N. Ches.* ii. 211; iii. 300, for *Olerton Harewood* and Ollerton meadow.
52 Mundret probably held part of Whitby; Hugh (FitzNor-man), Brimstage and Oxton; William (Malbank), parts

of Whitby and Tranmere; Hamon (de Massy), Bidston, Birkenhead, Claughton, Moreton, and Saughall Massie. One Robert may be identified as Robert of Rhuddlan with ½ hide at Tranmere. The other Robert may be the same man. Apart from Eastham itself and Bromborough, the earl's demesne probably included Childer Thornton and perhaps Higher Thornton: *Dom. Surv. Ches.* iii; J. Brownbill, 'Ches. in Dom. Bk.' *T.H.S.L.C.* li. 21–5.
53 The Domesday name could be a defective abbreviation of Ordmaer.
54 That it was Hadlow, unlocated in S. part of Willaston township, appears certain, despite Tait's doubts: *P.N. Ches.* iv. 232; *Dom. Surv. Ches.* 113.
55 Godric held another virgate in Marton: no. 223.

There [is] 1 virgate of land that pays geld. The land is for 1 plough. It was and is waste. There [are] 20 perches of wood.

(64) The same earl holds HUNGREWENITUNE [unidentified, in Lower Withington, Prestbury parish].[56] Godwin held it. There [is] ½ hide that pays geld. It was and is waste.

(65) The same earl holds CELEFORD [Chelford in Prestbury]. Brun held it. There [is] ½ hide that pays geld. The land is for 2 ploughs. It was and is waste.

(66) The same earl holds HAMETEBERIE [Henbury in Prestbury] of ½ hide, COPESTOR [Capesthorne in Prestbury] of ½ hide, and HAMEDEBERIE [Henbury in Prestbury] of 1 hide that pays geld, and HOFINCHEL [unidentified][57] of 1 hide, and TENGESTVISIE [Tintwistle, in Mottram in Longdendale] of 1 virgate of land, and HOLISURDE [Hollingworth, in Mottram in Longdendale] of 1 virgate, and WARNET [Werneth in Stockport] of 1 virgate, and RUMELIE [Romiley in Stockport] of 1 virgate, and LAITONE [Leighton in Marple, Stockport parish][58] of 1 virgate of land. All paid geld. Eight free men held these lands as [8][59] manors. In all there is land for 16 ploughs. The whole was and is waste. In Hofinghel is wood 2 leagues long and 2 wide. In Tengestvisie is wood 4 leagues long and 2 wide. In Warnet is wood 3 leagues long and 2 wide. T.R.E. this hundred was worth 40s., now 10s.

IN MILDESTUIC HUNDRED

(67) The same earl holds ELEACIER [Alsager in Barthomley]. Wulfric (*Ulvric*), a free man, held it. There [is] ½ hide that pays geld. The land is for 1 plough. It is waste. T.R.E. it was worth 3s.

(68) The same earl holds SANBEC [Sandbach] of 2½ virgates that pay geld, and CLIVE [Clive in Middlewich] of 1 virgate that pays geld, and SUTONE [Sutton in Middlewich] of 4 bovates of land that pay geld, and WIBALDELAI [Wimboldsley in Middlewich] of 1 virgate that pays geld, and WEVRE [Weaver in Middlewich] of 1 virgate of land that pays geld, and ACULVESTUNE [Occlestone in Middlewich] of 1 hide that pays geld.[60] Six free men held these lands as 6 manors. In all there is land for 7 ploughs. The whole was and is waste. In Wibaldelai is 1 acre of meadow, and a fourth part of a wood which has 1 league in length and 4 perches in width. In Wevre ½ acre of meadow, and a fourth part of a wood which has 1 league in length and as much in width.

IN WILAVESTON HUNDRED

(69) The same earl holds OPTONE[61] [Upton by Chester in St. Mary on the Hill]. (Earl *interlined*) Edwin held it. There [are] 4½ hides that pay geld. The land is for 12 ploughs. In demesne is 1 [plough] and 2 oxmen, and 12 villeins and 2 radmen with 5 ploughs.

Of this land of this manor Hamon[62] holds 2 [third] parts of 1 hide, and Herbert ½ hide,[63] and Mundret 1 hide. There are in demesne 4 ploughs and 8 oxmen, and 2 villeins and 2 bordars with 1 plough. There [is] 1 acre of meadow. The whole manor T.R.E. was worth 60s. Now the earl's demesne is worth 45s. and [the land] of his men 40s.

(70) The same earl holds STANEI [Stanney in Stoke] and Restald [holds it] of him. Ragenald held it as a free man. There [is] 1 hide that pays geld. The land is for 2 ploughs. In demesne is 1 [plough] and 2 oxmen, and 2 villeins and 2 bordars, and 1 fishery. T.R.E. it was worth 12s., now 14s. Of this land the fifth acre belonged and ought to belong to (*fuit et esse debet in*) the church of St. Werburgh, by witness of the county. The canons claim it because they lost it unjustly.

IN TUNENDUNE HUNDRED

(71) The same earl holds ENTREBUS [Antrobus in Great Budworth].[64] Leofnoth (*Levenot*) held it and was a free man. There [are] 1½ virgates of land that pay geld. The land is for 1 plough. It was and is waste. There [is] wood 1 league long and ½ [league] wide. T.R.E. it was worth 4s.[65]

[f. 264 col. 2]

IN DUDESTAN HUNDRED

(72) ROBERT FITZHUGH holds BEDDESFELD [Bettisfield in Hanmer, Flints.] of (Earl *interlined*) Hugh. (Earl *interlined*) Edwin held it. There [are] 7 hides that pay geld. The land is for 8 ploughs. In demesne is 1 [plough] and 2 serfs, and 3 villeins with 1 plough. There [is] ½ acre of meadow. Wood 3 leagues long and 2 wide. In this land 3 knights (*milites*) have 3 ploughs in demesne, and 9 villeins and 5 bordars, and 2 serfs, and 3 other men. Between them all they have 3 ploughs. A priest has 1 plough. The whole was worth £18 17s. 4d. T.R.E. It was waste. Now it is worth in all £3. Besides wood this manor has 2 leagues in length and as much in width.

Of this manor the bishop of Chester claims 2 hides which St. Chad held in the time of King Cnut, but which, he complains, have been lost from that time until now.

(73) The same Robert holds BURWARDESTONE [unidentified, in Is-coed, Flints., Malpas parish].[66] (Earl *interlined*) Edwin held it. There are 5 hides that pay geld. The land is for 14 ploughs. In demesne is 1 [plough], and 12

---

[56] *Dom. Surv. Ches.* 115; *P.N. Ches.* i. 89.
[57] Presumably in the Prestbury area: cf. *P.N. Ches.* i. 282.
[58] The name apparently survived as the field names Low and Old Leighton: *P.N. Ches.* i. 282.
[59] MS. has no figure and no space for one: cf. no. 68.
[60] Bigot had land in 4 of these places: nos. 242–5.
[61] Name not rubricated.
[62] Hamon de Massy: *Dom. Surv. Ches.* 117.
[63] Probably the 4 bovates in Hoole in Plemstall, given by Herbert the jerkin maker (*wambasarius*) to Chester abbey

before 1119: *T.H.S.L.C.* cxxxi. 159–60.
[64] See no. 36.
[65] Rest of column, 11 lines, left blank.
[66] The position of the entry between Bettisfield and Worthenbury suggests that the place lay, like them, in Maelor Saesneg (Flints.), where an Old English place name might well have fallen into disuse after 1086. The salthouse was probably that at Foulwich, later Lower Dirtwich, in Is-coed township, given to Chester abbey by Robert FitzHugh: *Dom. Surv. Ches.* 121.

villeins and 2 bordars with 3 ploughs, and 1 knight (*miles*) has 1 plough there, and another knight (*miles*) holds ½ hide which renders 12s. to him. There [is] a salthouse (*salina*) worth 24s. T.R.E. the manor was worth £6 4s., now 54s. He found it waste. This manor has 2 leagues in length and 1 in width. The bishop of Chester claims 1½ hides of this manor and 1 salthouse.

(74) The same Robert holds HURDINGBERIE [Worthenbury, Flints.]. (Earl *interlined*) Edwin held it. There [are] 5 hides that pay geld. The land is for 10 ploughs. In demesne is 1 [plough] and 1 serf, and 3 villeins and 3 Frenchmen and 1 radman with 4 ploughs. There [is] a new mill and 1 acre of meadow. Of this manor a knight (*miles*) holds 1½ hides, and has there 1 plough with his men. T.R.E. it was worth 12 ounces (*oras*) which the villeins rendered. Now it is worth 30s. He found it waste. It has in length 2 leagues and 1 in width.

(75) The same Robert holds DEPENBECH [Malpas]. (Earl *interlined*) Edwin held it. There [are] 8 hides that pay geld. The land is for 14 ploughs. In demesne are 3 [ploughs] and 1 bordar and ½ acre of meadow. Of this land 5 knights (*milites*) hold 5½ hides of Robert, and have there 3 ploughs, and 7 villeins with 2½ ploughs. There [are] 2 acres of meadow. T.R.E. the whole was worth £11 4s. It was afterwards waste. Now, all included, it is worth 52s. It has 2 leagues in length and 1 in width.

(76) The same Robert holds TILLESTONE [Tilston]. (Earl *interlined*) Edwin held it. There [are] 4 hides that pay geld. The land is for 8 ploughs. In demesne is 1 [plough] and 2 serfs, and 4 villeins and 2 bordars and 4 radmen and a reeve and a smith and a miller with 4 ploughs between them all. There [is] a mill worth 8s. Of this land Ranulph holds ½ hide of Robert, rendering 6s. 8d. T.R.E. the whole was worth £6, now 30s. He found it waste. It has 1 league in length and another in width. Of the land of this manor the bishop of Chester claims ½ hide, but the county does not testify that it belongs to his bishopric.

(77) The same Robert holds CRISTETONE [Christleton]. (Earl *interlined*) Edwin held it. There [are] 7 hides that pay geld. The land is for 14 ploughs. In demesne is 1 plough and 2 bondwomen, and 12 villeins and 5 bordars and 2 reeves with 8 ploughs. There [is] a mill worth 12s. and 2 radmen there. Of this manor Ranulph holds 2 hides of Robert; he renders 12d. to him. The whole was worth £6 T.R.E., now it is worth £3. He found it waste. It has 2 leagues in length and 1 in width.

(78) The same Robert holds CALMUNDELEI [Cholmondeley in Malpas]. Edwin and Dot (free men *interlined*) held it (as 2 manors *interlined*). There [are] 2 hides that pay geld. The land is for 4 ploughs. Edwin and Drew (*Drogo*) hold it of Robert. In demesne is 1 plough and 5 serfs, and 1 villein and 3 bordars and 1 reeve and a smith with 1 plough, and there [is] wood 1½

leagues long and 1 [league] wide. There [are] 3 hays. T.R.E. it was worth 13s., now 6s. 3d. It has ½ league of open country (*de plano*).[67]

(79) The same Robert holds EGHE [Edge in Malpas].[68] Edwin held it and still holds it of Robert. He was a free man. There [are] 2½ hides that pay geld. The land is for 1 plough. There are moors (*morae*). In demesne is 1 plough and 3 serfs. Two acres long and 1 wide of wood. It was waste and he found it so, now [it is worth] 4s.

(80) The same Robert holds HANTONE [Hampton in Malpas] and Edwin and Drew (*Drogo*) [hold it] of him. The same Edwin held it (as 2 manors *interlined*) and was a free man. There [are] 2 [and ½ *imperfectly erased*] hides that pay geld. The land is for 4 ploughs. There are 3 settlers (*hospites*) who have nothing. There [is] wood 5 acres long and 2 wide. The whole was worth 5s. T.R.E., now it renders 2s. and a sparrowhawk (*sprevarium*).

[f. 264v. col. 1]

(81) The same Robert holds LAVORCHEDONE [Larkton in Malpas] and Edwin and Drew (*Drogo*) [hold it] of him. The same Edwin held it. He was a free man. There [is] 1 hide that pays geld. The land is for 3 ploughs. One man is there and renders 12d., and 1 bordar renders 2s. It was worth 8s. T.R.E. It has 4 leagues in length and 4 in width.

(82) The same Robert holds DOCHINTONE [Duckington in Malpas] and Edwin [holds it] of him. He himself held it as a free man. There [is] 1 hide that pays geld. The land is for 2 ploughs. It is waste.

(83) The same Robert holds EGHE[69] [Little Edge in Edge, Malpas parish] and Edwin [holds it] of him and held it as a free man. There [is] ½ hide that pays geld. The land is for 1 plough. It is waste. There [is] wood 2 acres long and 1 wide. It is worth 12d.

(84) The same Robert holds CELELEA [Chowley in Coddington] and Mundret [holds it] of him. Wulfgifu (*Ulveve*) held it and was a free woman. There [is] 1 hide that pays geld. The land is for 1 plough. It is there with 2 radmen. Wood ½ league long and 1 acre wide and 2 hays. T.R.E. it was worth 10s., now 5s. He found it waste.

(85) The same Robert holds BROSSE [Broxton in Malpas] and Roger (and Picot *interlined*) [hold it] of him. Brihtmar (*Brismer*) and Raven, 2 free men, held it as 2 manors. There [are] 5 hides that pay geld. The land is for 6 ploughs. In demesne is 1 plough, and 3 villeins with 1 plough. One league of wood. T.R.E. it was worth 10s. 8d., now 18s. 8d.

(86) The same Robert holds OVRETONE [Overton in Malpas]. Wulfwig (*Ulvoi*) held it. He was a free man. There [are] 1½ hides that pay geld. The land is for 2 ploughs. In demesne is 1

---

[67] Sense of *de plano* obscure.
[68] See following note.
[69] Name not rubricated. If the 2 Domesday manors

called Edge were distinct settlements, they were probably Great and Little Edge, recorded by 1200: *P.N. Ches.* iv. 31.

[plough]. Wood 2 acres long and 1 wide. It was worth 5s., now 6s.

(87) The same Robert holds CUNTITONE [Cuddington in Malpas]. (The above *interlined*) Wulfwig (*Ulvoi*) held it. There [is] ½ hide that pays geld. The land is for 1 plough. There are 2 bordars ploughing with 2 oxen. It is worth 16d. It was waste.

(88) The same Robert holds SOCHELICHE [Shocklach] and Drew (*Drogo*) [holds it] of him. Dot, a free man, held it. There [are] 3 hides that pay geld. The land is for 4 ploughs. In demesne are 2 [ploughs] and 2 oxmen, and 2 villeins with 1 (plough *interlined*). There [is] ½ acre of meadow. T.R.E. it was worth 8s., now 12s.

(89) The same Robert holds TUSIGEHAM [Tushingham in Malpas] and Humphrey[70] [holds it] of him. Earnwine (*Ernuin*) (a free man *interlined*) held it. There [is] 1 hide that pays geld. The land is for 2 ploughs. In demesne is 1 [plough], with 1 bordar. Half a league of wood. T.R.E. it was worth 10s., now 4s. It was waste.

(90) The same Robert holds BICHELEI [Bickley in Malpas] and Fulk [holds it] of him. Wudumann (*Udeman*) held it and was a free man. There [is] 1 hide that pays geld. The land is for 2 ploughs. In demesne is 1 plough, and a reeve and 2 bordars with 1 plough. T.R.E. it was worth 5s., now 8s. He found it waste.

(91) The same Robert holds BICRETONE [Bickerton in Malpas] and Drew (*Drogo*) [holds it] of him. Dot and Edwin and Earnwine (*Ernuinus*), 3 thegns, free men, held it (as 3 manors *interlined*). There [are] 3 hides that pay geld. The land is for 4 ploughs. There are 2 villeins with 1 plough. Half a league of wood. T.R.E. it was worth 18s., now 11s. It was and is for the most part waste.

(92) The same Robert holds BURWARDESLEI [Burwardsley in Bunbury] and Humphrey [holds it] of him. Aelfric (*Alvric*), Colbert, and Ravenkel held it (as 3 manors *added in the margin*) and were free men. There [are] 3 hides that pay geld. The land is for 3 ploughs. There are 3 bordars with 1 plough and wood 1 league long and ½ [league] wide. It was worth 2s. T.R.E., now 5s. It was waste. Of this land 1 hide was taken from the church of St. Werburgh. This the reeves of Earls Edwin and Morcar sold to a certain Ravenkel (*Ravechel*).

(93) The same Robert holds CREUHALLE [Crewe Hall in Farndon], and Eli [holds it] of him. He himself held it and was a free man. There [is] 1 hide that pays geld. The land is for 1 plough. It is there in demesne with 2 bordars, and ½ fishery. It is worth 10s. It was waste and he found it so.

IN RISEDON HUNDRED

(94) The same Robert holds TIDULSTANE [Tilstone Fearnall in Bunbury] and William [holds

it] of him. Stenulf held it and was a free man. There [are] 2 hides that pay geld. The land is for 2 ploughs. In demesne is 1 [plough], with 1 bordar. There are coppices (*modicae silvae*). T.R.E. it was worth 6s. 8d., now 4s. He found it waste.

(95) The same Robert holds BUISTANE [Beeston in Bunbury]. Wulfwig (*Ulvoi*) held it and was a free man. There [is] 1 hide that pays geld. The land is for 2½ ploughs. In demesne is 1 [plough] with 2 oxmen. T.R.E. it was worth 10s., now 5s. He found it waste.

(96) The same Robert holds BOLEBERIE [Bunbury]. Dedol held it and was a free man. There [is] 1 hide that pays geld. The land is for 2 ploughs. In demesne is 1 [plough], and a priest with 2 villeins have 1 plough. Wood 1 league long and 1 acre wide. It was worth 4s., now 13s.

(97) The same Robert holds TEVRETONE [Tiverton in Bunbury]. Dedol and Hundulf held it as 2 manors and were free men. There [are] 2 hides that pay geld. The land is for 2 ploughs. There 3 villeins and 2 bordars have 1 plough. Wood 1 league long and another wide. It was worth 10s., now 25s.

[f. 264v. col. 2]

(98) The same Robert holds SPURETONE [Spurstow in Bunbury]. Wulfric (*Ulvric*) held it and was a free man. There [are] 1½ hides that pay geld. The land is for 3 ploughs. There 2 radmen and 3 bordars have 1 plough. There [is] wood 1½ leagues long and ½ league wide, and 1 acre of meadow. T.R.E. it was worth 16s., now 6s. He found it waste.

(99) The same Robert holds PEVRETONE [Peckforton in Bunbury]. Wulfric (*Ulvric*) (a free man *interlined*) held it. There [is] 1 hide that pays geld. The land is for 2 ploughs. There is 1 villein with 1 plough. It was worth 8s., now it renders 20s.

IN WILAVESTON HUNDRED

(100) The same Robert holds SUDTONE [? Guilden Sutton].[71] Toki held it and was a free man. There [is] 1 hide that pays geld. The land is for 3 ploughs. In demesne is 1 [plough], and 3 bordars with 1 villein. There [are] 6 acres of meadow. T.R.E. it was worth 40s. and afterwards 6s., now it renders a farm of 64d.

IN HAMESTAN HUNDRED

(101) Robert[72] holds BUTELEGE [Butley in Prestbury] of the earl. Hunding held it and was a free man. There [is] 1 hide that pays geld. The land is for 5 ploughs. It is waste except 12 sown acres (*acras satas*). T.R.E. it was worth 30s., now 2s. There [are] 2½ acres of meadow. There

---

[70] Humphrey de Costentin, who also held land of Earl Hugh at Coppingford (Hunts.). By the late 12th century the lords of Malpas were also lords of Coppingford: Farrer, *Honors and Kts.' Fees*, ii. 23, 27.

[71] As in H. C. Darby and G. R. Versey, *Dom. Gazetteer*, 36, but not *P.N. Ches.* iv. 126. FitzHugh's tenure is to be traced neither there nor in Sutton in Eastham: *Dom. Surv.*

Ches. 131.

[72] Omission of 'the same' may mean that in nos. 101-2 the scribe was not certain that the tenant was Robert FitzHugh. There are gaps, less than the height of a line, before no. 101 and after no. 102, and those entries were perhaps inserted later.

[is] wood 3 leagues long and 1 wide and 1 hay there.[73]

(102) Robert holds CROENECHE [Cranage in Sandbach]. Godric held it and was a free man. There [is] 1 hide that pays geld. The land is for 1½ ploughs. There 1 radman and 1 villein have ½ plough. There [is] wood ½ league long and 40 perches wide and 1 hay there. It was waste, now it is worth 3s.

IN WILAVESTON HUNDRED

(103) ROBERT OF RHUDDLAN [Rodelent] holds MOLINTONE [? Great Mollington in Backford][74] of (Earl interlined) Hugh. Godwin held it and was a free man. There [are] 1½ hides that pay geld. The land is for 3 ploughs. In demesne is 1 [plough] and 3 serfs, and 3 villeins and 3 bordars, and 2 acres of meadow, and 2 acres of wood. T.R.E. it was waste. It was worth 20s. when he received it, now 15s.

(104) The same Robert holds MOLINTONE [? Mollington Banastre in St. Mary on the Hill] and Lambert [holds it] of him. Gunnar (and Ulf interlined) held it (as two manors interlined) and were free men. There [is] 1 hide that pays geld. The land is for 2 ploughs. There is (1 interlined) [plough] in demesne with 2 serfs, and there [are] 2 acres of meadow. It is worth 14s. It was waste and he found it waste.

(105) The same Robert holds LESTONE [Leighton in Neston] and William [holds it] of him. Leofnoth (Levenot) held it and was a free man. There [is] 1 hide that pays geld. The land is for 2 ploughs. In demesne is 1 plough with 1 serf, and 1 Frenchman and 2 bordars, and 2 fisheries. It was and is worth 15s.

(106) The same Robert holds TORINTONE [Thornton Hough in Neston] and William [holds it] of him. Ulfketel[75] held it and was a free man. There [is] ½ hide that pays geld. The land is for 2 ploughs. There 1 radman and 1 villein and 1 bordar have ½ plough. It was worth 10s., and afterwards and now 5s.

(107) The same Robert holds GAITONE [Gayton in Heswall] and William [holds it] of him. Leofnoth (Levenot), a free man, held it. There [is] 1 hide that pays geld. The land is for 2 ploughs. There 2 villeins and 3 bordars have 1 plough, and there [are] 2 fisheries. It was worth 15s. and afterwards 2s., now 3s.

(108) The same Robert holds ESWELLE [Heswall] and Herbert [holds it] of him. Ulfkel[76] held it and was a free man. There [are] 2 hides that pay geld. The land is for 4 ploughs. In demesne is 1 plough and 2 oxmen, and 3 villeins and 1 bordar with 1 plough. T.R.E. it was worth 16s. and afterwards 20s., now 22s.

(109) The same Robert holds TURSTANETONE [Thurstaston] and William [holds it] of him. Leofnoth (Levenot) held it. He was a free man. There [are] 2 hides that pay geld. The land is for 4 ploughs. In demesne is 1 [plough] and 2 oxmen, and 4 villeins and 4 bordars with 1½ ploughs. T.R.E. it was worth 30s. and afterwards 8s., now 16s.

(110) The same Robert holds CALDERS [Caldy in West Kirby].[77] Leofnoth (Levenot) held it. He was a free man. There [are] 3 hides that pay geld. The land is for 10 ploughs. There 5 villeins and 5 bordars have 2 ploughs, and 1 Frenchman with 1 serjeant (serviens) has 2 ploughs. In demesne [are] 2 oxen, and 2 acres of meadow. T.R.E. it was worth 50s. and afterwards 10s., now 24s.

(111) The same Robert holds MELAS [Great Meols in West Kirby]. Leofnoth (Levenot) held it. There [is] 1 hide that pays geld. The land is for 1½ ploughs. There 1 radman and 2 villeins and 2 bordars have 1 plough. T.R.E. it was worth 15s., now 10s. He found it waste.

(112) The same Robert holds MELAS [Little Meols in West Kirby]. Leofnoth (Levenot) held it. There [is] 1 hide that pays geld. The land is for 3 ploughs. There 1 radman and 3 villeins and 3 bordars have 1 plough. T.R.E. it was worth 10s. and afterwards 8s., now 12s.

(113) The same Robert holds WALEA [Wallasey]. Uhtraed (Uctredus) held it and was a free man. There [are] 1½ hides that pay geld. The land is for 4 ploughs. There [are] 1 villein and 1 bordar with ½ plough, and 1 Frenchman has 1 plough with 2 oxmen, and 1 radman and 1 bordar.

(114) ROBERT THE COOK (cocus interlined) holds NESTONE [Little Neston in Neston] of the earl. Osgot held it and was a free man. There [is] 1 hide that pays geld. The land is for 3 ploughs. In demesne are 2 [ploughs] and 1 serf, and 2 villeins and 4 bordars with 1 plough, and 1 Frenchman [is] there. T.R.E. it was worth 13s. 4d., now 16s. He found it waste.

(115) The same Robert holds HAREGRAVE [Hargrave in Little Neston, Neston parish]. Osgot held it. There [is] 1 hide that pays geld. The land is for 2 ploughs. There 3 villeins and 2 bordars have 1 plough. T.R.E. it was worth 6s. 8d., now 10s. It was worth (when he received it interlined) 4s.

[f. 265 col. 1]

IN RISETON HUNDRED

(116) RICHARD DE VERNON holds ESTONE[78] [Ashton in Tarvin]. Thorth (Toret) held it and was a free man. There [are] 4 hides that pay geld. The land is for 5 ploughs. In demesne is

---

[73] No. 307, though differently ordered, has identical information, apart from the names of tenants before and after the Conquest and the extent of the sown acreage. The differences suggest that the entries are not duplicates; the similarities indicate a remarkably even, and therefore possibly recent, division.
[74] It is uncertain which of nos. 103 and 104 represents Great Mollington and which Mollington Banastre, or Little Mollington. Ormerod, *Hist. Ches.* ii. 378, 573, assigned no. 103 to Mollington Banastre, but the recorded population, ploughlands, and assessment suggest that no. 103 was Great Mollington.
[75] Probably same man as in no. 108.
[76] See preceding note.
[77] Formerly Little Caldy.
[78] Name not rubricated.

1 [plough] and 2 serfs, and 5 villeins and 2 radmen and 3 bordars with 2 ploughs. There [is] wood ½ league long and 1 acre wide. T.R.E. it was worth 16s., now 20s. He found it waste.

IN WILAVESTON HUNDRED

(117) The same Richard holds PICHETONE [Picton in Plemstall]. Toki held it and was a free man. There [is] 1 hide that pays geld. The land is for 3 ploughs. In demesne is 1 [plough] and 2 oxmen, and 1 radman and 3 bordars with 1 plough. There [is] ½ acre of meadow. T.R.E. it was worth 40s. and afterwards 5s., now 20s.

(118) The same Richard holds HOTONE [Hooton in Eastham]. Toki held it. There [are] 1 hide and 2 [third] parts of 1 hide that pay geld. The land is for 3 ploughs. There [are] 4 radmen and 1 villein and 4 bordars with 2 ploughs. T.R.E. it was worth 30s. and afterwards 5s., now 16s.

IN TUNENDUN HUNDRED

(119) The same Richard holds COCHESHALLE [Cogshall in Great Budworth] and Pain (*Pagen*) [holds it] of him. Leofnoth (*Levenot*) and Dedol (*Dedou*) held it as 2 manors and were free men. There [is] ½ hide that pays geld. The land is for 1 plough. It is there with 1 radman and 1 bordar. Wood 1 league long and ½ [league] wide. T.R.E. it was worth 2s., now 5s.

IN MILDESTUICH HUNDRED

(120) The same Richard holds SIBROC [Shipbrook in Davenham]. Osmaer held it. He was a free man. There [are] 2 hides that pay geld. The land is for 5 ploughs. In demesne is 1 [plough] and 2 serfs, and 2 villeins with 2 ploughs. There [are] 3 acres of meadow and 2 acres of wood. T.R.E. it was worth 20s., now 10s. He found it waste.

(121) The same Richard holds SURVELEC [Shurlach in Davenham]. Alweard [*Eluuard*] and Bers held it as 2 manors and were free. There [is] 1 hide that pays geld. The land is for 2 ploughs. In demesne is 1 plough and 2 serfs, and 2 villeins with ½ plough and 1 bordar, and 1 fishery, and 3 acres of meadow. T.R.E. it was worth 8s., now 7s. He found it waste.

(122) The same Richard holds WICE [Leftwich in Davenham]. Osmaer and Alsige (*Alsi*) held it as 2 manors and were free. There [is] 1 hide that pays geld. The land is for 3 ploughs. In demesne is 1 [plough] and 2 serfs, and 3 villeins with 1 plough, and 4 acres of meadow. T.R.E. it was worth 12s., now 6s.

(123) The same Richard holds MOLETUNE [Moulton in Davenham]. Leofnoth (*Levenot*) held it and was a free man. There [is] 1 hide that pays geld. The land is for 2 ploughs. There 1 villein and 1 bordar have ½ plough. There [is] 1 acre of meadow. Wood 1 league long and 1 wide. There [is] 1 hay. It was and is worth 5s.

(124) The same Richard holds WANETUNE [Wharton in Davenham]. Arngrim (*Haregrim*) and Alsige (*Alsi*) held it as 2 manors. (They were free men *interlined*). There [is] ½ hide that pays geld. The land is for 1 plough. It is there in demesne and 2 serfs, and 2 bordars. T.R.E. it was worth 4s., now 6s. He found it waste.

(125) The same Richard holds DEVENEHAM [Davenham]. Osmaer held it. He was a free man. There [is] ½ hide that pays geld. The land is for 2 ploughs. In demesne is 1 plough and 2 serfs, and a priest with a church, and 1 villein and 1 bordar with ½ plough. It was worth 8s., now 5s.

(126) The same Richard holds BOTESTOCH [Bostock in Davenham]. Osmaer held it. There [is] 1 hide that pays geld. The land is for 2 ploughs. They are there with 3 radmen and 2 serfs, and 2 acres of meadow, and 2 acres of wood. T.R.E. it was worth 3s., now 10s. He found it waste.

IN WARMUNDESTROU HUNDRED

(127) The same Richard holds ALDELIME [Audlem]. Osmaer held it. There [are] 2 hides that pay geld. The land is for 5 ploughs. In demesne is 1 [plough] and 1 serf, and 1 villein and 1 radman and 1 bordar with 1 plough. There [are] 2 acres of meadow. Wood 2 leagues long and 1 league wide, and 2 hays and a hawk's eyrie. T.R.E. it was worth 20s., now 8s. He found it waste.

(128) The same Richard holds CREU [Crewe in Barthomley]. Osmaer held it. There [is] 1 hide that pays geld. The land is for 2 ploughs. There [are] 1 radman and 1 villein and 2 bordars with 1 plough. There [are] 1½ acres of meadow. Wood 1 league long and ½ [league] wide. T.R.E. it was worth 10s., now 5s. He found it waste.

IN HAMESTAN HUNDRED

(129) The same Richard de Vernon[79] holds BRETBERIE [Bredbury in Stockport] and Wulfric (*Ulvric*) [holds it] of him, who also held it as a free man. There [is] 1 hide that pays geld. The land is for 3 ploughs. There 1 radman and 6 villeins and 2 bordars have 1 plough. Wood 1 league long and ½ league wide, and 3 hays and 1 hawk's eyrie. T.R.E. it was worth 10s., now the same.

[IN DUDESTAN HUNDRED][80]

(130) RICHARD THE BUTLER (*pincerna* interlined) holds PONTONE [Poulton in Pulford]. Edwin held it and was a free man. There [is] 1 hide that pays geld. The land is for 5 (*altered from 2*) ploughs. In demesne are 3 ploughs and 6 oxmen, and a reeve and 3 bordars with 2 ploughs. There [are] 8 acres of meadow. T.R.E. it was worth 40s. and afterwards as much, now £4.

(131) The same Richard holds CALVINTONE [unidentified].[81] Dot held it and was a free man.

---

[79] Entry added at foot of column after nos. 130-1, which is why the name is given in full.
[80] No hundredal rubric, so nos. 130-1 appear to be assigned to Warmundestrou, the rubric for no. 127. Dudestan is supplied on the assumption that *Pontone* is Poulton in Pulford.
[81] *P.N. Ches.* iv. 2 rejects identification with Carden. Another hundredal rubric may have been omitted.

There [are] 2 hides that pay geld. The land is for 2 ploughs. It was waste and he found it waste. Now it is at farm for 60s.

[f. 265 col. 2]

In Riseton Hundred

(132) WALTER DE VERNON holds Winfle-tone [Willington] of (Earl *interlined*) Hugh. Earngeat (*Erniet*) held it and was a free man. There [is] 1 hide that pays geld. The land is for 2 ploughs. There 2 villeins have 1 plough. There [is] wood ½ league long and 1 acre wide. T.R.E. it was worth 8s., now 10s. He found it waste.

In Wilaveston Hundred

(133) The same Walter holds Nesse [Ness in Neston]. Earngeat (*Erniet*) held it. There [are] 1½ hides that pay geld. The land is for 2 ploughs. In demesne is 1 [plough] and 2 oxmen, and 5 villeins and 3 bordars with 2 ploughs. There [is] ½ acre of meadow. T.R.E. it was worth 20s., now 16s.

(134) The same Walter holds Levetesham [Led-sham in Neston]. Earngeat (*Erniet*) held it. There [is] 1 hide that pays geld. The land is for 2 ploughs. In demesne is ½ plough and 1 serf, and 1 radman and 1 bordar with ½ plough between them all. T.R.E. it was worth 5s. and afterwards 8s., now 10s.

(135) The same Walter holds Prestune [Prenton in Woodchurch]. Wulfgeat (*Ulviet*), Eadric, and Luvede held it as 3 manors and were free. There [are] 1½ hides that pay geld. The land is for 3 ploughs. In demesne is 1 [plough] and 2 oxmen, and 2 bordars. There is a mill serving the hall (*curia*). Wood 1 league long and 1 [league] wide. It was worth 7s., now 5s.[82]

In Dudestan Hundred

(136) WILLIAM MALBANK (*Malbedeng*) holds of (Earl *interlined*) Hugh Tatenale [Tatten-hall]. Earnwine (*Ernuin*) held it and was a free man. There [are] 5 hides that pay geld. The land is for 6 ploughs. In demesne is 1 [plough], and 2 villeins and 2 bordars have another, and 1 Frenchman a third. There [is] 1 league of wood. T.R.E. it was worth 20s., now 26[s.]. It was waste.

(137) The same William holds Colburne [Gol-borne Bellow in Tattenhall]. Loten held it. There is ½ hide that pays geld. The land is for 1 plough which is there in demesne and 2 oxmen, with 1 villein and 3 bordars. There [is] a winter mill. It was worth 5s., now 6s. He found it waste.

In Riseton Hundred

(138) The same William holds Ulure [uniden-tified].[83] Wulfheah (*Ulfac*) held it and was a free man. There [are] 2 hides that pay geld. The land is for 4 ploughs. There 1 radman and 2 villeins and 3 bordars have 2 ploughs. There [are] 2 acres of meadow. Wood 1 league long and ½ [league] wide. T.R.E. it was worth 40s., now 10s. He found it waste.

In Wilaveston Hundred

(139) The same William holds Wivrevene [Wer-vin in St. Oswald's]. Colbert held it and was a free man. There [is] a third part of 1 hide that pays geld. The land is for 1 plough. There are 2 villeins with ½ plough. It was worth 8s., now 4s.

(140) The same William holds Pol [Overpool in Eastham]. Earnwine (*Ernuin*) held it as a manor. There [is] land of 4 bovates that pays geld. There 1 villein and 1 bordar have ½ plough. It was and is worth 4s.

(141) The same William holds Salhale [Saugh-all in Shotwick]. Lyfing (*Leving*) held it and was a free man. There [are] 6 hides that pay geld. The land is for 6 ploughs. In demesne are 1½ [ploughs] and 1 serf, and 7 villeins and 1 radman and 4 bordars with 3½ ploughs. There [is] a fish-ery. T.R.E. it was worth 20s. and afterwards 22s., now 45s.

(142) The same William holds Landechene [Landican in Woodchurch]. Aescwulf (*Essul*) held it and was a free man. There [are] 7 hides that pay geld. The land is for 8 ploughs. In de-mesne is 1 [plough], and a priest and 9 villeins and 7 bordars and 4 Frenchmen with 5 ploughs between them all. T.R.E. it was worth 50s., now 40s. He found it waste.

(143) The same William holds Optone [Upton in Overchurch] and Colbert [holds it] of him, who also held it as a free man. There [are] 3 hides that pay geld. The land is for 5 ploughs. In de-mesne is 1 [plough] and 4 serfs, and 2 villeins and 1 radman and 4 bordars with 1 plough. There [are] 2 acres of meadow. T.R.E. it was worth 25s., now 20s.

(144) The same William holds Tuigvelle [Thingwall in Woodchurch] and Durand [holds it] of him. Wintrelet held it and was a free man. There [is] 1 hide that pays geld. The land is for 2 ploughs. In demesne is 1 [plough] and 2 serfs, and 1 villein and 1 bordar have another. T.R.E. it was worth 8s., now 5s.

(145) The same William holds Chenoterie [Noctorum in Woodchurch] and Richard [holds it] of him. Colbert held it and was a free man. There [is] ½ hide that pays geld. The land is for 1 plough which is there in demesne with 2 ox-men, and 2 villeins. It was worth 15s., now 10s. It was waste.

In Mildestuic Hundred

(146) The same William holds Eteshale [Hassall in Sandbach]. Auti (*Outi*) held it and was a free man. There [is] ½ hide that pays geld. The land is for 2 ploughs. There [is] 1 radman with ½ plough and 1 serf, and 1 radman and 2 villeins and 3 bordars with 1 plough. Wood 1 league long and a hay there and a hawk's eyrie. T.R.E. it was worth 4s., now 5s.

---

[82] Next 2 lines left blank.
[83] Perhaps a moiety of Wardle and Calveley, both in Bunbury: *Dom. Surv. Ches.* 145–7; 3 *Sheaf*, iv. 132.

(147) The same William holds ETESHALE [Hassall in Sandbach]. Godric held it and was a free man. There [is] ½ hide that pays geld. The land is for 2 ploughs. There 1 radman with 1 bordar has ½ plough. T.R.E. it was worth 5s., now 5s. It was waste.

[f. 265v. col. 1]

(148) The same William holds MANESSELE [Minshull Vernon in Middlewich]. Leofnoth (*Levenot*) held it and was a free man. There [is] 1 hide that pays geld. The land is for 1 plough. There 1 radman and 2 serfs and 2 bordars have 1 plough. There [is] 1 acre of meadow. Wood 1 league long and 1 [league] wide and 4 hays and a hawk's eyrie. It was and is worth 4s. It was waste.

(149) The same William holds MANESHALE [Church Minshull]. Deorc (*Derch*) and Arngrim (*Aregrim*) held it as 2 manors and were free men. There [is] 1 hide that pays geld. The land is for 2 ploughs. They are there with 3 radmen and 2 bordars. There [is] 1 acre of meadow and wood ½ league long and ½ [league] wide and a hay and a hawk's eyrie. It was worth 4s., now 8s.

(150) The same William holds SPROSTUNE [Sproston in Middlewich]. Almaer [*Elmaer*] held it and was free. There [is] ½ hide that pays geld. The land is for 1 plough. It is there with 1 radman and 1 serf and 2 villeins and 2 bordars. There [is] ½ acre of meadow. Wood 2 furlongs long. T.R.E. it was worth 5s., now 4s. He found it waste.

IN WARMUNDESTROU HUNDRED

(151) The same William holds ACTUNE [Acton]. (Earl *interlined*) Morcar[84] held it. There [are] 8 hides that pay geld. The land is for 30 ploughs. In demesne are 3 [ploughs] and 2 serfs, and 13 villeins and 15 bordars with 7 ploughs. There [is] a mill serving the hall (*curia*), and 10 acres of meadow. Wood 6 leagues long and 1 wide and 1 hawk's eyrie. There [are] 2 priests with 1 plough, and 3 Frenchmen having 1½ ploughs and 1 serf, and 6 villeins (*villanos*) and 7 bordars with 4 ploughs.

This manor has its court in the hall (*aula*) of its lord, and in Wich [Nantwich] 1 house quit [of dues] for the making of salt. The whole was worth £10 T.R.E., now £6.

(152) The same William holds ESTUNE [Aston in Newhall, Wrenbury parish].[85] Dot held it and was a free man. There [is] 1 hide that pays geld. The land is for 2 ploughs. In demesne is 1 [plough] and 2 oxmen, and 2 villeins and 3 bordars have another plough. There [is] wood 1 league long and as much wide. T.R.E. it was worth 10s., now 5s. He found it waste.

(153) The same William holds WILAVESTUNE [Willaston in Wybunbury]. Wulfgeat (*Ulviet*) (a free man *interlined*) held it. There [is] 1 virgate that pays geld. The land is for ½ plough. There is 1 bordar. It was worth 5s., now 2s.

(154) The same William holds WARENEBERIE [Wrenbury]. Carle held it and was a free man.

There are 1½ hides that pay geld. The land is for 2 ploughs. In demesne is 1 [plough] and 2 oxmen, and 1 bordar. There [is] wood 2 leagues long and 1 [league] wide and 2 hays and a hawk's eyrie. It was and is worth 5s. He found it waste.

(155) The same William holds CERLETUNE [Chorlton in Wybunbury]. Frani held it and was a free man. There [is] ½ hide that pays geld. The land is for ½ plough. There is 1 villein with 2 oxen. It was and is worth 2s. He found it waste.

(156) The same William holds MERBERIE [Marbury] of 1½ hides, and NORBERIE [Norbury in Marbury] of 1½ hides, and WIRESWELLE [Wirswall, Ches., in Whitchurch, Salop.] of 1 hide. These lands pay geld. They were berewicks. They lay in WESTONE [Whitchurch, Salop.]. (Earl *interlined*) Harold held them. The land is for 5 ploughs. In demesne is 1 [plough] and 2 oxmen, and 2 villeins and 3 bordars with 1 plough. Wood 2 leagues long and 1 league and 40 perches wide. The whole was worth 21s. T.R.E., now 10s. Wiresuelle is waste.

(157) The same William holds WALCRETUNE [Walgherton in Wybunbury]. Gunning and Healfdene (*Alden*) held it (as 2 manors *misplaced at end of sentence and directed here by transposition signs*) and were free men. There [are] 1 hide and 1 virgate that pay geld. The land is for 2 ploughs. There is 1 [plough] with 1 oxman, and 1 radman and 2 bordars. T.R.E. it was worth 9s., now 5s. He found it waste.

(158) The same William holds SANTUNE [Shavington in Wybunbury].[86] Godwin and Dot held it (as 2 manors *misplaced at end of following sentence and directed here by transposition signs*) and were free. There [are] 3 virgates that pay geld. The land is for 1 plough. There 1 rad(man *interlined*) has ½ plough and 2 bordars. T.R.E. it was worth 4s., now 3s. He found it waste.

(159) The same William holds BURTUNE [Buerton in Audlem]. Siward held it and was a free man. There [is] 1 hide that pays geld. The land is for 3 ploughs. In demesne are 2 [ploughs] and 1 oxman. There [is] wood ½ league long and as much wide and 3 hays and a hawk's eyrie. It is worth 10s.

(160) The same William holds HARETONE [Hatherton in Wybunbury]. Ulfketel held it and was a free man. There [is] 1 hide that pays geld. The land is for 5 ploughs. In demesne is 1 [plough] and 2 oxmen, and 2 villeins and 1 bordar with 1 plough. There [is] wood ½ league long and as much wide. There [is] 1 hay.

(These 2 manors were worth 40s. T.R.E., now 10s. *in margin against entries 159 and 160*).

(161) The same William holds WISTANESTUNE [Wistaston]. Wulfric (*Ulvric*) held it and was a free man. There [is] 1 hide that pays geld. The land is for 5 ploughs. In demesne is 1 [plough] and 2 oxmen, and 2 villeins and 1 radman and 2 bordars with 1 plough. There [is] ½ acre of meadow. Wood 1 league long and ½ league wide and 2 hays. T.R.E. it was worth 30s., now 10s.

---

[84] Cf. no. 316: Acton said to be held by Earl Edwin.
[85] Other parts of Newhall were in Audlem and Acton.

[86] Cf. *Dom. Surv. Ches.* 155; *P.N. Ches.* iii. 69–70.

(162) The same William holds BERCHESFORD [Basford in Wybunbury]. Owain (*Ouuin*), Erlekin, and Leofric (*Levric*) held it as 3 manors and were free men. There [is] 1 hide that pays geld. The land is for 2 ploughs. There 3 radmen and 2 villeins and 3 bordars have 1 plough. There [is] 1 virgate of meadow. Wood 4 furlongs long and 1 wide. It was worth 5*s*., now the same. (They were waste. *in the bottom margin*)

[f. 265v. col. 2]

(163) The same William holds BERDELTUNE [Batherton in Wybunbury]. Healfdene (*Halden*) and Deorc (*Derch*) held it as 2 manors and were free men. There [is] ½ hide that pays geld. The land is for 2 ploughs. In demesne is 1 [plough] and 2 oxmen, and 1 villein and 2 bordars. There [are] 40 perches of wood. T.R.E. it was worth 6*s*., now 3*s*. He found it waste.

(164) The same William holds WERELESTUNE [Worleston in Acton]. Hacon, Alweard (*Eluuard*), and Alric (*Elric*) held it as 3 manors and were free. There is ½ hide that pays geld. The land is for 2 ploughs. In demesne is 1 [plough] and 2 oxmen, and 1 villein and 1 radman and 2 bordars with 1 plough. There [is] wood ½ league long and ½ [league] wide and 1 hay. T.R.E. it was worth 7*s*. 4*d*., now 8*s*. It was waste.

(165) The same William holds BERTEMELEU [Barthomley]. Siward held it and was a free man. There [is] 1 hide that pays geld. The land is for 3 ploughs. In demesne is 1 [plough] and 2 oxmen. [There are] a priest and 1 radman and 1 villein and 2 bordars with 2 ploughs. There [is] 1 acre of meadow. Wood 1 league long and ½ [league] wide and 1 hay and a hawk's eyrie. It was and is worth 20*s*. He found it waste.

(166) The same William holds ESSETUNE [? Austerson in Acton].[87] Osmaer and Owain (*Ouuinus*) held it as 2 manors and were free men. There [are] 3 virgates that pay geld. The land is for 5 ploughs. In demesne is 1 [plough] and 2 oxmen, and 3 bordars with 1 plough. There [is] 1 acre of meadow. Wood 1 league long and ½ [league] wide. There [are] 3 hays and 1 hawk's eyrie. T.R.E. it was worth 20*s*., now 10*s*. He found it waste.

(167) The same William holds WIVELESDE [Wilkesley in Audlem]. Dot and Godric held it as 2 manors and were free men. There [are] 1 hide and 1 virgate that pay geld. The land is for 3 ploughs. There 1 radman and 1 villein and 6 bordars have 1 plough. There [is] 1 acre of meadow. Wood 1 league long and as much wide and 5 hays and 1 hawk's eyrie. T.R.E. it was worth 18*s*., now 5*s*.

(168) The same William holds TITESLE [Tittenley in Audlem]. Eadric held it and was a free man. There [are] 3 virgates that pay geld. The land is for 1 plough. It is there with 2 villeins and 2 bordars. There [is] wood ½ league long and as much wide. It was worth 4*s*., now 5*s*.

(169) The same William holds STEPLE [Stapeley in Wybunbury]. Aelfric (*Elvric*) and Dot held it as 2 manors and were free men. There [is] ½ hide that pays geld. The land is for 2 ploughs. There is 1 [plough] with 2 oxmen, and 1 villein and 1 bordar. There [are] 1 (and ½ *interlined*) acres of meadow. Wood ½ league long and as much wide. T.R.E. it was worth 10*s*., now 6*s*. He found it waste.

(170) The same William holds WISTETESTUNE ['Wisterson' in Willaston, Nantwich parish].[88] Leofwine (*Leuuinus*) and Osmaer held it as 2 manors and were free. There [are] 3 virgates that pay geld. The land is for 2 ploughs. In demesne are 1½ [ploughs] and 3 oxmen, and 1 villein with ½ plough and 1 bordar. There [is] 1 perch of meadow. Wood ½ league long and as much wide. It was worth 8*s*., now 10*s*.

(171) The same William holds BRUNHALA [Broomhall in Wrenbury]. Eadric and Eadric held it as 2 manors and were free. There [is] ½ hide that pays geld. The land is for 1 plough. In demesne ½ [plough] with 1 oxman. Wood is 1 league long and ½ [league] wide and a hay there. T.R.E. it was worth 4*s*., now 2*s*. He found it waste. One virgate lay in Pol [Poole in Acton] manor.

(172) The same William holds POL [Poole in Acton]. Hacon held it and was a free man. There [is] ½ hide that pays geld. The land is for 1 plough. It is in demesne with 2 oxmen, and 3 bordars. There [is] ½ acre of meadow. It was worth 5*s*., now 8*s*.

(173) The same William holds TERETH [Frith in Wrenbury]. Leofwine (*Leuuinus*) and Osmaer held it as 2 manors and were free men. There [is] 1 virgate that pays geld. The land is for 2 ploughs. There 3 villeins have 1 [plough], and there [are] 4 acres of meadow, and wood ½ league long and 3 furlongs wide. T.R.E. it was worth 7*s*., now 5*s*.

(174) The same William holds CERLERE [Chorley in Wrenbury]. Aelfric (*Alvric*), a free man, held it. There [are] 3 virgates that pay geld. The land is for 1½ ploughs. There are 2 villeins and 1 bordar with ½ plough. Wood ½ league long and 2 furlongs wide. There [is] a hay. It is worth 3*s*.

(175) The same William holds BEDELEI [Baddiley]. Aelfric (*Alvric*), a free man, held it. There [is] ½ virgate that pays geld. The land is for 1 plough, which is there in demesne. Wood ½ league long and as much wide. There [is] a hay. It was worth 10*s*., now 5*s*.

(176) The same William holds 1 berewick [in] STANLEU [Stoneley Green in Burland, Acton parish]. This belonged to WESTONE [Whitchurch, Salop.].[89] (Earl *interlined*) Harold held it. There [is] ½ virgate that pays geld. The land is for 2 oxen. There is 1 radman. Wood ½ league long and ½ [league] wide. There [is] a hay. It was and is worth 2*s*.

---

[87] *P.N. Ches.* iii. 130 rejects the identification, which may be possible if the Domesday name form is one of the more eccentric ones.

[88] 'Wisterson' was the last recorded 19th-century form of the name for that part of Willaston township in Nantwich parish: *P.N. Ches.* iii. 42–3. [89] See no. 156.

(177) The same William holds COPEHALE [Coppenhall]. Healfdene (*Halden*) and Wulfheah (*Ulfac*) held it as 2 manors and were free. There [is] 1 hide that pays geld. The land is for 4 ploughs. In demesne is 1 [plough] and 2 oxmen, and 1 radman and 1 villein and 1 bordar with 1 plough. There [are] 3 acres of meadow. Wood 1 league long and 1 [league] wide. There [are] 2 hays. T.R.E. it was worth 24*s.*, now 12*s.*

[f. 266 col. 1]

(178) The same William holds POL [Poole in Acton]. Wulfgifu (*Ulveva*) held it and was free. There [is] 1 virgate that pays geld. The land is for 1 plough. There is 1 villein and 3 bordars with ½ plough. There [are] 2 acres of meadow, and 1 acre of coppice (*silva modica*). It was and is worth 3*s.*

(179) The same William holds ESTONE [Aston juxta Mondrum in Acton]. Ravenkel (*Ravecate*) held it and was free. There [is] 1 virgate that pays geld. The land is for 1 plough. There 1 radman has ½ plough with 2 bordars. There [are] 1½ acres of meadow. Wood 1 league long and ½ [league] wide. It was worth 5*s.*, now 3*s.* It was waste.

(180) The same William holds CHELMUNDESTONE [Cholmondeston in Acton]. Wulfgifu (*Ulveva*) held it and was free. There [is] 1 hide that pays geld. The land is for 2 ploughs. There [is] 1 radman having 1 plough, and 3 villeins with 1 plough. T.R.E. it was worth 10*s.*, now 6*s.*[90]

IN CESTRE HUNDRED

(181) WILLIAM FITZNIEL (*filius Nigelli*) holds of (Earl *interlined*) Hugh NEWENTONE [Newton by Chester, in St. Oswald's]. Arni (*Erne*) held it. There [is] 1 hide that pays geld. The land is for 3 ploughs. In demesne are 2 [ploughs] and 4 oxmen, and 6 villeins with 1 plough. T.R.E. it was worth 20*s.* and afterwards 10*s.*, now 20*s.*

(182) The same William holds LEE [Netherleigh in Chester]. Arni (*Erne*) held it. There [is] 1 virgate that pays geld. The land is for ½ plough. It is there with 3 villeins. It was worth 5*s.*, now 8*s.*

(183) The same William holds 1 carucate of land in BRUGE [Handbridge in Chester] that pays geld. Arni (*Erne*) held it as a manor. There are 3 bordars having ½ plough. It was worth 10*s.*, now 4*s.*

IN DUDESTAN HUNDRED

(184) The same William holds CLUTONE [Clutton in Farndon]. Edward and Wulfwine 'chit' (*Uluuinchit*) held it as 2 manors and were free men. There [is] 1 hide that pays geld. The land is for 2 ploughs. In demesne is ½ plough, and 1 Frenchman with 3 villeins has ½ plough. There [is] ½ acre of meadow. Half a league of wood. T.R.E. it was worth 20*s.*, now 8*s.*

IN RISETON HUNDRED

(185) The same William holds BERO [Barrow]. Thorth (*Toreth*) held it and was a free man. There [are] 3 hides that pay geld. The land is for 8 ploughs. There is 1 [plough] in demesne and 2 oxmen, and 2 villeins and 4 bordars and 2 Frenchmen. Between them is 1 plough. There [are] 2 mills worth 10*s.*, and 1 acre of meadow. Wood 1 league long and ½ [league] wide. T.R.E. it was worth 30*s.*, now as much. He found it waste.

IN WILAVESTON HUNDRED

(186) The same William holds NESTONE [Great Neston in Neston]. Arni (*Erne*) held it and was a free man. There [are] 2 [third] parts of 2 hides that pay geld.[91] The land is for 4 ploughs. In demesne are 2 ploughs and 1 serf. A priest and 4 villeins and 2 bordars have 3 ploughs there. T.R.E. it was worth 20*s.* and afterwards as much, now 25*s.*

(187) The same William holds RABIE [Raby in Neston] and Hardwin [holds it] of him. Arni (*Erni*) held it. There [is] ½ hide that pays geld.[92] The land is for 1 plough. It is there in demesne and 1 serf, and 2 villeins and 2 bordars with 1 plough. T.R.E. it was worth 10*s.*, and afterwards 14*s.*, now 20*s.*

(188) The same William holds CAPELES [Capenhurst in Shotwick] and David [holds it] of him. There [is] ½ hide that pays geld. Arni (*Erne*) held it. The land is for 1 plough. It is there with 1 villein and 2 bordars. T.R.E. and afterwards it was worth 5*s.*, now 8*s.*

(189) The same William holds BERNESTONE [Barnston in Woodchurch] and Ralph [holds it] of him. Ravensward (*Ravesvar*) and Leofgeat (*Leviet*) held it as 2 manors and were free men. There [is] 1 hide that pays geld. The land is for 2 ploughs. In demesne is 1 [plough], and 2 oxmen, and 3 bordars. It is worth 10*s.* He found it waste.

IN BOCHELAU HUNDRED

(190) The same William holds WAREBURGETUNE [Warburton]. Earnwig (*Ernui*) held it and was free. There [is] ½ hide that pays geld. The land is for 1 plough. There is 1 radman with 2 oxen. It was worth 5*s.*, now 2*s.*

(191) (The same William holds TATUNE[93] [Tatton in Rostherne]. Erchenbrand (*Echebrant*), a free man, held it. There [is] 1 hide that pays geld. The land is for 3½ ploughs. There [are] 3 villeins and 4 bordars. It is worth 4*s. in the bottom margin with marks to indicate the correct place for entry*).

(192) The same William holds MULINTUNE [Millington in Rostherne]. Dot [held it and] was a free man. There [is] ½ hide that pays geld. The land is for 1 plough. It was and is waste.

(193) The same William holds CUNETESFORD [Knutsford] and Erchenbrand (*Erchebrand*)

---

[90] Next line left blank.
[91] The remaining third was described in no. 26.
[92] The other half was described in no. 27.
[93] Name not rubricated.

[holds it] of him, who also held it as a free man. There [is] ½ hide that pays geld. The land is for 2 ploughs. It was and is waste. Wood ½ league long and 2 acres wide. It was worth 10s.

(194) The same William holds STABELEI [Tabley Superior in Rostherne]. Leofwine (*Leuuinus*) held it and was free. There [is] a third part of 1 hide that pays geld. The land is for 1 plough. It was and is waste. There [is] wood ½ league long and 40 perches wide. It was worth 10s.

(195) The same William holds in the same vill 1 bovate of land and a third part of 1 hide that pay geld. Sigrith (*Segrid*) and Wulfsige (*Ulsi*) held [them] as 2 manors and were free. The land is for 1 plough. It was and is waste. T.R.E. it was worth 7s.

(196) The same William holds PEVRE [Nether Peover in Great Budworth]. Edward held it (and was a free man *misplaced after the next sentence*). There [are] 2 [third] parts of 1 hide that pay geld. The land is for 1 plough. It was and is waste. There [is] wood 1 league long and 1 acre wide. It was worth 5s., now 12d.

[f. 266 col. 2]

IN TUNENDUNE HUNDRED

(197) The same William holds HELETUNE [Halton in Runcorn]. Orme held it and was a free man. There [are] 10 hides. Of these 5 pay geld and the others do not pay geld. The land is for 20 ploughs. In demesne are 2 ploughs and 4 oxmen, and 4 villeins and 2 bordars and 2 priests with 5 ploughs between them all. Two fishermen there render 5s., and [there is] 1 acre of meadow. Wood 1 league long and ½ league wide. There [are] 2 hays. In Wich [?Northwich] [there is] 1 waste house.
Of this land of this manor Odard holds ½ hide, Geoffrey 2 hides, Aitard 1½ hides, Humphrey 1½ hides, Odard ½ hide, Hardwin ½ hide. There are in demesne 3 ploughs, and 12 villeins and 1 radman and 5 bordars with 5 ploughs between them all, and 6 oxmen, and ½ acre of meadow, and 18 acres of wood. The whole manor T.R.E. was worth 40s. and afterwards was waste. Now what William holds is worth 50s., and what his knights (*milites*) [hold] is worth 54s.

(198) The same William holds WESTONE [Weston in Runcorn]. Gruffudd (*Grifin*) held it as a free man. There [are] 2 hides that pay geld. The land is for 5 ploughs. Odard and Brihtric [*Brictric*] hold it of William and have 2 ploughs in demesne there and 3 oxmen, and 5 villeins and 3 bordars with 3 ploughs, and 2 fishermen, and 2 acres of meadow, and 1 league in length and ½ [league] in width of wood, and a hay. T.R.E. it was worth 8s., now 35s. He found it waste.

(199) The same William holds ESTONE [Aston by Sutton, in Runcorn] and Odard [holds] of him. Leofric (*Levric*) (a free man *interlined*) held it. There [is] 1 hide that pays geld. The land is for 2½ ploughs. In demesne are 1½ ploughs, and 3 oxmen, and 1 villein and 1 bordar with 1 plough. There [is] a mill serving the hall (*curia*), and a fisherman, and 1 acre of wood. T.R.E. it was worth 5s., now 20s.

(200) The same William holds NORTUNE [Norton in Runcorn] and Ansfred [holds it] of him. Uhtraed (*Uctred*) and Toki held it as 2 manors and were free men. There [are] 2 hides that pay geld. The land is for 6 ploughs. In demesne is 1 [plough] and 2 serfs, and 3 villeins with 1 plough. There [is] 1 fisherman, and 3 acres of meadow, and 4 acres of wood and 2 hays. T.R.E. it was worth 16s., now 9s. 4d. He found it waste.

(201) The same William holds ENLELEI [Eanley in Norton, Runcorn parish]. Wicga (*Wighe*) held it. There [is] ½ hide that pays geld. The land is for ½ plough. It was and is waste.

(202) The same William holds DUNTUNE [Dutton in Great Budworth]. Edward held it as a free man as 1 manor. There [is] ½ virgate that pays geld. The land is for 2 oxen. There is 1 radman and 1 villein. It is worth 6d. It was waste.

(203) The same William holds LEGE [Little Leigh in Great Budworth]. Edward held it as a free man. There [is] 1 hide that pays geld. The land is for 1 plough. It is there with 1 radman and 1 serf and 2 villeins and 1 bordar. It is worth 4s. It was worth 5s. Earl Hugh has 1 virgate of this land which renders 3s.

(204) The same William holds ESTONE [Aston by Budworth in Great Budworth] and Pain (*Pagen*) [holds it] of him. Leofnoth (*Levenot*) held it as a free man. There [are] 2½ virgates that pay geld. The land is for 1 plough which is there in demesne and 2 oxmen, and 1 radman and 1 bordar and 1 serf. There [is] wood 1 league long and 40 perches wide and there are 2 hays.

(205) The same William holds BUDEWRDE [Great Budworth] and Pain (*Pagen*) [holds it] of him. Edward held it as a free man. There [is] 1 hide that pays geld. The land is for 2 ploughs. In demesne is ½ plough and 1 serf, and a priest and 2 villeins and 1 bordar with 1 plough, and a mill serving the hall (*aula*). There [are] 1½ acres of meadow. T.R.E. it was worth 6s., now 8s.

(206) The same William holds WITELEI [Whitley in Great Budworth] and Pain (*Pagen*) and Odard [hold it] of him. Leofnoth (*Levenot*) held it as a free man. There [are] 2 hides that pay geld. The land is for 2 ploughs. In demesne is 1 [plough] with 1 serf. There [is] 1 acre of meadow. Wood 1 league long and ½ [league] wide. It is worth 6s.

[IN MILDESTUICH HUNDRED *in the margin*]

(207) The same William holds GOSTREL [Goostrey in Sandbach] and Ralph [holds it] of him. Colben held it as a free man. There [is] 1 virgate that pays geld. The land is for 2 oxen. It was and is waste.[94]

---

[94] Entry rather compressed, perhaps added later in space between nos. 206 and 208.

In Hamstan Hundred[95]

(208) William[96] holds of the earl ALDREDELIC [Over Alderley in Alderley]. Brun held it and was a free man. There [is] 1 hide that pays geld. The land is for 4 ploughs. It was and is waste. Wood 2 leagues long and 2 wide. T.R.E. it was worth 20s.

In Mildestuic Hundred

(209) William holds of the earl LECE [Lach Dennis in Great Budworth]. Hasten held it and was a free man. There [is] ½ hide that pays geld. The land is for 1 plough. It was and is waste.[97]

[f. 266v. col. 1]

In Cestre Hundred

(210) HUGH DE MARA holds of (Earl *interlined*) Hugh LEE [Overleigh in Chester]. Leofwine (*Leuuinus*) held it. There [is] 1 virgate of land that pays geld. There are 2 villeins and 1 bordar with ½ plough. It was worth 10s. T.R.E., now 8s. He found it waste.

(211) The same Hugh holds BRUGE [Handbridge in Chester]. Leofwine (*Leuuinus*) held it. There [is] 1 carucate of land that pays geld. There 2 bordars have ½ plough. It was and is worth 3s.

(212) The same Hugh holds RADECLIVE ['Redcliff' in Chester]. Gunnar held it. There [is] a third part of 1 hide that pays geld.[98] There is 1 plough in demesne with 2 oxmen. It was waste when he received it. T.R.E. it was worth 10s., now 6s. 8d.

In Wilaveston Hundred

(213) The same Hugh holds CALDERS [Grange in West Kirby].[99] Earngeat (*Erniet*) held it and was a free man. There [is] 1 hide that pays geld. The land is for 3 ploughs. In demesne is 1 [plough], with 1 bordar. It was worth 5s., now 10s.

In Mildestuic Hundred

(214) HUGH[1] holds of the earl LAUTUNE [Church Lawton]. Godric held it and was a free man. There [is] 1 hide that pays geld. The land is for 3 ploughs. It is waste. There [is] wood 1 league long and 1 wide, and 1 acre of meadow. T.R.E. it was worth 16s.

(215) Hugh holds of the earl LAUTUNE [?Buglawton in Astbury].[2] Godric held it. There [is] ½ hide that pays geld. The land is for 3 ploughs. It is waste. There [is] wood 2 leagues long and 1 wide. T.R.E. it was worth 20s.

(216) Hugh holds of the earl BEVELEI [Byley in Middlewich]. Godric and Godwin and Archil held it as 3 manors, and were free. There [is] 1 hide that pays geld. The land is for 2 ploughs. There 2 radmen and 2 bordars have 1 plough.

There [are] 2 acres of meadow, and 2 acres of wood. T.R.E. it was worth 10s., now as much.

(217) Hugh holds of the earl GOSTREL [Goostrey in Sandbach]. Godric held it and was a free man. There [are] 3 virgates of land that pay geld. The land is for 1½ ploughs. It was always waste and is.

[In Cestre Hundred][3]

(218) HUGH FITZOSBERN holds of the earl (in *interlined*) BRUGE [Handbridge in Chester] 1 carucate of land that pays geld. Wulfnoth (*Ulnodus*) held it. There are 2 bordars with 3 oxen. It is worth 3s.

In Dudestan Hundred

(219) The same Hugh holds CALDECOTE [Caldecott in Shocklach]. Wulfgar (*Ulgar*) (the priest *interlined*) and 3 other thegns (*teini*) held it as 3 manors and were free. There [is] 1 hide that pays geld. The land is for 2 ploughs. They are there with 1 radman and 2 villeins and 3 oxmen. There [is] ½ fishery. T.R.E. it was waste yet rendered 2s., now 15s.

(220) The same Hugh holds PULFORD [Pulford]. Wulfric (*Ulvric*) held it as a free man. There [are] 1 (and ½ *interlined*) hides that pay geld. The land is for 1 plough and it is there with 2 radmen and 1 villein and 2 bordars. This land was waste, now it is worth 5s.

In Riseton Hundred

(221) The same Hugh holds WARHELLE [Wardle in Bunbury]. Alweald (*Aluuold*) held it as a free man. There [is] ½ hide that pays geld. The land is for 1 plough. There 1 villein has ½ plough. There [is] wood ½ league long and 1 acre wide. It was and is worth 3s.

In Hamstane Hundred

(222) HUGH[4] holds of the earl BOSELEGA [Bosley in Prestbury]. Godric held it and was a free man. There [is] ½ hide that pays geld. The land is for 4 ploughs. It is waste. There [is] wood 2 leagues long and ½ league wide. T.R.E. it was worth 20s.

(223) Hugh holds of the earl MERETONE [Marton in Prestbury]. Godric held it and was a free man. There [is] 1 virgate of land that pays geld. (The land is for ½ plough *in the margin*). It was always waste. There [is] wood 20 perches long and as much wide.

(224) Hugh holds of the earl 1 berewick CERDINGHAM [Kermincham in Swettenham]. Godric held it. There [is] ½ hide that pays geld. The land is for 2 ploughs. It was and is waste. It was worth 5s.

---

[95] Hundredal heading not rubricated.
[96] Omission of 'the same' may mean that in nos. 208–9 the scribe was not certain that the tenant was William FitzNiel.
[97] Bottom of column, 6 lines, left blank.
[98] See note 2, above.   [99] Formerly Great Caldy.
[1] i.e. Hugh FitzNorman, nos. 214–17, who gave Lawton and Goostrey to St. Werburgh's: *Dom. Surv. Ches.* 50; *Cart. Chester Abbey*, i, p. 40.

[2] Cf. *Dom. Surv. Ches.* 177.
[3] Rubric omitted.
[4] i.e. Hugh FitzNorman, nos. 222–5, to judge by the interest of his descendants in the places: Ormerod, *Hist. Ches.* iii. 736. The entries do not have the same alignment in the left margin as the preceding part of the column, perhaps deliberately to signal the separation of two parts of one fief: *Dom. Surv. Ches.* 50.

[IN MILDESTUIC HUNDRED *in the margin*]

(225) Hugh holds of the earl SUMREFORD [Somerford in Astbury]. Godric held it as a free man. There [is] ½ hide that pays geld. The land is for 1 plough. It was waste and still is.[5]

IN WARMUNDESTROU[6] HUNDRED

(226) HAMON[7] holds of Earl (Hugh *interlined*) POTITONE [Puddington in Burton]. Wulfric [*Ulvric*] held it and was a free man. There [are] 2½ hides that pay geld. The land is for 3 ploughs. In demesne is 1 [plough] and 1 serf, and 4 villeins and 4 bordars and 1 radman with 1 plough. It is worth 20*s*. It was waste.

IN BOCHELAU HUNDRED

(227) The same Hamon holds DONEHAM [Dunham Massey in Bowdon]. Alweard (*Eluuard*) held it and was a free man. There [is] 1 hide that pays geld. The land is for 3 ploughs. In demesne is 1 [plough] and 2 oxmen, and 2 villeins and 1 bordar, and 1 acre of wood. In the city[8] 1 house. T.R.E. it was worth 12*s*., now 10*s*. It was waste.

(228) The same Hamon holds BOGEDONE [Bowdon]. Alweard (*Eluuard*) held it and was a free man. There [is] 1 hide that pays geld. The land is for 2 ploughs. Two Frenchmen there have 1 plough. There [is] a priest and a church to which ½ of this hide belongs. There [is] a mill rendering 16*d*. It is worth 3*s*. It was waste and he found it so.

(229) The same Hamon holds HALE [Hale in Bowdon]. Alweard (*Eluuard*) held it. There [is] 1 hide that pays geld. The land is for 2½ ploughs. There 3 villeins with 1 radman have 2 ploughs. There [is] wood 1 league long and ½ [league] wide and a hay and a hawk's eyrie, and ½ acre of meadow. T.R.E. it was worth 15*s*., now 12*s*. He found it waste.

[f. 266v. col. 2]

IN HAMESTAN HUNDRED

(230) The same Hamon holds BRAMALE [Bramhall in Stockport]. Brun and Hacon held it as 2 manors and were free men. There [is] 1 hide that pays geld. The land is for 6 ploughs. There 1 radman and 2 villeins and 2 bordars have 1 plough. There [is] wood ½ league long and as much wide and ½ hay, and 1 acre of meadow. T.R.E. it was worth 32*s*., now 5*s*. He found it waste.

IN BOCHELAU HUNDRED

(231) The same Hamon holds ASCELIE [Ashley in Bowdon]. Alweard (*Eluuard*) held it and was a free man. There [is] 1 virgate of land that pays geld. The land is for 2 oxen. It was and is waste.

(232) The same Hamon holds ALRETUNE ['Alretunstall' unidentified in Timperley, Bowdon parish].[9] Alweard (*Aeluuard*) held it. There [are] 1½ virgates of land that pay geld. The land is for 6 oxen. It was and is waste.

IN DUDESTAN HUNDRED

(233) BIGOT[10] holds of (Earl *interlined*) Hugh FERENTONE [ALDFORD].[11] (Earl *interlined*) Edwin held it. There [are] 4 hides that pay geld. The land is for 8 ploughs. In demesne are 2 [ploughs], and 7 villeins and 3 bordars with 2 ploughs. There [is] a mill and a fishery with 2 fishermen, and 1 acre of meadow. T.R.E. it was worth 40*s*., now £6. He found it waste.

(234) The same Bigot holds LAI [Leahall in Lea Newbold, St. Oswald's parish].[12] Ansgot held it as a free man. There [is] 1 hide that pays geld. The land is for 2 ploughs. There are 2 bordars and 1 acre of meadow. It is worth 2*s*. It was waste.

[IN ROELAU HUNDRED][13]

(235) The same Bigot holds TORENTUNE [Thornton le Moors]. Steinketel held it and was a free man. There [are] 2 hides that pay geld. The land is for 2 ploughs. In demesne is ½ [plough], and 2 villeins and bordar(s) (*duo villani et bord'*)[14] have ½ plough. There [is] a church and a priest, and 1 acre of meadow. T.R.E. it was worth 20*s*., now 10*s*. He found it waste.

IN BOCHELAU HUNDRED

(236) The same Bigot holds MOTBURLEGE [Mobberley]. Dot held it and was a free man. There [are] 1½ hides that pay geld. The land is for 4 ploughs. There a thegn has ½ plough and 1 serf, and 1 villein and 2 bordars. There [is] 1 acre of meadow, and wood 2 leagues long and as much wide and 2 hays. T.R.E. it was worth 12*s*., now 5*s*. He found it waste.

IN HAMSTAN HUNDRED

(237) The same Bigot holds NORDBERIE [Norbury in Stockport]. Brun held it and was a free man. There [is] 1 hide that pays geld. The land is for 4 ploughs. There 1 radman with 3 bordars has 1 plough. There [is] 1 acre of meadow. Wood 5 leagues long and 3 leagues wide and 3 hays there. T.R.E. it was worth 10*s*., now 3*s*. He found it waste.

(238) The same Bigot holds ALDREDELIE [Nether Alderley in Alderley]. Godwin held it as a free man. There [is] 1 hide that pays geld. The land is for 8 ploughs. In demesne is 1 [plough] with 2 oxmen, and 3 villeins and 1 radman with 1 plough. There [is] 1 acre of meadow. Wood 1½ leagues long and 1 league wide and 2 hays there. T.R.E. it was worth 20*s*., now 10*s*. He found it waste.

[5] Next line left blank.
[6] Apparently in error for Wilaveston: above.
[7] Hamon de Massy: above.
[8] Chester.
[9] *P.N. Ches.* ii. 31.
[10] Bigot de Loges: above.

[11] *P.N. Ches.* iv. 77.
[12] See note to no. 49.
[13] Thornton le Moors has been considered a detached part of Dudestan hundred: *Dom. Surv. Ches.* 183. More probably a hundredal rubric has been omitted: above.
[14] A second figure may have been omitted.

(239) The same Bigot holds SUDENDUNE [Siddington in Prestbury]. Brun held it and was a free man. There [are] 1½ hides that pay geld. The land is for 7 ploughs. A Frenchman there has ½ plough, and 1 villein and 1 bordar with ½ plough. There [is] wood 1 league long and ½ [league] wide. T.R.E. it was worth 20s., now 5s.

(240) The same Bigot holds RODO [North Rode in Prestbury]. Beornwulf (*Bernulf*) held it and was a free man. There [is] ½ hide that pays geld. The land is for 2 ploughs. It is waste and he found it so. T.R.E. it was worth 8s. Wood 1 league long and ½ league wide.

IN MILDESTUICH HUNDRED

(241) The same Bigot holds COGELTONE [Congleton in Astbury]. Godwin held it. There [is] 1 hide that pays geld. The land is for 4 ploughs. There are 2 [ploughs] with 2 villeins and 4 bordars. There [is] wood 1 league long and 1 wide and 2 hays there. It was waste and he found it so. Now it is worth 4s.

(242) The same Bigot holds SANBECD[15] [Sandbach]. Dunning held it and was free. There [is] 1 hide that pays geld, and 1½ virgates that likewise pay geld. The land is for 2 ploughs. There is 1 Frenchman with ½ plough and 3 serfs, and 2 villeins with ½ plough. There [is] a priest and a church. Wood ½ league long and 40 perches wide. T.R.E. it was worth 4s., now 8s.

(243) The same Bigot holds SUDTUNE [Sutton in Middlewich]. Alstan and Beollan (*Belam*) held it as 2 manors and were free men. There [are] 3 virgates (and 16 acres *interlined*) of land that pay geld. The land is for 1½ ploughs. In demesne is ½ plough and 2 oxmen, and 2 villeins have ½ plough. T.R.E. it was worth 4s., now 3s. It was waste.

(244) The same Bigot holds WIBALDELAI [Wimboldsley in Middlewich]. Leofwine (*Leuuinus*) held it and was free. There [is] 1 virgate of land that pays geld. The land is for 1 plough. There 1 radman has ½ plough and 2 serfs, with 1 villein. It is worth 2s. It was waste and he found it so.

(245) The same Bigot holds WEVRE [Weaver in Middlewich]. Stenulf held it and was free. There [is] 1 virgate of land that pays geld. The land is for ½ plough. It is there with 1 radman and 1 villein and 2 bordars. Wood 1 furlong long and as much wide and a hay there. It was worth 2s., now 3s.

IN RISETON HUNDRED

(246) BAUDRY (*Baldricus*) holds of (Earl *interlined*) Hugh COCLE [unidentified].[16] Wulfheah (*Ulfac*) held it and was a free man. There [is] 1 hide that pays geld. The land is for 1 plough. It is there in demesne and 1 serf. T.R.E. it was worth 40s., now the same. He found it waste.

(247) THORTH (*Toret*) (a free man, *interlined*) held ALENTUNE [Allington in Gresford, Denb.]. There [are] 3 hides that pay geld.[18]

(248) In EITUNE [Eyton in Holt, Denb.] St. Chad held 1 hide[19] and in SUTONE [Sutton in Holt, Denb.] the same saint held 1 hide that paid geld. These 3 manors were waste when (Earl *interlined*) Hugh received them. Now Hugh (FitzOsbern *interlined*) holds them of him and has ½ plough in demesne and 3 serfs, and 7 villeins and 5 bordars and 2 Frenchmen. They have 1½ ploughs between them all. There [is] a mill worth 4s., and ½ fishery, and 4 acres of meadow. Wood 2 leagues long and ½ [league] wide. There [are] 2 hays. It is worth 30s. Four ploughs more could be there. T.R.E. it was worth 20s.

[f. 267 col. 1]

IN DUDESTAN HUNDRED

(249) GILBERT DE VENABLES holds of (Earl *interlined*) Hugh ECLESTONE [Eccleston]. Edwin held it and was a free man. There [are] 5 hides that pay geld. The land is for 6 ploughs. In demesne is 1 [plough] and 2 serfs, and 4 villeins and 1 bordar with 1 plough. There [is] a boat (*navis*) and a net, and ½ acre of meadow. T.R.E. it was worth 10s., now 50s. It was waste.

[IN RISETON HUNDRED][20]

(250) The same Gilbert holds ALBURGHAM [Alpraham in Bunbury]. (Earl *interlined*) Edwin held it. There [are] 2 hides that pay geld. The land is for 4 ploughs. There 3 villeins with 6 bordars have 1 plough. There [is] wood 2 leagues long and 1 wide, and 2 acres of meadow. T.R.E. it was worth 20s., now 8s.

IN RISETON HUNDRED

(251) The same Gilbert holds TORPELEI [Tarporley]. Wulfgeat (*Ulviet*) held it and was a free man. There [are] 2 hides that pay geld. The land is for 4 ploughs. In demesne is 1 [plough] and 2 serfs, and 4 villeins and 2 bordars with 1 plough. Wood 1 league long and 1 wide, and 1 acre of meadow. T.R.E. it was worth 20s., now 10s. He found it waste.

(252) The same Gilbert holds WATENHALE [Wettenhall in Over]. Glewin (*Gleuuinus*) held it and was a free man. There [is] 1 hide that pays geld. The land is for 2 ploughs. There 1 radman with 1 villein and 2 bordars has 1 plough. There [are] 2 acres of meadow. Wood 1½ leagues long and 1 league wide. It was and is worth 5s. He found it waste.

IN ROELAU HUNDRED

(253) The same Gilbert holds HERFORD [Hartford in Great Budworth and Weaverham]. Doda

---

15 The final letter was evidently an afterthought.
16 Just possibly Kelsall in Tarvin or a location in Over: *Dom. Surv. Ches.* 189; *P.N. Ches.* iii. 160-1.
17 Nos. 247-8 are compressed into foot of column.
18 Whether the assessment applies to T.R.E. or 1086 is unclear.
19 See no. 7.
20 Alpraham has been considered a detached part of Dudestan hundred: *Dom. Surv. Ches.* 191. More probably the rubric for Riseton was placed one entry too low.

(*Dodo*) held it (as 2 manors *in the margin*) as a free man. There [are] 2 hides that pay geld. The land is for 2 ploughs. There are 4 villeins and 2 bordars and a smith having 1 plough. In Wich [Northwich] 1 salthouse renders 2*s.*, and another ½ salthouse [is] waste. There [is] 1 acre of meadow. Of this land a knight (*miles*) holds ½ hide and has there 1 plough and 2 oxmen and 3 bordars. T.R.E. it was worth 20*s.*, now 10*s.*

IN BOCHELAU HUNDRED

(254) The same Gilbert holds LIME [Lymm]. Wulfgeat (*Ulviet*) held it and was free. There [is] 1 hide that pays geld. The land is for 2 ploughs. There are 3 bordars. There [is] ½ church with ¼ virgate of land. Half a league in length and as much in width of wood. T.R.E. it was worth 10*s.*, now 12*d.* He found it waste.

(255) The same Gilbert holds LEGE [High Legh in Rostherne]. Wulfgeat (*Ulviet*) and Dot held it as 2 manors and were free men. There [is] 1 hide that pays geld. The land is for 2 ploughs. There 1 man of his has ½ plough and 3 serfs. There [is] a priest and a church with 1 villein and 2 bordars having ½ plough. There [is] wood 1 league long and ½ league wide and a hay there. T.R.E. it was worth 10*s.*, now 5*s.*

(256) The same Gilbert holds WIMUNDISHAM [Wincham in Great Budworth]. Dot held it and was a free man. There [are] 1½ hides that pay geld. The land is for 2 ploughs. In demesne is 1 plough with 1 serf. There [is] 1 acre of wood and a hawk's eyrie, and 1 house in Wich [Northwich], and 1 bordar. It is worth 10*s.* It was waste and he found it so.

(257) The same Gilbert holds MERA [Mere in Rostherne]. Wulfgeat (*Ulviet*) held it and was a free man. There [is] 1 hide that pays geld. The land is for 2 ploughs. It was and is waste. There [is] wood ½ league long and 40 perches wide. There [are] 2 acres of meadow. T.R.E. it was worth 8*s.*

(258) The same Gilbert holds PEVRE [Peover, unidentified].[21] Dot held it. There [are] 2 bovates that pay geld. It was and is waste.

(259) The same Gilbert holds RODESTORNE [Rostherne]. Wulfgeat (*Ulviet*) held it. There [is] 1 virgate of land that pays geld. The land is for 1 plough. It was waste. There [are] 2 acres of wood. T.R.E. it was worth 4*s.*

IN EXESTAN HUNDRED

(260) The same Gilbert holds HOPE [Hope, Flints.]. Edwin held it and was a free man. There [is] 1 hide that pays geld. The land is for 1 plough, and it is there with 2 villeins, and 2 acres of wood. It is worth 7*s.* It was waste and he found it so.

IN MILDESTUIC HUNDRED

(261) Gilbert (the Hunter *interlined*) (*Giselbertus venator*)[22] holds of the earl NEUBOLD [Newbold Astbury in Astbury]. Wulfgeat (*Ulviet*) held it and was a free man. There [are] 1½ hides that pay geld. The land is for 5 ploughs. One radman there has 1 plough, and a priest 1 plough, and 3 villeins and 2 bordars. There [is] 1 acre of meadow, and wood 1 league long and as much wide and 2 hays there. T.R.E. it was worth 20*s.*, now 8*s.*

(262) The same Gilbert holds BRETONE [Brereton]. Wulfgeat (*Ulviet*) held it. There [are] 2 hides that pay geld. The land is for 4 ploughs. In demesne is 1 [plough] and 2 oxmen, and 2 villeins and 3 bordars. There [is] 1 acre of meadow. Wood 1 league long and ½ [league] wide, and a mill worth 12*d.* Of this land 2 of his men hold 1 hide and have 1 plough with 2 serfs, and 2 villeins and 4 bordars. T.R.E. the whole was worth 20*s.*, now the same. He found it waste.

(263) The same Gilbert holds CINBRETUNE [Kinderton in Middlewich]. Godwin held it and was a free man. There [are] 3 hides that pay geld. There is land for 5 ploughs. In demesne is 1 [plough] and 2 serfs, and 3 bordars. There [is] 1 acre of meadow. Wood ½ league long and as much wide and 1 hay there. It is worth 10*s.* It was waste and he found it [so].

(264) The same Gilbert holds DENEPORT [Davenport in Astbury]. Godwin held it. There [is] ½ hide that pays geld. The land is for 1 plough. It is there with 1 radman and 2 oxmen and 3 bordars, and 1 acre of wood. It is worth 3*s.* He found it waste.

[f. 267 col. 2]

(265) The same Gilbert holds WITUNE [Witton in Great Budworth]. Dot held it and was a free man. There [are] 1½ hides that pay geld. The land is for 2 ploughs. There 1 Frenchman has 1 plough and 2 oxmen and 1 bordar. There [is] a mill worth 3*s.* It is worth 7*s.* He found it waste.

IN WARMUNDESTROU HUNDRED

(266) The same Gilbert holds BLACHENHALE [Blakenhall in Wybunbury]. Godwin held it and was a free man. There [are] 4 hides less 1 virgate that pay geld. The land is for 5 ploughs. There 4 radmen and 2 bordars have 2 ploughs. There [is] wood 2 leagues long and 1 league wide. There [is] a hay and a hawk's eyrie. T.R.E. it was worth 10*s.*, now 12*s.*[23]

IN MILDESTUIC HUNDRED

(267) JOSCELIN (*Gozelinus*) holds of (Earl *interlined*) Hugh NEUTONE [Newton in Middlewich]. Gruffudd (*Grifin*) held it and was a free man. There [is] 1 hide that pays geld. The land is for 3 ploughs. In demesne is 1 [plough] and 2 oxmen. A priest with 1 bordar has 1 plough. There is ½ acre of meadow. T.R.E. it was worth 4*s.*, now 10*s.*

(268) The same Joscelin holds CROSTUNE [Croxton in Middlewich]. Godwin held it and

[21] *Dom. Surv. Ches.* 193 locates it in Nether Peover without good reason for such precision.
[22] i.e. Gilbert de Venables. The title Hunter seems to refer only to the holder of Newbold Astbury, which included part of Leek and Macclesfield forest: Ormerod, *Hist. Ches.* iii. 21; *Dom. Surv. Ches.* 54-5.   [23] Next 2 lines left blank.

was a free man. There [is] 1 hide that pays geld. The land is for 1 plough, which is there with 1 radman and 2 serfs, and 2 villeins and 1 bordar. It was worth 4s., now 10s.

IN BOCHELAU HUNDRED

(269) The same Joscelin holds STABLEI [Tabley Inferior in Great Budworth]. Uhtbrand (*Ostebrand*) held it and was a free man. There [are] 2 bovates of land that pay geld. The land is for ½ plough. It was and is waste.[24]

IN WILAVESTON HUNDRED

(270) RANULPH holds of (Earl *interlined*) Hugh BLACHEHOL [Blacon in Holy Trinity]. Thorth (*Toret*) held it and was a free man. There [are] 2 hides that pay geld. The land is for 4 ploughs. In demesne are 2 [ploughs] and 4 oxmen, and 4 villeins and 4 bordars have 1 plough. There [is] a fishery. T.R.E. it was worth 14s., now 40s.

IN ROELAU HUNDRED

(271) Ranulph holds WENITONE [Winnington in Great Budworth]. Leofnoth (*Levenot*) held it and was a free man. There [is] ½ hide that pays geld. The land is for ½ plough. There is 1 radman and 1 villein. It is worth 2s.

IN BOCHELAU HUNDRED

(272) Ranulph holds of the earl TATUNE [Tatton in Rostherne]. Leofwine (*Leuuinus*) held it. There [is] a sixth part of a hide that pays geld. The land is for ½ plough. It is there with 1 radman and 2 serfs, and 2 villeins and 4 bordars. There [is] wood 1 league long and as much wide. In Wich [?Northwich] 1 waste house. It is worth 3s.

(273) The same Ranulph holds PEVRE [Peover Superior in Rostherne]. Earngeat (*Erniet*) held it and was free. There [is] ½ hide that pays geld. The land is for 1 plough. There a certain man of his has 2 oxen and 2 serfs, and 2 villeins. There [is] wood ½ league long and 40 perches wide and a hawk's eyrie. T.R.E. it was worth 15s., now 4s. It was waste.

(274) The same Ranulph holds WAREFORD [Warford in Rostherne] and Godgyth (*Godid*) [holds it] of him. She held it herself and was free. There [is] ½ hide that pays geld. The land is for 1 plough. There she has 2 oxen and 4 serfs and 2 bondwomen. It is worth 3s. It was waste.

(275) The same Ranulph holds PEVRE [Peover, unidentified][25] of 2 bovates of land that pay geld. The land is for ½ plough.

(276) The same Ranulph holds CEPMUNDEWICHE ['Chapmonswiche', unidentified in Peover Superior, Rostherne parish][26] of ½ hide that pays geld. The land is for ½ plough. Godgyth (*Godid*) held it and was a free woman. This land was and is waste.

(277) The same Ranulph holds ALRETUNE [Ollerton in Knutsford] of ½ virgate of land that pays geld. Godgyth (*Godid*) held it. The land is for 2 oxen. It was and is waste.

(278) The same Ranulph holds SENELESTUNE [Snelson in Rostherne]. Leofnoth (*Levenot*) held it. There [is] 1 virgate of land that pays geld. The land is for ½ plough. It was and is waste.

IN TUNENDUNE HUNDRED

(279) The same Ranulph holds COCHESHALLE [Cogshall in Great Budworth]. Wulfgeat (*Ulviet*) held it and was a free man. There [is] ½ hide that pays geld. The land is for 1 plough. From the pastures comes 3s. The [arable] land is waste.

IN MILDESTUICH HUNDRED

(280) The same Ranulph holds Hoiloch [WHEELOCK in Sandbach]. (Earl *interlined*) Morcar held it. There [are] 3 hides that pay geld. The land is for 4 ploughs. In demesne is 1 [plough] and 4 serfs, and 2 radmen with 1 plough. There [is] wood 3 leagues long and 1 wide. T.R.E. and afterwards it was waste. Now it is worth 20s.

(281) The same Ranulph holds TADETUNE [Tetton in Warmingham]. Godgyth (*Godid*) held it. There [are] 1 hide and 1 virgate that pay geld. The land is for 2 ploughs. One Frenchman has there 1 plough and 2 oxmen, and 1 radman with ½ plough and 3 bordars. There [is] wood 40 perches long and 1 acre wide and a hay there. T.R.E. and afterwards it was waste. Now it is worth 10s.

IN DUDESTAN HUNDRED

(282) RALPH (THE HUNTER *interlined*) (*Radulfus venator*) holds of (Earl *interlined*) Hugh STAPLEFORD [Foulk Stapleford in Tarvin]. Wulfsige (*Ulsi*) held it and was a free man. There [are] 2 hides that pay geld. The land is for 3 ploughs. In demesne is 1 [plough], and 1 radman and 2 villeins and 5 bordars with 3 ploughs. There [is] wood 2 acres long and 1 wide. There [is] a mill. It was and is worth 16s.

[f. 267v. col. 1]

IN EXESTAN HUNDRED

(283) RAINALD (*Rainaldus*)[27] holds of (Earl *interlined*) Hugh GRETFORD [Gresford, Denb. and Flints.].[28] Thorth (*Toret*) held it and was a free man. There [are] 1½ hides that pay geld. The land is for 2 ploughs. There 1 villein with 2 bordars has 1 plough. It is worth 20s. Of wood which is 4 leagues long and 2 wide he has as much as belongs to 1½ hides. (*Whole entry cancelled.*)[29]

(284) The same Rainald holds ERPESTOCH [Erbistock, Denb.]. Rhys (*Rees*) held it as a free man. There [is] ½ hide that pays geld. The

---

[24] Next 2 lines left blank.
[25] *Dom. Surv. Ches.* 199 locates it in Nether Peover without good reason for such precision.
[26] *P.N. Ches.* ii. 86; Ormerod, *Hist. Ches.* i. 478.
[27] Probably Rainald de Bailleul, sheriff of Salop.: above.

[28] Gresford township lay wholly in Denb.
[29] The entry was probably cancelled because no. 314 gives a fuller account of Gresford, of which Rainald held only part. Hundredal heading and name of manor not rubricated.

land is for 1 plough. It is there with 1 radman and 1 villein and 1 bordar. T.R.E. it was waste, and afterwards it was worth 10s., now 9s.[30]

In Dudestan Hundred

(285) ILBERT[31] holds of (Earl *interlined*) Hugh Wavretone [Waverton]. Earnwine (*Ernuin*) held it and was a free man. There [are] 3 hides that pay geld. The land is for 4 ploughs. In demesne is 1 [plough], and 3 Frenchmen with 3 villeins have 3 ploughs. T.R.E. it was worth 20s. and afterwards 6s. Now 16s.

(286) The same Ilbert holds Etone [Hatton in Waverton].[32] Alnoth and Earnwine (*Ernuin*) held it as 2 manors and were free men. There [are] 2 hides that pay geld. The land is for 3 ploughs. There is 1 villein with 1 plough. T.R.E. it was worth 20s., now 9s. 4d. It was waste.

In Riseton Hundred

(287) The same Ilbert holds Clotone [Clotton in Tarvin]. Stenulf held it and was a free man. There [are] 3 hides that pay geld. The land is for 6 ploughs. There are 6 villeins and 2 bordars and 4 radmen having 5 ploughs. It was and is worth 12s.[33]

In Dudestan Hundred

(288) OSBERN FITZTEZZON (*filius Tezzonis*) holds of (Earl *interlined*) Hugh Hanlei [Handley]. Grimkel (*Grinchel*) held it and was a free man. There [is] 1 hide that pays geld. The land is for 4 ploughs. In demesne is 1½ ploughs with 1 serf, and 2 villeins and 1 bordar have ½ plough. T.R.E. it was worth 13s. 3d., now 15s.

(289) The same Osbern holds Colborne [Golborne David in Handley]. Edwin held it and was a free man. There [is] 1 hide that pays geld. The land is for 3 ploughs. In demesne is 1 [plough], and 1 villein and 1 bordar. There [is] ½ acre of meadow. It was and is worth 16s.

In Wilaveston Hundred

(290) The same Osbern holds Pontone[34] [Poulton in Bebington] and Roger [holds it] of him. Gamel held it and was a free man. There [are] 2 hides that pay geld. The land is for 4 ploughs. In demesne is 1 [plough] and 2 serfs, and 1 radman and 1 villein and a priest and 4 bordars with 1 plough between them all. T.R.E. it was worth 25s. and afterwards it was waste. Now it is worth 25s.

In Roelau Hundred

(291) The same Osbern holds Wenitone [Winnington in Great Budworth]. Hunding held it and was a free man. There [is] ½ hide that pays geld. The land is for ½ plough. There is 1 radman with 1 villein. It is worth 2s.

In Bochelau Hundred

(292) The same Osbern holds Lime [Lymm]. Edward held it and was a free man. There [is] 1 hide that pays geld. The land is for 4 ploughs. Edward holds it of him. He has there 1 plough and 2 oxmen, and 2 villeins and 4 bordars, and ½ church with a priest with ½ virgate of land quit [?of geld]. Wood ½ league long and as much wide. T.R.E. it was worth 10s., now 8s. He found it waste.

(293) The same Osbern holds Warburgetone [Warburton]. Raven held it and was a free man. There [is] ½ hide that pays geld. The land is for 1 plough. There [are] 1 radman and 2 villeins and 1 bordar with ½ plough. It was worth 5s., now 2s. It was waste.

In Tunendune Hundred

(294) The same Osbern holds Duntune [Dutton in Great Budworth]. Edward held it. (He was a free man *interlined*.) There [is] ½ hide that pays geld. Edward holds it of Osbern. There is 1 radman and 1 villein and 3 bordars with 1½ ploughs. T.R.E. it was worth 12d., now 2s.

(295) The same Osbern holds Epletune [Appleton in Great Budworth]. Dot held it and was a free man. There [is] 1 hide that pays geld. The land is for 4 ploughs. It was and is waste. T.R.E. it was worth 16s. There [is] wood ½ league long and 40 perches wide.

(296) The same Osbern holds Gropenhale [Grappenhall] and Edward [holds it] of him. He and Dot held it as two manors and were free men. There [are] 1 hide and ½ virgate of land that pay geld. The land is for 2 ploughs. In demesne is 1½ [ploughs] and 2 serfs, and 1 villein and 3 bordars. There [is] wood 1 league long and 40 perches wide. There [are] 2 hays. T.R.E. it was worth 5s., now 6s. It was waste.

[f. 267v. col. 2]

In Riseton Hundred

(297) NIEL (*Nigellus*)[35] holds of (Earl *interlined*) Hugh Altetone [Oulton in Little Budworth].[36] Dunning (*Donning*) held it and was a free man. There [is] ½ hide that pays geld. The land is for 1 plough. It renders in farm 5s. 4d. T.R.E. it was worth 20s. He found it waste.

In Wilaveston Hundred

(298) The same Niel holds Gravesberie [Greasby in Thurstaston and West Kirby]. Dunning held it. There [are] 2 hides that pay geld. The land is for 3 ploughs. In demesne is 1 [plough] and 2 serfs, and 3 villeins and 2 Frenchmen and 1 bordar with 1 plough between them all. T.R.E. it was worth 25s. and afterwards 10s., now 20s.

(299) The same Niel holds Stortone [Storeton in Bebington]. Dunning held it. There [are] 2

---

[30] Next line left blank.
[31] Ilbert de Rullos: above.
[32] *Dom. Surv. Ches.* 205; *P.N. Ches.* iv. 100.
[33] Next line left blank.
[34] Name not rubricated.
[35] Niel de Burcy: above.
[36] *P.N. Ches.* iii. 165, 185.

hides that pay geld. The land is for 3 ploughs. In demesne is ½ plough and 1 serf, and 5 villeins and 3 bordars with 1½ ploughs. T.R.E. it was worth 15s., now 20s. It was waste.[37]

[?IN HAMESTAN HUNDRED][38]

(300) TEZZELIN (*Tezzelinus*) holds of (Earl *interlined*) Hugh SUMREFORD [?Somerford Booths in Astbury]. Ravensward (*Ravesve*) and Ketel (*Chetel*) and Morfar held it as 3 manors. Two were free men; Morfar could not leave his lord. There [is] 1 virgate of land that pays geld. It was divided into 3 portions. The land is for 3 ploughs. There is 1 radman having 1 plough and 2 serfs. There [is] wood 40 perches long and as much wide. It was worth 6s., now 4s.

IN TUNENDUNE HUNDRED

(301) ODARD holds of the earl DUNTUNE [Dutton in Great Budworth]. Raven held it and was a free man. There [are] 1½ virgates of land that pay geld. The land is for 1 plough. There is 1 radman with 1 serf. Wood 1 league long and ½ [league] wide. There [is] a hawk's eyrie. T.R.E. it was worth 5s., now 12d.

(302) MUNDRET holds of the earl BERTINTUNE [Bartington in Great Budworth]. Dunning held it. There [is] ½ hide that pays geld. The land is for 1 plough. It is there with 1 radman and 1 serf and 1 bordar. T.R.E. it was worth 3s., now 64d.

(303) WULFGEAT (*Ulviet*) holds of the earl BERTINTUNE [Bartington in Great Budworth]. Leofnoth (*Levenot*) held it. There [is] ½ hide that pays geld. The land is for 1 plough. It is waste. It was worth 2s.

(304) A SERJEANT (*Unus serviens*) of the earl holds a piece of land [unidentified] in this hundred of Tunendune. This land was never assessed in hides. He has there 1 plough with 1 oxman. It is worth 4s.

IN ROELAU HUNDRED

(305) DUNNING holds of the earl CHINGESLIE [Kingsley in Frodsham]. He himself held it as a free man. There [is] 1 hide that pays geld. The land is for 2 ploughs. In demesne is 1 [plough] and 5 serfs, and 1 villein and 3 bordars. There [are] 1½ fisheries. There [is] wood 1 league long and 1 [league] wide. The earl put this into his forest, and there [is] a hawk's eyrie and 4 hays for roe deer. T.R.E. it was worth 30s., now 6s.

(306) LEOFRIC (*Levric*) holds of the earl ELVELDELIE [Alvanley in Frodsham]. Earnwig (*Ernui*) held it and was a free man. There [is] ½ hide that pays geld. The land is for 4 ploughs. In demesne is 1 [plough] with 1 villein and 2 bordars. Wood ½ league long and ½ [league] wide.

IN HAMESTAN HUNDRED

(307) WULFRIC (*Ulvric*) holds BOTELEGE [Butley in Prestbury]. He himself held it as a free man. There [is] 1 hide that pays geld. The land is for 5 ploughs. It is waste except 7 sown acres (*acras seminatas*). There [is] wood 3 leagues long and 1 wide, and a hay there, and 2½ acres of meadow. T.R.E. it was worth 30s., now 2s.[39]

(308) GAMEL holds of the earl CEDDE [Cheadle].[40] His father held it as a free man. There [are] 2 hides that pay geld. The land is for 6 ploughs. In demesne is 1 [plough] and 2 oxmen, and 4 villeins and 3 bordars with 2 ploughs. There [is] wood 1 league long and ½ [league] wide and a hay and a hawk's eyrie, and 1 acre of meadow. It was and is worth 10s. The whole manor has 2 leagues in length and 1 in width.

(309) The same Gamel holds MOTRE [Mottram St. Andrew in Prestbury]. His father held it. There [are] 1½ hides that pays geld. The land is for 4 ploughs. It is waste. There [is] wood 3 leagues long and 2 [leagues] wide and 2 hays and a hawk's eyrie.

(310) WULFRIC (*Ulvric*) holds of the earl ALRETUNE [Ollerton in Knutsford].[41] He himself held it as a free man. There [are] 2 [third] parts of 1 hide that pay geld. The land is for 3 ploughs. One is there with 1 oxman, and 1 villein and 2 bordars. There [is] 1 acre of meadow and 3 acres of wood. It is worth 5s. It was waste T.R.E.

IN MILDESTUIC HUNDRED

(311) MORAN holds of the earl LECE [Lach Dennis in Great Budworth]. Colben held it as a free man. There [is] ½ hide that pays geld. The land is for 1 plough. It is there in demesne and 2 oxmen, and 1 bordar. There [is] ½ acre of meadow. It is worth 8s. It was waste T.R.E.

[f. 268 col. 1]

IN BOCHELAU HUNDRED

(312) RANULPH and BIGOT hold of the earl NORWORDINE [Northenden]. Wulfgeat (*Ulviet*) held it as 1 manor and was a free man. There [is] 1 hide that pays geld. The land is for 2 ploughs. It is waste. There [are] a church and 2 furlongs of wood. It is worth 3s. T.R.E. it was worth 10s.

(313) GILBERT and RANULPH and HAMON hold SUNDRELAND [Sinderland in Dunham Massey, Bowdon parish] and BAGELEI [Baguley in Bowdon]. Alweard (*Eluuard*) and Sucga (*Suga*) and Wudumann (*Udeman*) and Pat held it as 4 manors and were free men. There [is] 1 hide that pays geld. The land is for 1½ ploughs. It is entirely waste. T.R.E. it was worth 3s.

---

[37] Next line left blank.
[38] A hundredal rubric has clearly been omitted here, at the start of the description of the fiefs of the earl's serjeants and thegns. Though Hamestan is the correct hundred for Somerford Booths, *Sumreford* could also be Somerford in Middlewich hundred: cf. no. 225.

[39] See no. 101.
[40] Doubts about the identification have been largely dispelled: *Dom. Surv. Ches.* 213; *P.N. Ches.* i. 246–7, 253.
[41] Hundredal heading for *Bochelau* may have been omitted: *Dom. Surv. Ches.* 236; or part of Ollerton may have lain in Hamestan hundred: *P.N. Ches.* ii. 79.

In Extan Hundred

(314) HUGH and OSBERN and RAINALD[42] hold GRETFORD [Gresford, Denb. and Flints.].[43] Thorth (*Thoret*) held it as a free man. There [are] 13 hides that pay geld. The land is for 12 ploughs. Hugh has 5 hides, Osbern 6½ hides, Rainald 1½ hides. In demesne are 1½ ploughs. There [is] a church and a priest and 7 villeins and 12 bordars and 1 Frenchman. Between them all they have 2½ ploughs. In the whole of this manor wood 4 leagues long and 2 wide and 2 eyries of hawks. Osbern has a mill grinding corn for his hall (*curia*). The whole was waste T.R.E. and they received it waste. Now it is worth 65*s.* in all. Of this land of this manor 1 hide lay in the church of St. Chad T.R.E., ½ [hide] in CHESPUIC [unidentified], and ½ [hide] in RADENOURE [Radnor, unlocated near Gresford, Denb. and Flints.].[44] To this the county testifies, but it does not know how the church lost it.

In Mildestuic Hundred

(315) HUGH and WILLIAM[45] hold of the earl RODE [Odd Rode in Astbury]. Godric and Ravensward (*Ravesva*) held it as 2 manors and were free men. There [is] 1 hide that pays geld. The land is for 3 ploughs. It is waste except that 1 radman has under them [*blank*] plough [*or* ploughs] and ½. It is worth 2*s.* T.R.E. it was worth 20*s.* There [is] wood 2 leagues long and 1 [league] wide and 2 hays and a hawk's eyrie.[46]

[f. 268 col. 2]

(316) T.R.E. there was in WARMUNDESTROU HUNDRED a WICH [Nantwich] in which there was a brinepit for making salt, and there were 8 salthouses (*salinae*) so divided between the king and Earl Edwin that of all the issues and renders of the salthouses the king had 2 [third] parts and the earl the third. But besides these the said earl had a salthouse of his own which belonged to his manor of ACATONE [Acton].[47] From this salthouse the earl had sufficient salt for his own house (*domus*) throughout the year. If however any was sold from that source, the king had 2*d.* of the toll and the earl the third [penny].

In the same Wich many men of the country (*patria*) had [*blank*][48] salthouses, from which there was the following custom: from the Ascension of Our Lord to the feast of St. Martin anyone having a salthouse might carry his own salt to his house [without paying toll], but if he sold any of it either there or elsewhere in the (entire *interlined*) county of Chester, he paid toll to the king and earl. After the feast of St. Martin anyone who carried salt thence, whether his own or purchased, paid toll, the above-mentioned salt-

house belonging to the earl excepted, as having its own custom.

In each week in which the aforesaid 8 salthouses of the king and earl were employed in boiling salt, on the Friday they rendered 16 boilings, of which 15 made a packload of salt. Other men's salthouses did not give these boilings on Fridays between the Ascension of Our Lord and the feast of St. Martin, but from the feast of St. Martin to the Ascension of Our Lord they all gave the boiling custom like the salthouses of the king and earl.

All these salthouses, both common and demesne (*salinae et communes et dominicae*),[49] were surrounded on one side by a certain stream[50] and on the other by a certain ditch. Anyone incurring a forfeiture within this boundary was allowed to make amends with 2*s.* or 30 boilings of salt, except for homicide and theft where the thief was adjudged to die. If these [offences] were committed here, amends were made as in the rest of the shire.

If anyone were proved to have taken the toll from the aforesaid boundary of the salthouses to anywhere else in all the county, he returned and made amends there with 40*s.* if he were a free man, with 4*s.* if he were not free. But if he took this toll to some other shire, he made amends where it was claimed.

T.R.E. this Wich rendered £21 in farm, including all the pleas of the same hundred. When (Earl *interlined*) Hugh received it, it was waste, except only 1 salthouse. William Malbank (*Malbedeng*) now holds the same Wich of the earl with all the customs belonging to it, and the whole of that hundred, which is valued at 40*s.*, of which sum 30*s.* is charged upon the land of the same William, the remaining 10*s.* upon the land of the bishop[51] and upon the lands of Richard [de Vernon][52] and Gilbert [de Venables][53] which they have in the same hundred, and the Wich is at farm for £10.

(317) In MILDESTUIC HUNDRED there was another WICH [Middlewich] [shared] between the king and the earl. There were no demesne salthouses there (however *interlined*) but the same laws and customs were in force there as have been mentioned under the previous Wich, and the king and the earl took their shares in the same way. This Wich was at farm for £8, and the hundred in which it lay for 40*s.* The king [took] 2 [third] parts; the earl the third. It was waste when (Earl *interlined*) Hugh received it. Now the earl holds it himself and it is at farm for 25*s.* and 2 cartloads (*caretedes*) of salt. The hundred is however worth 40*s.*

(318) Whoever carried away bought salt in a cart from these two Wiches paid 4*d.* in toll if he had

---

[42] Probably Hugh FitzOsbern, Osbern FitzTezzon, and Rainald de Bailleul. See no. 283 and above.

[43] Gresford township lay wholly in Denb.

[44] Radnor, 'at the red bank or slope', alludes to the scarp running through Hoseley and Marford (Flints.) and Bieston (Denb.). It was almost certainly near the later settlement of Rossett (Denb.), a name which derives from *yr orsedd goch*, 'the red mound': *Clwyd Historian*, iv. 13–14. Thanks are due to Mr. D. Pratt for the reference.

[45] Hugh FitzNorman and William FitzNiel.

[46] Entry written more spaciously than earlier part of

column. Rest of column originally left blank but later partly used for no. 319 with marks to indicate that it followed on from foot of second column.

[47] See no. 151.   [48] Number omitted.

[49] The phrase may reflect the contrast made earlier between those held by *homines patriae* and those held 'in demesne' by king and earl: *Dom. Surv. Ches.* 219.

[50] The river Weaver.

[51] Wybunbury: no. 8.

[52] Audlem and Crewe: nos. 127–8.

[53] Blakenhall: no. 266.

4 oxen or more in the cart; if 2 oxen, he paid 2d. toll if there were 2 packloads of salt.

A man from another hundred paid 2d. for a horseload. But a man from the same hundred paid only ½d. for a packload of salt. Anyone who so loaded his cart that the axle broke within a league of either Wich paid 2s. to the official (*minister*) of the king or the earl, if he could be overtaken within a league.

Similarly he who so loaded a horse as to break its back paid 2s., if overtaken within a league; beyond a league [he paid] nothing.

Anyone who made 2 horseloads of salt out of one made amends with 40s., if the official could overtake him. If he was not found, he did not make amends through any other person.

Men on foot from another hundred buying salt there paid 2d. for 8 men's loads; men of the same hundred [paid] 1d. for 8 loads.[54]

[f. 268 col. 1]

(319) In the same MILDESTUIC HUNDRED there was a third Wich which was called NORWICH [Northwich] and it was at farm for £8. There were the same laws and customs there as there were in the other Wiches and the king and earl similarly divided the renders.

None of the thegns who had salthouses in this Wich gave boilings of salt on Fridays in any part of the year. Anyone who brought a cart with 2 or more oxen from another shire paid 4d. in toll. A man from the same shire paid 2d. for a cart within the third night after his return home. If the third night passed [without payment], he made amends with 40s. A man from another shire paid 1d. for a horseload, but [one] from the same shire [paid] a mite [*minuta*] within the third night as aforesaid.

If a man living in that hundred carted salt about the same county to sell, he paid 1d. for each cart as often as he loaded it. If he carried salt on a horse to sell, he paid 1d. at the feast of St. Martin. Anyone who failed to pay at that date made amends with 40s. All the other [customs] in these Wiches are the same. This one was waste when (Earl *interlined*) Hugh received it; it is now worth 35s.

[f. 268v. col. 2][55]

IN ATISCROS HUNDRED

(320) (EARL *interlined*) HUGH holds HAORDINE [Hawarden, Flints.] in demesne. (Earl *interlined*) Edwin held it. There [are] 3 hides that pay geld. The land is for 4½ ploughs. In demesne are 2 ploughs and 4 serfs. There [is] a church to which ½ carucate of land belongs, and there [are] 4 villeins and 6 bordars with 2 ploughs. There [is] ½ acre of meadow. Wood 2 leagues long and 1 wide. It is worth 40s. Two waste houses (*masurae*) in the city[56] belong there.

(321) The same earl holds RADINTONE ['Rading-ton', unlocated, near Flint in Holywell,

Flints.].[57] (Earl *interlined*) Edwin held it. There [is] 1 hide that pays geld. The land is for 1 plough. It was and is waste.

(322) ROBERT OF RHUDDLAN (*Roelent*) holds of the earl BROCHETUNE [Broughton in Hawarden, Flints.]. Leofnoth (*Levenot*) held it and was a free man. There [are] 1½ virgates that pay geld. The land is for ½ plough, which is there with 1 villein. One and a half virgates of meadow. It is worth 3s. and has a third part of a wood 1 league long and wide.

(323) The same Robert holds there[58] 1 manor of ½ hide that pays geld. Wulfmaer (*Ulmer*), a free man, held it. The land is for ½ plough. There 1 radman has this [½ plough] with 1 villein and 1 bordar. It is worth 3s.

(324) The same Robert holds ULFEMILTONE [Golftyn in Northop, Flints.] and Ascelin (*Aze-linus*) [holds it] of him. Leofnoth (*Levenot*) held it. He was a free man. There [is] 1 hide that pays geld. The land is for 1 plough. There are 2 villeins and 1 bordar with 6 oxen. Wood 1 league long and as much wide. It is worth 10s.

(325) The same Robert holds LATBROC [Lead-brook in Northop, Flints.]. Leofnoth (*Levenot*) and Wulfbert (*Ulbert*) held it as 2 manors and were free. There [is] ½ hide that pays geld. The land is for 1 plough. Two radmen have this [plough] there with 2 bordars. Wood 1 league long and as much wide. It is worth 10s.

(326) The same Robert holds BACHELIE [Bagillt in Holywell, Flints.] and Roger [holds it] of him. Arni (*Erne*) held it. There [is] 1 hide that pays geld. The land is for 1 plough. Two villeins and 4 bordars have this [plough] there. It is worth 8s.

(327) The same Robert holds COLESELT [Coles-hill in Flint, Holywell parish, Flints.] and Edwin [holds it] of him, who also held it as a free man. There [is] 1 hide that pays geld. The land is for 1 plough. It is there with 1 radman and 4 villeins and 2 bordars. It is worth 10s. It was worth 6s.

(328) WILLIAM MALBANK (*Malbedeng*) holds CLAITONE [unidentified] and Richard [holds it] of him. Ravenkel (*Ravechel*) held it and was a free man. There [is] 1 hide that pays geld. The land is for 1 plough. It is there in demesne with 2 bordars. There [is] 1 acre of meadow. Wood 1 league long and as much wide. It is worth 10s.

(329) The same William holds WEPRE [Wepre in Northop, Flints.]. Earnwig (*Ernui*) held it and was free. There [is] a third part of a hide that pays geld.[59] The land is for a third part of a plough. This, 1 radman has there with 1 villein. It is worth 10s.

(330) WILLIAM FITZNIEL (*filius Nigelli*) holds MERLESTONE [Marlston in St. Mary on the Hill]. Arni (*Erne*) held it. Ansger holds it of William and has there ½ plough. There [is]

---

[54] The entry continues into the bottom margin and the next entry was placed in the blank lower half of the previous column.

[55] The first column was left blank.   [56] Chester.

[57] In 1360 Redynton lay within the borough of Flint's

boundaries, on the south side of the town: H. Taylor, *Historic Notices of Flint* (1883), 34, 42.

[58] Broughton, as in the preceding entry.

[59] The other two thirds of Wepre were described in no. 34.

1 virgate of land that pays geld. There is 1 serf. It was waste. Now it is worth 4s.

(331) HUGH FITZOSBERN holds BROCHE-TONE [Broughton in Hawarden, Flints.]. Ravensward (*Ravesvardus*) held it and was free. There [are] 1½ virgates of land that pay geld. The land is for ½ plough. There 1 radman has this [½ plough] with 1 villein and 2 bordars. Wood 1 league long and 1 wide. It is worth 5s.

(332) The same Hugh holds CLAVENTONE [Claverton in St. Mary on the Hill].[60] Osmaer held it and was a free man. There [are] 2 hides that pay geld. The land is for 2 ploughs. One is in demesne and 2 oxmen, and 4 villeins have the other [plough] with 3 bordars. To this manor belong 8 burgesses in the city and 4 over the river,[61] and they render 9s. 4d., and in NORUUICH [Northwich] [there is] 1 salthouse worth 12d. There [are] 3 acres of meadow. It was and is worth 40s. He found it waste.

(333) The same Hugh holds EDRITONE [unidentified][62] and Richard [holds it] of him. Almaer (*Elmer*) and Ravenkel (*Ravechet*) held it as 2 manors and were free men. There [is] 1 hide (and ½ *interlined*) paying geld. The land is for 1 plough. This is there with 2 radmen and 3 bordars. There [is] 1 acre of meadow. It is worth 10s. Of this land Osbern FitzTezzon holds 1 hide and Hugh FitzNorman ½ hide.

(334) OSBERN FITZTEZZON (*filius Tezonis*) holds DODESTUNE [Dodleston]. (Earl *interlined*) Edwin held it. There [are] 2 hides that pay geld. The land is for 2 ploughs. In demesne is 1½ [ploughs] with 3 oxmen, and 4 villeins with 3 bordars have ½ plough. To this manor belong 15 burgesses in the city[63] and they render 8s. Wood 1 league long and as much wide. It is worth 40s.

(335) HAMON[64] holds ESTONE [Aston in Hawarden, Flints.]. Edwin and Thorth (*Toret*) held it as 2 manors and were free. There [is] 1 hide that pays geld. The land is for 1 plough. This is there with 2 radmen and 2 villeins and 3 bordars. There [is] wood 1 league long and as much wide. It is worth 10s. Of this land Ranulph holds 1 virgate.

(336) The same Hamon holds CASTRETONE [? Llys Edwin in Flint, Holywell parish, Flints.][65] and Osmund [holds it] of him. Edwin held it as a free man. There [is] ½ hide that pays geld. The land is for 1 plough. There 2 villeins have ½ [plough] with 1 bordar. Wood 1 league long and as much wide. It is worth 5s.

(337) RALPH (THE HUNTER *interlined*) (*Radulfus venator*) holds of the earl BROCHETUNE

[Broughton in Hawarden, Flints.]. Wulfheah (*Ulfac*) held it and was a free man. There [is] 1 virgate of land that pays geld. The land is for 1 plough. This is there in demesne with 2 serfs. There [is] 1 virgate of meadow. It is worth 5s.

(338) Ralph holds SUTONE[66] [Soughton in Northop, Flints.]. Esbern (*Sberne*) held it and was a free man. There [is] 1 hide that pays geld. The land is for 1 plough. This is there with 1 radman and 4 bordars. It is worth 5s. There [is] wood ½ league long and 4 acres wide.

(339) Of these 20 hides[67] the earl has placed all the woods in his forest, whereby the manors are much depreciated (*peiorata*). This forest has 10 leagues in length and 3 leagues in width. There are 4 eyries of hawks.

[f. 269 col. 1]

IN ATISCROS HUNDRED

(340) EARL HUGH holds of the king ROELEND [Rhuddlan, Flints.]. ENGLEFELD [Englefield] lay there T.R.E. and the whole was waste. Earl Edwin held it. When (Earl *interlined*) Hugh received it, it was likewise waste. Now he has in demesne half of the castle which is called Roelent and it is the chief place (*caput*) of this district (*terrae*). He has there 8 burgesses, and half of the church and mint, and half of every ironmine wherever discovered in this manor, and half of the river Cloit [Clwyd] and of the mills and fisheries which shall be made there, that is to say, in that part of the river which belongs to the earl's fief, and half of the forests which did not belong to any vill of this manor, and half of the toll, and half of the vill which is called BREN [Bryn in Rhuddlan, Flints.]. There is land for 3 ploughs and they are there in demesne with 7 serfs. To BREN belong these 5 lands: CAUBER[68] [Cwybr in Rhuddlan, Flints.], KEVEND [Cefn Du in Rhuddlan, Flints.], BRENNEHEDUI [Brynhedydd in Rhuddlan, Flints.], LEUUARLUDAE [Llewerllyd in Diserth, Flints.], and half PEINTRET [Pentre in Rhuddlan, Flints.]. It is worth £3.

(341) To this manor of ROELENT belong these berewicks: DISSAREN [?Diserth, Flints.],[69] BODUGAN [Bodeugan in St. Asaph, Flints.], CHILUEN [Cilowen in St. Asaph, Flints.], and MAINEVAL [Maenefa in Tremeirchion, Flints.]. In these is land for only 1 plough, and wood 1 league long and ½ [league] wide. There 1 Frenchman and 2 villeins have 1 plough.

(342) Also WIDHULDE [unidentified], BLORAT [Blorant in Maesmynan, Denb., Bodfari parish, Denb. and Flints.],[70] DINMERSH [Tremeirchion,

---

[60] Claverton was sometimes regarded as extra-parochial: *V.C.H. Ches.* ii. 212; *P.N. Ches.* iv. 141.

[61] Presumably in Handbridge.

[62] Wrongly suggested to be Kinnerton in *Dom. Bk.: Ches.* ed. P. Morgan, FD 5,3. Possibly Bretton in Hawarden (Flints.): *Flints. Hist. Soc.* xi. 19.

[63] Chester.

[64] Hamon de Massy: above.

[65] Assuming that the Edwin from whom the 'court' at Llys Edwin took its name was the Edwin who held *Castretone* T.R.E.

[66] Name not rubricated.

[67] The total assessment for Atiscros hundred, recorded in nos. 320-38 and 34-5, is only 19½ hides.

[68] From here the only rubricated names are those of the hundreds and Roelend/Roelent, Mostone, Pichetone, Biscopestreu, Nortwales/Nortwalis, Ros, and Reweniou, but for the sake of clarity and consistency small caps. have been used for the names of all berewicks.

[69] Identified with the hill called Moel Diseren in Cwm parish, rather than Diserth itself, even though the hill was probably named from Diserth: J. Tait, 'Flints. in Dom. Bk.' *Flints. Hist. Soc.* xi. 23, n. 4.; Davies, *Flints. P.N.* 47.

[70] Although in the 17th century used as an alternative name for Maesmynan township, Blorant had been a distinct manor in the 14th century: E. Lhuyd, *Parochialia* (Cambrian Arch. Assoc. 1909-11), i. 68; Richards, *Welsh Administrative Units*, s.v.; *Blk. Prince's Reg.* iii. 169, 182, 191, 221.

Flints.],[71] and BRENUUEN [Bryngwyn in Tremeirchion, Flints.]. The land is for 1 plough, which 2 villeins and 1 serjeant of the earl have there. Wood 1 league long and ½ [league] wide.

(343) In TREVELESNEU [Trellyniau in Cilcain, Flints.], and SCHIVIAU [Ysgeifiog, Flints.] is land for 1 plough which 3 villeins have there. Wood 40 perches long and as much wide.

(344) In LESTHUNIED [Llystyn Hunedd in Cilcain, Flints.] and MOCLITONE [?Mechlas in Cilcain, Flints.][72] and LESSECOIT [Llys y Coed in Cilcain, Flints.] is land for 1 plough which 3 villeins have there and [there is] 1 acre of wood.

(345) In BRUNFORD [Brynford in Holywell, Flints.] and HELCHENE [Halkyn, Flints.] and ULCHENOL [unidentified] is land for 1 plough which 5 villeins have there. Wood 1 league long and 2 acres wide.

(346) In FOLEBROC [Greenfield in Holywell, Flints.][73] is land for 1 plough which 3 villeins and 2 bordars have there. Wood ½ league long and 40 perches wide.

(347) In MERETONE [Mertyn in Whitford, Flints.] and CALDECOTE [Calcot in Holywell, Flints.] and a third part of WIDFORD [Whitford, Flints.] is land for 1 plough which a priest with 6 villeins have there, and a church. Wood ½ league long and 20 perches wide.[74] Odin holds [this land] of the earl.

(348) In ASKETONE [Axton in Llanasa, Flints.] and CHESLILAVED [Gellilyfdy in Ysgeifiog, Flints.] is land for 1 plough. Marcud holds [it] of the earl and there are 3 villeins and 1 bordar ploughing with 10 oxen.

All these berewicks were waste T.R.E. and when Earl (Hugh interlined) received [them]. Between them all they are now worth 110s.

(349) ROBERT OF RHUDDLAN (Roelent) holds of (Earl interlined) Hugh half of the same castle and borough, in which the same Robert has 10 burgesses, and half of the church and mint, and of [any] iron mine found there, and half of the river Cloith and of the fisheries and mills made or to be made there, and half of the toll, and of the forests which do not belong to any vill of the aforesaid manor, and half of the vill which is called BREN [Bryn in Rhuddlan, Flints.] with these berewicks: LAUARLUDON [Llewerllyd in Diserth, Flints.], PENEGORS [unidentified in Rhuddlan, Flints.],[75] REUUORDUI [Rhydorddwy in Rhuddlan, Flints.], TREDUENG [unidentified],[76] and LITTLE CAUBER [Cwybr Bach in Rhuddlan, Flints.]. In these is land for

only 3 ploughs and they are there in demesne with 6 serfs, and there [is] a mill rendering 3 bushels (modii) of corn. It is worth £3.

(350) In DISSARD [Diserth, Flints.] and BOTEUUARUL [Bodfari, Flints.][77] and RUARGOR [unidentified] the land is for 1 plough. It is there in demesne and 2 serfs, and a church with a priest, and 2 villeins and a mill worth 3s. and 2 bordars. Wood 1 league long and ½ [league] wide and there [is] a hawk's eyrie. It is worth 30s.

(351) In RADUCH [Hiraddug in Cwm, Flints.][78] and PENGDESLION [unidentified] is land for 1 plough. It is there in demesne with 3 villeins. It is worth 10s.

(352) In RIVELENOIT [Trelawnyd, Flints.][79] is land for 1 plough and it is there in demesne with 2 serfs, and 5 bordars. It is worth 20s.

(353) In CAIROS [Caerwys, Flints.] and LANUUILE [St. Asaph, Flints.][80] and CHARCAN [Cyrchynan in St. Asaph, Flints.] is land for 1 plough and it is there with 1 serf and 6 bordars. Wood 40 perches long and 40 wide. It is worth 15s.

(354) In MEINCATIS [unidentified] and TREVERI [Trefraith in Ysgeifiog, Flints.] and COIWEN [?Trefedwen in Caerwys, Flints.][81] is land for 1 plough, and it is there in demesne with 2 serfs, and 4 bordars and 2 villeins. It is worth 25s.

(355) In INGLECROFT [unidentified] and BRUNFOR [Brynford in Holywell, Flints.] and ALCHENE [Halkyn, Flints.] is land for 1 plough. It is there in demesne with a church and a priest and 3 bordars. There [is] a mill worth 5s. Wood ½ league long and 40 perches wide. It is worth 10s.

(356) In WIDFORD [Whitford, Flints.] and PUTECAIN [Bychton in Whitford, Flints.][82] is land for 1 plough. It is there with 2 villeins and 12 serfs and bondwomen (inter servos et ancillas). There [is] a fishery, and wood ½ league long and 40 perches wide. It is worth 20s.

[f. 269 col. 2]

(357) In MOSTONE [Mostyn in Whitford, Flints.] is land for 1 plough. It is there with 4 villeins and 8 bordars. Wood 1 league long and 40 perches wide. It is worth 20s.

(358) In PICHETONE [Picton in Llanasa, Flints.] and MELCHANESTONE [unidentified] is land for 1 plough and it is there with 2 villeins and 2 bordars. Wood ½ league long and 40 perches wide. It is worth 15s.

(359) In DANFROND [?Tan y Fron in Llanasa, Flints.],[83] CALSTAN [Kelston in Llanasa, Flints.],

---

[71] Formerly Dymeirchion.

[72] Doubts about the identification were presumably based upon etymological difficulties: Flints. Hist. Soc. xi. 25; Dom. Surv. Ches. 235.

[73] Formerly Fulbrook: Davies, Flints. P.N. 77.

[74] perticas lata written twice.

[75] The name, meaning 'top of the bog', points to a location north of the borough of Rhuddlan: Davies, Flints. P.N. 125.

[76] Unconvincing identifications include Ednywain (formerly Trefednywain) in Whitford and Trellewelyn in Rhuddlan: Dom. Surv. Ches. 235.

[77] The identification has been unconvincingly rejected because of Bodfari's remoteness from Diserth: Dom. Surv. Ches. 237; Davies, Flints. P.N. 11.

[78] The former names Upper and Lower Hiraddug were perhaps later represented by Uchglan and Isglan townships. In 1985 the earlier name survived only in Moel Hiraddug: Flints. Hist. Soc. xi. 27.

[79] Known officially as Newmarket 1700–1954: Davies, Flints. P.N. 119, 165.

[80] Llan Elwy and St. Asaph are the same: Davies, Flints. P.N. 151.

[81] Trefedwen appears as 'Coegan' in the early 15th century: Clwyd Historian, xiii. 14–16. Thanks are due to Mr. K. L. Gruffydd for the reference.

[82] Davies, Flints. P.N. 24–5, dispels doubts in Dom. Surv. Ches. 237.

[83] Davies, Flints. P.N. 160.

and WESBERIE [Gwesbyr in Llanasa, Flints.] is land for 1 plough. There are 2 radmen and Tual, a certain Frenchman with 7 bordars, and 1 church. It is worth 15s.

(360) In CANCARNACAN [Carnychan in Gwaunysgor, Flints.] and WENESCOL [Gwaunysgor, Flints.] is land for 1 plough and it is there in demesne with 2 Frenchmen and 2 villeins, and 1 waste church. It is worth 15s.

(361) In GRONANT [Gronant in Llanasa, Flints.] and ULVESGRAVE [Golden Grove in Llanasa, Flints.] the land is for 1 plough. This is there with 2 villeins and 5 bordars. It is worth 16[s.; *MS. reads* car.].

(362) In WENFESNE [unidentified] is land for 1 plough and it is there in demesne with 2 serfs. It is worth 40s.

(363) In PRESTETONE [Prestatyn in Meliden, Flints.] and RUESTOCH [Meliden, Flints.] is land for 1 plough and it is there in demesne with 2 oxmen, and 2 villeins and 4 bordars. There is a church. It is worth 20s.

(364) In DICOLIN [Dincolyn in Trecastell, Diserth parish, Flints.][84] and RAHOP [unidentified][85] and WITESTAN [unidentified] is land for 1 plough and it is there with 2 villeins and 2 bordars. There [is] wood 1 league long and ½ [league] wide. It is worth 12s.

All these aforesaid berewicks of Englefeld lay in ROELENT T.R.E. and were then waste, and when (Earl *interlined*) Hugh received them they were waste.

(365) The land of this manor of ROELEND and ENGLEFELD or of the other aforesaid berewicks belonging thereto, never paid geld nor was it hidated.

(366) In this same manor of ROELEND a castle, likewise called Roelent has lately been made. There is a new borough and in it 18 burgesses [divided] between the earl and Robert, as has been said above. To those burgesses they granted the laws and customs which are [enjoyed] in Hereford and Bretuill [Breteuil, Eure] that is to say that throughout the year they shall pay only 12d. for any forfeiture, except homicide and theft and premeditated hamfare (*heinfar*).[86] In the year of this inquest (*descriptio*) the toll of this borough was let to farm at 3s.

The receipts of (Earl *interlined*) Hugh from Roelent and Englefeld are valued at £6 10s., Robert's share at £17 3s.

IN ATISCROS HUNDRED

(367) BISCOPESTREU [Bistre in Mold, Flints.] was a manor of (Earl *interlined*) Edwin T.R.E. It never

paid geld nor was it hidated. It was then waste and it was also waste when (Earl *interlined*) Hugh received it. Now Hugh FitzNorman holds of the earl half of this manor and the whole of LEGGE [? Leeswood in Mold, Flints.][87] and SUDFELL [unidentified]. The land is for 1 plough which is there in demesne with 2 bordars, and there [is] 1 acre of meadow. It is worth 10s.

(368) The other half of this manor and half of MULINTONE [unidentified] and the whole of WISELEI [unidentified] Odin holds of the earl. The land is for 1 plough which is there with 2 serfs and 1 bordar. It is worth 10s.

Berewicks of the same manor:[88]

(369) Hugh FitzNorman holds of the earl HENDREBIFAU [Hendrebifa in Mold, Flints.] and WELTUNE [unidentified][89] and MUNENTONE [unidentified] and (2 *interlined*) HORSEPOL [unidentified] and (½ *interlined*) MULINTONE [unidentified]. The land is for 2 ploughs. These 2 ploughs are there with 3 villeins and 2 bordars. It is worth 18s.

(370) Warmund (the Hunter *interlined*) holds of the earl BRUNCOT [Broncoed in Mold, Flints.]. The land is for 1 plough. There is 1 villein with ½ plough and 2 oxen. It is worth 10s.

(371) Ralph holds of the earl RISTESELLE [?Rhos Ithel in Nercwys, Mold parish, Flints.][90]. The land is for 1 plough. It is there with 4 bordars. It is worth 8s.

(372) William holds of the earl QUISNAN [Gwysaney in Mold, Flints.]. The land is for 1 plough. It is there with a priest and 2 villeins. There [is] wood 1 league long and ½ [league] wide. It is worth 10s.

All this land belongs to BISCOPESTREU [Bistre in Mold, Flints.] and was waste. It never paid geld nor was it hidated. In this same manor there is 1 wood 1 league in length and ½ league in width. There is a hawk's eyrie. The earl has this wood, placed in his forest.

(373) In the same hundred of ATISCROS King Gruffudd (*Grifin*) had 1 manor BISCOPESTREU [Bistre, Flints.] and had 1 plough in demesne and his men [had] 6 ploughs. When the king came there, every plough rendered him 200 loaves (*hesthas*)[91] and 1 vat (*cuvam*) full of beer and 1 firkin (*ruscam*) of butter.

(374) ROBERT OF RHUDDLAN (*Roelent*) holds of the king NORTWALES [North Wales] at farm for £40, except that land which the king gave him in fee, and except the lands of the bishopric.[92]

(375) The same Robert claims a hundred [called] ARVESTER [Arwystli] which (Earl *inter-*

[84] One of the names for the 13th-century Diserth castle, north of the village: D. J. C. King, *Castellarium Anglicanum*, i. 152.
[85] Gop Hill in Trelawnyd has been suggested: *Flints. Hist. Soc.* xi. 31.   [86] See no. 1b and note 4.
[87] Welsh Coed-llai. Identified by inf. from Dr. H. W. Owen.
[88] Because of a general change from English to Welsh place names in the region around Mold after 1086 very few of the following place names have been identified.

[89] The first element of the name may have survived in translation as Maes y ffynon, near Mold: Davies, *Flints. P.N.* 105.
[90] The modern name bears some resemblance to the Domesday form, but no intermediate forms are known: Davies, *Flints. P.N.* 144. If the Domesday form is Old English, the modern name does not have the same meaning.
[91] The word's meaning is uncertain, but it is related to the Welsh *gwestfa*, the ancient food rent.
[92] Evidently Bangor (Caern.).

lined) Roger[93] holds. The Welsh testify that this hundred belongs to this NORTWALIS [North Wales].

(376) In the fee which the same Robert holds of the king, ROS [Rhos] and REWENIOU [Rhufoniog] are 12 leagues of land in length and 4 leagues in width. The land is for only 20 ploughs. It is valued at £12. All the rest of the land is in woods and moors, and cannot be ploughed.

[ff. 269v.–270, comprising the land between the Ribble and the Mersey (*Inter Ripam et Mersham*), are translated and treated in *V.C.H. Lancs.* i. 269–87.]

---

[93] Roger de Montgomery, earl of Shrewsbury.

INDEX

Note. The following abbreviations used in the index, sometimes with the addition of the letter s to form the plural, may require elucidation: abp., archbishop; boro., borough; bp., bishop; bro., brother; cast., castle; cent., century; ch., church; co., county; coll., college; ct., court; dau., daughter; fam., family; fl., flourished; Gilb., Gilbert; Gt., Great; ho., house; Humph., Humphrey; hund., hundred; man., manor; Mat., Matthew; Mus., Museum; n, note; par., parish; pl., plate; Ric., Richard; riv., river; rly., railway; Rob., Robert; Rog., Roger; s., son; sch., school; Sim., Simon; sta., station; Thos., Thomas; w., wife; wid., widow; Wm., William.

A personal name followed by (T.R.E.) indicates that the bearer held land in Cheshire in 1066, while (fl. 1086) denotes a tenant or undertenant holding at the time of the Domesday survey.

An italic page number denotes an illustration on that page.

INDEX OF PERSONS AND PLACES MENTIONED IN DOMESDAY

References are to the entry numbers, not to pages. An italic *n* indicates a footnote. 'T.R.E.' after a personal name indicates a person entered as having held land in 1066. Names in italic type are in the form given in the original text.

Acatone, see Acton
Acton, 151 and *n*, 152 *n*, 316
Actune, see Acton
Aculvestune, see Occlestone
Adlington, 61
Aelfric, T.R.E., 92, 169, 174-5
Aescwulf, T.R.E., 38, 142
Aitard, tenant of Wm. FitzNiel, 197
Alburgham, see Alpraham
Alchene, see Halkyn
Aldelime, see Audlem
Alden, see Healfdene
'Alderley', 45
Alderley, Nether, 238
Alderley, Over, 208
Aldford, 233
Aldredelic, see Alderley, Over
Aldredelie, see 'Alderley'; Alderley, Nether
Alentune, see Allington
Allington (Denb.), 7 *n*, 247
Almaer, T.R.E., 150, 333
Alnoth, T.R.E., 286
Alpraham, 250 and *n*
Alretone, unidentified, 55
Alretune, see 'Alretunstall' in Timperley; Ollerton
'Alretunstall' in Timperley, 232
Alric, T.R.E., 164
Alsager, 67
Alsi, see Alsige
Alsige, T.R.E., 122, 124
Alstan, T.R.E., 243
Altetone, see Oulton
Aluuold, see Alweald
Alvanley, 306
Alvric, see Aelfric
Alweald, T.R.E., 221
Alweard, T.R.E., 121, 164, 227-9, 231-2, 313
Ansfred, tenant of Wm. FitzNiel, 200
Ansger, tenant of Wm. FitzNiel, 330
Ansgot, T.R.E., 50, 234
Antrobus, 36, 71
Appleton, 295
Archil, T.R.E., 216
Aregrim, see Arngrim
Arngrim, T.R.E., 124, 149
Arni, T.R.E., 52, 181-3, 186-8, 326, 330
Arvester, see Arwystli
Arwystli, 'hund.', 375
Ascelie, see Ashley
Ascelin, tenant of Robert of Rhuddlan, 324
Ashley, 231
Ashton in Tarvin, 116
Asketone, see Axton
Astbury, Newbold, 261 *n*
Aston by Budworth, 204
Aston by Sutton, 199
Aston in Hawarden (Flints.), 335
Aston in Wrenbury, 152
Aston juxta Mondrum, 179
Atiscros, hund., 34-5, 320-73; *and see* Englefield
Audlem, 128, 152 *n*, 316 *n*

Austerson in Acton, 166 and *n*
Auti, T.R.E., 146
Axton (Flints.), 348
Azelinus, see Ascelin

Bachelie, see Bagillt
Baddiley, 175
Bagelei, see Baguley
Bagillt (Flints.), 326
Baguley, 313
Bailleul, Rainald de, *see* Rainald de Bailleul
Baldricus, see Baudry
Bangor (Caern.), bishopric of, 373 *n*
Barnston, 189
Barrow, 185
Barthomley, 165
Bartington, 302-3
Basford, 162
Batherton, 163
Baudry, 246
Beddesfeld, see Bettisfield
Bedelei, see Baddiley
Bedesfeld, see Bettisfield
Beeston, 95
Belam, see Beollan
Beollan, T.R.E., 243
Beornwulf, T.R.E., 62, 240
Berchesford, see Basford
Berdeltune, see Batherton
Bernestone, see Barnston
Bernulf, see Beornwulf
Bero, see Barrow
Bers, T.R.E., 121
Bertemeleu, see Barthomley
Bertintune, see Bartington
Bettisfield (Flints.), 13, 72, 73 *n*
Bevelei, see Byley
Bichelei, see Bickley
Bickerton, 91
Bickley, 90
Bicretone, see Bickerton
Bidston, 57 *n*
Bieston (Denb.), 314 *n*
Bigot de Loges, 68 *n*, 233-45, 312
Birkenhead, 57 *n*
Biscopestreu, see Bistre
Bistre (Flints.), 340, 367, 372-3
manor, 367-73
Blachehol, see Blacon
Blachenhale, see Blakenhall
Blacon, 270
Blakenhall, 266, 316 *n*
Blorant (Denb.), 342 and *n*
Blorat, see Blorant
Bochelau, hund., 44, 190-6, 227-9, 231-2, 236, 254-9, 269, 272-8, 292-3, 310 *n*, 312-13
Bocstone, see Boughton, Gt.
Bodeugan (Flints.), 341
Bodeurde, see Budworth, Little
Bodfari (Flints.), 350 and *n*
Bodugan, see Bodeugan
Bogedone, see Bowdon
Boleberie, see Bunbury
Boselega, see Bosley
Bosley, 222

Bostock, 126
Botelege, see Butley
Botestoch, see Bostock
Boteuuarul, see Bodfari
Boughton, Gt., 18
Bowdon, 228
Bramale, see Bramhall
Bramhall, 230
Bredbury, 129
Bren, see Bryn
Brennehedui, see Brynhedydd
Brenuuen, see Bryngwyn
Brereton, 262
Bretberie, see Bredbury
Breteuil (Eure), 366
Bretone, see Brereton
Bretton (Flints.), 333 *n*
Bretuill, see Breteuil
Brictric, see Brihtric
Brihtmar, T.R.E., 85
Brihtric, tenant of Wm. FitzNiel, 198
Brimstage, 57 *n*
Brismer, see Brihtmar
Bromborough, 57 *n*
Broncoed (Flints.), 370
Broomhall, 171
Brosse, see Broxton
Broughton (Flints.), 322-3, 331, 337
Broxton, 85
Bruge, see Handbridge
Brun, T.R.E., 65, 208, 230, 237, 239
Bruncot, see Broncoed
Brunfor, see Brynford
Brunford, see Brynford
Brunhala, see Broomhall
Bryn (Flints.), 340, 349
Brynford (Flints.), 345, 355
Bryngwyn (Flints.), 342
Brynhedydd (Flints.), 340
Budewrde, see Budworth, Gt.
Budworth, Gt., 205
Budworth, Little, 54
Buerton, 159
Buglawton, 215
Buistane, see Beeston
Bunbury, 96, 138 *n*
Burcy, Niel de, *see* Niel de Burcy
Burton, 9
Burton in Tarvin, 9 *n*
Burton in Wirral, 9 *n*
Burtone, see Burton
Burtune, see Buerton
Burwardeslei, see Burwardesley
Burwardesley, 92
Burwardestone, unidentified, 73
Butelege, see Butley
Butley, 101 and *n*, 307 and *n*
Bychton (Flints.), 356 and *n*
Byley, 216

Caerwys (Flints.), 353
Cairos, see Caerwys
Calcot (Flints.), 347
Caldecot, see Calcot
Caldecote, see Caldecott